THE LIFE OF BILLY YANK

A BILLY YANK AND HIS AIDE

The soldier is a private of the Second Rhode Island Infantry Volunteers.

The Life of
BILLY YANK

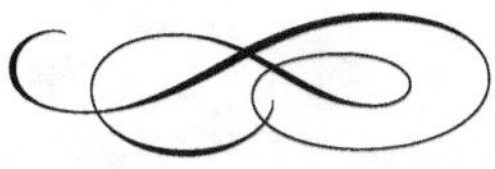

The Common Soldier of
the Union

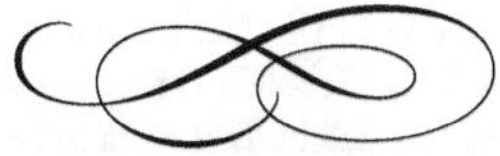

BELL IRVIN WILEY

With a Foreword by James I. Robertson, Jr.

UPDATED EDITION

LOUISIANA STATE UNIVERSITY PRESS
BATON ROUGE

To
Jennie, Henry and Jennie Lee

Published by Louisiana State University Press
lsupress.org

Updated edition, 2008

Library of Congress Cataloging-in-Publication Data

Wiley, Bell Irvin, 1906–1980.
 The life of Billy Yank : the common soldier of the Union / Bell Irvin Wiley. — Updated ed. /
with a foreword by James I. Robertson, Jr.
  p. cm.
Includes bibliographical references and index.
 ISBN 978-0-8071-3375-0 (pbk. : alk. paper) 1. United States. Army—Military life—History—
19th century. 2. Soldiers—United States—History—19th century. 3. United States—History—
Civil War, 1861–1865—Personal narratives. I. Title.
 E607.W49 2009
 973.7'83—dc22

                                                                              2008024243

CONTENTS

Foreword by James I. Robertson, Jr. 3

Preface 11

Introduction 15

  I Southward Ho! 17

 II From Reveille to Taps 45

III The Supreme Test 66

 IV In Dixie Land 96

  V Along Freedom Road 109

 VI The Depths of Suffering 124

VII Gay and Happy Still 152

VIII Toeing the Mark 192

 IX Hardtack, Salt Horse and Coffee 224

  X Evil and Goodness 247

 XI The Spirits Ebb and Flow 275

XII The Men Who Wore the Blue 296

XII Billy Yank and Johnny Reb 346

    Notes 365

    Bibliographical Notes 438

    Index 447

LIST OF ILLUSTRATIONS

A Billy Yank and His Colored Aide . . . . *Frontispiece*

FACING
PAGE

Mournful Ones at Sick Call 30

Digging In 31

"Dear Folks" 64

Items of Soldier Equipment 65

Hardtack 96

Some Soldier Types 97

William Black: A Boy Soldier Who Was among the Wounded . 106

John L. ("Johnny") Clem, the Drummer Boy of Shiloh and
    Chickamauga 106

The Coffee Call 107

Army Punishment 118

A Friendly Game 119

"Wild Blue Yonder" Boys of the 1860s 128

Portrait of a Zouave 129

A Cockfight in the Army of the Potomac 160

Union Soldiers Playing Baseball 161

Western Soldiers on Parade 192

Soldiers of Company F, Fourth Vermont, in Camp 193

Camp of Sixteenth Vermont at Union Mills, Virginia . . . 224

"California Joe" of Berdan's Sharpshooters Watching for Rebs . 225

Artillery Practice, Near the Gaines House 256

LIST OF ILLUSTRATIONS

On the Threshold of Freedom 257

Religious Service in Camp 288

Soldiers' Friends 289

Billy Yank Poses with the Brass 320

In the Ditches before Atlanta 321

On the Road to Recovery 352

Dispensers of Army Justice 353

FOREWORD

The name Bell Irvin Wiley is now synonymous with the common soldiers of the Civil War, because he was their close friend and their finest spokesman. Among American historians in the twentieth century, Wiley's populist voice was singular. Yet his energies, and his inspiration, gave rise to a veritable school of Civil War socio-military historians.

His own academic career was a rags-to-riches story. Born January 5, 1906, in the west Tennessee village of Halls, Wiley was the sixth of eleven children in a family poor but industrious. His father, Ewing Baxter Wiley, was a minister/ teacher/farmer; his mother, Ann Bass Wiley, taught school. Their farm home had neither electricity nor indoor plumbing.

Wiley grew up in a devout and abstemious atmosphere. The family farm was next door to a community church; his father was a puritanical Methodist; and young Wiley was not allowed to read novels. The idea of drinking an alcoholic beverage in the family was unimaginable. Wiley always retained some of that religiousness. A lifelong friend saw "ever present" in Wiley "a streak of the proselytizing evangelical, extremely sensitive to wrongs, indignities, and in- justice (John Barnwell, "Bell Irvin Wiley," *Dictionary of Literary Biography*, 1983, 17: 424).

In summertime the Wiley children lived by turns with their maternal grand- mother, Fredonia Abernathy Bass, who was the widow of a Confederate soldier. Wiley remembered her as "a splendid Christian woman, but her Christianity was never broad enough to embrace love of Yankees" (*Army Museum Newsletter*, July 19, 1980, 4).

From his grandmother, young Wiley heard stories of the ebb and flow of four years of fighting, Union soldiers marching across the land, and depriva- tions levied upon civilians by troops on both sides. Often invited to Sunday dinner were Confederate veteran Will Martin and Union veteran George Bun- ker. Naturally, the two old soldiers would relate war experiences. "Everything would go along amicably," Wiley recalled, "until and unless the conversation happened to drift to the question of the comparative fighting qualities of the two armies. Then . . . my father would have to invoke his ministerial tact to restore harmonious relations" (Barnwell, "Wiley," 424). Such were the beginnings of Wiley's lifelong fascination with Civil War history.

Wiley (as well as four of his brothers and sisters) enrolled in Asbury College, a fundamentalist school in nearby Kentucky. He graduated in 1928 and intended to become a teacher in public schools. Yet a public debate instructor, Zachary T. Johnson, was instrumental in getting Wiley appointed assistant professor of history and debate coach at Asbury. Wiley never forgot Johnson's helpfulness: "Not only was he an inspiring teacher, but he also took a great personal interest in his students. I am indebted to him more than to any other person, save my mother and father, for the things that have happened to me in my career" (ibid.).

Wiley began graduate studies in history at the University of Kentucky while still on the Asbury faculty. His M.A. thesis was a study of cotton and slavery in antebellum Kentucky. He received his master's in 1931 and then headed northward in quest of a doctorate at Yale University.

Still affected by his strict religious upbringing, Wiley was a somewhat solitary figure in the doctoral program. Friends remembered him as tall and lanky, with thick, dark hair. He had a strong Southern accent and engaging manners. Yet he was hard working and diligent to a fault. This proved to be an asset, particularly when his mentor, U. B. Phillips, contracted fatal throat cancer. Completion of the dissertation became a race with time, and Phillips did not live to see the study become Wiley's first book, *Southern Negroes, 1861–1865* (1938).

In 1934 Wiley began his major career as professor and departmental chairman at Hattiesburg State Teachers College (now the University of Southern Mississippi). He spent many of the Great Depression summers teaching at Peabody College in Nashville. It was there, while breakfasting as usual in a drugstore, that he met Peabody student Mary Frances Harrison. The couple married in December 1937 and moved the following year to the University of Mississippi, where Wiley assumed again the dual role of professor and department head.

An Oxford neighbor, William Faulkner, took a liking to the young professor. Friendship developed, according to Mrs. Wiley, because, "Bell didn't constantly bring up the great novelist's work" (James I. Robertson, Jr., and Richard M. McMurry, eds., *Rank and File*, 1976, 4). The two men spent time together fishing, but neither seemed to have influenced the other's approach to his professional pursuit—be it fiction or history.

The more Wiley probed into Civil War history, the more fascinated he became with the Southern "civilians on loan to the military": the common folk who formed the ranks of the Confederate armies. Research in earnest on these soldiers began during the Oxford years. Wiley and his wife crisscrossed the South, examining thousands of unpublished letters and hundreds of manuscript diaries both in archives and private possession. Wiley flagged the material he wanted to use; Mrs. Wiley did the copying.

Having outlined the proposed book in advance, Wiley then used soldiers' quotations to insert life into the text. A colleague noted, "Wiley examined and described a wide range of Johnny Reb's experiences in war: the mundane and the spiritual, the macabre and the humorous, the ridiculous and—very rarely— the sublime" (ibid., 425–426).

Wiley himself was aware of the pioneering nature of the efforts he was making. "In the flood of history and near-history published during the past half-century," he wrote, "the doings of common soldiers have usually served as a hazily sketched backdrop for dramas featuring campaigns and leaders. The present work is an attempt to give the man of the ranks, who after all was the army, something of his rightful measure of consideration" (Bell Irvin Wiley, *The Life of Johnny Reb*, 1943, 13). The book's appearance instantly established Wiley as a leading social historian of the Civil War period.

In 1943 Wiley also gave the Walter Lynwood Fleming Lectures at Louisiana State University. The three essays he presented appeared in print as *The Plain People of the Confederacy*. For the first time, Wiley stated what would become his recurring theme: class conflict within the Southern nation.

World War II interrupted his studies, and Wiley entered military service as a lieutenant and staff historian for the Second Army. His war service was in Washington, where his major duty consisted of writing required but unexciting manuals. Years later, Wiley admitted, "One of the monographs was so dull that I cannot endure looking back over it today" (Barnwell, "Wiley," 426). Nevertheless, Lt. Col. Wiley received the Legion of Merit in 1945 and left the army a year later. (He remained in the reserves until his 1966 retirement as full colonel.)

The Wileys then moved to Baton Rouge, where he became professor and department head at Louisiana State University. One of his first graduate students was Charles P. Roland (later an eminent historian in his own right). Roland too had just been discharged from service and arrived penniless to begin graduate studies at LSU. Wiley quietly offered to lend him money until his GI Bill funds arrived (Interview with Charles P. Roland, November 27, 2006).

Writing a book on Billy Yanks was a next and natural step in Wiley's career. Still, the Tennessee native could not help but experience feelings of uncertainty about the topic itself, as he confessed in one of his last public utterances. "When I began research on *The Life of Billy Yank*," he recalled, "I was apprehensive, owing to my Southern background, about my ability to deal fairly with the men who wore the Union blue. But after I had read many letters written by Billy Yanks, this fear vanished, for I found that most Northern soldiers, like their Southern counterparts, were genuinely admirable men. One of the things that impressed me most was the strong similarity between Rebs and Yanks. They thought and acted alike, and their letters were so similar that if the identifying marks were removed, the letters mixed together and thrown into the air to let the wind scatter them at will, no one could tell which were written by Southerners and which by Northerners" (*Army Museum Newsletter*, July 19, 1980, 30).

Despite his short tenure at LSU, Wiley received a year's leave to do research. Graduate students such as Roland assisted by thumbing through published memoirs and marking pages of interest. Meanwhile, Wiley and his wife traveled from Maine to Minnesota to Maryland in search of material for *Billy Yank*. When in a sizable city, Wiley went to great lengths to be interviewed on radio or for a newspaper. This announced what he was doing and produced a surprising number of Civil War manuscripts held in private hands.

However, the division of labor that had worked so well for the husband-and-wife team was not the same as it had been for *Johnny Reb*. The birth of their first son, George, made it difficult for Mrs. Wiley to sit by her husband's side and work. Now Wiley had to wade through manuscripts and flag material he wanted transcribed. In the evenings he babysat while his wife typed notes on 5 x 8 file cards. Wiley never typed well and thus took notes in longhand, which, he freely admitted, were impossible to read, even for him. When little George would cry at night, Wiley sat by the bedside and sang somber tunes. "George likes doleful Methodist hymns," he explained to a friend (Roland interview).

In the meantime, Wiley created a stir in the academic community by accepting a new job. LSU had granted him a year's absence under the expectation that he would resume his duties there. Instead, Wiley accepted an offer to become an anchor for the new doctoral program in history at Emory University. In 1949 the family moved to Decatur, Georgia. There, Wiley would spend twenty-five years as one of Emory's most distinguished professors.

The Life of Billy Yank appeared in 1952 and joined *The Life of Johnny Reb* as the basic reference on the three million men who served in the Civil War. Neither book could be termed military history. Wiley's intent in *Billy Yank*, as in *Johnny Reb*, was "to write a social history of men in arms" (Bell Irvin Wiley, *The Life of Billy Yank*, 1952, 13). He was not concerned with causation or consequences. Rather, Wiley concentrated on the war in the field, the trenches, and the hospitals. His interest was not only in what the soldiers did but more so in what they felt and thought.

Wiley refuted Walt Whitman's assertion that the real war would never get into the books. He focused on army discipline, routines, food, clothing, religion, medical practices, hardships, high jinks, the humorous, and the ridiculous. Soldiers' quotations filled every page. Indeed, Wiley quoted so freely from the colorful language, remarked one reviewer, "as to add to the value of the book by getting it banned in Boston" (Barnwell, "Wiley," 427).

A difference between *Johnny Reb* and *Billy Yank* is readily noticeable. The story of Federal soldiers, and Wiley's own recent military experiences, gave *Billy Yank* an air of nationalism not found in his earlier publications.

Reviews of *Billy Yank* were often glowing. The *New York Times* called it a work of "admirable objectivity . . . fabulous learning and considerable pace and humor . . . the finest memorial the Union soldier is ever likely to have." Bruce Catton, then the most popular writer in Civil War history, exclaimed that he was "filled with admiration" for the book and wished "he had written it himself" (Bell Irvin Wiley, *The Common Soldier in the Civil War*, 1963, 65).

Catton and Wiley were close friends; they also shared a deep esteem for Billy Yanks. However, they disagreed in their writings over the motivation of Union soldiers. In Catton's three-volume history of the Army of the Potomac, Federal volunteers slowly but steadily embraced the role of liberators and became champions of the emancipation cause. The righteousness of Catton's Union soldiers seemed to increase with the civil rights movement of the mid-twentieth century.

In contrast, Wiley found Northern enlistees largely unconcerned about ideology. Love for the Union was always there, Wiley stated, and it was vastly more important than any desire to end slavery or befriend blacks. "One who reads letters and diaries of Union soldiers encounters an enormous amount of antipathy toward Negroes. . . . Many whites remained deeply antagonistic to the end of the war" (Wiley, *Billy Yank*, 109, 121). That judgment has recently come under strong but unconvincing challenge.

Wiley hoped that his two studies might trigger a strong shift of attention to the common soldiers. Quite the opposite occurred. His research was so thorough that it took the discoveries of material in the Civil War Centennial and the passage of thirty years before historians would venture down the Wiley path.

The Emory professor remained a champion of America's common masses. "Despite the fact that the lowly people have always constituted the overwhelming majority of our population," he declared, "they appear only hazily on the pages of history, as a dim backdrop against which are projected the doings of the politicians, the statesmen, the generals, the planters, and the business titans. The history books are written about the bigwigs; the common folk are crowded into the background—or worse, distorted into impossible caricatures" (Hill Jordan et al., *Bell Irvin Wiley Reader*, 2001, 63).

Wiley firmly believed that writing made him a better teacher and that teaching made him a better writer. He proved that by becoming one of Emory's most popular lecturers. His undergraduate Civil War history course regularly attracted more than two hundred students. Imposing and soft spoken, his silver-gray hair worn in a John C. Calhoun haircut, he had the enviable teaching ability to carry a class on emotional waves ranging from laughter to tears. Classroom presentations seemed to grow better with each new book, essay, or discovery of Civil War letters. Wiley's voice chuckled or quivered, depending upon the content of the quotation. His exams, on the other hand, were notoriously long and weighted heavily with what students regarded as minutiae. That Wiley graded on a curve did little to lessen the foreboding at an approaching examination.

With graduate students, Wiley was far more demanding. His rationale was simple: each M.A. and Ph.D. candidate would be a reflection of Wiley himself. Hence, he demanded sweeping research into primary sources as well as impeccable writing. If his exactions as a mentor were severe, his encouragements were genuine. One doctoral candidate recalled a progress-report meeting in which Wiley displayed "that engaging laugh and those big hands slapping one on the knees and . . . urging one on to his task" (Barnwell, "Wiley," 430).

A polished speaker who loved his subject, Wiley accepted as many invitations as his schedule would permit. Civil War round tables, historical societies, colleges, and universities were favorite speaking sites. He taught summer school at such faraway places as Alaska and Hawaii; he traveled internationally as a Department of State American specialist leader; and from 1965 to 1966 Wiley held the Harmsworth Professorship of American History at Queens College, Oxford University.

Wiley was a rare scholar "in favor of anything that made history more accessible and interesting to nonacademic Americans," a colleague observed (Jordan, *Wiley Reader*, 10). He served a term as president of academia's Southern Historical Association, and he held a similar position later on the "layman's" National Historical Society.

Appointed by President Dwight Eisenhower in 1957 as a charter member of the U.S. Civil War Centennial Commission, Wiley became chairman of that body's executive committee. His lifelong liberal beliefs influenced much of the commission's direction and accomplishments. That political bent also cost him a number of friends.

A son of the South, Wiley was never a diehard Southerner. This first became apparent in 1956, when he published three essays on the causes of Confederate defeat. *The Road to Appomattox* packed a greater wallop than its small size indicated. A long essay on Jefferson Davis bordered on an indictment of the Confederate president. More irritating to many readers, another Wiley essay attributed Confederate defeat not to external Union might but to interior factors: disharmony among the people, exaggerated individualism nurtured in the plantation system of the Old South, and the Southern government's failure to take its citizens more into confidence.

Wiley was not by nature a crusader, but the civil rights movement of the 1960s made him so. Although a courtly speaker in private and in the classroom, in public utterances he pulled no punches. To a stunned Southern audience he asserted, "One of the basic troubles in Alabama and Mississippi is that many of the residents, especially some of the leaders, have not fully accepted the result of the Civil War" (*Washington Post*, April 7, 1980). Racial discrimination he found "illogical, contrary to common sense, and indefensible." On another occasion, he received boos after stating, "I consider it gross and utterly reprehensible for the Confederate flag to be used as an adornment in which despicable demagogues seek to wrap themselves to acquire respectability" (Jordan, *Wiley Reader*, 52).

Often attacked verbally and in print, Wiley never wavered in his social beliefs. However, in the late 1960s he began to suffer bouts of depression. They came at intervals, without apparent cause. Occasionally Wiley became so melancholy that other faculty would have to lecture in his stead.

In 1974 Wiley retired from Emory. He had written or edited thirty-three books, seventy-three articles, and hundreds of book reviews. In all, he had studied thirty thousand letters, a thousand diaries, and hundreds of printed sources. Among his awards were five honorary doctorates. Wiley remained academically active, with visiting professorships at the University of South Carolina, Tulane University, Agnes Scott College, and the University of Kentucky, and he began research on a book about the black settlers of Liberia. Yet declining health took its toll. Wiley died April 4, 1980, in Decatur. By his request, his remains were donated to the Emory University School of Medicine for research.

To the end, Wiley regarded the lowly folk as the bulwark of American democracy. A statement in one of his final interviews serves as a fitting valediction: "Basic to all my research and writing is a deep interest in the character of the common people and their role in the nation's history. . . . Never before nor since were they called on to endure as much suffering and hardship as during the Civil War. The magnificent way in which most of them acquitted themselves in this, their greatest test, reflected great credit on them as a people and justified the faith that had been reposed in them by Thomas Jefferson and the other founding fathers. They were, and they are, a great people. My most earnest hope is to be remembered as their historian" (*Army Museum Newsletter*, July 19, 1980, 31).

James I. Robertson, Jr.
April 2008

MY IMMEDIATE reason for undertaking this book was to get acquainted with the foes of Johnny Reb. I wanted to know what sort of men they were, what caused them to fight, how they reacted to combat, what they thought about the land and people of Dixie, how well they stood up under the strain of prolonged conflict, what they thought of their leaders, and how they compared with their opposites in gray. All of this, and more, I wanted to learn and write down in a companion volume to *The Life of Johnny Reb.*

A remoter aim was to pursue further an inveterate interest in the humble folk, the little people, who have always comprised the bulk of our population, but who for that very reason, and for being relatively inarticulate, have appeared only hazily on the pages of history.

The Civil War affords an unusually good opportunity for the study of the plain people, for during that conflict unprecedentedly large numbers of them were away from home. Absence from loved ones caused lowly folk who rarely took pen in hand during times of peace to write frequent and informative letters and to keep diaries, and thus to reveal themselves in rare fullness. More than that, their war experience caused them to be written about to an unusual extent, in newspapers, court-martial proceedings, hospital records and official reports. The Civil War, coming as it did when the picture-making art was attaining a practical basis, also resulted in producing the first large-scale photographing of America's humbler citizens.

True, larger numbers of this class were to be taken from home in the world wars of our generation, but by that time censorship and other restrictions, which for all practical purposes were nonexistent during the Civil War, had made letters and diaries less meaningful as social documents.

My main concern in this study, as in *The Life of Johnny Reb,* has been social rather than military. To put it another way: I have been trying to write social history of men in arms.

In choosing the title for the present work I am not on as firm historical ground as in that of the earlier volume. The term Johnny Reb had considerable usage during the conflict; so did the designation Yank.

But the name Billy Yank seems to have been a postwar creation. I have adopted it for euphony and balance and in so doing I have followed the example of one of Lee's veterans, Alexander Hunter, who in 1905 published his Confederate memoirs under the title *Johnny Reb and Billy Yank.*

Many types of material have been used but the basic source has been the undoctored writings of the soldiers themselves, especially the manuscript letters. In quest of these fascinatingly human documents I traveled twenty-three thousand miles and visited twenty-four states. In addition, material was borrowed in microfilm, photostat or typescript from several depositories not visited, including the Huntington Library, the Western Historical Manuscripts Collection of the University of Missouri, Luther College Library, Washington and Jefferson College, the New York State Historical Association at Cooperstown and the Nebraska Historical Society.

During these travels I became indebted to many people. Custodians of manuscripts kept extra hours to expedite research and in some cases obligingly lent keys so that I might work at odd times. Historians along the way extended courtesies far beyond the call of duty. Numerous private collectors and descendants of Union soldiers generously placed their treasured holdings at my disposal. These and others assisted immeasurably by their active interest and friendly encouragement. Limitations of space preclude individual mention of those whose kindness I received. I can only state that their help is deeply appreciated and that without it this book could hardly have been written.

I cannot refrain from making specific acknowledgment of the great value to this project of the inventories and guides prepared under the auspices of the Historical Records Survey of the Works Progress Administration. Use of these aids made possible a detailed planning of the research itinerary and saved many precious hours.

I am indebted for indispensable financial assistance to the Rockefeller Foundation, whose directors awarded me a Post-War Fellowship; the Social Science Research Council for two grants-in-aid; Louisiana State University; Emory University; and the Carnegie Foundation for the Advancement of Teaching.

The experience of looking at "the war" from the Northern point of view and through the eyes of the men who wore the blue has been enormously interesting and stimulating to one who was nurtured in Confederate tradition and whose focus has been on the Southern side. In the initial stage of research I was fearful that my long attachment to

Johnny Reb would prevent my treating his foe with the sympathy that he deserved and fair historical treatment required. But this anxiety was short-lived. For as I came to know the Northern soldier through his diaries and letters, I came to respect him, and as the acquaintance ripened I developed a genuine affection for him. I mean to pay him a high compliment when I state that he was no less admirable than the man he fought. Indeed, the two were so much alike that the task of giving this book a flavor and character distinct from *The Life of Johnny Reb* has at times been a difficult one.

Emory University, Georgia   BELL IRVIN WILEY
5 January, 1952

ACKNOWLEDGMENTS

The author wishes to express appreciation to the following persons and firms for permission to reprint material as indicated:

Louisiana State University Press, Baton Rouge, *With Sherman to the Sea: The Journal of Theodore F. Upson*, edited by Oscar O. Winther.

University of California Press and Harold A. Small, Berkeley, *The Road to Richmond: The Civil War Memoirs of Major Abner R. Small*, edited by Harold A. Small:

Yale University Press, New Haven, John William De Forest, *A Volunteer's Adventures: A Union Captain's Record of the Civil War*, edited by James H. Croushore.

Abraham Lincoln Association, Springfield, Illinois, Bell I. Wiley, "Boys in Blue," *Abraham Lincoln Quarterly*, December 1951.

American Association for State and Local History, Sturbridge, Massachusetts, Bell I. Wiley, "Men in Blue," *American Heritage*, winter 1952.

Association for the Study of Negro Life and History, Incorporated, Washington, D. C., Bell I. Wiley, "Billy Yank and the Black Folk," *Journal of Negro History*, January 1951.

John D. Barnhart, Bloomington, Indiana, letters of "Prock" and other articles in the *Indiana Magazine of History*.

State Historical Society of Iowa, various articles in the *Iowa Journal of History and Politics*.

Virginia Quarterly Review, Bell I. Wiley, "Billy Yank Down South," autumn 1950.

Wisconsin Historical Society, "A Badger Boy in Blue: The Letters of Chauncey H. Cooke," in the *Wisconsin Magazine of History*, Volumes IV and V.

TWENTY-EIGHT years ago, when I had completed research for *The Life of Billy Yank*, I estimated that I had read twenty thousand letters written by the men who wore the blue. These personal documents, along with the ten thousand Confederate letters that I had examined while preparing *The Life of Johnny Reb* (plus several hundred diaries of participants on both sides), while admittedly a small sampling, afford a more intimate and revealing insight into the mind and character of the American masses than any body of material treating of any other period of the nation's history. More letters were written by ordinary Americans who served in World War I and World War II, but censorship, which was practically nonexistent in the Civil War, and the greater degree of sophistication in the twentieth century, make the letters of latter-day soldiers considerably less informative than those of the men who fought for Grant and Lee.

The many letters and diaries that I have read since *The Life of Billy Yank* and *The Life of Johnny Reb* were first published have confirmed impressions formed while the books were in preparation. The differences and similarities of Northerners and Southerners, outlined in the concluding chapter of *The Life of Billy Yank*, were substantiated, and further support was found for the conclusion that Yanks and Rebs were far more alike than not. For the common soldiers of both sides the qualities that stand out were: pride in themselves and their families; a strong sense of duty; courage; a capacity for suffering; a will and strength to endure; and, for most, a devotion to country and cause which exceeded that of the folk at home.

Patriotism appears to have been deeper and more enduring among Yanks than among Rebs, and it was the devotion of the masses to the Union, coupled with the leadership of Abraham Lincoln, whom they regarded as their representative and champion, that sustained the Northern cause during the bloody reverses of 1861 and 1862, and which in all likelihood would have enabled it to withstand further setbacks, say at Gettysburg, Atlanta, or in the Valley of Virginia in 1864. Devotion to the Union found abundant expression in soldiers' letters, but few if any exceeded in eloquence that written by John F. Brobst of the 25th Wisconsin Regiment to his sweetheart early in 1863: "Home is sweet, and friends are dear, but what would they all be to let the country go to ruin and be a slave. I am contented with my lot . . . for I know that I am doing my duty and I know that it is my duty to do as I am now a-doing. If I live to get back, I shall be proud of the freedom I shall have, and know that I helped to gain that freedom. If I should not get back, it will do them good who do get back."

A regrettable gap in personal documents, which handicapped me in preparing the original edition and which I have not been able to repair in subsequent research, is a dearth of letters written by the 200,000 blacks who donned the blue. A careful search has turned up less than a score of these sources. Most of the Negro Yanks were ex-slaves condemned to illiteracy by state law; many of them learned to read and write after they became soldiers and some, recruited from among free blacks residing in the North, were literate when they enlisted in the army. But practically all of the letters that they wrote apparently were lost or destroyed. This is the more regrettable because other records bearing on their service, as indicated in Chapter 12 of *The Life of Billy Yank* and Chapter 9 of my *Southern Negroes, 1861–1865*, show that the black soldiers, struggling against gross discrimination and other serious handicaps, gave a good account of themselves and contributed immeasurably to the freedom and Union for which they fought.

BELL I. WILEY

Emory University
1 July 1978

CHAPTER I

SOUTHWARD HO!

THE South's attack on Fort Sumter fell like a thunderclap on the country north of Dixie. True, there had been talk of war, especially since the secession of the cotton states and the organization of the Southern Confederacy, but the agitators, consisting mainly of politicians, journalists, preachers and reformers, many of whom were on the make, were relatively few. A substantial portion of the population still hoped for a peaceful solution of the sectional crisis even after Jeff Davis set up his rival government.[1]

Fort Sumter changed all this. The flag had been affronted. Men wearing the American uniform had been forced by hostile fire to surrender a Federal fort and march out in acknowledged defeat. And with that humiliating incident peaceable secession lost all respectability. The die was cast.

Lincoln's request for troops was in a sense an anticlimax. The roar of cannon at Charleston, like the crash of bombs eighty years later at Pearl Harbor, was the country's call to arms.

During most of the war the raising of troops was a slow and painful process. But in the weeks following Fort Sumter the opposite was true. From Lake Superior to the Ohio, from Maine to Minnesota, and even from far-off California men rushed to arms with camp-meeting fervor. "Everybody eagerly asks everybody else if he's going to enlist," wrote a Detroit reporter on April 19, and the same might have been said of almost any other town or city in the North.[2]

The tremendous surge of patriotism manifested itself in various ways. In Bangor, Maine, schoolgirls pounced on a boy who came among them wearing a palmetto flag and destroyed the despised emblem. At Pembroke, Maine, a lawyer of alleged Southern sympathies was threatened with a ducking in a river, and at Dexter, Maine, a group of volunteers "rode a Mr. Augustus Brown . . . on a rail for . . . saying that he hoped every one of them would be shot." [3] Elsewhere Southern sympathizers, real or imagined, were pelted with rotten eggs or otherwise put in their places. And if traitors could not be found, patriots full of excitement and liquor often fell to fighting among themselves.[4]

Epidemics of "Star-Spangled Fever" struck many communities. The Detroit *Free Press* noted on April 18:

> The Star-Spangled Banner rages most furiously. The old inspiring national anthem is played by the bands, whistled by the juveniles, sung in the theatres . . . sentimentally lisped at every piano by patriotic young ladies, ground out on church organs . . . hammered on tin pans by small boys, and we had almost said barked by the dogs. The banner itself . . . floats proudly and beautifully in every direction . . . from the roofs of houses . . . from all public places. . . . Omnibus men decorate their vehicles and horses.

Little wonder that the same article announced: "The supply of bunting is rapidly becoming scarce."[5]

Preachers catching the spirit of the hour, and perhaps not unmindful of the drawing power of martial themes on sinners as well as saints, proclaimed the gospel of patriotism from the pulpit. In Bath, Maine, the Episcopal rector was the first to enlist, and in Madison, Wisconsin, on the Sunday after Lincoln's call for troops the Reverend William Brisbane of the Baptist church, a recent volunteer in a local company, preached his farewell sermon in his shiny new uniform.[6]

The women were the most spirited of patriots. Usually their activities consisted of displaying flags, singing martial songs, raising funds and making clothing for the volunteers. But occasionally they chose more aggressive roles. The ladies of Skowhegan, Maine, for example, on a Saturday afternoon in April rolled out the village artillery piece and treated their neighbors to "a salute of thirty-four guns."[7]

For males the order of the day was volunteering, and the fever extended to all ages and classes. At Shenango, Pennsylvania, the young boys organized a "company," elected a thirteen-year-old captain and held weekly drills in the schoolyard to the accompaniment of a dinner-bucket drum corps.[8] And in Belfast, Maine, thirty-odd veterans of the War of 1812 responded to Lincoln's initial call by forming themselves into a company and tendering their services to the state.[9]

Nowhere was the war spirit more rampant than in the classrooms. At Bowdoin College the students on hearing of Sumter's fall rang the chapel bell, displayed the national colors, defiantly waved a skull-and-crossbones banner and shortly began daily drills on the campus.[10] In Oxford, Ohio, Ozra J. Dodds, a senior in the college, rose in the chapel and proposed organization of a University Rifle Company. Within a few minutes 160 students and local boys signed up for service in what was to become Company B, Twentieth Ohio Volunteers. Girls of the neighboring female college, not to be outdone, set themselves to making red shirts, flannel underclothing and a flag for the volunteers.[11]

From the University of Wisconsin a student wrote his parents on April 20: "Madison is in a great state of military excitement. The fever has penetrated the University walls. Seven of the boys have enlisted in the Governor's Guards." Four days later he reported the dismissal of his geometry class "to see the soldiers off." At the University of Michigan five companies were organized within a fortnight of Sumter's surrender.[12]

The war fever was rampant at Oberlin College where the quick formation of a company among the boys was matched by the organization of a "Florence Nightingale Association" by the girls. Effects of martial activities on the academic program were vividly revealed by a student who wrote on April 20 to his brother: "War! and volunteers are the only topics of conversation or thought. The lessons today have been a mere form. I cannot study. I cannot sleep, I cannot work, and I dont know as I can write." [13]

In most cases college authorities seem to have admonished their students against hasty enlistment. One faculty, with a view to satisfying the martial urge of their charges without forfeiting their presence in the classroom, hired a drillmaster to conduct military exercises on the campus.[14] But in a few instances college authorities took the lead in the patriotic movement. President Burgess of Eureka College in Illinois became the first captain of a company made up largely of his students, and President Hovey of the Illinois State Normal College took command of the Thirty-third Illinois Infantry, the roster of which included so many faculty and students that it came to be known as the "Normal Regiment." [15] President Hovey eventually became a general.[16]

The action of the colleges was not without parallel among lower-ranking institutions. The lone teacher in a log school near Wayzata, Minnesota, a boy not yet twenty years old, responded to the Fort Sumter crisis by immediately suspending operations, though the regular closing time was only a week away, and taking about half of his "grown" students to Fort Snelling to enlist.[17]

The war spirit reached far beyond the halls of learning. Jacob Dodson, a colored man employed in the United States Senate, offered to the Federal authorities 300 free Negroes for defense of the nation's capital. And a few days later the Secretary of War received from far-off

Minnesota a message stating that Chief Pug-o-na-ke-shick, or Hole-in-the-Day, of the Chippewa Nation, "deeply impressed with the sentiments of patriotism, and grateful for the aid and protection extended to him and his people . . . desires . . . to tender . . . the services of himself and 100 [or more] . . . of his headmen and braves to aid in defending the Government and its institutions against the enemies of the country." [18]

The problem of responsible authorities during this flood tide of patriotism was not to obtain men but to hold volunteers to manageable numbers. Governor Dennison of Ohio, of whom Lincoln on April 15 requested thirteen regiments, wrote a week later that "owing to an unavoidable confusion in the first hurry and enthusiasm of . . . our people," a much larger force had already mobilized. Indeed, he added, "without seriously repressing the ardor of the people, I can hardly stop short of twenty regiments." [19] What a pity that the government did not accept and constitute as a national reserve this horde of men who in the spring of 1861 so eagerly sought service! More than a million recruits could have been had without difficulty then. But within a year volunteering had slowed down to a trickle and before Second Manassas, despite all sorts of inducements in the form of bounties, authorities had to resort to threats of draft in order to meet the President's modest calls for troops.[20]

The first men who went to war usually entered the service as members of militia companies. These organizations were for the most part military only in name, their peacetime activities rarely going beyond holiday parades and ceremonial functions. Of later recruits, some were inducted into Regular Army units and others went as conscripts or substitutes. But the overwhelming majority of those who wore the blue entered the army as members of volunteer regiments formed under state auspices and mustered into Federal service for periods ranging from three months to three years.

Going-away experiences of the volunteer organizations were very much the same throughout the country, and except for a decline in enthusiasm the pattern did not greatly change with the passing of time.

The lead in forming units was usually taken by men who aspired to be officers. Often governors promised colonelcies to prominent citizens who would raise regiments, and the prospective colonels in turn offered captaincies to friends on condition that they recruit the minimum number required for a company. In some cases the impetus came from the other direction, with would-be officers signing up men and then using the lists as claims for commissions.

Those attempting to organize units, whatever their authority, solicited recruits by personal appeal, broadsides and advertisements in newspapers. After bounties became the vogue, these were given prominent place in all promotional activities. Sometimes commission-bent recruiters supplemented authorized bounties with financial inducements of their own, though this practice on occasion resulted in men playing one promoter against another to force up the bid.[21]

Mass meetings were a standard feature of recruiting efforts. Here leading citizens joined prospective officers in regaling audiences with oratorical outbursts full of allusions to country and flag and breathing defiance at slaveholders and traitors. Between speeches, brass bands played patriotic airs. If veterans of former wars were available they were featured as speakers or as adornments for the platform. The total effect of these influences was sometimes tremendous, especially in the early days of the war, so that when the cry "Who will come up and sign the roll?" was given at the end, men rushed to the front like seekers at a backwoods revival, each vying with the other to be first on the list.[22]

Once a nucleus was signed up, the recruits were put to the task of bringing in others. At speakings, picnics and other public gatherings volunteers were given special recognition. The girls helped recruiting efforts mightily by showing a preference for those who responded quickly to the country's call. A timid young Hoosier, delightfully surprised at the attention received from a local belle after volunteering, wrote in his journal: "If a fellow wants to go with a girl now he had better enlist. The girls sing 'I am Bound to be a Soldier's Wife or Die an Old Maid.'"[23]

An effective means of adding members was demonstrated by the Eighth Kentucky Regiment, which in the process of recruitment made the rounds of the community picnics. Here, as one of the veterans recalled, "we hoisted our flag, headed by our three amateur musicians, playing their one and only tune, 'Sally is the gal for me.' As each recruit fell into the moving line, loud cheers rent the air."[24]

The filling up of units was accompanied by steps for provision of clothing and equipment. From necessity and inclination commanders looked to state and local sources for initial outfitting. Some of the governors were able to provide their units with handsome and durable suits of uniform pattern, color and material. But many of the early organizations had to go to war in their gaudy militia regalia. Heavy reliance for initial needs was placed on women's sewing groups and while the results sometimes were gratifying, in many cases the handiwork indicated more zeal than skill.[25]

In consequence of these various expedients Federal encampments of 1861 and even later were marked by the greatest diversity of clothing. Almost every conceivable color and shade was represented. Materials ranged from broadcloth to satinette, and styles from the outlandish fezzes and bloomers of the Zouaves to "stiff and old-fashioned" suits of ancient militia organizations. In some regiments each company had a distinctive uniform.[26]

Soldier letters and diaries indicate that gray was a favorite color among early volunteer units. Indeed, in the first months of the war gray seems to have been almost as popular in Northern as in Southern camps. This circumstance led to unfortunate results on more than one battlefield. At First Manassas the gray-clad soldiers of the Second Wisconsin were said to have been mistaken for Confederates and fired on by their comrades, and at Cheat Mountain a similar circumstance caused Ohio troops to shoot at soldiers of the Thirteenth Indiana, killing and wounding several of them.[27] At Wilson's Creek early in 1862 Louisiana and Arkansas troops were allowed to maneuver within musket range of Sigel's command because the opposing troops wore the same color.[28] Three days before Shiloh, Grant reported that some of his men were "still in the gray uniform," owing to their reluctance to swap the good-quality gray garments for the shoddy blue dispensed by the quartermasters.[29] Not until the summer of 1862 could the term boys in blue be applied accurately to the Union forces, and deviations were to be found occasionally until the close of the war.

The story of equipment was about the same as that of clothing. Shifting in large measure for themselves in the early days, commanders armed their men with a miscellany ranging from modern Sharps rifles to obsolete muskets hardly less dangerous to the wielder than to the target. Ignorance of the volunteers combined with the generosity of local donors to weight the soldiers down with such extras as dueling pistols, drinking tubes, havelocks, nightcaps, bulletproof vests and vicious-appearing daggers.[30]

Sometimes failure of authorities to provide necessary clothing and equipment forced the disbandment of volunteer organizations. Several three-month Massachusetts regiments were discharged in August 1861

after vainly waiting eight weeks for arms. Some of the members registered their protest by sending a box of wooden muskets to the governor.
And one of them had his say on the clothing situation by covering a
gaping hole in his trousers with a shingle on which was inscribed "The
Last Shift of a Soldier." [31]

Recruits were supposed to be checked for physical fitness, but apparently among early volunteers this provision was sometimes overlooked.[32]
And in many cases where it was observed the examination was a farce.
Private Charles Barker of Massachusetts wrote in November 1861 that
the examining surgeon felt his collarbones and said, "You have pretty
good health don't you?" When Barker replied affirmatively the doctor
remarked, "You look as though you did." After inquiring if the recruit
had fits or piles the examiner marked him able for service.[33]

Leander Stillwell of Illinois gave the following account of his examination:

The surgeon, at that time, was a fat, jolly old doctor by the name of
Leonidas Clemmons. I was about scared to death when the Captain
presented me to him, and requested him to examine me. I reckon the
good old doctor saw I was frightened, and he began laughing heartily
and saying some kind things about my general appearance. He requested
me to stand up straight, then gave me two or three little sort of "love
taps" on the chest, turned me round, ran his hands over my shoulders,
back, and limbs, laughing and talking all the time, then whirled me to
the front, and rendered judgment on me as follows: "Ah, Capt. Reddish!
I only wish you had a hundred such fine boys as this one! He's all right,
and good for the service." [34]

But the crowning commentary on the ineffectiveness of the examining
system is the number of women who, passing for males, succeeded in
entering the volunteer ranks.[35]

Little wonder that Frederick Law Olmsted after a fifteen-month investigation of recruiting conditions in the army reported to Lincoln in
July 1862: "The careless and superficial medical inspection of recruits
made at least 25 per cent of the volunteer army raised last year not
only utterly useless, but a positive incumbrance and embarrassment." [36]
Subsequently detailed examining procedures were prescribed by the medical department, but these were in large measure nullified by failure to
provide anything like an adequate staff of examiners.[37]

Not the least important of organizational activities was the selection
of an appropriate name for the volunteer company. Among early choices

were to be found such inspiring designations as "Union Clinchers," the "Oxford Bears," the "Douglas Guards," the "Cass Light Infantry," the "Huron Rangers" and the "Detroit Invincibles." [38]

At some point in the process of organization the volunteers moved to camp. Usually the initial encampment was a temporary one located in the home community, but occasionally the regimented life was begun at points of rendezvous or camps of instruction farther removed, though normally not so far away as to prevent exchange of visits with the home-folk. Indeed, some of the volunteers loaded wives and children on company wagons and took them along to camp, though a short stay among the soldiers usually sufficed to demonstrate the impracticability of this procedure.[39]

Among initial activities of camp was the designation of commissioned and noncommissioned officers. Election of captains and lieutenants by the men and of colonels and majors by company officers was common practice, with governors issuing commissions to those so selected. But frequently, if not usually, the voting was a mere formality, it being a foregone conclusion that persons responsible for recruiting the units, or previously approved by the governor, would become the officers. That highhanded tactics were not unknown is evidenced by an Illinois soldier's notation in his diary: "In the evening Col. Cumming meets us in our barracks and tells us that Adj. Gen. Fuller insisted on hurrying up our regimental organization—*that he (Col. C.) not knowing of any objection on our part (?) (!) had our acting officers . . . mustered into the U. S. Service . . .* that an election was only a matter of *form* (!) then put it to us by *word of mouth*, whether or not we would sustain him, and no one *daring* to object, he was sustained—This is called an election! What a farce!" [40]

Freedom of choice was allowed most often for lieutenancies, and the filling of these lowly positions, which some of the men referred to as disparagingly as "pumpkin rinds" (suggested by the appearance of the shoulder straps), might be accompanied by lively electioneering on the part of the candidates.[41] It was not uncommon for defeated aspirants to quit the service.

Elections, whether free or rigged, were often followed by speechmaking, feasting and drinking, with successful candidates serving as hosts to both officers and men.[42]

Induction into Federal service, preceded in some cases by muster in as state troops, was another incident of early camp life. The Federal ceremony, conducted by a Regular Army officer, was an impressive one.

After being formed by company the men and officers were inspected individually and collectively, following which they were required to take the oath of allegiance as prescribed in the tenth article of war. Then came the reading of the articles of war, a long and tedious exercise which regulations required to be repeated twice each year.[43] Sometimes reading of the articles preceded the swearing in, but the inadvisability of this procedure was indicated by an Iowa volunteer who wrote in his diary in June 1861: "The fact that nearly all violations . . . called for the death penalty or some other severe punishment so depressed a number of the boys that six of them hurriedly made their exit and were not thereafter heard of in connection with the company."[44]

The parting words of many mothers to their soldier sons were "Send me your picture." And during their first weeks in uniform countless soldiers visited the "daguerrean artists" who set up shop in camp or in near-by towns.[45] Many Yanks had never before confronted a photographer, and this no doubt accounts for the stiffness which characterized the "likenesses" or "shadows" sent back to the homefolk.

No one could consider himself a soldier until he learned to march and use his weapons. Hence instruction in the drill and the manual of arms as laid down by Winfield Scott, William J. Hardee or Silas Casey was an important part of initial activities. Since volunteer officers usually were chosen for popularity or political prestige rather than military accomplishment, guidance in rudimentary training frequently had to be sought from other sources. Fortunately most units had in their ranks veterans of the Mexican War or immigrants with European service who could act as drillmasters. The aid rendered by foreigners, schooled in the excellent systems of Prussia, France, Switzerland and other Western European countries, in training the Union forces was tremendous, and their service in this connection deserves far more recognition than it has received.

One of the greatest obstacles to training was the lack of system and direction. The present generation, accustomed as it is to an elaborate hierarchy of schools and a profusion of literature covering in detail all phases of training, has difficulty in appreciating the vastly different situation prevailing in Civil War times. Officer-training schools worthy of the name did not exist. Leaders had to learn their duties on the job from poorly written and skimpy manuals. Many regiments set up their own schools for officers and noncommissioned officers, but these, owing to lack of guidance and experienced personnel, often hobbled along in the fashion of the blind leading the blind. The manuals outlined fundamentals for the school of the soldier and for company, battalion and brigade, but uniform progressive-training programs prepared in higher headquarters, with time allotments for the various subjects and stages, were unknown. The same could be said of charts, models, slides and other streamlined training aids which did so much to simplify and vivify instruction in World War II.

The training problem might have been eased had the Regular Army been distributed among volunteer organizations as cadremen or instructors, but the War Department elected to keep regular organizations intact for use as a steadying or saving leaven in battle. Occasionally West Point cadets and Regular Army sergeants were used, apparently on a loan basis, for instructional purposes.

For the most part early volunteer organizations had to work out their own salvation, though some higher commanders, notably McClellan, and some lesser ones, with Sherman affording a good example, gave effective guidance to subordinate units.

A few of the volunteer organizations had the benefit of systematic preparation in their home states. In Michigan, Fort Wayne, near Detroit, was designated in June 1861 as a camp of instruction for the Fifth, Sixth and Seventh Regiments. Officers and noncommissioned officers were sent to this camp in advance of the privates. Here in skeleton groups, after being instructed by the most accomplished drill sergeants chosen from among their number, the leaders took turns commanding one another. Thus by the time the fillers arrived the instructors had acquired both a knowledge of fundamentals and a degree of self-confidence.[46]

But such well-conceived procedure was highly exceptional. As a general rule, officers and men started out together in equal ignorance and blundered along with inadequate equipment through varying periods of training. The results were pitiful. Infantrymen trying to execute the order to charge bayonet stuck one another, and cavalrymen drilling with sabers frightened their horses into running away.[47] Typical conditions among early volunteer units were described by a Pennsylvania soldier in the summer of 1861: "Col. Roberts has showed himself to be ignorant of the most simple company movements. There is a total lack of system about our regiment. . . . Nothing is attended to at the proper time, nobody looks ahead to the morrow, and business heads to direct are wanting. . . . We can only be justly called a mob & one not fit to face the enemy." [48]

One of the most grievous deficiencies of early training—and it persisted to an amazing extent throughout the war—was the lack of target practice. A few regiments did have systematic instruction in musketry and one commander even had enough imagination to set up replicas of Jeff Davis for his men to shoot at, but references to marksmanship exercises are notable chiefly for their absence.[49]

In some instances training was not only poor but woefully abbreviated. Of a unit organized as late as August 1862 a soldier wrote: "Within three weeks from the day this regiment was mustered into service, and before it had ever had what could properly be called a battalion drill, it was in the battle of Antietam." [50]

Activities on the drill grounds were accompanied by indoctrination in less formal aspects of camp life. Individuals of like habits and tastes soon discovered one another and formed messes, the members of which ate together and took turns in preparing meals. Often they occupied the same quarters and some even adopted nicknames. Private James Snell and his twelve associates in Company A, Eighty-second Illinois Regiment, called themselves the "Hyena Mess," with individual designations as follows:

Soldier	Nickname	Position
Snell	Elephant	President
Murray	Bulldog Clipper	Correspondent
Ellis	Greyhound	Grand Scribbler
Barnes	Rhinoceros	Reporter (Shorthand)
Leslie	Piss-ant	Artist
Murphy	Spaniel	Fry-master
Harrington	Jackal	Historian
Kutcher	Weasel	Absent, in his hole, asleep
Lane	Buffalo	Inspector-General
Swanson	Tiger	Scout & Foragemaster
Simpson	Monkey	Acrobat & Tumbler
Sanderson	Fox	Chesterfield gent.
Miller (cook)	Chicken	Caterer General [51]

Individual reactions to the new way of life were generally favorable. "I and the rest of the boys are in fine spirits . . . feeling like larks," wrote a New Yorker shortly after enlistment, while an Illinois youth reported: "I never enjoyed anything in the world as I do this life." [52] Youngsters, especially those from the country, were more enthusiastic than older men. Rural boys were thrilled by the new sights, the teeming crowds and the constant activity, and most of them found camp conditions no more uncomfortable and military duties no more onerous than those known at home. Some were startled by the abundance of material things which army life afforded. An Iowa farmer recently inducted wrote his homefolk that "I have got the best suit of clothes that I [ever] had in my life"—a statement often heard among rural recruits—and a little later he added, "I was perfectly surprised to find such good accommodations." [53] This rustic, like thousands of his kind, found in soldiering a thoroughly agreeable life.

At the other extreme were men who utterly detested the army. A few objected to the lack of privacy, some to the rampant ungodliness, others to the discipline and still others to the deprivation and hardship. "The way we have been treated is enough to make a preacher swear almost," wrote Private O. W. Norton from a camp in Pennsylvania. "We are cheated in our rations about half the time. Our clothes are all dropping off from us." [54] Another Yank of five weeks' service featured by long marches complained: "If there is anything peculiarly attractive in marching from 10 to 20 miles a day under a scorching sun with a good mule load, and sinking up to one's knees in the 'Sacred Soil' at each Step, my mind is not of a sufficiently poeticle nature to apreciate it." [55] So strong was aversion to the new order in some instances, owing to the combined influences of poor leadership, discomfort and homesickness, that units almost disintegrated before their officers could get them accepted into Federal service. In such cases a hard rain at a critical juncture would probably have spelled the difference between going south or going home.

But a majority of soldiers were neither exuberant nor mournful in their initial reactions. And whatever their first attitudes, the passing of time tended to bring all to the common denominator of good-natured conformity—though not without the chronic growling that has ever characterized the American soldier.

At some time during the course of their early training, officers and men put on their best appearance and manners for the flag presentation. The colors were often the handiwork of local women, and the donor almost invariably was one of the feminine patriots. The presentation ceremony was frequently the occasion of a vast assembly of relatives and friends.

When the Fourth Michigan received its colors at Adrian on June 21, 1861, special trains brought in hundreds of citizens from the surrounding country. At 2:30 in the afternoon the regiment in full uniform and "with such equipment as it had" formed in a hollow square on the local parade ground. Presently a carriage brought to the platform within the enclosure Mrs. Josephine Wilcox, accompanied by three maids of honor and the regimental color sergeant. Following the unfurling of the flag, made by the ladies of Adrian, Mrs. Wilcox addressed the soldiers:

When you follow this standard in your line of march or on the field of battle, and you see it waving in lines of beauty and gleams of brightness, remember the trust we have placed in your hands. We will follow you in our hearts with our hopes and our prayers. You are the sons of brave men, who under this banner achieved the glorious victory of our national independence. . . . We are the daughters of the brave women of '76. . . . Our trial has come, our spirits waken and we feel the blood of heroes stirring in our veins. The eyes of the world are placed upon our republican institutions. . . . Sustain this banner for the love you bear to woman, for under no standard in the wide world is woman so blessed as are Columbia's daughters. . . . You are to go forth to the conflict to strike for . . . our noble Constitution, for freedom of speech, for freedom of thought, for God and the right.

Then Mrs. Wilcox soared to her climax:

The eagle of American liberty from her mountain eyrie has at intervals during the past few years given us faint warnings of danger. Now she swoops down on spreading pinions with unmistakable notes of alarm; her cries have reached the ears of freemen, and brave men rush to arms. She has perched on this banner which we now give to your keeping. Let your trust be in the God of battles to defend it.

Colonel Woodbury, responding for the regiment, promised that the trust reposed in him and his men would not be abused; that the flag would "never be given up to traitors" or disgraced, but would be defended by himself and his associates with their lives and its luster increased by deeds of valor. The colonel's stirring pledge was endorsed by prolonged cheering of the men.

After other speeches by prominent citizens the soldiers treated the crowd to a series of battalion and regimental maneuvers.[56]

At Detroit the Ninth Michigan's colonel, W. W. Duffield, received the regimental colors from the hand of his father, the eminent minister, George Duffield, who made a long speech closing with the words: "Human government . . . is the ordinance of God. . . . Rebellion therefore against a lawful government, lawfully administered, is rebellion against God." The son in receiving the emblem remarked: "We wish no conquest. We desire no subjugation. . . . Our swords are drawn for the Union and our watchword shall be 'the Union, now and forever, one and inseparable.' " [57]

These scenes and these sentiments were repeated with only slight variation throughout the length and breadth of the land as the volunteers were mobilized for the mission before them. "The University Recruits" of Upper Iowa University were presented colors made by the girls of that institution. In appreciation of this service the boys permitted the girls to choose the color sergeant. At the balloting held in the reception room of the Ladies' Hall, Henry J. Grannis was elected standard-bearer. As it turned out the girls chose the regimental color-bearer, for when the university boys became Company C of the Twelfth Iowa, Grannis was elevated to that position.[58]

Not all the ceremonies were marked by the eloquence or beauty which characterized those described above. One of the less pretentious affairs was described by a Massachusetts lieutenant who participated in it:

This eve we were presented with a flag by the ladies of this town. A very homely young lady (though she was the best looking one in town) made a speach which she learned (at least she thought so, but I did not for she went through with [it] about as smooth as one might come down a rocky hill in the dark). Col. Gordon then answered it. Three cheers were then proposed for him which sounded a good deal as old bad Fali [the lieutenant's cat] did when her tail was stepped on. The officers of the regiment then gave the ladies three cheers which made them turn pale. The band play[ed], we took the [flag] . . . and went home.[59]

After varying periods of training in home areas came the trip to a camp near the scene of hostilities. The general direction of the "seat of war," as the fighting zone was usually called, for most units was southward—to the environs of Washington for Eastern regiments and to Missouri, Kentucky or Tennessee for Western organizations. But there was considerable deviation from this general pattern, with Western troops making the long journey to Maryland or Virginia and Eastern units going to Tennessee or Kentucky.

The southward move was usually preceded by rumors and false starts. During the final days before departure many Yanks received furloughs to bid their families good-by. The home farewells were solemn occasions often marked by tears of mothers or wives and painful silence on the part of male members of the household.

Public leave-taking of the unit, when finally the day of departure came, presented a different appearance. At the depot or wharf, speeches,

MOURNFUL ONES AT SICK CALL
Drawing by Charles W. Reed

DIGGING IN

Drawing by Charles W. Reed

music, bouquets and farewell gifts were the order of the day. The first troops to leave Madison, Wisconsin, in April 1861 were addressed at the depot "by Judge Vilas & Gov. Randall & the Star Spangled Banner was sung by Miss Susan Devin, actress. . . . Norcross & Ball of the Univ. boys stood it well, but Miller Wyse & Smith were much affected." [60]

In August 1861 the citizens of Kalamazoo gave the Sixth Michigan Regiment a tremendous send-off. The long train consisting of five baggage cars, twenty-two first-class passenger coaches and "the magnificent directors' car" was pulled by the railroad company's two crack engines, the "Ranger" and the "Stag Hound." The lead locomotive was elaborately decorated with banners "and a neatly executed head ornament consisting of two clasped hands supporting a shield, the whole being surmounted with a circular piece on which was painted 'death to traitors.'" The directors' car was occupied by the officers while the men rode the coaches. The railroad's favorite conductor was in charge of the train, and the superintendent went along to see that everyone was made comfortable.[61]

Incidents of departure ranged from the ridiculous to the sublime. When the Second Massachusetts entrained at Boston a mother said earnestly to the commander, "We look to you, Col. Gordon, to bring all of these young men back in safety to their homes." [62] A few hours' delay in the departure of the Sixth Massachusetts was utilized by one of the members for arranging a last-minute marriage. Accompanied by his lieutenant this soldier went to the city hall for the license, engaged the services of a clergyman and set out for the home of his lady love. And there, according to the lieutenant, "At the Early morning hour while all were moved to tears the marriage rite was performed." The ceremony was completed in time for the groom to leave with the regiment at nine o'clock.[63]

Once the train or ship was under way, the soldiers' spirits took an upward turn. Joking, pranking and general merriment became the order of the day. In many instances the festive bent was helped along by drinking. A New York volunteer wrote his mother on arrival in Virginia: "After we got out of their hearing the boys acted as if they had forgoten their mothers and . . . wives, that they had just . . . left . . . with tears in their eyesNot but a few minutes before the band boys handed wround the whisky bottle among themselves . . . one of the members of the band got drunk." [64] Another New Yorker who made the southward trip by boat in 1863 wrote: "Whiskey was freely used. . . . I 'piled in' down in the hole with a man half tight, while those that were wholly so made merry until a late hour . . . poor liquor was sold for a dollar a pint." [65] Now and then a volunteer made bold and unsteady by liquor would fall from the top of the cars or tumble overboard with fatal consequences. On rare occasions some sot would go berserk. A Connecticut sergeant en route to Annapolis recorded such an instance: "During the night a man on board was taken with the tremens and of all the Horrid noises and actions I ever saw . . . it took five strong men to hold him." [66]

If drink was not provided by friends at the parting or if the initial supply needed replenishing, soldiers now and then made raids on taverns along the way. A Pennsylvania regiment bound for Baltimore stole a keg of beer at "little York" and took it aboard their train. Here one of the soldiers beat the head in with the butt of his musket, but with disappointing results. "The beer shot up into the air 15 feet like a fountain & fell foaming on everything & person . . . very little of the beer was left." [67]

It is not meant to imply that southward movements were liquor orgies or that drinking was universal. Many soldiers deplored the conviviality and some took refuge in spiritual contemplation. But the number of these who resorted to the Bible seems less than those who sought the bottle.

The festive mood of the war-bound volunteers frequently found expression in song. Some regiments moved south to the strains of "The Star-Spangled Banner," while others tauntingly blended their voices in "Dixie." The 116th Pennsylvania sang "Johnny Is Gone for a Soldier" as their train rattled southward, while Germans of the Ninth Ohio made the coaches ring with their native "Morgenroth." [68] After Lincoln's call of July 1862 for 300,000 troops, departing volunteers began to sing,

> We are coming Father Abraham
> Three hundred thousand more.[69]

But the favorite going-away song for the war as a whole was the soul-stirring "John Brown's Body." [70]

Some units needed all assistance that song or stimulants would afford to alleviate the discomfort and hardship of travel. Few volunteers journeying by train enjoyed the luxuries provided for the Sixth Michigan as already described. In a far greater number of instances, accommodations consisted of boxcars equipped with backless benches of rough plank and inadequately, if at all, provided with heat, ventilation, food, water and sanitary facilities. Inferior tracks and poor roadbeds made for rough riding. Breakdowns were commonplace and wrecks frequent. Soldiers often cleared the stuffy atmosphere of the crowded cars by "smashing a good allowance of holes through the sides and ends."[71] On reaching their destination officers and men were sometimes so exhausted that they threw themselves on the station platform and slept for several hours.[72]

Soldiers traveling by river boat seem to have been relatively comfortable, but those who made long journeys by coastal craft were often subjected to extreme hardship because of crowded quarters, inadequate provisioning and rough seas. A soldier borne by steamer from Portland, Maine, to Fort Monroe with "men packed in a nasty hold so close that they could scarcely lie down . . . a part of them a drunken boisterous pack" compared his experience with that of slaves transported from Africa as human cattle.[73] And another whose route was from New York to Annapolis wrote: "We were huddled together more like a lot of pigs than human beings. . . . I was compelled to sleep on the floor. . . . Our rations we could hardly force down. In fact, most of it was rotten or nearly so. The water was very dirty. Yet we were glad to get enough of it."[74]

To some expeditions hurricanes and seasickness brought peril and misery. "It bloud up a storm and knocked us about," a Pennsylvanian wrote after landing in South Carolina, "and made some of the boys very sick and ye gods what a time some was praying and some was swaring and others wanted to be throd overboard."[75]

Some of those who made the long voyage from the East in Butler's Louisiana invasion of 1862 seem to have suffered most. One of the ships, the *Mississippi*, ran aground near Port Royal in sight of Rebel guns, forcing the dumping of many provisions and requiring a whole company to pump day and night to keep the vessel afloat.[76] Deprivation, sickness, gloom and death marked the cruise of the transport *North America*. The letter-diary of a Maine officer on board gave the following account:

Feb. 8th [1862] Saild. . . . Quite a number crazy drunk. . . . 300 men sea sick.

Feb. 12th. We have at least 300 men on board more than the ship can decently accommodate in the morning the air & filth between decks is enough to sicken a dog.

Feb. 15th. Making no progress. Uncomfortable hot could not sleep last night. . . . We have plenty of provisions but the arrangements for cooking are insufficient & the men complain bitterly for want of 'Grub'

. . . today we find that we are short of water & commenced dealing it out by the pint. . . .
Feb. 16th. . . . The man that died [of diphtheria] was buried in the Sea. . . .
Feb. 24th. . . . We feel anxious about our provisions & water—dirt & disease the men between decks are getting lousey. O horrid I imagine they are on me every day.
Feb. 26th. . . . Another man died of lung fever. . . .
Feb. 28th. . . . it is a hard place for a sick man between deck when 900 are crowded in—dirty, lousey, bad air it is a wonder how they live. . . .
March 4. . . . The squall struck us with terrible force. . . . No one could walk or stand without holding on with both hands. . . . Night came upon us without any abatement. . . .
March 6th. Another man died yesterday. . . . We are all getting heartily tired of the voyage.
March 8th. Made . . . [Ship] Island this morning. . . . We rent the air with cheers.[77]

A Vermont corporal on board the *Wallace*, another ship in the Butler expedition, revealed similar experiences in his journal:

March 12th. Sick myself. O dear, sick enough: sea-sick and sick of the sea. Wish I was home sugaring off for Aunt Elvira, or some of the girls. Wind due South and . . . hot as harvest.
March 13th. Dead calm, and all hands dead sick. . . .
March 18th. . . . A sad sight this evening;—a poor old father burying his son at sea. . . . The body was wrapped in a blanket, with iron slugs tied to the feet and slid over the side on a plank.
April 5th. Made Ship Island, after having sailed four weeks with almost nothing to eat, and much of the time with only a half pint of water per day. . . . Much of the time we had a little hard bread and salt, two or three times, boiled potatoes and salt, sometimes a little meat with our "white oak chips" [hardtack]. . . .[78]

Volunteers who traveled southward by land or river early in the war had their journey lightened by enthusiastic attentions of people along the way. For many the trip was a series of ovations, marked by speeches, music, feasting, handshaking and kissing. Members of the First Vermont, as they proceeded from Bradford to New York in May 1861, at Bellows Falls were "met by the citizens. The [town] Band and the Fire Company . . . escorted [us] through the streets . . . to partake of refreshments prepared by the ladies." At other villages cannon were fired and at Troy, New York, the townsmen fed the soldiers at the depot and the officers at a hotel.[79] A soldier of the Second Michigan wrote of his trip from Detroit to Washington in June 1861: "We was treated as good as a company could bee at every station their was a crowd to cheer us and at about every other one they had something for us to eat. We got kisses from the girls at a good many plaises and we returned the same to them." At Baltimore, where the Sixth Massachusetts had been attacked by a mob in April, he reported "a little fus with the rebles" during which one of his comrades was hit with a stone, but the soldier shot his assailant "ded on the spot," after which the regiment moved on to its destination.[80]

None of the early organizations was sent southward more enthusiastically than the First Minnesota, concerning whose river-land journey a supernumerary wrote:

After leaving Has[tings] we landed at Red Wing, Lake City, Wabashan and Winona, at which places great scenes were Enacted. . . . The good steamer Northern Bell kept us upon the *Father of Waters* until Eleven O'clock that night. We were transferred to a train of cars immediately and started for Chicago. . . . All along the road through Wis., Ill., Ind., Ohio, Penn., Md, we were cheered from almost every home. The boys tired themselves more yelling than from any thing they had to perform. In Pitts. we were treated to a supply of warm coffee. . . . At every station we found old men and women ready to greet us . . . and in one instance an old lady, grey headed and trembling sat in her door as we passed and blessed us in words & actions so fervently that she resembled a spiritual medium passing through her gyrations.[81]

Many soldiers from both West and East passed through Philadelphia, and most of them who stopped in the City of Brotherly Love seem to have enjoyed the hospitality of the Cooper's Shop, the Civil War's most famous volunteer way station, where within a year 87,518 transient soldiers were fed and refreshed.[82] The dining room, sleeping quarters and other facilities were operated on a twenty-four-hour basis, and apparently no man in uniform was turned away. Soldier letters and diaries paid the highest tribute to the fare and the treatment.

Other way stations maintained a high order of hospitality throughout the war, but the same could not be said of the citizenry as a whole. For as the conflict extended from months to years and the moving of soldiers from the hinterland to the front became a common occurrence, the enthusiasm of the people subsided and patriotic endeavor lost its sharp edge. The changed situation is vividly reflected in a Hoosier's description of his experience in Cincinnati while en route to war in September 1863:

We slept a little that night in the depot. Next morning . . . [we] had no breakfast as our haversacks were empty. About 7 o'clock we were marched to the principal part of the city . . . where we sat down in the street to wait for further orders. After waiting awhile some of the kind and benevolent Buckeyes were so generous as to pass each one of us an advertisement of a patent medicine. it was a noble present to hungry Hoosiers but poorly appreciated. In the course of time another very *savory dish* was served up to us in the shape of an advertisement telling us where we could make splendid bargains by buying rich military goods at high costly prices. . . . After a while some patriotic citizen made us each a present of Gen Logan's famous speech. Not long after American Messengers Tracts, Soldier Hymn Books &c &c were passed around. . . . About I o'clock we partook of bread, half boiled ham—coffee and an onion. . . . After our meal was finished we stood around in the market house until the rain was over when we marched to the ferry crossed over to Covington, Ky.[88]

But in the early period going to war was a tremendous picnic. The battlefield if given a thought seemed remote, and lack of martial experience made its horrors incomprehensible.[84] Hence, most Yanks gave themselves to enjoyment of the movement. Country boys, many of them having their first trips, marveled at the mysteries of trains and boats and gawked at the sights along the way. At the first opportunity they took pen in hand to tell the homefolk of the wonders of nature and the miracles of man. Struggling mightily with spelling and grammar, an Ohio rustic recently arrived in Maryland wrote to a friend:

Frank since I seen you last I hav seen the elephant. We started from urbana [Ohio] at three oclok p m . . . we run that night and the next day till ten oClock am We got to bellair on the bank of the ohio river then the thing was to get rit over again We got over and in the Cars . . . we past within 4 mils of Whelling virginia. we past through some of the damdes plases ever saw by mortel eyes. We run under som of the god dames hills it was dark as the low regeons of hell We past through one tunel too miles long . . . as we was passing from tunelton to New Crick the cars run onto a stone that would weigh 500 lbs it was put on the track by rebels it was just whair the track runs close to the river if the engen had not bin so hevy we would hav all went to hell in a pile or some other seaport. We went in to Camp four days after we left urbana.[85]

A Wisconsin boy wrote his parents on completion of the first stint of his trip:

We came in the cars to Madison from La Crosse. It was a new experience for me, I was wide awake the whole day. I was afraid we were off the track every time we crossed a switch or came to a river. At the towns the girls swarmed on the platforms to ask the boys for their pictures and to kiss the best looking ones. A young Frenchman . . . small and quick, got the most kisses. He was so short the boys held him by the legs so he could reach down out the windows to kiss the girls. Many times some old fellows held the girls up so she could be reached. It was fun anyway.[86]

Many Yanks compared what they saw with what they left behind and the new usually came off second best. "Since I left Nineveh everything has been new," wrote a provincial New Yorker, "but I must say deliver me from citty life." [87] Even Washington, to which countless Yanks eventually found their way to roam public buildings and gape at the great, proved disappointing to some. A New Englander who stopped off in the capital en route to Virginia in September 1861 noted in his diary:

We strolled from one end of the city to the other . . . we went into the Capital and in the picture galery. . . . Then ascending the stairs to the top of the building . . . had a fine view of Washington and the neighborhood, but I was struck with the mean appearance of the city of Washington with the exception of the Government Buildings there is not a building in the whole city which can be called a good one in comparison with the Stores and dwelling houses of Boston.[88]

Arrived at their southern destinations, the volunteers—now usually a part of large organizations containing a sprinkling of Regular Army officers—got down to the business of preparing for war.

At this point it is appropriate to raise the question of motives. Why did the men in blue go to war? For what were they fighting? Immediate impulses were varied. As already intimated the prevailing excitement, the lure of far places and the desire for change were dominant factors in the enlistment of many. Countless men joined up because of the example of friends and associates. A young Vermonter tied to his home by the illness of a parent revealed the force of the martial tug: "I was glad . . . to here that you had Enlisted," he wrote to a friend in June 1861. "Oh how I wish i could go I can't hardly controll myself I here the solgers druming round. If you get your eye on old Jef Davis make a cathole threw him. I am agoing to join a training Company that they are a getting up here so that I can realise a little of the fun that solgers have." [89]

The economic motive influenced many. At first thought it seems preposterous that thirteen dollars a month, the pay of infantry privates during most of the war, should be an attraction. But the first months of the war were marked by depression, and unemployment recurred periodically until 1863. Too, bounties early became a part of the recruiting system and these were steadily increased until early in 1864 a soldier was able to write: "I receive for reenlisting nearly . . . Eight hundred dolars which I shall devote to straightening things at home." [90]

If soldier pay was low, so were wages in general, and army employment had a certainty and permanence rarely found in field or factory. Duplicated frequently throughout the land was the situation of a Pennsylvanian who wrote to his wife in November 1861: "It is no use for you to fret or cry about me for you know if i could have got work i wood not have left you or the children." [91]

Financial inducement seems to have been especially cogent among the immigrants, about two million of whom had flocked to the North in the 1850s. Poverty, difficulties of employment, prior acquaintance with military life and a strong desire to acquire property combined with other influences to drive thousands of them into the army. A good case in point is that of William O. Wettleson, a Wisconsin Norwegian who wrote to his parents shortly after enlisting: "It seemed as if I were compelled to go in order to get out of debt and to buy Heddejord [a farm, apparently] which is Ingeborg's dearest wish." [92]

After resort to conscription the urge to avoid the stigma of forced service plus the desire to obtain certain privileges allowed only to volunteers, such as bounties and choice of unit, caused thousands to enlist. A leading Civil War historian, referring specifically to Ohio, characterizes the desire to avoid the draft as "the great spur to enlistment." [93]

Combination of a sense of duty and a fear of compulsion in inducing enlistment is well illustrated in the instance of a Vermonter who wrote in his diary on August 18, 1862: "Made application for membership in the 'Rutland Light Guard.' . . . God knows that the country needs men and I regard it as the duty of every able bodied man who can possibly do so to enlist at once—the sooner the better, and it is better by far to enlist voluntarily than to be dragged into the army a conscript. Nothing to me would appear more degrading." [94]

Love of country and hatred of those who seemed bent on destroying its institutions impelled many to enlist, though often patriotism was indistinguishably blended with practical urges. Sometimes idealistic sentiments were vaguely comprehended if at all, though their utterance by orators undoubtedly helped to stimulate emotions favorable to volunteering. A Detroit journalist wrote of encountering at a mass meeting in 1861 "a mild-looking blue-eyed little man [who] told us . . . that he was going to 'have his rights and stick to the constitution.' " The same reporter said of other recruits, "[They] expect to have a fight with somebody, but they dont exactly know who or what for." [95]

But some gave serious thought to their reasons for going to war and revealed considerable appreciation of the issues involved. Among these was Philip Smith, an immigrant member of the Eighth Missouri Regiment, who on July 22, 1861, wrote in his diary:

As I lay in my bed this morning I got to thinking. . . . I have left home and a good situation . . . and have grasped the weapon of death for the purpose of doing my part in defending and upholding the integrity, laws and the preservation of my adopted country from a band of contemptible traitors who would if they can accomplish their hellish designs, destroy the best and noblest government on earth, merely for the purpose of benefiting themselves on the slave question.[96]

Similar sentiments were expressed by Samuel Storrow, a Harvard student who against his parents' wishes enlisted as a corporal in the Forty-fourth Massachusetts in the fall of 1862. In a letter to his father Storrow justified his action thus:

I went to Cambridge and resumed my studies with what zeal I could. During that week we heard that the rebel forces were pushing forward and Northward. . . . I assure you, my dear father, I know of nothing in the course of my life which has caused me such deep and serious thought as this trying crisis in the history of our nation. What is the worth of this man's life or of that man's education if this great and glorious fabric of our Union . . . is to be shattered to pieces by traitorous hands. . . . If our country and our nationality is to perish, better that we should all perish with it.[97]

Hence, original impulses of individuals ranged from material considerations and a mere craving for excitement to profound idealism and hatred of traitors. It seems clear, however, that the great bulk of volunteers responded to mixed motives, none of which was deeply felt.

The same was generally true of the more permanent or basic influences. One searches most letters and diaries in vain for soldiers' comment on why they were in the war or for what they were fighting. While the men in blue were not so irreverent toward high-sounding appeals to patriotic sentiments as were their khaki-clad descendants in World War II, yet American soldiers of the 1860s appear to have been about as little concerned with ideological issues as were those of the 1940s.[98] For Billy Yank, as for his great-grandsons, the primary interests were physical comfort, food, drink, girls, furloughs, mail and gambling, in about that order, and ultimate objectives sooner or later simmered down to finishing an unpleasant though necessary job as soon as possible and getting home.

Of soldiers who did indicate personal commitment to broad issues, a few professed to be fighting for such concepts as law, liberty, freedom and righteousness. The phrase "fighting to maintain the best government on earth" was found in a number of letters. An Iowan who declared it his aim to "fight for my country so long as I can shoulder my musket" specified his objectives as "free Speach, free press and free Governments in General." [99]

Some fought to free the slaves, but a polling of the rank and file through their letters and diaries indicates that those whose primary object was the liberation of the Negroes comprised only a small part of the fighting forces. It seems doubtful that one soldier in ten at any time during the conflict had any real interest in emancipation per se. A considerable number originally indifferent or favorable to slavery eventually accepted emancipation as a necessary war measure, but in most cases their support appeared lukewarm. Even after the Emancipation Proclamation zealous advocates of the Negro's freedom were exceptional.[100]

The hordes of young men whom the historian James Ford Rhodes represents as roused to Republicanism and emancipation by *Uncle Tom's Cabin* seem either to have stayed home or to have lost the sharpness of their enthusiasm before joining the army.[101] Yanks who in their war letters and diaries revealed even a knowledge of Mrs. Stowe's hero were rare.

Among the minority whose mainspring was freedom was Chauncey H. Cooke. When Cooke, a mere boy, left home with the Twenty-fifth Wisconsin in November 1862 he was told by his father: "Be true to your country, my boy, and be true to the flag, but before your country or the flag be true to the slave." Cooke, like many other abolitionists, saw in Frémont's removal after the premature emancipation order a threat to the cause of freedom. In January 1863 he wrote: "I am awful sorry that Fremont was set down on by Lincoln. . . . I have no heart in this war if the slaves cannot be free. . . . I am disappointed in Lincoln." [102]

His first contact with Negroes in Kentucky two months later elicited the comment: "The slaves, contrabands we call them, are flocking into Columbus by the hundred. . . . I never saw a bunch of them together but I could pick out an Uncle Tom, a Quimbo, a Sambo, a Chloe an Eliza or any other character in *Uncle Tom's Cabin.*" [103]

As the regiment continued its southward course, the Negro's relation to the war was frequently discussed and Cooke often found himself on the defensive. After the fall of Vicksburg he wrote from Mississippi: "I tell the boys right to their face I am in the war for the freedom of the slave. When they talk about the saving of the Union I tell them that it is Dutch to me. I am for helping the slaves if the Union goes to smash. Most of the boys have their laugh at me for helping the 'Niggers.' " [104]

This youngster was from the Midwest whence came many others strongly imbued with antislavery principles. The cause of freedom was especially strong among Scandinavians and other immigrant groups noted for their individualism and democracy. "Is it not unnatural and inhuman," wrote a Norwegian after a close-up view of slavery in Maryland, "that in a family where there are twenty siblings of about the same color of skin, the father keeps fifteen as slaves; whereas the five are pampered dolls of fashion?" [105]

The antislavery urge was also strong among some of the native New Englanders. "Slavery must die," wrote a Vermont corporal from Louisiana, "and if the South insists on being buried in the same grave I shall see in it nothing but the retributive hand of God." [106] A Maine soldier viewed the North's failure in arms early in the war as divine punishment for acquiescing in slavery. "We well deserve it," he wrote in October 1862; "god punished Phario for keeping the children of israel in bondage and why should we go unpunished for we have committed a like sin." [107]

Massachusetts soldiers had a reputation for abolitionism which made them targets of many a jibe about the campfire. But one of the most intense enemies of slavery encountered among diarists and correspondents was Urich N. Parmelee of Connecticut who went out from Yale in 1861 as a private "to free the slave." Like other abolitionists he chafed enormously at the failure of the government to avow emancipation as an object of the war, writing bitterly to his mother before Antietam, "You cannot expect me . . . much longer to remain with this army as it is. If it does not change *soon*, either in its principles or its actions I trust in God that I shall have the moral courage to desert it." [108]

When the Emancipation Proclamation was issued Parmelee was doubtful of its execution, but as the reality of a change in the direction of the war toward freedom dawned upon him he became enthusiastic. "I do not intend to shirk now there is really something to fight for," he wrote on March 29, 1863. "I mean *Freedom*. . . . I do not expect any great success at present, but so long as I am convinced that we are on the right side I trust that no failure will dishearten me." [109]

He proved as good as his word, this earnest young follower of Henry Ward Beecher. Somewhat of a misfit in the rough and tumble of camp life, he made up in devotion what he lacked in camaraderie. Not once in his long service did he ask for a furlough, and on the field of battle he fought with reckless abandon. Gallantry in action brought promotions to captain, but he did not live to celebrate the victory he helped win. One week before Appomattox he died a hero's death at the head of his company.[110]

In marked contrast to those whose primary interest was in freeing the slaves stood a larger group who wanted no part in a war of emancipation. A soldier newspaper published at Williamsburg, Virginia, in 1862, which carried on its masthead the motto, "The Union Forever and Freedom to all," stated in the first issue: "In construing this part of our outside heading let it be distinctly understood that 'white folks' are meant. We do not wish it even insinuated that we have any sympathy with abolitionism." [111]

Some Yanks opposed making slavery an issue of the war because they thought the effect would be to prolong the conflict at an unjustifiable cost in money and lives. Others objected on the score of the slaves' ignorance and irresponsibility, while still others shrank from the thought of hordes of freedmen settling in the North to compete with white laborers and to mix with them on terms of equality. The opposition of many seemed to have no other basis than an unreasoning hatred of people with black skins.

The issuance of the Emancipation Proclamation aroused opponents of a "Negro War" to the highest level of bitterness. "Lincoln's proclamation . . . meets with denouncement among the men of the Army," wrote a soldier shortly after Antietam. "They do not wish to think that they are fighting for Negroes, but to put down the Rebelion. We must first conquer & then its time enough to talk about the *dam'd niggers*." Early in 1863 this man remarked: "I . . . would like to see the North win, but as to any interest in freeing the Negroes or in supporting the Emancipation Proclamation I in common with every other officer & soldier in the Army wash my hands of it. . . . I came out to fight for the restoration of the Union and to keep slavery as it is without going into the territories & not to free the niggers." [112]

While many men registered their protest against the proclamation by threatening to desert, and officers to resign, few appear to have taken these extreme steps.

Opposition to emancipation sometimes manifested itself in vehement denunciation of abolitionists. A Massachusetts soldier who by the summer of 1862 had come to the conclusion that the war was caused by "old fusty abolishionists like Sumner and Wilson" thought that "they ought to be made to go into the ranks and be put in the front and have to work in the trenches." [113] A like-minded New Yorker wrote from McClellan's army in July 1862 that "the men are all exasperated against the Tribune and would hang Greeley if they had their way." Of abolitionists in general he added, "The army would hang them as quick as they would a spy." [114] An Ohioan, with more brevity and less delicacy, blurted: "If some of the niger lovers want to know what the most of the Solgers think of them they think about as much as they do a reble. they think they are Shit asses." [115]

In some instances those who entered the army to fight for freedom experienced a change of heart. A Massachusetts sergeant in July 1862 stated that he had "good reason to believe there are *thousands* of men who came out here as rabid abolitionists whose ideas are now *entirely* changed." [116] This estimate appears exaggerated, but there can be no doubt that many faltered in their opposition to slavery and a few were converted to its defense. Discovery that slavery was not so bad as represented had a softening effect on some. "The more I see of slavery the more I believe we have been deceived at the North," wrote a New Hampshire private after a brief residence in Virginia. "You had ought to have seen the darkes going to church," he added, "they were as happy as clams in high water." [117]

Others were influenced by finding Negroes less ready for the responsibilities of freedom than they had expected. Some, while holding to the desirability of emancipation, became doubtful that it was worth the blood being spilled for its accomplishment. A New York artilleryman wrote in July 1863: "I am not so friendly to the Negro race as when I first read 'Uncle Tom's Cabin.' Too many good men have been killed to Establish their freedom. . . . Nearly 100 of my Battery have lost their lives." [118]

A far greater number changed in the other direction. Abolitionists usually became more intense in their hatred of bondage; many mild opponents of the institution and some who had sat on the fence became ardent advocates of freedom. And some were converted from support to denunciation of slavery. One of the factors in the metamorphosis was the shock of slavery's inhumanity as evidenced by mulattoes, shackles, scarred bodies and ignorance. But a growing belief that emancipation was essential to victory appears to have been the most cogent influence. A Minnesotan in March 1863 explained his change thus:

> I have never been in favor of the abolition of slavery until since this war has detirmend me in the conviction that it is a greater sin than our Government is able to stand—and now I go in for a war of emancipation and I am ready and willing to do my share of the work. I am satesfied that slavery is . . . an institution that belonged to the dark ages—and that it ill becomes a nation of our standing to perpetuate the barbarous practice. It is opposed to the Spirit of the age—and in my opinion this Rebelion is but the death strugle of the overgrown monster.[119]

For every Yank whose primary goal was emancipation were to be found several whose chief goal was the Union and the system of government that it represented. The objective often was imperfectly expressed, but the ideal shines through in unmistakable clearness. Devotion to the Union was strong among immigrant groups such as the Germans who had seen the unhappy effects of division in their native land and who felt a special responsibility for preventing a similar fate from overtaking their adopted country. Then, too, the Union was associated with ideals and opportunities which had helped pull them across the sea and which they felt were now imperiled.

Native Americans associated the Union with the struggles of the Revolution and with the greatness achieved in the period of independence. Immigrants and natives alike deemed perpetuation of the Union important as a proof to the world of the soundness of the democratic experiment.

The rallying cry of some was "the Union and freedom" and this combination carried unusual appeal. But the men in blue, save for very brief periods of threatened invasion, had no cause so dynamic as that of the Confederates in defending their homes. "John Brown's Body" and "Hail Columbia" were stirring songs, but neither possessed the emotional tug of the Rebel favorite "The despot's heel is on thy shore, Maryland! My Maryland!"

CHAPTER II

FROM REVEILLE TO TAPS

Soldier life was an ordered life and the instruments of regimentation
were the bugle and drum. Each activity in the day's routine had a dis-
tinctive "call" sounded by the buglers or tapped out by the drummer
boys.[1] In an infantry camp daily calls normally aggregated about a
dozen; in the artillery and cavalry, owing to additional signals for the
care of horses, they sometimes ran to more than a score.[2] During a
period of intensive refresher training in 1863, a cannoneer of Meade's
army complained: "26 bugle calls to attend every day keeps us so [busy]
we dont have much time to ourselves." [3]

The soldier's day began with the reveille, sounded usually about five
o'clock in summer and an hour later in winter.[4] This was the signal for
morning roll call, and as failure to answer meant extra duty or a stint
in the guardhouse, Yanks were reasonably prompt in shaking off their
blankets, donning shoes, blouses and hats (seasoned campaigners com-
monly slept in their trousers and shirts) and taking their allotted places
on the color line in front of the camp. Of course almost every company
had its quota of laggards who lingered in their bunks to the last minute
and had to throw on their clothes as they rushed frantically to their
posts.[5]

Some commanders required their men to turn out in full dress and
equipment; others permitted them to appear in semiundress and without
arms. The young correspondent George Townsend who late in 1861
witnessed soldiers of an Eastern regiment assembling at reveille reported:
"Some wore one shoe and others appeared shivering in their linen. They
stood ludicrously in rank, and a succession of short, dry coughs ran up
and down the line." [6]

As the sleepy soldiers stood in their places the first sergeant of each
company called the roll, after which the men usually were allowed to
return briefly to their quarters to complete their toilet or perhaps to
snatch a few extra minutes of sleep while the sergeant prepared the
morning report. But some commanders, especially during the breaking-in

period, insisted on putting their men through a brisk drill immediately after morning roll call.

Approximately thirty minutes after reveille came the breakfast call, commonly known as "Peas on a Trencher," followed shortly by sick call for the ailing and fatigue call for the well.[7] When the sick call sounded, the first sergeant or one of the company's duty sergeants lined up all the ambulatory patients and marched them to the regimental surgeon for examination and prescription. Later in the morning bedridden patients were visited by the surgeon in their quarters or in the regimental hospital. Fatigue duty consisted in policing the company grounds and tidying up the quarters, digging drainage ditches, cutting wood and similar activities.[8]

About eight o'clock the musicians sounded the call for guard mounting, at which the first sergeant of each company turned out his detail for the next twenty-four hours' duty, inspected them carefully and marched them out to the regimental parade ground. While the regimental band or drum-and-fife corps provided appropriate music, the sergeant major formed the company details into line, after which the adjutant supervised their inspection and then sent them to their respective posts. Details were so arranged that each member stood guard only two hours out of every six.[9]

The next call was for drill which commonly lasted until the welcome notes of "roast beef," as the dinner call was usually termed, summoned the men to the noon meal. Then came another period of free time, followed by additional drilling. In the latter part of the afternoon companies were dismissed, and the quarters began to hum with activity as men brushed their uniforms, blacked their leather and polished their brass. This was in preparation for retreat exercises which consisted of roll call, inspection and dress parade. The last, held sometimes by regiment and sometimes by brigade and accompanied always by music, was the day's climactic and most impressive ceremony.[10]

A typical dress parade, as observed by an infantry regiment early in the war, was described thus by a soldier:

The troops are drawn up in line of battle and the order "Parade rest!" given by each Captain to his command. The band "beats off"; that is, marches down and back in front of the regiment, playing slowly down and a quick step back. The officers step four paces in front, the Major and Lieutenant-colonel in advance of the rest. The sergeants march to the centre of the column, and make their report to the Adjutant. He reports to the Colonel and steps behind him. There is then a brisk exercise in arms, and the order of "Parade rest!" is repeated. The officers sheath their swords, proceed to the centre, face the Colonel, and under the lead of the Adjutant march up to him touching their hats as they approach, and, encircling him, hear his remarks and orders. Returning to their posts, the regiment breaks up into companies, each of which marching to its quarters under the lead of the sergeants is disbanded.[11]

Dress parades were the occasion for reading orders, such as the findings of courts-martial, and other official communications. They were sometimes attended by civilian visitors and high-ranking officers. All in all they were colorful, dignified affairs conducted in a manner calculated to inspire in the soldiers a pride in the bearing of arms.

Supper call came shortly after retreat, followed not long after dark by tattoo, which brought another roll call and an ordering of the men to their quarters. The final call of the day was taps, at which signal "all lights must go out, all noises cease and every enlisted man be inside his quarters." [12]

This was the typical routine of an infantry regiment in camp during a period of relative quiet. As previously intimated, artillery and other branches followed a slightly different system. Among units of the same branch practices varied with the season and with the inclinations of individual commanders. Some colonels and brigadiers held dress parades both morning and afternoon and a few required their men to answer roll five times a day.[13] During periods of active campaigning the number of calls was reduced and life became considerably less formal. When on the move with battle in prospect, it was not uncommon for reveille to be sounded at two or three o'clock in the morning.

Sunday routine in all units was different from that of other days. The Sabbath was synonymous with inspection.[14] Hence, after breakfast Yanks busied themselves cleaning up the company streets, sweeping out their quarters, arranging their bunks and accouterments and putting a shine on all their leather and metal equipment. "Spit and polish" had literal meaning in the 1860s, for soldiers of that period, lacking such conveniences as blitz cloths, had to scrub their buttons and buckles with whatever they could improvise. Dust and chalk were commonly used abrasives, applied sometimes with brushes and again with corncobs or sticks.[15] Saliva was the most convenient solvent. Mess equipment was scoured with dirt—knives and forks by simply plunging them a few times into the ground.[16]

Following some two hours of preparation including preliminary inspections by first sergeants and captains, soldiers marched to the drill ground and formed by company—Company A on the right, B on the left, and the others in between—to await arrival of the visiting inspector who was usually the brigade commander or one of his staff. After scrutinizing field and staff officers and taking a summary view of the regiment by walking down the open column, the inspecting officer, beginning with Company A, minutely inspected the arms, equipment and dress of each soldier. Then, to appropriate orders of their captain, the men stacked arms, unslung and opened their knapsacks and laid them on the ground for examination. The inspector checked the contents of each knapsack by poking among them with the tip of his sword. If perchance he found a dirty sock or handkerchief concealed beneath the immaculate top layer of garments, he reprimanded the offender on the spot which, while embarrassing enough, was usually mild in comparison with the tongue-lashing administered by the captain after return to the company area. When the inspection of a company was completed, the men reslung knapsacks, recovered arms and marched back to quarters. Usually about an hour was required for examining the knapsacks of the ten companies, during which the unfortunate members of Company B had to stand in line. Few enjoyed "knapsack drill," as this phase of the Sunday morning exercise was called, and Company B least of all.[17]

After the last company had been examined, the inspecting officer made the rounds of the hospital, guardhouse, sutler's shop, kitchens and such other facilities as he chose to see. He then proceeded to the company quarters where, with the men standing in their allotted places, he examined floors, bunks and furnishings to see that everything was in the order prescribed by regulations. Completion of this, the final part of the inspection, usually consumed the remainder of the morning.[18]

Sunday afternoon, until retreat, was normally free time, though some commanders required that their men attend religious services.

Every other month soldiers were mustered for pay, usually by an inspector general or by an officer specially designated by the army commander.[19] Muster exercises commonly included a review and inspection, but the muster proper consisted of calling the names on the company roll by the visiting officer. When a soldier heard his name he replied "here," brought his gun snappily to the "carry" position, and then dropped the butt to the ground and held it in the position of "order arms." After the mustering officer had accounted for every man on the roster he forwarded a copy of the muster roll to The Adjutant General in Washington.[20] Soldiers were not paid at the time of the muster, but information was provided on which payments were based. The "here" which Billy Yank rendered at the muster was doubtless delivered with more than the usual enthusiasm because this act put him on record for pay and reminded him of the pleasant fact that a visit from the paymaster was forthcoming.

Pay was commonly tardy, sometimes more than six months, and in comparison with that of World War II it was lamentably low. Privates received only thirteen dollars a month during most of the war and a meager sixteen dollars a month after the final raise of May 1, 1864.[21] But dollars had more purchasing power in the 1860s than now, and Civil War soldiers, being unaccustomed to "the abundant life," probably did not consider themselves any less well paid than did their great-grandsons of World War II. Under a voluntary system of allotment initiated in 1861, many Yanks found it possible to send home a portion of their earnings.[22]

However tardy or paltry the pay, Yanks were glad to receive it. One of them irreverently opined that "a paymaster's arrival will produce more joy in camp than is said to have been produced in heaven over the one sinner that repenteth." [23]

Musters and pay were infrequent occurrences and full inspections rarely exceeded one a week. But during initial months of service and at times thereafter, as when preparing for active operations following a season of quiet, drill was a daily event.

In new units drill consisted mainly of exercise in the handling of arms, practicing various positions and facings and performing the simple maneuvers of squad or comparable unit as laid down in the manuals. These elementary exercises, grouped in the manuals under the heading "school of the soldier," taught the men such fundamentals as to stand erect; face left or right; salute; march forward, to the rear, by the flank and obliquely; shift arms to the various positions; load "in nine times," "in four times," or "at will"; fire in standing, kneeling and prone positions; and parry and thrust with the bayonet. As soon as recruits became reasonably proficient in individual and squad tactics they were introduced to company exercises. Then, as rapidly as their development allowed, they were launched into skirmish drill, school of the battalion and eventually, where circumstances permitted, into maneuvers by brigades or larger unit.[24]

This procedure applied specifically to the infantry, but other branches followed a comparable scheme of training.

Initiation of advanced training did not necessarily mean discontinuance of the more elementary types. Rather, the change was one of a gradually shifting emphasis from the simple to the complex.

In a unit that had been in service for two or three months, typical routine consisted of an hour or so of squad drill early in the morning, an equal stint of company drill just before noon and about an hour and a half of battalion drill in the late afternoon. More advanced units commonly omitted the squad drill, had an hour or two of company drill in the forenoon and of battalion drill after lunch. Following a few weeks of this routine, company drill might be dispensed with or held only on alternate days, and brigade drill introduced in the afternoon.

In the artillery the usual routine after the first few weeks of training was instruction of gun crews in the manual of the piece in the morning and drill by battery and battalion in the afternoon.

The training day for privates closed with retreat. But noncoms and officers of many units were required to go to night schools conducted by their superiors. Lessons, based on the manuals, usually emphasized subjects to be covered in the next day's training. A Massachusetts corporal noted in his diary in 1863 that the noncommissioned officers of his company "have lessons in tactics every night at the Captain's quarters to fit them to drill the privates in squads according to the book." [25] And an Ohio sergeant wrote his homefolk in December 1862: "Every night I recite with the other 1st Sergts and 2nd Lieutenants. We shall finish Hardee's Tactics and then study the 'Army Regulations.' Theory as well as practice are necessary to make the perfect soldier." [26]

Night sessions were usually conducted by captains, but colonels and even generals sometimes took an active part in them.[27]

Evening schools were sometimes supplemented by day rehearsals at which noncoms and officers, organized into skeleton units (pivot men holding strings or poles across the space normally occupied by privates), took turns in putting one another through various maneuvers of platoon, company or battalion. Commanders fortunate enough to have on their rosters men with prior military experience frequently called on the veterans to act as instructors in these exercises.[28]

Skirmish drill was sometimes enlivened by the firing of blank cartridges. Practice with live ammunition was a rarity, though diaries and letters now and then tell of men going out in small groups on their own, or with their officers, and trying out their muskets or carbines on fence posts, trees or small game. Perhaps one of the reasons for neglect of target practice early in the war was the notorious inaccuracy of the anti-

quated muskets with which many soldiers were armed at that time.
Some Illinois soldiers who with smoothbore muskets fired 160 shots at
a flour barrel 180 yards away registered only four hits.[29] These were not
new troops but men who had been in uniform at least six months. The
performance of their weapons can hardly be imagined as making these
men eager for battle. If the captain afterward was no more than luke-
warm about target practice, his attitude was to say the least understand-
able.

In at least one instance advanced training included drill in amphibi-
ous operations. Private M. L. Gordon, who participated in the exercises
held on an island off the South Carolina coast in March 1863, wrote
of the experience:

> We had been thinking for some time that we had drilled in every-
> thing, but the past week we had "something new under the sun." We
> drill in getting on and off Transports. A Regt is taken on board & then
> put in small boats they are then formed in line and all strike for the shore
> —the moment the boats touch [land] the men spring out fix bayonets
> and make a charge. It is a good deal of fun, but we may see they day
> when it will not be quite so amusing.[30]

Some commanders supplemented training in the separate arms with
combined exercises in which infantry, artillery and cavalry worked to-
gether in practice attacks, withdrawals and other battle maneuvers, or
opposed one another in simulated combat. Such activities, when fea-
tured by the use of blank ammunition and accompanied by piercing yells,
as was sometimes the case, were excitingly realistic and hence thoroughly
enjoyed by both participants and spectators. A private in the Army of
the Potomac who saw a brigade stage a sham fight in Virginia in De-
cember 1861 described it thus:

> Infantry, cavalry and artillery were doing their best. The regiment
> of infantry were blazing away at each other when a squadron of cavalry
> dashed around a piece of woods and charged down on them with the
> wildest yells. Then the artillery commenced firing on them (the cavalry)
> and they gave it up, wheeled and retreated. . . . Quite a number of
> carriages were up from the city and I saw ladies watching the sport with
> a good deal of interest. They would start at the report of the cannons
> and give a nice little city scream, as ladies will. . . . I am getting some
> accustomed to the smell of powder.[31]

This soldier regarded the mock fight more as an amusement than
a training exercise. His reference to getting accustomed to the smell

of powder was an afterthought. But the opportunity to obtain an idea ahead of time of the atmosphere of battle—the noise, confusion, as well as the smell—and to carry out assigned duties under simulated combat conditions was the most valuable of training. It was especially beneficial to officers in that it taught them to maneuver and control their commands when orders could hardly be heard and when their men were keyed to a high pitch of emotion.[32]

Not the least of the returns from such exercises was the confidence that they gave to the men in their own effectiveness and in the co-operation of the other arms. A young soldier of a Western command, reporting in November 1862 on a recent series of exercises in which his regiment formed in hollow square to receive cavalry charges, stated: "When they charge us with wild yells (some of them get aufully excited, so do the horses) it takes some nerve to stand against them, although it is all a sham. But we have found out one thing—horses cannot be driven onto fixed bayonets and I dont believe we shall be as affraid of a real charge if we ever have to meet one in the future. We are learning a good deal, so are the Cavelry." [33]

A few weeks later a young infantryman stationed in Kentucky wrote his homefolk: "We had our first Brigade drill day before yesterday. There were in one field four Regts of Infantry, a Battery of Artillery, and a Squadron of Cavalry. . . . The Cavalry charged down on us and for the first time I saw something that looked like fighting. The artillery blazed away, and we had a regular sham battle. It was a beautiful sight, and our officers expressed themselves well satisfied with the drill." He then added significantly: "We began to think we can whip twice our weight in Rebels." [34]

Sometimes the sham fights were held in connection with grand reviews of several divisions. One of McClellan's men stated in November 1861: "One maneuver we pass through at these reviews . . . is this, we advance in line of battle and at a given signal, the men all lie down and the artillery come up and fire directly over our heads. This is done in order that if the enemy either Cavalry or infantry attempt to charge upon and take the cannon, we can rise up and protect them or charge upon the enemy if necessary." [35]

While the type of load used by the artillery in these particular exercises is not specified, the charges were unquestionably blanks. No instance was found of the firing of live ammunition over the heads of soldiers in Civil War training.

It would be misleading to leave the impression that combined or realistic exercises were commonplace. One gets a strong impression from letters and diaries of participants that training rarely was carried beyond the level of the regiment, and that few officers or men had the benefit of practicing the military art in joint exercises with members of other branches.

Some higher commanders realized the importance of large-unit training. Sherman, for example, wrote Thomas in April 1864, "to encourage drill by brigades and divisions and let the recruits practice at the target all the time." [36] But there is little ground for believing that brigade and division exercises in Sherman's or any other command often went beyond ceremonial parades and reviews.

One reason for this situation doubtless was the reluctance of brigade and division commanders to tackle the direction of large-unit maneuvers. Few of them had backgrounds commensurate with such responsibilities. Then, many must have felt, owing to such factors as lack of time and inexperience of regimental and lower commanders, that it was best to concentrate on more elementary matters.

Fundamental to the whole problem of training was the lack of high-level direction and co-ordination. As previously noted, the manuals prescribed certain basic principles and procedures, but lack of uniform training programs and a well-defined system of supervision naturally led to countless variations and numerous irregularities. To a large extent, especially in the crucial first year of the war, each colonel trained his regiment pretty much as he saw fit.

Hence, it is not surprising that in some units men were "burned out" by six or eight hours of drill a day, and in others they received not enough to harden their muscles; that some units had an overamount of company drill and insufficient practice in battalion maneuvers; and that some acquired proficiency with the bayonet while others had no more than a cursory knowledge of this form of training.

In all units drill was greatly curtailed during seasons of active campaigning. The same was generally true of the period when troops were holed up in winter quarters. One Yank wrote from Lookout Valley, Tennessee, in January 1864: "After breakfast there is little for the well men to do. . . . The forenoon is spent in poke, poke, poking around till the appetite says it is dinner time." [37]

Veteran units had considerably less drill than new ones, except when commanders ordered refresher exercises in anticipation of renewal of active operations or when large groups of filler replacements were being broken into the units. Replacement-training practices varied considerably. In some cases recruits before joining tactical units were drilled in fundamentals at a special camp of instruction, such as that set up near Annapolis in 1862 with a capacity of 50,000 men, "cavalry, artillery and infantry in due proportions." [38] In other instances new troops were sent directly from points of rendezvous to field commands for immediate assignment and training in the unit. The latter procedure was favored by Sherman who on August 7, 1864, wrote Grant: "Get the War Department to send us recruits daily as they are made, for we can teach them more war in our camps in one day than they can get at a rendezvous in a month." [39]

Replacements who came to their regiments with little or no prior instruction were usually placed under veteran noncommissioned officers for intensive segregated drilling in squad and company movements and then put in their regular places for training along with their seasoned comrades in battalion and higher exercises.[40]

Long hours on the drill field, the newness of soldiering, and the good-natured but brutal treatment by the veterans made the life of most recruits a hard one. An insight into the experience of one who joined a Massachusetts regiment in the late summer of 1862 is afforded by a letter which he wrote to his homefolk a short time afterward:

We recruits are getting kicked around pretty well now; we do all the duty in our company, and they call us d—d recruits. . . . I put up with things from minor officers . . . and even privates without a murmur, which I would have resented with a blow if I had been at home. . . . Our drill master (Sergeant William Salter), has gone to the hospital sick, and *common privates* grown old in sin and musty in discipline, are detailed to go through the movements with us. They are sick of soldiering and have no ambition to teach others.[41]

Drill to most Yanks, whether new or old in the service, was a dull, dreary chore and the more they had of it (except for the sham battles where realism relieved boredom) the less they liked it. A Pennsylvanian wrote after about six months' service: "The first thing in the morning is drill, then drill, then drill again. Then drill, drill, a little more drill. Then drill, and lastly drill. Between drills, we drill and sometimes stop to eat a little and have a roll-call." [42]

Combat veterans were especially unenthusiastic about tramping parade grounds under a crushing load of equipment; they had seen the elephant and were in no mood to "play soldier." An Ohioan of Hooker's army reflected a sentiment widely held among hardened campaigners when he wrote after an epidemic of refresher training in 1863: "Brigade drill and review today i dont know what will cum tomoror and dont cair one god dam sir." [43] But the discipline that was part of being a veteran caused the old-timers dutifully to take their places when the bugler's note rang out the unpleasant call to drill.[44]

An important aspect of the soldier's daily life was his shelter. The type of shelter varied considerably with time, season, location and other circumstances.

Except during periods of active campaigning, quarters were commonly arranged after a pattern specified in army regulations. In an infantry regiment, which at full strength approximated 1,000 men, tents or huts of privates were grouped by company with a street running between. Perpendicular to the company streets at the front of the camp was the color line, and at the rear in rows paralleling the color line were the quarters of the noncommissioned officers, then those of the company officers and finally those of the regimental commander and staff. Back of the officers' quarters were the baggage trains.[45]

Yanks who were stationed in permanent or semipermanent establishments such as Jefferson Barracks, in Missouri, had the privilege of living in frame buildings equipped with stoves and two-tier bunks.[46] But such installations were rarely to be found outside the North, and since they were used mainly as camps of rendezvous, sojourns in them usually were brief.

The normal home of a soldier in summer was a tent. During the early part of the war nearly all tents occupied by enlisted men were either the Sibley or the wedge type. The first of these was a bell-shaped structure supported by a center pole which rested on a tripod. It was equipped with a stove the pipe of which passed through an opening at the apex.[47]

The Sibley tent was designed for the accommodation of about a dozen men, but the emergency of war frequently resulted in the crowding in of a score. Inmates arranged themselves for sleeping in the manner of wheel spokes, with feet at the center and heads near the circumference.[48] In good weather the canvas was raised at the edges for ventilation, but when rain or cold required the capping of the apex and the closing of all other openings the air became stuffy and foul. One Yank stated in his reminiscences that "to enter one of them of a rainy morning . . . and encounter the night's accumulation of nauseating exhalations from the bodies of twelve men (differing widely in their habits of personal cleanliness) was an experience which no old soldier has ever been known to recall with any great enthusiasm." [49]

The wedge or "A" tent, which from the front looked like an inverted "V," was a piece of canvas stretched over a horizontal bar and staked to the ground on either side, with extensions for closing front and rear. The floor space, some seven feet square, was adequate for accommodation of four men; but when six were crowded in, as was frequently the case in the first months of war, soldiers had to sleep "spoon fashion" and when one Yank turned over all had to turn. Congestion brought greater discomfort in the daytime as there was no spot within where a tall man could stand erect, and the farther away from the ridge pole he moved the more he had to stoop. Furnishings, beyond an occasional box, were out of the question because of the space requirements of the six men and their "trappings." [50]

Wall tents, which were box-shaped structures with sloping roofs, were a common sight in most camps during the war's early years. But these were a luxury enjoyed only by the officers and Yanks sick enough to be sent to the hospital.[51]

After the first year of the conflict the standard field habitation of the rank and file was the shelter or dog tent. This was ordinarily a two-man dwelling made by buttoning together the half-shelters carried by the occupants as standard equipment and stretching them over a horizontal pole held in place by two upright sticks, or more commonly by muskets stuck into the ground with bayonets fixed. Ends were left open or draped with blankets or coats.[52]

In warm weather some Yanks elevated their shelter tents by tying the four corners to the upper ends of long stakes rather than fixing them flush with the ground. Others arranged the canvas in lean-to fashion or simply stretched it in a gentle slope over four uprights.[53] When they so desired, three or more soldiers could button their half-shelters together for a tent of larger size.

Occupants of shelters, and other type tents as well, sometimes built brush arbors either as porches or as separate structures, where in favorable weather they could lounge in greater comfort than that afforded by regular quarters.[54]

Many Yanks held the shelter tents in low esteem when first they were issued, one soldier writing in 1862 that he wished "the man who invented them had been hung before the invention was completed," as they reminded him "forceably of a hog pen." [55] The nickname "dog tent" reflected initial attitudes with a fair degree of accuracy. But disparagements declined in vehemence as the men became accustomed to their tiny dwellings, and in time references to them usually revealed more of affection than of disdain.

During the winter months inclemency of weather and the tendency toward a more settled mode of life combined to produce a great change in soldier dwellings. In areas where trees abounded and low temperatures were common, log huts built by the men were the vogue. Construction was commonly of the "pen" type, after the fashion of frontier cabins, with slanting roofs of board or thatch, but some Yanks preferred walls of stockade design.[56] In either case, cracks were filled with mud. If logs were not available, and sometimes when they were, Yanks might erect frame huts with materials obtained by wrecking abandoned Southern dwellings.[57]

Perhaps the most common type of winter quarters was a hybrid structure, part wood and part fabric, made by superimposing wedge or shelter tents on log bases. These "winterized," "stockaded" or "barricaded" tents, like the log huts, were usually designed for the accommodation of four men. Sometimes the occupants enhanced roominess and warmth, by digging out several feet of dirt. Roofs might be made more impervious by stretching rubber blankets or ponchos over the canvas.[58]

Both log cabins and winterized tents were commonly heated by fireplaces built of sticks and daubed with clay; but some Yanks preferred the "California" type of furnace which was made by digging a hole in the ground, covering it with a removable stone and tunneling the smoke to an outside flue.[59] Chimneys were usually of sticks and daubing topped by one or more barrels. The advantage of increased draft was offset to some extent by the tendency of the barrels to catch fire. A common occurrence in winter was the routing of soldiers from their quarters by the cry "Chimney afire!" The peril could usually be met by simply knocking the burning keg to the ground with a pole. Replacements were readily obtainable from the commissary, and the excitement produced by the conflagration afforded momentary relief from boredom.[60]

Floors were normally of boards or split logs laid with the flat side up. Some Yanks, however, simply covered the soil with straw or left it bare.

The average hut contained two bunks, one above the other, extending from wall to wall across the rear. The framework of the bunks was usually of boards or logs, while the bottoms were of barrel staves, slender poles or some other material flexible enough to give the effect of springs. Mattresses were improvised by adding a layer of pine needles, leaves or straw. Knapsacks were ordinarily kept at the head of the bunks, while other equipment and extra articles of clothing were hung from rails or pegs driven into logs along either side of the room.[61]

The lower bunk was used as a seat in daytime, though some soldiers objected to this practice on the ground that lice-laden callers might leave unwelcome reminders of their visits. Stools were made of pine slabs, boxes or upended logs, and tables of inverted hardtack cases mounted on legs. The customary candlestick was a bayonet with the candle fitted into the opening made for the gun barrel and the sharp end stuck into wall or floor. If candles were lacking, slush lamps might be made by filling a sardine container with grease and dropping a rag in one corner for a wick. Shelves were placed about the cabin as needed for pipes, books, papers, daguerreotypes and other possessions.[62]

These arrangements and furnishings sufficed for the general run of soldiers, but almost every camp had a few irrepressible "fixer-uppers" who insisted on papering their quarters, building fancy articles of furniture or adding other luxuries and adornments. One of these zealots wrote his homefolk: "We have our hut nearly finished. We have split little cedar for the floor they make a neat floor with their clean red and white, split them through the heart. Have been much reminded of Solomon's temple in the construction of this frail tenement, have used so much cedar." [63]

Decorative tendencies sometimes extended to the placarding of huts with high-sounding labels such as "The Astor House," fanciful designation of company streets, and even the erection of tremendous evergreen arches over thoroughfare entrances bordering the parade ground. The number of the regiment was frequently woven into the design and sometimes that of the brigade, division and corps, along with the names of the commanding officers.[64]

Whether their handiwork was pretentious or humble, Yanks usually regarded it with pride, and letters home were replete with details of construction and furnishing. "We want no better quarters than we now have," was written by a Massachusetts soldier shortly after completion of his hut in Virginia in the first year of the war, but the same statement might have been penned by almost any Yank during any winter of the conflict.[65]

Another basic item in the soldier's daily life was his clothing. Early in the war types of habiliment, as already noted, were so diverse as to make mockery of the term "uniform." But variation decreased with the passing of time and by 1863 a fair degree of standardization had been achieved.

In the infantry the uniform in its ultimate version consisted of a blue cap with black visor; a long single-breasted dress coat of dark blue with stand-up collar; a dark-blue jacket called a blouse; light-blue trousers; rough black shoes, known in soldier parlance as gunboats; wool flannel shirt; cotton flannel drawers; socks; and a long blue overcoat with cape. Artillery and cavalry regalia were the same as the infantry except that dress coats were shorter, boots were worn instead of shoes and trousers were reinforced in seat and legs.[66]

Black felt hats were an authorized item of issue and army regulations specified that they be worn for dress purposes. But many soldiers did not like them, one Yank writing to his homefolk, "My new hat looks as near like the pictures that you see of the pilgrim fathers landing on plymouth, tall, stiff, and turned up on one side with a feather on it. . . . I dont wear it any more than I am obliged to." [67] Another soldier described his hat as "rediculous." [68] Such attitudes were not universal and photographs, even of the late war period, reveal a number of hat wearers.[69] The most common headpiece for both formal and informal purposes, however, was the cap, worn with the crown sloping forward.

Another item prescribed in army regulations, but rarely used, was a cravat or stock made of stiff leather and fastened about the neck with a buckle. Soldiers called these uncomfortable articles "dog collars," and after the war one Yank stated that he never recalled seeing one worn "except as a joke." [70]

The short blouse was the favorite coat for field service, one veteran stating in his reminiscences that "Many regiments never drew a dress coat after leaving the state." [71] Overcoats also had only a limited use outside of camp owing to their cumbersomeness and weight. Drawers appear to have been regarded as superfluous by some. A young Hoosier, describing the initial issue of clothing to his unit, wrote: "Most of the boys had never worn drawers and some did not know what they were for and some of the old soldiers who are here told them that they were for an extra uniform to be worn on parade and they half believed it." [72]

Many Yanks commented on their poor luck in obtaining proper fits. The Indianian, quoted above, described his first experience with the quartermaster thus: "We had quite a time with our uniforms. . . . If they fit, all right; if not we had to trade around till we could get a fit as they are in different sizes. Being of medium size I got a fair fit but some of the very tall or short men were not so fortunate." [73] One Yank of low stature wrote after the war: "I . . . could never find in the quartermaster's department a blouse or a pair of trousers small enough, nor an overcoat cast on my lines. The regulation blue trousers I used to cut off at the bottoms and the regulation overcoat sleeves were always rolled up, which gave them the appearance of having military cuffs." [74]

In the latter part of the war some regiments were provided in the hot season with linen pants, light blouses and straw hats but, as a general rule, the present-day practice of issuing special summer uniforms appears not to have been followed in the Union Army.[75] Yanks adapted themselves to high temperatures by shedding all that commanders would allow, but even the most indulgent officers balked at the idea of letting their men go about in their underclothing. From June to September wool shirts and trousers were extremely uncomfortable in most parts of Dixie.

Uniforms were trimmed with cords or stripes in color and design appropriate to branch and rank. Infantry trimmings were blue; artillery, scarlet; and cavalry, yellow. Branch was also designated by brass insignia worn on the hats—a bugle for infantry, crossed sabers for cavalry and crossed cannon for artillery. After corps badges were introduced in 1863—for example, a sphere for the First Corps, cloverleaf for the Second, crescent for the Eleventh, star for the Twelfth, with a different color for each division—these were placed on top of the cap. Noncommissioned officers wore chevrons on their sleeves with ratings indicated by the same number of stripes as today. Insignia for the various commissioned ranks were also the same as today except that the bars of captains and first lieutenants were golden rather than silver and second lieutenants wore no bar, that rank being distinguished by the unadorned shoulder straps. Rank, rating and branch were distinguished also to some extent by design, arrangement and number of buttons, cut of coats and type of sash. Field-grade officers, for example, wore two rows of buttons on their dress coats, while captains, lieutenants and enlisted men had only a single row.[76]

During the early period of the war much of the clothing issued to the men in blue was of inferior quality. Unscrupulous contractors and corrupt officials frequently took advantage of the government's dire need and pawned off on the army at fantastic prices the most worthless of materials. The story of shoddy uniforms and imitation-leather shoes, some of which fell apart during the first heavy rain, has been fully told by Professor Fred A. Shannon and need not be repeated here.[77] Suffice to say, the contract situation was eventually cleaned up and after the first year or so of the conflict Billy Yank had relatively little ground for complaint as to the quality of clothing received from the quarter-master.

The same was generally true of quantity, though official reports and soldier accounts reveal numerous instances of raggedness and shortage. Deprivation was most common in periods of hard campaigning when rapid movement enhanced wear and made replenishment difficult. After Antietam, McClellan reported a serious deficiency of shoes and other articles of clothing in some of his corps;[78] and a soldier told of seeing "men with no coats, no underclothes, in rags, no shoes." [79] This Yank also stated that when Lincoln reviewed his regiment at this time "those who had overcoats were ordered to put them on, to hide the rags & make him believe that they had Jackets." [80]

During the Fredericksburg operations of December 1862, a New York surgeon reported that 200 of the men in his regiment were without shoes, and the next year while the Mine Run movement was in progress a sergeant of Meade's army wrote: "We had a light fall of snow last night. A great many of the troops are in want of clothes and shoes." [81]

The long marches of the Gettysburg campaign were exceedingly hard on clothing, one participant writing on July 8, 1863, that "the boys [are] almost wore out and a grate many shiewless," while another reported a little later: "I am awful ragged Imagine a modest, timid, & retiring young man like your son walking through the thickly populated land of Virginia . . . with a pair of pants on with a hole in the seat which like a broken window needs two old pots to stick through . . . to keep the cold out & the bottoms waving in rags between the knee and feet." [82]

The prolonged fighting in Virginia the next summer brought a recurrence of shortage, a New York *Tribune* correspondent reporting from Grant's headquarters on June 6, 1864, that "actual marching has worn out 50,000 pairs of shoes" and that "more than 100,000 have not changed a garment . . . [for] thirty days." [83]

Western soldiers suffered more from lack of clothing than did those of the East because of greater problems of distance and supply. In the Western armies, as in Eastern commands, deficiencies were most common during seasons of arduous campaigning. In May 1862, following a period of intensive operations in North Alabama, an Ohioan wrote a friend back home: "Our reg is purty naked they look moor like a reg of secesh than northern troops soom barfootted, soom with out coats soom with a citazens soot on. . . . I have ben barfooted evry sens we got back from brig porte." [84]

The long race through Kentucky after Bragg in the fall of 1862 was a severe strain on the wardrobes of Buell's men. The surgeon of an Ohio regiment wrote from Louisville in September that the hard stone pike had soon played havoc with leather and that some of his regiment had marched 200 miles without shoes.[85] The situation grew worse on the return, Rosecrans reporting to Halleck on December 4, 1862: "Many of our soldiers are to this day barefoot, without blankets, without tents." [86]

The strenuous operations about Vicksburg also produced instances of raggedness. One participant in the Port Hudson siege stated, "My shirt is more like a necklace than a shirt." [87] But the warmth of the climate prevented great discomfort save for those who had to march without shoes.

Sherman's long trek through Georgia and the Carolinas was marked by some raggedness and want of shoes.[88] The greatest hardship from lack of clothing on the Union side, however, seems to have occurred in the East Tennessee campaigns of November and December 1863.[89] Suffering was especially acute among members of the expedition to relieve Burnside, hundreds of soldiers marching entirely barefooted from Knoxville to Chattanooga over icy roads. A New Jersey sergeant wrote at the conclusion of this experience: "We reached our old camp [after] . . . 26 days march, without a blanket or shelter, barefooted and half pint of flour a day to live on. I wore raw cow skin shoes for ten days." [90]

Such experiences were exceptional and were due mainly to temporary failures of distribution rather than to shortages of stock. Some of the hardship was of the soldiers' own making, for Billy Yanks, like American soldiers of all time, were notoriously improvident of government issues.[91] They were especially resistant to lugging heavy loads for long distances; hence, a route of march during the winter season, particularly if the goal was a battlefield, was sure to be lined with an abundance of overcoats and blankets. Commanders railed against such profligate waste and recurrently made splurges of bringing offenders to justice, but their best efforts were no more than partially successful.

A number of items other than clothing figured prominently in the soldier's daily existence. The most important of these was his gun. As noted elsewhere the standard infantry arm, after a period of unhappy experience with antiquated American smoothbores and offcasts of European arsenals, was a Springfield or Enfield rifle musket.[92] The Springfield was of slightly larger caliber than the Enfield (.58 and .577 respectively) but was lighter and hence generally preferred by the soldiers. The difference in bore was not so great as to prevent use in both of the same bullet, which was an elongated, hollow-based cone commonly known as a Minié ball after the name of its French inventor. Both types of guns were muzzle-loaders. Breechloaders—and repeaters at that—were used by a few infantrymen in the latter part of the war and with great effectiveness, as for example by Wilder's brigade in the fighting about Chattanooga. But they were not an item of general issue to foot soldiers and their use was restricted largely to cavalrymen.[93]

The pride with which the few lucky possessors of the repeaters regarded their weapons was revealed by one of Sherman's soldiers who wrote in his journal on May 11, 1864: "I got a Henry rifle—a 16 shooter—yesterday. . . . I gave . . . 35 dollars—all the money I had for it. . . . I am glad I could get it. They are good shooters and I like to think I have so many shots in reserve." Ten months later he noted: "I think the Johnnys are getting rattled; they are afraid of our repeating rifles. They say we are not fair, that we have guns that we load up on Sunday and shoot all the rest of the week. This I know, I feel a good deal more confidence in myself with a 16 shooter in my hands than I used to with a single shot rifle." [94]

The muzzle-loading Springfields and Enfields were accurate guns, and most of the Yanks who carried them regarded them with affection and pride. A typical attitude was that of a New Hampshire private who wrote his parents in October 1861: "We have not got the enfield rifles but the spring field they are just as good and a good deel lighter. We went out the other day to try them We fired 600 yds and we put 360 balls into a mark the size of old Jeff, they will range 1500 yards with considerable certainty." [95]

Dependable as they undoubtedly were, these muzzle-loaders were far from being as good weapons as Billy Yank was entitled to expect. One of the major tragedies on the Union side was the failure of responsible authorities, with all the resources and talent which they had at their command, to provide the men in blue with more effective weapons.[96]

Artillerymen served a vast assortment of guns ranging from light fieldpieces loaded with canister, grape, shrapnel and solid balls, to enormous siege cannon hurling monstrous missiles over tremendous ranges.[97]

The cavalryman's gun was a pistol or carbine. Some of the early troopers carried cumbersome horse pistols, but these and similar types gradually were replaced by revolvers. The revolvers included products of Remington and Savage, but the prevailing model seems to have been the Colt six-shooter. Among carbines of the early war period were to be found the Gallagher, "Joslyn Patent" and Hall, but the Sharps apparently became the most widely used of the single-shot models. As already noted, repeating carbines had rather extensive use in the cavalry in the latter part of the conflict.[98] Favorite makes were the seven-shot Spencer and the sixteen-shot Henry. A young member of the Fourth Michigan Cavalry, who wrote home in March 1864 that his unit was about to swap its five-shot repeaters for a type that would shoot nine times, reported that a short time before some Confederates had given themselves up just to see the Yankee guns. "The rebs that we took while on a scout from Rossville said they dreaded to come across our brigade," he added, "for we kept shooting all of the time, when they see our guns they say 'no wonder *yourns* shoot so fast if *weuns* had such guns we'd fight longer.'" [99]

Billy Yank's other impedimenta consisted of a haversack or "bread bag"; cartridge box in which were carried his "forty dead men"; bayonet and scabbard; cap box; rubber and woolen blanket; canteen; and knapsack. The last-named article, called by some a "patent bureau," was packed with such items as underclothes, stationery, photographs, toothbrush, razor, soap, books, letters, and a mending kit known as a "housewife." Mess equipment, comprising a metal plate, knife, fork, spoon and cup—and sometimes a light skillet—was usually divided between knapsack and hooks attached to the belt. In winter an overcoat, tied above the knapsack while on the march, was an extra burden.[100]

The weight of all this equipment ranged in soldier estimates from forty to fifty pounds. A Yank who accepted the latter figure gave detailed estimates as follows: "40 rounds ammunition, belt &c . . . . 4 lbs; canteen of water, 4 lbs; Haversack of rations, 6 lbs; Musket, 14 lbs; Knapsack at least 20 lbs, besides the clothes we have on our backs." [101] Another soldier, after a similar listing, noted: "In addition to the actual weight the five different straps which passed over every part of our bodies produced unpleasant touches of cramp now & then. I can appreciate the feelings of an animal in harness now." [102]

Most Yanks eventually found means of reducing the load. Indeed, the process of becoming a veteran was in large measure one of shedding.[103] Reference has already been made to the tendency to get rid of overcoats and dress coats. Another item which disappeared at a fairly early stage was the knapsack, its contents—considerably reduced—being rolled into the blanket. Many soldiers also dispensed with the canteen, carrying in its stead a small bottle of water, stored in pocket or haversack, and trusting to luck for quick refills from springs and branches

"DEAR FOLKS"
Drawing by Charles W. Reed

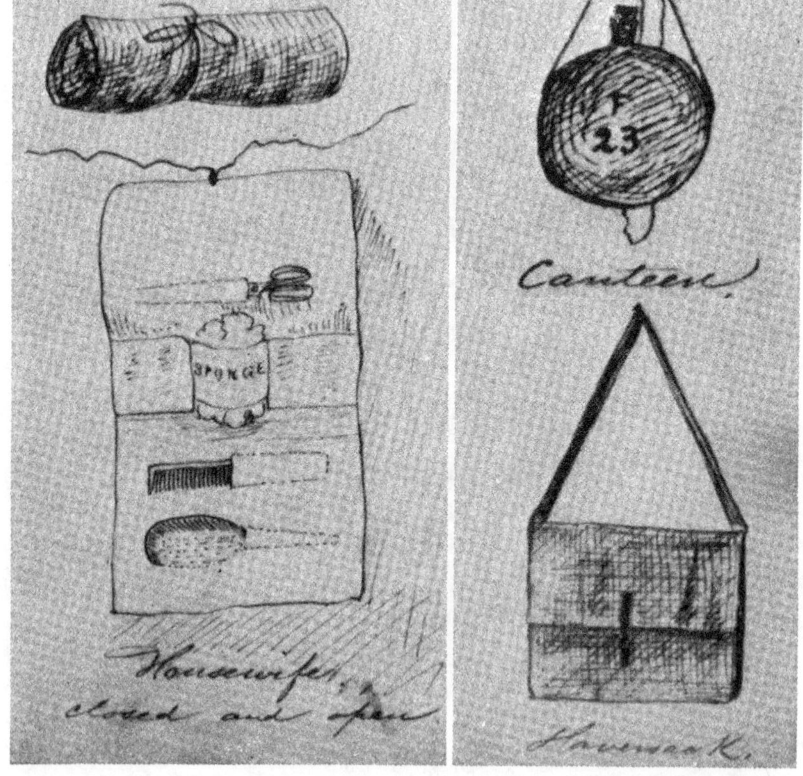

Courtesy Essex Institute

ITEMS OF SOLDIER EQUIPMENT

Drawings by Herbert E. Valentine, Company F, Twenty-third Massachusetts Regiment along the way. The tin cup or dipper did triple service as a coffee boiler, stewpot and drinking vessel, while a canteen could be blown apart with a small charge of powder to make a handy pair of combination plates and frying pans. Billy Yank model-1864, "in light marching order," was a lean, weather-beaten creature, topped by a battered cap and clad in a faded jacket, shaggy trousers—also considerably less blue than when first issued—and scuffed brogans.[104] Draped across his right shoulder with ends tied at hip level on the opposite side was a woolen blanket rolled in rubber within which was carried one or two extra garments and a minimum of small articles. On his right shoulder was his musket, and from his belt hung a sheathed bayonet, cartridge box, cap box, tin plate and cup. This with the haversack completed his load, except perchance there dangled from the musket barrel a portion of some yearling or shoat that had refused to take the oath or give the proper countersign.

CHAPTER III

THE SUPREME TEST

Battle is the ultimate of soldiering. All else in warfare is but incidental to the vital closing of opposing forces in conflict.

In recent times, owing to the tremendous increase in the range of weapons and introduction of such revolutionary instruments as radar, planes and rockets, "closing with the enemy" has lost much of its reality. Only a small portion of those who don uniforms ever draw a bead on an enemy or, for that matter, even have the field of combat as an objective. While the man with the rifle has proved less dispensable than was predicted before World War II, conflict has become increasingly mechanistic and impersonal.

In the Civil War, however, fighting was an intimate, elemental thing, with infantry bearing the brunt, and artillery and horse-mounted cavalry fighting, normally, in near support. The enemy could be seen with the naked eye by soldiers of all branches, and contests usually culminated in head-on clashes of yelling, shooting, striking masses. Closing with the enemy was more than a figure of speech.

Some Billy Yanks went into battle very soon after enlisting—a Federal brigadier after the Richmond, Kentucky, fight of August 30, 1862, reported that most of his command "had been less than a fortnight away from their homes." [1] Others waited many months for the fiery ordeal. One battle comprised the entire fighting experience of some, while many faced the jaws of death repeatedly. Regardless of when the test came or how many times, soldier reaction and experiences followed the same general pattern.

When circumstances permitted, certain preliminaries, more or less standard, were observed. [2] Among these was the issuance of three days' rations, sometimes more, with instructions to cook the meat immediately so that nourishment might be assured during the emergency. Benefits of this well-conceived measure often were lost, owing to the soldier's irrepressible bent for traveling light, eating when he was hungry and taking no thought of the morrow.

Next came the dispensing of ammunition. The usual allotment was sixty rounds of the paper cartridges—with bullets at one end and a plug or twist at the other to contain the powder—used in the muzzle-loading Springfield and Enfield rifles, the standard shoulder arms of both Federals and Confederates. Forty rounds filled the leather cartridge boxes carried on the belt; the others had to be carried in pocket or knapsack. Percussion caps, issued in about the same quantity as the cartridges, were carried in a small leather container also fastened to the belt. If, when battle was imminent, guns contained charges inserted a long time before or if the weapons had been exposed to rain or mist, barrels were cleared by firing or by removing the damaged loads with special instruments designed for the purpose (carried as standard equipment by noncommissioned file closers), and new charges inserted. Soldiers took seriously the matter of readying their weapons, as they wanted no failures when the shooting started. On the eve of combat Yanks were considerably more provident of bullets than of biscuits.

Following these preparations, and assuming that the initiative lay with the men in blue, units were marched to their assigned positions on the field. Then followed, usually, a period of waiting while final dispositions were being made for the "opening of the ball."

Colonels, if they had not previously done so, took advantage of this lull to whip up the emotions of their men. Sometimes the prebattle exhortation consisted of the reading of a circular previously issued by a higher commander; in other instances the address was original and impromptu. Whatever the source, it usually included instructions and sentiments such as these: Men, the hour which you have so eagerly awaited has arrived. We are about to engage the enemy. Let every man do his duty. Be cool. Keep ranks. If any of your comrades fall, do not stop to help them; leave them to the care of the men who have been specially detailed for removal of the wounded. The best way to protect the wounded, and yourselves as well, is to press forward and drive the enemy from the field. Hold your fire until the Rebels are in easy range, then aim low, fire deliberately. Close steadily on the enemy, and when you get within charging distance, rush on him with the bayonet. If you do this, you are sure to win.[3]

When veterans were addressed, reference was almost sure to be made to their former exploits. And speeches tended to become shorter and more pointed with the passing of time. At Antietam a colonel, pacing up and down before his regiment and speaking in jerks, said: "Men you are about to engage in battle. You have never disgraced your State; I hope you won't this time. If any man runs I want the file closers to shoot him; if they don't, I shall myself. That's all I have to say." [4] When the signal came to advance at Fredericksburg, the colonel of another regiment took the flag out in front of his command and waving it said: "Now boys is the time to write your names. Let every man do his duty. Follow me!" And with that he led off in the assault.[5]

At Murfreesboro the commander of the Twelfth Ohio, who was a minister, had his address cut short and its character changed by a Rebel thrust. The colonel began quietly: "Now boys fight for your country and your God, and . . ." At this point the Confederates fired a volley and the colonel, instead of ending with an Amen! as his men expected, concluded by shouting "AIM LOW!" For weeks afterward, whenever he passed through the camp he was hailed from behind trees and tents with the cry "AIM LOW!" [6]

After the speeches by higher commanders, captains, if time permitted, walked about among the men of their companies advising and exhorting them. Now and then officers or chaplains led the men in prayer or other religious exercises.[7] Considerable praying was done by the men themselves, and supplication was by no means confined to the righteous. Prayers were usually offered in silence, though now and then some frightened individual would audibly beseech divine aid. At Fredericksburg a brigadier on coming up to tell a colonel to take his regiment forward noticed a soldier "half raised up from his laying position with his open bible in one hand in loud and earnest prayer." The general withheld the order to advance until the prayer was finished.[8]

Some of the waiting men would attempt to break the tension by laughing and joking, but their efforts, strained and hollow, would elicit small response. Silence—awful, impenetrable, lonely silence—was the prevailing mood.

What were the sensations of these Yanks as they lingered on the threshold of battle? Were they afraid? Yes—at least most of them were. "If you see anyone that says that they want any afraid, you may know that it want me," wrote a Maine soldier after his baptism of fire at Fredericksburg, "but I want so frightened but I obaid all the orders." [9]

Among soldiers untried in combat, the fear was often not so much of death or injury as of inability to stand up under the awful and unknown test that lay ahead. Better a thousand times to fall facing the enemy, they thought, than to play the coward and bring humiliation or shame to the folk back home.[10] But could their spirits compel their bodies to go forward into the hell of screeching missiles, thundering

cannon, screaming wounded and bristling bayonets? That was the
burning question.

"I have a mortal dread of the battle field," wrote Private Edward
Edes to his father before his first entry into combat, "for I have never yet
been nearer to one than to hear the cannon roar & have never seen a
person die." He added: "I am afraid that the groans of the wounded
& dying will make me shake, nevertheless I hope & trust that strength
will be given me to stand up & do my duty." [11]

Veterans of prior conflicts were spared the novices' anxiety about
standing the gaff, but their fear was no less. They knew what a battle
was like, and their knowledge brought more of dread than of reassur-
ance. Too, the matter of diminishing odds entered into their thinking.
Did not each battle survived reduce the chance of living through an-
other? How long, after all, could good luck last? Declining eagerness for
the fray among the battle-wise was noted by Colonel Jacob Ammen at
Shiloh. "The Twenty-fourth Ohio . . . has been under severe fire
several times and behaved well," he wrote in his diary as troops of
Buell's command approached the field of action, "but does not appear
as anxious as the other regiments to get into a fight." After remarking
on the anxiousness of new units to "see the elephant" he added: "The
Twenty-fourth Ohio Volunteer Infantry had seen the elephant several
times, and did not care about seeing him again unless necessary." [12]

The two most noticeable differences in the prebattle mood of vet-
erans and nonveterans was a greater reticence of the old-timers when
confronting danger and their ability to postpone acute concern about
conflict much longer than their inexperienced comrades. Thus some
of them could relax even to the point of drowsing, until the shells
falling near proclaimed the actual beginning of hostilities.

Fear, whatever its basis and whenever it came, manifested itself in
various ways. But the most obvious effects were dryness of the throat
and lips; a sense of heaviness in the area of vital organs, as if a stone
were weighing on the chest, making breathing difficult; and excessive
perspiration. Some soldiers noted a sharpening of recollective powers
with the result that many long-latent memories of home and childhood
passed in rapid succession across the canvas of consciousness.

How did these men nerve themselves for the ordeal that lay ahead?
Resort to Providence has already been noted, and of the bolstering ef-
fect of religion on sincere believers there can be no doubt. Others
placed their hopes on chance, while still others found comfort in the
fatalistic view that no harm could come to one until his allotted time

was up.[13] A Maine soldier must have reflected a widespread sentiment when he wrote of his own attitude: "Death is the common lot of all and the diferance between dyeing to day and to morrow is not much but we all prefer to morrow." [14]

In the hour of crisis the thoughts of nearly all soldiers turned to loved ones at home, and the consciousness of their deep affection and concern gave heart to many. Still others found considerable strength in the conviction that they were doing their duty to family, friends, country and God.

Here and there among the impatient ranks might be found a soldier whose spirit was heavy with the conviction that he would not survive the fight. Thomas B. Barker must have felt thus as he stood in line on July 21, 1861, at Manassas, for at Centerville on the previous day he had written his younger brother: "We are to move on to attack them to-morrow. . . . Many will be slain . . . and I am as likely to fall as any one. But . . . I am content to take whatever is to come. Should I be slain you will then be the eldest left and I doubt not you will fill my place. On you will fall the delightful task of maintaining Father's and Aunt Charlotte's declining years. You will be kind to Walter & Abbey . . . forget my faults & forgive. . . . Good bye and God bless you. Tom." On the back of the letter Barker wrote: "If I am slain, whoever finds this will please to state the fact in this & forward it & confer a favor on the ashes of Thomas B. Barker." [15]

Many who entertained such sentiments lived to fight again, but not Barker. He died, and a Rebel surgeon who found his remains sent the farewell missive on its way. But before forwarding it he added this note: "This letter was found on the body of a man sacrificed by the Lincoln government in its unpatriotic, unholy, and hellish crusade against a people struggling for their rights under the Constitution. . . . A sad fate to fall in an unglorious cause." [16]

If the waiting troops were subjected to enemy fire as was sometimes the case, the suspense became almost intolerable. An Illinois sergeant, who experienced such a situation pending the deadly assault of May 22, 1863, at Vicksburg, wrote: "We lay there about eight minutes and yet it seemed an age to me, for showers of bullets and grape were passing over me . . . and not allowed to fire a single shot. . . . Oh how my heart palpitated! It seemed to thump the ground (I lay on my face) as hard as the enemy's bullets. The sweat from off my face run in a stream from the tip ends of my whiskers. . . . Twice I exclaimed aloud . . . *'My God, why dont they order us to charge!'* " [17]

Finally after a period ranging from a few minutes to several hours—but which in any case seemed interminable—came the order "fall in," followed by the command "forward, march." As the men moved out toward the Rebel position, officers kept shouting the words "center dress," "close up those gaps." Now that they were actually in motion the troops would feel better, though at first there would be considerable ducking and dodging as shells screeched close. Now and then a man would falter, but usually he responded readily to the officers' admonition to keep moving. If he did not, he would be helped into place by the spank of a sword and a resounding oath.[18]

At first the advancing men would not be allowed to fire. The inability to retaliate, especially after enemy shells began to cut down comrades, was a severe trial. When the whiz of bullets was added to the scream of shells, bringing an increase of casualties, the restraint became almost unbearable. In one engagement the suspense was so great that a calm corporal, about whose bravery there could be no doubt, was heard to exclaim, "Oh, dear! when shall *we* fire?" [19] And in others, the troops began to pop away without waiting for the command.

With the first shot would come a tremendous relief. "After the first round the fear left me," wrote a soldier to his mother after his initial battle, "& I was as cool as ever I was in my life. I think I have been a great deal more excited in attempting to speak a piece in school or to make remarks in an evening meeting." [20]

The sense of calm would be accompanied by an apparent indifference to the ghastly work in progress on every side, a circumstance which in reflection was both surprising and shocking. The day following Shiloh, Private Franklin Bailey wrote his parents: "I did not think any more of seeing a man shot down by my side than you would of seeing a dumb beast kiled. Strange as it may seam to you, but the more men I saw kiled the more reckless I became." [21]

The first shot would be followed by others, the soldiers dropping down after each round to reload, with many of them rolling over on their backs to ram the charge home and then rising to their feet to send the bullets on their way. Some fired from kneeling and prone positions, the latter gaining favor as the war progressed.

As the men tore open cartridge after cartridge with their teeth, black powder would spill out on their faces, forming dark circles around their mouths and giving their countenances a weird appearance befitting the fiendish task which now absorbed them.

The conduct of the men as they banged away at the Rebels was such as to belie the calm which seemed to follow the first fire. The air would be filled with profanity. Officers would urge their men on with oaths. Soldiers would swear at one another and to themselves in sheer excitement. The first indication of a missile finding its target was often a profane exclamation from the man who was hit. Cursing was by no means restricted to the habitually profane, for pious men from whose lips no oath was ever heard in camp sometimes became surprisingly eloquent swearers in battle.[22]

The continued firing would bring exhilaration to some, causing them to punctuate their shots with cries of satisfaction and defiance. At Opequon, for instance, after the fight got under way men praised a comrade's act of gallantry by shouting as they next pulled their triggers, "Here's one for Corporal Gray." Other volleys were accompanied by the cries, "Here's one for Sheridan," "Here's one for Lincoln," and "Here's one for Jeff Davis." [23] After Brandy Station a cavalryman wrote his parents, "I never felt so gay in my life as I did when we charged with the Sabre," and following Gettysburg an artilleryman remarked: "I felt a joyous exaltation, a perfect indifference to circumstances through the whole of that three days fight, and have seldom enjoyed three days more in my life." [24]

For others the prevailing mood was anger. Sometimes anger sprang from the failure of the attack or from the cowering of comrades. Of his sensations at Fredericksburg when enemy fire and faltering associates slowed the advance, a Massachusetts soldier later wrote: "I went so far ahead when I fired that I was ordered back by our major and lieutenant. I was mad, yet calm; how I itched for a hand-to-hand struggle." [25] More commonly the anger was inspired by the sight of fellow soldiers falling before the enemy fire. After Shiloh, Franklin Bailey recalled: "When George Gates who . . . stood next to me on my right hand, was shot, I was so enraged, I could have tore the heart out of the rebal could I have reached him." [26] And following Gaines's Mill, O. W. Norton wrote:

My two tent mates were wounded, and after that . . . I acted like a madman. . . . I was stronger than I had been before in a month and a kind of desperation seized me. . . . I snatched a gun from the hands of a man who was shot through the head, as he staggered and fell. At other times I would have been horror-struck, and could not have moved, but then I jumped over dead men with as little feeling as I would over a log. The feeling that was uppermost in my mind was a desire to kill as many rebels as I could. The loss of comrades maddened me.[27]

In the heat of fighting strange thoughts coursed through the minds of some. A Maine soldier who months before had received a letter from a girl back home urging him to gallantry had one of her phrases flash vividly in his mind in the advance at Brandy Station. "I heard her say as plain as day," he wrote his father after the fight, " 'I am confident that you will make a *brave and noble soldier.*' " [28] Others testified to recalling snatches of poetry, and interestingly enough the passages which raced through the minds of at least two Yanks, one at Fredericksburg and the other at Haines's Bluff, were the booming lines of Tennyson's "The Charge of the Light Brigade." [29]

The thoughts of many remained focused on religion. William O. Wettleson described his first engagement thus: "Strange feelings come over one when he is in battle and bullets are whizzing around one. . . . It is a wonderful place for one who believes he is a Christian to test his faith. I found my hope much weaker than I had thought, and I made good promises." [30]

As the men fired they would continue to move toward their objective. When a suitable position was reached officers would call a halt to re-form their lines, which in the course of the advance had become disorganized, and to prepare for the final dash on the Rebel works. During the lull, as the blood cooled, the spirit tended to weaken. A few, unable to steel themselves to a continuance of the ordeal, would take advantage of the interval to slip away to the rear. Some of the shirkers would use the excuse of assisting wounded comrades; others would claim the necessity of replacing damaged weapons or replenishing ammunition. Still others would take leave without any pretext. More would steal away were it not for the vigilance of officers and file closers.

But the majority would stay by their posts, however great their dread of the final assault. The force that compelled them, above all else, was the thought of family and friends and the unwillingness to be branded as cowards.

At this point, if not before, the men would receive the order to "fix bayonets," and steel would grate against steel as the sharp instruments were fitted over the ends of the rifle barrels. Then when all were ready would come the fateful command "charge," and the Yanks would spring forward with a cheer.

What sort of cheer? The battle cry of the men in blue was different from that of the Rebels. The standard Yankee version was a deeply intoned hurrah or huzza, while the Southern cry was a wild, piercing yell.[31] The contrast must have been a marked one, for it was the subject of considerable comment. A New York colonel testifying at the Fitz John Porter trial in 1862 remarked: "Our own men give three successive cheers, and in concert, but theirs is a cheering without any reference to regularity of form—a continual yelling." [32] An Ohio surgeon, commenting on an engagement near Chattanooga, stated: "I could hear the sharp, shrill *yells* of the rebs, so different from the *cheer* which our men use." [33] Another surgeon, who was at the Wilderness, was more specific: "I could easily tell whether our troops or the enemy were making a charge by the peculiar character of their outcry," he stated. "On our side it was a resounding, continuous hurrah," he added, "while the famous dread inspiring 'rebel yell' was a succession of yelps, staccato and shrill." [34] Junius Browne, correspondent of the New York *Herald*, noted at Vicksburg that the Rebel yell was "shrill, exultant, savage . . . different from the deep, manly, generous shout of the Union soldiers." [35]

But the Federal cheer, like the Rebel yell, had variations. Sometimes it was a "hi! hi!" Again it was an "Indian war whoop." [36] The commander of the Seventy-seventh Pennsylvania Regiment reported after Murfreesboro that his men had pitched into the Rebels "with a whoop and a yell," while an Indiana officer stated that in the same engagement: "We went forward toward a Rebel regiment . . . double quick, and uttering these unearthly Hoosier yells that have been heard so often on the Battlefields." [37]

Occasional reference in official reports to the men in blue charging with "furious yells" and "wild cheers" suggests that now and then the cry of the Federals bore some resemblance to that of the Rebels. However that may be, it is certain that the hurrahs and huzzas which distinguished the Yankee cry were sometimes shouted with savage abandon.[38]

Since the principal function of the battle cry was to relieve tension, it was usually spontaneous. But sometimes commanders specifically ordered their men to shout with the view of frightening the foe. At Antietam, Colonel Cross of the Fifth New Hampshire added another detail. "As the fight grew furious," according to one of his men, "the colonel cried out, 'Put on the war paint.' . . . Taking the cue . . . we rubbed the torn end of the cartridges over our faces, streaking them with powder like a pack of Indians, and the colonel to complete the similarity, cried out, 'Give 'em the war whoop!,' and all of us joined him in the Indian war whoop." In the ensuing fracas the whoopers were successful and the man who told the story was inclined to give some credit to the savage make-up and shouting.[39]

Whatever the nature or purpose of their shouting, the consuming impulse of the charging men was to reach the Rebel lines. This burning urge sprang in part from a hot-blooded desire to kill, and in part from a desperate eagerness to get beyond the flaming mouths of hostile guns, to strike danger at its source, to meet the worst that the battle had to offer and force a quick decision.

As the surging attackers closed on their objective, they would encounter an increasing flood of lead. At Lookout Mountain the fire was so intense that one charging Yank "thought it was raining bullets," and at Jackson, Mississippi, according to another, the balls "Sung Dixey around our years" while "the grape and Canister moed our Ranks Down like grass Before the Sithe." [40] Still another stated that at the Wilderness Confederate bullets rushed by in such swarms that it seemed "I could have caught a pot full of them if I had had a strong iron vessel rigged on a pole as a butterfly net." [41]

The fire might become so heavy that the men in blue would lean forward as they advanced, as if walking against a gale. At Fredericksburg a Yank found himself drawing his head down into his collar "the same as I would go through a storm of hail and wind." [42]

Minié balls, canister and grape would cut holes in the advancing lines. Officers would try to close up the gaps, but their efforts would have little effect. Eventually each man would fight on his own.[43]

The tempo of the assault would increase in the final stages and the last few yards be covered on a run. As the attackers threw themselves against the defending lines, shouting on both sides would rise to a tumultuous climax. Bayonets now came into play, though few of them actually pierced enemy flesh, and muskets were fired at such close range as to burn the faces of the contestants.[44] In the heated tussle men would pitch into one another with stones and fists, but most of the close-up fighting would be with the clubbed musket.[45]

At first the gray lines would bend back under the force of the assault. But if the defense was strong and the attack unsupported, the blue-clad survivors would fall back after a few minutes of desperate struggle and thus bring an end to this phase of the contest.

But before the battle was decided the Yanks might repeat the assault several times, as at Fredericksburg. Again they might have the defensive role as at Gettysburg. Or yet again, the contest might take the form of attack by one side and then the other as at Donelson and Shiloh.

The character of attacks varied greatly. Sometimes the only preliminaries were a hurried beating of the long roll, a quick forming of lines and a hasty dispensing of ammunition. Again, no distinct break occurred between advance to position and final charge. Many attacks were repulsed before reaching the assault stage, and some assaults were transformed into routs before hostile positions were ever reached. Some battles of course were more in the nature of piecemeal fire fights than of assaults and defenses. In almost any contest there was much more of waiting and maneuvering than there was of actual shooting.

Along with the variations, battles had a number of things in common. From the point of view of the man who carried the musket they were extremely exciting affairs. The mere rumor that a fight was in prospect would lift soldiers from the doldrums, and sustained firing on the picket line would affect a camp like an electric shock. Animation would redouble with the beating of the long roll and the rushing of men into line. And while the curve of emotions would show peaks and valleys as the drama was further unfolded, its general course would continue upward until clash with the foe brought thrill to a climax.

The thrill was the thing most remembered, but the sensational aspects were only the surface of the battle. The essence of fighting was hardship and discomfort. Owing to prior marching, soldiers were often tired when they entered combat. At Gettysburg and the Wilderness some units covered more than thirty miles in a stretch to reach the scene of action. Men advancing to battle commonly shed much of their equipment and clothing, as the littered approaches to almost any field would testify, and this practice, while affording some temporary relief, in the end frequently led to extreme discomfort. Soldiers at Donelson, for example, who had thrown away their overcoats as they marched in balmy weather from Fort Henry, suffered terribly when a cold snap overtook them on the eve of the battle. After the fort was taken a soldier wrote: "Wee had a hard time geting this place I beleave that we endured the most intence Sufering that ever an army did in the Same length of time. . . . We were bound to lay for fore days and knights without Sleeping and most of the time nothing to eat and raining and snowing a portion of the time with out any covering whatever was what I cald a bitter pill." [46]

But most fighting occurred in seasons other than winter, and heat rather than cold was the usual curse. Lying in the hot sun awaiting attack was enervating enough, but the yelling, rushing, shouting and excitement of the fighting itself caused the perspiration to run in streams and consumed one's energy at a fearful rate. Dust, kicked up by tramping feet and striking missiles, added to the discomfort, as did the thickening smoke that hung over the field like a cloud.[47] Exertion and tension brought enormous thirst which often could not be quenched because canteens had been discarded early in the battle. At First Manassas, when the Federal advance reached Sudley Ford, countless Yanks stopped to drink, dipping up the muddy water in their hands, their hats and their shoes.[48] A youngster who fought at Antietam wrote back to his father who had just joined the army: "If you ever go into battle, have your canteen full. I was so dry at one time I could have drank out of a mud puddle—without stopping to ask questions." [49]

Sometimes heavy rain beat down on the soldiers, increasing the weight of their clothing, making them uncomfortable by day and disturbing their rest at night. The constant seething of an army in motion soon converted the battlefield into a sea of mud which made marching difficult and clogged roads with stuck vehicles and swearing drivers.

Under any conditions fighting was extremely exhausting. A participant in First Manassas stated that before the Federal rout began he and the other members of his brigade "were so tired that we couldn't have left the field as fast as we had come to it." He added: "Men near me were plodding heavily and panting. Their faces were all sweat and grime, their eyes red from dust, their lips black with . . . powder. . . . They were dirty and weary and angry." [50] Another said of that engagement: "It was the hardest day's work I ever Expect to do." [51]

If the action extended over a considerable period, as in the Seven Days' and the Wilderness campaigns, weariness became so great that men plodded along numbly and without spirit, responding to orders like so many automatons.[52] A Vermonter wrote shortly after the Seven Days' battles that he was "so completely worn out that I can't tell how many days the has been in the last two weeks . . . five days . . . I went without sleeping or eating." [53]

A battle was also a chaotic event and especially so to the man in the ranks. As one soldier expressed it, "Nobody sees a battle." Regardless of how well-ordered the beginning or how thorough the over-all direction, most engagements seemed eventually to break up into innumerable small encounters, without shape or form, in which mixed units battled on their own against foes who could hardly be seen.

The confusion was disillusioning to some. Private William Brearley wrote after Antietam: "I have heard and seen pictures of battles—they would all be in line, all standing in a nice level field fighting, a number of ladies taking care of the wounded, &c &c. but it isent so . . . the rebels had Stone walls to get behind and the woods to fall back in." [54] Sergeant Matthew Marvin of the First Minnesota noted in his diary that at the conclusion of the Fredericksburg fight his regiment "was scattered from Hell to Breakfast." [55] Many soldiers commented on their inability to describe a battle, a circumstance which undoubtedly was due in no small part to the utter disorder which seemed to prevail.

Above all a fight was a noisy experience, and hardly any phase was the subject of so much comment as the sound of battle.[56] The blended fire of small arms was usually described as a rattle and that of artillery as a roll or a roar. The commingling of musket and cannon fire commonly suggested thunder; a New Yorker reported that the effect at Antietam was "not a noise, but a savage continual thunder that cannot compare to any sound I ever heard." [57]

The flight of bullets was variously described as a hum, whiz, whistle, whine and shriek, and some soldiers referred to the Minié balls as bumblebees, while others called them "swifts." Captain Oliver Wendell Holmes noted that at Seven Pines the Minié balls had "a most villainous greasy slide through the air." [58] Another Yank, telling of the fighting before Atlanta, stated: "We were sometimes amused by the music of musket balls. One would come along with the '*meow*' of a kitten, and the men would declare the rebels were throwing kittens at them. Another would come with an angry howl, as if seeking its Yankee victim. And we listened to others that had the wailing sound of a winter's wind. All these sounds were more musical than the 'zip' of the bullet at short range." [59] The sound of artillery missiles, to which soldiers gave such nicknames as "camp kettles," "cook stoves," "lamp posts," "iron foundries," "tubs" and "bootlegs," was most frequently referred to as a scream.[60] After Antietam a surgeon wrote: "You can have no idea of the horrible noise the shells make—when one passes over your head with its scream as if 50 Locomotive Whistles were blowing at once, no man can help dodging." [61]

The end of the battle brought various reactions. Perhaps the dominant feeling was one of relief at having come through the ordeal unharmed. But the satisfaction springing from personal safety was often marred by the wounding or death of beloved comrades. Indeed, one of the most trying aspects of combat was the moaning and screaming of the wounded that came in the wake of fighting; the situation was doubly grievous if, as was sometimes the case, one had to search among the casualties for a missing kinsman or friend.

Sadness over the loss of comrades combined with lingering weariness and the cooling of battle emotions to produce in some a sense of deep depression. Gloom was increased when the result of the fight was a humiliating defeat.

But as soldiers became accustomed to battle, the shock of both the fighting and the aftermath was considerably lessened. The degree of detachment attained by some was vividly revealed by a Yank who wrote after Antietam: "We dont mind the sight of dead men no more than if they was dead Hogs. . . . The rebels was laying over the field bloated up as big as a horse and as black as a negro and the boys run over them and serch their pockets as unconcerned. . . . I was going through a Cornfield and I run acros a big graback as black as the ase of spade it startled me a little at first but I stopt to see what he had but he had bin tended too so I past on my way rejoicing." [62]

The gathering of trophies, whether from dead bodies or the general litter of the fighting zone, was a standard feature of postbattle activity. A Yank who plundered a Rebel casualty in Virginia early in 1862 gave his homefolk the following report: "I give the slide 2 a division General, some of the butons 2 another general and the envelop 2 another general the slide I did not want 2 part with but I knew it wouldnt do 2 say no. . . . I will send some of the buttons in this letter and I may send the tooth brush in a paper if I dont conclude 2 use myself I also took one of his suspenders which was leather & I shall make a canteen strap of that a General tooke the other one." [63]

The souvenir mania was sometimes carried to ludicrous extremes. A New Yorker reported that at Fredericksburg some of his comrades came out of abandoned Rebel houses "with large doll babies & children's toys, whigs [wigs] on and white beavers & bonnets." [64]

For days after the fight, highlights of battle provided the theme of campfire discussions. Here hindsight tacticians told off the generals to their hearts' content. After Big Bethel a soldier reported, "Some who were in the Mexican and Crimean Wars say that we should not have made the attack without a good supply of artillery." [65]

Private Thomas N. Lewis must have echoed a sentiment often expressed over coffee cups by Shiloh survivors when he wrote on April 10, 1862: "Buell was the saving of Grant's army. . . . Grant is played out with me we wer strong enough to drive the rebells if we wer managed right, but no he would bring us up in a Single line when the rebells were 6 or 8 deep and any fool would know we could not stand then." [66]

Incidents of battle were the meat of these afteraction talks. Such dramatic episodes as Private Riley of the Ninth New York Heavy Artillery having his son slain by his side, and of a New Yorker who had joined the Confederate Army killing his youngest brother at Fredericksburg—and discovering the fact only when he turned his victim over to strip him—must have been often recounted.[67] But soldiers preferred to dwell on less tragic notes. Braggarts would sometimes wax eloquent on their exploits, though such claims were apt to be heavily discounted by the listeners. Lieutenant Henry Clune wrote after Shiloh that he had "been searching diligently during the past five days for the man who didnt kill Gen'l Johnston," adding: "He is the same individual who winged Genl Beauregard." [68]

Badger State soldiers never tired talking of the antics of "Old Abe," the eagle that accompanied the Eighth Wisconsin on its campaigns in the West. This mascot, the most famous of the war, usually behaved himself creditably on the march and in battle, but at Corinth, Mississippi, his courage suffered a lapse. When yelling Rebs charged the portion of the line where he was poised, wounding him slightly under the wing, "he hopped off his perch to the ground and ducked his head between his carrier's legs. He was thoroughly demoralized and the same feeling suddenly extended itself to the line and they broke and ran . . . the carrier of the Eagle picking him up and carrying him under his arm as fast as he could run." [69]

Mascots were not the only representatives of the bird and animal world that acted strangely on the battlefield. At Murfreesboro, according to a Union correspondent, flocks of sparrows from the cedar thickets "fluttered and circled above the field in a state of utter bewilderment, and scores of rabbits fled for protection to our men lying down in line on the left, nestling under their coats and creeping under their legs in a state of utter distraction. They hopped over the fields like toads, and as perfectly tamed by fright as household pets." [70] At the fighting about Spottsylvania Court House in May 1864 a flock of little chickens, according to Captain Oliver Wendell Holmes, came "peeping and cheeping" about his division's headquarters, completely ignoring the bullets whistling above their heads.[71]

Soldiers liked to recall the coolness and bravery with which their officers conducted themselves in battle. Members of the Fifteenth Iowa who gathered about campfires after Atlanta must have commented appreciatively on the feat in that engagement of their Colonel Belknap who, in the thick of fighting, took prisoner Colonel Lampley of the Forty-fifth Alabama by pulling him over the intervening works by his coat collar.[72] Hardly less amazing was the bold act of Colonel Isaac Suman of the Ninth Indiana at Chickamauga who, walking unexpectedly into a nest of Rebels and being called on by a gray-clad officer to surrender, coolly replied that he had surrendered some time before. The Rebel appeared satisfied at the moment and before he had time to discover the ruse Suman slipped away, organized some help and came back and drove his near captors away.[73]

But all officers were not brave, and soldiers probably had more fun talking about instances of their quaking than of their heroism. Private Frank Wilkeson got a hearty laugh from his comrades when he told them of catching an infantry colonel at Spottsylvania in a discreditable act. While walking to the rear on a water-hunting detail, Wilkeson espied the blond, bewhiskered wearer of eagles sitting behind a large oak tree "putting on his war paint." The officer "took a cartridge out of his vest pocket, tore the paper with his strong white teeth, spilled the powder into his right palm, spat on it, and then, first casting a quick glance around to see if he was observed, he rubbed the moistened powder on his face and hands and then dust-coated the war paint. Instantly he was transformed from a trembling coward who lurked behind a tree into an exhausted brave taking a little well-earned repose." [74]

Postbattle anecdotes had to do mainly with colorful incidents involving the rank and file. Ripples of laughter must have run through more than one campfire group when the story was told of the soldier who called on the file closer to unclog his rifle which he had inadvertently stuck in the mud, and the ensuing operation disclosed that the barrel contained very little mud but was full of unfired charges. In the excitement of fighting, this Yank had been loading and pulling trigger, but apparently had failed to put on new caps; and instead of mowing down the Rebels, as he thought, he had simply been stuffing his musket.[75]

Other soldiers made themselves vulnerable to teasing by pulling triggers before withdrawing ramrods and thus sending strange-looking missiles through the air. At the battle of Corinth a fast-firing Frenchman became so excited that he sent a bullet against the rifle of the man in front of him. The latter was so infuriated by this careless shooting that he laid down his gun and began to pommel the Frenchman, who returned the blows. After a brief duel of fists, while hostile bullets flew thick on all sides, honor was satisfied, the injured weapon was replaced by one picked up from the field and the two Yanks resumed their attack on the common foe.[76]

Private Dave Burns, an Irishman of the Fifth New York Regiment, afforded his comrades much amusement by a verbal exchange with a Rebel Irishman wounded and captured at Gaines's Mill. While the fight was still raging, Burns, noting that the prisoner had a revolver in his hand, asked him what he was doing with it. The Reb replied that the gun was for protection against Yankee bayonets. According to a comrade:

Burns waxed wroth at the idea of one of the Fifth doing anything so cowardly and berated him soundly; getting warmed up, he wished that the Confederate was a well man, and he would knock all the secesh blood out of him; that he was a disgrace to the Irish people for fighting against the flag, etc. Finally he took the revolver away from him and removed the caps, but the man begged so hard for it, as it was a present from one of his officers, he gave it back to him, and also a drink of water, and went at the fighting again, as if he had merely stopped work for a few moments to have an argument with a friend.[77]

Narrow escapes also figured prominently in the afteraction sessions. Soldiers must have chortled over such "mortal woundings" as that suffered by Iola Caleb of the Seventeenth Maine who at Chancellorsville lost part of his whiskers, though the ball doing the damage did "not bring more blud than many a barber." [78]

As soon after the fight as circumstances would permit, most Yanks took pen in hand to write their homefolk. The item of first priority, after the usual stereotyped opening, was the fate of the addressor: "I came out saft," or "I was slitely wounded in the rist." Then came an account of what befell soldier neighbors and relatives, followed in some cases by attempts to tell what the fight was like; the part played by the writer, how he reacted to the noise, the horror and the bloodshed; what unusual incidents he observed; the outcome of the encounter; and finally an expression of wonderment and thankfulness that the writer survived, and a hope that the war would soon come to an end.

Some soldiers told proudly, and no doubt with some exaggeration, how many shots they had fired. One Yank wrote of giving the Rebs forty rounds in a single advance at Mine Run, and another boasted that he shot eighty rounds "rite in frunt" before the repulse at Haines's Bluff.[79] "Sich firen a regiment never dun," he added, "the ginerl Swore he never Saw a rigment lode and fier So faste." [80] After Gettysburg, Private

George Milledge of the Sixty-sixth Ohio Regiment reported to his wife: "i fired about two hundred rounds." [81] A number of Yanks stated that their guns became so hot from the rapid firing as to make them temporarily unusable. In any circumstances, much of the firing was wild and reckless and considerably more injurious to treetops than to Rebels.

Occasionally a Yank would keep tab of his marksmanship. Private W. O. Lyford informed his father after First Manassas that "I had the pleasure of shooting three rebels dead and wounding another." [82] But the man who could say with confidence after a fight that his bullets hit any foe, much less several, was an exception. Indeed, some, fearful of conscience, preferred not to know the results of their fire.[83]

Many Yanks passed on to their folk gruesome details of slaughter and horror—of screaming comrades, severed limbs, splashed brains, bodies blown to pieces by exploding shells, and the nauseous stench of the dead. After Seven Pines, Alfred Davenport wrote his father of seeing piles of slain Rebels with horrible expressions on their faces, "as if they had seen something that scared them to death," and Cyrus Stone, who went over the field after Antietam, informed his parents: "The rebel dead lay in winrows and both our men and the rebels lay in every direction. . . . We were glad to march over the field at night for we could not see the horrible sights so well. Oh what a smell some of the men vomit as they went along." [84]

One Yank recounted seeing Federal dead that had been overrun by wagons as the Rebels withdrew, "mangled and torn to pieces so that Even friends could not tell them." [85] But the soldier who merited the prize for gruesomeness was the one who wrote after Fredericksburg: "There was a Hospital with in thirty yards of us . . . about the building you could see the Hogs belonging to the Farm eating arms and other portions of the body." [86]

Little wonder that some manifested strong revulsion at the scenes forced upon them. Three days after Shiloh an Illinoisan wrote: "I wish it was over with I am tired of seeing dead and wounded men." [87] Later in the year an Eastern soldier commented: "The sight of Fredericksburg and the battlefield presented on the 14th inst. would have made even the old hell-hound Horace Greeley cry—peace!" [88] Others found in the profligate slaughter a shocking evidence of the cheapness of human life.[89]

Most Yanks who commented on their individual reactions and performances gave a favorable report. But some confessed flying lead made them terribly afraid. A Vermonter who was at Mine Run wrote shortly afterward to his wife: "I tell you Sally if I ever lay clost to the ground it was at this time." [90] And a New Jersey soldier, reporting to his homefolk on an engagement in North Georgia in May 1864, stated that he came near being taken prisoner and "if I hadent seen the fix I was in, and run like blazes I would have been a goner by this time." [91] Of his part in an engagement near Petersburg in September 1864, a Maine Yank wrote: "They came in on us in 5 lines of batel so sum of the boys say but I did not stop to count I limbered up for the rear as fast as legs cood cariery and that was prety fast." [92]

Soldier accounts of combat were as varied as the personalities and experiences of the men who wrote them. Typical of battle descriptions by more articulate Yanks was the following report of Antietam which sixteen-year-old William Brearley made to his father:

> . . . the next morning we had our Second battle—it was rather Strange music to hear the balls Scream within an inch of my head. I had a bullett strike me on the top of the head just as I was going to fire and a piece of Shell struck my foot—a ball hit my finger and another hit my thumb I concluded they ment me. the rebels played the mischief with us by raising a U. S. flag. We were ordered not to fire and as soon as we went forward they opened an awful fire from their batteries on us we were ordered to fall back about ½ miles, I staid behind when our regiment retreated and a line of Skirmishers came up—I joined them and had a chance of firing about 10 times more— . . . Our Generals say they (the rebels) had as strong a position as could *possibly* be and we had to pick into them through an old chopping all grown up with bushes so thick that we couldent hardly get through—but we were so excited that the "old scratch" himself couldent have stopt us. We rushed onto them evry man for himself—all loading & firing as fast as he could see a rebel to Shoot at—at last the rebels began to get over the wall to the rear and run for the woods. the firing encreased tenfold then it sounded like the rolls of thunder—and all the time evry man shouting as loud as he could—I got rather more excited than I wish to again. I dident *think* of getting hit but it was almost a miricle that I wasent the rebels that we took prisoners said that they never before encountered a regiment that fought so like "Devils" (so they termed it) as we did—every one praised our regiment—one man in our company was Shot through the head no more than 4 feet from me he was killed instantly. after the Sunday battle I took care of the wounded until 11 P.M. I saw some of horidest sights I ever saw—one man had both eyes shot out—and they were wounded in all the different ways you could think of—the most I could do was to give them water—they were all very thirsty— . . . Our Colonel (Withington) was formerly a captain of the Mich 1st—he is just as cool as can be, he walked around amongst

us at the battle the bullets flying all around him—he kept Shouting to
us to fire low and give it to them——[93]

One important fact seems to have been only vaguely comprehended
by the soldiers in their home letters. This was the change which occurred
in the character of fighting. The last two years of the war witnessed a
decline of exposed, open conflict and an increase of protective procedures
and trench operations. In the shift the cannon and the rifle lost some
of their prestige and the mortar and the spade gained in importance.
Troops and officers who at Shiloh were disdainful of digging in had by
the opening of the Georgia campaign become eager and adept at throw-
ing up hasty fortifications. Trench modes, introduced on a large scale at
Vicksburg in 1863, were transferred to the East the following summer,
where, with certain refinements in detail, they became the prevailing
pattern of subsequent operations about Richmond. Sapping, mining and
use of hand grenades were important features of the new order.

This metamorphosis and the soldiers' reaction to it was reflected in
the reports of officers. Captain Frederick E. Prime, commenting on op-
erations at Vicksburg, noted the reluctance of work details from the line
to wield the pick and shovel and stated that their aversion to labor fig-
ured prominently in the decision to try to carry the works by assault.[94]
The engineer of the Thirteenth Corps reported the construction of
springboards, and the improvising of mortars from tree trunks, to lob
shells into the Rebel trenches.[95] Several officers in their accounts of
operations near Richmond in the summer of 1864 remarked on how
quickly soldiers dug in with whatever was at hand, including bayonets,
tin cups and plates.[96] On June 25, 1864, a brigadier of the Fifth Corps
wrote from before Petersburg to a friend: "We have never before used
the Spade as we have this summer. In any two days of the campaign
we have constructed more works than were thrown up by us two years
ago during the whole time we were in front of Richmond." [97] General
W. T. Sherman, in reporting a shift of positions before Atlanta, July
27-28, 1864, stated: "About 10 a.m. all the army was in position, and the
men were busy in throwing up the accustomed pile of rails and logs,
which after a while assumed the form of a parapet. The skill and rapidity
with which our men construct these is wonderful and is something new
in the art of war." [98]

Resort to trenches made warfare considerably less bloody, but danger
became more constant. As one of Sherman's generals, commenting on

the Atlanta campaign, put it: "No one could say any hour that he would be living the next. Men were killed in their camps, at their meals, and . . . in their sleep." He added: "So many men were daily struck in the camp and trenches that men became utterly reckless, passing about where balls were striking as though it was their normal life and making a joke of a narrow escape or a noisy, whistling ball." [99]

"In the Trenches before Petersburg" headed innumerable letters written during the last months of the war by Grant's soldiers. The contents told of watching the fiery trails of mortar shells on their arched flights through the air, the calling of shots, the scampering to bomb-proof shelters, the ever-present menace by day of the sharpshooters' bullets and the stifling heat of the trenches on summer nights. They also deplored the dullness of the dug-in existence and recounted the occasional exchange of taunts and pleasantries with Rebs across the way— Rebs whose lives were very much like their own, save for the Southerners' dearth of food and clothing and their ever-diminishing hope of victory.

Whatever the mode or period, the fighting of Billy Yanks was marked by varying degrees of proficiency. There was much of heroism and of cowardice and more of the solid, unsensational performance that lies between these two extremes.

In most engagements cowardice reared its ugly head before the shooting commenced. Some of the craven species resorted to self-mutilation in an effort to forestall exposure to enemy bullets. Shooting off toes and fingers became so flagrant in one division of the Army of the Potomac early in 1863 that the commanding general in May issued an order on the subject, requiring surgeons to make a complete report on such cases and threatening soldiers found guilty of the offense with severe punishment.[100] Another ruse frequently used for avoidance of battle was playing sick. A month before First Manassas an officer stationed near Washington noted in his diary: "Long Roll was beat about 11 oclock P.M. The Regt turned out to a man and were in line of Battle in 7 minutes, and ready for the enemy. Yet there was a number who were suddenly taken with a *pain in the stomach* and felt like going back to their tents. The trouble evidently was cowardice." [101]

Some cowards invariably felt a pressing "call of nature" as lines formed for advance against the enemy, and then turned up after the fight with glib stories of getting lost, fighting in other regiments or being called to help out with the wounded. Others, as previously mentioned, used the excuse of damaged weapons—the unserviceability of which had escaped notice until the moment of attack—to abandon their posts. A lieutenant testifying at the trial of a soldier who had slipped off from his company at Chickamauga, after being refused permission to leave the ranks on the plea of a clogged gun, made the revealing statement: "It was expected of every man to ask leave to leave ranks under every circumstance." [102]

Cowards usually had a better opportunity to abandon their posts after the fighting got under way, because of the smoke and confusion, and in every major engagement large numbers sought the protection of trees, dived into ditches, cowered behind stumps or headed openly for the rear. Soldiers were quick to note that skulkers frequently included those who had been most vociferous in proclaiming their desire to meet the enemy.[103]

Many of those who showed the white feather apparently felt little shame. Others wanted to be brave but were hopelessly immobilized when confronting a maelstrom of fire and lead. Abner R. Small related the following incident from his own experience at Fredericksburg.

In the charge I saw one soldier falter repeatedly, bowing as if before a hurricane. He would gather himself together, gain his place in the ranks, and again drop behind. Once or twice he fell to his knees, and at last he sank to the ground, still gripping his musket and bowing his head. I lifted him to his feet and said "Coward!". . . His pale distorted face flamed. He flung at me, "You lie!" Yet he didn't move; he couldn't; his legs would not obey him. I left him there in the mud. Soon after the battle he came to me with tears in his eyes and said, "Adjutant, pardon me, I couldn't go on, but I'm not a coward." Pardon him! I asked his forgiveness.[104]

Some were pitiful in their fright; others were ludicrous. Thomas L. Livermore told of a soldier who after contriving successfully to avoid all prior fights finally was compelled to undergo the ordeal at Chancellorsville. "When the shells came screaming over and through our lines here," Livermore stated. this man "got an empty cracker box, the boards of which were not over half an inch thick, and setting it up in front of him crouched behind it to shelter himself from the shells. . . . Colonel Cross saw it and became so indignant that he strode up to —— and kicked him clear out of position . . . saying, 'You will disgrace my regiment.' " [105]

Soldiers who played the coward sometimes had to endure the jeers and taunts of their comrades. A Yank who slipped out of line at Corinth and came back after the fight with a story of being detailed to guard the water tank was mercilessly ridiculed by members of his company who afterward on the march would cry out "Who guarded the water tank at the battle of Corinth?" and then shout the offender's name.[106] When soldiers of a Pennsylvania regiment, whose conduct at Fredericksburg left much to be desired, boarded the train for home at the expiration of the unit's term of service, other Yanks impudently sent them on their way with the cry "Who run at Fredericksburg?"[107]

Defection in battle varied in character and extent from individual skulking and running on a small scale to wholesale straggling and mass panic. The stampede which took place at First Manassas is so well known that it need not be recounted here. The next notable instance of large-scale demoralization was at Shiloh. Grant's force did not stampede en masse as did McDowell's at Manassas, but running, individually and in groups, was commonplace and the total number who abandoned their posts in the course of the fight ran well up into the thousands. The report of a colonel told of an Ohio regiment breaking and running "in a manner that can only be stigmatized as disgraceful and cowardly . . . their officers . . . setting them an example of speed in flying from the enemy that even Floyd might envy."[108] General Stephen A. Hurlbut stated that on Sunday, April 6, 1862, "A single shot from the enemy's batteries struck in Myer's Thirteenth Ohio Battery, when officers and men, with a common impulse of disgraceful cowardice abandoned the entire battery, horses, caissons and guns and fled, and I saw them no more until Tuesday."[109] Other official reports gave similar examples. The cumulative results were vividly described by officers who came up at the end of the first day with advance units of Buell's command. General William Nelson reported: "I found cowering under the river bank when I crossed from 7,000 to 10,000 men frantic with fright and utterly demoralized, who received my gallant division with cries, 'We are whipped; cut to pieces.' They were insensible to shame or sarcasm."[110] Colonel Jacob Ammen told much the same story, though he estimated the number of skulkers at 10,000 to 15,000. "In crossing the river," Ammen stated, "some of my men called my attention to men with uniforms, even shoulder-straps making their way across the stream on logs and wished to shoot the cowards. Such looks of terror, such confusion, I never saw before, and do not wish to see again."[111]

At Seven Pines and again during the Seven Days considerable demoralization was reported in some units, but such instances were exceptional.[112] At Second Manassas panic occurred among Pope's troops, but it was not nearly so pervasive as that of the previous year and appears to have been due more to mismanagement and confusion of high command than to shortcomings of men in the ranks.[113] Running to the rear was relatively rare at Antietam, but straggling appears to have been woefully common in some parts of McClellan's army.[114] Fredericksburg, while demonstrating extremes of gallantry under the most trying conditions, was also marked by instances of shameful conduct. Lieutenant Henry Ropes wrote his father on December 16, 1862: "Hooker's men ran by us like Sheep. I saw a whole Brigade of Pennsylvania cowards (Tyler's Brigade) break and run in total disorder when they were brought up to our relief. Our men cursing them most heartily." [115] And Captain Henry Abbott reported to his brother: "The army generally didn't fight well. The new regiments behaved shamefully, as well as many of the old ones. The 15th Mass. was seized with a panic at nothing at all and broke like sheep. . . . Hooker's troops broke and ran." [116]

In the West in 1862 the story was very much the same as that in the East. While wholesale melting away such as occurred at Shiloh was not repeated, considerable demoralization occurred in every major engagement. Rosecrans charged the Seventeenth Iowa Regiment with disgraceful stampeding at Iuka,[117] and a signal officer who witnessed the Perryville fight wrote that when new troops under General Jackson encountered the Rebels "many of the Regts turned and fled at the first fire." [118] The officer reporting the incident placed the major blame on the officers, some of whom, from colonels on down, broke before their men and led them in disgraceful flight. The "wildest confusion" ensued, he stated, the panicky units completely overrunning the older ones behind them. "I saw one Regt. (a new one)," he added, "deliver its fire into another of our Regts and then turned and fled. . . . Men were flying in all directions from the field." [119]

At Murfreesboro a rout occurred in the right wing among troops commanded by McCook, and two days later panic seized Van Cleve's division on the opposite end of the line.[120] Colonel W. B. Hazen who was sent to support the portion of the line held by Van Cleve later reported: "It was difficult to say which was running away the more rapidly, the division of Van Cleve to the rear or the enemy in the opposite direction." [121]

The most notorious instance of mass demoralization in 1863 was at Chancellorsville, following Jackson's surprise attack on the Union right and rear. Details of the defeat, including the degree of panic, have been the subject of considerable controversy. But the fact remains that a panic did take place and that troops of the Eleventh Corps, while not universally guilty of arrant cowardice and not the only ones demoralized, had a prominent part in the rout.[122] At Gettysburg where the general circumstances of fighting were markedly different, the most notable case of demoralization occurred in Sickles' Corps when that unit bore the brunt of Longstreet's attack of July 2.[123]

The great battles fought in the West in 1863 also had their share of demoralization. Skulking and cowardice were much in evidence in Banks's assault of Port Hudson on May 27.[124] In the attack of May 22 at Vicksburg, where performance was generally gallant, an Ohio regiment "faltered and gave way" under a fire which was "far from being severe." [125] Chickamauga, like Fredericksburg, was marked by extremes of valor and demoralization, the superb performance of Thomas' men offering a distinct contrast to mass flight in some other commands. Reporting the effects of the Confederates' overpowering attack on the portion of the line held by Sheridan and Davis, Charles A. Dana wrote: "Before them our soldiers turned and fled. It was wholesale panic. Vain were all attempts to rally them." [126]

While large-scale demoralization was considerably less common during the last year and a half of the conflict and usually was in the nature of straggling and skulking rather than stampedes, panic continued to occur occasionally until the very end. One of the most frantic "skedaddles" of the whole war was that which took place among Banks's troops at Sabine Cross Roads, near Mansfield, Louisiana, when the vanguard of the Union force, estimated at 8,000 to 10,000 troops, fell back in "utter disorder and confusion" on the troops behind them, yelling "all is lost," and, according to Admiral David D. Porter, "such a scene ensued as was never seen before except at Bull Run." [127] Another panic took place at Brice's Cross Roads in North Mississippi in June 1864, when Forrest pounced upon Sturgis and sent his expedition flying back to Memphis.[128]

At Cedar Creek on October 19, 1864, near Winchester, Virginia— the fight made famous by Sheridan's anxious ride—two veteran divisions were demoralized by the surprise Confederate attack and "after a few minutes of fighting . . . fled in such dismay as to be of no further use that day except as a reserve late in the afternoon." [129] A lesser rout occurred in the Fourteenth Corps at Bentonville on March 19, 1865; and a Union general reporting the action of March 31, 1865, at White Oak Roads, Virginia, stated that when his troops reached the bank of Gravelly Run they met "the Third Division running to the rear in a most demoralized and disorganized condition." [130]

Demoralization, to be sure, was only one phase of Billy Yank's battle performance and, when the whole record is considered, a minor one at that. Individual acts of cowardice were paralleled by shining deeds of heroism and wholesale panics by brilliant displays of mass gallantry.

Of the countless feats of individual valor cited in official records, none was more remarkable than that of Private Samuel E. Eddy of the Thirty-seventh Massachusetts Regiment who voluntarily went beyond the Union line at Sailor's Creek, Virginia, in April 1865, to rescue his adjutant who had been wounded and was still being fired on by the Rebels. After killing one of the officer's assailants, Private Eddy was attacked by several Confederates, one of whom ran him through with a bayonet. While pinned to the ground Private Eddy shot and killed the man who bayoneted him. For his conspicuous gallantry he was awarded the Medal of Honor.[131]

At Spring River, Arkansas, on March 13, 1862, Sergeant Moody of the Sixth Missouri Cavalry saved a howitzer and wrote his name on the roll of heroes. After close pressure of the Confederates had driven the gun crew back, Sergeant Moody, lacking the rammer which had been carried away in the retreat, forced a canister down the barrel with his saber, touched off the charge and scattered the foe.[132]

In the fight at Hanover Court House, May 27, 1862, Private Leland of the Forty-fourth New York Regiment fired over twenty shots after losing a finger and receiving two head wounds. Another soldier of this regiment, mortally injured in the same engagement, called feebly to his colonel near the close of the battle. The officer approached the wounded man with the expectation of receiving a last message for a loved one, but instead was asked, "Colonel, is the day ours?" "Yes," responded the officer. "Then I am willing to die," was the soldier's reply.[133]

At Seven Pines, William Clemens, a bugler of whom no fighting was required, took the gun of the first casualty and gave a good account of himself on the firing line until killed near the close of the action.[134] Corporal Foreman and Private Samuel French, comrades of Clemens who were both shot in the leg in this engagement, continued to fight until they fainted from exhaustion and loss of blood; and Private Todd, after being mortally wounded, fought on till the close of the battle, then died on the field.[135]

Private Murray of the Fifty-second Illinois staged a one-man rally at the battle of Corinth. When the regiment fell back from the redan, Murray refused to withdraw, stating that the colonel's orders were to hold the fort to the last. A Rebel captain ordered Murray to surrender, but he refused and received a shot in the hand from the officer's revolver. But Murray killed the captain, took his revolver and then turned to meet another assailant whom also he quickly dispatched. His signal bravery was rewarded by a return of his comrades, and the Confederates were driven out of the redan.[136] This feat bears resemblance to one performed on the second day at Gettysburg by an unnamed artillery sergeant. When during the heat of fighting the infantry assigned to support his battery fell back and threatened to leave the field, the sergeant, who belonged to the Excelsior Brigade, "dashed along the line like an infuriated tiger, halted, and cried, 'Boys you said you'd stick to us. . . . There's the Guns . . . if you're men come on,' and with that he wheeled around, struck the spurs deep into his horse and dashed into the enemy's disorganized ranks, his sword flashing . . . as his brawny arm laid about with mad recklessness. With one impulse the whole line yelled 'Charge,' " dashed after the sergeant and saved the battery.[137] At Chickamauga, when a demoralized brigade came flying back through Captain Frank C. Smith's battery, one of the artillerymen, Private Savage, became so infuriated with one of the officers leading the rout that he struck him with his sponge "and damned him for running against his gun." [138]

Private John Kistler of the 132nd Pennsylvania established a record for coolness under duress. As his regiment moved into the attack at Fredericksburg, Kistler's arm was blown off at the elbow by a cannon ball. But instead of heading for the rear he had the stump tied up on the spot, and when the regiment returned after being repulsed he slipped up to the commander munching a cracker and said, "Colonel, I hope we shall whip them yet." [139]

When Sergeant George G. Sinclair of the Eighty-ninth Illinois fell with a serious chest wound in the advance at Liberty Gap, Tennessee, in June 1863, he refused to let his comrades take him from the line of fire, but urged them on with the shout "Let me alone, and hold that fence." In that same action, Corporal Philip Grub, mortally wounded, cried out to a dying comrade lying by his side, "Have I not always done my duty?" and then expired.[140]

At Lookout Mountain, Private Clark Thornton of the Ninety-ninth Ohio, under arrest for desertion, "voluntarily went with the regiment and engaged in the fight, acting with great coolness and bravery, always being in the front rank." [141] Deserters also distinguished themselves in several other engagements.[142]

Reference has been made to the gallantry of a bugler at Seven Pines. The valorous conduct of another at Chickamauga merits special notice. On September 19 when his unit, a brigade of regulars, was falling back, Private William J. Carson with a sword in one hand and his bugle in the other constantly sought to turn the tide by blowing the "halt," the "rally" and the "forward" calls. Then, noticing the colors of a near-by regiment, he rushed to them and sounded "to the color." This heroic performance was repeated on the following day, to the admiration of the entire brigade.[143]

Most conspicuous of all for heroism were those charged with bearing and guarding the colors. In numerous instances the color-bearers continued defiantly to wave their cherished emblem in front of the enemy after the cloth had been shot into shreds by enemy fire; and official reports cite repeated instances of mortally wounded standard-bearers trying desperately to hold the colors aloft and refusing to give them up except to another member of the guard or until death relaxed their stubborn hold. To one of these heroes the colonel of the Forty-second New York Regiment paid the following tribute in his official report of Gettysburg:

The color-bearer, Sergt. Michael Cuddy, who established his great and superior courage in the Fredericksburg battle on this occasion displayed the most heroic bravery. When he fell, mortally wounded, he rose by a convulsive effort and triumphantly waved in the face of the rebels, not 10 yards distant, that flag he loved so dearly of which he was so proud and for which his valuable life, without a murmur, was freely given up.[144]

The colors were an especial object of enemy fire, and casualties among the standard-bearers were unusually heavy. But one who seemed to live a charmed life was Sergeant Henry J. Grannis of the Twelfth Iowa who left Upper Iowa University to join the army when only twenty years old, carrying with him to camp a flag made by the girls of the college. He bore the regimental colors through many hot battles from Donelson to Nashville, being under fire for a period exceeding in the aggregate 100 days. Although the flag he carried was often riddled by Rebel fire he escaped without a scratch, though on the second day at Nashville he had a remarkably close call. While the regiment was charging across the field in that action a Confederate shell burst in the folds of the flag, tearing it to pieces and enveloping standard and bearer in a cloud of smoke. This seemed to be the end of Grannis, but even while his comrades were bemoaning his fate the noble Grannis emerged from the haze holding the tattered emblem proudly aloft.[145]

Repeatedly during the conflict individual exploits of men like Grannis were matched by heroic performances en masse. To recount all of these would be to tell again the story of the war. It must suffice here merely to note that every major engagement was marked by meritorious conduct of regiments, brigades and other large units.

In general, the battle performance of Billy Yank improved as the war progressed. Factors in his developing prowess were increasing experience, the weeding out of inferior officers, a growing confidence of the fighting men in one another and in their leaders, and—especially after Vicksburg and Gettysburg—an ever-deepening faith in the eventual triumph of the Union cause.

This progress in arms was observed and commented on by a number of participants. Colonel W. M. Stone in his report of Port Gibson remarked with pride on the improvement of his troops since Shiloh. "We fought the veteran troops of the Confederacy . . . hand to hand," he stated, "and demonstrated the fact beyond all dispute that the fiery valor of the South is no match for the cool and stubborn courage of the Western soldier." [146] And another brigadier, in his report of the desperate attack of May 22 on Pemberton's works, wrote: "This assault, though unsuccessful, demonstrated that the command possessed the most reliable characteristics of soldiers, implicit obedience to orders, undaunted courage, and great endurance. Not a gun was fired during the entire assault, although the most earnest appeals were made to the commanding general to do so, and when at length the command was ordered to retire, the men did so under the control and direction of their officers." This, indeed, was a high order of soldiering.[147]

Perhaps an even more convincing proof of the volunteer's developing effectiveness in combat was the ability evidenced at Gettysburg—and commented on by Captain Henry Abbott—to acquit himself well when the confusion of battle temporarily separated him from his fellows and forced him to fight on his own, and then quickly to join them again while the contest was still raging.[148]

After Chickamauga, Rosecrans remarked on the rapid improvement evidenced by the artillery, and an infantry colonel reported how completely his men had mastered the art of firing by volley.[149] Many officers commented with pride, following the November battles about Chattanooga, on the infrequency of straggling and the eagerness of their men to close with the enemy.

The general effectiveness—in supply, support, and co-operation of the various arms and services, as well as on the firing line—manifested in the spring and summer of 1864 by Western soldiers in Georgia and Eastern troops before Richmond was nothing short of superb. Indeed, soldierly performance on the Northern side seems to have reached its peak in these campaigns.[150] In the East, especially, several factors tended in the last year of the war to dull the army's sharp edge of combat efficiency. Outstanding among these were the dilution of experience owing to the discharge of many three-year veterans, the terrific slaughter of May and early June which took away many of the best officers and men, and finally the softening influence of long months in the trenches.

CHAPTER IV

IN DIXIE LAND

DURING the course of the war nearly two million Yanks crossed Mason and Dixon's line for sojourns varying from a few months to several years. Most of them approached the South with prejudices born of ignorance and nurtured by years of sectional controversy. Their opportunities for observation were restricted and their views were distorted by war psychology and the uncongeniality of army service. Even so, their comments as put down at the time in letters and diaries throw valuable light both on the observers and the observed.

The character of the Southern country was the subject of extensive comment on the part of the Northern soldiers, and the reaction of most was unfavorable. The thing that impressed the visitors most was the general backwardness of the South. "The country is behind the times 100 years," observed a New York soldier stationed near Richmond, while a New Hampshire man writing from Bladensburg, Maryland, remarked that "they dont have eny stoves here and half of them have no wagons but go horse back it is at least 150 years behind new england." [1]

A Norwegian boy serving in a Wisconsin regiment wrote from Dalton, Georgia, that "everything is a hundred years behind the times. . . . The land is very uneven and ugly. . . . I would not give one farm in Koshkonong for the whole South." [2] This Wisconsin-reared lad, in comparing the South with his own community, indulged in a practice that was widespread among the invading soldiers. And it goes without saying that the land of Dixie suffered considerably by the contrast. A Michigander serving in Northern Virginia found the land miserable and farming methods wasteful and antiquated. "A man is no farmer at all," he said, "unless he has fifteen hundred acors of land, 60 or 70 nigers and the same amount of Jack-asses. The man licks the nigers and nigers the jasacks, and in that way drive business. . . . It is like spring here all winter," he concluded, "but I would rather live in Mich or even at the Nort pole than here." [3]

A Minnesotan's appraisal was even more damning. "I dont like this country nor the people that live here at all," he wrote from Chattanooga,

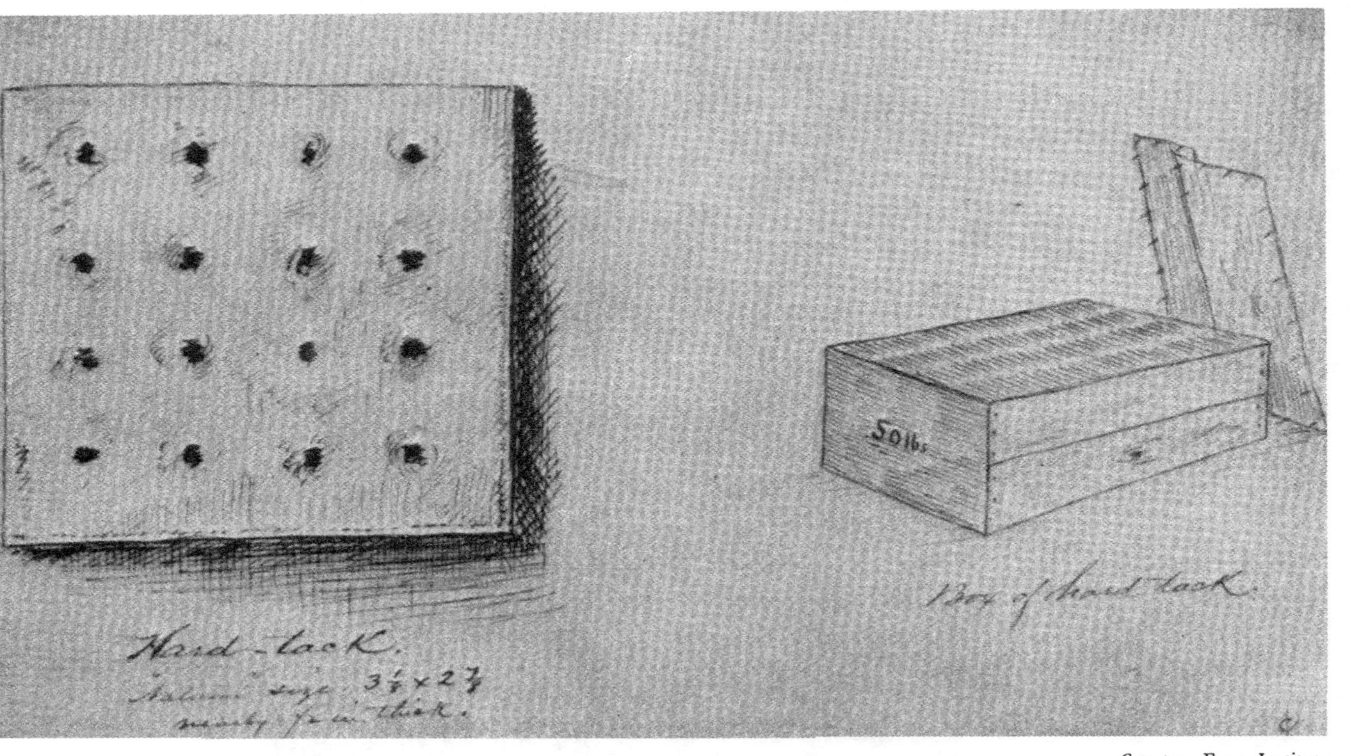

HARDTACK

Drawing by Herbert E. Valentine, Company F, Twenty-third Massachusetts Regiment

SOME SOLDIER TYPES
Drawings by A. R. Waud

"and wouldn't live here if they would give me the best farm in the State and the prettiest Girl in the State for a Wife throwd in. No not I. I had rather live in Minn. with no farm at all." [4]

The Midwesterners were hard enough on the South, but disdain reached its peak among the New Englanders. "You would laugh to see their wagons and harness tied up with leather strings," remarked one Massachusetts soldier, while another observed loftily that "it will probably be more than one generation before any of these slave-cursed states will rival New England in those elements which have made that little corner of the world of so much importance as affecting the human race." A third son of the Old Bay State hit the jack pot of disparagement; writing from near Opelousas, Louisiana, this man observed: "There is a good deal of this part of the world that the Lord has not finished yet. He meant the snakes & aligators to hold possession for a thousand or two years more before man [was allowed] to occupy it. The region from N.O. to Berricks bay is a part of this unfinished section. It is half land & half water." [5]

But from whatever part of the North they came, most of the soldiers who commented on the country conceded that it had tremendous potentialities. They found no deficiencies that could not be overcome by Northern energy and enterprise. As a Maine soldier writing from Virginia expressed it to his mother: "In the hands of New England people this country might be converted into a garden." [6]

The Southern climate inspired a considerable amount of growling. It is not at all surprising to find sarcastic allusion to the "Sunny South" in letters written by homesick Northerners shivering from the cold waves which in Civil War days, as now, occasionally gripped the upper South. An Illinois soldier, writing from a ragged tent in Memphis in December 1864, reported a thermometer reading of "full 250 miles below *Cairo*. . . . If this is a specimen [of Southern winter]," he added, "I want to winter at home next winter." But protestations of cold were mild in comparison to anathemas hurled at the heat. "The country about here reminds me more of New England than any place I have seen," wrote a New England sergeant from Fredericksburg in August 1862, "and the climate reminds me more of that infernal place down below that I have not seen but often heard of." And a Minnesotan, writing from Memphis in June 1864, remarked that he was "intirely cured of the old pashion for a warm Climate. . . . I had rather forego the fruit," he added, "and be where I can breath air that will not scorch my lungs when it goes down." [7]

Many complained of the enervating, depressing effects of the hot and humid atmosphere. A Massachusetts recruit recently come to Virginia wrote his homefolk in August 1862: "This climate is making me terribly lazy. I lose all my strength here, and feel dumpish continually; I want to lie down constantly; there seems to be something in the atmosphere that absorbs all my vitality." [8]

Expressions of opinion concerning Southern people were more frequent and in general more extensive than those about the country. In view of the emotion-charged atmosphere of the late fifties and early sixties in which Billy Yank's attitudes had been shaped, and considering the fact that during the war he was away from home, in a hostile country, and engaged in an unpleasant task, it is not surprising that most of his comment was unfavorable.

In considering Billy Yank's opinion of Southerners, however, it should be kept in mind that common soldiers had relatively little contact with the upper classes. The privileged groups constituted only a small part of the population; a goodly portion of them lived in isolated dwellings; and because of their way of life they were not generally as accessible to the man in the ranks as were people of lesser means and lower social standing. It was the common folk whom Billy Yank most frequently observed and hence who provided the basis of his estimates of the Southern people. But this is an advantage to one seeking information about the South's past, as the plain folk comprised the overwhelming majority of the population and less is known of them than of the upper classes.

No quality of the Southern inhabitants elicited more frequent or more disparaging comment than ignorance. Innumerable soldiers remarked on the dearth and poor quality of schools in Dixie. Further evidence of ignorance was found in the Southerner's rustic speech, his provincialism and his unawareness of time and distance. John P. Sheahan of the First Maine Cavalry reported that residents of Maryland "dont know anything atall, they dont know a mile from two miles, ask them how far it is to such a place they will at once say, 'well right smart distance I reckon,' and that is all that you can get out of them for that is all they know, and you can't get more out of anyone than what they know." Of Marylanders, also, another Yank remarked: "I dont believe the inhabitants even know the day of the week." [9]

A Connecticut soldier who on a short raid below Portsmouth, Virginia, in 1863, encountered people who ate their food with their hands and who never read newspapers was told by a comrade that the farther south he proceeded the less learning he would find. Pondering this suggestion, the New Englander concluded: "I cant form an Idea what they are in New Orleans if they continue 2 grow ignorant as they go South recollecting we onley went 26 miles from our Camp." [10]

When letters written by Southerners fell into Northern hands, great amusement was had in passing them about and making fun of their shortcomings in grammar and spelling. After such diversion a young Connecticut officer wrote his mother: "The ladies are so modest that they write of themselves with a little i. . . . Southern babies send their papas 'Howdy,' . . . a certain perfidious [stay-at-home] . . . is 'cortin the gall' of one of the brave palmetto soldiers." He concluded with the comment: "Above all penmanship, spelling and composition showed that the greatest need of the South is an army of Northern Schoolmasters." [11]

It is an interesting commentary on human nature that some of the most earnest critics of Southern culture were men who themselves were scarcely literate. Indeed, in the very act of disparaging they sometimes committed travesties that must have exceeded those of the ignoramuses whom they scorned. A striking example is afforded in the case of Private William B. Stanard of Michigan who wrote his sister from Bell's Tavern, Kentucky, in February 1862:

The Cuntry hear is the hardest plase that I ever Sea Wea Do Not Sea a Scool house near in one hundred Mills and you ask a man if they Go to Meaten they Say they Dont No What it is there aint one in 20 that Can tell one Leter from a Nother and every thing els in CordenCee with thear Lurnen.[12]

Another fault found with the Southern people was physical frailty which in some instances was attributed to the climate and in others seems to have been regarded as a congenital condition aggravated by bad habits. One soldier depicted men of the New Bern, North Carolina, area as being "all tall, lean, sallow, ugly-looking fellows," while another described Middle Tennesseans as "the poorest looking specimens phisically that I have ever seen—tall, thin, sickly looking mortals with hardly life enough to move." But the most expressive commentary on this trait was that of a Michigander serving near Little Rock who wrote that "the people look as though they have had the ague all their life." [13]

An impressive number of Yanks found Southerners to be lazy and indolent. An Ohioan whose comment is typical of many stated, after a tour of duty in Kentucky, Tennessee and Alabama: "The men are a very lazy trifling set; too lazy to work themselves but willing to sit around the store-doors whittling, smoking, and drinking. . . . The money comes from the labor ot *women* of all ages from fifteen to fifty years and upwards, *in the field*, hoeing, plowing, and planting." This man found evidences of indolence among all classes. On one occasion he wrote of having viewed some splendid houses, but added:

With all the elegance and appearance of wealth, there is an air of "shiftlessness" around, hardly perceptible at first, but which never fails in forcing itself on you after looking closely. There is a paling out here, a window-blind hanging by one hinge there, a gate propped up with *both* hinges gone; and I have seen in some of the finest dwellings a sunbonnet, or *something* else with ruffles on it, stuck into the window where a pane of glass is broken.[14]

Southern women often were special targets of the Yankee disparagers. Some Yanks thought the "Secesh" women, as they usually referred to them, forward and immodest (one offered in evidence their overfondness for kissing games), while others condemned them as coarse and immoral. A considerable number attributed to the feminine portion of the population a sickly paleness which made them less appealing than the girls back home. For example, one soldier remarked: "They are void of the roseate hue of health and beauty which so much adorns our Northern belles." A youngster from Ohio carried the comparison farther. "The southern girls are quite different from the northern," he wrote; "they (the southern) are not as healthy and robust as the northern but are thin and pale, but are very sociable." [15]

Lack of shapeliness was also a fault cited by some. "They look more like polls than any thing else," observed one Yank, while another remarked disgustedly: "The women here generally are shaped like a lath, nasty, slab-sided, long haired specimens of humanity. I would as soon kiss a dried codfish as one of them." [16]

Other points cited in derogation of Southern womankind included their lack of accomplishment in household duties, the crudeness of their speech, their lack of education, or, if schooled, the superficiality of their learning and their poor taste in reading. Of a Virginia belle a New York soldier wrote: "She might have been a smart girl, but she has never done anything but read novels and she is a novel educated thing and all she knows is what she has learnt from reading novels. This is a specimen of Virginia Ladies." [17]

But more frequent than any of these was the charge of slovenliness in dress and lack of concern for cleanliness. An Indiana soldier wrote from near Vicksburg: "The women wear their dresses without any hoops & they only come about 3 inches below their knees & and they had peaks to their dresses about 7 inches & it is so slick with grease that it looks like an alligator's head. . . . their shoes look like bred trays & their tracks like sowbeds." [18]

Summarizing his impressions of the unattractiveness of women in a North Mississippi town, one dour Yank with a bent for exaggeration wrote: "[They are] sharp-nosed, tobacco-chewing, snuff-rubbing, flax-headed, hatchet-faced, yellow-eyed, sallow-skinned, cotton-dressed, flat-breasted, bare-headed, long-waisted, hump-shouldered, stoop-necked, big-footed, straddle-toed, sharp-shinned, thin-lipped, pale-faced, lantern-jawed, silly-looking damsels." [19]

An amazing number of soldiers commented on the prevalence of the tobacco habit among Southern women, especially the use of snuff. An Illinois captain wrote from Scottsboro, Alabama: "I went to the nearest house to camp today, to beg a little piece of tallow. . . . I sat down by a fire in company with three young women, all cleanly dressed, and powdered to death. Their ages were from 18 to 24. Each of them had a quid of tobacco in her cheek about the size of my stone inkstand, and if they didn't make the extract fly worse than I ever saw in any country grocery, shoot me. These women here have so disgusted me with the use of tobacco that I have determined to abandon it." The surgeon of an Illinois regiment wrote his wife from Western Tennessee: "As I walked the streets on Memphis I met a lady . . . quite finely dressed . . . [with] a little stick in her mouth. . . . As I approached her she removed it and spit upon the pavement a great stream of *Tobacco Juice*. She then returned the little stick which I saw had a little swab on the end of it. *She* was dipping." [20]

Even the children were said to be addicted to the habit. Corporal Edward Edes of Massachusetts wrote his sister from Lookout Valley, Tennessee: "The little girls in these parts about seven or eight years old chew tobacco like veterans and babies smoke before they are weaned." But it was the fondness of the "courting-age" females for tobacco that seemed to be most disturbing to the Yanks—especially the young ones. Wrote Private John Tallman from Vicksburg: "Thare are some nice looking girls, but they will chew tobaco, Sweet little things. Don't you think 'I' for instance would . . . *make* a nice show rideing along in a carrage with a young lady, me spiting tobacco juce out of one side of the carrage and she out the other . . . wall aint that nice, oh, cow!" [21]

A young Illinois officer stationed in North Mississippi informed his homefolk: "Snuff-dipping is an universal custom here, and there are only two women in all Iuka that do not practice it. . . . Sometimes girls ask their beaux to take a dip with them during a spark. I asked one if it didn't interfere with the old fashioned habit of kissing. She assured me that it did not in the least, and I marvelled." [22]

Soldier references to smoking, chewing, and especially to "dipping" among Southern women could be cited almost indefinitely, but further piling up of evidence on the subject seems pointless. Suffice to say that so much independent testimony is given in Union soldier letters and diaries of the use of tobacco in all parts of the country and among all classes that, even with due allowance for prejudice, revision of ideas as to the prevalence of the tobacco habit among the Old South's women is suggested.

Among traits of Southerners in general the penchant for military titles did not escape notice. "To give you an idea of Southern love for titles," wrote a Yank from near Scottsboro, Alabama, in April 1864, "I'll name part of the citizens who help to form our party next Wednesday. Colonel Cobb, Colonel Provinse, Colonel Young, and Majors Hall and Hust. Every man who owns as many as two negroes is at least a colonel. None of them rank as low as captains." [23]

Not a few invading soldiers found the South to be a land abounding with sin. From Baton Rouge, Louisiana, a Massachusetts sergeant wrote to fellow members of a temperance organization back home that "almost every one (I do not know of an exception) drink their wine or their beer. . . . Even the women drink in the bar-rooms here, it is of common occurrence, & they must do it to be fashionable & respected." Another soldier from the Bay State noted that many Southern women "can swear like troopers," and "the children swear and smoke precociously. . . . Children get blase at the age of 10." [24]

An animal quality in sexual relations was seen by some in the unusual fertility of the Southern race. An Illinoisan after citing an instance of a Georgia woman with eleven children, the eldest of whom was nine years old, remarked: "This is a great stock country." But the evidence most commonly offered of impure and unrestrained passion among Southerners was the multitude of mulattoes encountered throughout the country. An Illinois surgeon was "quite sure" that he could see white blood in half the Negro children about Pulaski, Tennessee, while a chaplain from Massachusetts reported that the streets of Thibodaux, Louisiana, "were full of its hybrid population." [25]

Instances of horrible treatment of slaves were cited by some to illustrate Southern brutality. These included the tying of a Negro to a tree by a Georgian, who first turned his dogs loose on the hapless slave, then lighted fires about him, and finally suspended him from a limb; a planter's wife who "kept her hand in practice by flogging some mulatto girls"; and an owner who punished his Negroes by nailing their ears to a tree, and by flogging them and leaving them tied naked to trees for the flies and mosquitoes to feed on their lacerated flesh.[26]

With such stories as these circulating in Union camps, it is not surprising to find a Massachusetts blue blood exclaiming: "Honestly, papa, I do not see how anyone can say that the Southern people are civilized." [27]

The Southern social system was the subject of occasional comment. The prevailing impression seems to have been the erroneous one held by many both North and South even to the present day that the white population consisted of two classes, one made up of wealthy, slave-owning aristocrats and the other of shiftless, down-at-the-heels, poor white trash, who were worse off than the slaves. The planters were represented as utterly despising those lower than themselves in the social scale and grinding the poor under their heels.

A Wisconsin Yank who marched with Grant's forces from Port Gibson to Jackson, Mississippi, noted that farmers who owned a few Negroes "scorn[ed] work themselves," made themselves ridiculous, and ran their property to waste "trying to ape the lordly owner of a hundred slaves." A young Massachusetts officer serving in South Carolina was even more strongly impressed by the force with which the idea of caste gripped the South. "I have grown immensely aristocratic since in South Carolina," he wrote his mother. "There is something in the air that's infectious. A few more weeks here, and I'll be able to stomach even a Bostonian." [28]

This man's attitude toward the South was softened by a sense of humor. But in many cases censure of the invaded land was accompanied by expressions of unmitigated hatred. As a Michigander put it: "Everything looks as if it is going to the devil & I know the citizens ought to, & I have faith they will." [29] Interesting for the light thrown on later Reconstruction policies was the satisfaction manifested by some of the soldiers at the destruction being wrought in Dixie, and the sentiment evidenced by them that the work should be continued until full penance had been done for the South's sins against the nation and against humanity. An Illinois soldier declared: "I think it perfectly right to take the hog and leave them none and then if they ain't Satisfied I am fore banishing ever Rebel and rebel simpathiser from the U. S. I . . . belive in giveing the rebels a lesson to be rememberd in after generations then we will never be troubled with Civil War again." [30] A Yankee diarist of rhyming bent stated his position thus:

> Emancipation without deportation
> Sequestration without Litigation
> Condemnation without mitigation
> Extermination without procrastination
> Confiscation without Botheration
> Damnation without reservation
> And no hesitation until
> there is a Speedy termination
> to this Southern Confederation. [31]

Certain Southern groups elicited more vengeful utterances than others. South Carolinians were singled out for special damnation because of the leading part borne by them in the secession movement. An Ohioan who had just entered South Carolina in February 1865 wrote his homefolk: "We will make her suffer wors than she did the time of the Revolutionary war we will let her know that it isened So Sweet to Secede as She thought it would be." And a Hoosier whose sister informed him that she had named her newborn son for him wrote in reply: "I fear you cannot get him into the service soon enough to help us in this war, but theare may be other wars hearafter be sure you teach him to despise South Carolinians & there is no danger of his ever fighting on the wrong side." [32]

Against the politicians who were deemed guilty of bringing on the war, and against Jefferson Davis in particular, many denunciations were hurled. A Michigan private, through the medium of his diary, vented his spleen against the Rebel President thus:

I pray God that I may be one of the men who will pull the rope to hang Jeff Davis and that the spirits of Washington, Jefferson and Jackson and Adams may look over the Batalments of Heaven down upon the Bleaching Carcuss as the flesh Drops from the Bones and Listen to the Winds Whistleing Hail Columbia and Yankee doodle through the Decaying ribs which once enclosed his corrupt and Traitirous heart—for causing this war and Still Caring on this Wicked and Cruell War and Keeping W. E. Limbarker from his Dear Wife and Daughter. [33]

While dislike of the South and its inhabitants was unquestionably the prevailing attitude among Union soldiers, a considerable number of them reacted favorably to the country and the people. Some even had kind words to say about the climate, though it is interesting to note that none of the complimentary references bear midwinter or midsummer dates. A Connecticut corporal was inspired by the charm of the country near Alexandria, Virginia, to exclaim: "This country is so beautiful I wish I had been born here." [34]

Certain areas elicited especially enthusiastic comment. The Florida coast and the country between Nashville and Chattanooga were rated as particularly attractive. Of Louisiana a Midwesterner said: "Louisiana is the Prettiest State that ever I Saw flowers of all kinds are out everything are green and nice." [35]

Occasionally Yanks reported evidences of refinement and culture in Southern homes. A Chicago artilleryman paid high tribute to the elegance and good taste in furnishings and grounds observed in the Lake St. Joseph area of Louisiana; and of planter dwellings in North Mississippi he remarked: "Everything about their places has a good old fashioned air of comfort, neatness and refinement; in the most unpretending houses we find generally a good library & piano, and a great deal of taste displayed inside and out of doors." [36]

While the majority of such comment was directed at the planter class, humbler groups were not entirely overlooked. Concerning homes observed in Thibodaux, Louisiana, a Massachusetts chaplain stated: "Each little cottage had its garden; . . . every window and pilaster buried in vines; every garden gilt-edged with ripe oranges along the borders." A New Yorker whose associations were with the middle and lower strata wrote from Florida in 1862: "I never met with a class of people who were more refined, friendly and hospitable." [37]

Indications of friendliness toward Southern civilians appear with impressive frequency in the letters and diaries of Billy Yank. For example, one file of manuscripts reveals a sergeant protesting vehemently the cruelty of a proposal of General Hunter to expel from his department all persons having husbands, sons or brothers in the Rebel Army; and another tells of a group taking up a collection for a poor Georgia woman reduced to the verge of starvation by the fortunes of war. A private's diary cites this instance in North Alabama: "Wensday we went up in to the mountains after a team it belonged to a widow woman it was all the team she had the lieutenant put it to vote whater [whether] we should take it or not we voted not to take it she came out and thanked us."

Another private, wounded at Brice's Cross Roads, lying in a hospital at Gunntown, Mississippi, reported: "Visited today by several Southern ladies with such delicacies for our wounded as they could raise. God bless them for their kindness." [38]

Revealing also is the instance of Northern soldiers pitching in to help a South Carolina woman put out the fire set to her cotton by less considerate comrades; of an Ohio farm boy turning aside from his military duties to help some Tennesseans plant potatoes; and a Massachusetts youngster trimming a grapevine for a "Secesh" woman of Maryland, "for which I got a pint of milk, which was a luxury for our coffee." [39]

Southern women, though more often maligned than praised, were not without admirers among wearers of the blue. Sometimes approval of Dixie's offerings in feminine charm was registered by such brief comments in letters or diaries as these: "Got some milk from a minister. . . . pretty lady." "Like Arkansas first-rate . . . good farms and orchards—pretty girls." "Thar is Som durnde good looking girls in the Soth." "Squads of 'em (some confounded good looking ones, too) were on dress parade." [40] But in other instances their estimates were couched in rapturous phrase. Private Isaac Taylor of the First Minnesota Regiment, while doing sentry duty on the Rappahannock River near Fredericksburg in March 1863, noted in his diary: "A pair of Secesh damsels promenade up & down the island opposite our post. . . . I call Sergt Wakefield down to the river bank & he goes into ecstacies at the sight of the fair ones, & sighs, 'oh this war.'" [41] And an Illinois captain on the eve of his departure from Savannah, Georgia, in January 1865 wrote his sister: "I found the sweetest girl here that ever man looked at. She is just your size & Form, with large very deep brown eyes, almost black that sparkle like Stars. I swear I was never so bewitched before." That the recipient considered this statement as heretical is suggested by the fact that when fifty years later she edited her brother's papers for publication the complimentary passage was deleted.[42]

Sometimes women encountered by Union soldiers insisted on making displays of their Rebel sentiments by singing Confederate songs or by cheering Southern leaders. But, if they were pretty enough, or if it had been an unduly long time since the Yanks gazed on a feminine form, such demonstrations would be overlooked; or they might even be regarded as commendable indications of spunk.

After a tour of duty in Paducah, an Illinois sergeant wrote his homefolk: "I fell in love with Paducah while I was there, and I think I will settle there when the war is over. I never saw so many pretty women in

JOHN L. ("JOHNNY") CLEM, THE DRUMMER
BOY OF SHILOH AND CHICKAMAUGA

WILLIAM BLACK: A BOY SOLDIER WHO WAS
AMONG THE WOUNDED

THE COFFEE CALL

From Winslow Homer, *Campaign Sketches* (Copyright, L. Prang and Co., Boston, 1864) my life. . . . They hollered 'Hurrah for Jeff' at us . . . but that's all right. I could write until tomorrow morning about Paducah." Other soldiers made similar statements about the girls of Murfreesboro, Franklin and Jackson, Tennessee; New Orleans; Winchester, Virginia; and Raleigh, North Carolina. The reaction of a captain to flauntings of disloyalty by some Tennessee girls is especially interesting. "Camped three miles from Somerville," he recorded in his diary, "on the farm of one Mitchell. His daughter gave us some chicken, coffee, mush & milk & 'Dixie' & the 'Bonnie Blue Flag' . . . but who cares. The music was good & the girls intelligent and kind hearted. Let the dear little rebels have their way in this respect." [43]

On many occasions the coming together of Federal soldiers and Southern women was marked by verbal jousts. These varied in intensity, but most of them seem to have had the character of good-natured banter. With Billy Yank performing the role of reporter of such contests, he usually emerged the victor, but occasionally he conceded himself the vanquished. A soldier named Dave Murphy, on meeting a sprightly young student of an Athens, Alabama, "female academy," took her to task for her Rebel sympathies. He told her of his hardships, of sleeping on the ground and marching over strange country, but said that these were freely endured for love of the cause and the old flag. She told him that she had brothers in the Confederate Army who likewise were suffering hardship. He said that he thought he loved his whole country as much as her brothers loved the half of it. To which she retorted half piqued, half defiantly: "Mr. Murphy, if you love your country as well as that, you're not a bit too good to sleep on it"—a reply that left Mr. Murphy speechless.[44]

The charm of Southern girls for Federal soldiers became so noticeable in some cases as to excite jealousy among the women of the North. In most instances the fears of lasting attachments being formed in Dixie did not materialize, but in a considerable number of cases, wartime acquaintances ripened into romances leading to marriage. And hundreds of Billy Yanks, some with Northern wives, settled permanently in Dixie after the war.

But wherever they took up their peacetime abode, and whatever their *post-bellum* attitudes, the men in blue left an enduring record of their wartime impressions in their letters and diaries. The South as portrayed in these documents, many of which are now fragile and faded, was in the main a land of extremes: the people were wealthy or poor, well-educated or illiterate, refined or crude, righteous or sinful. The country was one of light and darkness, with far more of the latter than the former. Intermediate shadings were only rarely discerned. This is not surprising, however, in view of the emotion-charged atmosphere of the period in which the impressions were formed and recorded. It is worthy of note that tolerance increased with continuing service in the occupied country, and soldiers who remained in Dixie for two years or more often were able to achieve a fair degree of objectivity and accuracy in their observations. Certainly their attitudes were more friendly than those of later years, when hatreds were aroused to unprecedented intensity by scheming politicians waving bloody shirts. On the whole the wartime reactions of Billy Yank compare favorably in interest and accuracy with those of other nineteenth-century visitors, and even with some of recent times.

CHAPTER V

ALONG FREEDOM ROAD

ONE WHO READS letters and diaries of Union soldiers encounters an enormous amount of antipathy toward Negroes. Expressions of unfriendliness range from blunt statements bespeaking intense hatred to belittling remarks concerning dress and demeanor.

"I dont think enough of the Niggar to go and fight for them. I would rather fight them," wrote an Ohioan shortly before enlisting, while a New Yorker after a few months' service remarked to his homefolk: "I think that the best way to settle the question of what to do with the darkies would be to shoot them." [1]

One of these men was middle-class and the other of humble station. But the meanest statement of all came from a young Boston blue blood who early in 1863 wrote his brother from New Orleans: "As I was going along this afternoon a little black baby that could just walk got under my feet and it look so much like a big worm that I wanted to step on it and crush it, the nasty, greasy little vermin was the best that could be said of it." [2]

Several factors contributed to anti-Negro feeling in the army. Many soldiers were deeply prejudiced before entering the service. This was especially true of those of border-state or Southern background and of Irishmen; it was apparently true of men belonging to lower educational and economic groups. Initial prejudices sometimes were softened by army experience, but usually the reverse was true.

A considerable amount of ill feeling sprang from the impression that military authorities were partial to Negroes. After a stint of shoveling mud a New Hampshire Yank observed disgustedly: "No matter, nothing but a soldier. Some of the Boys say that the Army Moto is First the Negro, then the mule, then the white man." [3] A Minnesota sergeant complained of the preferred status of a colored aide attached to General Howard's headquarters: "Their [are] 3 Dr. 3 chaplins & one of his Staff to look after the wants of the nigar. Their has been moore sympathy lavished on him than I ever saw on 20 white men. I guess the day is not distant when a white man will be as good as a Nigar." [4]

Similar sentiments were voiced by a Connecticut infantryman who wrote from Virginia, "A Negro here can ride a horse a private Soldier can walk"; and by a Maine cavalryman who complained, "Contrabands . . . have better places to sleep in and better grub than we do and that is the way all through the niggers . . . fare better than the soldiers do." Even more bitter was a New Yorker who growled: "Each one of them [officers] having a Nigger servant . . . whom they generally feed out of our Rations, it is a well known fact that they are treated better than we are, & in this very camp some of our men were turned out in the Rain from some Rebel Barracks . . . in order to accommodate the niggers." [5]

Many professed to dislike Negroes because they found them lazy and shiftless. "We have four nigger wench's to do our washing at no expense to us," wrote Private C. B. Thurston of Maine, "and as a general thing the clothes are not much dirtier when they come back from the wash than they were when we took them off. They are about as full of dust as an old carpet, from washing in Missippi river water." Another soldier remarked of the colored cook employed by his mess: "[He is] worth about as much as if he was blind for he hardly ever gets his eyes open." Still another Yank, after admitting that the freedmen had saved the soldiers much hard labor, had the following comment to make: "They are much more willing to work than I supposed, but a lasy white man will do more work in a day than half a dozen of the smartest specimens." [6]

Numerous Yanks, weighing laziness of Negroes against the cheapness of their labor, considered sending contrabands home for use as domestic servants and a number actually did so. A Hoosier captain who entertained the idea for a time, but who apparently decided against it, wrote his wife: "I dont know now but I may bring home a little contraband to nurse Aggy and tote up wood and help about the kitchen, but they are all so lazy I dont know about it . . . the niggers down here are not worth 3 cents . . . some of them [are] willing to work but you have to tell them every thing you want done. I have to tell the oldest monkey (about 6 years old) to keep the flies off the table every time I set down. They and their mother lays around on the ground like hogs and only gets up to Cook when told." [7]

A Michigan officer who appears to have entered the army without strong prejudice, after a few months' service in Kentucky noted in his diary:

Christmas. So the niggers all say, for it is a holiday with them in reality. From Christmas to New Years they are free to dance, make love, ride like mad, race horses and raise the devil generally——On the whole I think a system of servitude & serfdom better for both whites & blacks than immediate emancipation. It is true there are many of the blacks well qualified to take care of themselves, but the masses are lazy and shiftless & would become worthless vagabonds if free. They think to be free is to be free from labor. . . . A large portion of the blacks would very soon become intolerable nuisances. They have been for generations dependent & treated like children & mentally they are nothing else.[8]

Even among avowed emancipationists lapses of confidence in the Negro's sense of responsibility sometimes were evidenced. James T. Ayers, a somewhat erratic but usually intense friend of the freedmen, wrote while recruiting colored men in Alabama: "I feel now much inclined to go to Nashville and throw up my papers and Resign as I am hartily sick of Coaxing niggers to be Soaldiers Any more. They are so trifleing and mean the[y] dont Deserve to be free." [9]

Occasionally soldiers found fault with the Negroes on the score of lying and thieving, but more frequently their antipathy was based on what they regarded as insolence or sauciness. "I perfectly Detest the sight of them," wrote an Illinois private to his brother from Vicksburg in 1864. "You cant speak to them and have a civil answer. The smarter they are the worse they are." In like vein a Connecticut soldier wrote from New Bern, North Carolina, in 1862: "If a soldier goes down Town, ten to one he doesent get insulted by nigers! & he can't open his head because if he does, or insults a niger back, touches or strikes him . . . [he] is sentanced to Fort Macon for 6 months with a ball & chain to his leg to live on hard tac & water and Pay stoped. . . . I for one do not like niger society." [10]

The Negro's changing status aroused in some a fear of social equality enforced by Federal authority. A Massachusetts captain after observing a celebration honoring Negro soldiers of B. F. Butler's command on Christmas Day 1864 commented:

The "nigger" in this department is supreme and it is policy for those who desire to bask in the smiles of official favor to be its very devout worshippers. The darkeys make good soldiers enough, but the attempt to mix them up with white soldiers and people is productive of mischief, they are very arrogant and insolent, presuming altogether too much on their social position. Republican as I am, keep me clear of the darkey in any relation. My repugnance to them increases with the acquaintance, they have their place and their work, but the time is not yet, in my judgement, when they can strike hands with the whites.[11]

Social equality became even more of a bugaboo when associated with the thought of large-scale migration of freedmen to the North, as many predicted, to intermingle with the whites and compete for their jobs. A Hoosier private wrote from a hospital shortly after the Emancipation Proclamation: "As soon as I get my money . . . i am coming home let it be deserting or not, but if they dont quit freeing the niggers and putting them in the north i won't go back any more . . . it is very wrong to live with the niggers in freedom." [12]

The support given to colonization in the army sprang in part from a desire to prevent inundation of the North by equality-minded blacks. Some who strongly endorsed emancipation did so on the assumption that freedmen would be sent out of the country. Among soldiers having this view was J. R. Barney of Illinois who closed a letter praising the Emancipation Proclamation with the postscript: "I am not in favor of freeing the negroes and leaving them to run free and mingle among us nether is Sutch the intention of Old Abe but we will Send them off and colonize them. the government is already making preparations fore the Same and you may be assured it will be carried into Effect." [13]

The factor which probably contributed most to anti-Negro sentiment among the rank and file was the association of colored folk with the war itself. War was fun at first, but after a while it was grim and eventually it became for most a dull and wearisome chore. Bored by the routine, tired of the hardship, disgusted by mud, lice, mosquitoes, heat and hardtack, longing for home associations and unhappy at the prospect of continued peril, Yanks found it natural to seek out a pretext for their misery and heap on it their accumulated displeasure. The Negroes who flocked to the Union lines, identified as they were with the conflict, became scapegoats on whom the soldier could spill his hatred of the war.

Denunciations of the Negro were more frequent and more violent after long, hard and unsuccessful campaigns. The peaks of anti-Negro feeling in the Army of the Potomac seem to have been reached in the wake of McClellan's repulse before Richmond in the summer of 1862 and Burnside's bloody failure at Fredericksburg the following winter.

Manifestations of anti-Negro sentiment usually took the form of disparagement or denunciation. Occasionally a soldier made sly comments about physical peculiarities attributed to the colored folk. "If

I marry any one at all I believe I'll marry one of these nigger wenches down here," wrote a New Englander from Louisiana. "One that grease runs right off of one that shines and one that stinks so you can smell her a mile, and then you can have time to get out of the way." A barely literate Ohioan, writing home about "alegaters" in Southern swamps, observed with apparent seriousness: "Thay ar dangres thay will take a niger quicker than thay will a white man thay can smel them farther." [14]

It is plain that many Yanks regarded the colored folk as belonging to a lower physical order than the whites. A Massachusetts soldier remarked of a Negro child: "If her mouth had been two inches longer her head would have been an Island," while a Pennsylvanian reported his observations in South Carolina thus: "They are the genuine Negro here . . . as black as tar and their heels sticks out a feet behind and the young ones . . . butt each other like rams." Another soldier noted of freedmen near Washington: "Their physiognomy is a broad flat nose with thick lips and a very black complection." [15]

Prejudice and hostility frequently asserted themselves in abuse. Sometimes mistreatment was no more than a semi-good-natured playing on the freedmen's gullibility and ignorance. An Ohioan wrote his mother of an experience with a colored woman who came near his tent picking up cracker scraps:

i got my hat foo [full] and giv her and tolde her to eat them and then die i ast her whie she wasent with her Master. . . . she sede that proclemation of Masey lincon sat us all free free the devil I told her affter the war was all over and the nigers was all free us Northern people lode [allowed] to make the men work for us and the wiman and children we lode to blinde fold them and drive them in to the river she rolde the white of her i up to me and sede mye god Masey i never go up dar i give her som mo crackers and then buted her of[f]. [16]

At Huntsville, Alabama, in May 1862, Union soldiers nabbed a sanctimonious-looking old Negro who came to their camp and compelled him to preach them a sermon. When early in his discourse, delivered from a stump, he stated that the Lord had been very kind to him and he could never repay Him for His goodness, the audience interrupted with "Never pay the Lord. . . . Oh, you wicked nigger! Just hear him! He says he is never going to pay the Lord!" The minister tried to explain, but the soldiers, ignoring him, chided: "Here is a nigger who will not pay the Lord. . . . Oh! Oh!" and vowed that they never before had seen such a wicked man. [17]

A Wisconsin Yank wrote from Columbus, Kentucky, of soldiers vulgarly taunting a mulatto girl who delivered laundry to their tents. Another Badger reported from near Vicksburg: "I have seen some of the soldiers of the so-called *gallant 28 Wis.* as well as others insult, by disrespectful & indecent language many, very many, blacks *men & women. . . .* On the contrary I have yet to see the first disorderly act & to hear the first insolent word from any of the many blacks which I have seen." [18]

Soldier ideas of fun were sometimes crude and the results brutal. A Connecticut soldier wrote from Virginia that his comrades had taken two "niger wenches . . . turned them upon their heads, & put tobacco, chips, sticks, lighted cigars & sand into their behinds." [19]

At Hampton, Virginia, in 1861, soldiers tied a rope around the neck of an officer's servant and hilariously drummed him about the camp with drawn bayonet, and at Paducah the next year, Midwestern troops pelted with stones colored fugitives who tried to enter their lines. In a few instances Negro camp followers were shot by Yanks whose hatred they had aroused to extreme heights.[20]

Court-martial proceedings and other records reveal occasional cases of assault and rape of Negro women. An Illinois chaplain told of a soldier who on a raid "stepped up to a colored lady who had come out of her cabin and grasping her round the waiste, forcibly marched off with her under his arm, while she struggled to get loose, and a hundred voices cheered." [21] One of the most shocking cases of maltreatment, occurring in connection with the invasion of the South Carolina coast in 1862, was described by a German soldier thus: "While on picket guard I witnessed misdeeds that made me ashamed of America. . . . For example about five miles from the fort about 8-10 soldiers from the New York 47th Regiment chased some Negro women but they escaped, so they took a Negro girl about 7-9 years old, and raped her." [22]

An Ohioan told of a comrade removing Negro babies from a cabin in Mississippi and riding off to camp with them, "gust taken them along for develment." [23]

More common forms of mistreatment were pillaging, theft and fraud. On Sherman's Carolina expedition both Generals O. O. Howard and A. S. Williams complained of the robbing of Negroes, Williams reporting that houses were "stripped of the necessary bedclothes and of family apparel." Soldiers in Louisiana in one instance sold unsuspecting Negroes worthless passes to or from the camp at one dollar each, and in another persuaded them to give up several hundred dollars in gold by telling them that "Massa Lincoln" wanted to borrow the money, issuing as guarantees of repayment soap-wrapper certificates.[24]

Considerable meanness and some outright fraud was practiced in connection with employment of Negroes as camp helpers and personal aides. A Massachusetts soldier writing from Louisiana summed up the situation thus: "Every private wants & Every officer has his colored servant whom he feeds scantily, clothes shabbily, works cruelly & curses soundly & in his curses includes the whole race." [25]

In view of the treatment accorded them by some who wore the blue, it is not surprising that Negroes occasionally became extremely dubious of freedom's blessings.

But the picture of soldier-Negro relations had its bright side. Many Yanks were favorably disposed toward the colored folk and dealt decently with them. Friendliness for the blacks in many instances had its springs in pity for a downtrodden people.

Stories heard in the North of suffering under slavery—sometimes confirmed by firsthand observations in the South—aroused the deep sympathy of humanitarians and promoted kindly relations with the freedmen. True, starry-eyed abolitionists were now and then "taken in" by the Negroes who, sensing the eagerness of their deliverers for horror stories of slavery, gave them an overflowing measure. But barbarism of masters, while undoubtedly not the rule, had been frequent enough to provide a bona-fide basis for earnest solicitude. One man in blue, not an extremist, gave his reaction to the sight which met his eyes when colored recruits were stripped for examination in Louisiana: "Some of them were scarred from head to foot where they had been whipped. One man's back was nearly all one scar, as if the skin had been chopped up and left to heal in ridges. Another had scars on the back of his neck, and from that all the way to his heels every little ways; but that was not such a sight as the one with the great solid mass of ridges from his shoulders to his hips. That beat all the antislavery sermons ever yet preached." [26]

Another Yank, who was hostile to slavery but who appears to be a credible witness, wrote of an experience near New Orleans: "Visited during the day several plantations and saw enough of the horrors of slavery to make one an Abolitionist forever. On each plantation . . . may be seen the stocks, gnout, thumb screw, ball and chain, rings and chain, by which victims are fastened flat to the floor; and others by which they are bound to perpendicular posts; iron yokes of different pattern, hand cuffs, whips and other instruments of torture, for the benefit of those who had been guilty of loving liberty more than life." On several occasions this man told in his diary of sawing heavy chains and weights from colored refugees. One entry stated: "Released another Negro from his iron yoke, and ball and chain, with which he had traveled 18 miles. His ear had been cut off, to mark him, and he had been well branded with the hot iron. His flesh was badly lacerated with the whip and torn by dogs, but he escaped and I have just dressed his wounds with sweet oil. There is little hope that he will live." It is not strange that this soldier professed a deepening hatred of slavery and gave himself to increased effort for ameliorating the condition of the freedmen with whom he came in contact.[27]

Further cause for kindly attitudes toward the Negroes was found in the good qualities manifested by many of those who came under Federal control. Many Yanks testified to their amiability, piety, intelligence, resourcefulness, eloquence and eagerness to learn. Evidence of these and other virtues tended to promote good will toward the colored folk and to stimulate confidence in their ability to pay their way in a free society.

Another influence working for a kindly disposition toward the Negroes was the support given by them to Union soldiers and their cause. All along the route of invasion, with some exceptions, slaves told what they knew about the strength and disposition of Rebel forces and revealed the location of valuables hidden by their owners.[28] The information was not always accurate, but the spirit of helpfulness which prompted the informers was nonetheless appreciated. Many an escaped prisoner owed his successful passage Northward to effective assistance given, sometimes at considerable risk, by colored bondsmen.[29]

Finally countless Yanks, hungry for hoecakes and for companionship, visited Negro cabins and were amply provided with both.[30] The welcome given by the Negroes was all the more appreciated because of the opposite treatment sometimes accorded by the whites.

Good will of soldiers toward the Negroes manifested itself in various ways. Many Yanks implemented their kindliness by teaching the freedmen to read and write. In some cases educational effort was in regular schools, but usually soldier instructors worked informally, sitting with one or more pupils under a tree, giving out words for spelling, setting copies on slates or shingles, or teaching the ABC's. The spelling and grammar used in home letters raise serious doubts as to the scholarly qualifications of some of the blue-clad dispensers of learning, but of their sincerity there can be no question.

Religiously inclined Yanks took delight in offering spiritual instruction to the Negroes and in sharing their church services. Laymen often taught Sunday schools, while ministers filled pulpits. Nearly all who worked among the freedmen were enthusiastic about their spiritual interest and progress. Some marveled at the eloquence and power of the colored exhorters and most were thrilled by the singing. A New York sergeant who went often to Negro churches wrote his parents after one visit: "I tell you they had a noisy time, but still there was apparently much of the spirit of the Master amoung them. I was very much surprised at the intelligence which they displayed in their remarks and exhortations. They show great knowledge of the Scriptures and in relating their experience use some beautiful illustrations." [31] A Massachusetts soldier who attended a Negro service in Virginia thought that the colored minister preached a much better sermon in fifteen minutes than the regimental chaplain could deliver in an hour.[32]

Interest in promoting the educational and spiritual progress of the colored folk was especially strong among soldiers of antislavery background. An Ohio company made up largely of Oberlin College boys sent one of the first fugitives who came under their control to Oberlin for education.[33]

Friendly relations between Yanks and Negroes sometimes took the form of intermingling at social functions such as parties and balls. A Pennsylvanian wrote of attending a Christmas Eve party in Fernandina, Florida, in 1864, where men in blue danced with colored women. The soldier historian of a New York artillery regiment told of a similar party in Danville, Virginia, in the spring of 1865, but the Virginia affair was allegedly brought to a premature end by colored friends of the Negro women visiting the dance hall and informing the Yanks "Dat de presence of de white gemmen was offensive to de ladies for dey couldn't stan' der odor." [34]

An indeterminable number of Yanks cohabited with colored women. A Pennsylvanian wrote his wife from Winchester, Tennessee: "I won't be unfaithful to you with a Negro wench . . . though it is the case with many soldiers. Yes, men who have wives at home get entangled with these black things." [35] Practices of this sort were by no means confined to the rank and file, for a number of instances were found of officers sharing their quarters with colored concubines.[36]

Usually such relations were without benefit of legal ceremony, but in a few instances marriage vows seem to have been exchanged by white soldiers and colored women. A Nashville newspaper in 1864 reported the trial of "Ellen and Sally, two Negroes," in the Recorder's Court for fighting. "Sally told her Union friend [Ellen] that she supposed she thought herself better than other niggers bekase she was the wife of a white soldier, but so far from any decent nigger thinking she had elevated herself thereby Sally thought her nothing but a ——." A fine of ten dollars was levied on each.[37]

Whether favorably or unfavorably disposed toward the colored folk, Yanks usually found them entertaining. When first they arrived in Dixie the invaders were exceedingly curious about the Negroes and would walk miles to get a close-up view of them. Eager for souvenirs, like American soldiers of all times, they would trade for articles of Negro clothing and other curiosities with the result that slave communities, sprinkled with Yankee blouses, trousers, hats and Zouave fezzes, sometimes acquired a military air. That the newcomers, despite their reputation for driving close bargains, occasionally met their matches among the colored folk is suggested by the fact that a venerable bondsman, claiming to be the original "Uncle Tom," sold a New Englander the lash with which he was so cruelly beaten.[38] Another instance of shrewdness, this time on the part of an urchin who sold milk at an exorbitant price, was reported by a Massachusetts soldier: "Some one asked him what made him sell so cheap! he said well gemmin, I tell you the truth. If I sell cheap one man he takes all I have for his ready money while the rest have to go without. So I charge twenty-five cents a quart so they all can have a little." This story must have made the rounds of the campfire with many an appreciative chortle.[39]

Yanks delighted in the quaint talk of the Negroes and many of them passed on to their homefolk choice samples of the slaves' vernacular. One of the reasons for the great popularity of Negro church meetings among the Yanks was the colorful phraseology heard there. A Hoosier sergeant was much impressed by this prayer: "O, Lo'd, Massa, come to dis e'th; an' when yo' do come, git on de fas'es' hoss yo' kin fin'; an' O, Lo'd, don' run ner gallop, but jest trot all roun' dis e'th, till des aw sinnehs is converted an' Massa Linkum's sojers whip all de secesh!" [40]

A Massachusetts soldier was amused by a prayer heard at a Negro revival in which the worshiper pleaded: "De good Lord take dese 'ere mourners & shake em over hell but dont lieff em go." This Yank also told of hearing one song with the lines:

> The devil's mad & I am glad—Glory Hallelujah!
> He's lost a soul he thought he had—Glory Hallelujah!

and another beginning:

Carrying a Log   Wearing a Placard

Bucking and Gagging

Drawings by Charles W. Reed from John D. Billings
Hard Tack and Coffee (Copyright, George M. Smith, Boston, 1888)

ARMY PUNISHMENT

Courtesy National Archives

A FRIENDLY GAME
Private J. H. Carpenter and comrades

Jesus said he'd come again
The devil's gone a howling.

In describing his reaction which, except for scoffers, must have been typical, he stated: "One of them would lead off and the rest join in the chorus at the top of their voices and though it made me laugh at first at the comical way they did it, yet I soon got over it and could join with them in spirit if not in words." [41]

A less reverent man from the Bay State gave his impression of another service: "We have been to the niger meeting tonight the Sprit mooved in one old lady and I guess it hurt her by . . . [the way] she hollered." [42]

Countless soldiers commented on the Negroes' accomplishments in music and dancing, and many an evening was enlivened by their impromptu performances about the campfire. An Illinois soldier wrote from Tennessee: "It would make you laugh yourself blind almost if you could see a lot of 'ebonics' congregated by moonlight or candlelight, one fiddling, another 'patting' (a mode of keeping time to music by patting with the hands & feet) and four or five dancing in their style." And a New Englander who apparently had paid to see minstrels at home reported from Virginia: "There were five negroes in our mess room last night, we got them to sing and dance! Great times. Negro concerts free of expense here . . . hope I shall not be obliged to leave." [43]

Even on the march soldiers were sometimes entertained by colored performers. After the campaign through Georgia a Minnesotan wrote his wife: "There were many comic occurrences on the Journey. At Shady Dale a large plantation about 35 miles West of Milledgeville there was 15 young Wenches came out and danced for every Regiment that passed the Brigade Band playing wile Each Brigade passed and the next one in turn taking its place. The way the[y] hoed down was caution and extremely ludicrous." He added: "We have a couple of little darkies with the Brigade that are called Tater Boys that can Beat anything in the Plan[t]ation dance I ever seen the[y] make their own music Singing the Melancholy Ya Ha all the time they are dancing." [44]

The attitude and demeanor of white Yanks toward the 200,000 Negroes who served in the Union Army deserves special mention. When enlistment of colored men first became an issue in Congress in the summer of 1862, the overwhelming majority of Union soldiers appear to have been against the proposal. The opposition of some was violent. A typical reaction was that registered by Sergeant Enoch T. Baker, a Pennsylvanian serving in Virginia, who in July 1862 wrote his wife:

Thair is a great controversy out hear about the nigger Question at present if they go to Sending them out hear to fight thay will get Enough of it for it Will raise a rebelion in the army that all the abolisionist this Side of hell Could not Stop the Southern Peopel are rebels to the government but they are White and God never intended a nigger to put white people Down if they would hang a few of the Speculators and leading politicians who are trying to make Presedents instead of good generals the War Wood Soon be over without the help of niggers.[45]

This Yank was averse to putting Negroes in uniform because he thought the measure unnecessary and especially because he saw in it a threat to white supremacy. His views were shared by countless Northerners in and out of the army. Others objected to arming the blacks because they thought them deficient in soldierly qualities. A Connecticut infantryman on hearing that colored regiments were being recruited wrote: "I think a drove of hogs would do better brought down here for we could eat them and the nigers we can't, the negroes are about as contrary as a hog since they have been free & as for fighting they wont be enclined that way I am afraid. I know they are all for getting out of the way when there is a battle afoot or any signs of it." [46]

Some were repelled by the prospect of having to serve in the same units with colored soldiers. This attitude was exemplified by some Kansas soldiers who, when an unusually dark-complexioned recruit joined their company in 1862, petitioned his transfer because "firstly we believe him to be a 'nigger'; secondly . . . he was . . . refused in several other companies." These men, while professing willingness to serve their country, declared that "to have one of the company . . . pointed out as a 'nigger' while on dress parade or guard is more than we like to be called upon to bear." [47]

Now and then a Yank talked of deserting when he heard that Negroes were coming into the army, but such threats rarely if ever were executed.

Opposition to colored soldiers subsided as recruiting progressed. One factor in this trend was the government's change in 1863 from hesitancy to aggressiveness in promoting Negro enlistments.[48] When white soldiers learned that high authorities were determined black men should be accepted and respected they tended to go along with the policy.

The fact that Negroes were used mainly for fatigue and garrison duties, thus relieving whites from these unpleasant chores, made many converts to Negro enlistment. Still others were won over by good reports of Negro performance under fire at Fort Wagner, Milliken's Bend and other engagements.

A considerable number of Yanks were moved to support the Negro soldier policy by the desire to secure commissions in colored units. Scores of enlisted men who never would have risen from the ranks in their own organizations found their way into the shoulder-strap fraternity through examination for commissions with the United States Colored Troops. By no means all who traveled this course were favorably disposed either toward the colored race or Negro soldiers, but a goodly portion were friendly to both.

Perhaps the most important influence of all in breaking down opposition to Negroes was the simple fact that Yanks grew accustomed to the sight of black men wearing the Federal uniform.

But it would be misleading to convey the impression that Negro soldiers won universal acceptance in the army. Many whites remained deeply antagonistic to the end of the war. An Ohio sergeant wrote from Beaufort, South Carolina, in January 1865: "The colored troops are very much disliked by our men & several affrays have taken place in town between them, in which the darkeys have always got the worst of it, two or three of them having been killed & several wounded." In New Orleans, colored soldiers occasionally were pounced on by white Yanks who stripped them of their clothing and forced them to return to their quarters naked. At Ship Island, Mississippi, white gunners on a boat (some of whose crew had recently been embroiled with the blacks), when ordered to support the advance of three colored companies, fired at the Negroes instead of the Rebels.[49]

Such instances of violence between white and black troops were matched, for the most part, by acts of genuine co-operation and friendship. Some Yanks, delighted by the government's decision to enlist the Negroes, sought earnestly to promote their well-being after they became a part of the armed forces. Among these was Rufus Kinsley of Vermont who, while serving in Louisiana in the early part of the war as a corporal in a white regiment, worked zealously for the improvement of the freedmen. In his spare time he taught scores of them the alphabet and on Sundays worked for their spiritual betterment. He also gave much attention to the care of the sick and needy. On one occasion he wrote: "In the education of the black is centered my hope for the redemption of the race and the salvation of my country." [50]

When the government began to organize Negro units Kinsley applied for a commission and was appointed lieutenant in the Second Regiment, Corps d'Afrique. In his new position he devoted himself unstintedly to making good soldiers and good citizens out of his men and to increasing his fitness to command them. On June 1, 1864, he wrote: "I have . . . [been] instructing as many of the soldiers as my time would allow, in the rudiments of an education. Have been very busy. Time has passed very pleasantly. No occasion to regret that I came here." [51]

Another consistent supporter of the colored folk, civilians as well as soldiers, was Henry Crydenwise of New York. His experience was similar to Kinsley's. After two years of enlisted service with white troops, marked by many acts of kindness toward the ex-slaves, he was in December 1863 commissioned captain of Company A, First Regiment, Corps d'Afrique (later the Seventy-third Regiment, United States Colored Troops). Shortly before receiving his captain's bars he wrote his parents:

I dont know what your feelings or prejudices may be in regard to colored troops. I am well aware that many are strongly prejudiced against colored soldiers and that with some I should loose caste by becoming an officer in a colored regiment. but I cannot think that the petty prejudices or even the frowns of others should deter us from persuing what we conceive to be a line of duty. The class of men who are engaged in this enterprise are certainly a superior class. Though there may be exceptions most of the officers of colored regiments are moral and intellectual men In organizing these regiments the Government is very careful to officer them with strictly moral men. and before one can get a position there he must pass a rigid examination and show testimonials of his good character. The association with such officers will be very pleasant. Then there is a system of instruction kept up in these regiments and the Government while it makes use of the negro in crushing out this rebellion also seeks to elevate and enlighten him that he may be prepared for the future which shall open before him Here then is a great field for Christian & philanthrophic labor. a field where great good may be accomplished. Then in a pecuniary view to one in humble circumstances like myself dependant upon my own hands for future support the prospect of permanent position at $120. or $130 per month is no small temtation By what I have written you will understand somewhat the motives which influence my choice.[52]

That the pecuniary motive was secondary in Crydenwise's case is attested both by his prior and subsequent conduct. He strove mightily to make his company a model of excellence, and had the satisfaction of twice having it commended for presenting the best appearance at regimental inspection. He never spoke disparagingly of his colored command. His culminating experience was the leading of his men in a charge at Blakely, Alabama, on the day of Lee's surrender. Of this engagement he wrote his homefolk:

O! My God how the rebs did sweep that line with those screeching, devilish shells & it seemed that nothing could live under such a fire. . . . The rebs still held that part of the works in our front & continued to fire upon us my boys wanted to go forward & capture it. But as my orders were to hold that line I told them to wait for orders. At that moment cheer after cheer went up from the line held by the colored troop & forward came the darkie boys. When my regt came up to where I was we all rushed togather for the rebel works & the old 73rd was the first to plant its flag upon that portion of the line captured by the colored troops. . . . I am proud Thankful & happy that my company did so well. Never have I known a company to do as well before under such circumstances.[53]

CHAPTER VI

THE DEPTHS OF SUFFERING

"I AM NOT very well and I do not think I ever will be again," wrote a New Yorker in December 1861, a few weeks after his arrival in Dixie. A year and a half later an Ohioan serving in Tennessee informed his parents: "Christopher Dimick was ded that makes 3 of the Dover boys that has died out of 42 and one killed. that is about the way there is more dies by sickness than gets killed." [1]

Statistics compiled by the Army Medical Department after the war confirm the observations of these soldiers as to the deadliness of disease.[2] In the Federal forces four persons died of sickness for every one killed in battle, and deaths from disease were twice those resulting from all other known causes.[3]

It is a sad fact of Civil War history that more men died of looseness of the bowels than fell on the field of combat. The best available figures show 57,265 deaths from diarrhea and dysentery as against 44,238 killed in battle.[4]

Disease was woefully prevalent. It was not uncommon for new regiments to have two thirds of their strength on the sick list, and among older units the ratio of one sick man to four or five well ones seems to have been fairly normal.

In the Union Army as a whole the heaviest incidence of disease came early in the war, and individual units suffered most during the first few months of their service. The sick rate for the year ending June 30, 1861, was 3,882 cases for each 1,000 soldiers and for the next annum 2,983. The trend thereafter was generally downward, the rate for the last year of the war being 2,273. The peak of sickness each year usually came during July and August. In 1862 two peaks were experienced, the second coming in October, owing to a large influx of new troops.[5]

Colored troops proved considerably more susceptible to disease than their white comrades. The average annual rate for whites was for each 1,000 of mean strength 2,435 cases of sickness and 53.4 deaths, while for Negroes the figures were respectively 3,299 and 143.4. To put it another way, each white soldier on the average was sick about 2½ times a year and each Negro about 3⅛ times; and the death rate from disease was nearly three times as great among Negro soldiers as among whites.[6]

Several factors contributed to the scourge of illness which bedeviled Federal camps. Basic among these was the failure to sift out unfit men at induction. This was especially true in the early part of the war. Of some 200 regiments investigated in the latter months of 1861 by the United States Sanitary Commission, 58 per cent were reported as having "had no pretence of a thorough inspection of recruits on enlistment," and in only 9 per cent "had there been a thorough inspection when or after they were mustered in." Not only did scores of weaklings enter the ranks under this loose system, but many men with hindering maladies, including hernia, varicose veins, tuberculosis and syphilis, donned uniforms and went hopefully to war.[7]

The associate secretary of the United States Sanitary Commission reported after an extensive visit to volunteer camps in the fall of 1861 that one tenth of the men in units observed by him "would be rejected on a thorough and rigid examination." Eventually most of these substandard specimens broke down and thus increased the burden of an already overloaded hospital system.[8]

Smallpox vaccination was known long before 1861, but the failure to make immunization a standard part of induction procedure led to many needless cases of this disease. Disregard of army regulations concerning both vaccination and physical examination was in large measure chargeable to the pre-eminent role of the states in the mobilization process. As a medical historian put it, "Regiments were raised by the various States and rushed to the front under the successive calls of the President for men without a thought of small pox or vaccination." A Sanitary Commission representative, who in late 1861 inspected thirteen Midwestern regiments stationed in Kentucky, found only one that had been "systematically vaccinated." About the same time the medical director of the Army of the Potomac reported some Eastern regiments with more than half of their men unprotected by vaccination.[9]

Ignorance of the cause of disease was, of course, a fundamental factor in epidemics and death. A veteran of the Union Medical Corps, contrasting in 1918 practices of the Civil War and World War I, stated: "In the Civil War we knew absolutely nothing of 'germs.' *Bacteriology—the youngest and greatest science to aid in this conquest of death—did not exist.* . . . Sanitation . . . was crude and unsatisfactory . . . research had not discovered any of the antitoxins nor the role of the insect world in spreading disease." [10]

Contaminated water sent thousands of men to the hospital. Troops in the vicinity of Cairo, a concentration point for Western forces, regularly drank the impure water of the Ohio and Mississippi rivers, and a like practice was followed throughout the army with rivers, creeks, ponds, springs and shallow wells constituting the principal sources.[11] Purification units were unknown. Medical authorities in some instances recommended that drinking water be boiled or filtered but the advice seems rarely to have been heeded.

The direful ignorance of water contamination even in supposedly informed circles was revealed by the following inspection report by the president of the United States Sanitary Commission:

The Mississippi water has a general reputation for wholesomeness. The Missouri mud, with which it is charged, in settling carries down whatever vegetable or animal substance may exist in the water and leaves it, though still colored, comparatively pure. The Ohio water, being more conveniently reached, is, however, chiefly used by the troops. They had all suffered diarrhoea from the use of this water, or from change. It took about a fortnight to accustom them to it. The surgeons were doubting the expediency of going into the use of the Mississippi water from fear that another change might produce another access of the same complaint.[12]

It is doubtful if the doctors received any help from their distinguished inspector in solving their problem.

Pitching of camps in swamps, poor provision for drainage and crowding together of tents occurred with shocking frequency. But far more injurious to health was the filth in which soldiers lived, especially in the early days of the conflict.[13] Latrines, or "sinks" as they were called in Civil War times, were standard camp fixtures, but often these were shallow trenches left uncovered for long periods of time and located so near the quarters as to subject the occupants to nauseous odors. Many Yanks from rural areas, accustomed at home to following the rule of convenience in answering nature's calls and shrinking from immodest exposure, declined using the sinks. Unfortunately the normal trend of camp life was in a back-to-nature direction; and some who at home had been fastidious in the observance of toilet practices, in the army became as indifferent as the most confirmed frontiersman.

An inspector of camps in the Washington vicinity in July 1861 reported: "In most cases the only sink is merely a straight trench some thirty feet long, unprovided with pole or rail; the edges are filthy, and the stench exceedingly offensive; the easy expedient of daily turning fresh earth into the trench being often neglected. . . . From the ammoniacal odor frequently perceptible in some camps it is obvious that men are allowed to void their urine, during the night, at least, wherever convenient." [14]

Garbage disposal left much to be desired. A survey of 200 regimental camps in the latter part of 1861 revealed that 26 per cent of them were "negligent and slovenly" in this respect, and 24 per cent "decidedly bad, filthy and dangerous." Among evils reported were: "Camp streets and spaces between the tents littered with refuse, food and other rubbish, sometimes in an offensive state of decomposition; slops deposited in pits within the camp limits or thrown out broadcast; heaps of manure and offal close to the camp." [15]

Neglect of personal cleanliness further darkened the picture. Army regulations prescribed daily washing of hands and faces, biweekly ablutions of the feet and complete baths once or twice a week. But few were the companies early in the war that complied fully with these provisions, and neglect was common in some units throughout the conflict. In 1861 men often went for weeks without bathing and without washing their clothing. For the latter, lack of a change of suits was sometimes given as an excuse.[16]

Inadequacy of clothing and shelter was also a factor in poor health. This was especially true of the first winter of the war, when production and supply lagged considerably behind the enormous needs resulting from rapid mobilization and when ruthless contractors so frequently defrauded the government with inferior materials. Inspectors during this period often noted a shortage of overcoats as well as insufficient shelter against cold and rain.

Exposure to the elements, while injurious enough, produced far less illness than did food. The ration specified in army regulations authorized both fresh and "desiccated" vegetables, and it was contemplated that regular allowances would be supplemented by purchases from company funds obtained by credits for unused portions of the issue.[17] But surpluses were commonly wasted instead of being applied to company funds, processed foods were spurned as unpalatable and fresh vegetables were hard to get. The net result was to confine camp fare largely to salt pork, bread and coffee. Yanks frequently supplemented commissary issues by purchases from sutlers and peddlers but since the standard items in stock were pies and cakes, or "pi-zan cakes" as the colored venders' cry was sometimes translated, the results were more harmful than helpful.[18] The widespread deficiency of vegetables and fruits not only helped swell the sick list but slowed down recovery from illness and wounds and increased mortality.

Despite persistent efforts by higher authorities to have food prepared in company quantity by experienced men detailed for the purpose, cooking was usually done by small groups or messes with each man taking his turn at the skillet. The results were deplorable, owing to ignorance, lack of sanitation and a propensity for frying everything in a sea of grease. Even the flour was commonly mixed with water and fried as flapjacks.[19] Culinary procedures improved with experience, but the general level of efficiency in food preparation remained lamentably low throughout the war.

As already implied, a basic factor underlying most unhealthful practices was incompetent leadership, especially on the regimental and company level. Discipline was especially poor during the early part of the war and to this circumstance, probably more than to any other, must be attributed the high tide of sickness which engulfed Federal camps in 1861 and 1862.

Volunteer officers, ignorant of their responsibilities and fearful of offending the men who elected them, were slow to lay down rules of sanitation and diet and even more reluctant to enforce them.[20]

The vital cog in the disciplinary system was the company commander. Initial concepts of this leader's role were based primarily on the militia system, in which the captain's duties were restricted largely to assembling his men on ceremonial occasions and leading them in parades. Hence, it was difficult for the captain in wartime to adjust to a situation which required him to become a father to his men—to live intimately with them, see that they bathed frequently, ate properly and reported to the surgeon when ill; and some captains, deeming such responsibilities and relationships unbecoming to their position, refused to accept them.[21] Only after much bearing down from above, considerable weeding out of incompetents and extensive instruction in the hard school of experience did the idea take hold that close attention to detail was not degrading and that a loose disciplinarian was an enemy rather than a friend of his men.

Eventually, and by a gradual process, a substantial portion of officers and men came to realize what the astute Frederick Law Olmsted had proclaimed in 1861: that there was "no disease so destructive to an army as laxity of discipline." [22] The decline in the sick rate which paralleled the rooting of this concept was no accident. It was regrettable for all concerned that the close correlation between discipline and health was

"WILD BLUE YONDER" BOYS OF THE 1860s
Cavalrymen of the Army of the Potomac

PORTRAIT OF A ZOUAVE
Drawing by Charles F. Johnson

not sooner understood and when at last comprehended not more generally followed by remedial action.

Listing of factors contributing to the prevalence of disease would be incomplete without reference to medical personnel and administration. The war was begun with a pitifully small staff, heavy at the top with old men who had attained their eminence solely by virtue of seniority. The system was based on peacetime conditions and was lamentably slow in gearing itself to the emergency needs of a great war, the greatest by far that the world had ever known.[23]

Deficiencies and delays were by no means the exclusive fault of the Medical Department. Congress held appropriations to miserly limits, and high army leaders sometimes displayed amazing unconcern and ignorance when reform measures were urged on them. But that the top leadership in the medical organization was notoriously weak during the war's first year is beyond question. Only after the death of one Surgeon General and the retirement of another was a man of real ability, William A. Hammond, placed at the head of the medical establishment; and his appointment, in April 1862, over the heads of less competent seniors, required the utmost exertion of the politically powerful United States Sanitary Commission. Even so, the pressure was not great enough to enable the new regime to function as it should. Hammond was defeated in his effort to appoint medical inspectors on a merit basis, and in less than a year and a half difficulties with Secretary of War Stanton drove him from his position.[24]

Hammond, though laboring under difficulty—some of which was caused by his own lack of tact—accomplished wonders, and by contrast brought into bold relief the weakness of his predecessors. Under his able administration, field surgeons and commanders for the first time received from the highest medical office effective advice and stimulating assistance. This, together with increases in personnel, selection of capable men for key positions—the most outstanding of whom was Jonathan Letterman, appointed Medical Director of the Army of the Potomac in June 1862—and important reforms in organization and procedure led to decided improvement in prevention and treatment of disease.[25]

Personnel weaknesses at the top of the medical organization in the early days were matched by deficiences even more grievous on the lowest level. In each regiment a surgeon and assistant surgeon were authorized and it was to these officers that the men looked immediately for medical care. The surgeons and their assistants, like other officers in volunteer organizations, were as a general rule commissioned by state governors.

Many appointments were based on political influence rather than on professional accomplishment and, while most of the regimental surgeons appear to have been well-meaning, a considerable number were utterly incompetent.[26] Data compiled by the United States Sanitary Commission on 200 regimental surgeons in 1861 indicated that 129 of them had discharged their duties with "competence, . . . creditable energy and earnestness" and 25 with "tolerable attentiveness," while 19 were reported as "negligent and inert."[27] In July 1861 an inspector reporting a visit to a volunteer regiment near Washington stated: "There is one surgeon and one assistant, father and son, who were appointed by the colonel and have not been examined by any medical board. . . . [I was told] that the former had been a barber . . . and an occasional cupper and leecher, and had no medical degree. The son's medical education was also doubted. . . . On examining the file of prescriptions at the hospital, I discovered that they were rudely written and . . . consisted chiefly of tartar emetic, ipecacuanha, and epsom salts, hardly favorable to the cure of the prevailing diarrhoea and dysenteries."[28]

Incompetence was even more prevalent among the contract physicians who were hired as occasion required to supplement the regularly commissioned medical staff.[29]

Surgeons who met desired professional standards were handicapped on first entering the service by ignorance of army procedure. Many regiments limped along with insufficient medical supplies through the peaks of illness which commonly followed induction simply because the doctors did not know what items were stocked by purveyors or how to make out the necessary requisitions.[30]

The life of a regimental surgeon was a trying one. This fact, coupled with easy access to liquor, caused some doctors to lean too heavily on the bottle. A division medical director reported after Fort Donelson that the senior medical officer of the Fifty-second Indiana Regiment, "an efficient and skillful surgeon when sober, was so much under the influence of liquor for twenty-four hours as to be incapable of discharging the responsible duties of his office." During the Atlanta campaign an assistant surgeon in the Army of the Tennessee was dismissed from the service "for habitual drunkenness while on duty and for leaving his command and abandoning the sick and wounded men of his regiment while on an active campaign and in the face of the enemy."[31]

An Ohio surgeon abandoned fifty-three sick men of his regiment in January 1862 and went North with his wife. The sick were left without a change of clothing and not "a particle of medicine, food, delicacies . . . & about half blankets enough." Before his departure the surgeon became so intoxicated that "he went staggering through the camp . . . with one man on each side of him." He was dismissed from the service ten months later, but in other instances drunkards of the Medical Corps were permitted to resign or had their offenses whitewashed.[32]

It is not meant to leave the impression that Union doctors in general were an incompetent, drunken lot. The majority were undoubtedly men of solid ability and character. It was inevitable that among the more than 5,000 surgeons and assistant surgeons who served in volunteer regiments some sorry specimens should be found, and, since misdeeds tend to attract more attention than everyday devotion to duty, care must be exercised in judging them and their work. Even in the war's first year many good doctors could be found for each worthless sot, and the passing of time brought steady improvement. Some incompetents resigned or were dismissed, while others by diligent application were converted into creditable practitioners.[33]

Heroism of the highest order was displayed by some of the surgeons. Indeed, the martial spirit was so strong in a few that in the heat of battle they swapped scalpel for musket and by so doing won official commendation.[34] Medical Corps casualties showed that 42 were killed in battle, 83 were wounded, 290 died of disease or accident and 4 died in Confederate prisons. Doctoring in the Union Army was dangerous business.[35]

Whatever their abilities, doctors were so frequently held in low esteem by officers and men as to lessen their usefulness in combating disease. Typical of the attitude of many officers was that registered by Captain E. G. Abbott of the Second Massachusetts Regiment in December 1862: "I pray the regiment may improve," he wrote his father, "but with our present surgeon I see no prospect of good medical attendance in case of sickness. He is a jackass—a fool—and an ignorant man—three quarters of the sickness could have been prevented by a good physician." [36]

Enlisted men were usually less restrained in their comment on surgeons, whom they variously nicknamed as "sawbones," "opium pills" and "quinine." [37] An Illinois soldier wrote disgustedly on June 7, 1861: "The Doctors are no acount the[y] cannot cure the Ague and be with the patient all the time." A comrade of the same regiment observed: "Our doctor knows about as much as a ten year old boy." Members of a New York regiment dubbed their doctor "Long John the Shoemaker" in tribute to the profession which they claimed he followed before joining their organization.[88]

An Ohioan, plagued by mud and mosquitoes near Vicksburg and alarmed by the tide of sickness, in March 1863 wrote in plaintive wrath: "The docters is no a conte . . . hell will bea filde with doters and offersey when this war is over." Another Ohioan in May 1864 reported a recent experience near Chattanooga: "The surgeon insisted on Sending me to the hospital for treatment. I insisted on takeing the field and prevailed—thinking that I had better die by rebel bullets than Union Quackery." [39]

The note stressed by all of these soldiers was inefficiency. Others based their objections on inhumanity. "Our Regimental doctor has no more respect for a sick soldier than I would have for a good dog," observed a Tennessee Unionist in his diary; "no not near so much, for if my dog was sick or wounded I would spend some little time in relieving him. Our doctor will not." A Massachusetts soldier reporting the death of a young comrade stated: "He never received humane treatment from the docters & I believe they thought no more of his death than they would of that of a sheep." [40]

Much of the complaint against doctors was nothing more than a manifestation of the soldiers' chronic bent for growling and was based on no deep antipathy. Moreover, some of the protest came from deadbeats whose shirking designs had been thwarted. But aversion to doctors, whether real or feigned, kept many men away from sick call who if promptly attended, even by less than perfect surgeons, might have avoided serious illness or dangerous complications. The all-too-prevalent attitude, "If a fellow has to [go to the] Hospital, you might as well say good bye," as expressed by one Yank, undoubtedly sent many soldiers prematurely to their graves.[41]

Disease began its onslaught soon after units were organized. Sometimes attacks approached epidemic proportions just as regiments moved to the seat of war, thus causing unusual suffering. In August 1861 an Indiana regiment arrived in Washington with thirty-six ill men isolated in a hot, dirty car, the toilet of which was "beyond use or endurance." These men had been deprived of medical treatment because the surgeon's chest was unavailable in the baggage car, and their only nourishment for twenty-four hours had been hard bread and water. Crowded conditions in the capital forced the men to remain in the car for the rest of the night while the surgeons went in search of medicine and quarters. Fortunately a Sanitary Commission agent, on a routine visit to the station, found the men early the next morning. He had the car cleaned up and distributed tea, bread and butter among the sick.[42]

In its initial attacks illness fell with unusual vehemence on rural units. Prior exposure to contagious disease and a more favorable attitude toward vaccination gave greater immunity to city-reared soldiers. Too, men of urban background were more adaptable psychologically to army life and, except for slum dwellers, were generally more sensitive to sanitary conditions. A Pennsylvania officer stationed near Washington observed in 1862:

Doctor Fulton today reported Bell's camp among others for bad sanitary arrangements. It is strange to see Bell's Company, 83 strong, rough back-woodsmen with 15 men sick, several cases serious, while Widdis' just along side, delicate, city bred men 85 strong have but 3 sick men, all light cases. The difference is no doubt mainly due to the great care Widdis forces his men to take in cleansing and airing their tents and blankets and ditching and policing his street, while the country officers almost entirely neglect all this.[43]

The disease which usually struck first in epidemic proportions was measles. Medical reports show that attacks usually came within a few months of a unit's organization and recurred after each large addition of recruits.[44] Among new regiments cases numbered from twenty to three hundred, the principal factor in the variation being the proportion of country troops. A private in a recently organized rural regiment wrote his parents in December 1861: "The measles went through our Reg. in such a manner that out of 560 men only some 250 are on duty." [45]

Measles showed a preference for the winter months. Ordinarily it ran its course in three or four weeks. Usually it was mild, but undue exposure and improper care frequently led to pneumonia and other serious complications. Private John McMeekin wrote his mother from near Vicksburg in February 1863: "We burred Simon Groves yestery he dide with the mesels that is what kilde the moste of our boys thay wod take the measels and haft to lay out in the rane and storm and thay wod only laste a bot 2 days." The disease was considerably more prevalent and more fatal among colored troops than among whites.[46]

"We are more afraid of ague here than the enemy," wrote an Illinois Yank from Cairo two weeks after Sumter's fall.[47] The observation was an apt one, for malaria, popularly known as ague or "the shakes," was distressingly common from the beginning to the end of the war. The malady's prevalence was due in no small part to ignorance of its cause, the accepted idea being that it resulted from poisonous vapors emanating at night from swamps. Some soldiers attempted to close their quarters to the miasma and incidentally they shut out the mosquitoes, but in so doing they made the atmosphere unhealthfully stuffy.

Mosquito bars were used by some, but the protection sought was against bites rather than the malaria that followed. In diary after diary the sad sequence was recorded of units arriving in low Southern areas, such as Baton Rouge, Ship Island and Key West, the appearance of clouds of mosquitoes and then in due time the outbreak of what the surgeons called "simple intermittent fever."

One out of every four cases of illness reported in the Union Army was malarial in character. The disease was so common, indeed, that a standard greeting in some camps was "Have you had the shakes?" If the vibrations of the more than one million cases of malaria that plagued the men in blue could have been synchronized the South might have been shaken into submission.[48]

The malarial graph prepared by the Army Medical Department shows peaks in the late summer or early fall and troughs in midwinter. Heaviest incidence of the disease came in August 1863.[49]

Less prevalent than malaria but far more deadly was typhoid. Owing to confusion in terminology, figures on this disease are not so reliable or meaningful as for most others. But "camp fevers" or "continued fevers," undoubtedly typhoid in the overwhelming majority of instances, comprised about one fortieth of total sickness and caused one fourth of all deaths from disease. Prevalency among white and colored troops was about the same, but the mortality rate for Negroes was 19.24 per thousand cases as against 13.27 for whites.[50]

Typhoid, like malaria, had its peak in summer or fall and its low in winter. The highest rate of prevalence during the war came in November 1861 following a rapid increase over the prior six months. It is noteworthy that during this period the troops on whom statistics were based increased from 16,000 to 300,000. No more striking commentary could be found on the poor state of discipline and sanitation among the first volunteers than is afforded by the sharp and lofty ascent of the typhoid frequency curve in the war's initial period.[51]

General trends become more appalling when viewed on the level of regiments and individuals. A colonel stationed in Kentucky reported to General George H. Thomas in December 1861: "Typhoid fever is striking our men a heavy blow; 233 of my regiment now down, and dying daily. My loss is greater here than during all the preceding service. Unless we are moved, the regiment will soon become greatly weakened. . . . We would rather die in battle than on a bed of fever." [52] From Louisiana in August 1863 the soldier-novelist John William De Forest wrote of companies appearing on dress parade with only fourteen men, and a little later his gifted pen spelled out the distressing details: "Two-thirds of the regiment are buried or in hospital. It is woful to see how nearly destitute of comforts and of attendance the sick are. They cannot be kept in their wretched bunks, but stagger about, jabbering and muttering insanities, till they lie down and die in their ragged, dirty uniforms. . . . We can distinctly hear the screams and howls of the patients in their crazy fits. It is woful to see a battalion of four hundred choice veterans thus ruined in a few weeks." Still later he reported: "Swamp fever has turned our fine regiment into a sickly, dispirited, undisciplined wreck. . . . Forty-two deaths in forty-two days; barely two hundred and twenty-five men left for duty; and most of those staggering skeletons covered with fever sores; if they were at home they would be in bed and asking the prayers of the congregation." [53] Little wonder that the well and the near-well turned to whisky for solace!

An Illinois private wrote from Camp Butler in November 1861: "Tiford fever is Rageing here verry much their has been several deaths of it . . . they hardley ever get over it." [54] Here, as in many other camps, alarm and depression were enhanced by the frequent carrying away of fever victims by burial details to the mournful cadence of muffled drums beating out the dead march.[55]

Yellow fever, while causing considerable apprehension from time to time, attained serious proportions in only three instances, the worst outbreak occurring at New Bern, North Carolina, in the fall of 1864 with 763 cases and 303 deaths. Of scarlet fever, only about 700 cases were reported for the entire war.[56]

Figures on certain other diseases of lesser prevalence during the period May 1, 1861—June 30, 1866, are tabulated below:

Disease	Cases			Deaths		
	White	*Colored*	*Total*	*White*	*Colored*	*Total*
Rheumatism	254,738	32,125	286,863	475	235	710
Pneumonia	61,202	16,133	77,335	14,738	5,233	19,971
Scurvy	30,714	16,217	46,931	383	388	771
Tuberculosis	13,499	1,331	14,830	5,286	1,211	6,497

This table shows that, except for pneumonia where the difference was not so striking, the diseases listed were far more fatal among colored than among white troops.[57]

Shortly after joining the army a Midwestern rustic informed his homefolk: "There is but one kind of Sickness here, and that is the diarhoea, and everybody has it." While some allowance usually has to be made for exaggeration when soldiers comment on their woes, it is entirely possible that this Yank was telling the truth. Certainly diarrhea or dysentery in one form or another made a complete run of some of the early camps, and the Yank who went through the war without a siege of flux —a term applied by doctors to bowel disorders in general—was indeed exceptional. Innumerable cases never came to the attention of surgeons because of widespread indulgence in self-treatment, but even so, more cases were reported of flux than of any other disease and no malady caused more deaths.[58]

No other ailment was so frequently mentioned in soldier letters and diaries. "My bowels trouble me a great deal," wrote a Massachusetts sergeant from Harrison's Landing, Virginia, in July 1862. A New Yorker in a diary comment of the previous year was more specific: "On as Corp. of the Guard . . . sick with diarhea. Sickest I ever was. My bowels moved 18 times in 3 hours." [59]

Various euphemisms were coined for the malady, the most popular of which was "the quickstep." Soldiers serving in the Old Dominion reported the "Virginia Quickstep"; those in the Volunteer State, the "Tennessee Quickstep"; and so on down through the list of states in which Union camps were found.[60]

Like most other diseases, diarrhea and dysentery struck most heavily during the early months of the conflict, the wartime high coming in midsummer 1861. The general pattern thereafter was a declining succession of summer peaks and winter lows, the one exception being a slightly higher rate in July 1864 than in the previous summer. This variation was no doubt attributable to the long, strenuous campaigns in Northern Virginia, before Atlanta, along Red River and in various other areas.[61]

Statistics compiled by the Medical Department show for the period May 1861—July 30, 1866, a total of 1,739,135 cases of diarrhea and dysentery with 57,265 deaths. These figures are obviously low, owing to the previously noted tendency of soldiers not to report bowel disorders and occasional crediting to other causes of death for which diarrhea and dysentery were responsible.[62]

Bowel diseases became increasingly deadly with the continuance of the war, owing to the cumulative tendency toward chronic conditions. The ratio of deaths to army strength during the last year of the war was more than five times that of the first.[63]

Diarrhea and dysentery were more prevalent among colored troops than among whites, and decidedly more fatal. During the year ending June 30, 1864—the first for which satisfactory figures on Negroes are available—the annual ratio of deaths per thousand of mean strength among colored soldiers was 43.54 and among whites only 15.78. For the next year the respective figures were 36.29 and 21.29.[64]

Medicine was in a relatively undeveloped state during the Civil War.[65] For this reason, treatment of illnesses in the Union Army often appears absurd to one accustomed to modern practice. Archaic concepts of the 1860s are strikingly illustrated by a statement of J. S. Newberry, one of the most eminent medical scholars of the period, following a visit to Western camps in 1861: "Bowel complaints . . . might still further be reduced," he reported, "by the general adoption of the habit of wearing flannel body bandages or stomach belts, of which there is a large number [on hand]." [66]

Diarrhea victims frequently had their bowels further irritated by heavy drafts of whisky and repeated doses of salts or calomel, though many doctors discountenanced such procedures and followed milder practices. Opium was widely used in combating dysentery and some chronic cases were treated with strychnine. Other medicaments for bowel disorders were turpentine, castor oil, camphor, ipecacuanha, laudanum and blue pills (blue mass) of mercury and chalk.[67]

Whisky and quinine was the standard treatment for malaria, but clinical records show use of a wide variety of other remedies, including iodide of potassium, sulphuric acid, syrup of wild cherry, blue pills, morphine, ammonia, iron, cod-liver oil, soda, sweet spirits of niter, cream of tartar and cinnamon.[68] Combinations in which these were used, as well as the effects, may be illustrated by a chills-and-fever case in the Twenty-ninth Michigan Regiment. Treatment began in quarters on October 10, 1864, with "eight grains of blue pill and a Seidlitz powder," which produced a bowel movement but caused nausea and vomiting. The next day the patient was taken to the hospital. Clinical records give his subsequent history as follows:

On admission he had fever, anorexia, great thirst, offensive breath, white furred tongue, constipated bowels and headache . . . pulse 120, respiration 30. Sweet spirits of nitre and extract of ipecacuanha, barley-water and cream of tartar were given, with a Dover's powder at bedtime;

next day quinine was administered. The fever, headache and constipation continued, and on the 14th the patient was delirious during the greater part of the day. Eight grains each of calomel and rhubarb were given, followed by a saline cathartic, which moved the bowels. Next day he was conscious, his pulse regular and slow. Tea, toast, soups and panada were given. After this he improved in condition; but on the 25th he had symptoms of cerebral congestion, which were relieved by cold to the head and mustard to the feet. These attacks recurred during the early part of November, but by avoiding excitement and errors of diet they ceased to trouble him. On October 31 Fowler's solution was given in fluid extract of cinchona and continued for three weeks.

Presumably the patient recovered and was returned to duty.[69]

For typhoid, one surgeon gave his remedy as "blue pill and quinine," while another reported: "Treatment is alterative, tonic and stimulating by blue mass, carbonate of ammonia, turpentine, quinine and brandy." [70] The methods of these two surgeons seem fairly representative. In coping with typhoid, as in treating diseases in general, army doctors relied heavily on stimulants and purges. Resort to calomel became so excessive in the opinion of Surgeon General Hammond that he issued a circular in May 1863 striking that medicine from the supply table of the army.[71]

Reactions of the men to army medical treatment, as might be expected, was predominantly unfavorable. One Yank who rose to the rank of major recorded his impressions after the war:

The regular prescriptions were numbered six, nine and eleven, which were blue pill, quinine, and vinum. We soon learned that "vinum" meant either wine or brandy. I have seen men count from right to left, "six, nine, eleven—six, nine, eleven—six, nine, eleven," and step into the line just where "eleven" would strike. It was a sure thing, since the surgeon gave in regular order, as the men filed past him, something as follows: "Well, what's the matter with you?" "I don't know, Doctor, I've got an awful pain in my bowels; guess I've got the chronic diarrhoea." "Let's see your tongue! Give him number six! Next, what's the matter with you?" "I was took with an awful griping pain in my bowels —guess I've got the chronic diarrhoea." "Give him number nine! Next, what ails you?" "I've g-g-got an almighty b-b-bellyache, g-g-guess I've got the chronic d-d-diarrhoea." "Run out your tongue! Give him number eleven!" [72]

Another soldier wrote while serving in Virginia: "A man might as well die as 2 go through the rounds for [he is] . . . stufed with all kinds of poison & then Sent 2 the Invalid Corps . . . & if he is not able 2 do duty there, he is stufed with Poison agen 2 months longer. . . . I had rather be here 10 years than 2 run the risk for I know what the medicine is they give, dont make [any] difference what ails you the same dose cures all blue Pills & other stufe as bad." [73]

"He prescribes 'salts' to everbody," complained a Pennsylvanian of his doctor, while a Connecticut Yank who had been on the sick list for three days wrote his sisters: "The first day Dr. gave me a powder that came very near turning my stomach inside out and today he gave me 20 drops of Aromatic Sulforic Acid 3 times a day; that goes better. . . . I will inclose one of my powders. It will cure any ails that flesh is heir to, from a sore toe to the brain fever." A third soldier noted in his diary: "Sick did nothing went to Dr he gave me a powder wonder it want a pill." [74]

Sometimes Yanks went to their captains for treatment rather than risk the doctor's cures. Members of Edward S. Redington's Company D, Twenty-eighth Wisconsin, received the benefit of an original remedy, hit upon by their captain in circumstances and with results stated thus by him:

Have a slight attack of Helena Quickstep, but feel much better tonight and think I shall be all right in the morning. I have been taking quinine, pain-killer, and whiskey and my head feels rather large and rings like a kettle. The way they all got mixed was in this way: a bottle of quinine and pain-killer got broken in my medicine chest; the quinine soaking up the pain-killer, so I put them in another bottle and filled up with whiskey. A more villianous compound to swallow never passed a man's lips. I have given several of the boys out of the same bottle and it has always cured them without fail. I think I shall apply for a patent on it as a cure for all the ills the flesh is heir to from colic to cholera.[75]

As previously noted, Yanks often chose to be their own doctors, and most who treated themselves claimed good results. One attributed robust health to keeping himself "dosed full of red pepper." Another cured his diarrhea with a patented product known as "Radways Ready Relief." The practice of one recuperating from "Yaller Janders," as he put it, is indicated by a plea to the homefolk to "Please send me some Flower and some salurates and Rusey save." [76]

While the confidence of soldiers in their own curative efforts was undoubtedly exaggerated, still it cannot be denied that owing to the backwardness of medical science, shortage of supplies and professional incompetence Yanks sometimes were as well off with home remedies as with the surgeon's services.

Deficient facilities combined with exigencies of the service to produce instances of unusual suffering among the sick. The period after Shiloh affords an example of extreme misery in the West. Medical supplies greatly depleted by battle requirements could not be immediately replenished because of confusion and lack of transportation. Disorganization ensuant to fighting, and exposure to the unfavorable weather which followed, led to an enormous swelling of the sick rolls. Despite this situation, Halleck in late April decided to move toward Corinth, and as a first step he ordered transfer of the sick to Hamburg, about six miles up the river from the Shiloh battleground. The sad consequences were described by Surgeon Charles McDougall who took over at this time as medical director: "Before the medical officers and attendants arrived at Hamburgh, the sick were pouring in from all quarters, and the hospital boats on the river were fast filling up. . . . For five days from morning until night, the unfortunate sick were thrown on the bank of the river in parties of from two to fifty, and in most instances, without any report in their cases, other than that they were sick." [77]

Suffering was enhanced by the shortage of doctors and attendants since regimental surgeons and their assistants had to join their units for the projected advance. Surgeon McDougall did the best he could with the three or four assistants available, but until receipt of additional help and supplies the woes of the sick were terrible.[78]

A similar circumstance marked McClellan's campaign of 1862 on the Virginia peninsula. When the forward movement was ordered after capture of Yorktown, regimental surgeons left their sick by the hundreds on the riverbank. Here the unfortunate men lay for days in poorly placed tents or completely exposed to sun and rain, without adequate attendance or food until boats came to remove them.[79]

Those who became ill during the subsequent campaign against Richmond suffered much from exposure to the frequent rain, shortage of food and medicine and lack of attention. When the army retired to Harrison's Landing after the Seven Days' battles, the plight of the ill, who increased greatly in number as a result of the hard campaign, became even worse.[80]

Other peaks of suffering were experienced during the Perryville campaign in 1862 when defective planning and rapid movement resulted in shameful neglect; the operations against Vicksburg early in 1863 when Grant's army was bedeviled by mud, mosquitoes and despondency; and the offensive efforts against Richmond of May and June 1864 when sustained fighting and enormous casualties created excessive burdens for medical authorities.[81] But, in general, care of the sick improved with the progress of the war.[82]

The same may be said of the care of the wounded, though battle casualties as a rule suffered more than the sick. In early engagements the wounded often had to get to hospitals under their own power or lie for long periods without succor. Commitment to medical care was by no means a guarantee of relief, for often during the war's first years hospitals were crowded, poorly run, ill equipped, dirty dens of butchery and horror.[83]

Several factors contributed to this sad situation. Basic among them were the lethargy and lack of vision which have already been noted as prevailing among responsible authorities, both in and out of the Medical Department. Realization was slow in dawning that a great war calling for swift and far-reaching adjustment was at hand. When the idea did begin to take hold, poor planning, competition for facilities and jealous clinging to prerogative often hamstrung efforts to meet the emergency.[84]

Much unnecessary suffering was caused by slowness in providing hospitals. At the outbreak of the war the only installations for treatment of the wounded were regimental hospitals consisting usually of one or more tents situated at the rear during combat and staffed by the regimental surgeon; the assistant surgeon normally followed the troops as they went into action.[85] When these facilities soon proved inadequate, general hospitals were established in cities and towns. The first general hospitals were improvised from schools, churches and other large buildings, expanded when necessary by erection of tents in the yards. To these makeshift affairs, manned by soldier details and volunteer nurses, came wounded from regimental hospitals or directly from the field of action. Provision for sanitation and comfort usually left much to be desired.[86]

Typical of early institutions was the Alexandria Hospital in which wounded from First Manassas were treated. Located in an old seminary this establishment was described thus in late July 1861:

It is an irregular structure, and badly adapted to hospital purposes. Its halls and stairways are narrow and abrupt, and many of its wards small and difficult of access. Its immediate precincts are damp . . . and the wood-work of its piazzas and sheds is rapidly decaying. Ventilation is even now very defective and an unhealthy odor pervades the building. The latter is due in a measure to the fact that troops recently quartered in the building, had been allowed to accumulate filth in some of the upper rooms and the cellar. . . . There being no in-door water-closets or baths, the same necessity for conveying close-stools through the house induces the risk that obtains in the Union Hotel and other Hospitals. . . . There is no dead-house. This Hospital now contains ninety-six patients.[87]

During McClellan's peninsula campaign, barracks in the vicinity of Washington and Baltimore, recently vacated by units moving to the front, were adapted for hospitalization of the flood of casualties pouring in from Virginia. These facilities were intended merely as makeshifts but many of them remained in use for the rest of the war.[88]

Importunities of wide-awake medical officers like Letterman and Hammond and pressure from the Sanitary Commission eventually caused the government to undertake erection of pavilion hospitals on the order of types developed in the Crimean War. The first hospitals of this model were completed in the spring of 1862 in Western Virginia and in Washington.[89]

These and similar hospitals built later in the year were not without structural defects, but improvements came with increasing experience. The basic type proved so satisfactory that it was followed in designing the famous Letterman General Hospital of Spanish-American War times and the "A" and "B" hospitals of World War I.[90]

Implementation of new developments, however, was generally slow. Not until July 1864 did the War Department get around to issuing comprehensive instructions embodying improved practices for guidance of the Quartermaster Department in building general hospitals. This was too late to be of much use.[91] All too many Yanks who went to general hospitals had to be treated in improvised and inadequately equipped facilities.

But the worst suffering was usually experienced before arrival at general hospitals. During the first year of the war, and to a considerable extent thereafter, wounded were collected on the battlefield by musicians, soldiers temporarily detailed from the line and self-appointed aides who frequently were shirkers. These men had little or no training for their duties and control over them was haphazard and ineffective.[92]

Wounded were removed by litter, crude ambulances or wagons to regimental hospitals where surgeons rendered first aid and operated on the most urgent cases—which usually meant amputation. The next step, early in the war, was evacuation to general hospitals by ambulance, wagon, train or boat. As the war progressed brigade and division hospitals were established, first informally and then by higher authority, as intermediate institutions.[93]

This system worked poorly. Transportation of the wounded was a quartermaster function and medical authorities often were unable to secure the needed ambulances, boats and other equipment.[94] Despite the vigorous protest of surgeons, ambulances often were used as personal conveyances for line and supply officers; and sometimes during evacuation crises quartermaster authorities peremptorily diverted to other service boats that had been fitted at great labor and expense for transportation of the wounded.[95]

Volunteer state agencies sometimes complicated the situation by appearing on the scene, as at Shiloh, with boats and medicines reserved for the use of soldiers from specific areas. These well-meaning efforts played into the hands of skulkers who, once aboard a locally sponsored transport and in the hands of friends, headed home for indefinite sojourns. The evil became so great in the West that Grant once issued an order forbidding removal of the wounded of his command beyond Memphis.[96]

The inadequacy of the system as it existed in the first part of the war may well be illustrated by some typical experiences. After First Manassas many men with bullet holes in their legs walked over twenty miles to Washington without prior treatment. A volunteer surgeon abandoned by his supposed helpers at Ball's Bluff had to force soldiers at the point of his revolver to aid in the removal of wounded; even so, many lives were lost for lack of evacuation facilities. At the battle of Belmont in November 1861, many wounded suffered prolonged exposure and neglect because the only transportation furnished the medical authorities by the quartermaster consisted of "two or three ordinary army wagons." [97]

After Shiloh, Grant's medical director, J. H. Brinton, told of "thousands of human beings . . . wounded and lacerated in every conceivable manner, on the ground, under a pelting rain, without shelter, without bedding, without straw to lay upon, and with but little food . . . the circumstances . . . were fearful, and the agonies of the wounded were beyond all description. They were, moreover, fearfully increased by the dearth of those nourishments and stimulants essential to relieve the shock of injury." [98]

Brinton attributed the unusual suffering mainly to lack of ambulances and medicine. The Army of the Ohio, coming by forced march from Nashville, had been compelled to leave most of their medical equipment behind, and in the Army of the Tennessee long-standing and oft-repeated requisitions remained unfilled because, as Brinton put it, "the medical department of the United States army had not yet freed itself from that system of blind routine," which, while adequate in peace, "failed utterly to meet the necessities of a gigantic war." [99]

During McClellan's peninsula campaign the story of Shiloh was in a measure repeated, though suffering was to some extent reduced owing to more ample supplies. At Seven Pines or Fair Oaks the need of a regularly constituted ambulance corps, trained ahead of time in its duties, was again brought into bold relief. According to an assistant surgeon who was there, "The bands of the various regiments proved utterly worthless in bringing off the wounded, behaving with the utmost cowardice, and required more persons to watch and see that they did their duty than their services were worth. As a natural consequence of this, whenever a man fell out of the ranks wounded four and sometimes six of his comrades would fall out for the purpose of carrying him away, thus seriously depleting the ranks and affording opportunity to the skulkers and cowards to sneak away." [100]

Eventually the wounded of Seven Pines arrived at the field hospitals, were treated and then carried to a depot a half mile to the rear for transfer by rail to points of embarkation. But for some reason the trains were slow in arriving, and suffering soldiers, their wounds teeming with maggots "as though a swarm of bees had settled" on them, "lay by the hundreds on either side of the railway track . . . exposed to a drenching rain . . . shivering from the cold, calling for water, food, and dressings . . . the most heart-rending spectacle. Many died from this exposure, and others prayed for death to relieve them from their anguish." [101]

Misery did not cease with removal, for on the peninsula as elsewhere during this period, wounded transported by rail "were placed in common burden cars, where, like so many sheep, jarred and jolted by every movement . . . without proper food, clothing or attention, they often passed hours and even days in indescribable agony." [102] Not until the autumn of 1862 were specially equipped hospital cars made available in anything like adequate numbers.[103]

After the Seven Days' battles, many wounded were forced to lie on the wharves for unduly long periods, owing to failure of the Quartermaster Department to provide needed boats.[104]

At Second Manassas confusion in arrangements, failure of the commanding general to inform medical authorities of his movements, and shameless behavior on the part of ambulance drivers led to deplorable neglect and suffering of the wounded, hundreds of whom lay on the battlefield for days without sufficient food and attention. Of the ambulance drivers the surgeon in charge of evacuation stated: "It was with the greatest difficulty that I could put a reasonable limit to their stealing from my commissary and hospital stores. . . . Very few would assist in placing the wounded in their ambulances; still fewer could be induced to assist in feeding them or giving them water. Some were drunk; many were insubordinate; others when detected with provisions or stores would not surrender them until compelled to by physical force." [105]

Once they got to Washington, where they flocked in the retreat, few of the drivers could be persuaded to return to the battlefield. As a last resort, five days after the battle a train consisting of "about one hundred hacks, forty omnibuses, wagons, and other vehicles" was dispatched from Washington to Centerville to bring in the wounded. The jolting and jarring of these crude conveyances must have brought indescribable agony to soldiers already miserable from nearly a week of torture and neglect.[106]

At Perryville terrible suffering was caused by Buell's refusal to permit surgeons to carry their ordinary stock of supplies and by the Quartermaster Department detaining for two weeks at Bardstown a shipment of medical stores sent out by the purveyor from Louisville.[107]

Unusual misery befell the wounded in a number of subsequent engagements, especially at Gettysburg where Union facilities already heavily strained were overtaxed by the responsibility of caring for several thousand Confederates left behind in Lee's retreat, and at Chattanooga where closing of supply lines caused a shortage of food and medicines.[108] But the fall of 1862 marked a turning point in the care of the wounded, and the person most responsible for the change was Jonathan Letterman who became Medical Director of the Army of the Potomac. In his reform efforts Letterman was strongly supported by Surgeon General William A. Hammond who shares with him the distinction of making the medical system of the Union Army a model of excellence. Letterman had already distinguished himself by taking the lead, while medical director for Western Virginia, in constructing general hospitals of the type later adopted throughout the army. Now, as chief medical officer of the Army of the Potomac, thirty-eight years of age, full of confidence, ability and enthusiasm, he at once ordered the setting up of an ambulance corps consisting of permanently detached men trained in their duties, commanded by line officers and all under the control of the Medical Department. He next worked out an effective supply plan which was put in operation in the East on October 9, 1862. The culminating step in his thoroughgoing reform was the institution of a field-hospital system centering in the division which provided a pooling of supplies and personnel at that level and permitted most effective utilization of available surgical skill.[109]

Letterman's new system required some time for implementation, but at Fredericksburg, where it received its first full trial, wonders were performed. Wounded were not only promptly collected and moved to tented field hospitals, but were quickly treated and well cared for until transferred to general hospitals.[110]

Surgeon General Hammond in August 1862 tried to get Halleck to adopt for all the Union forces an ambulance system similar to Letterman's but that officer, with a lack of vision too often found on high staff levels, turned it down on the amazing ground that the presence on the battlefield of noncombatants would encourage stampedes and panic! In March 1863, General Grant ordered establishment of an ambulance corps throughout the Army of the Tennessee. Finally in March 1864, by act of Congress and a War Department order, a uniform ambulance system, modeled after Letterman's plan as improved by experience, was prescribed throughout the Union Army.[111]

Medical service in the field, as ultimately perfected, comprised the following:

The personnel of the division hospital consisted of a Surgeon in charge, with an Assistant Surgeon as executive officer and a second Assistant Surgeon as recorder, an operating staff of three Surgeons aided by three Assistant Surgeons, and the requisite number of nurses and attendants.

The division ambulance train was commanded by a First Lieutenant of the line, assisted by a Second Lieutenant for each brigade. The enlisted men detailed for ambulance duty were a sergeant for each regiment, three privates for each ambulance, and one private for each wagon. The ambulance train consisted of from one to three ambulances for each regiment, squadron, or battery, a medicine wagon for each brigade, and two or more supply wagons. The hospital and ambulance train were under the control of the Surgeon-in-Chief of the Division. The division hospitals were usually located just out of range of artillery fire. Sometimes three or more division hospitals were consolidated under the orders of a Corps Medical Director, who was assisted by his Medical Inspector, Quartermaster, Commissary, and chief ambulance officer.

The medical officers not employed at field hospitals accompanied their regiments and established temporary depots as near as practicable to the line of battle.

As soon as possible after every engagement the wounded were transferred from the division or corps hospitals to the base or general hospitals.[112]

The system pioneered by Letterman and contributed to by many Civil War surgeons has no more eloquent testimonial than the fact of its remaining the basic structure of military medical care through World War II.[113]

Revision of general plans and procedures was paralleled by many improvements in detail. These included replacement of antiquated two-wheeled ambulances and rough wagons used for transporting wounded by smoother riding and more amply equipped vehicles, introduction of specially devised hospital cars on railroads and provision for more comfortable and better-staffed hospital boats. In general medical supplies became more plentiful and gross neglect less frequent.[114]

Surgical practice also improved as doctors gained experience and as the most competent were selected for wielding of the scalpel.[115] Another factor contributing to surgical progress was the periodic meeting of doctors in various commands to exchange experiences and to discuss new techniques.[116] Interest of medical men in enlarging the body of medical knowledge is attested by the careful and complete records which many kept of the wartime cases, and the specimens they sent in to the Army Medical Museum founded by Hammond in 1862.[117]

Despite earnest application and commendable progress, surgery in the Union Army was often painful and barbarous. Serious operations were sometimes performed by men sadly deficient in professional skill. Chloroform was widely used as an anesthetic and ether to a lesser extent, but sometimes neither was available and patients had to submit to the most painful operations without any deadening influence except such as could be obtained from a bottle of whisky.[118] When anesthesia was available some soldiers refused it for fear of never regaining consciousness, but medical records show relatively few cases of death from anesthesia alone.[119]

Army surgeons argued long and earnestly over the relative merits of amputation. Piles of severed arms and legs about field hospitals after any battle testified to a large membership in the school of the saw. But the frequency of gangrene, even in minor injuries, gave considerable support to advocates of radical surgery.[120]

Sometimes soldiers slated for loss of a member took things into their own control. An artillery corporal wounded in the knee at Hatcher's Run on being told that his leg must come off borrowed a pistol from his comrade and put it under his pillow. When the surgeon came to take him to the operating room the Yank drew the gun and exclaimed: "The man that puts a hand on me dies." The surgeon was momentarily taken aback, but recovering his poise he tried to convince the soldier that his only hope of survival lay in parting with the injured leg. The corporal adamantly held that if he died he wanted to take both limbs with him to the promised land. Finally the doctor, losing his patience, exclaimed: "Let the d— fool keep it and die." Since the story as here told was first related by the soldier himself, it goes without saying that he kept both his life and his leg.[121]

A close-up view of hospital experience near the middle of the war was related by a colonel who was wounded at Port Hudson and evacuated to Baton Rouge. On June 25, 1863, this officer wrote his wife:

I never wish to see another such time as the 27th of May. The surgeons used a large Cotton Press for the butchering room & when I was carried into the building and looked about I could not help comparing the surgeons to fiends. It was dark & the building lighted partially with candles: all around on the ground lay the wounded men; some of them were shrieking, some cursing & swearing & some praying; in the middle of the room was some 10 or 12 tables just large enough to lay a man on; these were used as dissecting tables & they were covered with blood; near & around the tables stood the surgeons with blood all over them & by the side of the tables was a heap of feet, legs & arms. On one of these tables I was laid & being known as a Col. the Chief Surgeon of the Department was called (Sanger) and he felt of my mouth and then wanted to give me cloriform: this I refused to take & he took a pair of scissors & cut out the pieces of bone in my mouth: then gave me a drink of whiskey & had me laid away.[122]

Ignorance was a prime factor in the deplorable conditions which prevailed in Union hospitals. A Federal surgeon, who lived through the revolution in medical science which came in the half century following Appomattox, in 1918 spoke thus of his Civil War experience:

We operated in old blood-stained and often pus-stained coats, the veterans of a hundred fights. . . . We used undisinfected instruments from undisinfected plush-lined cases, and still worse, used marine sponges which had been used in prior pus cases and had been only washed in tap water. If a sponge or an instrument fell on the floor it was washed and squeezed in a basin of tap water and used as if it were clean. Our silk to tie blood vessels was undisinfected. . . . The silk with which we sewed up all wounds was undisinfected. If there was any difficulty in threading the needle we moistened it with . . . bacteria-laden saliva, and rolled it between bacteria-infected fingers. We dressed the wounds with clean but undisinfected sheets, shirts, tablecloths, or other old soft linen rescued from the family ragbag. We had no sterilized gauze dressing, no gauze sponges. . . . We knew nothing about antiseptics and therefore used none.[123]

Little wonder that gangrene, tetanus and other complications were so frequent and that slight wounds often proved mortal.

Suffering of the sick and wounded would have been infinitely greater had it not been for the work of civilian agencies. True, voluntary effort occasionally was characterized by an overamount of state consciousness; and sometimes failure to take a realistic view of war and reluctance to work within the military framework caused more harm than good.[124]

It is also true that well-meaning exertions of individuals sometimes were carried to the point of absurdity—which fact did not escape the comment of soldiers. "There is lots of ladies comes here to the Hospital," wrote a New York private from Baltimore in 1862, "but they have not rubbed the skin off of any of the patients' faces yet." [125] A Missouri infantryman who was taken north during the Vicksburg campaign on a hospital boat noted that a slightly wounded patient received an embarrassing amount of attention from volunteer nurses and doctors. "Every one had eather a fan, and was fanning the poor man with such vivacity that had he not been a tolerable fat man [he] would have been blown off," he wrote, "or [was offering] a cup of tea, water, coffee or the devil Knows what all, and the doctors were discoursing wether the poor defender of his country ought to have his leg or arm . . . amputated or have some castor oil or some other damn stuff." [126]

An Indiana volunteer, describing the various classes of visitors who flooded Washington hospitals in 1864, wrote:

First, and least important, are the wordy sympathizers—of both sexes —the male portion of these "drones" are generally composed of broken-down, short-winded, long-faced, seedy preachers of all denominations. They walk solemnly up and down the wards, between the couches of patient sufferers; first casting their cadaverous looks and ghostly shadow upon all, and then, after a *whispered* consultation with the surgeon of the ward, offer to pray; do so, and retire, without having *smiled* on a single soldier or dropped a word of comfort or cheer. The females belonging to this (the "first class") go gawking through the wards, peeping into every curtained couch, seldom exchanging a word with the occupant, but (as they invariably "hunt in couples") giving vent to their pent up "pheelinks" in heart-rending(?) outbursts of "Oh, my Savior!" "Phoebe, do look here!" "Only see what a horrid wound!" "Goodness, gracious, how terrible war is!" "my! my!! my!!! Oh, let's go—I can't stand it any longer!" And as they near the door, perhaps these dear creatures will wind up with an audible—"Heavens! what a smell! Worse than fried onions!"

Class No. two is composed chiefly of flashy youths, got up in the latest style, and "perfectly regardless of expense," and every "har" in its proper place, kids, canes, and patent leathers, seal rings, and an odor of musk. Accompanying these are wasp-waisted, almond-eyed, cherry-lipped, finely-powdered damsels, carrying tiny baskets, containing an exquisitely embroided handkerchief, highly perfumed, and a vial or two of restoratives (to be used in case of sudden indisposition). This batch of "sight seers," do-nothings, idlers, time-killers, fops, and butterflies skip through the hospital, and like summer shadows, leave no trace behind.[127]

In the vast majority of instances, however, the assistance proffered the sick and wounded was well directed and helpful. In the field of nursing the Sisters of Charity and in the realm of general assistance the Sanitary and Christian Commissions were especially well organized and effective.[128] The United States Sanitary Commission was far and away the most outstanding of volunteer benevolent organizations. Ably directed by Henry W. Bellows as president, Frederick Law Olmsted as general secretary and J. S. Newberry as secretary of the western department— all of whom were advised and actively supported by some of the country's most distinguished doctors and philanthropists—it co-ordinated and turned into useful channels the activities of hundreds of small groups, raised millions of dollars, purchased and distributed vast amounts of food, clothing, medicines and supplies, provided scores of nurses and doctors at critical times, and equipped, staffed and put into operation hospital boats, trains and numerous other facilities. Its agents conducted innumerable inspections, collected valuable data and kept the country informed as to the needs and conditions of the sick and wounded. Its usefulness was enhanced by its studied policy of conforming to military practices and winning the good will and support of responsible commanders.[129]

Not the least of the contributions of the Sanitary Commission was the lead which it took in pointing up shortcomings and forcing corrective action. As already noted it was the moving spirit behind the house cleaning in high administrative circles in 1862 and the appointment of Hammond as Surgeon General. It also played a conspicuous part in modernizing the system of general hospitals and securing for the Medical Department adequate control over evacuation personnel, supply and transportation.[130]

Soldiers sometimes complained that Sanitary Commission representatives showed partiality to officers, and it may be that in efforts to promote good will in key places some of its representatives were overly sensitive to shoulder straps.[131] Its accomplishments far outweighed its shortcomings, however, and its efforts eased the suffering of countless wearers of the blue.

But all the zeal and competency marshaled for the great emergency— and the amount contributed of both was impressive—could not overcome the scientific lag of the age. The result was suffering on a scale without parallel in American military experience save in the Confederacy where equal ignorance and inferior resources led to even greater woe. In both armies the greatest heroes were not those who died at the cannon's mouth, but those who endured the lingering agonies of the sick and wounded.[182]

GAY AND HAPPY STILL

A LONG MARCH might be hard work, but changing scenery and exciting prospects afforded relief from boredom. Battles, while nerve-racking and exhausting, were lively and absorbing, so much so that hours sometimes seemed to pass as rapidly as moments. But active campaigning, except in the last two years when entrenchments and sustained offensives gave a foretaste of future modes, comprised only a small part of Civil War operations. Warfare in the sixties consisted in the main of close engagements, each lasting only a short time, spaced by long static intervals devoted to recuperation, reorganization and waiting to see what the enemy was going to do.

Between November and April both sides usually suspended operations and holed up in winter quarters. Two major exceptions were Grant's Donelson campaign which after great suffering from exposure succeeded by the narrowest margin, and the Fredericksburg disaster following which Burnside became so hopelessly mired in Virginia clay that opposing Rebels tauntingly displayed placards reading: "Burnside's Army Stuck in the Mud." [1] After these discouraging experiences the seasons received their due respect.

What to do in the long periods between campaigns when dullness, homesickness and despondency hung like dark clouds over encampments, threatening to make life intolerable and to destroy the army's will to fight? In our day this question is a vital concern of command, and special staff sections devote full time to recreational functions. Civilian agencies join in with an impressive program featuring canteens, lounges, libraries and star-studded shows. As a result Yanks of World War II, whether in Fort Bragg or in Burma, could take their choice of a wide assortment of tedium-easers ranging from volleyball to variety shows, doughnuts to dominoes and colas to Crosby.

The situation was quite different in the 1860s—and the contrast is sharply reflected in the enormously higher desertion figures of that period. Command in Civil War times was literally a matter of discipline, drill and fight. Officers, if they gave a thought to recreation for their men, regarded the planning of such activities as extraneous if not down-right unbecoming to their positions.

The net result was to leave the soldiers largely to their own devices in seeking relaxation. And the men in blue, like their gray-clad opponents, displayed considerable ingenuity in meeting the problem. If their achievements seem meager in the light of present standards, let it be remembered that, because of a marked difference in taste and tempo, soldiers of the sixties were more easily satisfied than those of today.

Of the many diversions enjoyed by Billy Yank, reading was perhaps the most common. "Everybody has taken to reading," wrote one soldier, while another declared that he "longed more for something to read than for something to eat." [2] These men were undoubtedly stretching the truth, but an enormous craving for reading matter did exist. Readers were considerably more numerous in Union than in Confederate camps, owing to greater abundance of material and a higher degree of literacy.

Newspapers, rarely seen by Johnny Rebs, had a wide circulation among men in blue and headed the reading list of most. Local weeklies, sent by the homefolk, appear to have been the most popular. "The most satisfaction I have is in reading the news from home," wrote an Urbana, Ohio, Yank from Virginia. "I would like to have the Urbana paper sent me once in awhile I would sooner read it than any paper I can get hold of." Foreign-born soldiers found special delight in home papers printed in their native tongue. "As soon as 'Emigranten' arrives there are always many hands to grab for it," wrote a Norwegian from Maryland in 1861. "The condition imposed," he added, "is that he who gets it must read it aloud to his comrades." [3]

Metropolitan dailies such as the New York *Herald* and *Tribune*, the Boston *Transcript* and the Cincinnati *Commercial* also had many eager readers. Sometimes the city papers came by individual subscription, but more frequently they were distributed by sutlers or newsboys.

In June 1863 Hooker, in a competitive bidding, sold to John M. Lamb for $53.20 per day the exclusive privilege of supplying newspapers to the Army of the Potomac. Lamb agreed to provide all newspapers requested by the different commands at five cents a copy.[4]

Before the making of this contract New York papers had sold in Virginia for ten cents a copy. Soldiers earning only thirteen dollars a month could not afford to purchase many issues at this price. Newsboys did a thriving business immediately following payday, but after a short time sales fell off so sharply that they sometimes ceased making their rounds.[5]

One paper usually was made to serve many readers. Sometimes a group of soldiers would agree to share issues bought by each in turn. Again, a Yank with ready cash and good voice would read his paper aloud to a large audience of comrades. In any event, newspapers, like most other reading materials, were passed from one soldier to another until literally worn out.

The illustrated newspapers, especially *Frank Leslie's*, were eagerly sought by soldiers who were quick to discover errors in features about their own units.[6] Soldier letters leave the impression that journalistic art, especially that portraying combat operations, was notoriously inaccurate. But some allowance must be made for the exaggerated unit pride of Yanks who denounced artists for miscrediting feats of gallantry.[7]

Literary periodicals also had a wide following in Federal camps, though readers were confined largely to the cultural uppercrust. *Harper's* and the *Atlantic* are most frequently mentioned in letters and diaries, though considerable popularity seems to have been enjoyed by the *Continental Monthly, Littell's Living Age,* the *Eclectic Magazine* and the *North American Review.*

Religious periodicals and tracts, distributed by earnest individuals and by organizations such as the Christian Commission, were more widely read by soldiers than civilians. This was not because of a greater spiritual interest in camp, but was due rather to a greater dearth of other types of literature.

Books read by soldiers ranged from such classics as the *Divine Comedy, Macbeth* and *Paradise Lost* to trashy comics and cheap, yellow-backed thrillers. Extremes of taste may well be illustrated by some specific references in letters and diaries.

A Minnesota boy wrote his parents in March 1863 from Fredericksburg: "P H. & Fowler go down to the R. R. depot. They bring home 'Harper's Weekly,' 'Nix-Nax,' 'Budget of Fun,' 'Phunny Fellow' &c." About the same time a Massachusetts corporal who had come to the army by way of Harvard requested his parents to "send by the earliest opportunity Casey's Tactics & Mahan's Field Fortifications. I also want Hamlet & Macbeth. . . . I want something to read & know of nothing so condensed as Shakespeare."[8]

One youthful soldier who before the war had attended Washington and Jefferson College, revealed a varied appetite. On November 12, 1863, he wrote: "I read Jean Valjean through and think it splendid." A month later he reported: "I received the Dime Novel and will commence to read it as soon as I am done this letter. There is a good article in Littels Living Age about the *Millenium* you should read." In February

1864 he stated: "I received . . . the books. I have not forgotten my Horace yet but I need a lexicon very badly. I want to read all of Horace." Early in March he noted: "I have read a good part of Horace. . . . We have a splendid lot of novels, almost all of Sir Walter Scot's, and some of Cooper's." Later in the month he wrote: "I receive a Dime Novel occasionally and I find them very interesting. I have read all of Sir Walter Scott's novels within the last month, also a great many of Cooper's . . . [and] a novel called Earnest Linnwood by Mrs. Lee Hentz." An important factor in this soldier's volume of reading was his assignment to garrison duty where work was relatively light and permanency of station facilitated shipment of materials by his homefolk.[9]

Among readers of better taste, inclinations turned most commonly to history, drama and fiction, with Sparks, Parton, Shakespeare, Hugo, Dickens and Thackeray as favored authors. Foreign-born soldiers, while not nearly so well supplied with books and papers as their American comrades, took great delight in reading works of their homeland.[10] The Bible was a favorite among religiously inclined Yanks, and one soldier of college background found great satisfaction in reading his testament in the original Greek.[11] But devotees of good literature constituted only a small minority of soldier readers.

Yellow-covered, twenty-five-cent thrillers and Beadle's famous "Dime Novels," sold by sutlers, peddled by news venders or brought in by the soldiers themselves, fairly flooded some Yankee camps.[12] A Hoosier recalled after the war that in Middle Tennessee in 1863 "miserable worthless . . . novels . . . were sold by the thousand" and that men paid one dollar for "three worthless novelettes which contained a love story or some daring adventure by sea or land." Disapprovingly he added: "The minds of the men were so poisoned that they almost scorned the idea of reading a book or journal which contained matter that would benefit their minds. I can remember when the Atlantic and Continental Monthlies were considered dull reading, while the more enticing literary productions, such as Beadle's novels, novelettes and other detestable works were received with popular favor." [13]

Another soldier wrote that "high way stories and Beadle's dime novels with now and then a True Flag &c, form the principal part of reading." Unfortunately diarists and correspondents usually did not specify individual titles, though one revealed that he read Beadle's *East and West* and another the *Gold Fiend*, which he declared "the best Novelette story I ever saw." [14]

Chaplains and Christian Commission agents, fearing baneful effects of trashy writings on soldier morals, fought a hard but losing fight against them. But to one chaplain who scored a notable victory in Chattanooga we are indebted for an unusually revealing view of camp reading. This divine, meeting on a street a soldier loaded with twenty-five-cent novels —bought in the city at thirty cents each and to be sold in camp at forty— talked him into swapping the fiction for tracts and other "clean" litera- ture. More than that, he obtained from the repentant Yank a pledge not to read or deal in novels again. The chaplain closed his account of the incident with the following inventory of confiscated books: "2 'Dick Turpin'; 2 'Pirates Son'; 4 'Flying Artillerist' and 1 each of 'Red Rover,' 'Iron Cross,' 'Red King' and 'Jacob Faithful.' " [15]

Reports of religious workers also indicate that "licentious books" and "obscene pictures" had some circulation among Yanks, but references are vague and give no information concerning authors, titles, publishers or content.[16]

War experience was not always degrading to reading habits. Some who at home would never have got around to good books were driven by the boredom of camp to read everything that came to hand including the works of the literary masters. In some cases first reactions to the classics were so favorable as to suggest a continuing interest in them.

One Yank predicted improvement of his own practices but on a negative basis. "I think by the time that the war is over," he wrote in February 1864, "I shall get so disgusted with light trash that I shall take to solid reading and hard study with much greater zeal than ever be- fore." [17]

Various means were used to facilitate reading. The Christian Com- mission established in many hospitals loan libraries, each consisting of 125 volumes; publishers provided books at half price and the Adams Express Company transported them without charge. In 1864 the Chris- tian Commission made a similar arrangement with publishers and shippers to furnish the Army of the Cumberland 25,000 magazines, mostly of the literary type.[18]

A number of regiments during winter months organized literary asso- ciations, the chief function of which was to maintain libraries or reading rooms. Often the chaplain was the moving spirit in such projects. A Chelsea, Massachusetts, soldier wrote from Maryland in February 1862: "I have joined the 'Fay Literary Institute' [named for the mayor of Chelsea], a sort of Lyceum. We have a library of about 500 or 600 volumes of good reading. . . . It is very pleasant all the boys in my section belong." [19] The next winter a Connecticut soldier reported from

Virginia: "We have a Library for the Regt. Maj. Lane elected president. Chaplain Welch elected librarian. . . . Books to be issued Tues & fri. Eve'gs of Each week." [20] Libraries were commonly housed in regimental chapels which ordinarily were tents or log structures.

Now and then a Yank would operate an informal library on his own.[21] Book collections of both individuals and organizations were occasionally supplemented by items confiscated from Rebels. One soldier wrote after the fall of Vicksburg that he had "plenty of papers and captured books to read," while another told of "picking up" numerous volumes in Florida. Corporal Samuel Storrow of Massachusetts, who on a raid in North Carolina appropriated a copy of the Rebel Pollard's *History of the First Year of the War*, stated of his prize: "The book pitches into Jeff Davis & his dictatorial power mercilessly & is really of a good deal of interest as a South Side view of the war. I intend to preserve it until we return home." [22]

Most reading was for entertainment but some was for self-improvement. A few soldiers wrote of studying such subjects as Greek, Latin and arithmetic. The most numerous and earnest pursuers of learning were the Negro soldiers recruited from the ex-slaves, and their emphasis was, of course, on elementary subjects.[23]

Ranking close to reading among camp diversions was music. On the march, sitting about the campfire, riding trains or transports, at home on furlough—wherever Yanks assembled—the strains of popular tunes were sure to be heard. The men who wore the blue, and the butternut Rebs who opposed them, more than American fighters of any period, deserve to be called singing soldiers.

Some Yanks on leaving home for the war took violins, guitars and other instruments along with them and entertained their comrades at informal camp sessions. These impromptu affairs were supplemented by band concerts featuring martial airs, patriotic selections and sentimental melodies. In the early part of the war each regiment was authorized a band, but in July 1862 a law was passed prohibiting bands below the brigade level; some regiments, however, found means of evading the act.[24] Since the best of the regimental musicians usually were transferred to the brigade bands, the effect was to improve the quality of the playing. When not on the march, brigade bands commonly gave twilight concerts which were greatly enjoyed by the soldiers. On holidays and other festive occasions the bands gave special programs. Now and then they serenaded high-ranking officers, much to the pleasure of the rank and file, after which the honorees commonly treated the

musicians to drinks. Not the least appreciated of the bands' perform-
ances were those given during the course of fatiguing marches.

Soldier appreciation of a good band is exemplified by the comment
of an unidentified member of the Twenty-fourth Massachusetts Regi-
ment who wrote from the North Carolina coast in April 1862:

I dont know what we should have done without our band. It is
acknowledged by everyone to be the best in the division. Every night
about sun down Gilmore gives us a splendid concert, playing selections
from the operas and some very pretty marches, quicksteps, waltzes and
the like, most of which are composed by himself or by Zohler, a member
of his band. . . . Thus you see we get a great deal of *new* music, not-
withstanding we are off here in the woods. Gilmore used to give some of
the most fashionable concerts we had at home and we lack nothing but
the stringed instruments now. In their place however we have five reed
instruments, of which no other band can boast.[25]

This band was no doubt exceptional both in the nature of its selec-
tions and the quality of its performance.[26] More typical from the stand-
point of pieces played was a concert reported while it was in progress in
1863 by an officer stationed at Folly Island, South Carolina: "The band
are just now playing 'Love Not.' It is a sweet air but the words are rather
heathenish. . . . They must be playing a medley of airs, for they have
just passed to 'Katy Darling' and are even now changing to 'Annie
Laurie.' . . . At this point they suddenly started off into 'Ain't you
glad to get out of the Wilderness.' . . . Here comes 'Pop Goes the
Weasel.' . . . They are winding up with the Lancers." [27]

In the peninsula campaign and at Shiloh, Cedar Mountain and
Chancellorsville men were urged to feats of valor by musicians playing
patriotic and martial airs.[28]

Soldiers transported on river steamers were sometimes treated to
calliope concerts. A member of a Tennessee River expedition to Shiloh
early in 1862 told of the calliopes playing "Starry Flag," "Red, White
and Blue," "The Old Folks at Home," "The Girl I Left Behind Me"
and "My Old Kentucky Home." [29]

The music enjoyed most was that made by the soldiers' own voices.
Yanks went to war with songs on their lips. They sang on the march, in
the trenches, on fatigue, in the guardhouse, on the battlefield and espe-
cially in bivouac. The urge to sing was so irrepressible that men on out-
post duty sometimes had to be reprimanded for lifting their voices and
giving away their positions.[30]

Yanks sang individually as they puttered about the camp. They sang in duets, trios, quartets and glee clubs; and sometimes the country-side at night was made to reverberate with thousands of voices uniting in the strains of some cherished melody.[31]

Soldiers sang mostly for the sheer joy of making music. But they also sang to combat homesickness, to buoy drooping spirits, to relieve bore-dom and to forget weariness. The harder the going the more lustily they sang. After a rapid march into Murfreesboro early in 1863, one regiment struck up the song:

> Sometimes we have to double-quick;
> This Dixie mud is mighty slick.
> The soldier's fare is very rough,
> The bread is hard, and beef is tough,
> That's the way they put us through,
> I tell you what, it's hard to do.
> But we'll obey duty's call,
> To conquer Dixie, that is all! [32]

In response to the enormous demands of soldiers and the folk at home, publishers in New York, Philadelphia, Chicago and other cities ground out thousands of songs on broadsides, in folding cards much after the fashion of scenic sequences sold in modern tourist centers, in sheet folios and in pocket songbooks.[33] The name of Beadle adorned several of the songsters, in such titles as "Beadle's Dime Songs for the War," "Beadle's Dime Union Song Book" and "Beadle's Dime Military Song Book and Songs for the War." [34] Other booklets issued with the soldier market in view were "The Camp Fire Songster," "The Flag of Our Union Songster," "Tony Pastor's New Union Song Book," named for the famous singing showman of the period, "The Little Mac Songster," published during McClellan's heyday, "Nat Austin's New Comic and Sentimental Song Book," "Fred May's Comic Irish Songster," "The Frisky Irish Songster," "Shoddy Songster," "Stars and Stripes Songster," "Camp Fire Companion," "Dawley's Ten-Penny Song Book," "Union League Melodies," "Bugle Call," compiled by the famous composer George F. Root, "The American Union Songster," "War Songs for Free-dom" and "The Yankee Doodle Songster." [35]

Only a few of the mass of songs hopefully launched by the publishers became popular in camp. A careful check of soldier references to music in all the letters, diaries and reminiscences used in this study indicates that the number-one song in Federal camps was "John Brown's Body." Yanks enjoyed especially the line beginning "We'll hang Jeff Davis," completing it with whatever tree came to mind but usually a sour apple or a palmetto.[36]

Parodies and variations were innumerable. One of the first to gain popularity was "Ellsworth's body lies a mouldering in the grave," sung in tribute to the famous Zouave leader killed in May 1861 while taking down the Rebel colors from a house in Alexandria, Virginia.[37] Another song sung to the John Brown tune by the soldiers was entitled "Song of the Volunteers," beginning "The bugle blasts are sounding, 'tis time to be away." [38]

Late in 1861 Julia Ward Howe wrote new words for this popular tune in order to provide a song of greater power and dignity. The resulting "Battle Hymn of the Republic," while a tribute to Mrs. Howe, never gained among soldiers anything like the popularity of the original "John Brown." [39]

Other martial songs which soldier accounts credit with a high degree of popularity were: "Happy Land of Canaan," "Yankee Doodle," "The Battle-Cry of Freedom," "The Star-Spangled Banner," "Weeping Sad and Lonely, or When This Cruel War Is Over," "The Girl I Left Behind Me," "Gay and Happy Still" and "Johnny Fill Up the Bowl." Of these one of the most stirring was "The Battle-Cry of Freedom," written by George F. Root, an outstanding composer of war songs, and popularized by the Lombard brothers and the Hutchinson family.[40] The soldiers usually referred to the piece by the opening words "We'll rally round the flag, boys." The appeal of the song was strikingly evidenced by an incident of the Wilderness fighting in Virginia in May 1864. At one point in the action a brigade of the Ninth Corps, after having broken the Rebel line, was thrown back in disorder by the threat of a flank attack. After the retreat the brigade re-formed and faced the enemy but apparently the prevailing mood was one of defeat. Just at this moment a soldier of one of the regiments—the Forty-fifth Pennsylvania—launched into the song:

> We'll rally round the flag,
> Boys, we'll rally once again,
> Shouting the battle-cry of Freedom.

The words were immediately picked up by the others, and soon the entire brigade was singing the defiant chorus:

> The Union forever,
> Hurray! boys, Hurrah!

Courtesy National Archives

A COCKFIGHT IN THE ARMY OF THE POTOMAC

Courtesy New York Historical Society, New York City

UNION SOLDIERS PLAYING BASEBALL

Confederate Prison, Salisbury, N. C. Drawing by Major Otto Botticher

> Down with the traitor, up with the star;
> While we rally round the flag boys, rally once again,
> Shouting the battle-cry of Freedom! [41]

"Weeping Sad and Lonely," which had a host of enthusiastic singers in both Union and Rebel camps, no doubt owed much of its popularity to the universality of the sentiment expressed in the doleful words:

> Weeping, sad and lonely,
> Hopes and fears how vain! . . .
> When this cruel war is over,
> Praying that we meet again. [42]

"Gay and Happy Still" appealed to soldiers because of its devil-may-care tone. A glimpse of its effect is afforded by the following reference of an Iowa soldier: "While passing through a deep ravine where clouds of dust rose in suffocating volumes to our faces, rendering breathing difficult, I began to doubt my ability to proceed, when suddenly the stillness of the scene was broken by Corporal N. B. Graham, of Company E, in a loud clear voice singing

> Let the wide world wag as it will,
> I'll be gay and happy still.

The sentiments of the song contrasted so strangely with our feelings and circumstances that we gained a momentary relief in a hearty laugh." [43]

An Indiana soldier, who after the war declared "Johnny Fill Up the Bowl" the "most popular of all the army songs," recalled that "While this was being sung, some would chime in with 'so ball, so ball.' Next time another would ring out, 'sow-belly! sow-belly!' . . . and so on, till every change was rung in on the refrain." [44]

Martial and patriotic hits of the period competed closely with sentimental, folk and religious favorites of the past for top rating. [45] The most popular of the old tunes was "Home, Sweet Home," but "Auld Lang Syne," "Annie Laurie," "Old Hundred," "I'm a Pilgrim," "There is a Happy Land," "Finnegan's Wake," "Bingen on the Rhine," "The Faded Flowers," "Go Tell Aunt Rhoda," "Pop Goes the Weasel" and "Come Where My Love Lies Dreaming" also had high standing among singers in blue.

Rating below songs of all types listed above, but still enjoying considerable popularity in Federal camps were: "Tenting on the Old Camp Ground," written by a draftee named Walter Kittredge; "When Johnny Comes Marching Home"; "Johnny Is Gone for a Soldier"; "Tramp, Tramp, Tramp" and "Just Before the Battle, Mother," both by the indefatigable George F. Root; "Grafted into the Army," and the Rebel-taunting "Kingdom Coming," by Henry Clay Work, another famous composer of the period; and "Who Will Care for Mother Now," by Charles Carroll Sawyer who also wrote the favorite "Weeping Sad and Lonely," and who shares with Root and Work highest honors as a producer of Civil War songs.[46]

Other selections rating as secondary favorites included: "Lilly Dale"; "Babylon Is Falling," which like "Kingdom Coming" was a thrust at slaveholders; the rollicking old army tune "Benny Havens, Oh!"; "Oft in the Stilly Night"; "Wait for the Wagon"; and "Poor Old Soldier." [47]

The Yanks, as if not content with their own tunes, appropriated a few songs from the Rebels. The "Homespun Dress" had appreciative singers among the men in blue, as did the "Bonnie Blue Flag," sung to the invaders by Southern girls in patriotic defiance, but in some cases liked so well by the Yankee listeners that they added it to their repertoire.[48] The "Bonnie Blue Flag," like some other tunes of the period, had both Northern and Southern versions.[49]

"Dixie" enjoyed considerable popularity in Northern camps, but since this song was of Northern origin, the men in blue cannot properly be charged with appropriating it.[50] Northern civilians were constrained by Rebel taint of the original to adopt a Yankee version, but soldiers seemed to prefer the original. Perhaps they regarded the taunting note which they injected as purifying enough to make it acceptable.[51] "Lorena," a song of Northern origin which became a favorite of Confederates, had many admirers among Federal troops.[52]

For "Dixie," as for many other songs, the soldiers improvised countless parodies. On the famous "mud march" after Fredericksburg, as men stumbled along in the mire with bodies weak and spirits depressed, an Illinois soldier heard some of his comrades up ahead singing:

> I wish I was in St Law County
> Two years up and I had my bounty,
> Away, Look away, Away, Away.

"The men kept stringing in yelling and hooting for miles back," he added, "and no trouble for those in the rear to know the way." [53]

An impressive proportion of war favorites had extremely doleful notes, but this does not necessarily mean that the ranks were filled with melancholy soldiers. Paradoxical as it may seem, carefree campaigners apparently derived satisfaction from dwelling on themes of suffering and death, enjoying their misery as it were, and emerging from excursions into gloom with hearts lighter than before.

But soldiers enjoyed many types other than lugubrious ballads, hymns and pure patriotics. The routine of camp life provided the theme for a number of lighter songs. Yanks readily found catchy words for the various bugle calls. A common accompaniment for reveille ran like this:

I can't wake 'em up, I can't wake 'em up, I can't wake 'em up in the
    morning,
I can't wake 'em up, I can't wake 'em up, I can't wake 'em up at all.
The corporal's worse than the private, the sergeant's worse than the
    corporal,
The lieutenant's worse than the sergeant and the captain's worst of all.
I can't wake 'em up, I can't wake 'em up, I can't wake 'em up in the
    morning,
I can't wake 'em up, I can't wake 'em up, I can't wake 'em up at all.[54]

Sick call would arouse a chorus:

> All ye sick men, all ye sick men,
> Get your calomel, get your calomel,
> Get your calomel, get your calomel.[55]

Still another sick-call accompaninent was:

> Are you all dead? are you all dead?
> No, thank the Lord, there's a few left yet,
> There's a few—left—yet! [56]

On the march, sounding of brigade call to fall in after a rest was sometimes greeted by the chant:

> Fall in, ye poor devils, as fast as ye can,
> And when ye get tired I'll rest you again.[57]

A popular adaptation to mess call was:

> Soupy, soupy, soupy, without any bean,
> Porky, porky, porky, without any lean,
> Coffee, coffee, coffee, without any cream.[58]

One of the most famous accompaniments of all was to a special brigade call used in Butterfield's command which ran:

> Dan, Dan, Dan Butterfield, Butterfield,
> Dan, Dan, Dan Butterfield, Butterfield.[59]

Army rations inspired a number of ditties. When the issue was reduced to a single cracker and when foraging "played out," an Illinois regiment sometimes struck up the refrain:

> Lord, what a wretched land is this,
> That yields us no supply! [60]

Hoosier soldiers, and others too, expressed their loathing of hardtack by parodying the song "Hard Times Come Again No More" in this fashion:

> 'Tis the song of the soldier, weary, hungry, and faint,
> Hardtack, hardtack, come again no more;
> Many days have I chewed you and uttered no complaint,
> O Greenbacks, come again once more.[61]

But it was to the old stand-by beans that most ration songs were inscribed. One of these, adapted to the religious air "The Sweet Bye-and-Bye," had these words:

> There's a spot that the soldiers all love,
> The mess-tent is the place that we mean,
> And the dish that we like to see there
> Is the old-fashioned, white Army bean.

Chorus:

> 'Tis the bean that we mean,
> And we'll eat as we ne'er ate before
> The Army bean, nice and clean;
> We will stick to our beans evermore.[62]

Favorite generals provided the theme for a few songs. While "Little Mac" was at the helm Eastern soldiers sang this piece with the chorus.

> For McClellan's our leader; he is gallant and strong.
> For God and our Country we are marching along.[63]

And after his removal a song came out with the title "Give Us Back Our Old Commander." [64] In the Western army admirers of Rosecrans, who were many in the period before Chickamauga, delighted in singing a tribute containing these words:

> Old Rosy is our man,
> Old Rosy is our man.
> He'll show his deeds, where'er he leads.
> Old Rosy is our man.[65]

In 1864 Grant was honored with a selection entitled "Ulysses Leads the Van." [66]

Some songs, such as "Chickamauga," had notable battles for their subjects, while others recounted in epic fashion high lights of a considerable portion of the conflict.[67] In the latter category falls E. W. Locke's "We're Marching Down to Dixie's Land." "Marching Through Georgia," written by Henry C. Work in honor of Sherman's famous expedition from Chattanooga to Savannah, also belongs in this group, but it was written too late to gain wide popularity before the end of the conflict.[68]

Various organizations had their special songs. "The Song of the Twentieth Corps" recounted the exploits of the famed unit that "wore a single star." [69] The "Song of the Michigan Second," set to the tune of "Drink Her Down," began with these lines:

> Of our regiment we will sing,
>> Bully boys!
> Join and make the chorus ring,
>> Bully boys!
> The "Michigan Second" is our name
> And we will sustain its fame,
> With our cool and deadly aim,
>> Bully boys!

Then followed a verse to each officer in the hierarchy of command, beginning with McClellan and coming on down through the regimental staff with a final verse paying tribute to company officers as a group.[70]

The First Arkansas, a colored unit, had a song written by one of its white captains to the tune of "John Brown's Body," the first verse of which ran:

> Oh! we're de bully soldiers of de
>   "First of Arkansas";
> We are fightin' for de Union, we are
>   fightin' for de law;
> We can hit a rebel furder dan a
>   white man eber saw;
> As we go marching on.[71]

Another group of songs lampooned unpopular aspects of army administration. Examples of this type are "Shoddy on the Brain," "Wanted a Substitute," "Our Brass Mounted Army" and "The Invalid Corps." [72] Foreigners in the service were good-naturedly caricatured in "I Goes to Fight Mit Siegel" and "Corporal Schnapps." [73] Confederate leaders came in for derision in a number of selections. An old English song, "Lord Lovel," was adapted to chide General Mansfield Lovell for his precipitate surrender of New Orleans.[74] General Bragg was satirized in several pieces, the most boisterous of which was "Bragg a Boo," the last verse and chorus of which were:

> Dear General Bragg, here's to your health,
> With Secesh script to swell your wealth;
> Your coat of arms, when Fortune deals,
> We trust will bear a pair of heels.

Chorus:

> Then shout, boys, shout! The foe is put to rout,
> And Bragg a Boo and Morgan, too,
> Have started on for Dixie.
> Hey, ho! we've laid them low,
> Se-cessh are blue as in-di-go.[75]

The first citizen of Confederate Virginia was satirized in the lines of

> Old Governor Wise
> With his goggle eyes[76]

while Jeff Davis, in a song by that name set to "Nell Flaughtery's Drake," was the object of this thrust:

> Bad luck to him early! Bad luck to him dearly!
> May the devil admire him, where'er he may be!
> May mosquitoes bite him, and rattlesnakes smite him,
> The traitor that brought these hard times unto me.[77]

The South in general was taunted in a parody to "Dixie" which began:

> Away down South in the land of traitors,
> Rebel hearts and Union haters,
> Look away, look away, look away
>   to the traitor's land.[78]

Yanks sang nonsense ditties, such as "Shoo Fly Shoo," and comic parodies galore.[79] They also delighted in giving roguish twists to old favorites. "Abraham's Daughter," not very reverent in its original form, was parodied by one group thus:

> I'm a raw recruit with a bran-new suit
>   Nine hundred dollars bounty,
> And I've come down from Darbytown
>   To fight for Oxford County.[80]

Even the sacrosanct patriotics did not escape the mischief-makers, as witness the following:

> Mary had a little lamb,
> Its fleece was white as snow,
> Shouting the Battle-Cry of Freedom!
> And everywhere that Mary went
> The lamb was sure to go,
> Shouting the Battle-Cry of Freedom! [81]

Hymns were occasionally used in a way that must have shocked the devout. Hardened soldiers of the West, when plodding wearily through rain and mud, sometimes would break out with "There is a land of pure delight," and their rendition must have been like that of World War II soldiers who in similar circumstances sang:

> I am Jesus' little lamb;
> Yes, by Jesus Christ, I am.
> I don't care if it rains or freezes,
> I am safe in the arms of Jesus.
> I am Jesus' little lamb;
> Yes, by Jesus Christ, I am.[82]

One night a group of Connecticut soldiers who had made a raid, apparently on a store reserved for officers, had trouble with the squawking of their quarry. The expedient to which they resorted, as recounted by one of them, was: "Of the first lot of hens, owls stole 7, brot them into tent & wrung their necks while others sang 'Come Holy Spirit Heavenly dove.' The job finished by roll call at 8." [83]

Yanks, like Rebs, had their off-color songs. Apparently they gave the famous ballad "Joe Bowers" a twist that jarred the chaplains. References to "vulgar songs" appear occasionally in letters and court-martial records, but unfortunately they do not give titles or words. Indeed, there is no more elusive phase of Civil War history than the seamy side of soldier life. In pursuing ribald music the researcher has to be content with such statements in letters as: "After the evening dress parade, some amuse themselves . . . in singing vulgar songs," and in official records: Captain James H. Slade, Thirty-eighth Massachusetts Volunteers, found guilty of entertaining two whores in his tent, serving them wine and having them sing "vulgar and secession songs." [84]

Music of national and racial groups deserves special notice. Colored aides or body servants of officers often entertained camp audiences with folk melodies and improvisations. A fourteen-year-old aide, who proudly bore the name Henry George General Washington, one evening near Memphis sang:

> Possum put on an overcoat,
> Raccoon put on gown,
> Rabit put on ruffled shirt,
> All buttoned up and down.
> Wait, Billy, wait, wait I say
> And I will marry you bime by.[85]

Nearly all Northern whites closely associated with colored soldiers commented appreciatively on their singing. An Amherst student, who worked among the wounded in Virginia in 1864, reported hearing several Negro casualties of the Crater fight singing in a field hospital:

> Times going away, why dont you pray,
> And end this cruel war in heaven,
> Oh my blessed Lord.
>
> I wish my Lord would come down
> And take us to wear the crown,
> Oh my blessed Lord.[86]

Lieutenant Colonel Charles B. Fox of the colored Sixty-sixth Massachusetts complimented the band of that regiment on a number of occasions for their rendition of such pieces as "Hail to the Chief," "Midnight Hour," "Gay and Happy Still," "Glory Hallelujah," and "Someone to Love." [87] He also told of the special enthusiasm with which Negro soldiers sang "Babylon Is Falling," and the beauty with which they rendered "All Hail" to the air "Greenland's Icy Mountains" at a festive meeting on Folly Island, South Carolina, in October 1864.[88]

Among foreign soldiers, the Germans were noted for their musical leaning and accomplishment. A New York private wrote "Friend Elvira" from Virginia in 1863: "I heard some splendid singing last night by the 20th N. Y. a German Regt. . . . They all belong to the society of Turners of which the celebrated Max Webber is leader. I went over to their camp and heard them and then they went over and Serenaded General Patrick." Another New Yorker, commander of an artillery unit, reported from Maryland: "We have pretty lively times in the evenings; the Germans of my company get together and sing very sweetly, and I try to join in with them. I send you a copy of one of their songs . . . it is simple but very sweet, I think, and shows a reflection and elevation of sentiment to be found only among the Germans." [89]

The favorite of the Germans seems to have been their stirring soldier song "Morgenroth," which they sang in their native tongue when on the march and about the campfire.[90] They also delighted in folk and national melodies of the homeland, and in patriotic and martial songs of their adopted America. Their bands were among the best in the army.[91]

Frenchmen, and their American-born comrades as well, sang the "Marseillaise" with gusto, especially when on the march.[92] The Irish had many native songs with which to entertain their fellow soldiers, and their broguish renditions were sure to bring smiles to all who listened.[93] The Scandinavians were accomplished in both secular and religious music. Colonel Hans C. Heg gave a glimpse of Norwegian proficiency in a letter from Louisville of September 1862, in which he stated: "My Regiment went through singing Norwegian Songs, and attracted more attention than any other regiment that passed." [94]

The Scots, the Italians and the many other nationalities represented in the Union Army had their special songs and music. Indeed, life in the Federal camps had no more enriching influence than the music contributed by the diverse and talented groups who wore the blue.

Sports and games were another very popular diversion. Foot races, wrestling, boxing, leapfrog, cricket, broad jumping and free-for-all scuffles helped Yanks while away many tedious hours. Football was occasionally mentioned in letters and diaries, but baseball, or "bass ball" as one Yank put it, appears to have been the most popular of all competitive sports. Baseball as played by Yanks differed considerably from that of today. A Vermont soldier gave this description: "The ball was soft, and a great bounder. To put a base runner out, he had to be hit by the ball, thrown by the pitcher." Another impressive difference was the score. A game between the Eighth and the 114th Vermont Regiments near Franklin, Louisiana, in February 1864 was won by the former 21 to 9. The "first team" of the Ninth New York Regiment beat the Fifty-first New Yorkers 31-34 at Yorktown, Virginia, in 1863. But a few days later the "second nine" of the two units played, with the Ninth Regiment triumphing by the fantastic score of 58-19! Soldier baseball must have been vigorous. One Yank noted after a contest in Tennessee, "We get lamed badly." [95]

In winter, snowballing was the order of the day. Sometimes units pitched into each other in regular battle fashion, led by their officers with bugles sounding and flags waving. A notable engagement was that between the Twenty-sixth New Jersey and a Vermont regiment near Fredericksburg early in 1863 when: "Both regiments formed a line of battle, each officered by its line and field officers, the latter mounted. At the signal the battle commenced; charges and counter-charges were made, prisoners were taken on either side, the air was filled with white missiles, and stentorian cheers went up as one or other party gained an advantage. At length victory rested with the Vermonters, and the Jersey boys surrendered the field defeated." [96] No mention was made of wounded casualties in this contest, but if Yanks battled with the same vehemence as Rebs—and there is no reason to believe that they did not— black eyes, bruised shins and gashed faces must have required the attention of first-aid men.[97]

Boating, fishing and hunting each had its followers among soldier sportsmen. Sometimes opossums, coons, squirrels and quail were the prizes sought by hunters, and less frequently deer, wild hogs, foxes and wild ducks. In coastal areas mammoth turtles and their eggs were objects of eager search. The usual weapon for small game was a gun, but now and then soldiers armed only with torches and sticks would bring in hundreds of birds knocked from their roosts in a thicket or canebrake. Next day camp fare would be varied by delectable servings of potpie.[98]

Rabbits abounded in most Southern areas, and it was to these fleet and savory animals that most seekers of game gave their attention. The sight of a cottontail in camp or on the march would almost invariably set off an epidemic of whooping and running, and if the terrain was favorable and the pursuers were numerous, the bewildered bunny would sometimes be surrounded and caught. Regardless of the outcome, the exciting chase was thoroughly enjoyed by all who participated.

In the long Southern summers every stream and lake of the invaded country was a swimming hole for men in blue, and sometimes Rebs and Yanks shared the same spot.[99] Bathing in some areas was not without its perils, as the diary of a private stationed in Louisiana pointedly disclosed: "Two men of the 8th Indiana killed by alligators. We saw the alligators and saw the boys go down, but never saw the bodies again. . . . There was great excitement for awhile as we were nearly all in the water." [100]

In the tent of an evening or any time on a stump or log, checkers, chess, dominoes or cards, the last usually for stakes but sometimes for fun, were the mode. When sedentary diversions lost their charm, a sham fight or a tug of war might be quickly arranged; or, better still, the sutler might be raided. One day a group of soldiers playing with an artillery rope, on a sudden impulse, headed for the brigade sutler's tent dragging the rope in a great loop between them. Soon, over went the tent and the vender's wagon with it, spilling out sutler, clerk, canned goods and knickknacks, all in a jumble. "All the boys ran to help pick up the scattered goods, but strange to say, no sooner were they picked up than they disappeared misteriously." The sutler stormed, and the colonel too. A detail was sent to search the quarters, but no rope or raider or lost delicacy was ever found.[101]

Billy Yank was an inveterate tease and prankster. A civilian who happened to come into camp wearing unusual attire or presenting any oddity of appearance was sure to be the victim of a chorus of derisive comments. One day near Atlanta a man riding a bony nag approached a large crowd of soldiers. The first Yank who noticed him let out a raucous "caw-caw-caw." Immediately others took up the cry and soon the whole camp joined in so that for several minutes it seemed that "10,000 crows were holding a jubilee." [102]

Recruits were of course a favorite target. A youngster who joined one unit, after drawing his clothing and equipment from the quartermaster, was asked by a veteran why he did not get his umbrella.

"Do they furnish an umbrella?" inquired the recruit naïvely.

"Why, certainly," replied the veteran. "It's just like that fraud of a quartermaster to jew a recruit out of a part of his outfit. . . . Go back and *demand* your umbrella."

Poor recruit! He returned only to find out how completely he had been taken in.[103]

First duty as sentry was an exceedingly shaky experience for new soldiers, as was attested by the number of cows and pigs that, mistaken for sneaking Rebels, became the targets of trigger-happy novitiates. The nervousness of new sentinels made them ready prey for pranksters who would dress themselves in awe-inspiring regalia, approach a post and when challenged with a palsied "Who goes there?" reply with some such nonsense as "The devil with the countersign" or "A flock of sheep." [104]

Fun seekers delighted in tying cans, baskets and other objects to the tails of stray animals and then helping the poor victim along its frenzied course by emitting loud whoops and setting off charges of powder. Men of one regiment adorned a mud turtle with a "Secesh" flag and laughed uproariously as they prodded him along the company street. Another group found great merriment in burning Jeff Davis in effigy while their band played "Yankee Doodle." [105]

The accent and unusual ways of foreigners often made them the victims of mischievous acts. Men of a New York artillery unit slipped a mouse into the little tin box which a German comrade used for carrying his fine plug tobacco—and then hid near his tent to hear the oaths that came when he reached for a chew.[106]

Negroes, as noted elsewhere, were favorite targets of pranksters. Civilian camp helpers, especially those who seemed inclined to take their freedom too literally, were commonly given the "blanket treatment," and the more aggravated the case the higher the toss. One victim, "elevated till the tossers themselves feared he would not come down," afterward "shook the dust of our camp from his feet, saying 'you tossed me too high entirely.' " [107]

As a rule Yanks confined their horseplay to civilians and fellow soldiers, but now and then they had fun at the expense of the "shoulder straps." Discomfiture of surgeons, owing to the low opinion which many soldiers had of them, afforded special pleasure. When an Illinois surgeon in full view of a marching regiment in North Alabama was pitched into a puddle by a stumbling mount "the boys," according to a captain who witnessed the incident, "consoled him with a clean 1,000 cheers, groans and sharp speeches." [108] But even a general might be considered fair game. When the new commander of a division in the West set out to curb the reckless firing of guns, for which the camps had become notorious, he found that he had taken a lion by the tail. His troubles were described by a soldier of the command:

The other night there were a number of loud explosions over in the Infantry camp. The boys take an empty canteen, put the powder from three or four catridges in it and cork it up tight, then throw it in the fire. It make considerable noise. The General (Harrow) called for the scouts and his horse. We started out. When we got to the Infantry camp all was quiet—men all asleep, Apparantly. Then it broke out over in the Artillery. Away we went, but could find no one there except the gaurd at the guns and he knew nothing about it. Could not leave his beat to find out. Then away over in the Cavelry—boom! boom! Another fast ride. No results—all quiet. My! but the General was hot. He left the scouts to look after things and went back to his Quarters.

The general eventually succeeded in catching two of the culprits and, by giving them a well-publicized ride on a wooden horse constructed especially for the occasion, brought the situation under control.[109]

Take-offs on army institutions and procedures relieved the tedium in a number of camps. In these burlesques, Yanks rarely passed up an opportunity to satirize the "brass." At a mock court-martial, staged with due regard for form as prescribed in regulations, soldiers of the Twenty-third Massachusetts tried one of their number on the following charges and specifications: "At supper, said Eben S. Perkins, with malice prepense and without provocation did throw into the face of one Alec Munroe a dipperful of hot tea, thereby burning him and stopping the growth (?) of a large pair of whiskers." After proceedings got under way, several officers joined the audience and immediately the trial took a new turn, featuring the quality of tea served to soldiers. One witness testified: "I saw the liquid thrown at Mr. M. Am not certain that it *was* tea, although it bore that name." Another stated that he "heard a sudden splash, and saw the hot water called tea." After further testimony along similar lines, the prisoner, who seems to have been so naïve as to think the trial a real one, was found guilty of a felonious assault with intent to kill. But leniency being recommended the sentence required only that the culprit ask pardon of his victim on bended knee and serve two weeks on the wood-and-water detail.[110]

The most common take-off was of dress parade. At these sham affairs, officers and noncommissioned officers were sometimes required to march in the ranks while privates with exaggerated shoulder straps, improvised from orange peelings and even canteens, gave the commands. Broom-

sticks and poles were substituted for muskets, and cannon were repre-
sented by logs borne on wagons or muskets laid across wheelbarrows.
Knapsacks were dry-goods boxes, and haversacks sometimes were re-
placed by tiny bags labeled "ten days' rations." Nondescript clothing,
blacked faces, "officers" riding broken-down horses or mules with saddles
hind part before, shirttail flags, tin-pan drums, knee-length havelocks,
candlesticks pinned on as medals and other ludicrous devices were
introduced to add to the comic theme.[111]

Mock dress parades usually came on holidays as part of extensive
programs featuring sports, horse races, competitive firing, feasting, drink-
ing and other activities. Christmas, New Year's Day, Washington's
Birthday, the Fourth of July and Thanksgiving were the most festively
observed by Yanks in general, while the Irish made much of St. Patrick's
Day and the other foreign groups celebrated occasions memorable in
their respective national histories. Frequently at Christmastime and
on St. Patrick's Day, regimental streets and quarters were elaborately
decorated with evergreen wreaths, arches and other appropriate orna-
ments.[112]

In shooting matches, foot races, hurdles, sack races and wheelbarrow
races, representatives of companies usually competed for cash prizes of
one to five dollars. Chasing greased pigs or climbing slick poles at the
top of which were nailed five-dollar bills were ordinarily free-for-all
affairs, with the porker or money going to the first successful contestant.
A special feature of some celebrations was a "scrape" in which "contra-
bands," with hands tied behind, rooted in tubs filled with meal or flour
for pieces of money placed on the bottom.[113] Whisky flowed freely on
these occasions, adding to the festivity and producing on the morrow
a heavy crop of hang-overs. Sometimes intoxicants were contributed by
officers.

Of a Christmas spree in 1864, Sergeant Onley Andrus of the Ninety-
fifth Illinois Regiment wrote: "Col. Tom turned out 15 galls of Rotgut
& several of the boys got Happy, and some got pugilistic, and as a con-
sequence some had Eyes Red & some Black and all felt as though they
had been poorly staid with at best." Another sergeant, of a New Jersey
regiment, related a New Year's experience thus: "Last night I had plenty
of Whiskey but to day I have none, we had five canteens full and we
had a merry old Time. they broke all my furniture, tore my table cloth,
and tore evry thing upside down, I thought I would fire a saulute, I got
my musket and fired it, and I set my tent a fire, and by the time I got

through, my tent was most burnt up. New Years dont come but once
a year, & tents are cheap." [114]

In their efforts to make life more tolerable in ordinary seasons, sol-
diers resorted to some unusual expedients. One Yank told of a mock
wedding of "J. Hamilton and V. Davy with B. Lee as chaplain," fol-
lowed by music and dancing. Womanless nuptials seem to have been
rare, but dances without benefit of ladies were common. Sometimes the
women were simulated by Yanks who sent home for bonnets and hoop
skirts or borrowed the finery of local Negroes; and when warmed by
generous swigs of "tanglefoot" wheedled from the commissary partici-
pants seemed hardly aware of the pretense. Certainly, whether with or
without resort to subterfuge and spirits, the dances were often lively
affairs with cotillions, polkas and jigs constituting the usual forms.[115]

"From many of the [company] streets," wrote a Wisconsin officer
from Milwaukee early in the war, "the sound of a violin in the last
agonies of the 'Arkansaw traveler' or the 'Campbells are coming' greets
the ear and following the sound one finds a ring formed and a merry sett
'going in' on a quadrille." [116] A few months later a New Yorker reported
from a camp near Washington: "We have a ball almost every night.
The ladies are personified by soldiers." [117] An Ohioan writing from Mur-
freesboro, Tennessee, in 1862 gave these details:

The boys are having a grand cotillion party on the green in front of
my tent and appear to have entirely forgotten the privations, hardships,
and dangers of soldiering. . . . The dance on the green is progressing
with increased vigor. The music is excellent. At this moment the gentle-
men are going to the right; now they promenade all; in a minute more
the ladies will be in the center, and four hands round. That broth of an
Irish boy, Conway, wears a rooster's feather in his cap and has for a
partner a soldier twice as big as himself whom he calls Susan. As they
swing, Conway yells at the top of his voice: 'Come round, old gal!' [118]

Billy Yank, like Johnny Reb, took considerable delight in exercising
his dramatic talents. Sometimes the performances were staged in the
open air on rough platforms and with meager properties. Again, when
stationed for long periods in cities like Atlanta or Chattanooga facilities
might be pretentious. Offerings of units, such as the Forty-fourth Mas-
sachusetts, composed largely of men from the Boston area who formed
a regimental dramatic association, were varied and good. The "Second
Dramatic and Musical Entertainment" given by this group consisted of
songs by the Quartette Club, musical selections by the band, the trial

scene from *The Merchant of Venice* by a cast from the regiment and a concluding number, " 'A Terrible Catastrophe on the North Atlantic R. R.' with Characters by the Company." [119]

The Forty-eighth New York Regiment, which also seems to have possessed unusual dramatic talent, gave a series of creditable productions at Fort Pulaski near Savannah, Georgia, in 1863. An officer of the regiment gave this account of the opening performance: "Address by Corporal Michaels. Singing by the members. Farce, 'Family Jars.' Song, 'The Flea,' by Owens, of Company H. Recitation by Hutchinson. Light balancing by Dr. Haven. Tragedy, 1st act of 'Richard III.' Song by Dickson. Concluding with the tableau, 'Washington's Grave.' The theatre was very pretty, and the performances excellent. The scene-painting was done by Harrison, who was by profession a scenic artist, and was very good." [120]

Minstrels and comedies seemed to be the most popular shows among both performers and audiences. Of a presentation by the Ninth New York Regiment's Zouave Dramatic Club, a soldier wrote: "Combastus De Zouasio, a burlesque performed well and after some very good comic songs and dancing the entertainment concluded with the farce 'Box & Cox'—the house was crowded to acces and the aristocracy of Roanoke was all there generally escorted by some members of our regiment. Gen. Hawkins atended and was receaved with enthusiastic cheers by the audience." [121]

Some of the most entertaining performances were those given about the campfire by talented individuals. Of one of these informal showmen, a comrade wrote: "Brown . . . is a perfect mimic, facile, quick, good looking . . . has a keen sense of the ridiculous & a good fellow for fun generally. Took off an old Orthodox nigger minister last night affected with bronchitis & applying his nostrils occasionally [to] his handkerchief in a professional way—got it all in—I haven't laughed so much since I came in the army." [122]

Occasionally, though rarely, soldiers in camp or hospital were treated to the offerings of itinerant entertainers. A nurse in the general hospital at Chester, Pennsylvania, told of visits to that institution by a Negro minstrel show from Philadelphia and by Antonio Blitz, the famous ventriloquist, bird imitator and sleight-of-hand artist.[123] Various singers gave camp performances, the most famous being the Hutchinson family troupe.[124] James Edward Murdoch, a notable tragedian of the time, entertained soldiers on a number of occasions, as did Thomas Buchanan Read, a famous poet, the two sometimes appearing together with Murdoch reading patriotic poems written by Read.[125] When Read himself attempted to perform, as he sometimes did, results were disappointing because his voice was weak and his material was over the heads of the listeners.[126]

Soldiers stationed near large cities now and then had the opportunity of attending the performances of leading actors and actresses of the period, but relatively few of them appear to have taken advantage of their privileged situation. When soldiers did attend good shows, they sometimes made things difficult for the artists by coarse and drunken conduct.[127] Farces, varieties and minstrel shows were far more attractive to soldier visitors to cities than were good plays.

A sample of dramatic offerings in Southern cities is afforded by the diaries of two soldiers. On August 21, 1863, an Ohioan noted at Vicksburg: "Went to the minstrels in town tonight . . . performances were good, it being the first night of the season. The female who performed the 'fancy dance' was very poorly formed, her limbs didnt amount to a cuss as far as beauty was concerned, but she handled them very gracefully, her face was pretty as she appeared on the stage. How it is naturally I can not say. The best thing of the evening was the map of the 'Southern Confederacy' with the nigger in the background. It was a soiled handkerchief all ragged held up before a darkey's face." [128] In addition to a tightrope walker and trapeze artists, seen at two different shows, an Illinois Yank reported the following from New Orleans:

Jan 4, 1865. Have been to the Varieties theater tonight. . . . The plays were Dot or the Cricket on the Hearth and Pocahontas. . . .

Jan 10, 1865. Went to the St. Charles Theatre in the Evening—Lucie De Arville & phenomenon in a Smock Frock . . .

Jan 24, 1865. Went to the morning Star Minstrels in the Evening. Damn poor show all of the performers drunk.[129]

Trips to towns and cities had attractions other than shows. Riding in the streetcars or rented hacks, gazing at the girls and gawking at the sights afforded diversion to many. Religiously inclined Yanks found pleasure in attending church and in mingling after the service with the members—especially the ladies. Seekers after more worldly pleasures commonly made a beeline for the barrooms, and some found their way to houses of prostitution. When money for drinks was exhausted before thirsts were quenched, saloons were sometimes raided in force. A jovial tippler from Chicago who frequented the gay spots of New Orleans wrote in his diary after one visit to the Crescent City: "Boys cleaned out a Bar up town, any amount of Whiskey, Rum, Gin, Brandy & Wine in camp. Most all got drunk as the Devil and had an awful time." [130]

Whether their excursions were to town or country, Yanks often managed to make the acquaintance of natives and to share their social activities. "You must not think you have all the fun at home," wrote a Philadelphian from a camp near Chambersburg, Pennsylvania, in 1864, "for I have been out several times and had a great deal of pleasure. I have been at a wedding and at Singing School and several places." [131]

Enterprising and attractive Yanks often gained entree to Southern homes. A young New Yorker confided to his diary while serving in Virginia: "At night after taps, run the Picets and went out in the cuntry to see the girls." [132] A Minnesotan, also youthful, wrote after a tour of guard duty on a planter's premises: "When not on post we sit in the house by the fire conversing with the old gentleman's daughters & enjoying ourselves hugely. It is a long time since I was in a private house and as the 'gals' are quite sociable I enjoy this treat 'right smart.' They amuse us with a warm dinner & 'Secesh songs.' . . . One of our special duties is to keep the boys from milking the old man's cow." [133]

Music was often the key which opened the door to acquaintance and provided the basis for continuing association. The talented and sociable Chicagoan, whose frequent trips to New Orleans have already been noted, wrote in his diary after one visit: "Dan and myself called on some of the town people who had a piano and amused ourselves for some time at music." Later he observed: "Called on Mrs. —— 4 Daughters . . . had quite a play on the Flute. Dyer played the Piano. . . . They have two splendid pianos. Old Lady very garrulous." Still later he reported: "Parker, Dyer, Robb & myself called on Miss Pfrang in the evening and had a sing." After moving to Franklin, Louisiana, in the autumn of 1863 he wrote: "Give Tracy 'Weeping Sad & Lonely' to give to a secesh wench that lives in town." [134]

Soldiers occasionally found diversion in calling on relatives or friends in other organizations, with eating, drinking and talk of home providing the principal activity. Once in a great while life might be brightened by visits from wives, fathers, ministers, politicians or other members of the home community. But in the main Yanks had to be content with such recreation as they themselves could provide in their own camps.

Debating afforded considerable fun in many organizations. Topics argued ranged from old favorites such as capital punishment and the relative pleasures of pursuit and possession to questions of the day such as "Resolved: That We Should Support the Constitution as It Is and the Union as It Was," and "Resolved: That the Present War Will Be More Productive of Good Than Evil." Members of the Twenty-fourth Iowa Regiment debated the proposition: "Which Has the Most Influence on Men, to-wit 'Money or Woman,'" and decided in favor of woman. They likewise found that the pen was mightier than the sword. The "Temperance Society" of the Sixteenth Connecticut Regiment weighed the relative influence on society of woman and man, but unfortunately no record was found of their conclusion. Other subjects discussed by this group were: "Resolved: That Public Speaking Is Not a Safe Rule of Action," and "Resolved: That Intemperance Is a Greater Evil Than War." With respect to the latter an hour and a half of serious argument resulted in the decision that Bacchus was more wicked than Mars.[135]

In some units debates, along with orations, recitations, spelling bees and other cultural exercises, were sponsored by "lyceums" and other imposingly named literary bodies. These organizations were usually much more active in winter than in summer because of the relatively stable conditions which prevailed during the cold season. A glimpse of one society's doings is given in a Hoosier sergeant's letter from Culpepper, Virginia, February 11, 1864: "We have built a hall that will hold about 125 men and organized . . . the 'Forest Lyceum'; order of Exercises—Declamations, Essays, Orations, Debate, Anonymous Communications &c. It is well attended and we have an excellent time. If you can find 'Poe's Raven,' a piece I used to declaim and copy it and Send it to me immediately I will be greatly obliged to you." [136]

Handicraft of various sorts, especially the carving of pipes and rings, was a favorite diversion in hospitals and prisons and was practiced to a considerable extent during periods of leisure in camp. For pipes, brier root was the usual medium and for rings and other ornaments, bone, sea shell or soft wood. Knitting had an occasional enthusiast among hospital patients, as did painting and drawing.

Nearly every regiment had one or more printers on its rolls and these, when circumstances permitted, delighted in teaming up with interested comrades to publish camp newspapers. Soldier papers ranged in character from elaborate dailies and weeklies extending over long periods of time to crude one-page affairs limited to a single issue. The strength of Billy Yank's urge to break into print is strikingly evidenced by the fact that soldiers established during the course of the war more than 100 different camp newspapers.[137] In addition to these, numerous papers were launched in Union hospitals and several by Yanks confined in Southern prisons. Moreover, soldiers had a part in publishing some of the official and semiofficial organs established in occupied areas for both military and civilian readers, such as the *New South* and the *Free South* issued in South Carolina and the *Union Appeal* in Memphis, Tennessee.[138]

The titles of the soldier papers throw some light on their character and are interesting in themselves. Three different organs, two published in camp and one in a New Orleans prison, bore the heading *Stars and Stripes*.[139] Several took their names from items of soldier equipment, as the *Buck and Ball*, *The Knapsack*, the *Union Guidon* and the *Camp Kettle*.[140] Some appropriated unit designations, as the *First Minnesota*, the *First Kansas*, the *Connecticut Fifth*, the *Pennsylvania Thirteenth*, the *Ohio Seventh*, the *New York Ninth*, the *Fifth Iowa Register*, the *Illinois Fifty-Second*, the *Dragoon*, the *Sixth Corps* and the *Letter H*.[141]

Patriotic themes provided the inspiration for a number of titles such as the *Whole Union*, the *War Eagle*, the *Union Volunteer*, the *Banner of Freedom* and the *American Patriot*.[142] Federal commanders were honored in three titles, namely, *Unconditional S. Grant*, *Grant's Petersburg Progress* and *Lauman's Own*.[143] Still other titles featured the names of camps, towns, states and rivers.

Hospital papers commonly had the same name as the institution in which they were issued, but interesting variations were found in such titles as the *Cripple*, the *Crutch* and the *Cartridge Box*.[144] One cannot but wonder whether the editors were trying to be witty or poetic when they issued to one group of patients a sheet headed the *Soldier's Casket*.[145]

A few organizations, such as the Thirteenth Pennsylvania Regiment, could boast of portable printing presses. In loyal areas local publishers sometimes made their facilities available without charge to soldier editors. But in the majority of cases camp papers were published on captured presses.[146]

When Federals occupied a Southern town soldier journalists usually made the newspaper office their primary objective, and as soon as other duties permitted they set up and published their own sheet. Sometimes, as in the case of the First Minnesota's occupation of Berryville, Virginia, in 1862, and the Twenty-fifth Ohio's entry into Manning, South Carolina, in 1865, the Yankee typographers, finding the local paper already in process of publication, simply let the Rebel portion stand and printed their own columns on the back or on additional sheets.[147]

When loyal soldiers of Missouri captured Boonville, Missouri, on June 18, 1861, and found one page of the "Secesh" paper, the *Boonville Patriot*, already in type they reset the title as *The American Patriot* and replaced four of the eight columns with Union material.[148] Occasionally the new editors chided their predecessor for urging his readers to defy the invaders to the last ditch and then taking inglorious flight before the men in blue came within gun range.

Most soldier editors aimed at a weekly schedule, though a number announced "semi-occasional" issues. The Corinth, Mississippi, *Chanticleer*, published by members of the Second Iowa Regiment, stated that it would appear "as often as possible," while editors of the *Union Advance Picket*, sponsored by the Third New York Cavalry at Washington, North Carolina, promised publication "whenever we have time." Ohio artillerymen who launched the *Battery Reveille* at Fayetteville, Tennessee, on June 7, 1862, informed their readers that issues would appear "as often as providence and the commanding general will permit." [149]

Whatever the announced intentions, most papers were issued irregularly and their life span was short. The *Badger Bulletin*, projected by a Wisconsin group, died with a single issue published at Iuka, Mississippi, on June 14, 1862. The editors explained the premature demise thus: Marching orders "nip our rising effort in the bud." [150] The same, no doubt, could have been said of scores of other papers.

Publication of the single issue, which comprises the career of many papers, sometimes was accomplished in the face of enormous difficulties. A case in point is the *Buck and Ball* printed by soldiers of the Eleventh Kansas Regiment at Cane Hill, Arkansas, in December 1862. This four-page paper bears the date of December 6 on the outside but an explanatory note inserted within indicates that printing begun on that date had to be suspended after setting up the first page, so that the staff could take part in the battle of Prairie Grove, December 7, 1862. The remaining portion, devoted largely to details of the fight, was not completed until December 15.[151]

Sometimes, when lack of facilities made printing impossible, determined Yanks wrote out their papers in longhand, passed the single copy about among their comrades and eventually sent it home for circulation.[152]

Content of the camp papers, whether printed or written, varied considerably. In some cases the columns were devoted almost exclusively to orders, reports of battles and other official matter. In others the publishers concentrated on editorials, essays, poems, jokes and stories and gave only scant attention to military items. In still other instances most of the space was devoted to lecturing local Rebels on the error of their ways and the blessings of Union.

Many papers carried advertisements. When these were genuine they consisted mainly of notices by sutlers, photographers and others attached to the military establishment who desired to do business with the soldiers. Illustrations were sparse, owing to limited facilities, and consisted largely of flags, mules, boots and other standard items which usually could be found in quantity in the morgue of confiscated journals. Sometimes considerable cleverness was demonstrated in adapting these stereotypes. Editors of the *Yazoo Daily Yankee* ran an elaborate cut of a cemetery scene, accompanied by these lines:

> Gentle stranger drop a tear
> The C.S.A. lies buried here;
> In youth it lived and flourished well
> But like Lucifer, it fell.
> Its body's here—its soul in . . . well,
> Even if I knew I would not tell.
> Rest from every care and strife,
> Your death were better than your life,
> And this one line shall grace your grave:
> Your death gave freedom to the slave.[153]

Poetic selections were standard features of many camp papers. Sometimes these were original pieces contributed by soldiers or their civilian friends, but more frequently they were borrowed from other sources. Popular songs such as "Weeping Sad and Lonely" were occasionally published, as were numerous parodies composed by the rank and file. One paper ran a parody on "Hard Times" under the title "Sow Belley." This song, as the title suggests, reflected the soldiers' disesteem of salt pork.[154]

Camp editors depended heavily on jokes, humorous stories and conundrums as fillers for their columns. Some of these were on the shady side. Readers of *Unconditional S. Grant* were treated to this tidbit: "If you wish to keep your oldest boy from walking in his sleep, let your servant girls be as old and ugly as possible." [155] The *Tri-Weekly Camp Journal*, under the heading "Insulting," carried the following:

"Have you a fellow feeling in your bosom for the poor women of Utah?" asked a speaker of the sister of Mrs. Parlington.
"Get out, you insulting rascal," said she. "I'll have you know I don't allow fellows to be feeling in my bosom. Oh, dear!" [156]

Editions varied in size from a few copies to thousands, and prices ranged from a penny to a quarter with a nickel being the usual rate. Of the first issue of the *Soldier's Letter* published at Harrodsburg, Kentucky, November 28, 1862, by the Ninety-sixth Illinois Regiment, 2,500 copies were printed at five cents a copy. Fourteen hundred copies of the *New York Ninth*, published at three cents in Warrenton, Virginia, on July 21, 1862, were exhausted so quickly that a second edition of 500 copies was run off. The *Sixth Corps*, published at Danville, Virginia, in the spring of 1865, had all the buyers it could accommodate at the high price of twenty-five cents a copy.[157]

Most soldier papers had as a partial aim the enlightenment and entertainment of the folk back home. At least two of them bore the title *Soldier's Letter*, and these along with many others were often used as substitutes or supplements for personal correspondence. Whether crude or elegant, these fugitive organs must have afforded keen pleasure to those who had a part in their preparation and must have had many interested readers both in camp and at home.[158]

Of far greater interest to the folk at home, however, were the personal letters of their soldier boys; and letter writing was one of the most pervasive of camp diversions. A civilian who visited many units in the autumn of 1861 reported that some regiments of 1,000 men had for weeks sent out an average of 600 letters a day.[159] This volume was probably not sustained, as soldiers usually carried on a more extensive correspondence during their first months of service. But outgoing mailbags were fat during any period of the war. One Yank with a penchant for record keeping reported the writing of 164 letters in 1863, 109 of which went to his homefolk and 55 "to other friends." In addition he wrote 37 letters "for other men" who presumably were illiterate comrades. Balanced against this impressive output was a total of 85 letters received.[160]

Letters were written under all sorts of conditions. In winter quarters, desks and other conveniences were usually available, but when life in the open was the vogue, as was the case most of the time, correspondents had to improvise much of their writing equipment. In 1861 Private Abraham Kendig began a letter to his homefolk: "By the light of a candle stuck in a pine stick, setting on the ground leaning against Bruce Wallace who is asleep . . . and two other fellows laying asleep in front of me I undertake to write you." Kendig was probably using his knapsack for a desk as this was a favorite makeshift, but he and other Yanks often rested their writing sheets on their knees, tin plates, books, cracker boxes or drumheads. The prone position was frequently employed, though not always with satisfactory results. "You must excuse bad writing," stated Bishop Crumrine to his brother on one occasion, "as I am almost dead lying on my belly." Another Yank who stretched himself out on the floor of his tent to write his wife had his effort brought to naught by the tramping feet of two scuffling comrades.[161]

Many Yanks interrupted their letters to take part in a skirmish or battle and some continued their scribbling even amid the confusion of screaming missiles. Most instances of writing under fire were during sieges or trench fights. "Not less than 50 balls have passed over me since I commenced writing," wrote a Yank from Vicksburg in 1863, and another, writing near Atlanta the next year, stated: "Sometimes a bullet comes a little to[o] near where I am writing and makes me spoil a letter; a man never gets so used to them but what he will dodge when they whistle past his ear." [162]

Stationery varied from fancy sheets adorned with patriotic emblems and verses (with envelopes to match) to ruled pages torn from army record books and rough paper taken from the Rebels. Ink was the preferred writing medium, but during periods of active campaigning pencils often had to be employed.

The form and content of letters varied greatly with the background and character of the writers. Some were models of literary excellence done in beautiful script, while others were so crudely written and so full of misspellings as almost to defy deciphering. The great majority of letters lay between these extremes, but since the typical private was of limited education the average was much nearer the lower than the higher end of the scale. It is not meant to imply that the polished missives were consistently superior to the roughhewn products in every respect, for sometimes the crudely scribbled and ungrammatical letters of semi-literate Yanks were absorbingly interesting, highly informative documents, rich in humor and replete with original and colorful phrase.

Often the letters of rustics told more of soldier life than did those of sophisticates, for the latter, assuming that their correspondents read the newspapers, touched certain subjects only lightly, while their less privileged comrades, unable to make such assumptions, would treat them extensively. Then, too, better-educated Yanks, because they had a more highly developed sense of delicacy, were more inclined to pass over the seamy side of camp life than were their less cultivated associates.

A characteristic letter of an average Yank would open with the words "Dear Wife [who sometimes was addressed as "Esteamed Friend"]: I seat myself and take pen in hand to drop you a few lines [or, I will take the present opertunity to drop you a few lines]. I am well at the present and hope you are injoyin a like blesson." Then would follow one or more pages of information about the writer and his comrades, interspersed with inquiries about home affairs. The writer would threaten recurrently to bring his note to a close, but other items of news coming to mind would set him going again. When finally he ran out of subject matter or writing space he would sign off with the words, "Your husband until deth [or, I remane yore afecshonet husban ontel deth do us part], John Jones to Elvira Jones." The correspondent might add a sentimental rhyme such as this: "When this you sea, remember me, though meny miles apart we bea." [163]

Favorite topics of soldier correspondents were battles, about which they wrote at great length; health; the weather; the land and people of Dixie, especially the Negroes who were a source of unusual curiosity; camp doings, particularly those involving residents of the writer's home community; rumors of future movements; food; and officers.

Sin was a subject on which both the ungodly and the righteous, especially the latter, liked to dwell. "George Farnum . . . has lost his Religion and Swars like a Salor," wrote one Yank, while another told what comrades had sired the crop of illegitimate babies recently born in the home community.[164] Others passed on information about fellow soldiers carrying on scandalously with Southern women. Young blades writing to male acquaintances of similar interests sometimes boasted of their own illicit doings, in phrases never intended for delicate readers.[165]

Tragedy was another favorite theme. Mortal illnesses and fatal accidents were recounted at length, and combat fatalities were reported in even greater detail. Executions, however, elicited the fullest descriptions, owing probably to the solemnly impressive manner in which they were staged.

Unpopular officers inspired some of the most expressive phrases of denunciation. One soldier wrote in disgust: "The Major is a hell of a man to go on a . . . [detail] with he dont no enough to learn a dog to bark." Another attributed the recent death of his general to an overdose of whisky and stated: "I did not see a tear shed but heard a great many speaches made about him such as he was in hell pumping thunder at 3 cents a clap." [166]

Writing came hard to most Yanks because of educational deficiencies, lack of experience and the seeming unimportance of camp routine. The tendency to regard as newsworthy only the unusual found frequent expression in the phrase, "I would have written before but I had nothing strange to tell you." Often those who maintained a considerable flow of correspondence, despite their handicaps, showed decided improvement in style during the course of their service.

As already noted and illustrated, letters of unsophisticated Yanks were replete with misspellings. Some of the most flagrant errors arose from efforts to tell about camp ailments. Pneumonia sometimes appeared as "nu mornia," again as "new mony," and one Yank put the word down as "new mornion." Diarrhea, a word formidable enough for educated Yanks, suffered all sorts of distortion at the hands of rustics; one victim of the disease wrote that he "had the camp Diary." Yellow jaundice was frequently "yaller ganders"; a Yank who served in General Landers' command wrote that "Landers has had the ganders." [167]

Among Northern soldiers as among their foes, "horsepittle" was standard spelling for hospital though occasionally variations were used. One Yank wrote that "James Swartz is some wares in the hose pittle." [168] Another reported that "they are deviding the Army up into corpses." [169] Typical misspellings included "stoode beanes" for stewed beans, "Hurey Can" for hurricane, "fortigg" for fatigue, "nea deap" and "axidently." "Haint" and "hant" had wide usage and the old English practice of prefixing a's to verbs, as in "agoing" (sometimes "agonter"), was common practice.

Difficulties of spelling and grammar did not prevent some Yanks from getting their ideas across with force, as witness the following outburst from an Ohioan to his sister:

Alf sed he heard that you and hardy was a runing to gether all the time and he thought he wod gust quit having any thing mor to doo with you for he thought it was no mor yuse. . . . i think you made a dam good chouis to turn of as nise a feler as Alf dyer and let that orney thefin, drunkerd, damed card playing Sun of a bich com to Sea you. the god damed theaf and lop yeard pigen tode helon, he is too orney for hel. . . . i will Shute him as shore a i Sea him.[170]

Some of the expressions used by soldier correspondents were original and vivid, while others were trite and colorless. Private Charles Babbott characterized a recently received letter as "Short and Sweet just like a rosted maget," while Henry Thompson, writing from "Camp Sh—t," informed his wife: "To tell the plain truth we are between a sh—t and a sweat out here." [171] An Ohioan stated that he had to answer roll call when it was "raining pitchforks," but, even so, he was "well, pot gugged and saucy." [172] Another Yank reported that he was "Hunkey Dora." [173]

An Ohio soldier wrote his wife that Rebel dwellings near Fredericksburg looked "like the latter end of original sin and hard times," and a Wisconsin Yank stationed in North Alabama informed a friend that "the folks [here] is pooer than skim piss." Private Michael Dresbach while convalescing in a Chattanooga hospital wrote his wife that he was so hungry that he "could eat a rider off his horse and snap at the stirrups." [174]

Other Yanks used the familiar phrases "snug as a bug in a rug," "chief cook and bottle washer," "sasia [sashay] around," "raise Ned," "raise the old hary," "let 'er rip," "midling peart," "i am well and a creking," "drunk as a fool," "scarce as hens' teeth" and "grab a root." Money was sometimes referred to as "rocks" and "spondulix."

Many slang terms which gained currency in the army also found their way into letters; included among these were "Who wouldn't be a soldier?" which meant, roughly, "Who cares?" and "Here's your mule," which was a nonsensical term used much in the same manner as soldiers of a later generation used the phrase "Kilroy was here."

A substantial portion of the letters written in camp were addressed to sweethearts who in camp parlance were known by such unflattering nicknames as "pigeon," "pig," "duck," "biddy," "jularky" and "hoosey dooksy." Correspondence between soldiers and the girls they left behind them was frequently formal and stilted, though now and then an established suitor would hazard the use of an endearing phrase. Despite the restrained tone dictated by usage of the time, a goodly number of Yanks were able, with the assistance of a timely furlough, subtle prodding by the girl and perchance a show of paternal opposition, to push their cases from a casual to a permanent basis.

Romantically inclined Yanks, like their opposites in gray, found poetry a convenient and effective agent in conveying the gentler sentiments, for poetry had the priceless quality of saying much or little, as the recipient chose; moreover, the ability to make verses was considered a mark of gallantry.

Francis S. Flint of the Second Minnesota Battery addressed these lines to his "Darling Jennie":

> Oh I wish I was and I know whare
> A sitting in an old arm chair
> And no boody thare but She & I
> The door locked & the key laid by
>
> Wouldnt we have a Gallant old
> time Well we would perhaps
> you'd like to know who she is well
> the first letter of her name is
> Jennie that's all I'll tell.[175]

From an unidentified Yank, Margaret McMeekin received the following verses which carried the bold heading "A Proposal to Maggie":

> 1 Do you darling do you Maggie
> in my absence think of me
> Think of him who loves you Maggie
> *And woud ever faithful be*
>
> 2 Does your heart beat with emotion
> Do the tear drops fill your eys
> When I proffer my devotion
> *Do you find relief in Sighs*
>
> 3 Tell me Maggie Darling tell me
> Coud you trew and constant be
> And whatever woses befell me
> *love me onely onely me*
>
> will you do hur Mag[176]

The most confirmed sentimental-verse addict encountered by the writer was Albert E. Trumble of the Fifteenth Illinois Regiment. Trumble's poetic flow, written in neat script and addressed to Amelia Boyce, began shortly after he joined the army and continued throughout his service. The first lines, sent as a postscript, were:

> My pen is poor
> My ink is pale
> My love to you
> As long as a rail.

As acquaintance ripened, Trumble waxed bolder in both his prose and poetry. From Bolivar, Tennessee, in August 1862 he penned the following:

> Though waters may between us roll,
> May friendship still unite our soul,
> Though far distant may be our lot,
> *Dearest friend for get me not.*

The next spring he wrote from Memphis:

> When the waning moon beams sleep
> At midnight on the lovely sea
> And nature's pensive spirits weep
> In all her dews remember me
>   do it Amelia

And in August 1864, while campaigning in Georgia, he wrote as a postscript:

> Way down here clear out of sight;
> Three little words I wish to write
> *Forget me not*

Trumble's capture a little later, followed by a long imprisonment, interrupted his poetic effusion. But after the war he renewed courtship of Amelia and apparently married her.[177]

Many Yanks advertised for feminine correspondents in the newspapers, but the tone of some of these notices is such as to suggest that they were inserted by pranksters.[178]

Regardless of whether or not they wrote to girls, nearly all unmarried soldiers wrote about "the dear little creeturs." A Missouri cavalryman directed his younger brother "to keep the Girls strate and wright to me and Let me now what Girl you are sparking," while a Kentucky Yank wrote his sister: "Give my love and respect to Miss Dumps Ritter tell her I feal mity like marying now. I would like to have a sweat buss from her rosy cheeks." Countless other Yanks enjoined friends at home to look after the girls for them until they returned to make up for lost time. "We have very good times here," wrote one soldier from deep in Dixie, "but i am agetting tired of dooing without girls. We dont have any women here in this wooden country." [179]

Far more diverting than the writing of letters was the reading of missives received from relatives and friends. The craving for correspondence was so great that Yanks would entreat, importune and even browbeat folk at home to write and to write fully and often. "FOR GOD-SAKE RITE" was a standard part of the letters of one soldier to his parents and another wrote his sister: "I like to get big letters i want you to fill up the whole Sheete." [180]

Sounding of the mail call—or as many Yanks put it the "male" call— would produce a most enthusiastic response, causing soldiers to stop any activity, even eating, and rush hopefully to the place of distribution. "When the lieutenant came to the door and told ous that the male had come Every one of the boys jumped up to heare his name called out," wrote Private John Herr to his sister; "it made the boys shout withe Joy to heare from home once more." Another Yank wrote his parents that he thought "more of a letter from home than I would a gold watch." [181]

The day following arrival of a long-delayed mail pouch in a North Carolina camp, a Norwegian Yank wrote his parents: "I got my hands on your letter . . . and one from my wife. . . . I can never remember of having been so glad before. I cried with joy and thankfulness." [182]

Soldiers read and reread many times their letters from home. It was not unusual for them literally to "wear out" the cherished missives; and nothing did more to make camp life tolerable for most of them than a regular flow of correspondence from loved ones.

When correspondence, journalism, music, reading, sports, horseplay and other activities could not be enjoyed, soldiers might always turn to conversation as a means of breaking the monotony. Chat sessions about the campfire or in quarters were indeed a favorite mode of diversion. Topics were as varied as the soldiers' interests, but talk seemed most frequently to turn to such subjects as home, women, religion, battles, officers, food, politics, slackers, profiteering, freedmen and Rebels. Discussion was frequently enlivened by rumors and the more fantastic they were the more diverting. Humor also added sparkle, especially when dispensed by masters of the storytelling art who were to be found in almost any company.

One of the favorite stories that made the rounds of the campfires had as its central character an awkward eccentric who was far better acquainted with the Bible than with tactics. In one version of the yarn, the hero was Hackett and the details were as follows:

The guard-house was located just inside the Fort entrance and a bridge spanned the moat to the entrance. Once, when Captain R was officer of the day, it was his duty to inspect the guard at least once after midnight. Hackett was at Post number one, near the gateway of the Fort. It was a dark, rainy night, when Hackett heard Capt. R. Approach, and called out, 'Who comes there?' Captain R. Being on one side of the bridge, stumbled and fell headlong into the moat; as he fell he exclaimed in a loud voice, 'J—s Ch—t.' Hackett faced about and called out promptly, 'turn out the Apostles. J—s Ch—t is coming.' Then the guard helped the Captain out of the moat.[183]

Another humorous item which must have produced hearty chortles was the famous saltpeter poem burlesquing Rebel expedients for making gunpowder.[184] Perhaps the favorite of all comic verses recited by the men in blue was a parody of the Lord's Prayer addressed to "Father Abraham," as the soldiers sometimes called Lincoln. As reported by a Connecticut soldier, the lines ran:

> Our Father who art in Washington,
> Uncle Abraham be they Name,
> Thy will be done at the South as at the North
> Give us this day our dailey rations,
> Of crackers salt horse and Pork,
> [For] Give us our short comeings,
> As we forgive our Quarter Master,
> For thine is the power,
> The soldiers and the Nigers,
> For the space of 2 Years,
> AMEN [185]

The urge to have fun in one form or another was irrepressible. And despite the lack of organized efforts to promote recreation, wearers of the blue, like the men in gray, were able to make tolerable a life which to most was thoroughly unattractive.

CHAPTER VIII

TOEING THE MARK

A few weeks after Gettysburg one of Meade's veterans wrote to his wife: "We are bound up pretty tight here . . . the military law is quite diffrent from Common law we have to toe the mark." [1]

The military system of control which, rather than military law, was the subject of this Yank's comment was indeed different, as soldiers of all periods have readily attested. The disciplinary setup as it existed in the American Army at the time of the Civil War may be summarized briefly.[2]

Closest to the soldier in the scheme of control were the commanders of small units and their noncommissioned agents. These authorities habitually administered as "company punishments" minor penalties for trivial breaches of discipline, such as absence from roll call, violations of uniform regulations, neglect of equipment, loud talking after taps and petty altercations. But in certain circumstances commanding officers held supreme authority over their men, as in battle, in time of mutiny, or in any other emergency requiring extreme and immediate action for protection of the life of persons under their control. And in a few instances this power of life and death was exercised by unit commanders, with the approval of their superiors. A most amazing example was the shooting on August 30, 1863, of two soldiers by Lieutenant Colonel H. Robinson, commander of the First Louisiana Cavalry Regiment. When Robinson attempted to enforce an order issued by General Banks to absorb into his command some 200 soldiers of the disbanded Second Rhode Island Cavalry, the Easterners resisted, some of them saying: "We enlisted in the 2nd R. I. Cavalry, we will by God, serve in no other." After unsuccessful efforts to persuade the mutineers to comply, Robinson had the consolidation order reread to them and then threatened to shoot on the spot those who still refused to obey. Under force of this threat nearly all of the men took their places with the Louisiana regiment. From the very few still holding out Robinson selected two whom he adjudged the ringleaders and within half an hour, without resort to any sort of trial, had them executed. While the offenders were no doubt

Courtesy National Archives

WESTERN SOLDIERS ON PARADE
Company H, Forty-fourth Indiana Regiment

SOLDIERS OF COMPANY F, FOURTH VERMONT, IN CAMP

guilty of mutinous conduct, there is no indication that life was in danger or the case so urgent as to admit of no delay. Certainly Robinson had at his disposal a sufficient force to overpower the mutineers and hold them in restraint until a court could be assembled or the case referred to higher authority. A military commission, however, which on September 5-6 investigated the affair, not only exonerated Robinson but commended him for the "prompt and efficient manner" in which he suppressed the mutiny. General Banks, commander of the Department of the Gulf, in endorsing the court's findings, admitted that order could probably have been maintained without resort to capital punishment but declared that he was "unable, with his knowledge of the facts, to say that it was not justifiable in consideration of all the circumstances of the case." General in Chief Halleck and the Secretary of War, though obviously disturbed by a strong protest of Governor Smith of Rhode Island, apparently agreed with Banks. At least no record was found of disapproval of the execution by any military authority.[3] The incident may not have been startling to people of the sixties, but in the light of present concepts it is inconceivable that a regimental commander would presume on his own authority to shoot men except in extreme peril, or that if he did his action would go unreproved by higher authority.

While commanding officers in the Union Army seem usually to have respected the spirit of army regulations requiring them to dispose of only minor breaches of discipline and refer serious offenses to courts-martial, exceptions were by no means rare. John W. Geary and Stephen Weld were among those who assumed far-reaching authority. Geary, while still a colonel, took the responsibility of shaving a soldier's head and drumming him out of camp. After he became a general, he once knocked down and choked a soldier whom he caught straggling. Lieutenant Colonel Weld, after shooting an insubordinate private in the arm, wrote: "I meant to kill him, and was very sorry I did not succeed. . . . I called him up a few days after shooting him and told him that I meant to have killed him . . . but that if he would promise to let rum alone, I would release him from the guard-house. I might have had him tried by court-martial and shot, but I thought I would give him another chance." Another lieutenant colonel, commander of a Negro regiment, followed the interesting practice of giving serious offenders a choice between being punished by him or having their cases referred to courts-martial.[4]

Next above company punishment in the disciplinary scheme were the regimental and garrison courts-martial. These courts, convenable by order of commanders of posts, regiments and comparable organizations, consisted of three officers. Their jurisdiction was restricted to enlisted men and to noncapital cases. Since the articles of war prohibited regimental or garrison courts from inflicting fines exceeding one month's pay or imposing hard labor or prison sentences exceeding a month's duration, offenses tried by these bodies were usually of a minor character, such as petty theft, brief absences without leave, straggling, skulking and brawling.[5] Some of the punishments habitually meted out by regimental courts, such as tying up by the thumbs, carrying heavy weights, bucking and gagging, and riding wooden horses, while not specifically violating the maximum penalties authorized by the articles of war, actually exceeded them in severity.

The next higher organization in the disciplinary system was the general court-martial. At the outbreak of war, power to convene this type of court was restricted to commanders of armies or departments. But the unusual needs growing out of the war caused Congress in December 1861 to extend the convening authority to commanders of divisions and separate brigades.[6]

General courts-martial consisted of five to thirteen officers, and their jurisdiction extended to all ranks and comprehended all types of cases, including capital offenses. Army regulations specified the following legal punishments dispensable by courts-martial: death; imprisonment; confinement on bread and water; solitary confinement; hard labor; ball and chain; forfeiture of pay and allowances; discharge from the service; reprimand; and, in cases of noncommissioned officers, reduction in grade. Solitary confinement of a prisoner, or confinement on bread and water, was restricted to a total of eighty-four days out of a year, and in a lengthy sentence had to be broken every fourteen days with a two weeks' respite. Until its abolition in August 1861, flogging was a legal punishment for desertion.[7]

General courts-martial often prescribed a combination of legal punishments, and it was not unusual for them to impose penalties which violated the spirit if not the letter of the law, such as branding and head shaving.

Comparable in authority and procedure to the general court-martial was the military commission, a judicial body designed for enemy areas where civilian agencies were inoperative or for other localities under martial law. Jurisdiction of military commissions comprehended both military and civilian personnel, and soldiers were occasionally tried before these bodies, especially for offenses against civilians.[8]

Courts-martial and military commissions followed a well-defined procedure designed to assure a full hearing and a fair trial for the accused.[9] Persons on trial were allowed benefit of counsel, could challenge members of the court and had the right to question witnesses. An extensive record was kept of proceedings.[10] In a great number of cases sentences were set aside by higher authority, and prisoners found guilty of the most serious offenses were often relieved of punishment because of minor deviations from prescribed procedure.[11] For example, a private, sentenced to be shot for striking a superior officer and deserting, was ordered released and returned to duty by General Hooker because the record of proceedings did not explicitly state that the sentence had been concurred in by two thirds of the court.[12] In the case of another soldier convicted of desertion, proceedings stating that the court and the judge were "duly sworn" failed to include the phrase "in the presence of the accused" as required by army regulations. The Judge Advocate General of the Army called General Banks's attention to the flaw and suggested that the court be reassembled to correct it. General Banks replied that the court had been dissolved and stated he intended to have the soldier shot, in accordance with the court's sentence, as he deemed the irregularity a purely technical one. The Judge Advocate General commended Banks's desire to exercise a firm discipline but held that the defect was "fatal," and on his recommendation President Lincoln remitted the sentence.[13]

Beyond the court-martial and the military commission was a chain of higher commanders, the Judge Advocate General of the Army (which office was created in July 1862) and the President of the United States.[14] The commander who ordered a court reviewed its proceedings and, except when the sentence was death (or dismissal of an officer from the service), ordered it put into effect, mitigated or set aside. Dismissal of officers had to be approved by army or department commanders, and early in the war these commanders had the power to confirm and order execution of the death penalty. But in July 1862 Congress passed a law requiring referral of all sentences of death and imprisonment to the President. Subsequently this provision was modified to give army and department commanders final authority in death sentences for certain types of offenses, including spying, desertion, mutiny, arson, burglary and rape. When cases were referred to the President they were forwarded through command channels and the Judge Advocate General of the Army.[15]

The disciplinary system as it existed in 1861, while adequate in times of peace, failed to meet the unusual circumstances created by the war. Rapid mobilization of hordes of civilians unaccustomed to discipline led to a volume of offenses which swamped the courts-martial. Moreover, when active campaigning began, with straggling an inevitable concomitant, officers were too vitally needed in their units to permit the frequent holding of courts-martial. The result was the accumulation of enormous backlogs of prisoners whose diversion from soldierly duties, along with that of the force required to guard them, seriously impaired the armies' effectiveness. Then, too, the failure to bring offenders promptly to trial violated fundamental principles of justice and had an adverse effect on discipline.

The situation was further complicated by the dearth of officers skilled in court-martial procedure. As a general rule, only the Regular Army officers were thoroughly acquainted with the system and these officers were too few, too poorly distributed and too badly needed for other functions to be frequently available for courts-martial. Early in the war the regiment that could provide officers sufficiently informed to conduct any kind of court was a rarity, and throughout the conflict higher commanders seem to have had difficulty in finding personnel who could operate general courts-martial in complete accordance with regulations. On August 10, 1863, N. P. Banks, commanding general of the Department of the Gulf, wrote the Judge Advocate General of the Army: "With the utmost care in the selection of officers, I have found it impossible to assemble a court whose proceedings will not in some way violate the rules of military jurisprudence." [16]

Owing to these considerations, a law was passed in July 1862 providing that cases hitherto brought before regimental or garrison courts-martial should be tried by a field-grade officer specially detached for the purpose. The same law created the office of Judge Advocate General of the Army and authorized appointment in each field army of a judge advocate with rank of major whose function was to advise and assist in the administration of justice.[17] These changes expedited action and increased the general efficiency of judicial machinery.[18]

Even so, military justice was sometimes so ineffective that impatient and angry soldiers took punishment into their own hands. In July 1863 a New York regiment, while on the march from Harrisburg to New York City, became so infuriated with a chronic thief that they seized him, put him under guard, shaved his head, poured tar on him, wrote the word THIEF in large letters on his back and after parading him before the regiment drummed him from their ranks. While the main body of the regiment proceeded on its way, a few members followed the culprit, stoning and jeering him until he sank down in exhaustion, begging for his life; and thus they left him.[19] But instances of this sort were unusual.

Probably the most common of all offenses was absence without leave. In the overwhelming majority of cases absences were of short duration. Running the guard, or taking French leave as the soldiers commonly put it, was most frequent while units were encamped near large cities or in the vicinity of such irresistible attractions as chicken roosts, stock pens or orchards. The usual punishments for absence without leave and the concomitant evil of missing roll call or drill were: confinement in the guardhouse, which more often than not was a guarded tent; marching about the camp carrying a log, a bag of sand, a knapsack filled with rocks or some other weight; riding the wooden horse, which consisted of sitting astride a horizontal pole held aloft by upright supports; digging stumps; and doing extra duty.

Some commanders kept a black list made up of absentees from roll call and other minor offenders. From this list drafts were made when some particularly disagreeable task had to be performed, such as burying dead horses, digging latrines or cleaning up the camp.[20]

Punishments were adapted to the gravity of offenses by adjustments in time or quantity. For a brief overstaying of a pass or failure to answer roll by a soldier whose conduct generally was good, the guardhouse confinement might be limited to an hour or two; if the sentence was carrying a log, the weight might be light and the period brief; or if the penalty was grubbing stumps, their size might be small and the number few. But for serious or chronic offenders the dosage of punishment would be increased to considerable severity. In the Sixth Michigan Regiment, for example, breaking guard became so prevalent during a period of encampment near Baltimore that offenders were required to carry twenty-pound bags of sand for several days, walking in a ring for alternate hours from six o'clock in the morning until six at night.[21]

When unauthorized absence from camp extended over a period of several days or weeks, heavier penalties were applied, such as forfeiture of pay, wearing ball and chain and imprisonment for one or more months, sometimes with the stipulation that during part of the confinement rations be restricted to bread and water. A private of the Seventh Massachusetts Regiment received this sentence for absence without leave: "Stand on a barrel in front of Guard house with stick of wood on his shoulder from Reveille to Retreat for 2 days." [22]

Fighting and brawling, usually inspired by liquor, were also common offenses. "When they can't get Johnny Rebs to fight, some of the fellows do a good deal of fighting among themselves," wrote Private Edward L. Edes from East Tennessee in March 1864.[23] Brawls were more frequent during periods of inactivity and when encampment near large cities gave easier access to whisky. For minor altercations punishments were about the same as for running the guard, but when fighting was persistent or general, heavier penalties were imposed.

Drinking, per se, when not on duty and when held to moderation, was usually not regarded as a breach of discipline. But army regulations made corporal punishment mandatory for drunkenness on guard;[24] and habitual intemperance sometimes led to dishonorable discharge. Typical instances of punishment for drunkenness are afforded by comments of two soldiers on the subject. Richard L. Ashhurst of the 150th Pennsylvania Regiment wrote his homefolk on November 6, 1862: "Three men sentenced to walk in barrels for six days for continuous drunkenness." [25] Joseph D. Galloway of another Pennsylvania regiment noted in his diary July 5, 1861: "Desher being quite [drunk] as a punishment . . . was compelled to carry a musket and a carpet bag strapped to his [back] containing fifty pounds of stones. Gus Goodwin was put on guard over him to see that he kept moving." [26]

Promiscuous firing of guns was a common violation in many units. This practice, objectionable both on the score of wasting ammunition and of endangering life, frequently occurred in connection with unauthorized invasion of civilian premises for such delicacies as pork or poultry. The evil became so widespread in the Army of the Potomac in April 1862 as to elicit a prohibitory general order, and during Sherman's Georgia campaign the commander of the Seventeenth Corps found it necessary to charge foraging parties fifty cents for each missing cartridge that could not satisfactorily be accounted for.[27] In the army as a whole the customary penalty for this offense seems to have been confinement in the guardhouse.

Insubordination was shockingly prevalent during the early period of the war, owing to the civilian soldiers' aversion to discipline and the incompetency of officers. The low esteem in which many volunteers held their leaders was pungently expressed by Private Charles A. Barker, who seems to have been a Civil War version of Bill Mauldin. In 1862 Barker wrote: "The officers consider themselves as made of a different material from the low fellows in the ranks"; and the next year he complained: "They get all the glory and most of the pay and don't earn ten cents apiece on the average, the drunken rascals." Another private, George Gray Hunter, hit the jackpot of disparagement. In response to an inquiry as to his having a commission, Hunter exploded: "I am vary glad to Be able to inform you that I have Not—and that ant all I would have for a Dollar, for if thare is one thing that I hate more than anothe[r] it is the Sight of a shoulder Strap, For I am well convinced in My own Mind that had it not Been for officers this war would have Ended long ago." [28]

In its most common form, insubordination consisted of the use of contemptuous or disrespectful language toward superiors. A Michigan private when ordered to extra duty for refusal to drill said to his captain: "You are God damned trash. You think you can do just as you God damn please because you are officers. I'll be God damned if I will [perform the duty]. . . . I'll see you in hell before I will." An Irish soldier of a Pennsylvania regiment when ordered by his adjutant to keep quiet while serving a sentence in the guardhouse replied: "I will not keep quiet for you, you God damned low-lived son of a bitch, you shit-house adjutant." An Ohio artilleryman when placed under arrest by his lieutenant remarked: "You order me! You aint worth a pinch of shit!," and another Yank chafing under reproof told a platoon leader, "You kiss my arse, you God damned louse." Other officers who sought to discipline refractory soldiers were dubbed with such uncomplimentary titles as "bugger," "dog," "green-horn," "whore-house pimp" and "skunk." But by far the most frequently applied expletive was the time-honored "son of a bitch." [29]

Occasionally soldiers flouted authority by refusing to obey orders or perform required duty. In less frequent instances insubordination was carried to the extreme of pushing, kicking, striking and even shooting officers. An unpopular colonel awoke one morning to find that the tail of his favorite horse had been shingled. Another officer narrowly escaped serious injury when a grapeshot hurled by an aggrieved soldier came flying through his tent at night, knocking over a candle. An Illinois sergeant who killed a captain bent on punishing him remarked after the fatal shooting: "I killed him. The company wanted him killed. . . . I killed the son of a bitch and I was the only man in the company who had the heart to do it." In numerous instances men stated their intention of shooting officers when they went into battle, but it is impossible to establish instances of the threat being executed.[30]

Insubordination declined in frequency and gravity with the passing of time. But it remained a serious problem throughout the war. Penalties most frequently meted out to soldiers who became disorderly and disrespectful to their superiors were "tying up" and bucking and gagging. These punishments, imposed usually by order of unit commanders, were sometimes deemed sufficient in themselves. In other instances, especially when the resistance was unusually violent or the offenders were chronic troublemakers, the cases would be referred to courts-martial for trial and further punishment.

Tying up usually meant suspension by the thumbs from a limb or pole in such manner as to permit only the toes to touch the ground. When left in this position for an hour or more, as was not unusual, the victim suffered extreme pain. The severity was enhanced if the punishment took place outside during cold weather. Other forms of tying up were the strapping of offenders to trees, posts or other stationary objects in such a way as to immobilize them, or binding arms to the body and roping the feet so that the victims could only sit or lie on the ground.

Bucking consisted of setting the offender down, tying his wrists together, slipping them over his knees and then running a stick or musket barrel through the space beneath the knees and over the arms. Gagging was the tying of a bayonet or piece of wood in the mouth. A surgeon who witnessed this type of punishment wrote of the results: "The culprit was completely subdued . . . having been tied some 4 hours. He was sobbing and crying as though suffering greatly. When untied he was not able to walk. . . . He was *carried* to his quarters." [31] Sometimes brutality of this punishment was increased by forcing large gags into the mouth, thus causing excessive strain on the jaws or laceration of the mouth. One case is on record of a soldier dying from bucking and gagging.[32]

An unusually testy and cruel lieutenant became so infuriated at a soldier who talked back to him that he gagged him by tying a large rope tightly in his mouth and suspended him by the thumbs. The Yank placed as guard over this soldier wrote: "It was a cold day & the blood running down from his hands and arms & the tight cord cutting through the skin made the man groan so that I was strongly tempted to cut him down myself. . . . The Lieut. [ordered] . . . me if he Struggled to release himself to put my Bayonet through him. Once in a while the said Brute would come & visit him & seemed to enjoy his torture exceedingly." Fortunately for the victim, the colonel commanding the regiment came by and ordered the prisoner's release, but not until he had

become so stiff and weak as to require assistance of two men in getting
back to the guardhouse.[33]

When insubordination went beyond threats and nasty talk and in-
volved physical violence against an officer, the offense assumed a graver
character and led to more serious penalties. The ninth article of war,
which can be traced directly to Prince Rupert's Code of 1672, stated
that "any officer or soldier who shall strike his superior officer, or draw
or lift up any weapon or offer any violence against him . . . shall suffer
death, or such other punishment as shall . . . be inflicted upon him by
the sentence of a court-martial." [34] But a sampling of courts-martial
records indicates that death sentences for violent action against officers
were rare; and executions were almost unheard of. An official list of
executions published by the War Department, which appears fairly
complete, shows only one instance of a soldier paying the extreme
penalty for violation of the ninth article of war. This compares with
twenty executions for mutiny.[35] The usual punishment for striking an
officer was a long term of imprisonment at hard labor followed by dis-
honorable dismissal from the army.

Various types of insubordination and the punishments incurred may
well be illustrated by a few specific cases. A Massachusetts private en
route to the guardhouse for snapping his gun repeatedly on drill became
so enraged at the sergeant escorting him that he called him a "God
damned little piss-pot" and attempted to shoot him. The sentence im-
posed on this soldier by court-martial was forfeiture of ten dollars of each
month's pay for one year and thirty days in the guardhouse. A
Kansas cavalryman, when asked by his lieutenant why he gave whisky to
some prisoners he was guarding, replied, "I thought I would give them a
dram—You may shove it up . . ." This bit of impudence was ad-
judged "conduct prejudicial to good order and military discipline" and
its perpetrator sentenced to confinement at hard labor and forfeiture of
pay for three months. Even more rambunctious was an Irish sergeant of
the Thirtieth Massachusetts Regiment who said to his first sergeant in
the presence of other enlisted men of the company: "You are a God
damned, white-livered, tallow-faced skunk, and if you say that again I
will knock every tooth down your throat and kick your arse through the
company streets if I lose the stripes by it." He did lose his stripes, ripped
from his uniform in the presence of his regiment, and in addition paid
a fine of twenty dollars.[36]

Private John Williams of the First New Jersey Cavalry, for striking
his lieutenant and saying to him, "If I ever get liberated I will shoot you

and all such sons of bitches," was sentenced to forfeiture of all pay, confinement in the penitentiary for the rest of his enlistment and dishonorable discharge from the service. A German private in the Twelfth Pennsylvania Cavalry became so insubordinate toward his major for tying up a comrade that the officer knocked him down. Afterward while the major was proceeding through the camp a shot was fired at him by a hidden assailant. The court had some difficulty establishing the insolence of the language since it was spoken in German and of definitely identifying the German as the person firing the shot, but the majority held him guilty and he was sentenced to five years in the penitentiary and dishonorable discharge.[37]

An Ohio artilleryman who cursed and twice struck in the face a lieutenant who was attempting to arrest him for disorderly conduct was sentenced to be shot. But President Lincoln, on recommendation of Army Commander George H. Thomas, commuted the sentence to forfeiture of all pay and imprisonment during the remainder of the offender's term of enlistment.[38]

Almost every regiment had a few rascals who were not above pilfering from their comrades. Punishments for this offense varied with the value of the articles stolen and with the reputation of the culprit, but dispensers of justice usually dealt more harshly with stealing (from soldiers) than with other noncapital crimes. Petty theft was often punished by unit commanders with such penalties as: marching about the camp in a "barrel shirt"—a commissary barrel slipped down over the offender's head—on which was painted THIEF; parading the drill ground or company streets with placards marked THIEF hanging front and back; standing on a barrel, a stump or other elevated place adorned with labels proclaiming their offense and displaying the stolen articles; and suspension by the thumbs. If the culprit was hailed before courtsmartial, heavier penalties usually resulted. An Iowa soldier who stole nearly fifty dollars from two comrades forfeited all pay due him, had his head shaved, was placarded THIEF and drummed out of the service through the ranks of his regiment to the tune of the "Rogue's March." A Pennsylvania private who stole $260.00 from his fellow soldiers suffered similarly, with the added penalty of five years' imprisonment at hard labor. For appropriating five government blouses worth about ten dollars, an Illinois artilleryman forfeited a month's pay and worked for thirty days on the Vicksburg fortifications during which time there hung from his back a board two feet long and one foot wide inscribed with the word THIEF.[39]

Pillaging of civilians, particularly those of Rebel sympathies, was a common practice. While high commanders usually deplored the practice and issued repeated orders against it and while a few plunderers were shot, various factors prevented the punishment of more than a small percentage of those who looted Southern premises. In the first place, soldier sentiment, while by no means consistently condoning the practice, certainly was not so strongly opposed to stealing from Rebels as from one another; and many Yanks who at home had the most scrupulous regard for private property took the view that things were different now that they were down south. Lower-ranking officers often shared the views of their men that Rebels were rightful objects of plunder and hence were lax in compelling compliance with the injunctions of superiors.[40] Indeed, some lieutenants and captains were not above leading their men in raids upon Southern wardrobes and treasure troves.[41] At any rate the difficulty of distinguishing between authorized foragers and private plunderers worked against a close control over the invading forces. The net result, especially on rapid movements such as those of Grant in North Mississippi in 1862 and Sherman in Georgia and the Carolinas in 1864-1865, was to afford relative impunity to "bummers" and others determined to prey on civilians.

Sleeping on post occurred with notable frequency, especially during the early part of the war. While theoretically this was one of the most serious military offenses, punishable under articles of war by death, in practice it was treated with shocking leniency. In September 1861 a general court-martial of McClellan's command found six soldiers guilty of this offense. The severest sentence handed down was a month at hard labor and forfeiture of three months' pay. One of the men received no punishment at all on the ground that he had been on sentry duty two successive nights.[42] Courts of other commands, in the war's first year, viewed sleeping on sentry duty with similar nonchalance, imposing repeatedly such sentences as short confinement with ball and chain and light fines.[43]

The case of Private Joshua C. Ward affords one of the most amazing commentaries on the casualness with which sleeping on post was sometimes regarded. In February 1862 Ward was tried by a general court-martial of Banks's division, Army of the Potomac, and found not guilty. McClellan's review of the proceedings brought out the fact that Ward, after being duly posted as a sentinel, was found lying asleep on the ground and that when finally aroused after much shaking and shouting he "arose in great wrath against those who had waked him." The commissioned officer of Ward's company who turned him in, later remarked: "Had I known that he would have been reported to General Court-martial I would not have reported him because I had reason to believe others had been asleep on guard and not been reported." The court in returning a verdict of not guilty cited as extenuating circumstances: The post was not an important one as it was not in the face of the enemy and other guards were situated near by; the accused had marched seven miles and had been on guard duty the previous day; discipline was poor in the offender's regiment and instructions concerning guard duty were imperfect and erroneous; and acquittal of Ward would probably cause the army commander to issue a needed order for proper instruction of sentinels. Little wonder that this finding called forth a blistering rebuke from McClellan! But he did not order a new trial.[44]

As the war progressed a general trend toward severer punishment of those who slept at their posts was apparent, but as late as 1864 a court of the Army of the Potomac gave two sleeping guards a sentence of a thirty-dollar fine and carrying a twenty-pound log eight hours a day for thirty days.[45]

Throughout the war, courts occasionally issued the death sentence in cases of sleeping on post, but in most such instances army commanders, when they had authority to do so, would lighten the penalty and this despite their own prior protests against treating lightly the "sacredness" of a sentinel's duty. The few capital penalties for sleeping sentries which came to Lincoln's desk for final action were disapproved by him. One Yank thus saved by Presidential clemency was Private William Scott of the Third Vermont Regiment. His pardon was dramatically delivered at the last minute while he stood in the presence of his assembled division and awaited the fatal blast of the firing squad.[46] No record was found of any Union soldier dying for sleeping at his post.

Another serious offense was misbehavior before the enemy. Cowardice and skulking in battle, like most other delinquencies, were sometimes punished on authority of company or regimental commanders. For example, a Vermonter who showed the white feather in the fighting before Richmond in June 1862 was required by his colonel to walk a beat in front of regimental headquarters wearing a coffee barrel on which was inscribed in huge letters, FIRST MAN LOST AT SAVAGE STATION. But more frequently those who failed to do their duty in combat were called before courts-martial and given such sentences as: a fine of forty dollars and standing on a barrel every alternate hour for four days; a year at hard labor with forfeiture of all pay; and dishonorable discharge, which usually was attended by such tokens of disgrace as head shaving and drumming out in the presence of comrades. Sometimes branding the letter C with a red-hot iron on the culprit's hip or cheek was made a part of the penalty.[47]

Two Vermont soldiers who played the coward during the Seven Days' battles were sentenced to have half their heads and faces shaved, to have the buttons cut off their blouses and then to be drummed out of camp. A Yank who witnessed the punishment wrote: "[The] sentence was duly carried out, in the presence of the brigade, which formed in hollow square, the culprits under a Strong guard with fixed bayonets were marched around the inside of the square, in the following order, first, a file of our men with arms reversed, [then] a file on Each Side of the prisoners, followed by a file with bayonets at the charge; the whole preceded by the drum corps playing the Rogue's March, to which someone set these words: 'Poor old Soldier, poor old soldier, tarred and feathered, and drummed out of camp, because he was a deserter.' " [48]

While these measures fulfilled the terms of the court's sentence, more humiliation was yet to be endured by the unfortunate cowards. Other men of the regiment, smarting under the disgrace which their unit had suffered as a result of the craven act, now dressed the culprits in castoff slave clothing, spread molasses on the ground "and gave them a thorough rolling in the Stuff, and from thence to the red clay dust. When the operation was complete, they looked as though they had been [in] the hands of the Phillistines, and were allowed to go where they chose." [49]

Other serious offenses included treason, murder and rape, all of which were punishable by death, and which, more so than other capital offenses, actually led to the supreme penalty. The War Department's official list of 267 Union soldier executions records three deaths for spying, eighteen for rape, two for the double crime of murder and rape, one for rape and theft and seventy for murder. Two of the "spies" were bounty jumpers, caught deserting and giving important information to one whom they supposed a Rebel. General Sheridan had them summarily shot on his own authority.[50] Eleven of the rapists were Negro soldiers, five of whom were executed by order of drumhead courts-martial.[51] Of the murderers one was hanged by order of a regimental court-martial, in violation of army regulations which reserved capital sentences to general courts-martial.[52] Another of the executions for murder was done apparently on the sole authority of a lieutenant of cavalry.[53]

By far the most common of capital offenses was that of desertion. And probably for no other offense was such a wide variety of punishments imposed. Early in the war punishments were amazingly light, often not exceeding the forfeiture of one to three months' pay. As in other types of offenses, penalties became more severe after the first year or two of conflict, but even then deserters occasionally drew relatively trivial sentences. In the summer of 1863 a general court-martial of the Department of the Gulf let several deserters off with fines of thirty-nine dollars each, and another court which met in Arkansas in September 1864 required of four deserters only that they forfeit varying amounts of pay and make up the time lost from service.[54]

Except during the initial period of the war, the most frequently applied punishment for desertion was imprisonment for from one to five years, sometimes at hard labor, preceded or followed by dishonorable discharge from the service. As in the case of cowardice, branding (with the letter D) on shoulder, hip or cheek, shaving all or parts of the head and drumming out of camp were sometimes included in the sentence. During hard labor and prison periods, culprits in some cases were required to wear ball and chain.

The percentage of Union deserters apprehended and brought to trial is not known.[55] But some idea of the frequency of conviction and the meting out of the death sentence is afforded by a report prepared at Lincoln's request in November 1863. This document revealed that in the Army of the Potomac between July 1 and November 30, 1863, 592 men were tried for desertion, 291 were found guilty, 80 received capital sentences and 21 were eventually shot. During this same period about 2,000 deserters had been returned to their regiments.[56]

The War Department list of Union executions shows 141 deaths for desertion. This represents more than half of the total number executed for all offenses during the war.[57]

Executions for desertion, as for other crimes, were usually carried out in such manner as to inspire as much awe as possible. For the gruesome occasion the brigade or division to which the culprit belonged was formed around what was called a hollow square but which actually was a rectangle open at one end. After the troops had taken their places an escort marched the prisoner out. At the head of the procession was the provost marshal on horseback; next came the band playing the doleful strains of the "Dead March"; then followed a guard of twelve armed men which was deployed diagonally across the open end of the formation as protection against the prisoner's escape; next in order were four soldiers bearing the coffin, and after them came the condemned man accompanied by a chaplain and flanked on each side by a guard. Last in the solemn procession came the firing party composed usually of twelve men, one of whom bore a musket containing a blank charge; but as none knew which was the innocuous weapon each could hope that it was the one he carried. Sometimes a reserve firing squad was brought along to act in case the first group failed to accomplish its mission.

When the procession reached its destination the prisoner was seated on a coffin placed near the grave in the open end of the rectangle. Following the chaplain's final ministrations, the provost marshal came forward, blindfolded the culprit and read the official order of execution. He then directed the firing party to carry out the order and after a painful last moment, broken by the clicking of hammers, the fateful command "Fire!" brought a merciful end to the suspense.

Following the surgeon's pronouncement that life was extinct, all the soldiers comprising the formation were required to march by the corpse so that a close-up view might be had of a deserter's fate. The impression was tremendous, as letters of the spectators vividly attest.[58] Even so, there is no indication that desertion was greatly deterred by these gruesome dramas.

Executions sometimes were marked by unanticipated details which added to their horror. In one instance, two of a firing squad of six failed to discharge their muskets, a third missed the target, a fourth fired a blank cartridge and a fifth inflicted an unmortal wound. Fortunately the shot of the sixth was fatal. The two who disobeyed the order to fire were placed in irons and held for severe punishment.[59]

In other instances executions were woefully bungled. A surgeon recounts such an occasion in his diary thus: "Sgt Walker Co. A, 3rd S. C. Inf. [Union, colored] was shot by sentence of court martial at 10:00 A.M. . . . 5 balls entered the body, one the head. Two vollies were fired 12 paces off. At the first the culprit staggered back one pace & fell. I examined his wounds briefly and retired and the other volley was fired as he lay on the ground." A Pennsylvanian reported a case in which three attempts were required to dispatch a deserter. After the first fire the culprit remained sitting upright on his coffin. "Another platoon of the firing squad was hurried up and when they fired the poor fellow fell; his elbow struck the rough box; he recovered himself and sat up for the second time. The third squad was ordered up; they fired and he fell into his box dead." In still another case, where execution was by hanging, the rope broke when the trap was sprung and the hapless victim, crying pitifully "Shoot me! shoot me!" had to be lifted up and dropped a second time.[60]

From what has already been stated it is apparent that for offenses as a whole the most common penalties were confinement in the guardhouse, ball and chain, carrying logs or weighted knapsacks, wearing barrel shirts or placards, doing extra duty, standing on a barrel or other eminence, public reprimand by a superior, bread-and-water diet, stoppage of pay, tying up and bucking and gagging.

Commanders and courts supplemented these common penalties with an impressive array of unusual punishments, some of which were highly original and a few extremely brutal. Despite the Congressional interdiction of August 5, 1861, flogging was practiced to a limited extent throughout the war. In February 1863 General Jefferson C. Davis had four of his soldiers, who molested a Tennessee girl, tied to the wheel of a cannon, their heads shaved, their bare backs beaten with fifty lashes of a rawhide whip and then drummed out of camp. A fifth soldier escaped the flogging by turning informer, but he was compelled to wield the lash on his fellows. Of the culprits' reaction to the whipping, a soldier who witnessed the punishment wrote: "The first one yelled and screamed and prayed lustily—the 2d never uttered a groan. The 3d stood it better than the 1st but he whined considerably." [61]

An Ohio colonel had four stragglers of his command march for three hours with a rail, attached by rope to their necks, dangling in front of them, their guns hanging from the rail and their hands tied behind them.[62]

In the Fifty-first Indiana a minor offender sometimes was required to stand on one foot atop a cracker box while a comrade likewise guilty of some slight fault was stationed near by and instructed to prod the living statue with a bayonet should he lower the other foot. In case of the guard's failure to prod as ordered, he had to mount the pedestal himself and another comrade took over the role of guard for both. Soldiers of the Fifty-ninth Illinois Regiment were treated one day to the sight of a comrade parading through camp with both hands tied fast to a singletree which was hitched to a mule. Guards with fixed bayonets flanked the soldier while behind him came a fifer and drummer playing the "Rogue's March." [63]

Musicians, like other soldiers, sometimes were punished by doses of extra duty. A Massachusetts fifer, caught in some minor violation, was sentenced by regimental court-martial to play on his instrument for two hours before regimental headquarters. Instead of varying the tune, as was expected, the fifer devoted his talents exclusively to the doleful air "On the Road to Boston," with the result that the staff suffered almost as much punishment as the culprit.[64]

A Pennsylvania soldier named Spotswood, whose sentence was to dig a pit behind his colonel's tent, also gave an amusing twist to his punishment. As Spotswood dug he piled the dirt in such a manner as to resemble a parapet. When the excavation was completed holes were made in the parapet after the fashion of embrasures and black bottles pointed through them toward the tent, much to the merriment of the enlisted men.[65]

In the cavalry petty offenders were sometimes required to carry saddles about the camp, and artillerymen, for violations both serious and trivial, were tied spread-eagle fashion to the spare wheel which habitually rode at an angle on the rear of caissons; and in rare instances they were bound to the tailboard or the forage rack of battery wagons.[66] These latter punishments were uncomfortable under the best conditions, and when prolonged or when the vehicles were driven over rough roads they became excruciating. Of the brutality of the wheel penalty an artillery private wrote: "Feet and hands were firmly bound to the felloes of the wheel. If the soldier was to be punished moderately he was left bound in an upright position on the wheel for five or six hours. If the punishment was to be severe, the ponderous wheel was given a quarter turn . . . which changed the position of the man being punished from an upright to a horizontal one. . . . I have frequently seen men faint while undergoing this punishment. . . . To cry out, to beg for mercy, to protest ensured additional discomfort in the shape of a gag . . . being tied into the suffering man's mouth . . . no man wanted to be tied up but once." [67]

For the army as a whole, other unusual punishments included isolation of trivial offenders on elevated platforms, confinement in stocks and encasement in sweat boxes. The last-mentioned device was described by a soldier as "a box eighteen inches square, and of the full height of a man into which the culprit was placed to stand until released." One of the most original penalties was that inflicted by the colonel of the Thirty-fourth Indiana Regiment who, when a soldier was brought before him for stealing a shirt, ordered him to "go with the guard, and stick your head into each and every tent in the regiment beginning at Company A, and tell them you stole a shirt." Finally the thief was required to return the shirt to the owner and ask his forgiveness.[68]

What of the general quality of military justice in the Union Army? As previously intimated, undue leniency was common during the early part of the war, and while the trend was toward greater severity, grave offenses throughout the conflict occasionally were treated with shocking softness. The unwillingness of courts to "bear down" and issue sentences commensurate with the crimes was the subject of repeated complaint by higher commanders. Following the issuance of trivial penalties for the most serious offenses by a general court-martial in Hooker's command in September 1861, McClellan remarked: "It has seldom happened that military delinquencies so grave have been visited with punishments having so much the appearance of intending to sanction future violations of good order and discipline. . . . Military crimes to which the articles of war annex the heaviest penalties are treated as if they were the most venial misdemeanors." [69]

Early in 1862 McClellan rebuked even more severely a court-martial for letting off with a five-dollar fine a soldier who struck two of his sergeants and sentencing to only a ten-dollar fine another man who entered a private home, cursed the occupants and at the point of a gun forced them to feed him and his comrades. "Such offenses are punishable *capitally*," wrote McClellan in his review of the proceedings. "The paltry penalty exacted of the prisoners . . . is a burlesque upon military justice." But McClellan, notwithstanding his protests against undue leniency, proved squeamish when faced with the unpleasant task of approving death sentences. Of twenty-seven capital sentences meted out by eleven courts of the Army of the Potomac early in 1862, only five were confirmed by McClellan.[70]

The effect of unduly light punishment was to encourage misconduct. A typical reaction was that of a Norwegian in a Wisconsin regiment who reluctantly returned to his unit at the end of his furlough while some of his companions elected to stay at home another month. Writing later to his uncle about the delinquents, the Norwegian remarked: "They have had their trial and . . . were let off with the mere loss of a month's pay. I should have been happy to be at home a month longer than I was if I had been sure of getting off with such light punishment." [71]

Except during the early months of the war, however, punishments were overly harsh about as often as they were unduly mild. Captain John William De Forest, after sitting on a court near New Orleans in September 1862, wrote his wife: "The punishments are terribly severe. One poor blockhead, who had merely been absent without leave for five days, was allotted three years at hard labor on fortifications with loss of all pay and allowances except enough to cover his washing bill." A few months later Brigadier General J. J. Bartlett of the Army of the Potomac wrote another officer: "I am Pres. of a Court martial, principally trying deserters, poor fellows! & most all of them because their families were suffering at home for the Soldiers' pay. I could hate myself for being a soldier at times, for having to sit in judgement in such cases, hampered and restricted by the arbitrary rules of military law, which crushes heart and soul out of one's identity." [72]

Sometimes ignorant and even mentally defective soldiers, who failed at duties they were not competent to perform, were given the most serious sentences by courts that were unable or unwilling to temper the stark severity of the military code with mercy and common sense.

The disciplinary system sometimes acquired added harshness from failure to bring prisoners promptly to trial. The seventy-ninth article of war forbade confinement beyond eight days without trial except when circumstances prevented the prompt assembling of a court-martial. The exception allowed a latitude which tended to invalidate the rule, since under the conditions prevailing during periods of active campaigning it was easy to justify failure to convene courts. Postponement of trials was undoubtedly necessary in some cases, but in others the principal factor in delay was the unconcern of responsible authorities or their unwillingness to be inconvenienced. For example, inexcusable indifference seems to be the only explanation for allowing soldiers encamped near Baltimore to lie for several winter months "in irons in the Guard House." [73] A general order of the Department of the Gulf dated September 13, 1864, indicated that in New Orleans "many prisoners" were "confined in the various jails of the city used by the military authorities without any charges and in many cases without knowledge on the part of the keepers . . . or . . . the Provost Marshals of any offense having been committed by them." Possibly some of these prisoners were civilians, but the wording of the order leaves no doubt of soldiers being among those detained without charge or trial.[74]

Some of the most cruel and unreasonable penalties were those imposed by unit commanders without resort to courts. In some instances the excessive severity sprang from the fact of the punishment being summarily applied while the officer's anger was at high pitch. In others, the motivating factor was the desire to set an example that would deter future wrongdoing, or a determination to prove the officer's mastery by bearing down on the culprit. In still other cases cruelty derived from sheer highhandedness or bestiality.

Two specific cases will serve to illustrate the brutality which men suffered at the hands of sadistic officers. In 1861 a court-martial found a captain guilty "without just cause" of cursing a private, striking him with a saber on the neck and head, causing the blood to flow profusely, tying his hands and feet with a rope, roughly forcing an excessively large gag in his mouth, and then throwing him out on the cold, damp ground.[75] But this captain's action was mild in comparison with that of a lieutenant colonel of Negro troops who frequently beat and kicked his men for failure to polish their buttons and who, for the offense of pilfering roasting ears, removed the shoes and stockings of soldiers, tied them down on the ground with arms and legs outstretched, covered their faces, hands and feet with molasses and left them exposed all day to the sun, flies and ants.[76]

Whether applied by courts or officers, punishments in the Union Army were so uneven as to appear utterly capricious. A soldier might be sentenced to death for an offense for which a month earlier one of his comrades had had to pay only a token fine.

Still another characteristic of punishments, and of the disciplinary system in general, was a marked slanting in favor of officers. Not only did officers guilty of serious offenses such as cowardice, desertion and theft frequently escape punishment by resigning, but in instances where they were brought to trial they often got off much more lightly than enlisted men charged with the same breaches of discipline. Since the making of arrests and the preferring of charges were exclusive officer functions, commissioned personnel sometimes were inclined to consider themselves a mutual protective association and hence beyond the reach of the disciplinary code.

A major convicted in 1861 of participating in a public disturbance in Washington, refusing to submit to arrest and using contemptuous language toward the provost marshal, was let off with a mere reprimand. McClellan, characterizing the sentence as "a burlesque upon military punishments," ordered the case remanded but the court refused to modify its action.[77]

A sergeant told in his diary of an officer of the day being ordered to break up an after-taps gambling party and arrest all the participants; but when the officer found that a fellow "shoulder-strap" was involved in the game he turned away without making an arrest. In view of such inequities it is not surprising to find a soldier complaining: "If these had been poor privates nothing less than two or three months in the Guard house or hard labor on the forts would have been the sentence. When shall such a cursed state of affairs cease to exist?" [78]

Discriminatory treatment by courts-martial is well exemplified by an incident which took place in the Army of the Potomac early in 1862. A private soldier called as a witness by a court-martial in Baltimore was found to be intoxicated. The court sentenced him to wear a ball and chain for thirty days. Later, when an officer appeared before the court in the same condition, he was excused from testifying and given no punishment. An even more striking example of the slanting of the disciplinary system in favor of officers is to be found in the action of two courts-martial which met about the same time in 1864 in the Army of the Potomac. One sentenced to be shot a soldier who had abandoned his post in battle; the other on finding an officer guilty of the same offense deemed cashiering a sufficient penalty.[79]

In 1861 a lieutenant who left his unit while it was under fire at First Bull Run drew the amazingly light sentence of fifteen days' suspension of rank and pay.[80]

Inclination of courts-martial to tip the scales of justice to the advantage of fellow officers is also evidenced by an occasional juggling of charges to permit a lightening of the sentence. For example, a New York lieutenant early in 1862 appeared before a court charged with "conduct unbecoming an officer and a gentleman." This charge, if sustained, made dismissal from the service mandatory. The specification given in support of the charge was the lieutenant's remark to his captain in the presence of enlisted men: "If it were not for the difference in rank I would . . . knock shit out of you." The court found him guilty of the specification but held that the appropriate charge was "conduct subversive to good order and military discipline" which, under the articles of war, was punishable at the discretion of the court. Using the discretion thus assumed the court sentenced the lieutenant to reprimand by the colonel of his regiment in the presence of the noncommissioned officers only and a month's suspension from rank and pay. The court's action drew a rebuke from McClellan who held that the lieutenant should have been found guilty of conduct unbecoming an officer and a gentleman on the basis of the language that he unquestionably used.[81]

An even more flagrant case was that of an Illinois lieutenant tried in February 1863 on the charge of conduct unbecoming an officer and a gentleman on the basis of having a lewd Negro woman in his tent, fornicating with her there, and encouraging a private soldier to do the same in his presence. The court, while finding the lieutenant guilty of the specifications, chose to interpret the charge as "conduct prejudicial to good order and military discipline," and instead of sentencing him to dismissal from the service required only that he forfeit a month's pay and allowances! This amazing sentence, even though accompanied by an endorsement of the commander of the post where the accused was stationed charging that he was "dangerously disloyal—flagitiously immoral—of evil example—health impaired by degrading vice—damaging to discipline—useless to the service—" was approved all the way up through the corps and army commanders (Hurlbut and Grant) only to be set aside by the Judge Advocate General of the Army on the ground that under established procedure a court-martial could not substitute one charge for another.[82] The lieutenant apparently escaped punishment altogether because of this procedural fault. The Judge Advocate General of the Army could have recommended dismissal to the President (who could dismiss officers on his own authority) and his explanation of the failure to do so is, to say the least, most interesting. "A recommendation for dismissal would be made," he wrote in an endorsement dated October 29, 1863, "but for the long time that has elapsed . . . and a doubt may be entertained whether meantime this officer may not have retrieved his conduct." [83] Little wonder that soldiers sometimes complained of the army being an officers' world.

Some officers while under arrest were not above bringing pressure on enlisted men likely to be called as witnesses. A captain was charged with visiting a house of ill fame while on command of a picket detail and telling the guards that they might all go to sleep just so they were awake when he made the rounds about ten o'clock. He visited the witnesses a few days before his trial and gave each of them a drink of whisky.[84] The extent to which men were influenced by such overtures, and by hope of favor or fear of reprisal, cannot be ascertained. But reading of courts-martial proceedings discloses occasional instances of such poor memory on the part of soldiers called as witnesses against their superiors that doubt about the free flow of justice is inescapable.[85]

It is not meant to leave the impression that discipline was always inequitable or oppressive, for such was not the case. Many officers were humane and generous in dealings with their men and some carried leniency to harmful extremes. Moreover, Yanks, like all other soldiers, found ways and means of evading restrictions. "The officers exercise all their ingenuity to keep the men within the lines," wrote a New Yorker from a camp near Baltimore in 1861, "but notwithstanding the strong guard of 100 men on night & day, the men slip out with the connivance of the sentries. I suppose there must be at least 30 or 40 go out and come in every night in this way." An Iowa private made an even more illuminating comment on the effectiveness with which soldiers shielded themselves: "The boys stand up for one another in all scrapes that any member may get into," he wrote, "so that if some ones does something that is against all rules such as knocking the lights out in a grocery and taking whatever is handy, or taking a milk pail from a pedlar wagon, any kind of stealing whatever is not reported." He added: "If any one gets drunk the orders are to report him so that he may be sent to the guard house. Instead of doing so we stow them away in some quiet place until sober." [86]

Sometimes men caught in the disciplinary net took their punishment with marked unconcern and even with levity. Such reactions were encouraged by the manner in which guardhouses occasionally were administered. Far from being dull and dreary, some of these institutions were lively places featured by card playing, laughing and singing. It must have been this sort of prison to which Private Wesley Armfield was sent for whistling after taps in the company streets, for when his colonel later offered him release on promise of good behavior Armfield replied: "I will not promise because the guard tent is more comfortable than my tent and I had rather stay here." [87]

Even the "Rip Raps," a prison near Norfolk which had an unenviable reputation, was so favorably regarded by one group confined there early in the war that they expressed regret at having to leave. But of the Dry Tortugas, a notorious prison situated off the coast of Florida, not one kindly comment was found. In general, guardhouses and other prisons were denounced by soldiers as filthy, loathsome places.[88]

The tendency of some soldiers to make a joke of their punishment is illustrated by the conduct of some New York soldiers sentenced to carry twenty-five-pound weights in front of the guardhouse. "They . . . have appointed a captain," wrote one of their comrades, "who with a stick to represent a sword, with the sole of an old shoe for a guard, is drilling in the most approved style. The man with the placard [marked 'Running Guard'] is in the middle to represent the color bearer. They seem to enjoy it." [89]

In some instances drumming out of the service, instead of being regarded as the shameful, humiliating ordeal contemplated in the articles of war, produced opposite reactions both on the part of the culprit and his comrades. A skulker who was drummed out of camp in March 1863 exclaimed at the conclusion of the exercises: "Who says I aint a citizen." Following the imposition of this penalty on two soldiers near Harrison's Landing, Virginia, a comrade wrote: "Instead of being looked on as a disgrace . . . by the majority of the men, they considered that they were better off and many almost envied them as they were free men as soon as outside of camp." [90]

The sympathy of soldiers for a comrade whom they thought unjustly ejected sometimes found tangible expression. A private in the Fifty-ninth Illinois Regiment who was drummed out of the service for insubordination received a considerable purse raised by his comrades to send him to parts unknown.[91]

Effectively registered group sentiment sometimes tended to restrain highhanded and brutal officers and to temper punishment. An extreme example was that of Kansas cavalrymen who, when one of their number was tied to a caisson and ordered whipped for some uncomplimentary references to the colonel, rushed out of their quarters shouting protests. The colonel and some of his officers drew their swords and dashed down the lines making threats and trying to quell the commotion. But the only response of the soldiers was to cry out, "Unloose the man or we'll blow you all to hell!" The man was released and the rioters were not punished.[92]

No discussion of factors mitigating the harshness of punishment would be complete without reference to the part played by Lincoln. Enlisted cases coming to his attention, as previously noted, consisted mainly of those involving long imprisonment or death sentences. Study of Presidential action in these cases reveals a rather well-defined pattern. In purely military offenses such as sleeping on post, insubordination and desertion where either a commanding general or the Judge Advocate General of the Army recommended clemency, Lincoln almost invariably accepted the recommendation. And in death sentences he frequently ordered mitigation or pardon on his own authority. In February 1864, by Lincoln's direction, the War Department issued a blanket order requiring mitigation of all pending sentences of death for desertion to imprisonment at the Dry Tortugas for the rest of the war. The order likewise empowered army and department commanders to restore to duty deserters under sentence when in their judgment the service would be benefited by the restoration. In pursuance of this order, sixty-two death sentences were commuted at one stroke in May 1864.[93]

Only in instances of crimes against civilians or those which civil courts treated as heinous was Lincoln consistently inclined to severity. When clear cases of rape, robbery, arson and the like came to him with the death penalty prescribed, the President usually approved them. But when all types of cases passed on by Lincoln are considered, it becomes readily apparent that his influence was a softening one.[94]

Sometimes Presidential clemency in capital sentences was initiated by the urgent request of a politically prominent person. A case in point is that of a private who deserted on August 26, 1863, from the Army of the Potomac. During the trial the accused testified that at the end of his tour of picket duty he chased a pig into a near-by wood. While he attempted to catch the pig, three Rebel cavalrymen approached, and to escape them he swam a river and concealed himself. When he came back later and inquired of the next picket detail as to the whereabouts of his unit he was arrested and charged with desertion. This was his story, but the court did not accept it and he was sentenced to die; the sentence was approved by the appropriate authorities and the execution ordered for the afternoon of September 25, 1863.[95]

On September 24 a Mr. Walsh, President of the Board of Aldermen of New York City, called at the White House bearing a note from the mayor asking Lincoln to look into the case. Walsh did not get to see the President personally, but left the mayor's note with one of his own which testified to the prisoner's good character, denied his intention to' desert and requested a Presidential stay of the execution pending an investigation. Later in the day Lincoln telegraphed Meade to give him the facts in the case, which the general promptly did. That night Lincoln dispatched a telegram ordering suspension of the execution. But learning of a break in the telegraph line, he sent another message over another route, the delivery of which required transmission a part of the way by a colonel riding a special locomotive. The order reached its destination in due time and the shooting was stayed. Later the President commuted the sentence to six months' imprisonment at Albany. Thus was a soldier snatched from the jaws of death because prominent politicians actively interceded for him and the President, after investigation, deemed a lighter punishment appropriate, apparently on ground of doubt as to the man's intentions.[96]

In another instance Lincoln overruled himself and commuted a death sentence on application of a condemned soldier's counsel. The facts of this case, an especially interesting one because of the light it throws on the seriousness with which Lincoln regarded his control over the life of a fellow man (who in this case seems not to have had influence in high places), were briefly as follows: Private Blank, as he may be called since his real name is immaterial, in September 1863 deserted his original unit, a New York artillery regiment, and enlisted as a substitute in another organization. Almost immediately he deserted again and remained absent until apprehended about a year later. While imprisoned at Elmira, in a futile move to effect his escape he inveigled his guards into drinking some poisoned whisky which caused the death of one of them. In

December 1863 a general court-martial found him guilty of desertion and murder and sentenced him to be hanged.

When the papers in the case were referred to Lincoln on April 14, 1864, he indorsed them: "Sentence approved and execution fixed for Friday, April 22, 1864." But on application of Blank's counsel, who apparently entered a plea of mental defectiveness, Lincoln stayed the execution and on April 25 called on a Utica physician to inquire thoroughly into the prisoner's sanity. The physician heard a number of witnesses, among them Blank's father who testified that the prisoner had suffered a severe head injury when five years old and had afterward been erratic. To the question "Have any of your relatives been insane?" the father replied: "My father's sister was wild for years. Would run around the fields howling." [97]

The doctor reported to Lincoln on May 13, 1864, that Blank was a borderline case but was not insane; and that there was no doubt of his being lucid when he killed the guard on October 31, 1863, and when the physician interviewed him on April 29-30, 1864. After receipt of the physician's report Lincoln on January 25, 1865, commuted Blank's sentence to imprisonment at hard labor for ten years.

Now that offenses and punishments, the machinery of control and the character of military justice have been discussed, some comment on the state of discipline in the Union Army is in order. In general, discipline was weak early in the war, improving as the officer corps acquired experience and sloughed off incompetents, and as men became habituated to military life. Evidences of poor discipline during the first months of conflict could be cited almost indefinitely, but the general pattern may be indicated by a few specific testimonials. In November 1861 General Joseph Hooker, then a division commander, wrote the adjutant general of the Army of the Potomac: "In some regiments there appears to be a total absence of anything like authority. The officers are on the same footing with the men." And from the Department of Missouri in December 1861 General H. W. Halleck reported to General Winfield Scott: "This, General, is no army, but rather a military rabble. . . . I am almost destitute of regular officers, and those of the volunteers are, with some exceptions, entirely ignorant of their duties." A few weeks later, General D. C. Buell, commanding the Department of the Ohio, registered a similar complaint, citing as a source of special difficulty the interference of state authorities in disciplinary affairs. [98]

These comments of higher officers were borne out by inspectors who made the rounds of the camps during the war's first year. The following

notations, taken from the report of an inspection of the Department of
Missouri, are typical:

12th Iowa Infantry. . . . A fine body of men but entirely with-
   out discipline.
Nebraska Cavalry. . . . Entirely without discipline.
23rd Indiana Infantry. . . . This regiment is entirely demoral-
   ized and discipline hopeless unless the colonel . . . is dis-
   missed.
2nd Missouri Infantry. . . . No discipline.
Jeff. C. Davis Brigade (8th, 18th, 22nd, 25th Indiana Infantry;
   Hauser's Battery). . . . The whole appearance of the troops
   is unsoldierlike showing an almost total want of discipline.

Of the 159 units covered by this report only 4 were rated as *superior*
in discipline, while 34 were *good,* 39 *fair,* 25 *poor;* no comment was
made concerning the remaining 57. The colonel making the report at-
tributed the low state of discipline primarily to the incompetence of
volunteer officers who seemed unaware of the importance of systematic
training, some even ridiculing drill as "playing soldier." [99]

Observations of commanders and inspectors were confirmed by in-
formal comments contained in letters of the period. A lieutenant wrote
his homefolk from a training camp in Albany, New York, on May 7,
1861: "You can hardly realize in what sort of a constant turmoil we live
here now. There are some 1800 men in all sorts of command, in all stages
of civilization and in all states of content. Hardly a meal passes when
there is not some sort of a muss at the tables. Dishes are overturned,
victuals thrown, men refuse to eat, disobey orders. . . . We live in con-
stant expectation of a general fight. . . . there has not been a day since
I have been here at the Barracks when we have not as officers taken our
pistols and gone out at some alarm to quell a riot." [100]

While the over-all trend was undoubtedly one of improvement, dis-
ciplinary lapses in specific units and areas were numerous and deteriora-
tion on an army-wide scale occasionally was apparent. Following the
retreat from Richmond in July 1862, the Army of the Potomac seems to
have experienced a disciplinary retrogression which persisted well into
1863, with lowest points occurring just before Antietam and just after
Fredericksburg. General orders of this period complain of infrequent in-
spections, neglect of drill, dirty clothing and equipment, omission of
officer schools, nonchalance in performance of guard duty and failure
to observe rules of military etiquette.

Soldier letters also noted a poor state of discipline. In September

1862 a Massachusetts private stationed near Falls Church, Virginia, wrote that "drill & saluting officers & guard duty is played out." About the same time a Michigander wrote from another Virginia camp that he had recently witnessed the passing of two divisions of the Army of the Potomac, and "it was almost impossible to tell which were the officers as they were all dressed alike, some of the privates had lost their muskets & had picked up swords on the Battlefield, and as most of the officers had lost their shoulder straps." A few days later this man reported: "I have never been told to salute an officer except when acting as a sentinel. I am just as free with those I am acquainted with as I would be at home." [101]

A similar deterioration of discipline appears to have occurred in Grant's army following the surrender of Vicksburg, though evidence is too sparse to permit a firm conclusion on the subject.

As a general rule, discipline was considerably worse among troops far removed from fighting areas and having little hope of combatant duty. Units held to service for long periods in Northern states, especially if stationed near the homes of the men, were frequently reported as sadly deficient in this respect. Colonel James Hardie of the Inspector General's Department in Washington wrote General Halleck in October 1864 that the Forty-third Indiana Regiment, on duty in its home state, was in a deplorable state of discipline. "They are little better than an armed mob. . . . New Enfield rifles issued to the men instead of making them clean their old arms. The officers are very negligent in the discharge of their duties. In my last month's report I had occasion to recommend them to be reprimanded—There is no improvement in them since last month's inspection." [102] Another inspector reported in January 1865 that Kentucky troops serving in their home state were "poorly officered . . . not at all instructed and destitute of discipline. . . . They are *a mere mob*. Less than half the aggregate reported are [present] for duty at any time of need; and this too when four fifths of the aggregate of troops from other states serving with them are [available] for duty." He added: "Their want of discipline and their serving at home are the causes conducing to such inefficiency." [103] Similar reports were found concerning locally recruited troops serving in Tennessee, Arkansas and Missouri.

Units assigned to garrison duty, especially in remote areas, were notably inclined to disciplinary deficiency. Of the Thirty-fifth Missouri Regiment stationed at Helena, Arkansas, Colonel D. B. Sackett of the Inspector General's Department in Washington reported in January

1865: "In service nearly 3 years . . . it is the poorest regiment in every respect I have ever seen since the commencement of the war. The Lt. Col. Commdg is wanting in nearly every quality that constitutes an officer. He has no force and is ignorant of the first principles of drill. The officers and men . . . have no energy or spirit in them; they move like drones . . . are not instructed in any kind of drill . . . arms and accoutrements . . . very dirty . . . clothing dirty and in many cases ragged . . . hair . . . very long." [104]

Reports of like tenor, dated for the most part in 1864, were found for garrison units in Minnesota, Western Virginia, Middle Tennessee, Mississippi, the Carolinas and the country along the Mississippi. Inspector William Sinclair in August 1864 found "two divisions of infantry . . . near Harper's Ferry . . . in a deplorable condition . . . commanding officers of regiments and companies generally ignorant of the condition of their commands . . . drills, parades and Sunday morning inspections . . . entirely neglected for months . . . orders not enforced . . . soldiers employed as servants and not mustered as such." Concerning his observations near Cumberland, Maryland, this officer reported a "large number of drunken ragged soldiers in the streets, and dirty officers about the hotels. . . . Many cases of officers and enlisted men wearing the grey pants of the rebel service . . . some enlisted men entirely dressed in rebel colors." [105]

Discipline became so lax among Nineteenth Corps troops stationed in the vicinity of Morganza, Louisiana, in the summer of 1864 that a general order had to be issued calling attention to the frequency with which men had been found playing cards while on picket and the failure to have "a man on duty either as a vidette in advance or on watch on the post." [106] Delinquency was hardly less flagrant at Fort Mitchell, South Carolina, where in August 1864 an inspector reported two large artillery pieces unserviceable from neglect and abuse. Rats and moths had been permitted to destroy the cartridges and spare powder bags. "The muzzles of the guns have not been kept depressed and the boxes have become rusted and covered with sand," he wrote. "In several pieces the elevating screws are broken. The guns have not been traversed and the traverse circles are so sunken as almost to make this impossible." [107]

Cavalry units as a rule were not so well disciplined as those of other branches, owing largely to the relative independence with which they operated and a certain jaunty, devil-may-care attitude which, while possibly adding to their effectiveness in combat, had the opposite tendency in other aspects of soldiering. It seems unquestionable that the poorest discipline in the entire Union Army was that of mounted units operating in remote areas on loosely defined missions. The following letter, written by an inspecting officer in September 1864 to the commander of the cavalry division stationed in Arkansas, speaks for itself:

> Gen'l . . . I visited the Stables of the 9th Kan. Cav. this morning . . . at least half an hour after reveille; and not one commissioned officer was present. . . . No stable call had been sounded. Most of the horses had been fed, many had not, and were restless and fretting for something to eat. Some of the horses were provided with feed boxes, the larger number had none. Upon inquiring of one of the men why all the horses had not been fed, his reply was that the men in charge of them had not got up, especially those under arrest. When I inquired of a private soldier present whether the officers were in the habit of attending stable calls, he laughed at the idea. . . . Horses unprovided with Boxes were obliged to eat their grain in the mud. . . . No provision is made for draining . . . the stables. . . .[108]

Even more damning to the cavalry was a report made by Colonel James Hardie in September 1864 concerning units of the Department of the Gulf. Of the Second New Hampshire Cavalry (dismounted) he stated: "Men in all kinds of rig on drill—officers and men surly. Discipline poor." The Eighteenth New York Cavalry had four field officers and one captain under arrest, and another field officer was absent, sick. Equipment was scant and in poor condition. "Most of the officers seemed careless and indifferent. . . . There seemed to be a total want of martial spirit and soldierly bearing such as springs from the heart of the true soldier. . . . The regiment can be of little service to the government in its present condition." But the Second Illinois Cavalry brought forth the most disparaging of all comments, which for emphasis was in part underscored by the inspecting officer: "*Nothing good can be said of them. Take officers and men, and they are the worst looking military organization I ever saw.* The only clean or respectable place I saw in camp was that occupied by their animals. . . . everything was uniformly in bad order." [109]

These examples, as previously noted, are from units which were assigned to outlying areas and performed for the most part noncombatant duties. But even when actively engaged in major operations, cavalry appear to have been inferior to infantry in discipline. It is worthy of note that in Sherman's campaign in Georgia and the Carolinas the command having the worst reputation for pillage was that of Kilpatrick.[110]

Some cavalry organizations, to be sure, were exceedingly well disciplined, for in the mounted service, as in any other branch, the state of discipline varied greatly from unit to unit and from time to time. Of the various factors influencing discipline such as character of duties, state of equipment, prospect of active service, background of the soldiers and quality of command, the last was far and away the most important. The nub of discipline was leadership, especially on the platoon and company levels. In fact, it hardly seems too much to say that a regiment was well disciplined if it had good lieutenants and captains and poorly disciplined if it did not. Good company officers could sometimes "carry" a weak regimental staff, but a good colonel, lieutenant colonel and major were of little avail if company officers were consistently weak.

In conclusion it should be stated that discipline was frequently not so bad as it seemed. Inspection reports as well as the informal comments of soldiers tended to stress deficiencies. A unit was expected to have good discipline; hence, failure to measure up to prescribed standards was more apt to attract attention and elicit remarks than was acceptable performance. This observation is likewise applicable to offenses and punishments. The unusual and the extreme tended more frequently to get into the record than the ordinary or the average. It is essential to consider all degrees and variations, but the mean must be ever kept in the forefront. Application of this formula to the present discussion requires the statement that while men were often intractable, officers incompetent, punishments unreasonable and discipline deficient, these facts are offset in large measure by opposite extremes of a positive character, and that the great bulk of instances lie in between. When the whole war, all the personnel and the complete system of control are considered, men were fairly orderly, officers generally creditable, punishments usually tolerable and discipline of most units passable. Otherwise the North would not have won the war. And despite the fact that a few Southerners have not yet "surrendered," the North *did* win.

CHAPTER IX

HARDTACK, SALT HORSE AND COFFEE

About the mid-point of the war a poetically inclined Yank sent to a Nashville editor a doggerel description of army life. The lines treating of food ran thus:

> The soldiers' fare is very rough,
> The bread is hard, the beef is tough;
> If they can stand it, it will be,
> Through love of God, a mystery.[1]

At the time this verse was published and throughout the war, except for the period before August 3, 1861, and after June 20, 1864, the daily allowance for each Union soldier was:

twelve ounces of pork or bacon, or, one pound and four ounces of salt or fresh beef; one pound and six ounces of soft bread or flour, or, one pound of hard bread, or, one pound and four ounces of corn meal; and to every one hundred rations, fifteen pounds of beans or peas, *and* ten pounds of rice or hominy; ten pounds of green coffee, or, eight pounds of roasted (or roasted and ground) coffee, or, one pound and eight ounces of tea; fifteen pounds of sugar; four quarts of vinegar; . . . three pounds and twelve ounces of salt; four ounces of pepper; thirty pounds of potatoes, when practicable, and one quart of molasses.[2]

In relative terms this was a generous allowance. It was about one fifth more than that of the British Army, almost twice that of the French, and compared even more favorably with that of the Prussians, Austrians and Russians.[3] It was also more liberal than the official diet of Confederates. The Southerners, after hopefully adopting the old army ration early in the conflict, were forced repeatedly to cut it, while the Federals in August 1861 effected a substantial increase. Surgeon General Hammond was on firm ground when he boasted after this augmentation that the men in blue had the most abundant food allowance of any soldiers in the world.[4]

Courtesy Vermont Historical Society

CAMP OF SIXTEENTH VERMONT AT UNION MILLS, VIRGINIA

"CALIFORNIA JOE" OF BERDAN'S SHARPSHOOTERS WATCHING FOR REBS

Indeed, Union subsistence authorities were to conclude after long experience that the issue was overly generous to the point of encouraging waste. On their recommendation Congress in June 1864 revoked the increase, but a provision was retained which allowed substitution of fresh or processed vegetables for other items in the ration.[5]

Throughout the conflict, regulations permitted company commanders to sell back to the subsistence department any portion of the authorized ration not used by their men, the money thus obtained to become a part of the company fund. It was the intent of higher authorities that company commanders use the money accumulated for supplying their men with items not obtainable from commissaries and thus add variety to camp fare. But it seems that this wisely conceived aim rarely materialized in actual practice. Some captains did not know about the company fund; others did not want to be bothered with administering it; and still others appropriated it to their own use.[6] One Yank of unusual intelligence and broad experience wrote after the war: "I have yet to learn of the first company whose members ever received any revenue from such a source, although the name of *Company Fund* is a familiar one to every veteran." [7]

The specification of abundant fare by high authorities did not necessarily mean that the rank and file were consistently well fed. Far from it. Reports of officers and comments of soldiers reveal the greatest variation in the quantity of food actually made available to the men who did the shooting. As one lowly consumer aptly put it early in the war: "Some days we live first rate, and the next we dont have half enough." [8]

Almost every regiment suffered occasional periods of hunger, though usually these did not last more than a few days. But the course of the war was marked by a surprising number of what might be called major food crises, when deprivation extended over a considerable period and involved large numbers of men.

In the West in the early part of 1862 there were numerous instances of prolonged hunger. A member of the Fourth Iowa Regiment wrote after a period of arduous service in Missouri and Arkansas: "We have marched hundreds on hundreds of miles and on Short rations all the time and about one third of the time we had nothing but a little coffe indeed we have not had half rations since the 2nd of last January." [9] A Yank serving in Kentucky complained: "A man that Enlisted in the 18th Regt Is of but few days & with hard rasions to live on. . . . The last few weeks past we only get about ½ Enough to eat . . . for the last 10 days

. . . we have been living on Slap jacks . . . one the sice of my two hands every meal with Coffee & a chunk of meat. . . . We realy are about half starved." [10]

Rations were uncomfortably short among some of Buell's soldiers in the Kentucky campaign. An Illinois corporal wrote from Perryville on October 26, 1862: "The boys say that our '*grub*' is enough to make a *mule* desert, and a *hog* wish he had never been born. . . . Hard bread, bacon and coffee is all we draw." The Goldsboro expedition of December 1862 also was marked by subsistence failures. Some of the participants reported that they had nothing to eat for two days but three crackers. Others declared that they robbed horse troughs of hard corn to allay the gnawings of hunger.[11]

Similar conditions were experienced by troops serving in the Shenandoah Valley in the late spring of 1862. On June 12 Carl Schurz reported to Lincoln: "This morning I found General Fremont in a somewhat irritated state of mind, and I must confess I understand it. The Government has plenty of provisions and our soldiers die of hunger; plenty of shoes, and they go barefooted; plenty of horses, and we are hardly able to move." The hard fighting about Richmond during the Seven Days' campaign was also accompanied by some hunger, but the principal complaint there was lack of fresh vegetables and other specific items rather than empty haversacks. On the whole, the Army of the Potomac fared well as to quantity while McClellan was at the helm.[12]

Soldiers of that army experienced under Burnside their first general food shortage in the war's second winter. A Massachusetts Yank wrote his father from near Fredericksburg on November 28, 1862: "Yesterday was thanksgiving at home, but a dismal day for us. Never since I have been in the army have I seen supplies so short. Now we see soldiers going round begging hard bread." This Yank and others told of comrades haunting the slaughter pens picking up the heads, feet and tails of steers and other scraps to supplement their meager fare. A Connecticut corporal reported on December 1 that "there was a fellow got a bone with a little meat on it, he picked the meat off it and threw it away; another fellow found it and worked away on it awhile and threw it away; well, there were four men who picked that old bone." Early in January 1863 a private closed a letter to his sweetheart with the statement: "I must fall in for my beans or lose them We have two beans to a pint of water." [13]

Hooker's replacement of Burnside in January led to a revolution in the food situation. One of the first acts of the new commander was to order the erection of bakeries so that the men might have soft bread. He also attacked the whole problem of supply with a vigor that soon un-choked subsistence lines and brought to the hungry soldiers an unprece-dented quantity and variety of food.[14] The results of his reforms are vividly revealed in the pages of a diary kept by a soldier detailed in one of the brigade commissaries. Following are some sample entries:

Feb 9, 1863. Dried apples and onions was issued to the brigade today.
Feb 15, 1863. Fresh bread was issued to the first and second regiments today from the ovens.
April 21, 1863. Supply train went to the landing and brought pork, bacon, sugar, hard bread and one day's issue of potatoes.
April 25, 1863. The supply train went to the landing and brought up sugar, coffee, candles, soap, carrots and turnips.
April 28, 1863. Supply trains went to the landing and brought hams and pork.
May 1, 1863. This morning went over the river with eight wagons and issued two days rations of pork, sugar, coffee, and one day's of soft bread.
May 6, 1863. Whiskey was issued twice today.[15]

Whatever they thought of Hooker's other qualities, soldiers highly approved his competency as a provider.[16]

Except for brief shortages during the Gettysburg campaign, the Army of the Potomac generally fared well through the summer and early fall of 1863, but the Mine Run campaign of November brought another "starvation time." [17] A New Yorker wrote his homefolk on November 18: "For six weeks past we have suffered a good deal from Fatigue and Hunger. . . . I *thought* I knew what hunger was before, but I did not." [18] Reopening of the railroad which had been cut by the Rebs and the return of more settled conditions brought an end to this emergency. And while the disorganization produced by the intensive operations of the next summer again caused some temporary hardship, soldiers in the East for the remainder of the war had little cause to complain about the quantity of their rations.

In the Western armies the story was different. Grant's soldiers in Tennessee and Mississippi were periodically hungry in late 1862 and early 1863, especially after Van Dorn's and Forrest's raids on their sub-sistence stores and supply lines. An Illinois Yank wrote his wife from Abbeville, Mississippi, on December 7, 1862: "I never thought I could relish a chunk of cold corn bread like I did last night; it was delicious sure. We have not been on full rations for several days." [19] After

Christmas another Illinois soldier stationed at Jackson, Tennessee, informed his father:

> We got half rations of coffee and quarter rations of hardtack and bacon. What we call small rations, such as Yankee beans, rice and split peas are played out. . . . The hardtack is so precious now that the orderly sergeant no longer knocks a box open and lets every man help himself, but he stands right over the box and counts the number of tacks he gives to every man. . . . And that aint all. The boys will stand around until the box is emptied, and then they will pick up the fragments that have fallen to the ground . . . and scrape off the mud with their knives and eat the little pieces and glad to get them.[20]

A third participant in Grant's operations wrote that men of his unit confiscated a huge coffee mill in which they ground hard corn, using the meal thus obtained for making mush. "This served to fill up with," he added, "but with the majority it did not agree . . . giving them . . . the 'Miss. Quick Step.' After the first day the Surgeon could not begin to prescribe for his many patients." [21]

The "cracker line," as the Yanks called their subsistence channel, was clogged occasionally during the operations about Vicksburg, especially during the march from Bruinsburg to Edwards. Resulting deficiences were frequently met—and more—by raids on civilians.[22]

Portions of Rosecrans' command suffered from hunger during the Tullahoma operations of June and July 1863, but the worst food crisis in the history of the Union Army came in connection with the ensuing Chattanooga and Knoxville campaigns. While the Army of the Cumberland was under siege in and about Chattanooga after Chickamauga, "starving soldiers would follow the wagon trains" that came in over the tortuous and uncertain route from Stevenson and Bridgeport, "hoping to pick up the few grains of corn that might fall in the road." Furthermore, "The feed troughs of the horses and mules had to be guarded to keep soldiers from taking the little allowance of grain that had to be given the animals to keep them going." [23]

A young Hoosier private wrote from Chattanooga on October 22, 1863, that since the Chickamauga fight he and his comrades were eating "but two meals per day, and one cracker for each meal." He added: "We generally draw five days' rations at one time and generally eat them up in three days and starve the other two. I was nearer starved here than ever, lived on parched corn. . . . You surely have heard the song entitled Hard Times, well we have seen 'em." [24]

The opening of the Tennessee River late in October to a point near Chattanooga removed the threat of starvation, but some units, at least, continued to feel the pinch of reduced rations for a long time afterward. An Ohioan stationed in Chattanooga complained on January 18, 1864: "When we came here we had about ½ rasion. . . . We were told that we would get more when the Boats came up the River. Then we got less & now as the Cars Comenced to run last Thursday we are still getting less. . . . If it keeps on like this we will starve to death Entirly." [25]

Actually this Yank should have considered himself fortunate. He doubtless fared much better than those soldiers who in December marched from Chattanooga to Knoxville and back with only three days' rations, supplemented as occasion would permit by contributions forced from farmers along the way.[26]

Some of Sherman's men complained of food shortages while pursuing Hood northward after the fall of Atlanta.[27] A Wisconsin soldier wrote from near Lafayette, Georgia, on October 18, 1864: "Some of the Boys got some corn along the Road and making their plates into graters they ground some corn and had some mush." [28] Short rations were even more common near the end of the march to the sea as foraging, in soldier parlance, "played out." Until the opening of water routes brought in a new stock of supplies shortly before Christmas, many veteran campaigners were reduced to a fare of coffee and rice.[29] The rice was issued unhulled, but the men soon devised means of meeting this situation. Some resorted to wooden pestles and mortars borrowed from slaves while others, according to an Ohio sergeant, hulled the kernels "by placing a handful in our haversacks which we lay on logs and pound with our bayonets. Then we pour the contents from hand to hand, blowing the while to separate the chaff from the grains." [30]

Even after the cracker line was opened, supplies were inadequate; as a result skimpy fare persisted until departure from Savannah brought better opportunity for foraging. But living off the country became difficult in North Carolina near the end of the march, and cries of short rations again became common. One Yank wrote from Fayetteville on March 12, 1865, that after crossing the South Carolina boundary he and his comrades had lived five days "on nigger Peas or Beans as the boys call them and were glad to get them." [31]

Several factors contributed to the food shortages experienced by the men in blue. Fare was often scant in the early part of the war because officers responsible for drawing and issuing rations were not fully acquainted with army procedure. Failure of supply agencies to have the necessary stocks at the right places at the right time also led to instances of want. This appears to have been the situation at Savannah during Sherman's sojourn in that city. An officer of the Inspector General's Department reported in February 1865: "There was an inexcusable neglect or delay in furnishing rations to the army. . . . Up to the time of leaving Savannah the QM & Commissary Depts failed most signally to supply this command with necessary subsistence. The men actually suffered." [32]

As previously intimated, shortages were most common during periods of rapid movement and active fighting. When intensive campaigns were in progress, or when the fortunes of war closed channels of supply, as at Chattanooga, reduced fare was unavoidable. But sometimes soldiers brought hunger upon themselves by the improvident practice of consuming several days' rations shortly after their issue.

Yanks frequently attributed their meager fare to corrupt officers, and unquestionably some of those involved in the procurement and distribution of food were dishonest.[33] It is improbable, however, that peculation was nearly so prevalent as the soldiers charged.

Two specific instances clearly demonstrate how selfishness, indifference and lethargy on the part of officers sometimes caused the enlisted men to receive less than their due allowance of food. In the second winter of the war a scurvy threat occurred in the Army of the Cumberland. Rosecrans was perplexed, since the commissary records indicated an issue of 100 barrels of vegetables daily in his command, and he had taken it for granted that this food was being consumed by the soldiers. But on investigation he was shocked to discover "that one fourth in amount of this issue went to the staff officers and their families at Head-Quarters, and that of the remaining three-fourths, the Commissaries of the various Corps, Divisions and Brigades obtained the larger portions, so that the Regimental Commissaries who supplied the wants of the private soldiers were left almost unprovided." Further inquiry by medical authorities "revealed the extraordinary fact that although this very liberal daily distribution was shown by the books . . . still the soldiers had not received on an average from the Government more than three rations of vegetables during the twelve months ending on the first of April, 1863." [34]

A similar instance occurred in the latter part of 1864 in the District of West Florida. There an investigation, inspired by appearance of scurvy, revealed that while officers were purchasing fresh vegetables and other choice items liberally for themselves they were not having comparable distribution made to the men. The table of returns for September showed that of 10,658 pounds of potatoes received by the Commissary Department the 250 officers received 1,850 pounds while only 165 pounds were issued to the 3,850 men; of 1,324 gallons of pickles, officers drew 190 gallons and the men 162 gallons; issues from a stock of 14,249 pounds of dried apples were 1,749 to officers and none to the men. The figures on whisky are especially interesting: From a store of 2,345 gallons the officers obtained 434 gallons and the men (who could not purchase commissary liquors as the officers but had to depend on commanders to order its issue as part of the ration) drew only 162 gallons; in other words, officers obtained on the average one and seven-tenths gallons of whisky each during the month, and the men forty-two one thousandths! [35]

The culpability of these officers was noted in Washington, a high-level staff member writing on a report forwarded from department headquarters: "The officers seem to have been most negligent of their men. . . . They seem to have appropriated the major portion of everything to their own use and let the men get along the best they could." Whether or not these or the officers involved in the Army of the Cumberland affair were disciplined is not known.[36]

The dietary deficiencies suffered by troops in West Florida in 1864 were due to failures of distribution. The same could be said of food shortages in general. Uncle Sam had at his command enough food to provide amply for all who wore the blue. The fact that soldiers were sometimes hungry was due to his inability always to make it available to them when they needed it.

Billy Yank was not solely dependent on Uncle Sam for his subsistence. His army rations were often supplemented by the homefolk. Soldier letters reveal a considerable flow of boxes, packed with all sorts of food, originating in every loyal state and extending to all areas where Federal troops were encamped. The most active channels of home-to-soldier supply were from Northeastern communities to the Army of the Potomac and from the Midwest to troops stationed along the Mississippi River and its tributaries. Rough handling along the way frequently jumbled contents of these shipments, but damaged boxes were better than none at all. Experience led to improvements in packing and recipients became experts at salvage.

"We have been living on the contence of those boxses you and George sent to us," wrote a New York soldier from near Fredericksburg, Virginia, March 8, 1863; "nothing was spoiled except that card of buiscuits . . . those wer molded some but we used over half of them this morning in a soup we made of potatoes and onions and a little flour to thicken it and then put the buiscuits in and it made a nice dish for a soldier." [87] Contributions to the box from various neighbors was indicated by a request to "thank Mr. Burdicks a thousand times for me also Mrs. Maxson for those pies . . . and those fride cakes and ginger snaps are first rate and the dried berries they are nice . . . and the dried beef . . . and aple sauce that was first rate." He added that the boxes had been opened at headquarters to see if they contained any whisky, that the investigators had sampled the apple sauce, "and a little of the juice run out on my paper as you will see when you get this." [88]

The Sanitary Commission and other volunteer organizations also distributed food from time to time. During the scurvy scare in Rosecrans' command early in 1863, the Sanitary Commission made available a vast quantity of vegetables, and in February 1865 Rebecca Usher, representing the Maine State Agency at City Point, Virginia, reported receipt of twenty-eight barrels of vegetables for Maine soldiers. "The soldiers roasted potatoes all day in the ashes in the reading room," she wrote. "The soldiers come in and ask for a potato as if it was an article of the greatest luxury." She also told of giving out mince pies, apples, sauerkraut and other items that must have brought delight to the recipients.[89]

Sutlers also helped relieve the scantiness and monotony of camp fare, but their cakes, pies, butter, cheese, apples and other delicacies were offered at prices which frequently placed them beyond the reach of the common soldier. Yanks often complained that sutlers were never around except for brief intervals following payday.

The food venders most often patronized by the soldiers seem to have been native peddlers who, as season, location and other circumstances permitted, went through the camps selling pies, bread, butter, milk, fruit, vegetables, watermelons and oysters. A Yank wrote from Savannah, Georgia, in January 1865: "The Negroes are selling all the oysters they can get to our men. The soldier takes the tin cup and dips it into the tub or bucket of oysters, fills it full and then drinks the oysters as if he was drinking water." [40]

In one instance at least, enterprising Negroes set up a short-order restaurant in camp. This institution, located near Louisville, Kentucky, was described by a soldier thus:

Two Collered men . . . bring out a kettle of Buckwheat batter and one corn batter and bake us cakes as we want them. I think them the best I ever tasted they are always light and nice he gives us three large cakes for 5 cts, Eggs in any style 3 for 5 cts, beef steak 10 cts he has for dinner several kinds of pudding with sauce and apple dumplings baked (which I have a weakness for) large home made pies 5 cts &c &c, so we have a little something to fall back on if our rations prove a little indifferent.[41]

As noted elsewhere, Yanks occasionally supplemented their fare by eating at Southern tables.[42] Sometimes they were fed without charge and again they dined as paying guests. Negroes, in view of their friendlier attitude toward the invaders, played host far more frequently than whites. The meals served in Negroes' cabins were normally simple, consisting usually of such items as hoecake, corn bread, field peas, sweet potatoes and turnip greens, and now and then a piece of pork. Sometimes the visitors brought with them flour, sugar, meat and other ingredients not easily obtainable by civilians. Whatever the nature of the meal thus obtained, it afforded relief from camp offerings and was consumed with relish.

The statements of two soldiers will suffice to illustrate experiences and reactions of those who dined at Negroes' homes. From Key West, Florida, a New York sergeant wrote in 1862: "I was on guard down town the other day I went into an old negro woman's house and had a fine breakfast consisting of roast Beef fried onions a sweet Johny cake smoking hot boiled homony butter good tea &c &c all for two bits. Cheap enough." It seems not unlikely in view of the tendency of the colored folk to look on the Yanks as God-sent deliverers that this woman "put on a special spread" for her blue-clad guest.[43] In March 1863 another Yank wrote from Maryland: "We went up to old Pools and got old Diner to get us some bread and milk. It was good if the blacks did get it for us; after we ate our bread and milk we sat down and talked with the nigs awhile then went back to camp after dark." [44]

Some Yanks followed the practice of selling parts of their rations and using the money thus obtained to buy food from sutlers or natives. A Vermonter who followed this practice wrote from Louisiana to his brother: "I draw my rations in the morning, take what I want for the day & sell the rest. I keep my bread & potatoes sugar; sell all my meat . . . part of my soap & candles & the most of my Coffee & this I take to by milk, blackberrys cornbread Eggs fish &c &c so you see I live pretty well just now." [45]

The most common method of supplementing army fare was by foraging—which usually meant drawing on Rebel civilians, without measure and without price. If the despoiled owner denied being a Rebel, as he often did, then a receipt might be given and the responsibility of proving loyalty and obtaining compensation placed on the unwilling provider. As a rule, however, receipts were given only when provisions were taken by authorized foraging parties.

Much of the foraging was done by regularly appointed groups, led by officers and operating under authority conferred by higher commanders. This was the procedure ordered by Sherman on his famous march, and official records indicate a sincere effort by most of his corps and division commanders to enforce it.[46] But regardless of the directives and desires of the generals, Billy Yanks contrived to do a vast amount of food gathering on their own authority. Even the regularly organized foraging parties sometimes were under little control owing to the officers in charge of them—who usually were lieutenants or captains deeply imbued with the attitudes of the men—making no effort to enforce discipline.[47]

Appropriation of civilian edibles whether by authorized or irregular procedure sometimes gave Yanks a richness of fare that made them spurn the comparatively unsavory commissary issues. Living was more bounteous, of course, in prosperous areas not previously ravaged by either army.

The fertile country about Warrenton, Virginia, provided sumptuous food for the invaders during the first years of the war. A Connecticut corporal wrote his homefolk from this region in November 1862 that "on our way here . . . the boys took anything they wanted and some things they did not want. . . . They took Horses, killed cattle and brought in the quarters, Sheep, Hogs, Honey." He also reported that measures taken by the officers to protect civilians, such as calling the roll every hour and posting guards, were only partially effective in restraining the men. "The boys get lots of Geese, Ducks and Chickens in spite of the Guards," he stated.[48]

The coastal region of North Carolina also made rich contributions to soldier larders. From New Bern a Massachusetts Yank wrote his parents late in 1862: "Whenever we neared a town where we were to halt, our approach was marked by a spattering fussilade, amid which the last dying squeaks of the unfortunate pigs far and near were heard, and then we would see soldiers and sailors coming forth from the barnyards bearing their game impaled on a bayonet & dangling over their shoulders." He added: "When we first started the colonel tried to prevent our foraging but he quickly found out that all that was nonsense & before we got back we were as expert at it as any of the old hands." [49]

Middle Tennessee was another garden spot that yielded bountiful fare to its early occupants. Soldier letters frequently reported rich hauls of smoked hams, chickens, ducks, geese and other delicacies from premises about Nashville, Pulaski and Murfreesboro.[50]

The same was true of many other localities. Captain John William De Forest wrote appreciatively from a camp near Thibodaux, Louisiana, in November 1862: "When mealtime comes . . . I seat myself on a log, or a pumpkin, and devour the richness of the land. For we forage here; we go without hardtack and salt horse for the present; we live on roast pig, turkey, geese, chickens, beef and mutton; as for hoecake and sweet potatoes, they are nothing." [51]

From North Alabama a Wisconsin artilleryman wrote in November 1863: "Foraging done on a large scale by our boys sweet potatoes and chickens in plenty. . . . So soon as we came in sight of camp the Infantry went out in squads in search of meat the woods were full of hogs and it soon sounded like heavy skirmishing, General Smith riding in great fury back and forth endeavoring to punish the guilty parties and put a stop to it he tied up several men by their thumbs all night but the boys got their hogs." The next afternoon he wrote:

As we approached camp guns were heard in every direction more than last night several bullets flew directly over camp but fortunately no body was hurt Officers of the day and staff officers galloped in every direction endeavoring to stop it a camp guard was thrown around the Infantry with orders to keep all men from going in with meat or guns But Gen Smith had commenced to late to stop this division from foraging the guards sat down and always looked the wrong way and meat in plenty was brought.[52]

Yanks who campaigned in North Mississippi in the latter part of 1862 and about Vicksburg the next summer also had a picnic at the natives' expense.[53] There, and elsewhere, some of the soldiers made great sport of foraging, referring to their domestic prizes as wild game. Sergeant Onley Andrus stated that when his comrades "find a hog they down him & skin him & call it possum & it is very good eating for a hungry man." [54] In similar vein another Yank wrote from Western Tennessee: "There is not much game around here there is . . . however . . . *Bear, Swamp Oppossom, Turkey, Tame phesant,* & Squirles & so-fourth. All I have to say is that when any of the above see fit to come onto our table in the place of *spiled beef* or salty middling we dont grumble but try to eat them." [55] Even the officers sometimes made a joke of the plunder. In January 1863 a Wisconsin surgeon wrote his wife from Missouri: "Hogs run wild in the woods here. . . . Every hog seen is 'a wild hog' of course & in soldier parlance 'a slow deer' and very few escape alive. . . . Col. Harris & myself were standing together & the men aimed at the hogs . . . but did not hit them. The col. in a low tone said you shoot with your pistol and see if *you* can hit one. I did So & succeeded & the men in Soldier Style cried out 'bully!' " [56]

An Ohio soldier wrote his cousin that he could not help chasing Southern chickens, and added, "they are always sure to cackle at the Stars and Stripes and that would not do." [57]

A story that must have produced many a chuckle about the campfire told of an Irishman coming into camp with a hen and a goose hanging from his rifle. When reproached by an officer for robbing civilians the soldier glibly replied: "Oh! bedad S-r-r-r, this goose came out as I was wending my way along *pacably* and hissed at the American flag, and bejabez I shot him on the spot . . . and I found this hin laying eggs for the Ribil Army, and I hit her a whack that stopped that act *of treason* on the spot, too." [58] Other tall tales recounted attacks on unoffending men in blue by hens, geese and all sorts of edible creatures, ending of course in the aggressors' paying with their lives—and their savory flesh —for their unwonted conduct. Literal reading of soldier accounts would leave the impression that Southern poultry and livestock were even more disloyal and vicious than the Rebels who owned them.

The most notorious instances of foraging came in connection with Sheridan's valley campaign of 1864 and Sherman's march through Georgia and the Carolinas.[59] Soldier accounts and official reports indicate, however, that participants in these campaigns lived no better than those who first tapped the larders of other unusually productive areas. But they lived well enough—so well, indeed, that some professed to tire of the rich fare of chickens, turkeys, hams and honey and to long for the plainer offerings of the subsistence department. One of Sherman's sergeants reported from near Orangeburg, South Carolina, that the men "will not take the trouble to kill cattle, & if it is killed for them, they will not cook it." [60]

This sort of sumptuous living at the expense of Rebel civilians, while immensely gratifying and much discussed both during and after the conflict, was a relatively rare experience. Foraging in any area yielded diminishing returns and most Yanks did the majority of their soldiering in regions where opportunities for living off the country were scant. Procurement of food from sutlers, homefolk and other extraneous sources was also subject to many limitations. Hence, the men who wore the blue had to depend chiefly on army fare.

The staples of army diet were bread, meat and coffee. Bread was sometimes of the loaf variety, but more often it was a flour-and-water cracker or pilot biscuit, known commonly among soldiers as "hardtack."

A Yank who preserved some hardtack as mementos gave their dimensions as three and one eighth by two and seven eighths by one half inch. Commissary authorities usually considered ten or twelve crackers a full bread ration.[61]

Soldier accounts leave little doubt of the cracker being hard. Derisive references ranged from "teeth dullers" to "sheet-iron crackers." One Yank reported that the hardtack made his teeth so sore he could scarcely eat. Another thought that the crackers "would make good brest works," as they would surely stop a musket ball. A third told of carving a durable violin bridge from one of them. Others testified to the necessity of beating the crackers with their musket butts to make them edible.[62]

An Ohio soldier wrote a friend: "Without joking any thing about it I have eat crackers here that I could not take in my hands and break into without getting a pry on something." [63] And a Kansan reported this camp dialogue:

Sergeant: Boys I was eating a piece of hard tack this morning,
            and I bit on something soft; what do you think it was?
Private: A worm?
Sergeant: No by G—d, it was a ten penny nail.[64]

Another Yank recommended as a soldier's "Grace" before eating:

> Oh! Lord of Love,
> Look from above,
> Upon we hungry sinners:
> Of what we ask 'tis not in vain,
> For what has been done can be
> Done again, Please turn
> Our water into wine, and bless
> And *break* these *crackers*.[65]

Soldiers found various ways of softening the crackers and making them palatable. A favorite practice was to crumble them in coffee, soup or milk. Other methods were to toast the crackers over coals; fry them in bacon grease; or beat them into a powder, mix with boiled rice and serve as griddle cakes. Some Yanks made a dish they called "skillygalee" by soaking the hardtack in cold water and then browning them in pork fat and seasoning to taste. Others who varied this procedure by pulverizing the crackers before soaking them called the product "hell-fired stew." [66]

Another improvisation was "hardtack pudding" which according to one Yank:

was made by placing the biscuit in a stout canvas bag, and pounding bag and contents with a club on a log until the biscuits were reduced to a fine powder; then we added a little wheat flour, if we had it . . . and made a stiff dough, which we next rolled out on a cracker-box lid, like a pie-crust; then we covered this all over with a preparation of stewed, dried, apples, dropping in here and there a raisin or two just for Auld Lang Syne's sake, rolled and wrapped it in a cloth, boiled it for an hour or so and ate it with wine sauce. The wine was usually omitted and hunger inserted in its stead.[67]

When circumstances precluded preparation of any sort, as was often the case, hungry Yanks ate the hardtack just as it came from the box, or in a sandwich form with a slice of fat pork (spread with sugar if convenient) as filler.[68]

Aversion to hardtack sprang in part from the poor quality of the product as issued in camp. Crackers often were stale from age or moldy from storage in exposed or damp places. In many instances they were infested with worms or weevils, a fact which gave rise to a flood of irreverent comment. "All the fresh meat we had came in the hard bread . . . and I preferring my game cooked, used to toast my biscuits," was the remark of one disgusted campaigner. Another observed: "We found 32 worms, maggots, &c in one cracker day before yesterday. We do not find much fault, however, but eat them without looking as a good way to prevent troublesome ideas." Still another testified after the war: "It was no uncommon occurrence for a man to find the surface of his pot of coffee swimming with weevils after breaking up hardtack in it; . . . but they were easily skimmed off and left no distinctive flavor behind." In view of the frequency of animal occupation, it is not surprising that some Yanks referred to their crackers as "worm castles," and that others parodied "John Brown's Body" with these lines:

> Worms eat hearty in the commissary stores
> While we go starving on.[69]

Much of the criticism was, of course, embellished with fiction. And however strong was the initial antipathy toward "Lincoln pies" or "McClellan pies," as the government crackers were sometimes called,

many Yanks came eventually to like them. Hunger compelled soldiers
to eat them and taste was acquired with use. One historian states: "In
the Eighth Iowa Regiment the first issue of hard tack 'nearly created
insurrection.' Later the men came to thank their stars they had even
hard tack . . . to eat." Sometimes conversion came quickly. After only
a few months of service a Pennsylvania soldier wrote: "I have got to like
the army crackers very much. I eat them in the place of bread altogether
now, though there is plenty of the latter." [70]

The meat portion of the army ration was normally pork or beef,
though fish was issued occasionally in some commands. Pork now and
then came in the form of cured bacon or ham, but, according to one
veteran, the issue in either case "was usually black, rusty and strong
and decidedly unpopular." [71] The meat served most frequently to Billy
Yanks was salt pork.

When served in company quantities the salt pork was commonly
boiled. But when the soldiers prepared rations individually or in messes,
they fried it, broiled it on forked sticks, baked it with beans or used
it as an ingredient of soup or stew. Soup seasoned with pork and thick-
ened with hardtack made a dish known as lobscouse which, while asso·
ciated traditionally with sailors, was relished nonetheless by Billy Yanks.

Seasoned campaigners, pressed for time or disinclined to cook,
thought nothing of throwing their pork ration between hardtack and
eating it raw.[72]

Men in blue, like their opponents, commonly referred to salt pork
as "sowbelly"; one Yank with a penchant for detail added parenthetically
"with the tits on." [73]

Beef was fresh or pickled. Fresh beef could be fried, broiled or cooked
in soup or stew; but pickled beef, known almost universally among Yanks
as "salt horse," presented special problems of preparation. Pickling as
done for the army meant preserving the meat in a solution so briny that
even the most hardened veterans would hardly presume to cook it with-
out a thorough soaking in water. "It was not an unusual occurrence,"
according to one experienced Yank, "for troops encamped by a running
brook to tie a piece of this beef to the end of a cord, and throw it into
the brook at night, to remain freshening until the following morning." [74]

The soaking took away the natural juices along with the surplus salt,
thus reducing taste as well as nutrition. Edibility was further impaired
in many instances by poor preservation, and this despite the fact that the
special pickling process was supposed to make the beef impervious to
decay in any sort of climate for at least two years. Even with due allow-

ance for soldier exaggeration, the conclusion is inescapable that "salt horse" dispensed in camp was commonly tainted and frequently, if not usually, tough enough to justify the soldier appellation of "old bull." [75]

Fresh beef was less than fresh at times and pork now and then was inhabited by worms. Hence, meat, like hardtack, came in for abundant reviling among consumers. "Fresh-killed beef . . . had to be eaten with the odor and warmth of blood still in it," wrote a soldier historian of his Louisiana experience, "under penalty of finding it fly-blown before the next meal." A Massachusetts Yank complained that the pickled beef "was ten times saltier than salt itself & almost blistered the tongue." A Pennsylvanian reported that smoked flitch which he received on one occasion "was so strong it could almost walk its self." [76]

"We drew meat last night that was so damd full of skippers that it could move alone," wrote an Ohioan, and a comrade reported: "Yesterday morning was the first time we had to carry our meat for the maggots always carried it till then. We had to have an extra gard to keep them from packing it clear off." An Illinois Yank stationed in Tennessee in 1862 found the so-called fresh beef so worthless "that one can throw a piece up against a tree and it will just stick there and quiver and twitch for all the world like one of those blue-bellied lizards at home will do when you knock him off a fence rail with a stick." [77]

Almost any camp contained wags who were ready to assert unequivocally that the stuff being issued as beef was not beef at all but mule. A camp newspaper in 1862 quoted a Connecticut soldier as stating "that the commissary at Annapolis has given the boys so much mule meat that the ears of the whole regiment have grown three and a half inches since their arrival at the Maryland capital." Sometimes Yanks who drew a particularly bad lot of meat would decide to lay it away with the honor due long service in the army. Hence, they would deposit the beef or pork in a hardtack box, surround it with scraps of harness for proper identity, bear it away with appropriate music and procession to a final resting place in the camp dump and fire the customary fusillade over the grave. Thus was hardship converted to merriment.[78]

Coffee was one of the most cherished items in the ration. Of this article the men in blue, in striking contrast with the experience of their opponents, usually had an ample supply. The effect on morale must have been considerable. And if it cannot be said that coffee helped Billy Yank win the war, it at least made his participation in the conflict more tolerable.

Soldiers who liked the beverage sweet commonly carried coffee and sugar ready mixed in a cloth bag.[79] At mealtimes, and often in between, they would bring water to a boil in pint dippers or tin cans rigged with wire bails and then dump in the mixture and let it boil until the desired hue was attained. As a general rule the longer a man served, the darker he liked his coffee.

The finished product was described by one of Sherman's veterans thus: "Black as the face of a plantation, 'strong enough to float an iron wedge,' and innocent of lacteal adulteration, it gave strength to the weary and heavy laden, and courage to the despondent and sick at heart." [80]

Now and then Yanks would lighten their coffee with milk "confiscated" from Rebel cows or with an evaporated product dispensed on rare occasions by commissaries; but usually army coffee was black.

Some soldiers consumed enormous quantities. "I can drink two and three quarts of coffee a day easily and want more," wrote a Pennsylvanian, "and I always was a fair coffee drinker." But his capacity was exceeded by an Ohioan who stated: "I have a large cup that holds nearly 2 qts. I now can manage that full 2 times a day and sometimes 3 of them a day." [81]

Yanks usually liked the coffee prepared in their individual pots much better than that brewed in large quantities by company cooks. An Irishman whose regiment followed the latter procedure wrote disgustedly: "The coffee is on the boarding house order. I find the greatest difficulty distinguishing between it and the soup. Therefore I . . . drink Adam's Ale instead." [82]

In the second year of the war the commissary department distributed to the field armies a product consisting of extract of coffee mixed with sugar and milk and known as "essence of coffee." This compound, according to a regimental adjutant, was packed in half-gallon tin cans and looked like axle grease. A teaspoonful mixed with a cup of hot water, he added, produced a beverage so villainous that the men would not drink it. This earlier version of "instant coffee" aroused similar reactions elsewhere; as a result it was shortly discontinued as an item of army issue.[83]

Essence of coffee was only one of several processed foods known to Billy Yank. The regulation ration in use at the outbreak of the war authorized desiccated potatoes as a substitute for beans; and revisions adopted during the conflict added desiccated vegetables and provided that either the potato or vegetable product might be substituted for beans, peas, rice, hominy or fresh potatoes. Late in the conflict a light ration, consisting in part of processed foods and known as "Dr. Horsford's Marching Ration," was approved, but this compound was not put into use until after the cessation of hostilities.[84]

Desiccated potatoes, which had been used by the British in the Crimea, were described by an Illinois veteran as "Irish potatoes cut up fine and thoroughly dried"; they "much resembled the modern preparation called 'grape nuts,'" he commented. Soldiers were hostile to this article at first but medical authorities, prompted by the erroneous belief that it would prevent scurvy, were so insistent on its use that many Yanks were forced to give it a trial. Some used it as an ingredient for soup while others converted it into small cakes. The cakes, when fried to a deep brown, came to be regarded by a few, at least, as "first rate." But the majority of soldiers seem never to have acquired a taste for desiccated potatoes in any form.[85]

The vegetable concentrate, specified in regulations as "desiccated compressed mixed vegetables" but commonly known by soldiers as "desecrated vegetables" or "baled hay," was made of an assortment of garden produce, including turnips, carrots, beets, onions and string beans. The compound was issued in hard, dry cakes. These when soaked would expand enormously, a circumstance which gave rise to the story of a Yank eating his ration raw, swelling up and almost dying.[86] About the only practical means of using the mixture was in soup.

The desiccated vegetables aroused even more consumer opposition than the potatoes. One factor working against them was their appearance; in solution they reminded an officer of "a dirty brook with all the dead leaves floating around promiscuously." Too, they were so heavily peppered (for antiseptic purposes), and so utterly insipid, as to repel most of "Uncle Sam's boarders." [87] But positive orders of commanders and periodic shortages of more palatable foods combined to compel a limited acceptance of the desiccated vegetables. Some of the reluctant consumers eventually found them tolerable—one even pronounced them "an excelent article." [88] But all were happier when sufficiency of regular rations made their issue unnecessary.

An often ridiculed but very important item of camp fare was the army bean. As a mainstay of diet it was outranked only by bread, meat and coffee.

New England soldiers, as might be expected, were especially fond of beans. When members of the Forty-fourth Massachusetts Regiment wrote an original comic opera for presentation before General Foster and other notables at New Bern, North Carolina, in March 1863, they included these lines:

> Beans for breakfast—breakfast,
> Beans for breakfast—breakfast,
> Beans for breakfast
>   Down on the Readville farm.[89]

The verse was repeated with substitution of dinner and supper for breakfast. The Readville farm represented the initial training camp, but beans accompanied the New Englanders on campaigns throughout Dixie and, while they rarely were dished out as often as three times a day, they were, indeed, a frequent item of issue.

Nor was their consumption limited to soldiers of the Northeast. Westerners and others adopted not only the beans but also the New Englander's favorite mode of preparing them. This method, as given by a young Minnesota private to his mother in 1863, was:

Take as many beans as you want for a mess and par boil or partly boil them then take a spade and dig a hole large aneugh for the pot you are going to cook the beans in and build a fire in it and get it as warm as you can, then take the pot of beans and put a peice of meat in the center of the pot then cover the pot over and put it in the hole covering the pot with the coals that are in the hole and shovel earth on top of them and in twenty four hours you have a soldiers dish of baked beans.[90]

Overnight, rather than twenty-four hours, seems to have been the usual baking period. That soldier was rare whose salivary glands did not begin an expectant flow when the beans were uncovered in the morning. "The best I ever eat," was the considered judgment of one who partook of this appetizing preparation.[91]

Beans were sometimes used in soup either as the principal ingredient or along with sundry other articles. Soup, in one form or another, was a common camp dish. To prepare it several soldiers usually pooled their rations, thus saving time and effort and securing maximum returns in savoriness and nourishment. Now and then a Yank would denounce the preparation as tasting more like dishwater than soup, but the majority judgment as recorded in letters and diaries was favorable.[92]

Shortage of rations and a bent for experimentation, common among amateur cooks, resulted in numerous variations and specialties. Hungry Yanks stationed in Louisiana, taking a cue from Seminole War experience, converted the tail of an alligator into soup. They pronounced it good, but the decision apparently was based more on necessity and pride than on taste; for, when after a brief interval the commissary dealt out a ration of bread and pork, the highly vaunted delicacy was quickly forsaken.[93]

Rattlesnakes also were killed and eaten in a few instances. But Sergeant Henry A. Buck apparently reflected prevailing opinion when he wrote: "The meat looked very nice and delicate, but I did not feel like trying it." Another dish of limited acceptance must have been the fried "jabird and a read headed wood pecker" which one Yank reported.[94]

Among miscellaneous delicacies receiving the favorable comment of soldier correspondents and diarists were hogs and chickens coated with clay and roasted in hot ashes; Indian pudding; doughnuts; and pies. Rebel apiaries were often raided to provide delicious sweetening; and Southern orchards and thickets yielded an abundance of apples, peaches, cherries, plums, blackberries and other fruits that were eaten as plucked or converted into pies or sauce. Typical of many soldier comments was that of Sergeant Onley Andrus written from the depths of Dixie in the spring of 1863: "I have been Blackberrying and Oh! I wish you was here to go with me. . . . I eat all the *black* ones & brot the red ones home to stew for *Sas!*" [95]

In the fall and early winter, Yanks frequently partook of the wild grapes and persimmons that grew in abundance in many parts of the South. Some even learned to relish the fruit of the lowly pawpaw tree.[96]

Culinary arrangements varied considerably from time to time and in different commands. But as a general rule the company plan, with cooking done for the whole group by a permanent or rotating detail, was followed during the period of initial training in home areas and in permanent camps and barracks. This system had the advantage of easier supervision and in theory, at least, conduced to more expert preparation.

When units moved to the field they usually went over to the mess or individual plan of cooking. Messes consisted normally of four to eight men, grouped on the basis of congeniality, each of whom took his turn in serving as cook—or "dogrobber" as some Yanks put it. The mess system worked well when troops were in a relatively settled state, as in winter quarters, but when on the march or in contact with the enemy they often found it more convenient to prepare their food individually.[97]

Sometimes members of a mess engaged the service of a Negro, obtainable from among the freedmen at nominal compensation, to relieve them of the drudgery of cooking and scrubbing. Frequently the blacks were better cooks than the soldiers, but a fault common to both was an overfondness for frying. It is only fair to add that commissary issues and field conditions were not such as to encourage artistry in cooking and that most camp chefs in time mastered essential principles.

Concern over the prevalence of disease in the army, which many civilians attributed to improper preparation of food under the mess plan, caused Congress in March 1863 to enact a law requiring cooking by companies and authorizing enlistment of Negroes to serve as assistants to soldier details.[98] But this legislation apparently had little effect outside the Northern states. Cooking in small groups or as individuals was the prevailing practice among seasoned troops in the field during any period of the war; and the tendency was toward the individual plan. A typical bivouac scene in the latter half of the conflict was a small party of Yanks hovering about a pile of burning rails or pine knots, each boiling his coffee in a dipper, broiling his sowbelly on a stick and, if hardtack happened not to be at hand, baking a flour-and-water dough ball on the end of a ramrod. Faces, already brown from exposure to wind, sun and dirt, grew darker as the veterans puttered about the fire, and "smoked Yanks" became something more than a catchy phrase.[99]

Many men were never able to adapt themselves with any degree of happiness to the rough fare of field and camp. Some, from much practice, achieved a high level of profane eloquence in denouncing it. One soldier wrote his brother: "We live so mean here the hard bread is all worms and the meat stinks like hell . . . and rice to or three times a week & worms as long as your finger. I liked rice once but god damn the stuff now." Another stated that "the butter we have had lately has been rather strong . . . if Samson had had a little to rub on his head after his hair was shaved off the Philistines never would have taken him prisoner." A third reported that owing to his inability to eat any of the beans, "rusty pork" or potatoes served in camp, he was forced "to live on faith and sour wheat bread." [100]

Numerous blasts were directed at the commissaries, whom the malcontents often envisioned as "damd old raskels" who cheated them out of their due allowances and fed them on condemned junk. In one instance about 300 soldiers gathered up the bread issued to them and "stormed the commissary with the sour loaves as ammunition." [101]

But outbreaks were rare and protests frequently reflected less of venom than a desire to keep alive a soldier's sacred right to grumble. The overwhelming majority of Yanks eventually learned to accept as a normal part of soldiering a fare considerably less attractive than that known at home. One factor working to this end was the natural tendency of human beings to adapt themselves to whatever they cannot avoid. Another was the stimulating effect of army life on appetite. Early in his camp career a Massachusetts man observed: "When I first came here I ate about one third of a ration but now neither coffee nor bread are long without a covering." After five months in service a Vermonter wrote his sister: "I'll bet when I get hom I Shall have an appetite to eat most anything . . . if a person wants to know how to apreciate the value of good vituals he had better enlist. . . . I have seen the time when I would have been glad to picked the crusts of bread that mother gives to the hogs." An Ohioan who had been through the strenuous Chickasaw Bayou and Fort Hindman campaigns informed his mother: "i often wish i hade to eate what ante poley doge gits and what you throe away." [102]

One of the most vivid glimpses of the impact of military life on appetite and eating practices was that given by a Pennsylvanian who wrote to his wife in 1864: "It goes perty greasey Some times but wee will have to be Satisfied. . . . When wee go to draw our Rashions it puts mee in mind as iff thare ware about Thirty hungray horgs In one pen and the trought onely Big a nough for about three to get in . . . that is the way it goes with us." [103]

In conclusion it may be said that as Billy Yank moved away from his civilian status he thought less and less about the quality of his rations and more and more about their quantity.

CHAPTER X

EVIL AND GOODNESS

"I WILL BE a perfect Barbarian if I Should Stay hear 3 years," wrote a Vermonter from camp near Burlington in June 1861, while a Minnesotan who marched with Sibley against the Indians in 1863 noted in his diary a short time after the expedition got under way: "I must confess that I have seen but little of the wickedness and depravity of man until I Joined the Army." In similar vein, an Illinois soldier reported from Corinth, Mississippi, after Shiloh: "If there is any place on God's fair earth where wickedness 'stalketh abroad in daylight,' it is in the army. . . . Ninety-nine men out of every hundred are profane swearers . . . hundreds of young men . . . devote all their leisure time to [gambling]." [1]

Countless other Yanks serving in widely scattered commands testified to the prevalency of evil and the degenerating influences of army life. Alfred Davenport, a city-bred Easterner not overly pious or easily shocked, wrote his homefolk from near Baltimore in December 1861 that camp was "a hard school" and that scores in his regiment had been "ruined in morals and in health for they learn everything bad and nothing good." A year later he reported from Fredericksburg: "The more vulgar a man is, the better he is appreciated and as for morals . . . [the army] is a graveyard for them." Still later he observed: "If you think soldiering cures anyone of wild habits it is a great mistake, it is like Sending a Boy in the Navy to learn him good manners. We have Drummer Boys with us that when they came at first could hardly look you in the face for diffidence but now could stare the Devil out of contenance and cant be beat at cursing, swearing and gambling." [2]

In like tone Private Delos W. Lake of the Nineteenth Michigan wrote in 1864 from Middle Tennessee to a brother about to become a soldier: "The army is the worst place in the world to learn bad habbits of all kinds. there is several men in this Regt when they enlisted they were nice respectable men and belonged to the Church of God, but now where are they? they are ruined men." [3]

Observations of religious workers, records of the Medical Department and official reports of commanding officers confirm soldier impressions of the pervasiveness of evil in Union camps. It is not that bad men flocked to the colors while good ones stayed at home, or that the army was the devil's own instrument for making sinners out of the righteous. Men did not grow worse from the mere fact of becoming soldiers, for there is nothing contaminating about an army uniform. Unquestionably some men were as good when they came out of the service as when they enlisted, and a few were even better. But in general, among Yanks as among Rebs, evil flourished more than good. The degeneration came from the removal of accustomed restraints and associations, the urge to experiment with the forbidden, the desire to escape boredom and the utter inadequacy of religious and recreational facilities for soldiers of the sixties.

One of the most common evils of the camp was profanity. A New Englander serving on Staten Island in the fall of 1861 reported that "swearing is almost universal," while a Chicagoan stationed near Memphis observed: "The swearing especially is terrific, and even to a man accustomed to hear bad language, and with sensibilities not very easily shocked, it is really disgusting. The worst characters of the worst dens up North, I am afraid, would have to yield the palm for profanity to the gallant army of the Southwest." [4]

Articles of war forbade the use of profanity and, in the case of officers, prescribed a fine of one dollar for each offense.[5] But little attention was paid to the prohibition, and commissioned personnel, far from enjoining their men, seem rather to have set an unwholesome example in the use of oaths and execrations.

Occasionally a pious commander would publish an order against swearing and chaplains consistently made it one of their principal targets. Religiously inclined soldiers sometimes rebuked comrades for their blasphemy, but more often than not such endeavors were squelched by a flood of ridicule.

The drift toward swearing was so strong that it drew in many good men. A Hoosier boy of exemplary background found after a few months' service that it was remarkably easy for a soldier to be profane, and an Ohio surgeon noted in December 1861 that while at first little swearing had been heard in his regiment, "of late oaths and gross profanity are painfully on the increase." Even more to the point was the observation of a Connecticut captain who wrote from Louisiana in 1862: "It is wonderful how profane an army is. Officers who are members of the church, . . . who would not even play a game of cards, have learned to rip out oaths when the drill goes badly or when the discipline 'gets out of kilter.' " [6]

The type of profanity used in Federal camps is revealed in some detail by courts-martial proceedings, which specify *ad literam* objectionable phrases of soldiers charged with disrespectful conduct toward their superiors. These records indicate that the swearing of Billy Yank did not differ greatly from that of his descendants in World Wars I and II. "Hell" and "damn" were the most common expletives, but "God damn," "son of a bitch," "Jesus Christ," "kiss my arse," "go stick it up . . ." and the age-old array of smutty, four-letter words, used singly and in varying combinations, also had frequent usage.

Now and then a soldier made exuberant by drink would step out of his tent and yell "Hurrah for hell!" [7] If some nosy sergeant or despised officer should call him to task, he might become considerably more profane. Private Charles N. Heath when threatened with arrest by his sergeant replied: "If you arrest me, I will rip your God damned guts out and scatter them over the parade ground." And Private John Killeen when ordered to guard duty blurted: "By my living Jesus Christ I will have your life the first chance, you son of a bitch." Another soldier was so provoked by a sergeant's order to keep still while in formation as to exclaim "that he wished the whole God damned Army and Navy and every other God damned thing was in hell" and that "no God damn man could make him keep still." [8]

These were statements made in anger against offending superiors. But most of the profanity heard in camp was of the idle, uninspired sort, thrown in to keep up a flow of chatter or from sheer habit. As such, it was uttered without intent or consciousness of offense either to God or man.[9]

Gambling was hardly less prevalent than swearing. One Yank, while stationed near Petersburg in October 1864, noted in his diary that "so far as my observation goes, nine out of ten play cards for money," and another, writing after the war, recalled that after Fredericksburg he once sat for twenty-four hours in a poker game.[10]

The peak of gambling came on payday when clusters of soldiers might be seen on every hand, intently trying to multiply their greenbacks by resort to chance. As the money gradually shifted to the possession of Dame Fortune's chosen few, the crowds thinned out and chance took a holiday until the next return of the paymaster.

The gambling urge of some Yanks was so strong that they would indulge in it at the risk of their lives as well as their fortunes. One group of poker zealots who found themselves a special target of Rebel gunners completed the hand, though swearing incessantly at the enemy for disturbing them, and then leisurely shifted to the unexposed side of a large tree to continue their play.[11]

At the other extreme from those who brazenly shuffled and dealt to the accompaniment of whining bullets was a group so sensitive to the evil of gaming that they took no chances of being killed with the instruments of sin on their bodies. Several soldiers bore witness to the fact that the line of march leading to battle was strewn with playing cards, tossed aside by conscience-stricken gamblers fearful of their future. But if they survived, "these same fellows," according to one observer, "would immediately gather up the cards until they had a full deck." [12]

The principal gambling medium was cards and the favorite game was poker, commonly called "bluff," which was played in several variations. Other card games included twenty-one, euchre, faro and seven-up or "old sledge."

Crap shooting had some practitioners, but the most common dice game seems to have been chuck-a-luck, also called sweat, which was a banking contest played by rolling three dice on a board or cloth marked off into numbered squares. This game became so popular in Grant's army during the early months of 1863 that soldiers gave a water-surrounded retreat opposite Yazoo Pass the name of Chuck-a-luck Island.[13]

Raffling—of objects ranging from watches to horses—cockfighting and horse racing provided other means of gambling, though none of these had anything like the following of cards and dice. Contests between game roosters sometimes aroused unusual interest from the fact of the feathered gladiators representing organizations strongly imbued with unit pride. General John Beatty reported a fight between cocks sponsored respectively by Company G of the Third Ohio Regiment and Company G of the Tenth Ohio, with a side bet of fifteen dollars. "After numerous attacks, retreats, charges and countercharges, the Tenth rooster succumbed like a hero," wrote Beatty, "and the other was carried in triumph from the field." Just as enthusiasm ran highest General Ormsby Mitchel, the division commander, came riding by; thinking that the cheering was for him he "passed on, well pleased" with both the soldiers and himself.[14]

Whatever the form of gambling, the stakes were usually small; considering that the maximum pay of an infantry private was only sixteen dollars a month, they could not often be otherwise. But occasionally well-heeled and reckless individuals would push the betting to fantastic heights.[15]

Gambling sharks trained in metropolitan dens frequented some of the camps and on payday made heavy inroads on the meager resources of un-suspecting soldiers.[16] Now and then a Yank of pious background suc-ceeded by diligent application in becoming so expert at games of chance as to live sumptuously at the expense of his fellows. Such a one was C. W. Bardeen, a teen-aged fifer who was introduced to gambling when he joined the army and who became so proficient that many comrades would not risk sitting down with him in a friendly game. The following entries from his diary afford glimpses of his gambling experience:

> Aug. 22, 1863, Riker's Island, New York—We were paid off to-day. I made considerable playing Bluff. $27.00 at Draw Poker.
> Aug. 24—Played Bluff of course. Made pretty well.
> Aug. 25—Played Bluff as usual. Sent $50.00 home.
> Aug. 27—Made 20.00 at Bluff. . . . Sent $50.00 home.
> Aug. 28—Lost $5.00 at Sweat this morning but won it back again at Bluff. I seem to have uniform good success at Bluff this payday.
> Aug. 30—Sunday. . . . Lost $10.00 at Bluff & Sweat and set up a board winning more than I lost. Paid $25.00 to Hull for a watch.
> Sept. 1—Won $20.00 at Bluff in a.m. A full hand, two Flushes. I held the Full. In p.m. won twenty dollars at Sweat Got a $30.00 draft.

Bardeen's winnings in August and September 1863 aggregated several hundred dollars, permitting him to take a trip to the city, have his pic-ture taken, see the sights, attend the opera and subscribe to three news-papers. He resumed his gambling full blast at Brandy Station, Virginia, in October, adding raffling and "props" (played with four shells, two red and two white) to his repertoire. But in the latter part of the year his conscience began to bother him, as his diary entry of December 31, 1863, reveals:

> The year that has passed was passed by me in the Army. I bear wit-ness to its contaminating effects. Many an evil habit has sprung up in me since Jan. 1st 1863. God grant that the year in which we now have entered may not be so.

In February 1864, Bardeen, then sixteen years old, started attending reli-gious services, took the temperance pledge and shortly gave up gam-bling.[17]

In his case, abandonment of gambling resulted primarily from immi-nency of the fighting season and concern for the soul. Other soldiers were constrained to reform by the quick loss of badly needed wages.

Typical of those impelled to better ways by bad luck was Jacob E. Hyneman of Grant's army who wrote in his diary on February 20, 1864, shortly after drawing four months' pay: "In camp. I must say that I feel down in the mouth, only paid a week ago and have not a cent now, having bluffed away all that I did not send home. I don't think I will play poker any more." [18]

Resolves to eschew chance, whatever the motivation, usually were ineffectual, and gambling, like swearing, was considerably more prevalent in 1865 than in 1861.

A frequent accompaniment of swearing and gambling was the drinking of intoxicating beverages. Whisky was the usual tipple, but gin, brandy, wine and—among German troops especially—beer were also consumed in large quantities. The cider stocked by sutlers sometimes had sufficient potency to make imbibers of a few glasses limber and joyful.

The prevalence of excessive drinking was such as to disturb moralists and greatly enhance the problem of discipline. After presiding over a court-martial session involving fifty men in July 1862, John William De Forest wrote that "every solitary case of misbehavior originated in whiskey. . . . It seems clear than an army of teetotalers would be one-fourth more reliable and effective than an army containing the usual proportion of hard drinkers." [19] And in reviewing a case of liquor-provoked insubordination in Hooker's division in February 1862, McClellan observed: "No one evil agent so much obstructs this army . . . as the degrading vice of drunkenness. It is the cause of by far the greater part of the disorders which are examined by courts-martial. It is impossible to estimate the benefits that would accrue to the service from the adoption of a resolution on the part of officers to set their men an example of total abstinence from intoxicating liquors. It would be worth 50,000 men to the armies of the United States." [20]

Drinking was more prevalent in some organizations than in others, owing to differences in the background of the men, the character of commanders, the effectiveness of chaplains and various other factors. Regiments from large cities, especially those with a heavy Irish or German admixture, often were more inclined to strong drink than were those composed mainly of rural men. But organizations distinguished for sobriety might, under unusual temptation, go on a roaring spree. Such was the case with the Forty-eighth New York Regiment, known as Perry's Saints, whose colonel, James M. Perry, was a prominent minister. In June 1862 while this unit was stationed on Tybee Island, a storm blew ashore a large quantity of beer and wine and Perry's Saints proceeded to get gloriously drunk. The incident must have upset the reverend colonel greatly, for he was fatally stricken on the very next day while sitting at his desk.[21]

Excessive drinking was undoubtedly more common among Yanks than among Rebs. This does not mean that the Southerners were naturally more abstemious than their Northern counterparts but rather that they had less opportunity to partake of Bacchus' offerings. Intoxicants were more abundant in the North than in the Confederacy; Yanks had more money than Rebs; they were more frequently stationed near large cities; whisky was more often an item of government issue; and the Federals had a more effective system of supply.

Since drinking was largely a matter of opportunity, intemperance was most common during changes of station, especially those requiring passage through cities, on holidays and at paytime. Colonel Hans Heg of the Fifteenth Wisconsin wrote his wife after taking his command south by way of Chicago that he lost three men en route and many others "got awfull drunk." [22] The comment "pay day—most of the boys drunk," or "Christmas—nearly all tight" appears so often in soldier letters and diaries as to become monotonous.

The quality of liquor drunk by soldiers ranged from choice to vile, with the vile being far more common than the choice. Commissary whisky, denounced with about the same degree of enthusiasm as consumed, was analyzed by a soldier journalist as "bark juice, tar-water, turpentine, brown sugar, lamp-oil and alcohol." And a Yank who on Christmas Day 1864 imbibed so heavily of the government issue that he was not able to entertain his dinner guests wrote in his diary on December 26: "Got up this morning with severe bee hives in my head." Perhaps the most revealing commentaries on the varying quality of intoxicants were the nicknames applied to them in camp. These included "how come you so," "oil of gladness," "tanglefoot," "the ardent," "Oh, be joyful" and "Nockum stiff." [23]

Effects of drinking sprees varied with individuals and beverages. Many Yanks were aroused to extreme pugnacity, as the full guardhouses and numerous bruised heads after payday readily attested. Others became exceedingly gay, lifting their voices in laughter or song, while still others were reduced to misery and tears. A few sank unobtrusively into peaceful stupor and some ran the entire gamut of physical and emotional reaction.

Numerous and varied efforts were made to combat the tide of drinking which beset Union camps. Sutlers and peddlers caught selling liquor in camp forfeited their trading privileges and some were summarily punished. The sutler of a New York regiment who sold a large quantity of whisky to soldiers was drummed out of camp with a dozen liquor bottles dangling from his neck. A peddler who bootlegged "condensed corn" in another camp was forced to stand on a barrel, while his wife, likewise apprehended, was compelled to carry a log.[24]

Some commanders hated whisky so thoroughly that they spilled every drop found in possession of their men, though such extremes were greatly deplored by devotees of drink. When one officer emptied a demijohn found cached in a wagon during a march up the Shenandoah Valley, a thirsty Irishman, who looked ruefully on what seemed to him an unwarranted sacrifice, was heard to remark to a comrade: "Dennis if I'm kilt in the next battle, bring me back and bury me here." [25]

Sundry disciplinary expedients were invoked to restrain drinking. An engineer commander in Grant's army on one occasion sent the numerous drunks corraled on the night following payday to a riverbank where each was stripped, a rope was tied around his waist and he was pitched into the water.[26]

Efforts of officers, chaplains and civilian reformers to combat drinking in the army often were paralleled by temperance activities of the soldiers themselves. Sometimes these were quite informal, consisting simply of a few soldiers resolving to abstain from drink. In other instances entire companies entered into an agreement not to partake of any intoxicant.[27]

Many regiments had temperance associations which solicited abstinence pledges and worked generally to restrict the use of liquor. In the spring of 1864 a temperance movement originating in the Fifth Maine Regiment was said to have spread to numerous other organizations of the Army of the Potomac.[28] But these and all other attempts to curb drinking among the soldiers appear to have been of little avail.

Stealing from comrades, Northern civilians and especially from Southerners was another evil which had considerable prevalency among soldiers, though thievery was never so widespread as profanity, gambling and drinking.[29] A Wisconsin captain wrote from Waterford, Mississippi, November 6, 1862: "Until lately no pig, chicken, cow or sheep stood one chance in ten for its life, if within a mile of camp. . . . Stealing is the most common practice in the army. . . . It will be a great wonder, indeed, if the army does not turn out hundreds of men perfectly irresponsible and thievish, not to speak of uncontrollable licentiousness, who before the war were not bad men." [30] Because of greater opportunity, cavalrymen were worse plunderers than infantrymen. One trooper who accompanied Sherman wrote in his diary while at Lawrenceville, Georgia: "In Covington, Oxford, and indeed all the towns in Georgia, the conduct of our Division has been disgraceful—homes plundered, women insulted and every species of outrage committed." [31] From both cavalrymen and infantrymen South Carolinians, owing to a widespread tendency of Yanks to place first blame on them for bringing on the war, suffered the greatest outrages of all.[32] But even the hapless Indians, whose war guilt could hardly have been used as a pretext, suffered greatly when exposed to soldier villainy and greed. Long after the conflict a woman who had lived in Indian territory invaded by Federal troops told a historical researcher: "During the Civil War the Northern men were so mean to the Choctaw women, they would jerk their earrings from their ears and lock them in one stuffy room together, keeping them there for days." [33]

Vulgarity and obscenity, though not so pervasive as some other evils, were more common than one whose knowledge of soldier life is based on published works might suspect. Nineteenth-century Americans, while in most respects a robust, earthy folk, usually were restrained by an exaggerated sense of delicacy from putting the seamy side of life into print. Soldiers occasionally recorded off-color doings and sayings in their letters and diaries, but when in later years they or their descendants prepared these documents for publication false notions of propriety inclined them to delete items offensive to Victorian tastes.

Reticence concerning evil is not necessarily a proof of righteousness, and ample evidence joins with common sense to justify the conclusion that soldiers of the 1860s differed little from those of today in basic morality.

As previously noted one of the forms in which vulgarity manifested itself was the singing of ribald songs.[34] Occasional references point also to the popularity among campfire groups of racy stories and obscene jokes. Reports of religious workers indicate the circulation among Yanks of licentious books, though details as to character and quantity are not given. A Christian Commission representative told of finding obscene pictures in a tent of some of Grant's soldiers that he visited early in 1865, and the availability of charm-revealing pin-up girls is indicated in the following advertisement from a Chattanooga paper published primarily for Federal troops:

PHOTOGRAPHS, RICH, RARE & RACY

A very beautiful picture of the handsomest woman in the world; a peculiar rich-colored photograph in oil, taken from life; beautiful to behold. This is really a magnificent picture, a perfect gem. She is a bewitching beauty. Price fifty cents. Sent free by mail in a sealed circular envelope.[35]

Some off-color poetry also made the rounds of the campfires, though relatively little of this type of literature has been preserved. Thomas B. Wetmore's saltpeter verses, which originated in the Confederacy as a result of Captain Jonathan Haralson's advertisement for "chamber-lye," crossed over to the Federal lines soon after their composition.[36] No doubt many Yanks recited or sang the racy stanzas to appreciative comrades and some made copies for their homefolk.[37] Northern publishers ran off broadsides of the poetry for circulation among both soldiers and civilians. The version published by H. De Marsan of New York City carried an illustration which is so flagrant in its vulgarity as to prove conclusively that delicacy was not a universal trait in the 1860s.[38] Perhaps the salaciousness was rendered more acceptable to Northerners because of its being pointed at "Secesh" women.

In the correspondence of an Ohio Yank was found a poem, "Jeff Davis' Dream," which for gross obscenity would stand high in erotic literature of any period. But no information was given concerning the source or circulation of this item.[39]

In view of the roughness of camp ways, it is not surprising that Yanks threatened with visits from their womenfolk sometimes revealed signs of panic. John B. Cuzner of the Sixteenth Connecticut Regiment wrote his sweetheart from Portsmouth, Virginia, on August 28, 1863: "Mother wanted to come down and see me she wrote and asked me what I thought of it but the camp is no place for Women there is so much vulgar talk I thought I had got toughened to it, but last night one of the boys got tight and his swearing made my hair stand straight up." A Pennsylvania Yank in reply to his wife's proposal to come to see him in 1861 wrote: "As much as I wood like to See you i must Say this Place is not fit for you to come to. Nearly 600 men 3 miles from Eney town. Some of them . . . are not very particular What they Say if a Strange face Comes among them." Another Yank whose wife had registered hurt at her husband's apparent reluctance to have her visit him offered the following explanation: "You say I don't want you 2 come & see me, that

Courtesy Vermont Historical Society

ARTILLERY PRACTICE, NEAR THE GAINES HOUSE

Courtesy Vermont Historical Society

ON THE THRESHOLD OF FREEDOM
Family of Negroes at the Gaines House

is not so, I should be as glad 2 see you as anybody would 2 see their wife but . . . it is not a fit place for any woman, for there is all kinds of talk, songs and everything not good for them 2 hear." [40]

It is not at all unlikely that the desire of wives to visit camp sprang in part from concern over the constancy of soldier husbands. Well might the home ladies have been alarmed, for association with lewd women was one of the most notorious of soldier sins.

Prostitution was most rampant in the cities frequented by soldiers. The raising of the Northern armies was paralleled by informal mobilization for active service of a vast horde of loose women anxious to capitalize on the sexual longings of the men who donned the blue. In every Northern metropolis these unsavory characters set up shop and peddled their tawdry wares. A Cincinnati newspaper complained in January 1864 that *femmes du monde* had "nearly succeeded in elbowing all decent women from the public promenade" of that city, and in Chicago in 1864 and 1865 an estimated 2,000 lewd women thronged the streets and filled the bawdy houses. Boston was said to have swarmed with strumpets and in New York loose females doubling as waitresses in "concert saloons" became such a nuisance that a state law was passed in 1862 closing these dens of debauchery; but the dispensers of sin evaded the prohibition by simply dropping the concerts, and by 1864 houses in the Broadway area specializing in liquor and lewdness were more numerous and active than ever before. [41]

Washington, because of its prominence as a military center, became a mecca for whores. The local provost marshal in 1862 reported the existence in the capital of 450 houses of ill fame, and the next year the Washington *Star* estimated after a vice survey that prostitutes in the capital area numbered no less than 7,500. This figure did not include mistresses whom some of the better-situated soldiers and officers maintained in such circumstances as to prevent their being counted.

A war correspondent, resident in the capital during the early period of the conflict, stated that at the time of his departure in the fall of 1862 Washington probably "was the most pestiferous hole since the days of Sodom and Gomorrah. The majority of the women on the streets were openly disreputable . . . in fine, every possible form of human vice and crime, dregs, offscourings and scum had flowed into the capitol and made of it a national catch-basin of indescribable foulness." [42]

In a colorful portrayal of the seamy side of life in wartime Washington, Margaret Leech calls the roll of some of the leading prostitutes and bordellos. "Entire blocks on the South side of Pennsylvania Avenue were devoted to the business," she states, while Marble Alley between Pennsylvania and Missouri avenues, a section east and west of the White House, Lafayette Square and portions of Twelfth and Thirteenth streets were other areas noted as resorts for bad women. "One whole section," she adds, "was christened Hooker's Division." Soldiers knew some of the disreputable establishments as "the Ironclad," "Fort Sumter," "Headquarters, U.S.A.," "the Devil's Own," "the Wolf's Den" (run by Mrs. Wolf), "the Haystack" (kept by Mrs. Hay) and "Madam Russell's Bake Oven." [43]

Yanks were almost as reticent as Johnny Rebs about their associations with loose women. But the comments of an exceptional few, mainly in letters to gay blades at home, afford glimpses of amorous adventures. A Massachusetts soldier stationed in Virginia wrote in April 1863 after a visit to Washington: "I had a gay old time I tell you. Lager Beer and a horse and Buggy [and] in the evening Horizontal Refreshments or in Plainer words Riding a Dutch gal—had a good time generally I tell you. I can take care of two correspondents for sometime. . . . I see . . . any quantity women around a Plenty whores. . . . [A] little toten Don't go Bad." [44]

In like vein an artilleryman reported a pleasure jaunt of the next year: "I have just returned from Baltimore where I have been on a short spree with one of our Wagon Masters; and you may guess that we had a good time, for you know it is a sporting place, and fast women are all the go now days. . . . We stoped in Washongton for two days and nights it is a hard place full of Officers, Soldiers and fast Women; we went into some hard places, but came out all right." [45]

Washington and the Northern cities held no monopoly on prostitution, for in the wake of the invading forces moved an army of harlots, with the result that every occupied city became a haven of vice. Louisville, New Orleans, Portsmouth and Norfolk, all of which were teeming with Federal soldiers during most of the war, were notorious centers of prostitution. Of the two last-named towns, a Connecticut soldier in December 1863 wrote: "They call the places sodom and Gormorrow on account of the wickedness . . . both plases are full of bad wimmen, lots of them from Conn." Early in 1865 this same Yank remarked of New Bern, North Carolina, another town noted for military activity: "I have got back from town. I went after a broom, but did not get any for there was so many wimen looking around after men that I bought a pie & got out of the place as quick as I could. Where so many wimen came from

I dont know, this place is worse by double than any place we were in before." [46]

From City Point, Virginia, which in 1864 was an important Federal base, a New Hampshire soldier wrote with more frankness than refinement: "We cannot get any thing here but f—king and that is plenty." [47] And a Pennsylvanian assigned to sentry duty in Savannah, Georgia, wrote a few weeks after the Federal occupation of that city: "I'm on duty every other day; but the reason of it is because there are so many hore houses in town which must have a Sentinel at each door for to keep them Straight." [48]

Chattanooga also had its quota of soldier-frequented bawdy houses, but in scarlet doings it appears to have run a poor second to Nashville and Memphis.[49] The Tennessee capital, which passed into Federal hands before the war was a year old, soon became a favorite resort of fancy women. Its underworld districts of "Slabtown" and "Smoky Row" were scenes of nightly orgies involving convalescent, transient and occupying soldiers. But in Nashville, as elsewhere, the character of worldly women, euphemistically dubbed "Cyprians" by police reporters, ranged from filthy slatterns who served their customers for nominal fees in alleys to tastefully attired and sophisticated concubines kept in comparative luxury by prosperous and discriminating clients. In January 1865 a surgeon in the provost marshal's office reported that in the past six months 393 prostitutes had been registered in Nashville but that, as a result of departures, deaths and ten marriages, the number had been reduced to 236. In concluding the report he stated: "The prostitutes complain that they are not making much money now, because of the scarcity of troops around the city. These women are rapidly leaving in all directions; some profess to be going home, while others are looking out for situations where more money can be obtained where with to bedeck and bedizzen themselves." [50]

In 1863 prostitution became such a problem in Nashville that the post commander, on the score of military necessity, loaded approximately 150 "Cyprians" on a boat and shipped them north. But the authorities of Louisville and Cincinnati raised such a howl that the expulsion order was revoked and after a brief excursion the unwanted cargo was returned by government steamer.[51]

The experience of these travelers was far less exciting than that of two of their associates who shortly after the battle of Nashville took a carriage out to the site of the engagement. As bold in their sightseeing as they were loose in their morals, they ventured so far out as to fall into the hands of some Rebel cavalrymen who, suspecting them to be spies, took them to Franklin and placed them under guard in a hotel. Shortly afterward, when a change in the fortunes of war restored Franklin to Federal control, Yankee horsemen mounted the whores on a mule and brought them safely back to Nashville.[52]

In Memphis prostitution became so flagrant during the Federal occupation that newspapers complained repeatedly of whores—many of them escorted by men wearing the Federal uniform—usurping the streets and monopolizing amusement places; and citizens threatened to rise in wrath and drive them out of the city. In April 1863 the Memphis *Bulletin* complained: "Our city . . . is a perfect bee hive of women of ill fame. The public conveyances have become theirs by right of conquest." A few weeks later an Ohio captain stationed in the city wrote in his diary: "Memphis . . . can boast of being one of the first places of female prostitution on the continent. Virtue is scarcely known within the limits of the city." [53]

The *nymphs du pave* were the more objectionable because of being the scum of the Northern underworld. "Memphis is the great rendezvous for prostitutes and 'pimps,' " the *Bulletin* observed on May 1, 1863. "When a woman could 'ply her vocation' no longer in St. Louis, Chicago or Cincinnati, she was fitted up in her best attire and shipped to Memphis, and in more cases than one to prevent the 'package' from being miscarried, was accompanied by gentlemen (heaven save the mark) with the insignia of rank." [54]

The provost marshal of Memphis in April 1863 issued an order closing houses of ill fame, threatening prostitutes with expulsion and warning military personnel that any of them caught in bawdy establishments would be reported to their commanders.[55] About fifty lewd women were said to have departed for the North after issuance of this order and newspaper comments indicate a general slowing down of vice activities for a period of several months; but by the autumn of 1863 prostitutes again were swarming the streets, and houses of ill repute were operating full blast.[56]

The lewd creatures who accommodated wearers of the blue were not all imported from the North. In all Southern cities, and especially in those that had been frequented by Rebel soldiers, the invading forces were greeted by numerous harlots who quickly saw the error of their past associations or whose loyalty to the Union had been temporarily thwarted. It is only fair to this class of Southerners to state that some of them chose to follow the Rebel armies rather than bow to the conquerors, and that among those who nominally submitted to Federal authority were inveterate Rebels who would occasionally sing the "Bonnie Blue Flag" and let out a whoop for Jeff Davis.[57]

One of the consequences of soldier association with immoral women was a costly tide of venereal infection. Reported cases of venereal disease among white troops whose mean strength for the period covered (May 1, 1861—June 30, 1866) was 468,275 aggregated 182,779 of which 136 proved fatal; colored troops, for whom figures are available only during the period June 30, 1864—June 30, 1866, from a mean strength of 63,645 reported 14,257 venereal cases with 32 fatalities. The breakdown of diseases was as follows:

	White		Colored	
	Cases	*Deaths*	*Cases*	*Deaths*
Syphilis	73,382	123	6,207	28
Gonorrhea	95,833	6	7,060	1
Orchitis	13,564	7	990	3 [58]

A statistician of the Union Medical Department found that during the first year of the war one Yank out of every twelve suffered from venereal disease, and that for the entire period of the conflict the annual venereal rate was 82 cases per 1,000 men.[59]

Prevalency of venereal disease varied with circumstances, the most important of which was the opportunity for lewd associations. Hence, the peaks of infection tended to come during encampments near cities and after furloughs, such as those given to units who signed up for additional terms of service. The incidence of disease was especially heavy among new units composed largely of rural men passing through metropolitan centers en route to the front. Freed of home restraints and facing an uncertain future, such men, inexperienced as they were in the ways of the world, often felt bound to taste the sweets of sin.[60]

Economics was another factor influencing venereal trends. Recruits on their way to war and veterans on re-enlistment furlough frequently had pockets full of bounty money which made them readier prey than usual for the fancy women who thronged metropolitan way stations.

While Confederate records are too scanty to permit a meaningful comparison of Northern and Southern experience, it seems reasonable to conclude that fornication and venereal infection were more common among Yanks than among Rebs. The men in blue were better paid, drew more generous bounties and had easier access to large cities than those who wore the gray. If Rebs had the better record, it was not from superior goodness—for available venereal statistics on a few regiments transferred from the deep South to the vicinity of Richmond in the summer of 1861 show a shocking fondness for the fleshpots—but rather the result of a more limited opportunity for indulging lustful appetites.[61]

Army surgeons deplored the ravages of venereal disease and on their suggestion controlled prostitution was instituted in at least two Southern cities—Memphis and Nashville—with good results. In both cities prostitutes were required to register, submit to periodic examinations and have certificates attesting freedom from infection. The Nashville project, more elaborate than that of Memphis, included the setting up of a hospital for treatment of diseased women. It was maintained from examining fees paid by registered prostitutes. Reports of the surgeon in charge indicate greater concern about soldiers contaminating the women than of the women infecting the men. Passage of the Eleventh and Twelfth Corps through Nashville in November 1863 was said to have caused cases treated in the hospital to jump from a daily average of twelve to twenty-eight. As to ameliorative effects of the system on forces garrisoned at Nashville, no figures are available on enlisted men; but a final report on commissioned personnel shows a decline from "ten to twenty officers at one time" before control was attempted, to no more than one case a month during the last half year that it was in operation.[62]

While evil undoubtedly abounded among the men who wore the blue, army life also had its better and brighter side. It is, of course, impossible to draw any firm conclusions as to the relative prevalency of good and evil. Contemporaries tended to exaggerate the rampancy of sin because wickedness made more of an impression than plain, everyday goodness. On the other hand, postwar commentators, influenced by the mellowing effects of time and anxious to enshrine the saviors of the Union in sacred halls of memory, were inclined to take a far more charitable view of soldier morals than the facts warranted.

No matter how pervasive the forces of darkness, they were always resisted and the usual medium of opposition was religion.

The religion of many Yanks was of the practical, unobtrusive sort, marked by little if any conformity to conventional practices. Of the Third Wisconsin Regiment, Private William F. Goodhue wrote in 1864: "I know but two men in it who are realy Christians by creed, yet I know a hundred . . . [who] like the good Samaritan will help a fellow being when in trouble. . . . the Boys are a good, honest, intelligent sett of men, some exceptions of course, full of fun & frolic; will share their last biscuit yet there is the least religion among them than any Regt I know of." [63] Among individuals who fitted into the pattern described by Private Goodhue was Theodore Upson of the 100th Indiana Regiment. Upson told in his journal of earnestly seeking religion before he joined the army, but without success. After long anguish over his soul's salvation he finally concluded not to worry any more. "I think God knows all about me," he wrote shortly after donning the uniform, "and if he wanted me to feel a change he would have changed me and if I go along trying to do right . . . that is the best I can do and I shall just leave it to Him." Upson's day-by-day record indicates that he lived up to his resolution and that, while never claiming to be religious in the usual sense, throughout his service he was a moral man and an exemplary soldier.[64]

For the most part, however, religion in the army, as among civilians, was of the conventional kind, stressing recognized forms and services, depending heavily for inspiration and direction on a properly accredited ministry and following closely orthodox views of a loving but jealous God.

The Union Army, like the mid-nineteenth-century America from which it was drawn, was overwhelmingly Protestant, with a strong leaning toward evangelical denominations, especially Baptist, Methodist and Presbyterian. Catholics were also well represented, especially among soldiers of Irish, French and Italian extraction. Units from large cities contained a considerable sprinkling of Jews. Among Germans, especially the "Forty-eighters," were to be found a goodly number of "freethinkers" who openly scoffed at orthodox religion of any sort.[65]

Scoffing was not confined to the Germans, however. In almost any regiment there were individuals who laughed at the pious endeavor of their comrades and some even made mockery of worship. An Ohioan told of "Major Tracey and Alf Burnett" of the First Tennessee Cavalry going on a Sunday spree, forming the regiment in a hollow square and holding service, with Burnett doing the preaching. Burnett announced as his text, "And the Whangdoodle mourneth for its first born and fleeth to Mount Hepsidam," and launched into the famous take-off of a frontier sermon. But the listeners, many of whom were piously disposed, were so infuriated by the sacrilege that they booted both offenders out of camp and told them never to return.[66]

Religious activity centered about the chaplains, one of whom was authorized for each regiment, for specified army posts and, after May 1862, for general hospitals. In the volunteer regiments chaplains were selected by vote of the field officers and company commanders, approved by the state governor and officially appointed by the War Department. Hospital chaplains and those serving posts and Regular Army units were designated by the President. Initially, qualifications of chaplains were not specified, but a general order of May 4, 1861, required that each appointee be "a regularly ordained minister of some Christian denomination." When a Jewish chaplain was forced to resign under the terms of this order and the War Department refused appointment to a rabbi selected by a Jewish regiment, a wave of protest arose as a result of which regulations authorized as chaplain the properly certified representative of any "religious denomination." At the same time that it made this change, Congress added the requirement that chaplains must have the endorsement "of some authorized ecclesiastical body or not less than five accredited ministers belonging to said religious denomination." This change was the result of an indiscriminate commissioning early in the war of persons without ecclesiastical standing, many of whom had been attracted to the ministry by the prospects of collecting a chaplain's pay.[67]

Soldier comment on chaplains, while not always reliable, was derogatory far more often than otherwise. The most frequent complaint was neglect of primary duties in favor of lighter activities, especially those that entailed absence from camp. "Our chaplain is not very popular," wrote Private C. B. Thurston from Louisiana in 1863; "he hardly ever has any religious exercises and spends a great part of his time in New Orleans getting the mail, which generally takes longer than most of us think necessary." Private Edward Edes, writing from Fredericksburg in 1862, was even stronger in his denunciation. "I have lost all confidence in the chaplain," he stated; "he lied to me about carrying the mail & does nothing at all but hang around his tent & sort the mail. He never goes around any amongst the men & I think he is nothing but a confounded humbug & nuisance." Along the same lines was the statement of a Hoosier who wrote from Nashville the same year: "Our chaplain . . . started home this morning. A chaplain in the army is usualy of little force except to attend to the mail. I suppose the reason is that the most worthless prechers, those who can not make a good living at home, are the ones who strive to secure the position for the money." [68]

Common soldiers were quick to denounce chaplains who proved battle-shy. Furthermore, they had little use for those who from undue delicacy or a sense of superiority seemed unable to tolerate the hard facts of camp life. "Mr. Cummings is not liked here," wrote a Vermonter to his sister from Virginia in 1863; "he [is] to big fealing and an old maid. the regt does not like him." [69]

Occasionally a Yank would condemn chaplains on the score of their poor sermons. An Illinois private wrote his homefolk that "our minister is no account. he will get up and prais himself and tell the Lord what he must do." A youthful Minnesotan who complained he did not "hear any very good preaching" thought "the people at home have an idea that the soldiers cannot appreciate a good chaplain so that the scum is sent to the army." [70]

Unit commanders sometimes found chaplains less than realistic in disciplinary matters, one colonel deploring their constant interference with every prisoner put in the guardhouse whom they all desired to have released immediately for his supposed penitence.[71] But among officers, as among men, the prevailing complaint was their lack of attention to spiritual duties. A Maine captain who wrote from near New Orleans in 1862 that "our chaplain . . . drives a fast Horse [and] has never spoken of religion . . . since he has been in the army," reported the following conversation between the delinquent minister and General B. F. Butler:

Butler: When did you preach last?
Chaplain: I dont recollect.
Butler: How many funerals have you attended?
Chaplain: I dont know.
Butler: Well, G—d d—n you. You are a disgrace to your profession.[72]

Another company commander, disgusted by the fact that "our chaplain in his usual romping style has been off at Martinsburg for the last ten days," was constrained to state: "Chaplains ought to be abolished in the Army, or else we ought to have a decent energetic one instead of the lazy fellow who pretends to officiate in that place now." [73]

Dislike of chaplains by the common soldier sometimes manifested itself in irreverent pranks. The sergeant major of an Illinois regiment on one occasion assembled the worst soldiers from each of the companies and ordered them to report to the chaplain for prayer. The colonel heard about the order but refused to countermand it, because he thought it an appropriate rebuke for a notorious neglect of duty that had aroused considerable resentment. The chaplain, much to the amusement of all, invited the "hard cases" into his tent and earnestly exhorted them to improve their ways. Even more impudent was an act credited to Bugler Buck Cole of the Seventh Kansas Cavalry. When the chaplain came to recover a book that the bugler had borrowed, Buck was carrying a rail in punishment for some minor breach of discipline. When approached about the book the soldier handed the chaplain his burden and asked him to hold it while he went to get the borrowed volume. But instead of returning he threw himself down on his bunk and went to sleep. On being rebuked by the captain, Buck roguishly answered that he thought the captain's idea was to have the rail carried and that he deemed the chaplain as capable of performing the chore as himself.[74]

Soldier disesteem of chaplains is also apparent in some of the nicknames which were applied to the spiritual counselors, though this was not necessarily true of "Holy Joe" and "Holy John." A Pennsylvania chaplain whose vociferous pledges to pray for the men, preach to them and even fight with them, were completely forgotten when the going became tough, was dubbed "the great thunderer." A New York chaplain who collected a penny for each letter that he carried for the soldiers was referred to as "One Cent by God," while a Massachusetts divine who confined his chaplain's activities almost exclusively to postal duties was hailed as "the postmaster." For reasons that are not ascertainable, but probably because of an undue dwelling on the uncertainty of life, a Maine chaplain was known by his charges as "Death on a Pale Horse." [75]

Antipathy of the soldiers, the dreariness and peril of camp life, homesickness and sundry other factors caused a heavy sloughing off of inferior chaplains after a brief period of service. This exodus together with the raising of standards for procurement led to an improvement in the quality of chaplains in the last two or three years of the war, though benefits were offset by inability of many regiments to keep spiritual counselors.

Many chaplaincies throughout the war were held by good men impelled by lofty motives and thoroughly devoted to the cause of righteousness. Such chaplains held services as regularly as military exigencies would permit, sought out the soldiers for individual counsel, shared fully the hardships and hazards of field service, were practical and discreet in their utterances, set a good example in their conduct and in general helped promote the physical and spiritual welfare of the organizations to which they were assigned.

The better chaplains, far from seeking shelter at the first sign of battle, went forward with their units, blessed the men as they prepared for the assault, nourished and comforted the wounded, performed last rites over the dead, wrote notes of condolence to the homefolk and collected and forwarded personal effects.

Billy Yanks were as quick to register approval of good chaplains as they were to condemn poor ones, and the qualities eliciting admiration were about the same in Civil War times as now. Not the least among these was proof of physical courage. "The new chaplain . . . is well liked by the boys," wrote Private Cyrus Stone shortly after Fredericksburg; "he kept long with the reg. all the time it was on the battle field." Another Yank, likewise stationed on the Virginia front, wrote in his diary on January 17, 1862: "The Rev. Dr. Strong has ben to See me this day and he wanted my Catrage Box and Belt and I gave them to him and I told him he aught to Shoot with Spiritual Balls in Sted of Lead but he says their [they] are not so good for Sesesh as lead ones. Buley for him." [76]

Unstinted devotion to duty, whatever the hazards or difficulties, was another quality highly appreciated by the men. Shortly after Chaplain John A. Brouse joined the 100th Indiana Regiment a private soldier wrote in warm approval of him: "Without a thought of his personal safty he was on the firing line assisting the wounded, praying with the dying, doing all that his great loving heart led him to do. No wonder our boys love our gallant Chaplain." Of another chaplain who faithfully attended his flock during the trying siege of Mobile late in the war, a New York lieutenant wrote: "I am particularly proud & thankful for him as some officers (nonprofessors) used to think & even say that a chaplain was a sort of fifth wheel . . . and even voted against having one, but now all are ready to admit that we could not get along without our Chaplain." [77]

Integrity, sympathy, goodness and a sincere interest in spiritual matters were also regarded as commendable if not essential traits. "He is truly a great and good man," wrote a sergeant of his chaplain in 1862, "an ornament to the cause of Christ and one in whose countenance is seen the radience of the inner light reflected through." Both men and officers, however, seemed to prefer chaplains whose righteousness was unostentatious and who could adapt religion to the realities of soldiering. A minister who deemed it not unbecoming to carry brandy along with the Bible when visiting the battlefield, if not acclaimed by all, was sure to win the hearty blessing of some. And the chaplain who was as zealous in helping the men with small problems of everyday living as he was in denouncing the sins of camp stood a good chance of being accorded a welcome place in the community of soldiers. If he could crown these virtues, as a chaplain of the Forty-fourth Massachusetts did, by the unselfish act of yielding his horse on a hard march to ailing privates while he himself plodded along with the rank and file, he was assured of an unassailable niche in the affections of his comrades.[78]

Of no less importance than the chaplains in influencing religious activities were the commanding officers, especially those of regiments, brigades and divisions. Spiritual efforts in many organizations were seriously hindered by the unco-operative attitude of tactical leaders who deemed religious exercises ineffectual if not a downright nuisance. Such officers were apt to make the chaplain's position an intolerable one by failing to allow time for services in the Sunday schedule and refusing to put at his disposal the necessary facilities for carrying out a constructive religious program.[79]

At the other extreme were officers who, because of pious inclination, belief in practical benefits or both, entered wholeheartedly into the religious activities of their commands. Such a leader was the Reverend Granville Moody, a distinguished minister who commanded the Seventy-fourth Ohio Regiment and who often preached to his own and other commands. An Illinois lieutenant who heard Colonel Moody preach to a soldier audience in Nashville in October 1862 stated: "It was one of the most eloquent sermons I ever heard, one which I shall always remember. I could have listened to him for hours without experiencing the least weariness." [80]

Preaching by commanders was usually limited to those of ministerial background, but laymen occasionally conducted prayer meetings and Bible-study sessions. Among higher commanders who frequently led divine service was General O. O. Howard. A Pennsylvania soldier who heard General Howard twice on the same Sunday said that he made "eloquent addresses and earnest exhortations, also a fervent prayer . . . thus showing to the world that though he ranked high among men, he humbled himself before God." [81] General William S. Rosecrans, a devout Catholic, aggressively promoted the spiritual interests of his men, and both Generals George B. McClellan and Ambrose Burnside, while commanding the Army of the Potomac, issued general orders stressing the importance of divine worship.[82]

Occasionally the religious activities of military personnel were supplemented by the ministrations of casual visitors and itinerant representatives of Northern churches and benevolent organizations. Among distinguished lecturers who toured the camps was Laura S. Haviland. Concerning her address at Ship Island, in 1864, a Vermont officer wrote: "I never listened to a more simple and at the same time more powerful sermon." [83]

Most of the civilian visitors who ministered to the spiritual needs of the soldiers in the latter part of the war were representatives of the Christian Commission. Some of these were full-time agents and others were ministers sponsored by the Commission for brief tours of duty in field and camp. Both types of representatives preached to the soldiers, visited them in their tents for individual conferences, distributed tracts, books, magazines and writing paper, dispensed hot drinks from "coffee wagons," acted as amanuenses and conducted elementary classes in reading and writing. They ministered also to the spiritual and physical needs of the wounded, maintained reading and writing rooms in cities and camps and dispatched soldier mail. Some of the representatives were of the opinion that the men whom they visited were interested only in the gifts distributed, but had they known the high esteem in which soldiers in general held the organization and its services they would have been reassured concerning the value of their work.[84]

Forms of worship varied with sects and circumstances, but the usual Sunday service, ordinarily held in the afternoon to avoid conflict with the weekly inspection in the morning, consisted of Scripture reading, songs and a sermon. Among Protestants, singing inclined to old favorites such as "All Hail the Power of Jesus' Name," "Blest Be the Tie That Binds," "Jesus Lover of My Soul," "Just As I Am without One Plea," "My Faith Looks Up to Thee," "On Jordan's Stormy Banks I Stand," "Rock of Ages," "Sweet Hour of Prayer" and "There Is a Fountain Filled with Blood." [85]

The heart of Sunday services was the sermon, delivered usually by the chaplain. Favorite texts were those stressing the homely virtues, warning against the evils of camp, proclaiming the transforming power of divine grace, calling attention to the precariousness of life and threatening sinners with eternal damnation. Some chaplains made a special point of identifying the Union cause with righteousness and hence bound to have God's blessing; when reverses were met they were interpreted as temporary setbacks resulting from sin, and the vicissitudes of the children of Israel in their epic struggles with ungodly foes were cited as examples.

Reaction of Yanks to camp sermons, as registered in their letters and diaries, ranged from enthusiastic approval to extreme derogation. "He done well" was a private's comment on a much-needed discourse about temperance heard by the Second Wisconsin Cavalry, and a lecture "on the use of tobacco and spirituous liquors" delivered to another group of Badgers was characterized by one of the audience as "real good." [86]

A Maine soldier noted appreciatively that "our chaplain is witty or rather he is brief and breavity is the soul of wit." These endorsements were much more restrained than those of a pious New Yorker who, after listening to sermons by chaplains in Sherman's command, entered in his diary such remarks as "felt much of influences of Spirits," "Received new strength from on high," "feel comforted," "a happy time," and "feel strengthened and blessed." [87]

In opposite vein, a lieutenant who served with Butler in Louisiana found almost intolerable the ill-adapted sermons which the chaplain of his regiment drew from prewar storage. On one occasion, according to the lieutenant, this minister "took an old piece of faded yellow manuscript and . . . discussed *infant baptism* and closed with an earnest appeal, touchingly eloquent, to *mothers*. . . . I'm sure there wasn't a mother in the regiment," added the officer sarcastically, "and not more than two or three infants." Of another chaplain's efforts, a Michigan colonel wrote protestingly to the governor: "He preaches doleful Sermons to the men about the hardships they will have to encounter, the Sickness & death and all the dificulties." [88]

Soldiers who found the chaplains' sermons uninspiring usually did not have to listen to them—a prerogative which most Yanks often chose to exercise—though some commanding officers made attendance of Sunday services compulsory. Members of the Third Pennsylvania Cavalry who indicated a desire to pass up the chaplain's ministrations on a December Sabbath in 1861 "were marched to the guard house where they had the articles of war read to them for punishment." Soldiers usually resented being mustered for church to the beat of drum and screech of fife, especially when the weather was foul and other duties onerous. A typical attitude toward mandatory worship was that expressed by M. P. Larry on a winter Sunday of 1863: "I scarcely write at all but what I expect to hear the bugle call for something and now I am waiting to hear the call to . . . a dry discourse from the chaplain. the sound will call fourth much profanity for it is a biter cold day and the Boys have just come in from inspection and have not had time to get diner or even to get warm." [89]

The religious zeal of a few commanders extended to the point of requiring the saying of prayers at daily dress parade which, according to a soldier, caused "some of the boys [to] sweare . . . cussing the minister the worst kind." [90]

Prayer meetings usually consisted of singing, Bible reading, supplication and testimonials of triumph over Satan. Sometimes these sessions

were led by a chaplain or officer, but frequently the men themselves
conducted the services. Most meetings were held at night and varied in
frequency from one to several times a week.

Another type of worship was the informal singing of sacred songs.
These sessions often had their origin in some lonely Yank lifting his
voice as he sat at the campfire in the evening and the chiming in of a
few comrades. Sometimes the tune was picked up by adjacent units and
even by Rebs with the result that a whole countryside would reverberate
with the strains of a majestic hymn. On such occasions the men "sang
merely because they liked it, the tone was pleasing and the volume of
sound was grand." [91]

In sad contrast to these spontaneous hymn fests were the services
held in burying the dead. These were usually brief, consisting of the
reading of prescribed ritual or simply the offering of a prayer. During
large-scale campaigns, however, casualties were often so numerous and
military exigencies so pressing as to prevent rites of any kind.

Places of worship varied with locale, season and other circumstances.
In balmy weather outdoor meetings were common. Sometimes brush
arbors were built for protection against rain and sun, and to afford
privacy. In winter, soldier worshipers built log chapels and covered them
with canvas or slabs. Late in the conflict the Christian Commission
undertook to furnish canvas roofing to every brigade that would agree
to erect chapel walls. As a result over 100 chapels were built in 1864
and supplied by the Commission with stoves, hymnbooks and other
equipment.[92]

Sometimes Rebel churches were appropriated for soldier use. A
private of the First Minnesota Regiment recorded in his diary on Sun-
day, March 9, 1862, that he went to services conducted by the chaplain
in the Presbyterian church of Charlestown, Maryland. "The fine organ
discoursed sweet music," he wrote. "The church is a fine brick building
with gallery. . . . The Min. 1st run the whole institution, organ & all."
An Ohioan recounted stumbling on a similar, though far less preten-
tious, service at the Cayuga Baptist Church in Mississippi during the
Vicksburg siege. "I expect you would have laughed . . . at the oddity
of the scene," he wrote his sister. "A house full of men in all styles
of military dress almost, some with canteens hung around them and the
most of them as dirty looking as they should be. The audience started
up a hymn, but no go. Some too high and others too fast, and so they
failed. But they succeeded at last. We had a very pleasant meeting
notwithstanding." [93]

Religious activities were promoted by organizations among both chaplains and men. In the spring of 1863, thirty-nine chaplains assembled in Nashville and organized the "Council of Chaplains of the Army of the Cumberland" to discuss common problems and consider means of furthering the spiritual welfare of their respective organizations. Similar groups were formed in other commands. Among the soldiers the most common form of organization was the regimental Christian association. The constitution of "The Christian Association of the Thirteenth Regiment Pennsylvania Volunteers" specified that the object of the organization was the moral and religious improvement of its members and of their fellow soldiers of the regiment and required that members take a pledge to live according to the rule of the Bible. "The Christian Association of the Sixteenth Regiment of Connecticut Volunteers," among other activities, sponsored a series of debates on topics that included: "Resolved: that the present war will be more productive of good than evil" and "Resolved: that Intemperance is a greater evil than war." The negative came off victorious in the first of these arguments, but in the second, after an hour-and-a-half discussion, the affirmative was adjudged winner.[94]

The influence of the Christian associations cannot be definitely stated, but indications point to a limited effectiveness. The same soldier who on January 9, 1864, told of the organization of the Sixteenth Connecticut Association within two weeks reported two drunken sprees, one involving "most of Co. D" and the other resulting in the destruction of "a part of the cook house." [95]

An important aspect of promoting the spiritual welfare of soldiers was the publication and dissemination of religious literature. Religious periodicals circulated in the army aggregated scores of titles and included the *Sunday School Times, Episcopal Recorder, Presbyterian Standard, German Reformed Messenger, Christian Times, Congregationalist, Independent* and *Morning Star.*[96] *The American Messenger*, published and distributed gratuitously by the American Tract Society, was said to have had a circulation in 1864 among soldiers and sailors of 195,000.[97]

Hymnbooks, testaments and scriptural selections were also made available to Yanks in large quantities by the American Bible Society and various other organizations. But tracts were by far the most common form of religious literature dispensed to the soldiers. The American Tract Society was one of the most active organizations in circulating this type of publication, but the United States Christian Commission,

the Young Men's Christian Association and various denominations and
sects also participated in the work.

Tracts varied greatly in character and content. Some pointed up
as pious examples the careers of great soldiers of former times, though
distortion used in a pamphlet like *The Religious Character of Washington* must have been shocking to Yanks who knew history. Others, such
as *The Gambler's Balance Sheet* and *The Temperance Letter* and *Satan's
Baits*, warned against camp vices. Still others were devotional in nature
while many were didactic essays on righteous living.[98]

Yanks showed a preference for tracts having a military slant, such
as *Masked Batteries, A Greater Rebellion, Halt, The Grand Army, The
Soldiers' Talisman, The Widow's Son Enlisting* and *A True Story of
Lucknow*. They also liked hymns and poetry better than prose forms.
Because of variety of content and greater convenience in handling, they
favored bound volumes over leaflets; accordingly, tract publishers issued
as little books with blue or red covers *Soldier's Pocket Book, Soldier's
Text Book, Soldier's Prayer Book* and *The Soldier from Home*, all of
which were well received, as was a bound collection of prize tracts issued
by the American Tract Society.[99]

Some tracts were printed in several languages to meet the needs of
foreign-nationality groups. German soldiers, who had a reputation for
unusual diligence in reading as well as a preference for "stronger meat"
than native Americans, found special pleasure in reading Hufacker's
sermon entitled *Wie die Religion taeglich zu ueben sey* (How to Practice Religion in Daily Life).[100]

The stock of some tract dispensers included large quantities of
Uncle Tom's Cabin and copies of this work apparently were made available to Yanks by the thousands in the latter part of the war. Records
of the United States Christian Commission show that the Protestant
Episcopal Book Society in August 1864 sent 47,000 copies of Mrs.
Stowe's book to the central office of the commission at Philadelphia and
that in August and September the central office forwarded 11,000 copies
to its representatives in St. Louis, 5,000 to Nashville, 2,000 to Baltimore
and 2,000 to Cincinnati.[101]

Distributing agents and some of the chaplains claimed that tracts
were eagerly received, widely read and productive of distinct improvement in religion and morals. But soldier letters and diaries do not sustain these conclusions. Billy Yanks hardly ever mentioned religious literature of any kind, and their comment on the general tone of camp life

leaves the impression that the combined influences of spiritual agencies operative in the Union Army were of little avail in combating the tide of evil.

This does not mean that religious endeavor was always defeated, for many organizations experienced periods of spiritual awakening. A "strong revival" was said to have occurred in the Fifth Maine Regiment during its encampment in Virginia in the second winter of the war, and a Hoosier sergeant stationed near Vicksburg noted in his diary August 8, 1863: "Have a protracted meeting in our Division. Very warm." [102]

Religious interest tended to quicken when large-scale fighting was in prospect. The imminence of an unprecedented spilling of blood was doubtless responsible in part for the unusual flurry of revivals that occurred in various parts of the army during the early months of 1864 and 1865. But these movements were local in character, usually restricted to regiments and brigades and rarely if ever overleaping the boundaries of divisions. They were also limited in duration and in harvest of converts. An Eastern soldier who in January 1865 wrote that "theaire is a great revival of religion here" added that eight or ten of his company had "got religion," and a Yank stationed in the Department of the Gulf, who about the same time reported "constant revival" in a camp comprising 6,000 soldiers, specified that "not less than 20 have received salvation." [103]

CHAPTER XI

THE SPIRITS EBB AND FLOW

BILLY YANKS, like Johnny Rebs, donned their uniforms in 1861 with tremendous enthusiasm. They rushed to arms in such numbers as to swamp state and Federal authorities who were trying desperately to provide equipment and to gear the nation for conflict. The Union volunteers, thinking that the Rebels would quickly be forced to submission, were extremely anxious to have a part in the first fight. For it was their strong opinion that the first battle also would be the last one, and hence to miss the initial encounter would be to have no sniff of powder.

This flood tide of enthusiasm was destined to be short-lived, and before many months had passed, the government, from rejecting clamors for service, was to be begging soldiers. In time conscription was to be invoked, but loopholes which allowed draftees to buy exemption from service for $300 or hire substitutes to go in their stead greatly impaired the effectiveness of this bungled first effort of the nation to press its citizens into uniform.

The morale of the army was nearly always better than that of the homefolk. But, even so, the spirit of the fighting forces drooped markedly after a few months of conflict and thereafter rose and fell periodically until the end of the war. Morale varied considerably among individuals and commands, but a general pattern existed, the tracing of which will be the first concern of this chapter.

Morale of some of the first volunteers began to sag before midsummer of 1861, owing to boredom of camp routine, discomfort of heat and pests and inability to engage the foe in the battle that would end the war and send the soldiers home in triumph. On July 14, 1861, a Pennsylvania private of a three-months regiment wrote:

The Erie Regiment is one grand fizzle out. We left home full of fight, earnestly desiring a chance to mingle with the hosts that fight under the Stars and Stripes. For two months we drilled steadily, patiently waiting the expected orders which never came but to be countermanded. We have now come to the conclusion that we will have no chance, and we are waiting in sullen silence and impatience for the expiration of our time.[1]

First Manassas satisfied the volunteers' craving for action but disappointed their expectations of bringing the war to a victorious conclusion. The immediate effect of the defeat was dispiriting, but after the initial shock had passed, soldiers in both East and West seemed to be seized with a stubborn determination to recover lost prestige and to push the conflict with enhanced vigor. Gone was the illusion of a quick and easy triumph, and in its place there developed a deep earnestness to prove the North's superiority. This sentiment was reflected by a Western soldier who wrote not long after First Bull Run: "I shall See the thing played out, or die in the attempt; I am not generally very free to pitch in; but I am awful to hang on." [2]

In the East, McClellan's rigorous training program breathed life into the army and helped sustain morale at a relatively high level through the autumn of 1861. But as fall passed into winter without major commitment of the large force that had been so zealously prepared, discontent was manifest and spirits began to droop. Morale was further depressed as the troops, many of whom were inadequately clothed, began to experience for the first time the unpleasantness of wintering in the field. An Ohioan wrote his homefolk from camp in mid-December that "when we get up here in the morning we shiver like Belshazzier did when he seen the vishion on the wall." [3] Countless other Yanks stationed in the North and along the far-reaching Southern border had similar misery.

Spirits took an upward turn in the early part of 1862, owing to the bustle and stir of preparations for the Gulf and Yorktown expeditions and the heartening triumphs in the West and along the Eastern coast. Shortly after Grant's capture of Forts Henry and Donelson one Yank wrote from the Virginia front that "the news of the late brilliant victories . . . had aroused the fighting spirits of the whole army," while another gloated: "The Old Flag waves in triumph oe'r its foes. Co E. give 3 cheers & a 'tiger.' . . . Big grist of glorious news for *one* morning. The 'Anaconda' tightens well. Secession soon will go to— . . . We are growing fat on hard bread, victory & hope." A month later a participant in the Western exploits informed his wife that "we are driveing things right endways I think they [the Rebs] will have to give it up for a bad job it is gratifying to us solgers to hear of so many victories." [4]

Union triumphs at New Bern, North Carolina, Fort Pulaski, Georgia,

New Orleans, Shiloh and Memphis, and McClellan's initial successes on the Virginia peninsula helped sustain morale throughout the spring of 1862. But the stalemate and failure, sickness and suffering, toil and weariness that came with the summer months caused a recession. Many a Yank lost his enthusiasm, if not his patriotism, in the steaming lowlands near Richmond and New Orleans and the hot hills and valleys of the country about Corinth, Mississippi. The depression which overtook the army during this period was strikingly evidenced in the instance of Alfred Davenport, a soldier of McClellan's force. On May 23, 1862, Davenport wrote his homefolk from Cold Harbor: "We are all now in hopes that our trials will soon be at an end & that Richmond will be taken & we will be discharged, which is looked forward to as a shining light & alone keeps us up." On June 1, the day after Fair Oaks, he urged his mother not to let a brother enlist, stating that it would be better for him to be dead. "There are men who have been all over the world, in every station in life, with us," he added, but "[I] have not seen one that does not pine to get away, but honorably." The Seven Days' fighting and the failure to take Richmond plunged him into deeper gloom. On July 8, 1862, he stated: "Sometimes I think that I will try to get away as many have done, it is a horrible life, worse than State Prison, & there are few here but what would like to have some wound to get out of it." Four days later, as the army lay in misery at Harrison's Landing, he wrote despondingly: "The ringing laugh is now seldom heard, but men go dragging along with their long, sad & careworn faces, nothing to do but kill time and answer Roll Calls, with occasionally a little fatigue duty . . . each man doing as little as he can and stealing away if possible." [5]

Gloom abated somewhat in the autumn with the stopping of Lee's and Bragg's offensives in Maryland and Kentucky. But the respite was only an Indian summer, for in the winter of 1862-1863 soldier morale reached its nadir.

The extreme spiritual defection manifested itself in a flood of desertion and absence without leave. In February 1863 Hooker reported that twenty-five per cent of his army was absent and that desertions averaged several hundred a day. Around Union campfires everywhere criticism of the government was rife, and talk of quitting the service was common. During Burnside's brief command of the Eastern army, efforts of regimental officers to elicit cheers from their men as he made the round of camps sometimes produced open manifestations of disrespect. [6]

Morale may have been worse among Eastern commands than in

others but in this critical period it sank to a deplorably low level everywhere. In Grant's army members of one regiment when ordered to embark for the Vicksburg area stacked their arms and swore that they would not go.[7]

Dissatisfaction with army service became so great during this period that a rash of self-mutilation broke out among the soldiers. An Illinois Yank shot off the trigger finger of his right hand and a Vermont soldier got rid of three fingers while on picket by setting off his musket with a stick. A Massachusetts private, after failing in an effort to blow his toe off, succeeded a few days later in injuring his right forefinger to such an extent that it had to be amputated. The evil of self-injury became so widespread that authorities ceased granting discharges to those found guilty of the practice.[8]

This morale crisis of the war's second winter was the result of several influences. First was the accumulation of military reverses. In the East the failure to take Richmond had been followed by the disaster of Second Manassas, the escape of Lee and his army after an auspicious beginning at Antietam and then the futile and blundering effusion of blood at Fredericksburg with the humiliating sequel of Burnside's notorious "mud march." In Middle Tennessee Rosecrans' long-awaited advance bogged down at Murfreesboro after an enormous spilling of blood in the battle of Stone's River. Farther West, Grant's two-pronged thrust at Vicksburg was thwarted by Van Dorn's surprise attack on the Federal base at Holly Springs and Sherman's failure to penetrate the Confederate lines at Chickasaw Bayou. The capture of Arkansas Post on January 11, 1863, brightened the outlook, but the effects were soon lost as Grant's men floundered in the mud trying unsuccessfully to get at Vicksburg by canals and passes.

These reverses were the more depressing because of their costliness in lives, the absence of major successes to offset them and the discouraging outlook which they and the long train of prior setbacks gave to the future. Gloom was further enhanced by signs of defection on the home front, dwindling confidence in political leadership and repeated demonstrations of incompetency among military commanders. The effect of these combined influences was to produce in the minds of many Yanks a conviction that the prospect of Northern victory was too hopeless to justify further slaughter and that the South's independence should be conceded.

The extreme demoralization and the various factors contributing to it were vividly revealed in letters issuing from camp in the period December 1862—March 1863. Three days before Christmas, M. N. Collins, a Maine officer, wrote from camp opposite Fredericksburg:

> The newspapers say that the army is eager for another fight; it is false; there is not a private in the army that would not rejoice to know that no more battles were to be fought. They are heartily sick of battles that produce no results.[9]

In like vein Edward Edes, a Massachusetts private, wrote a few days later:

> It is my firm belief that the war will be settled in some way by compromise. That will be better than for any more lives to be thrown away so extravagantly by incompetent leaders & ambitious politicians. As far as I can judge from what I have heard, there is very little zeal or patriotism in the army now, the men have seen so much more of defeat than of victory & so much bloody slaughter that all patriotism is played out. Even in this regiment only out five months . . . I dont believe there are twenty men but are heartily sick of war & want to go home.[10]

Letters written by Grant's soldiers had the same tone. On February 1, 1863, Private John N. Moulton wrote his sister from near Vicksburg:

> I am in moderate health . . . as to spirits I cannot Boast of their being very high. There is the most down cast looking set of men here that I ever saw in my life. the men are Beginning to talk opernly and to curse the officers and leaders and if the[y] go much farther I fear for the result. they are pretty well divided and nothing But fear keeps them under. . . . At Walnut hills . . . the whole thing was Badly managed by Sherman, and General Steel, my division commander, was drunk or he never would have ordered general Thayer to take us where he did. My regiment was within 70 yards of the Breast works at the Arkansas Post when the white flag was run up and we was preparing to make another charge. dam this charging I dont like it. More than that there was no kneed of it at the Post at all only to give certain men a Big name that was all.[11]

Six weeks later, after shivering through a long period of heavy rain which converted the low-lying country into a sea of mud, with disease rampant, rations short and recreational facilities severely circumscribed, this Yank lamented:

> The cannal is a failure, the men all dying off pretty fast if you call 47 in two days anything out of one regiment. The 34th Iowa lost that

amount. . . . I am lonesome and down hearted in Spite of my Self. I am tired of Blood Shed and have Saw Enough of it.[12]

Moulton's complaint was the more significant in that his morale during nearly two years of prior service had been consistently high.

That the gloom was not confined to Grant's and Burnside's armies is clearly indicated by the following letter, written from Nashville on February 3, 1863, by one of Rosecrans' soldiers:

The troops are becoming very much disheartened in consequence of recent disasters in the field and the bad management of the War Department. When we Enthusiastically rushed into the ranks at our Country's call, we all Expected to witness the last dying struggles of treason and Rebellion Ere this . . . But in these Expectations we have been disappointed. Over 200,000 of our noble soldiers sleep in the silent grave. Almost countless millions of treasure has been Expended in the Unsuccessful Effort of the Government to put down this Rebellion. But after all this sacrifice of valuable life and money we are no nearer the goal . . . than we were at the first booming of Sumter's guns. You can judge how we feel here in the 86th [Illinois] when I tell you that only 8 men in Co. K approve the policy and proclamation of Mr. Lincoln. Many are deserting 23 men from one Company in this brigade have deserted. . . . The unfortunate division at the North is the worst feature of the times. The army of traitors at the North is truly formidable. They ought to hang higher than Haman. Many of the boys here are in favor of a Compromise, some are of the opinion that the Southern Confederacy will soon be recognized by the U. S. Alas! for our beloved Republic! [13]

A recurring note in these and many other letters, written in the depths of gloom that marked the conflict's second winter, was loss of confidence in leadership, both political and military. Charges of incompetency, mismanagement and corruption were freely hurled at many incumbents in high position, though Lincoln usually was excepted from the roll of the damned. Two days before Christmas 1862 a Maine soldier stationed in Virginia wrote his sister:

I have nothing cheerfull to write. All though I am wel and able to do duty I am in a very unhapy state of mind. That delusive fantom of hope that has so long burnt dim has at last vanished and there is nothing to be seen in the distance but darkness and gloom. The great cause of liberty has been managed by Knaves and fools the whole show has ben corruption, the result disaster, shame and disgrace. . . . I am always ready to undergo the privations of a soldiers life if it is to do any good, but evry thing looks dark, not becaus the south are strong but becaus our leaders are incompitent and unprincipled. The whole thing is roton to the core.[14]

Admirers of McClellan—and no high-ranking general was so popular as he among the troops—saw in the removal of that leader an indication of evil influences in government.[15] Resentment of his final displacement was enhanced by the miserable failure of his successor and the general darkening of the military outlook. "I believe the wrong thing was done in the removal of McClellan," wrote Private Samuel Croft from Falmouth, Virginia, on December 21; " 'Little Mac' is the only man we have got who can match the Rebel Gen'l Lee. McClellan whipped the Rebs every time he fought them." On February 3, 1863, he added: "The North have kicked out the best and only man capable of copeing with Lee when they kicked out 'little Mac.' " In similar vein, Herman Chauncey Newhall wrote on December 28, 1862: "If we had the rebel generals to command this army more would be done. . . . They will have to give us McClellan before this army will be as efficient as it was before the last affair at Fredericksburg. . . . I am disgusted." [16]

Others regarded the Emancipation Proclamation and the calling of Negroes to arms as evidence that the radical element was corrupting the government and converting the war into an abolitionist crusade. The thought of fighting a "nigger war" was utterly abhorrent to some, and while the ultimate result of the policy of freeing and arming the blacks was helpful to morale, immediate effects, because of the state of mind which pervaded the country at the time, were probably more depressing than inspiriting. On February 22, 1863, a Pennsylvania private wrote that he was thoroughly tired of the war and that if he had known the issue was to be the freeing of the slaves, as he was inclined now to think it had become, he "would not have mingled with the dirty job." About the same time an Illinois soldier deplored the fact of the radicals having forced upon the administration the twin evils of emancipation and Negro recruiting. "I do not care how quick this war is brought to a close," he stated. "I have slept on the soft side of a board, in the mud & every other place that was lousy & dirty . . . drunk out of goose ponds, Horse tracks &c for the last 18 months, all for the poor nigger, and I have yet to see the first one that I think has been benefited by it." [17] The reactions of these soldiers to the change of policy toward the Negro, as previously stated, was mild in comparison with that of some of their comrades.

Further evidence of mismanagement was seen in the provisions of the conscription act which was going through the Congressional mill in the dark days of early 1863. Especially objectionable to soldiers, and extremely depressing to their morale, was the commutation clause which favored the rich over the poor. "I believe that a *poor* man's life is as dear as a rich man's," angrily wrote one Yank a short time after the law's enactment. "The blood of a poor man is as precious as that of the wealthy," he added, and the rich, having more at stake, "should sacrifice more in suppressing this infernal Rebellion and in restoring the Union and thereby save their property, homes and liberty." [18]

Though the cloud of gloom which engulfed the Union forces in the winter of 1862-1863 was larger, darker and more persistent than any that preceded or followed, it was finally dispelled, save for a thin mist and a few lingering thunderheads, by fresh breezes arising from the stubborn resolve, the reviving hope and the pure patriotism of the blundering but generally well-meaning devotees of the Union.

Several factors contributed to restoration of soldier morale. In the East, Hooker's dynamic leadership, which quickly manifested itself in such tangible matters as improvement of rations, replacement of worn-out clothing and equipment, renewal of ceremonies and drill and tightening of discipline, had a tremendous effect.[19] In the West the heartbreaking and ineffectual tussles with Ole Man River were finally abandoned in favor of a roundabout approach to Vicksburg by higher ground. Everywhere spring weather, increased activity and the prospect of aggressive campaigning helped Yanks to shake off their gloom and to get a new grip on life. Flurries of volunteering inspired by the draft act and the setting up of the Provost Marshal General's Bureau to implement conscription and apprehend deserters promised a strengthening of the armed forces.[20] Finally improvement of health which came with the passing of winter also helped mightily to restore drooping spirits.[21]

The brightening outlook was strikingly reflected in soldier letters. One of Burnside's New Jersey privates, who in January had despaired of victory, in April reported that "the blind acts of unqualified generals and statesmen" had not "chilled my patriotism in the least." A comrade from a Maine regiment, who in February had confessed that he and most of the other soldiers were in a deplorable state of morale, stated in April that "the Army is in as good if not better condition than I have ever before seen it." A third member of the Army of the Potomac whose spirit had sunk very low immediately after Fredericksburg wrote in the spring, "evry one seems ready to go into the fight with the note victory or death. this is fare different from the state of things before Hooker took command." [22]

Expressions of similar tone emanated from Western camps. For example, an Ohioan stationed at Milliken's Bend wrote on March 19,

1863: "A dark cloud has passed over and thank God the bright sky once more appears. You have no idea of the hard talk that I have heard come from the discouraged soldiers a short time since, but all that has passed. . . . You have never seen such a great change. . . . The men are in excellent spirits." [23]

The upward surge of spirit that came in the spring was so strong that it carried the Eastern army through the Chancellorsville disaster with flying colors. A typical reaction to this setback was that registered by a Minnesota participant who wrote in his diary on May 6, 1863: "It seems we have not *exactly* whipped the Secesh *this time*. The 11th Army Corps is said to have behaved badly. I suppose we will have to recruit up a little & 'try again.' " [24]

Two reasons for the failure of morale to sag in the East after Chancellorsville were the continuing activity and the shift of the battleground to the North, thus giving to Yanks the challenge of defending their homes against invasion. On July 1, 1863, a Federal surgeon wrote from near Gettysburg that "our men are three times as Enthusiastic as they have been in Virginia. The idea that Pennsylvania is invaded and that we are fighting on our own soil proper, influences them strongly. They are more determined than I have ever before seen them." [25] Still, as many Yanks realized, the thing most needed to buoy morale to a desirable level was success in the field.[26] That success came in overflowing measure at Gettysburg and Vicksburg.[27] The effects were tremendous. From Fort St. Philip, Louisiana, to cite only one of the many exultant expressions, a Maine Yank wrote:

Three times three for Grant and Banks! The Confederacy "played out!" Day before yesterday we received official news of the fall of Vicksburg, today we have news . . . that Hooker has whipped Lee. I wish you could have been here to see the boys when they got the news. Cheer after cheer for nearly an hour, one hundred guns from the two forts, everyone seemed as happy as they would be to hear of the death of a rich uncle making them his heirs.[28]

With these victories the lingering fear of Rebel invincibility that had bedeviled many Yanks was dispelled and in its place came a renewed faith in the triumph of Union arms. This confidence made hardships more tolerable and built up a spiritual reserve for the long pull ahead.

Morale receded considerably in the winter of 1863-1864, though it did not sink to nearly so low level as that following Fredericksburg. Factors in the decline were the failure of the Rebels to show the expected readiness to throw in the sponge, the setbacks at Chickamauga and Mine Run and the ensuant hardships experienced by many soldiers, especially those participating in the Chattanooga and Knoxville campaigns. Spirits rose with the coming of spring and the renewal of large-scale operations designed to break the back of Southern resistance.

But when these gigantic efforts of 1864 resulted in overt failure as in the Red River campaign, in blood-soaked stalemate as in Virginia and in only partial success as in Georgia, enthusiasm fell sharply and discontent again became rife in the army. The widespread defection on the home front did not help the situation. Especially dispiriting to the soldiers was the wholesale evasion of military duty by people of means who instead of taking their places in the ranks sent substitutes gathered from wharves and brothels or sorry specimens of humanity lured into the service by enormous bounties. Many of the recruits thus obtained were chronic "bounty jumpers" who had no interest in the war and who deserted soon after enlistment. Those who continued in the service were often despised as low characters and regarded more as liabilities than as assets. Frank Wilkeson after the war cited as the "potent cause of demoralization" in the last year of the conflict "the worthless character of the recruits who were supplied to the army" during that period. They were "the weak, the diseased, the feeble-minded," he added, "the scum of the slums of the great European and American cities . . . the rakings of rural almshouses and the never-do-wells of villages . . . the faint-hearted and stupid. . . . Many were irreclaimable blackguards. . . . They were moral lepers. They were conscienceless, cowardly scoundrels, and the clean-minded American and Irish and German volunteers would not associate with them." [29]

The capture of Atlanta early in September, Sheridan's victories in the Shenandoah Valley a few weeks later and Lincoln's decisive triumph at the polls in November lifted ebbing spirits enormously. Some complaint was voiced in the camps about persistent shirking on the home front as evidenced in the continuing poor quality of recruits, but the general tone of soldier letters in the latter part of 1864 evidenced a growing conviction that despite evasion, disloyalty, mismanagement and all other handicaps the North was bound to win the war and that soon.

Sherman's march through Georgia and South Carolina raised the morale of his men to unprecedented heights, and this spectacular feat, together with Thomas' thumping victory over Hood at Nashville, gave heart to soldiers everywhere. Then Grant broke through the Confederate lines at Petersburg and a few days later forced Lee's surrender at Appomattox. Spirits soared to their highest peak and joy in Federal camps was without restraint.[30]

In tracing the general course of morale, it has been indicated that important factors influencing soldier spirit were the military situation, attitude toward the government's conduct of the war, degree of confidence in civilian patriotism, attitude toward military leadership, discipline, health, comfort and home conditions. Some of these factors require additional comment, especially as they affected individual soldiers, and others need to be added to the list.

Health had a tremendous bearing on morale. The presence in camp of large numbers of ailing soldiers was depressing to those who were well, for extra duties were often required of them to maintain the usual routine and assist in the care of the sick. Moreover, the ill were a constant reminder of the precariousness of one's own health; and heavy mortality among those stricken, evidenced by numerous processions to burial grounds to the doleful tunes of the dead march, gave emphasis to the tenuousness of life.[31] The prospect of dying far away from home, in a hostile country and among strangers, was far more terrifying than that of perishing on the field of battle, and even the strongest soldiers became jittery and despondent during an epidemic of measles or typhoid.

The sick were especially prone to defection of spirit. Even the most patriotic and uncomplaining of Yanks sometimes were converted by illness into creatures of the most abject gloom. William A. Harper of the Forty-seventh Indiana Regiment is a case in point. Harper entered the service in 1861 with strong belief in the rightness of the Union cause and firm confidence in its success. His spirit remained high through the first nine months of service. But after his transfer to Memphis, in the summer of 1862, his health wavered and he began to find fault with the conduct of the war. Early in 1863, while stationed at Helena, Arkansas, he became seriously afflicted and had to go to the hospital. That his spirit suffered no less than his body is suggested by the following letter which he wrote to his wife shortly after entering the hospital:

This is a world of trouble, sorow and afliction. We must look forward to a beter day although it seems that the whole human rase is lost in sin. Our country it seems is allmost gon to ruin it looks too me when I get too studieing over maters and the condition of maters that there certainly [is] a downfall of this nation.[32]

After Harper rejoined his unit his outlook began to improve rapidly and by the time he recovered his full physical strength he had regained his high morale also. Vicksburg and Gettysburg doubtless aided in both physical and spiritual restoration, but his morale continued good, despite subsequent fluctuations in the fortunes of war, throughout the remainder of the conflict. In Harper's instance, as in many others, health was of transcendent importance to morale.

Some Yanks were exceedingly sensitive to the attitude and conduct of civilians with reference to the war. They bitterly resented able-bodied males buying exemption from service and money-mad scoundrels pawning off on the government at exorbitant prices shoddy uniforms, worthless guns and rotten food which undermined the health and endangered the lives of soldiers fighting on token wages to protect those very swindlers. But even more damaging to morale was the specter of disloyalty which appeared on the horizon in the form of Copperheadism and other movements that had, or seemed to have, compromise with Rebels as their end. These movements were regarded by most Yanks as stabs in the back in that they gave aid and comfort to the enemy and prolonged the war. "If the mouths of the Northern traitor could only be shut," wrote one of Grant's sorely tried veterans in January 1863, "the rebellion would not last Sixty days longer. The hope of Rebellion in the free States is the only thing that keeps them up," he added, "and our friends at home are injuring the efficiency of the Army every day." Another Yank wrote indignantly from Georgia in April 1864: "Dont send me the Standard any more as It Is too much Secession for me to read while I am fighting in the front & they a talking in the rear of us men." [33]

Other soldiers were less restrained in their denunciation of the appeasers. "I think the rebels at home far meaner than the rebels of the South," wrote an Illinois Yank from Middle Tennessee in March 1863. "The latter has courage enough to meet me in open conflict while the former poor miserable sneaking hound, seeks to creep up in the dark and strike his dagger at my heart." [34]

Another Illinois soldier delivered himself thus: "You may tell evry man of Doubtful Loyalty for me up there in the north that he is meaner than any son of a bitch in hell. I would rather shoot one of them a great teal [more] than one living here. . . . there may be some excuse for the one but not for the other." [35]

Scorching comments about home "traitors" were not confined to Midwesterners. A New Yorker's reaction to the report of Lee's move into Pennsylvania was this:

I rejoice, & hope Lee will invade all the Copperhead territory of those border free states. I think a little smell of gun powder & a good taste of the bitter realities of war will have a salutary Effect upon their treason loving souls. I want no innocent women & children to suffer, but those God provoking, hell-deserving "Copperheads"—"Vallandighammers," I fain would see weltering in their own gore—The Devil ought to be ashamed of them.[36]

Another New Yorker, who on March 3, 1863, had expressed a desire "to send a couple of double charges of cannister in amongst . . . the Copperheads," wrote a friend in New York City after the draft riots of mid-July 1863:

Hang the leaders . . . hang them, damn them hang them. . . . I would show them no mercy. . . . What a pity there was not force enough to cut them down in heaps. How I would like to stand by a gun and mow them down.[37]

The soldiers, whose denunciatory statements have been cited, were so infuriated by the thought of disloyalty on the home front that their anger seemed to kindle their resolve to push the war to a successful conclusion and then give Northern traitors their due. But in other instances, particularly where spirits were already sagging from other causes, reports of compromise activities had an opposite effect. An Ohioan of Grant's army, immersed in the gloom that accompanied the canal-digging ventures, wrote from Young's Point, Louisiana, on February 11, 1863:

We got a lot of Cinnati papers the other day. thay dun us a hepe of goode to reade them. thay hade a hepe of nues in them a bote peas. the peopple in the north donte like the idy of freeing the nigers and be gode i donte eather. . . . Vallandigham tolde them thay code make peas rite now as well as in a year or 2 years for to whipe the Soth thay never can doo it in the worlde nor thay cante eather. this hole armey is afel dissadesfide and donte cear how the war goes. thay all Say thay ar going home this Spring if things donte look beter than thay doo now.[38]

In other letters this soldier wrote of his intention to desert and even told how he proposed to get away. A shell killed him on May 1, 1863, and thus brought an honorable end to his service. It seems not unlikely that he would have taken leave of the army early in the year had not his home-folk manifested concern over his plans. Certainly the Copperhead-inspired talk of peace and of the futility of continuing the war helped break down his will to fight and contributed to the desertion of many of his fellows-in-arms.[39]

Hardship was another factor which had an important bearing on morale. A short period of service sufficed to convince many Yanks that military life was far more onerous than they had imagined and some of them began to pine for their former status. "Soldiering does well for a few months," wrote one volunteer after a brief residence in camp, but "it dont ware like farming." Another, chafing under the deprivations and discomforts of a winter on the Virginia front, remarked: "I aint home Sick, i dont no what home Sick is, but i no the diferens between home and Soldieren." [40]

Others were more acerb in registering their disillusionment. "Uncal Sam has [not] as much care for his Nefews as he has for one of his mules or horses," wrote an Eastern soldier disgustedly after several stints of standing out in the rain waiting for "read tape" to unwind itself. A Westerner exposed to similar trials stated: "You can compare the Soldier to a mule he has to go when he is told to and never knows when he will stop untill his driver tells him, it makes no difference how the roads is or how hard it rains nor whether it is light or dark and he eats what is given him without the power to get any better." Soldiers in eating "are like a hog," he added, "as every one tries to get it all and worse than the Devil in evry other respect." [41]

A goodly portion of Yanks thus depressed by initial hardships eventually achieved a tolerable degree of equanimity. But a few, unable to make the adjustment, wallowed in gloom during each recurring period of unusual discomfort, comparing themselves to prisoners, slaves or friendless orphans.

Hardship was the more difficult to endure when it seemed to be the result of mismanagement or evil design. Much of the suffering to which the soldiers were subjected could have been avoided, of course, had supply services been better organized, logistics more refined or officers more competent. Some soldiers, of course, were so constituted that they attributed any forced march or diminution of rations, however unavoidable, as willful mistreatment by malicious superiors.

On the other hand, occasional instances were to be found, in the ranks, of rugged souls seemingly impervious to hardship. Among these was H. R. Leonard of Indiana who wrote from Maryland in November 1861:

Courtesy Prints and Photographs Division Library of Congress

RELIGIOUS SERVICE IN CAMP

Chaplain L. F. Drake preaching to Thirty-first Ohio Volunteers at Camp Dick Robinson, Kentucky, Nov. 10, 1861

SOLDIERS' FRIENDS

U. S. Sanitary Commission Quarters, Brandy Station, Virginia

I have layed down in the rain and slep all night and got up in the morning driping wet cold and Hungry, but I would see my comrads in the same fix and think it no worse for me than for them. . . . We have all the chestnuts and persimmons we can Eate Every day. I have not been hungry cince we quit marching. We can live in the woods like hogs.[42]

Likewise of this stripe was C. B. Thurston of Maine who wrote his home-folk from Louisiana in 1863:

I expect that when my time is out I shall want to reenlist. I shan't feel at home out of the Army. I shall wake up in the morning and want to know if the drums have beaten and be asking for a pass when I want to go up town. . . . A greater part of the soldiers I have seen would leave the army if they possibly could. . . . I enlisted for three years and will stay my time out unless I am sick. I believe it to be the duty if not a pleasure . . . to help crush this rebellion.[43]

In this staunch group also was Vance Nelson of Ohio who remarked amid the discomforts of his first winter in camp:

We have some hard times but it is Nessary we should learn to indure hard ships in order that we may be good soldiers. We came out here to defend the best government that the sun ever shone on and this should stimulat any man to take misuseag if we have to eat hard crackers we must remembe that the union must be peserved the stars and stripes must Wave over the land of the free and the home of the brave. this is t[h]e sentiment union now and foreve one and inseparable.[44]

Home circumstances had an enormous influence on morale. A soldier who was confident that his loved ones were healthy, adequately provided with food, clothing and shelter, well treated by relatives and neighbors, constant in their affections and optimistic in their outlook was better satisfied with his lot than one whose family conditions were a source of anxiety. Letters bringing any sort of bad news from home were apt to be upsetting, and if they told of want, sickness, neglect or persecution by kinfolk, unfriendliness of neighbors, or indicated a weakening of marital bonds, they might lead to complete demoralization and desertion.

The wife of a Connecticut soldier undoubtedly was responsible for the chronically low state of her spouse's morale. The tone of her correspondence has to be inferred for the most part from her husband's replies, but there can be no question of its being generally plaintive. One of the few letters written by her that was preserved contains the statement:

> I have been to Williams . . . but he dont know anything about the war & cares less & that is the way withe the most of them hear. they have got you all into the scrape & that is all they care for. I dont think it will be half as much disgrace to you to have you come home as it will be to stay. . . . it is no worse for you than for thousands of others that is coming all the time. . . . dont stay for . . . a minute nor an hour if you see a chance . . . think not of the name in these times.[45]

Little wonder that the husband repeatedly reflected extreme dissatisfaction with his lot in the months following, though be it said to his credit that he served out his time.

Letters detailing home woes, while disturbing enough, were apparently not so demoralizing as no letters at all, especially if failure to receive them was interpreted as a token of marital infidelity, as was sometimes the case. A New Jersey Yank who failed to hear from his war bride for several weeks wrote angrily:

> I think it is damn mean. . . . Before we was married I heard from you every week and now we married I dont hear from you once a month. . . . it isnt Because you dont know where to write. . . . it seems as if you dont care the snap of your finger wether you write or not.

Ten days later he wrote again:

> I dont know what is the reason that I cant hear from the one that is nearest and dearest to me. it makes me feel down hearted and dull. . . . Mary I dont think you would deceive me so soon, if you have I am ashamed of you. I may be talking at random and I hope I am.

Failing still to get a letter, he wrote after the lapse of another week openly indicating his doubt of her faithfulness. When finally he heard from her he was reassured, but only for a little while, for in a subsequent note she made the mistake of asking permission to go out with male friends. This brought from the husband the blunt reply: "Go at your own risk. if I find out you go out with any one besides briggs or Jeff I will discard you for ever."

While being tortured by doubts of his wife's fidelity, this Yank was having other troubles, including reduced rations, disagreeable weather and uncongenial camp associations. All of these, coupled with what seems to have been a basic deficiency of spiritual stamina, caused him in October 1863 to send his wife the following remarkable message:

> I want to get out of this thing some way if I can, but I dont know how I will do it Hardley. there is no chance for deserting. I will have to work some plan to get my discharge. I have been stuffing medicine in myself since I been out here. I have been taking Pulsotil, Bryvina, Beladona, Acoute, Nuy Pom . . . Mucurins And Arsnic Poison when you write I wish you would send me some Arsnic or some other kind of stuff so as to make me look pale . . . find out at the druggist what will make you look pale and sickly . . . and send a small quantity in every letter. . . . If I aint Home . . . by next spring I dont care wether I ever get Home or not.

The recipient did not send the arsenic, but the husband contrived a visit home early in 1864, apparently by playing sick.

This case might be dismissed as that of a worthless character or hopeless psychopath were it not for the fact that he obviously had the respect of his associates, that he rose to the responsible position of orderly sergeant, and that, despite repeated talk of quitting the service and three unwarranted furloughs, he apparently acquitted himself creditably in combat and remained in the army until after Appomattox.[46]

Letters detailing home deprivations were especially depressing if the recipients' pay were in arrears, thus making it impossible for them to provide needed financial assistance. Failure to receive pay was the more disturbing in view of the uncertainty of aid from home-relief services which often were poorly administered. The worry experienced by unpaid soldiers over needy dependents was well illustrated in the instance of John N. Henry who in January 1863 wrote his wife:

> I have suffered more anxiety on account of my family for several weeks past than for the whole year. Six months pay behind & no knowledge of what the Forestville Committee were doing except the letter of Mrs. Pash to her [soldier] husband sometime ago that payment was refused her.[47]

Failure to draw wages when due was also hard on the morale of Yanks who had no hungry families looking to them for sustenance. In April 1864 an Ohio sergeant thus situated wrote in his diary near Chattanooga: "Weather cloudy and cold no news—Strapped for money, got the blues like a old maid." A year earlier a soldier correspondent wrote to a news-

paper from the Virginia front: "The shameful neglect of the proper offi-
cials at Washington to pay our brave soldiers has been the principal
means of causing the wholesale desertion in the army." [48]

Furloughs were hardly less important than pay as factors in morale.
Policies governing leave, haphazard throughout the conflict, were espe-
cially unsatisfactory during the first half of the war. Apparent hopeless-
ness of visiting home in the foreseeable future contributed much to the
depression which pervaded camps in the winter of 1862-1863; and the fre-
quency of furloughs resulting from the veteran re-enlistment program of
the next winter helped sustain morale during that period.

Many soldiers completed three years of service without getting leave.
A young Hoosier who requested and was refused a furlough in November
1863, after nearly two and a half years' absence from home, later wrote
his sweetheart: "You ask when I am going to get my furlough. I 'holler'
never and echo answers never—across Murphy Hollow [near Chatta-
nooga]. I expect to get one in eight months." [49]

This soldier was able to laugh at his failure to get leave. The same
was not true of most Yanks and especially of those with families. Gen-
eral Joseph Shields wrote General McDowell in June 1862 that volunteer
troops "if not allowed to go home and see their families . . . droop and
die. . . . I have watched this," he added. "The men who are denied this
permission cease to be of any use." [50]

A Michigan soldier sick in body and spirit, the father of several chil-
dren, wrote home from Alexandria, Virginia, in November 1862: "I sed
that I shuld get a furlow and com home if I could. I have given up the
Idea for it would cost me more figering & kiniving than it wold bea worth
and I wold stand ten chances to bea struck with lightning whare I wold
wone of getting a furlow." [51]

Still another consideration which greatly influenced morale was ad-
justment to unit, branch and associates. Some Yanks who were miserable
as infantrymen became happy soldiers when transferred to the cavalry.
Members of the mounted branch, on the other hand, sometimes were
thoroughly demoralized by the mere prospect of being reduced to a walk-
ing state.

Enforced association with strangers, through transfer or by consolida-
tion of units, also was apt to be demoralizing, especially during the period
of adjustment following the change. But where initial assignments were
uncongenial, transfers sometimes were the salvation of drooping spirits.
An excellent case in point is that of W. O. Lyford who left college in the
spring of 1861 to enlist in the Second New Hampshire Regiment. Dur-

ing the first few weeks he expressed contentment with his lot, but misconduct of some of his superiors at the First Battle of Bull Run undermined his confidence in them. A further source of discontent was the promotion over him of noncommissioned leaders whom he deemed less deserving than himself. In view of his changed attitude, it seems safe to assume that friction developed between him and those from whom he had to take orders. At any rate, from being a happy, eager soldier, he became a captious and dissatisfied one. On July 31, 1861, he complained about the excessive drinking of his officers and added, "I want my discharge right off, as soon as I can get it." A month later he wrote his parents: "I am satisfied that I cant live in the army. . . . I am tired and sick and hope it will be possible for me to come home and settle down."

In the autumn he transferred to the Fifth New Hampshire Regiment and was promoted from corporal to sergeant. The effect on his morale was revolutionary. In February 1862 he wrote his mother: "I have the care of the neatest and best boys in the company and I am contented as can be." The next month he devoted most of a letter to singing the praises of his captain whom he rated as by far the best in the regiment. "I would not be at home for anything," he stated, "for I am learning more about tactics than I ever knew." Shortly after the ordeal of Antietam he boasted to his father: "I am tough and rugged now and am willing to serve my country as long as I am able." [52]

Later in the year he received his lieutenant's bars. But illness overtook him soon afterward and he died before the end of the war.

In Lyford's instance the difference between poor morale and good morale was largely one of leadership. The same was true in countless other cases. Good leadership meant effective discipline, and effective discipline usually spelled high morale. Two regiments of the same brigade and even two companies of the same regiment might be poles apart in morale if one had superior officers and discipline while the other had ineffective leadership and loose discipline.

In August 1864 the close-observing John William De Forest, whose regiment had recently been transferred to Western Virginia from the Washington area, visited a near-by brigade of the Sixth Corps that had recently been through the hard fighting of Grant's "On to Richmond" campaign and had experienced an extreme deterioration of soldierly qualities. De Forest, coming from an organization where an opposite state prevailed, was shocked by the contrast. Irregular placing of tents, dirty guns, disregard of authority as manifested by a private telling a lieutenant "I'll slap your face if you say that again" and other conditions gave undeniable evidence that discipline had gone to pot and with it morale. Of the officers De Forest wrote: "Their talk about the war and our immediate military future had a tone of depression which astonished me."

"Don't you believe in Grant at all?" asked De Forest.

"Yes, we believe in Grant," a colonel answered, "but we believe a great deal more in Lee and in the Army of Virginia." [53]

And this was only eight months before Appomattox!

Yet another important factor in morale remains to be cited and this was age. Soldiers in their middle twenties and younger were of better spirit than older men; and men above forty had the lowest morale. Unmarried men, who for the most part were in the lower age groups, were less susceptible to depression than husbands and fathers. The youngsters pined less for home, endured privation more cheerfully, stood up better (if not so youthful as to be physically immature) under the wear and tear of strenuous campaigning, recovered more quickly from the shock of combat, manifested greater patience when sick or wounded and in general proved more adaptable than their elders.

One instance—that of Day Elmore—is cited elsewhere of a Yankee boy's unquenchable spirit.[54] Another shining example is found in Charles Ward, a Massachusetts lad who donned the uniform in his late teens and who, when offered a noncombatant post in regimental headquarters about the time of Antietam, turned it down with the comment: "I came to carry a gun and not to do the [clerical] work for others to fight." A little later, on the repeated urging of his officers, he accepted a clerkship, but he was troubled in conscience by not being in the ranks with his comrades at Fredericksburg. During the gloom of the war's second winter, while many wavered in spirit, his morale remained high. On one occasion, after marching fifty-five miles in three days, he boasted to his mother: "When we halted the first night I was the first man in the front rank and only 24 of us there. . . . They fell out one after the other, but I did not feel a bit tired."

At Chancellorsville he sneaked away from his desk and "fired one shot from a gun I picked up thrown away by one of our men who skedaddled." At Gettysburg, while performing the responsible duties of sergeant major of his regiment, he received a wound in the chest which caused his death on July 9, 1863. Two days before he died he wrote from his hospital bed this farewell message:

Dear Mother: I may not again see you but do not fear for your tired soldier boy. Death has no fears for me. My hope is still firm in Jesus. Meet me and Father in heaven with all my *dear friends.* I have no special message to send you, but bid you all a happy farewell.

Your affect. and soldier Son[55]

A happy farewell was in keeping with his unwavering cheerfulness, his noble character and his unsullied patriotism. To him and to the young Minnesota farmer, Ira Butterfield, who in 1863 dismissed the suggestion of a discharge with the statement, "I dont want a discharge by a long shot for if I were at home I could not take any comfort as long as there was men in the field doing Battle for me and my priveleges when I went in I goes the whole hog and never take hold of the plow and look back" [56] —to them and their kind for their dauntless spirit in fair weather or foul, in victory or defeat, the Union will ever owe a debt of gratitude.

CHAPTER XII

THE MEN WHO WORE THE BLUE

THE MOST STRIKING thing about Union soldiers was their diversity. The visitor to a Federal camp at any period of the war would encounter persons of many nationalities, races, creeds and occupations and observe great variations in dress, habits, temperament, education, wealth and social status. Indeed, there was hardly a type or class of any conceivable kind that was not represented in the Northern ranks.

Yanks ranged in age from beardless boys to hoary old men. The youngest wearers of the blue were the drummer boys and cavalry buglers. Apparently no minimum age was specified for the juvenile musicians until March 3, 1864, when an act of Congress prohibited the enlistment of any person under sixteen.[1]

The principal duties of the drummer boys were to sound the daily calls on drum, fife or bugle and to assist the band in providing music for ceremonies and drill. In addition, they performed sundry chores about the camp. The diary of William C. Richardson, drummer boy of the 104th Ohio Regiment, shows that he supplemented his musical activities with barbering, carrying water for the soldiers, honing the surgeon's instruments, assisting in removal and care of the wounded, helping bury the dead and drawing maps. Another drummer boy sold cakes, nuts, watermelons and other delicacies to the soldiers at a profit which infuriated the men and which permitted him to send home in one lump the then fabulous sum of sixty-five dollars.[2]

In view of their associations, it is not surprising that some of the youthful musicians acquired bad habits. A famous Civil War photograph shows a uniformed stripling playing cards with a whiskered sergeant, while an even younger boy looks over his shoulder. An Ohio cavalryman reported seeing a fifteen-year-old win $120 in one gambling session.[3]

Private Harvey Reid in a remarkable letter to a very young brother gave the following delightful glimpse of little Johnnie Walker, twelve-year-old drummer in the Twenty-second Wisconsin Regiment:

Johnnie is drummer for the band, and when they play at dress parade every evening lots of gentlemen and ladies come from the city to hear them play and see the little drummer and when we are marching, and the ladies see the little soldier-boy they always give him apples, cakes or something. . . . When we are marching Johnnie always keeps up with the big men, and is always singing and laughing but when he gets tired the big Colonel or Lieutenant Colonel or Adjutant will let Johnnie have his horse to ride. Everybody in the regiment likes Johnnie because he is a good little boy, is always pleasant and polite and not saucy like a great many boys. His mother sent him a suit of clothes made exactly like officer's clothes, and Lieutenant Baumman says he will get him a pair of shoulder straps with silver drum sticks upon them. Johnnie used to live in Racine and he has a half brother who is corporal in our company (but he is a mean bad man, don't take care of Johnnie, who lives with the Captain of Company B).[4]

Martial exploits of drummer boys must be considered with caution, owing to the appeal which the subject has had for balladists and romancers. The "Drummer Boy of Shiloh," for example, who supposedly furnished the theme for Will S. Hays's song of that title, has been traditionally identified as Henry Burke of the Fifty-eighth Ohio Regiment. But a careful investigation by the historian of Shiloh National Park revealed that the only Henry Burke carried on the official lists of Ohio soldiers was a private in the 148th Regiment who enlisted on May 2, 1864, long after Shiloh; and examination of the Shiloh cemetery records indicates that the "Henry Burke" there listed was added to the burial roll after the Shiloh drummer boy became a celebrity.[5]

Shiloh had its real drummer boys, of course, though the deeds of none seem to accord fully with those of song and story. The most famous of the Shiloh drummers, and probably of the whole war, was John L. (Johnny) Clem who ran away from home to join the army in May 1861, though only nine years old. When he offered his services as drummer to a company commander of the Third Ohio Volunteer Regiment, the captain looked him over, laughed and, according to Clem, "said he wasn't enlisting infants." Johnny then tried to join the Twenty-second Michigan Regiment and was refused. But he "went along with the regiment just the same as a drummer boy, and though not on the muster roll, drew a soldier's pay of thirteen dollars a month," which was contributed by officers of the regiment.[6]

The smashing of Johnny's drum by a shell at Pittsburg Landing won for him the sobriquet of "Johnny Shiloh." Shortly afterward he was regularly enlisted as drummer. Subsequently he exchanged drum for musket because, as he put it, "I did not like to stand and be shot at without shooting back."

So at Chickamauga, Johnny, though still carried on the rolls as drummer, went into the fight riding an artillery caisson and carrying a musket cut down to size. When a Confederate colonel dashed up and demanded, "Surrender you damned little Yankee!" Johnny gave him a blast that knocked him from his horse. For this feat Clem, then twelve years old, was made a sergeant and became known as the drummer boy of Chickamauga. Some Chicago ladies who heard of his bravery and promotion sent him a new uniform. In typical soldier fashion the young hero donned the fancy regalia, armed himself with a musket and posed for the photographer.[7]

Johnny carried dispatches for General Thomas during the Atlanta campaign, had his pony killed under him and before the end of his service was twice wounded. After the war was over he sought admission to West Point, but was rejected on account of deficiency of his prior schooling. He then appealed to President Grant who appointed him second lieutenant in the Regular Army. Clem retired from the Army in 1916 as a major general.[8]

Other boy musicians had less spectacular careers than Clem, but many followed his example of swapping drums for guns in the heat of conflict. The colonel of the Fifty-second Ohio Regiment told of one such instance in his official report of Perryville where "Charley Common, a little drummer-boy, having lost his drum, took a musket and fought manfully in the line." [9]

One drummer boy, Orion P. Howe of the Fifty-fifth Illinois Regiment, for gallantry at Vicksburg was awarded the coveted Medal of Honor. His citation stated: "A drummer boy, 14 years of age and severely wounded and exposed to a heavy fire from the enemy, he persistently remained upon the field of battle until he had reported to Gen. W. T. Sherman the necessity of supplying cartridges for the use of troops under command of Colonel Malmborg." [10]

By no means all the youngsters who wore the blue were musicians. Despite issuance of War Department orders as early as August 1861 forbidding acceptance without parental consent of minors under eighteen and an unqualified barring of them the next year, thousands of boys seventeen years and younger found their way into the ranks.[11] Benjamin A. Gould, a United States Sanitary Commission actuary who compiled vital statistics for 1,012,273 Union volunteers, reported that 10,233 of them were under eighteen at the time of their enlistment, with age groupings as follows:

Age	Number
13	127
14	330
15	773
16	2,758
17	6,425 [12]

Examination by the writer of the descriptive lists of 123 companies containing 14,330 men and representing 96 regiments of infantry, 15 of cavalry and 12 of artillery revealed 3 boys who were 12 years old when mustered into service, 12 who were 13, 4 who were 14, 5 who were 15, 62 who were 16 and 160 who were 17. Boys under 18 comprised 1.02 per cent of Gould's total and 1.6 of the writer's. While many of the youngsters in both groups were musicians, most of them apparently were full-fledged soldiers. Some who started out as drummer boys graduated, while still below the legal age, to positions in the ranks.[13]

The number of boys under eighteen was actually greater than that shown in the surveys, for the figures were compiled from muster rolls and many Yanks listed as eighteen and above in these records were in reality below eighteen; they misrepresented their age in order to get into the service.[14] Joseph T. Bushong of the Eighteenth Ohio Regiment, who claimed to have completed a three-year enlistment before his eighteenth birthday, declared that his false statement to the recruiting officer concerning his age was "the only lie I ever told in my life." [15] Chauncey H. Cooke of the Twenty-fifth Wisconsin Regiment, whose letters home are among the best of Civil War sources, wrote thus of his mustering-in experience:

Every one he suspicioned of being under 18 he would ask his age. He turned out a lot of them who were not quite 18. . . . Seeing how it was working with the rest, I did not know what to do. . . . I saw our Chaplain and he told me to tell the truth, that I was a little past 16, and he tho't when the mustering officer saw my whiskers he would not ask my age. That is what the boys all told me but I was afraid. I had about made up my mind to tell him I was going on 19 years, but thank heaven I did not have a chance to lie. He did not ask my age. I am all right . . . but the sweat was running down my legs into my boots when that fellow came down the line and I was looking hard at the ground fifteen paces in front.[16]

It is possible that boys even younger than twelve marched in the Union ranks, though the writer is not able to state this as a positive fact. The *Photographic History of the Civil War* contains the picture of William Black and describes him as the "youngest wounded soldier reported," but his age, unit and status are not given.[17] The Portland, Maine, *Transcript* of September 6, 1862, made a brief reference to the nine-year-old son of George H. Wilson who "went off without the knowledge of his parents with the 17th [Maine] Regiment and writes home that he 'likes the soldier's life' and is the pet of the regiment"; but this boy was undoubtedly a hanger-on rather than a soldier.[18] The claim to the distinction of being the "Youngest Yank" seems impossible of establishment.

Some of the boy soldiers deserted after a few months but most seem to have given a good account of themselves.[19] A Connecticut cavalryman who was at first skeptical of a group of recruits not big enough to "fill up the government breeches" that came to his unit in April 1864 wrote later of one of them: "He is about fourteen years of age . . . by occupation a shoemaker . . . a bright active boy full of enterprise & spirit. He had nearly or quite made his escape [when captured in a recent engagement] but went back to the rebel guard because his friend William Foley, also a young boy, who was to escape with him became exhausted on account of a wound. . . . I regard it as a remarkable instance of generosity & self sacrifice." [20]

On hard marches the ponies, as the boys were called, sometimes showed greater stamina than their mature comrades, a fact which afforded them much satisfaction. An Ohio lad wrote proudly to his parents after two days and a night of tramping through the rain in Virginia: "There was a grate many give out but i made the riffel some of the bigest men give out. . . . i told the boys that they ort to be ashamed of themselves for a boy like me to stand the march two days and not give out." [21]

The buoyancy and blitheness of the teen-agers often spread to their comrades and helped make soldiering more tolerable for all. The boys also carried their part of the load on the firing line. The colonel of the 102nd Pennsylvania Regiment reported after Seven Pines that "Privates W. C. Wall, Jr., and John Aiken, Jr., of Company M, two of the youngest soldiers bearing arms in the regiment . . . stood in a most exposed position . . . firing deliberately . . . and careful not to waste ammunition." Cited also for gallantry in action was Private David W. Camp who at Shiloh, "though a mere boy, only fourteen years old, served as No. 5 man at the left [artillery] piece with the skill and bravery of an old soldier," and Private Nathaniel Gwynne of the Thirteenth Ohio Cavalry who at Petersburg on April 2, 1865, was cautioned not to enter the action as he was only fifteen years old and had not been mustered; but Gwynne "indignantly protested," joined in the charge, lost an arm and was awarded the Medal of Honor.[22]

A substantial though indeterminable number of the boy soldiers paid the supreme price for their patriotism. Among the slain was W. W. Dutton of the Tenth Vermont Regiment who enlisted in December 1863 at seventeen, participated in the bloody battles of the Wilderness, Spottsylvania and Second Cold Harbor and was killed in July 1864 at Monocacy before attaining the age of eighteen.[23]

One of the most interesting things about the boy soldiers was the speed with which they matured under the stress and strain of army life. The quick metamorphosis was strikingly revealed in the letters of Charles Goddard who enlisted in the First Minnesota Regiment shortly before his sixteenth birthday. After only a brief period of service he wrote his widowed mother in paternal strain concerning a younger brother: "Tell him he must be a good boy and not trouble his mother as much as I did." Eight months later he replied to an indirect inquiry about correspondence with girls: "I have something els to do than to make love to the women"; at the same time he read his mother a lesson concerning her proposal to join his unit in the capacity of nurse: "I consider myself milatary General of our famly and I wont allow you to make such a rash move as that." Still a few weeks later he stated: "Tell brother that if any body abuses him to jest hint to them that he has a big brother in the army that may some day return when he will procede imediately to settle up all these little accounts." Following a wound at Gettysburg, though not far beyond the ripe age of seventeen, he wrote in old-soldier fashion: "My leg is a regular old weather clock for I can tell when it is going to be bad weather—it feels num and as if it had been froze and was not thourally thawed out yet." [24]

Goddard continued to grow in stature and wisdom, proving himself in every respect a worthy soldier of his country. His career in arms gave striking support to the observation that age is more a matter of experience than years. By the time of his return to civilian life in 1864 at the age of nineteen, he who had gone out three years before as a boy had unquestionably become a man.

Some of those who as boys donned the blue rose to high rank before the end of the war. Arthur MacArthur, father of General Douglas MacArthur, after being awarded at eighteen the Medal of Honor for carrying the colors of his regiment in the vanguard of a charge at Missionary Ridge was promoted to the command of the Twenty-fourth Wisconsin Regiment and led it through the bloody battles of Resaca and Nashville. After the conflict "the gallant boy colonel," as he was called by a superior during the war, rose to the grade of lieutenant general. Another brave soldier who commanded a Union regiment before his twenty-first birthday was Henry W. Lawton of Indiana. Still another boy colonel, James B. Forman of the Fifteenth Kentucky Regiment, was mortally wounded at twenty-one while leading his men in the thick of the fight at Stone's River.[25]

At the other extreme from the boys were the old men. Instructions issued by the War Department in September 1862 specifically forbade the mustering of persons above forty-five, but many men of middle age and beyond had already found their way into the ranks, and hundreds of others gained admittance after the prohibition by the simple expedient of putting up a bold front and lying.[26] Slightly more than one half of one per cent of the 1,012,273 Yanks surveyed by Gould were over forty-five when they entered the service and the writer's sample of 14,330 contained 85, or six tenths of one per cent, who were forty-six and older.[27] As previously suggested, the proportion of soldiers over forty-five was always greater than that shown on the muster rolls because older men, prompted by patriotism or bounty, sometimes overlooked one or more birthdays when they enrolled for service. The age distribution of the older men in the surveys of Gould and the writer was as follows:

Gould's			The Writer's	
Age	Number		Age	Number
46	967		46	21
47	712		47	11
48	699		48	12
49	469		49	7
50 and over	2,366 [28]		50	3
			51	4
			52	7
			53	3
			54	1
			55	2
			56	1
			57	3
			58	2
			59	2
			60	3
			62	2
			65	1 [29]

The sixty-five-year-old in the writer's survey was a musician in Company D, First Missouri Infantry.[30] Despite his advanced years he was by no means the eldest wearer of the blue. A chaplain encountered in an army hospital a septuagenarian who had been recruited "under a false representation of his age." [31] But the person who seems clearly entitled to the designation "oldest Yank"—and for that matter, "oldest Civil War soldier"—was Curtis King who was mustered into the Thirty-seventh Iowa Infantry on November 9, 1862, at the age of eighty and who was carried on the rolls until March 20, 1863, when he was discharged for disability.[32] The regiment to which King belonged was unique. Known as the Greybeards and organized for guard duty, this unit was composed mainly of men over forty-five. In its ranks were 145 men sixty years of age and older.[33]

The great mass of Yanks were neither very old nor very young but fell in the eighteen-to-forty-five group. Over 98 per cent of the million volunteers in Gould's survey were in this category and, despite some error resulting from false statements by those falling outside authorized limits, Gould's figures represent with reasonable accuracy the age pattern of the Union Army.[34]

On the basis of Gould's estimate it may be stated that in the first year of the conflict the largest single age group among the men who wore the blue was the eighteen-year-olds (even with due allowance for lying); that the next largest category was the twenty-one-year-olds, and that beyond twenty-one, as a general rule, age groups became progressively smaller.[35]

The average age of the men in blue increased slightly with the progress of the war. The age pattern of men coming into the service remained fairly constant, but as the old-timers matured they pushed the general age level upward. Gould estimates the average age of the army to have been 25.10 years in July 1862; 25.76 in July 1863; 26.06 in July 1864; and 26.32 in May 1865.[36]

The Union Army, then, was a youthful army.[37] At the mid-point of the conflict three out of every four Yanks were under thirty years of age and less than half of them had celebrated their twenty-fifth birthday.[38] This predominancy of youth was of incalculable moment both to the army and the nation. Youth gave a cheerful tone to camp life, made for generosity in human relations and provided a priceless core of ruggedness, optimism and resilience which a succession of defeats could not crush and which led eventually to victory, peace and Union.

Occupations and professions of the men in blue were considerably more varied than their ages. The writer's examination of 123 company rolls turned up more than 300 occupations and specialties. Alphabetically the vocations represented by the 14,000 Yanks considered extended from accountant to woodcutter and included such diversities as artists and barkeepers, brokers and brakemen, chemists and contractors, dancing masters and ditchers, grocers and glass blowers, hairdressers and heelers, Indian lecturers and ironworkers, landlords and locksmiths, miners and manufacturers, peddlers and pianists, surveyors and stonecutters, tinsmiths and teachers, varnishers and veterinarians and wheelwrights and waiters. Such well-known functionaries as the butcher, the baker and the candlestick maker stood side by side with oddities who classified themselves as gamblers, gentlemen and loafers. One Yank declared himself a "Jack of all traids." [39]

The most numerous groups were the farmers, who comprised nearly half the total, and common laborers, who accounted for more than a tenth. Other well-represented categories were carpenters who numbered 610; shoemakers, 374; clerks, 367; blacksmiths, 325; painters, 200; soldiers, 173; mechanics, 183; sailors, 178; machinists, 155; masons, 143; printers, 126; teamsters, 99; and teachers, 97.[40]

The varied accomplishment of the men in blue manifested itself in sundry and impressive ways. When the colonel of the First Michigan Regiment at dress parade called for printers to run off some official papers, eight men stepped forward to offer their services.[41] A Massachusetts colonel whose mobility was seriously impeded by Rebel destruction of transportation facilities in Maryland early in the war soon found that his men were equal to the emergency. Walking up to the debris of a dismantled locomotive one of the soldiers coolly remarked: "I made this engine and I can put it together again." Others of section-gang background soon had the rails relaid; and when an engineer was requested to start the train rolling, nineteen Yanks from this one regiment avowed themselves capable of taking over the throttle.[42] By these and countless other feats the citizen army mobilized by Lincoln demonstrated the genius and versatility of a people whose resourcefulness and energy carved a nation out of the wilderness, conquered its distances, harnessed its resources and ultimately made of it the arsenal of democracy in an epic struggle for individual freedom.

Educational backgrounds ranged from no schooling at all to the highest levels of specialized training, and intellectual qualities extended from imbecility to genius. Among the aristocrats of learning was Scotch-born Edward F. Reid of the Third Indiana Cavalry who began his soldier career as a private in 1861 and was commissioned second lieutenant in

January 1864. Reid's diary is sprinkled with quotations, some of them in Latin, Greek and German, from classical and contemporary literature. The first entry of his army service began:

> Came into camp—went home on furlough the same evg.
>> The Splendor falls on castle walls
>> And snowy summits old in story
>> The long light shakes across the lakes
>
> . . . .
>
>> Blow bugle blow. . . .
>> Blow bugle answer echoes dying, dying . . .

and concluded with a Greek quotation from the New Testament. On August 5, 1861, he wrote: "Eat, drank and drilled," and then transcribed extracts from Tennyson and other poets. On January 1, 1861, he summarized a *Harper's Monthly* article by Ruskin and two days later he copied excerpts from Seneca and Schiller.[43]

Another of the cultural upper crust was Samuel Storrow, a Harvard student who served as corporal in the Forty-fourth Massachusetts Regiment. Storrow's home letters indicate outstanding proficiency in Latin and Greek. They also show that familiarity with the classics tended to isolate the writer from the great mass of his comrades. "It has been one of the most unpleasant of my experiences as a private," he wrote in 1863, "to be unable to find any congenial companion and friend in my company, and to be obliged to associate with men whom nothing else could have forced me into such close intimacy with. . . . I do not regret having Entered . . . [the ranks], but I long ago found out that it was an uncongenial sphere, Even in the 44th, at least in Co. H." [44]

At the lower end of the educational and intellectual scale were the illiterates. Many of them were ignorant from lack of educational opportunity and some from native stupidity. In one notorious instance substitute brokers enticed an idiot from a New York asylum and palmed him off as a soldier.[45]

Among the illiterates were many Negroes recently redeemed from bondage and a considerable sprinkling of underprivileged whites from the large cities. A member of a Massachusetts company drawn largely from an industrial center stated that the only education found among his comrades was that which could be obtained "from a nail mill or rum shop," and a cavalryman from the New York City area reported that many of his company could neither read nor write. But such instances seem to have been exceptional. The average company in the Union Army had from one to a half-dozen illiterates. Many had none. A veteran corporal on encountering his first instance of a soldier requiring an amanuensis remarked: "There is not one in a thousand hardly but what can write." [46]

Schools were organized in many Negro regiments, and in some white ones, to teach the rudiments of learnii g on a voluntary basis. Both officers and men acted as instructors. A New York artillery captain described an educational enterprise in his own battery thus:

My school is in a flourishing condition; the boys built a table and desk, with forms out of split logs, and set it up under the shade of the trees, and every day at 2 P.M. the schoolmaster, an old corporal whom I detailed for the purpose, fetches the spelling-books and the writing materials, and sets his classes their lessons. You would be pleased to see the eagerness with which men from twenty to forty years of age seize upon this opportunity for repairing the defects of their early education, and the progress which they all make is most encouraging.[47]

While illiteracy was not so great a handicap to soldiers of the sixties as to those of today (since warfare is now far more technical), still it constituted a serious disadvantage and sometimes produced embarrassing and dangerous situations. Court-martial records tell of an illiterate Yank being assigned to guard a bridge leading into the nation's capital. When the soldier protested the order on grounds of his inability to read passes he was told by the sergeant, "Never mind, you only have to look at them." Instead of trying to conceal his ignorance the soldier left his post and got drunk, for which offense he was sentenced to two years of hard labor.[48]

Barely literate Yanks sometimes displayed an amusing sense of superiority over less polished comrades. An Ohio soldier, in a letter urging younger relatives to attend school, made the following statement:

i can see the good of what i have got now. there is lots of men here that cant wright and they have got to git somebody to wright there leters i wouldent take five hundred dolers for what learn i have got.[49]

The nativity of the Northern soldiers was an impressive conglomerate. Descriptive rolls show that every state in the Union and virtually every nation and province on the globe were represented in the Union ranks.[50]

The impression is strong and persistent that the Federal forces were made up largely of foreigners. Prevalence of this idea among Southerners is attributable in part to prejudice born of intersectional strife (the genuine Yankee had no love of fighting, suh, and if he had, he couldn't have whipped us; so in keeping with his scheming, cowardly nature, he took his filthy wealth, much of it ill-gotten from his less materialistic brothers in the South, and hired a horde of hungry foreigners to face the bullets for him, while he stayed at home and fattened his bank roll with war profits).[51] Another basis of the opinion is the ease with which foreign-born invaders could be distinguished by their speech and demeanor. A Southerner whose premises were visited by bluecoats was inclined to take more notice of one thick-brogued Irishman or guttural-speaking Teuton than a half-dozen smoothly articulating sons of America; and after the hostile forces passed on, he was apt to refer to them as horrible foreign scum.

Like many other stubborn traditions, the idea of foreigners constituting the bulk of the Northern Army is erroneous. The overwhelming majority of Yanks, probably more than three fourths of them, were native Americans. A sample of 14,330 cases taken from the descriptive books of 123 well-distributed regiments yielded 2,617 natives of New York, 1,808 of Pennsylvania, 1,751 of Ohio, 1,000 of Indiana, 474 of Illinois and lesser numbers born in other states. Every slaveholding state except Florida was represented in the list. Of the 14,330 men included in the sample, 814 were natives of the slaveholding states and 437 were born in the eleven states comprising the Southern Confederacy. Virginia, represented by 198 names, contributed more natives than any other Confederate state, Tennessee was next with 123 and North Carolina was third with 34. Louisiana led the Gulf states with 20 representatives, and Alabama was second with 17. A company raised in the Old Northwest or Middle West normally contained one or more sons of the Old Dominion in its ranks and frequently had representation from two or three other Confederate states.[52]

Germans were the most numerous of foreign-born Yanks. The Northern states in 1860 contained over a million persons of German birth, and the total number of German-born soldiers in the Union Army probably exceeded 200,000. Several divisions were made up largely of Germans, and the number of regiments comprised mainly of Teutons ran up into the scores. The State of New York raised ten regiments that were almost wholly German and many more that were predominantly so. Only a minority of the Germans, however, were grouped in foreign units. A majority, owing to the wide diffusion of the Teutons among the civilian population, were scattered throughout the entire army in quantities ranging from a dozen to several hundred per regiment. Indeed, it is hardly an exaggeration to state that the company which lacked a German-born member was a rarity among the Federal forces.[53]

Some of the Germans were less than admirable both as men and soldiers, but on the whole the contribution of this nationality to the Union cause was tremendous. Many Germans, and especially the Forty-eighters, were men of good education and refined tastes whose influence improved the cultural tone of the units to which they belonged. Their technical aptitude and skill helped meet specialist needs in artillery, engineer and signal units. The prior training of many of them in European organizations was utilized for instruction of vast levies of green recruits. Their neatness, precision and respect for authority was of infinite aid in molding a mob of individualists into an organized fighting force. What the Teutons lacked in quickness and glamour was more than offset by their patience and steadiness, not to mention the idealistic devotion of many of them to the cause of Union and freedom.[54]

Despite a reputation for cowardice, attributable largely to their alleged defection at Chancellorsville, the Germans were good fighters. Their effectiveness as artillerymen was well exemplified by Wiedrich's battery on the second day at Gettysburg. A Rebel officer who rushed up to this unit as its capture seemed assured crying "This battery is ours!" received the retort from a stubborn defender, "No, dis battery is *unser!*" and then was felled by a blow of this man's sponge staff.[55]

Second only to the Germans, among foreigners who fought for the Union, were the Irish. Native sons of Erin swelled the Northern ranks to the number of nearly 150,000. More than a score of regiments were pure Irish or nearly so when they donned the blue, and numerous others contained a heavy admixture of men born on the Emerald Isle. New York furnished more Irish than any other state. Among units raised in the Empire State was General Thomas F. Meagher's famous Irish Brigade, composed of the Ninth, Sixty-third and Eighty-eighth New York Regiments. This brigade covered itself with glory and blood in many battles and especially in the desperate assault on Marye's Heights at Fredericksburg. In New York also was recruited Corcoran's Irish Legion of five regiments whose original composition was predominantly Irish. Massachusetts, Pennsylvania, Indiana and Illinois each contributed two Irish regiments, and several other states each provided one. But the regiments tell only part of the story, as Irishmen in smaller units and individually flocked to the ranks from every part of the Union. Their motivation was less idealistic than that of the Germans and some of the other nationalities. It is quite possible that their predominant urge was the sheer love of combat.[56]

Certainly the sons of old Erin were among the most desperate and dependable of fighters. Their distinctive green flag, adorned with harp and sunburst, was usually to be found where the fire was hottest, giving assurance and inspiration to all who beheld it. Generals often called on them when the situation was most desperate, and comrades openly admired them for their reckless courage.[57] The reputation which they enjoyed is well illustrated by the statement of Corporal Charles Ward concerning the "Irish Ninth" of Massachusetts. "They fight like tigers," he wrote after Antietam, "& no regt. of Rebs can stand a charge from them. They have a name which our Regt. will never get." [58]

All Irishmen were not heroes, of course; nor were they faultless as soldiers. Some of them played the coward in combat and others carried recklessness to undesirable extremes. On the whole they were less effective in sustained defensive operations than in offensive spurts.[59]

Their pugnaciousness and the excessive fondness of many of them for strong drink sometimes made them difficult to discipline, but their troublesomeness was counterbalanced by their ready humor, sparkling repartee and matchless buoyancy.[60] Their joviality, aptitude for play and love of pageantry brightened camp life and made their festive days occasions which attracted hordes of visitors from far and wide. All in all their influence and example both in battle and in garrison was an immense asset to the Union cause.[61]

The same might be said of the other British peoples, from the mother isles and the various dependencies, who joined the Union ranks in large numbers. Their numbers and characteristics varied but their combined contribution was substantial. More than 50,000 Canadians wore the Federal uniform, along with 45,000 Englishmen and lesser numbers of Scotsmen, Welshmen and other natives of the empire.[62]

Germans, Irish, Canadians and British comprised about five sixths of the foreigners in the Union Army, but other nationalities were represented in impressive ratio to their part in the Northern population. Outstanding among the minor groups were the Scandinavians, who readily translated their ancient devotion to country and freedom into enthusiastic support of the Union cause. In numbers this group was small, but their hardihood and dependability as soldiers won for them a wholesome and far-reaching respect. The most famous Scandinavian unit was the Fifteenth Wisconsin, composed mainly of Norwegians with a sprinkling of Swedes and Danes and commanded by Colonel Hans C. Heg. The

Third Wisconsin Regiment contained one company known as the Dane Guards and another called the Scandinavian Guards. Several Illinois regiments had one or more companies made up largely of Scandinavians.[63]

The nativity of the Scandinavians was usually apparent from their names. One company of Colonel Heg's Fifteenth Wisconsin contained five Ole Olsens, another had three Ole Ericksons and still another included three Ole Andersons; in the whole regiment were at least 128 men who answered to the first name of Ole. Companies bore such designations as the St. Olaf Rifles, Oden's Rifles and the Norway Bear Hunters.[64]

Knute Nelson, a Norwegian youth, enlisted as a private in the Fourth Wisconsin in 1861, completed three years' service before his twenty-first birthday and after the war became governor of Minnesota and United States Senator. Nelson's war letters, some in English and others in Norwegian, reveal a deep love of Union, an abiding interest in emancipation and an earnestness about life in general that was far beyond his years. Sample glimpses of his attitudes and reactions may be had from two letters written while in Baton Rouge, Louisiana. In one of them, dated June 10, 1862, he said:

The careless reckless wild boy that left home a year ago will return home if Providence wills it, with more experience, and more thoughtful. He has at least learnt how to *associate* with his fellow beings. He has learnt that the world is not the school house nor the narrow limits of the litle farm. . . . I know that I caused you much grief in leaving you as I did; but my heart dictated it and I could not otherwise. Forgive me.

The other, written nearly two years later to a younger brother, lashes out at fellow immigrants who waited for rich bounties before entering the service:

You tell me that Lunner ag Björn Torsen have just enlisted and will receive 500 dolls Bonties each. Does it not look as though they inlisted for money rather than because they loved the Country? Why could not such big strapping fellows have gone to fight for their Country before now? [65]

Swiss, French, Italian, Mexican and Polish representation in the Union Army was indicated by such regimental designations as the Swiss Rifles (Fifteenth Missouri); Gardes Lafayette (Fifty-fifth New York), commanded by Regis de Trobriand; Garibaldi Guard (Thirty-ninth New York); Martinez' Militia (First New Mexico); and Polish Legion (Fifty-eighth New York). But, as in the case of other foreigners, most of the soldiers of these nationalities were scattered as individuals through units in which they were only a minority.

As a general rule regiments organized in the East had a heavier admixture of foreign-born members than did those formed in the West. The nationality profile of an Eastern unit may be illustrated by Company F, Forty-sixth Pennsylvania Regiment, which contained 78 natives of Pennsylvania, 33 of other American states, 11 Irishmen, 7 Welshmen, 4 Scotsmen, 2 Germans, 1 Frenchman and 1 Canadian; or Company B, Fifth New York Regiment, which had 67 New Yorkers, 8 other Americans, 35 Irishmen, 18 Germans, 14 Englishmen, 5 Canadians, 4 Scotsmen and 3 Frenchmen. The make-up of a Western regiment is exemplified by Company C, Second Illinois Cavalry, which had 30 natives of Illinois, 50 other Americans, 10 Germans, 6 Irishmen, 2 Englishmen, 1 Canadian, 1 Frenchman and 1 Swiss; or Company H, Eighth Michigan Infantry, which had 47 New Yorkers, 37 Michiganders, 26 other Americans, 7 Canadians, 5 Englishmen, 4 Germans, 2 Irishmen, 1 Scotsman, 1 Dutchman and 1 who gave his nativity as "the ocean." [66]

It seems probable that the portion of foreign-born in the army increased as the war progressed, because of the waning of the martial spirit among the domestic population and the greater susceptibility of immigrant groups to financial inducement and to the tricks and pressures of fraudulent recruiting agencies.[67]

The diverse national background of the Union soldiery manifested itself in many ways. One of the most noticeable of these was the babel of tongues that rose from the camps. The colonel of one regiment which included fifteen nationalities gave commands in seven different languages. In such an organization efforts of the various groups to hold conversation often led to ludicrous results. Americans derived much amusement from the speech gaucheries of foreign-born comrades wrestling with a strange language. The Yanks from distant lands also brought with them to camp peculiarities of dress which stubbornly resisted prescribed regulations; foods and beverages strange to the Federal commissariat; songs and music long cherished in the homeland; festivities and games better known to the Old World than to the New; and European practices in the arrangement of shelter and furnishings.[68]

These distinctive customs and traits gave color and variety to army life. They also aroused prejudice and friction. Taunts of "greenhorn" and the bandying of contemptuous epithets occasionally led to fisticuffs and riots. Some American-born officers complained of assignment to units composed largely of foreigners. A Yale-educated lieutenant who served in a battery of Germans and Irishmen wrote on one occasion: "What is most unpleasant to me of all, is, that I have to live with these men, to eat their onions and drink their lager and very rarely to hear a word of musical English from American lips as I am almost the sole specimen of a Yankee in the Company." Later he referred unhappily to "marching through much mud to this camp where the Teutonic element has its head-quarters, and revels in endless streams of lager, infinite plantations of sauerkraut, and strings of small but seductive sausages." Still later he noted: "This Division is called the German Division, and the officers at head-quarters have to do business in a polyglot fashion. I greatly outraged the assistant adjutant general by refusing to recognize a German order which was sent to me when I was in command." [69]

Even greater was the resentment manifested by some of the Americans in the ranks toward foreign-born officers. A tipsy Hoosier who was reprimanded by an Irishman recently elected lieutenant said: "I didnt vote for you and I . . . wouldn't vote for any damned Irish son of a bitch. I dont care a damn for you. . . . A damned Irishman always gets his ass up in about two days after he is promoted." And a German major who disciplined an unruly New York cavalryman was told to "Hold your barking and speak English, you damned Dutch son of a bitch." Another obstreperous citizen of the Empire State when placed in the custody of a detail of foreigners cried out in protest, "I am not going to be guarded by a lot of Dutch hounds." [70]

On June 23, 1861, Private Charles Wills of the Eighth Illinois Regiment wrote in his diary: "The Americans in our company think some of seceding, filling up from home with American boys, and letting the Dutch now in the company paddle their own canoe." [71] But this was early in the war, and the Americans instead of taking leave of the foreigners came to respect and like them and to take pride in the reputation which their soldierly qualities helped win for the unit. The experience of Private Wills's company was duplicated countless times throughout the army, and while prejudice existed as long as men of diverse nationalities remained in close association it was always accompanied by instances of camaraderie and mutual esteem. The most powerful influence in leveling barriers of nationality was the confidence and respect born of sharing hardship and danger. Courage in battle was the mark of a man, and the soldier who proved his bravery was not long disparaged for peculiarities of speech.

In sum, the ultimate standing of a foreigner, like that of an American, depended mainly on his character and habits. If he was shirking, filthy, dishonest or craven, he was held in low esteem and his deficiency associated with his foreignness. If he measured up well as a man and soldier, he stood a good chance of winning full acceptance by his comrades.

Whatever the reputation of foreign-born soldiers during the war, it can be unequivocably stated in the perspective of time that they compared favorably with their American associates in every respect and that their experience, talents and loyalty helped mightily in preserving the Union of their adopted country.

Racially the Northern Army was predominantly white. The largest non-Caucasian group were the Negroes, 186,017 of whom were carried on Federal muster rolls. Of these, 134,111 came from the slaveholding states and a substantial majority were bondsmen recently redeemed. Louisiana, with 24,052 Negro Yanks to her credit, headed the list of states whence Negroes were recruited, and Texas with 47 was at the bottom. Northern states contributing the most Negro soldiers were Pennsylvania (8,612), New York (4,125) and Massachusetts (3,966).[72]

Union authorities were slow in reaching the decision to arm the Negroes, but when policy finally crystallized early in 1863 recruiting was pushed with vigor and colored regiments were formed in the artillery, cavalry, infantry and engineer branches. Several divisions were composed in large part of Negro troops, and the Twenty-fifth Army Corps, organized in December 1864 and placed under the command of Major General Godfrey Weitzel, was predominantly Negro.[73]

A few of the Negro units were staffed initially with colored line officers—notably three regiments organized in Louisiana by General Benjamin F. Butler—but Federal policy was in general opposed to the commissioning of Negroes except as chaplains and surgeons; and most colored officers were eventually replaced by whites. An effort was made to fill noncommissioned positions in the colored units with Negroes, but educational deficiencies, especially among Southern recruits, worked against the realization of this goal. Some regiments of "United States Colored Troops," as all Negro soldiers except the Fifty-fourth and Fifty-fifth Massachusetts Regiments were ultimately designated, had only black noncommissioned officers, but this arrangement was by no means a satisfactory one. Colonel R. B. Marcy, who was favorably disposed toward the use of Negroes as soldiers, reported after an inspection of the Forty-ninth Regiment, United States Colored Troops: "All the noncommissioned officers were colored men, a few of which could read and write a little, but not sufficient to make out company papers, which gave the commissioned officers a great amount of office duty." Colonel Thomas Wentworth Higginson, prominent Massachusetts abolitionist and writer who commanded a regiment of Negroes recruited in South Carolina, stated: "I spend hours daily in doing what in white regts would be done by a secretary detailed from the ranks." Instruction in the three "R's" proved to be one of the major functions of officers assigned to colored units.[74]

Not all colored soldiers were at the bottom of the literacy scale. Some reared in the North or abroad had good educational background. A religious worker encountered in a Virginia camp a Negro soldier who as a merchant seaman had learned Spanish, Italian and Portuguese and another who could read Latin, Greek and Hebrew.[75]

Negro soldiers participated in several battles including Port Hudson, Milliken's Bend, Fort Wagner, Olustee, Fort Pillow, Brice's Cross Roads, the Crater and Nashville. The combat performance of the colored soldier is difficult to evaluate because of the prejudiced character of most of the evidence on the subject. Northerners who were unfriendly to Negroes or opposed to emancipation, and nearly all Southerners, tended to belittle the colored soldiers; while antislavery zealots and commanders of colored units were inclined to close their eyes to deficiencies of the Negro fighters and exaggerate their accomplishments. However, a careful sifting of available testimony indicates that some Negro soldiers conducted themselves heroically in battle while others skulked and ran; that leadership was a crucial factor in their combat performance; that units recruited in the North were more effective than those composed of recently freed slaves; that in offensive spurts the showing of Negroes compared favorably with that of whites of comparable background and training; and that the Civil War experience of colored troops was too limited to permit a meaningful conclusion concerning their ability to stand up against stubborn and sustained resistance.[76]

Because of its unusually calm tone the following statement about Fort Wagner, made by a young Massachusetts staff officer favorably disposed toward the colored race, is offered as a lone exhibit from a mass of conflicting evidence:

About the Negro troops, I find it hard to come to an opinion; no one says they behaved remarkably well. I think they did fairly, no better than the white troops and probably not so well, for they came back two hundred muskets short of the number of men, while the other regiments had a surplus. Tom Stephenson who has the 54th Massachusetts, [colored] in his brigade, spoke well of them but probably he would be slow to say anything in their disfavor. With long and careful discipline I suppose a regiment of negroes might do as well as a poor white regiment, but negro troops disciplined no better than many of our white regiments are would be useless.[77]

The principal use of colored soldiers was for garrison and labor purposes rather than for fighting. Their service in the lowlier capacities, while essential and valuable and while releasing thousands of whites for combat duty, was tedious, onerous and dispiriting. The lot of the Negro troops was made harder by an unbecoming discrimination on the part of the government in matters of equipment, clothing and pay. Not until 1864 did Congress get around to giving colored troops the same pay as whites.[78]

The Negroes, especially those from the North, protested discriminatory treatment, but in general they bore their lot with patience and good humor. Inspection reports and other comments testify to pride in their dress, aptitude and precision in drill, amenability to discipline, eagerness for the learning dispensed in unit schools, interest in religion and less addiction than white comrades to drinking, swearing, gambling and most other evils of camp.[79]

In addition to those who wore the Federal uniform, thousands of Negroes assisted the army in the capacity of personal servants, teamsters, laundresses and laborers. The servants, used for such purposes as foraging, cooking, cleaning and looking after horses, were usually the employees of officers, but occasionally the rank and file, individually or collectively, engaged a colored helper to lighten the drudgery of camp. A Connecticut cavalry sergeant wrote his sister from Virginia: "I have got a Slave boy about 16 years old who ran away from his master and offered to work for me for his rations and a small compensation a month. He takes care of my horse and Equipment and blacks my boots &c." Another Connecticut Yank, recently promoted from the ranks and of strong antislavery leanings, informed his brother: "I have a little nigger to wait on me and am growing quite respectably corpulent in my old age [he was 22]. How much easier it is to have a little nig to take your extra steps for you than it is to do it all yourself." [80]

Some of the blue-uniformed masters were no less harsh in their comments about colored servants than the most captious of slaveowners, but others praised highly their efficiency and devotion. A Massachusetts lieutenant who lost his colored aide and later discovered that he was dead wrote on locating the gravestone: "Poor Jack! if faithfulness has a reward in Heaven, Thou wilt surely find them." [81]

The aggregate of Negro helpers sometimes ran to considerable numbers. Captain John W. De Forest estimated that his regiment, while stationed in Louisiana in the summer of 1862, had fully sixty "contrabands" in its service.[82]

Ordinarily colored servants stayed in the rear during combat, but now and then they would succumb to the martial spirit, seek weapons and blaze away at the Rebels. De Forest stated that at the battle of Baton Rouge "the officers' waiters and other black camp followers picked up the rifles of the wounded and fought gallantly."[83] William Tecumseh Sherman, who in general was opposed to use of Negroes in combat, ordered the organization of plantation workers in Mississippi as "a kind of outlying picket." Concerning one such group, formed under their own leader, he wrote General John B. McPherson, half humorously, in September 1863:

There are about 100 negroes fit for service enrolled under the command of the venerable George Washington, who, mounted on a sprained horse, with his hat plumed with the ostrich feather, his full belly girt with a stout belt, from which hangs a terrible cleaver, and followed by his trusty orderly on foot, makes an army on your flank that ought to give every assurance of safety from that exposed quarter.[84]

Another racial group who wore the blue were the Indians. A brigade of red men was organized early in the war for service in the Indian country. This unit, commonly known as the Indian Home Guard, was composed of the First, Second and Third Indian Regiments. The First Regiment consisted mainly of Creeks, but had a sprinkling of Seminoles and other groups. The Second Regiment was comprised initially of Osages, Quapaws and "other broken fragments of tribes," but these Indians proved to be so unsatisfactory as soldiers that they were replaced by Cherokees, half-breeds and whites. The Third Regiment was a Cherokee organization whose ranks, like that of the Second, were filled largely with men won over from Confederate service. A Fourth and Fifth Indian Regiment were authorized at one time and their recruitment actually initiated, but the War Department reconsidered the action and assigned the recruits to other organizations.[85]

The Indian Brigade left a unique and interesting relic of its Civil War service in the form of muster rolls now preserved in the Oklahoma Historical Society. As one glances down the list of warriors he finds such distinctive names in the Second Indian Regiment as Captain Spring Frog and Private Arch Killer Clay and Bird Jones. In Company A, Third

Indian Regiment are listed Private Stephen Killer, John Bearmeat, Crying Bear, Little Dear, Alex Scarce Water, Spring Water, Wolfe, Poor Wolfe and Mixt Water. The file of Company B of the same regiment includes Big Mush Dirt Eater, Pot Falling, Oo-li-Skun-ee, Rabbit Jack, Soup, Swimmer Jack, Sharp and Warkiller Hogshooter.[86]

The Descriptive Book of Company F, Third Indian Regiment contains a tragic note concerning Sergeant Harrison Benge, a Georgia-born Cherokee listed as a farmer, who had joined the Union Army at Fort Gibson, Indian Territory, on May 1, 1863, at the age of thirty-two:

Murdered on the 17th day of August, '64 by an assasin during his sleep in his tent. Sergt Benge deserves the praze of Evry true Patriot and good Soldiers for his fadelity honisty & Valor and the Co feels his loss the more that his plase cannot be filled for in F Co. his Equel do not Exist.

Possibly the hand that wrote the above tribute was that of the Indian orderly sergeant, Samuel Beinstick. Or it might have been one of the other red-skinned comrades whose names are listed on the same roll as Tyer Bigfeather, Flying Bird, Arch Bigfoot, Chickiller, Camp Chicken, Wade B. Fish, Edward Duck, George Hogtoter, James Sweetcaller, Himman Sweetkiller, Bone Eater and Do You Ne Se. Or the eulogy might even have been the work of Second Lieutenant Jumper Duck.[87]

Company M of the Fourteenth Kansas Cavalry was composed of Delawares and Shawnees, and various other organizations contained a sprinkling of red men. A Union captain told of receiving a detail of Indians from the Fifth Wisconsin Regiment to help him destroy Confederate stores in Jackson, Mississippi. "No sooner had they comprehended the nature of the work we had to do," he wrote, "than they 'put their war paint on,' and with demoniac yells and all sorts of leapings and wild motions began putting the torch to every house they came to." The fire engines were summoned to put out the flames which the savages had set to dwellings and churches, but the rampaging Indians blocked the firemen's efforts by jabbing their bayonets into the hoses. Finally the captain in desperation called out a company of white soldiers to run down the berserks and send them back to their quarters under guard, while paleface comrades less susceptible to frenzy took over the work of destruction.[88]

The Indian soldiers took part in a number of border engagements, including those at Newtonia, Missouri; Prairie Grove, Arkansas; and Honey Springs and Perryville in the Indian Territory.[89] At Honey Springs, as in some of their lesser battles, the Federal Indians were arrayed against red men bearing the Rebel standard. Indeed, the Honey Springs fight was primarily an Indian affair, though the Northern force included a colored regiment, the First Kansas Cavalry, and the Southern contained some white units from Texas. Official reports indicate that the Indians here, as elsewhere, raised the savage war whoop when the contest grew hot.

Confederate Indians were said to have mutilated the bodies of white foes killed in some engagements and it is probable that the Northern Indians did likewise.[90]

The Indian regiments initially were staffed with white field officers and Indian captains and lieutenants. Except in a few instances, however, the red men proved disappointing in command positions, not for lack of bravery but mainly because they were deficient in stability, administrative capacity and discipline. As a result, the War Department replaced most of the Indian officers with whites. The Third Indian Regiment, last to be organized from among the red men, had white first lieutenants and orderly sergeants specially selected for their character and leadership. This regiment also made the best record of any Indian unit on the Federal side.[91]

The Indians maintained a good reputation as fighters. In his official report of Prairie Grove the commander of the First Indian Regiment stated: "Of the Indian officers, Captain Jon-neh of the Uches, and Capt. Billy Bowlegs of the Seminoles and Captain Tus-te-nup-chup-ko of Company A (Creek), are deserving of the highest praise." He reported two killed and four wounded, but expressed doubt as to the accuracy of those figures since "the Indians entertain a prejudice against speaking of dangerous occurrences in battle and report no wounds but such as the necessities of the case demand." [92]

The conduct of Indians in other engagements also won praise from their officers. But the same cannot be said of their performance in noncombatant aspects of soldiering. Between battles the red men were often slovenly in dress, careless of equipment, neglectful of camp duties and indifferent to prescribed routine, especially that governing furloughs and passes. They also seemed inclined at times to support the side which appeared in strongest force among them. Colonel William A. Phillips, who knew the Indian soldier as well as any Federal officer, said of them in 1863: "The besetting sin of Indians is laziness. They are brave as death, active to fight but lazy." He also observed that absence without leave was a "chronic Indian weakness." General James G. Blunt, another officer with much experience in the command of Indian troops, remarked in August 1863 that the red men "are of little service to the Government compared with other soldiers." He stated further that the Cherokees were "far superior in every respect" to other Indians of his command, but that the Cherokees were effective only so long as they had in view the specific objective of occupying their own country. "I would not exchange one regiment of negro troops for ten regiments of Indians," he concluded.[93]

Indians who wore the blue sometimes received shabby treatment by the government. Reports of inspectors and commanding officers indicate that their arms were often obsolete, their pay frequently in arrears while their families suffered for food, and that in general they were more often dealt with as stepchildren of the Great White Father than as fighting sons supporting the cause of Union and freedom.[94]

Whatever their nationality or race Billy Yanks were distributed by assignment or detail among several branches.[95] The overwhelming majority were infantry, as the Civil War was primarily a musketman's conflict. Union infantrymen comprised the equivalent of 1,696 regiments, while cavalry aggregated 272 regiments and artillery 78.[96]

The nucleus of the Federal forces was the Regular Army which numbered approximately 13,000 in March 1861, and during the war added about 67,000 recruits. Other components of the army at various times were the state militia called to Federal service; conscripts whose net number was about 46,000; substitutes who usually were inducted in the stead of draftees and who aggregated about 118,000; and volunteers who made up the great bulk of the army.[97]

An infantry regiment of volunteers, whose authorized strength in 1863 was 39 officers and 986 men, was divided into ten companies each having 3 officers and 98 men. Each company was divided into two platoons and each platoon into two sections. Above the regimental level was the brigade, composed of four regiments; the division, consisting of three or four brigades; the corps (authorized by Congress on July 17, 1862), made up of two or more divisions; and the army, having one or more corps. Combination of arms began at the brigade level, with the bringing together of infantry and artillery, but on higher echelons other supporting branches were added.[98]

As previously noted the various branches were designated by distinctive trimmings and insignia, and units above the company level by their own standards.[99] In March 1863 corps badges were instituted and thereafter this symbol, worn usually on cap or hat, became a standard feature of the uniform. As a general rule the predominating color of first-division badges in each corps was red; second division, white; and third division, blue.[100]

In the volunteer force each regiment of cavalry was divided into twelve companies or troops and each regiment of artillery into twelve batteries. Organization of Regular Army units was different in that infantry regiments comprised two or more battalions of eight companies each; cavalry regiments had three battalions of two squadrons each, with two companies in a squadron; and artillery regiments consisted of eight or twelve batteries. Furthermore, Regular Army divisions were composed of two brigades.[101]

These were the arrangements specified in War Department orders; but in actual practice variations were common. After a brief period of service units were habitually below strength. Thomas L. Livermore gave as the average regimental strength in the Union Army during various engagements the following: Shiloh, 560; Fair Oaks, 650; Chancellorsville, 530; Gettysburg, 375; Chickamauga, 440; Wilderness, 440; and Sherman's battles of May 1864, 305.[102]

The regiment figured prominently in Billy Yank's loyalties. Regimental pride was especially strong in some of the older organizations which won fame in early engagements and became exceedingly jealous of their reputations. Typical of the fierce loyalty of members of such units was that manifested by Sergeant Matthew Marvin of the First Minnesota who wrote after Fredericksburg: "I would rather be a private in this reg[imen]t than captain in any that I know of"; and Private E. A. Johnson of the First Massachusetts who declared in April 1862: "I had rather be a private in the Mass. 1st regiment than to hold the highest commission in any of the others, and I have heard many say the same." [103]

Regimental consciousness occasionally reached such a high degree as to cause men of different units to pitch into each other with bricks, clubs and fists, but rivalry usually found an outlet in friendly banter.[104] Loyalty to regiment increased with the passing of time and in the latter part of the conflict became so strong that proposals of the War Department to consolidate depleted organizations aroused a howl of protest. "If we lose our name and number," wrote one Yank whose regiment was threatened by consolidation, "our record would soon be forgotten." [105]

Attachment to brigade and division usually was nominal while loyalty to corps was often strong. In some instances corps sensitiveness manifested itself in the exchange of abusive language by members of different organizations and even in free-for-all fighting. A captain of the Fifteenth Corps in Grant's old army wrote in March 1864, after corps from

BILLY YANK POSES WITH THE BRASS
A Michigan Private and Lieutenant

Courtesy National Archives

IN THE DITCHES BEFORE ATLANTA

other commands had been brought in for the Chattanooga and Georgia campaigns: "Our corps dont get along well with these Cumberland and Potomac soldiers. To hear our men talk to them . . . you'd think the feeling between us and the Rebels could be no more bitter. We are well off by ourselves, but still we dont feel at home. We're too far from our old comrades, 13th, 16th, and 17th Corps. This feeling that grows up between regiments, brigades, divisions and corps is very strong and as strange." Soldiers of Burnside's Ninth Corps who served for a time with those of the Twenty-third in the West remarked of the latter that they were "the first to retreat and the last to advance . . . just what you might expect of the 23rd Corps." [106]

Many Yanks manifested outstanding pride in their army, but army consciousness was frequently so closely associated with sectional consciousness that the two were indistinguishable. Cleavage seems to have been primarily geographical, as between East and West, and secondarily organizational, as between the Army of the Potomac—which though heterogeneous in composition was regarded by outsiders as an Eastern group—and armies made up primarily of soldiers from other sections.

Eastern soldiers disparaged their Western comrades as crude, undisciplined and slovenly, while Yanks from Ohio, Michigan or Kansas denounced those of Massachusetts, New York or Pennsylvania as effete, liquor-soaked, money-mad dandies—"bandbox" troops, fit only for parade and garrison. Illustrative of Western attitudes (and the Westerners seem to have been the more outspoken of their prejudices) was that expressed by a Hoosier after attending a band concert by Maine troops at which the collection plate was passed: "D—n these 'Down East,' money-loving, Yankee band-box Provost Guard regiments," he stated. "Dressed out in full rig, with all the extra (brass) touches on, and polished boots, they take possession of the little towns along the line of march, *as fast as we run the rebels out—strut* about like turkey goblers with guns that have never fired a shot at secesh (nor never will)." [107] Even more pointed was the remark made after Antietam by one of Grant's Illinois soldiers: "Nobody in this country seems to care a cuss whether McClellan is removed or not," he disclosed. "General feeling is that the Potomac Army is only good to draw greenbacks and occupy winter quarters." [108]

The favorite theme of recrimination was relative fighting abilities. Soldiers of Western commands were convinced that they bore the brunt of the conflict while the Army of the Potomac was making no more than a halfhearted effort. An Indiana private of Rosecrans' army on hearing of Meade's victory at Gettysburg wrote: "Well it was a great wonder that the Army of the Potomac did not fall back, but it was time that they were doing something, this army . . . goes where it pleases . . . we have fought the most stubborn Battles of this war, but where has our praise gone to? why to the band box army on the Potomac, they needed it to keep up spirits, and we kept ours up by Victorious Battles . . . they have been in but one Confederate state while we have been through five." Repulse of the Eastern army in the Mine Run campaign provoked this soldier to state: "It is a most disgusting fact to again know that the *very grand army of the Potomac* have again been scared back to their old familiar haunts near Washington—the war would never end were it left to the fighting of the band box army in the east. Soon will be seen the Army of the Cumberland advancing upon Richmond from the Southwest leaving their many bloody battle fields, over which they have gained great victories, behind them." [109]

Western Yanks predicted that the assumption of command in the East by Grant, whom they esteemed as one of their own, would work a revolution in the Virginia theater, and when the offensive of 1864 bogged down they were not long in finding a scapegoat. "The final assault on Petersburg was rendered a failure by the gross cowardice of the Potomac Army which has ruined every Gen. before Grant," wrote an Illinois soldier in August 1864. But he confidently predicted that Grant would eventually "win the victory over all disaster" as "his grasp on the Rebel Capitol is like the hand of Fate." [110]

Some of the Westerners who marched triumphantly with Sherman through Georgia and the Carolinas became extremely cocky in their attitude. One of them, a Wisconsin private, went to Richmond and Petersburg just before the famous victory parade in Washington to look over the Rebel defenses that had thwarted the Easterners until the war was almost over. "I expected to see some big breastworks," he wrote, "but was disappointed. I have seen more works around Kennesaw Mountain than there are around both of these places." He concluded that "the Potomac Army has no doubt done some hard fighting, but it has been on a different scale than ours, and the most of it was done in the papers." [111]

When Eastern soldiers were transferred to Chattanooga and other Western points they were subjected to considerable abuse. A favorite form of insult was for the Westerners to greet the newcomers with such phrases as "Bull Run," "fall back on your straw and fresh butter," "advance on Washington," "Burnside crossing the Rappahannock," and "All Quiet on the Potomac." [112]

Such twitting and taunting often led to ill feeling and strife. "The 4th and 14th Corps Cumberland chaps, our men can endure," an Army of the Tennessee officer reported in March 1864, "[but] the 11th and 12th Corps Potomac men and ours never meet without some very hard talk." [113]

A Wisconsin private stationed in Louisiana noted in his diary in September 1863, shortly after some Nineteenth Corps troops from the East came to the Department of the Gulf: "They and the Western boys fight every time we meet. I think either side would rather shoot at each other than the Johnnies." [114]

Westerners had no monopoly on superiority complexes, for many Easterners were strong in the opinion that the "Potomac boys" were the bravest of the brave and that the battles fought in the hinterland were mere skirmishes compared to the bloody engagements of their own baili- wick. If perchance they conceded notable triumphs to the followers of Buell, Rosecrans or Sherman, they were apt to offer in explanation the comment that Western Rebs were far more docile than those led by Lee and Jackson. No less a personage than Grant was cited to support this claim by one Eastern veteran who wrote on June 12, 1864: "This last week Grant publicly acknowledged to our generals that he . . . *never knew what real hard fighting was until he came to the Army of the Potomac.* He says . . . that our Western army never had any *such men* to fight as we have, nor such able generals to contend against as Lee and his Lieuts. Ewell, Hill and Longstreet." This man added the observation that Grant's statement "but corroborates the opinion we have always had, and that was the Western rebels are nothing but an armed mob, and not anything near so hard to whip as Lee's well disciplined sol- diers." [115]

The Easterners were not above indulgence in name-calling and deri- sion. Ninth Corps troops sent to assist Grant's forces in the Mississippi campaign of 1863 chided their associates by asking, "Who had to come away out here to help you take a one-horse town like Vicksburg?" and "Who took Jackson for you?" [116]

It would be incorrect to assume, however, that troops from diverse organizations and areas were always hostile, for such was not the case. In many instances friendliness was predominant from the beginning of mixed associations. Much of the oral cross fire was idle chatter or good-natured banter. Even when relations were genuinely strained initially, tensions usually eased as the units intermingled; and if they became co-partners in battle antipathy frequently gave way to mutual admiration.

Moreover, rivalry and strife were by no means wholly reprehensible, for often they were but the obverse of a healthy pride and a high morale. The same Hoosier soldier who looked down his nose at the "band box army on the Potomac," wrote vauntingly: "I can (should I live to get home) be proud of being a soldier of Uncle Sam's a[nd] belonging to the best Army in the United States (not wishing to flatter any) but where has this Army of the Cumberland ever been defeated in all its travels from Kentucky, through Tennessee, Mississippi, Alabama and one corner of Georgia? Why no place, and that is not all we do not intend to be defeated with 'Rosie' in the lead." [117]

And who can say that this man was not a better soldier for his prejudice and pride?

State consciousness was strong in the Union Army though it was by no means so pronounced among the rank and file as among high-ranking officers. A Pennsylvania private observed in March 1862 that there was "no great love" between Keystone troops and those of certain New England states with whom they had the misfortune to be brigaded.[118] Similarly a Vermont lieutenant wrote in June 1861 that "We [of Vermont] are jealous of our honor and when Mass. cast any imputations upon us or our Col. they will be properly resented." The Massachusetts soldiers, he added, were offended that a Vermont colonel, and not their own, commanded the post, for to the Bay State men "Vermonters are bushwhackers." [119]

Actually there was no discernible difference in the fighting qualities of soldiers from the various sections. Nor were there any marked divergences in other basic characteristics. Eastern units, as already noted, normally had more foreigners than those recruited in the West, but this was due in large measure to the fact of the East having more large cities. A survey of 315,620 conscripts by the Provost Marshal General's Bureau indicated that Western Yanks were taller than those from the East, but the difference was negligible. Contrasts between city and country soldiers were greater than those between Easterners and Westerners. But the impressive diversity that existed among the Union privates was more a matter of individual differences than anything else.[120]

Another strong prejudice that existed in Federal camps, as in those of the Confederacy, was that of volunteers toward regulars. Here, again, the sentiment was not so marked among the men as among their leaders. Occasionally, however, the citizen soldiers would register resentment toward the professionals and the latter would look with contempt on the novitiates in arms. A Nashville newspaper in November 1864 reported a serious altercation in the bawdyhouse district of that city between regulars of the Thirteenth United States Infantry and volunteers of the Ninth Pennsylvania and Fourth Michigan Regiments. The point at issue was the respective fighting abilities of the two groups. The controversy moved swiftly from words to pistols and the regulars took refuge in a whorehouse. The volunteers soon drove their foes from this first line of defense to a second stronghold which also was a bawdyhouse, run by Dutch Lize. In the pitched battle that ensued before the provost guard intervened over a hundred shots were fired and some of the citizens were said to have concluded that "Hood with his whole army" was attacking the town. The fracas may have justified to each group its own martial superiority but outsiders were probably most impressed by the amazingly poor display of marksmanship, for the only casualty was one of the women who had part of her shoe cut away by a bullet.[121]

The volunteers' hostility toward the professionals was blended with admiration. "We're as good as the regulars," or, as some put it, "better," was deemed one of the highest tributes that the volunteers could pay themselves. One civilian soldier who visited a regiment of regulars in 1862 afterward wrote his homefolk: "Oh, father, how splendidly the regulars drill; it is perfectly sickening and disgusting to get back here and see our regiment and officers manoeuver, after seeing those West Pointers and those veterans of eighteen years' service go through guard mounting. . . . I am only glad I saw, for now I know I am a better soldier after seeing them perform." [122]

If this soldier was inspired thus by excellence in drill, how much greater must have been the admiration aroused in him, and in his comrades, by the performance of the regulars in combat! [123]

Some of the volunteers manifested strong bias against the conscripts. "Many of the boys sympathize with those who were drawn 'over the left,' " wrote a Michigander on hearing of the results of the draft in his home community, "and wish them all sorts of joy, such as long marches, heavy knapsacks, etc., saying it would have been much better to have volunteered and so got rid of the name of 'Conscript,' which they seem to dread more than the name of Convict in time of peace." Another Yank whose regiment was about to be replenished with draftees expressed great fear that "the 3d Wisconsin *volunteers* will be the 3d Regt. of *conscripts,*" and added, "I pity the conscripts that come into our Regiment, the boys will annoy them to death." [124]

Of course if the conscripts proved themselves worthy men and good soldiers, as they frequently did, they were usually able to overcome prejudice and win full acceptance among their volunteer associates.

In the realm of interbranch relations, the favorite objects of abuse were the cavalrymen and the principal dispensers of invective were the infantrymen. The cavalry, whose status and demeanor in Civil War times bears striking resemblance to airmen of World War II, were themselves responsible for much of the derision heaped on them by the foot soldiers—though undoubtedly some of the ridicule was born of envy. Wearing spurs and fancy hats, dashing about on gaily caparisoned horses, forcing plodding infantrymen off the roads and perhaps showering them with mud, charging in and out of battle while other soldiers stayed on to wrestle with the foe, and afterward swaggering about as if theirs had been the crucial role in the conflict—all of which, and more, cavalrymen did or seemed to do—was not the sort of conduct to win friends in other branches. Few of the infantry considered the fact that cavalrymen were frequently scouting while other troops lay quietly in camp. The thing that stuck in the riflemen's minds was the exaggerated estimate of enemy strength which reconnoitering expeditions occasionally turned in.

A mule-mounted infantryman, who in 1864 was swept onto a Western column by a cavalry force which came rushing rearward with reports of Forrest and 10,000 troops ahead, was much put out by being mistaken for a member of the scorned branch. "I'm no lying cavalryman, boys," he hurriedly explained, "there ain't over 5,000 of them, but their [they're] coming right along." All except the cavalry had a good laugh when the source of panic proved to be a foraging party returning to the Federal lines.[125]

Infantrymen commonly regarded the cavalry as playboys who roamed the country at will leaving to foot soldiers the mud, misery and peril; and they took out their spite on the boot-and-saddle fraternity by whatever means they could. A mounted regiment from New Jersey, noted for the multicolored gaudiness of its irregular uniform, was dubbed the "Butterfly Cavalry" by their walking comrades and, until the garish regalia was exchanged for that prescribed in regulations, members of this unit were greeted with taunts and jeers wherever they went.[126]

Typical of infantry attitudes was that registered by one of Sherman's men while the Army of Tennessee was en route from Mississippi to

Chattanooga in 1863. "We have considerable cavalry with us," he noted in his diary, "but they are the laughing stock of the army and the boys poke all kinds of fun at them." He added: "I really have as yet to see or hear of their doing anything of much credit to them." [127]

It was said to have been a standing joke in Sherman's command late in the war that General John A. Logan had offered a reward for a dead cavalryman, blue or gray.[128]

The infantrymen's disesteem of the mounted branch was not so deep or real as to prevent his yearning to "jine the cavalry." Indeed, the urge proved so strong in some instances that infantry commanders had to take extraordinary measures, such as placing a double guard around the camp, to keep their men away from cavalry recruiting officers.[129]

Relations between infantry and artillery seem to have been consistently cordial, and friendliness seems generally to have existed between the musket-bearing soldiers and members of the other branches. Two exceptions were surgeons and regimental quartermasters whom common soldiers of all arms frequently reviled, but these functionaries were denounced partly for being officers. The attitude of the private toward quartermasters was aptly represented by an unidentified soldier when he wrote in his diary at Baton Rouge, January 27, 1863: "Prayer meeting in Chapel tent. Q. M. gets up and asks the forgiveness of the whole Regt for his misdeeds, professes to be under conviction. Glory Halleluiah!" [130]

Scattered through the army as a whole were a number of distinct types. Perhaps the most despised, and certainly the most maligned, was the deadbeat. Almost every company had a drone who shirked his duties and lived off his comrades. Such a man was a chronic borrower of money, tobacco, equipment and food; refused to carry a canteen, choosing rather to depend on the generosity of his fellows; avoided menial tasks such as gathering wood and pitching tents; dodged guard and fatigue details, or else contrived to throw most of the work on associates. Some were so lazy that they would not rise from their seats to receive what they borrowed, but instead requested the lender to "chuck it" to them. A favorite ruse of the deadbeat was to play sick, and some were capable of feigning the most distressing illness or deformity.[131] A goodly portion of the deadbeats were cowards who, by hook or crook, managed to find a place in the rear when fighting was imminent. But some entered wholeheartedly into combat.

Closely akin to the deadbeat was the blowhard, otherwise known as the puffer. This type of Yank was a leader in gabfests and lost no opportunity for self-glorification. He bragged of his family background, his achievements as a civilian, his prowess as a lover and his numerous triumphs in affairs of honor. In battle he was usually inconspicuous, if present at all, but this did not prevent him afterward from proclaiming himself a hero of the first magnitude. If comrades seemed unimpressed by his exploits, the blowhard sometimes sought a more distant audience, such as the family circle or the hometown editor. A Buckeye braggart, who was published in a Zanesville newspaper as the heroic killer of two Rebs at First Manassas, was shortly afterward called on by comrades bearing shovels who mischievously announced that they had come to bury the dead about whom they had read in the paper.[132]

The blowhards usually did not fade away in the postwar years, but rather waxed bolder in recounting their martial accomplishments. Defined aptly by Senator Benjamin Hill of Georgia as "invincible in peace and invisible in war," some of them rode by way of their fictitious achievements into public office.[133]

Another species encountered occasionally in Federal camps was the rogue. This type varied in character from the genial rake to the vicious scoundrel, and included thieves, cutthroats, pimps, murderers and other offscourings of humanity. Among the better class of rogues was a group who might be called the hell-raisers—mischievous men who would provoke a fight for pure devilment; or hurl derogatory epithets at an officer from some concealed spot and then laugh at his embarrassment; or get down on hands and knees and yelp like dogs when a spit-and-polish colonel ordered a more uniform pitching of pup tents.[134] At the lower end of the scale was the hardened knave who would pilfer the pockets of his comrades, ransack civilian premises, abuse defenseless women and take base advantage of gullible Negroes.

A roster of rascals in blue would include Joe Boner of a Minnesota unit who in 1862, along with a comrade, died in a jail to which they had set fire with a view to effecting their escape. Boner was so frequently in confinement that his associates called him "Guardhouse Joe." After his death a comrade wrote: "Boner was a fideler . . . he was about 30 years of age a very small man he was allways drunk when he could get a chance." [135]

Of similar ilk was an unnamed member of a New York regiment who in 1861 was bayoneted to death by camp guards whose restraining order he refused to heed. Concerning this soldier a comrade remarked: "[He] was the worst man I ever saw. He was always drunk, fighting and threatening the lives of the soldiers, he has been in the guard house times without number." [136]

Occasionally rogues revealed themselves as such in their correspondence. A Vermont scamp, who was well along in years and a snuff addict, boasted of feasting on chicken, cakes, pies and other delicacies stolen from the wagons of peddlers who thronged the camps. "We don't pay out any money for our liveing," he stated, "and we live better than uncle sam can a ford and it tase better than hard tacks salt beef and pork." [137]

Early in his service this man secured a detail as surgeon's assistant and then as a hospital worker. Though he was said to be healthy and tough, he does not appear to have done any fighting. He was quite active, however, in money-making projects of various sorts, including laundering the apparel of his associates at five cents a garment and selling at a handsome profit various articles of food and clothing sent at his request by the homefolk.[138] He even did a bit of bootlegging, as the following instructions which he sent from Virginia in 1864 to his son indicate:

I want yo to Send me 10 Galones of hye wines or Elcoll [alcohol] I want it to sell i can git fore dollars a pint for it yo can put it in tin canes [cans] And pack it in Saw dust have the canes made so you can cork them tight And put them in A good Stout Box fille the canes full so it wont ratle now Send it as Sun as yo git this leter And Send . . . me the coss of it canes And all . . . And when yo Send it Send me A letter the Same time. . . . bee cufule And pack it so it wont wratle for they are gitin very strick . . . if I can git it heare it will bring me good too hundred dolars the minet I git it if yo cant git hy wines git what yo can eny thing that is licker when yo Send it Direct it to Docter Sawin Just as yo have the rest.[139]

The box arrived in due time, but whether it contained "hy wines" or some other kind of "licker" is not known; nor is the recipient's profit from it a matter of record. But available correspondence indicates that this private's side earnings from various enterprises aggregated about fifty dollars a month. Indeed, financial gain seems to have been the principal concern of his military service. A comrade wrote the homefolk on one occasion that the old soldier was "making money like dirt" and an adult son who received this report, fearful that his father might become so enthralled by his profits as to prolong his army connection, wrote: "You said something about Enlisting over again. Dont for God's sake even menchion anything of that kind again. Money is entresing I know but it is better to Di poor than to fasten yourself for any longer time than what you are Fastened for." The parent evidently followed his son's advice about re-enlistment, but near the end of his original stint of service he fell from a hospital boat and drowned.[140]

Another type whose presence in the Union ranks was deplored by the overwhelming majority of Yanks was the sot. This species would drink any sort of intoxicant, however vile, and would stay tight (the word was current in Union camps) as long as liquor could be had by begging, buying or stealing. A New York soldier, whose attachment to drink won for him the nickname Whisky Bill, amazed his comrades by his never-failing ability to elude the camp guards, slip into near-by towns and get roaring drunk. Sots were usually worthless as soldiers and their departure from the service, whether by desertion, death or dishonorable discharge, caused little if any heartache among their associates. The low esteem in which they were held by conscientious comrades was pungently, if not delicately, illustrated by the comment of an Ohioan concerning some sots in his organization: "tom is the ornryist shit in the regamment. . . . tom and Pet drinks every think [thing] in the shape of Whiskey tom is perfectly orny." [141]

Still another type was the chronic forager, the soldier who spent a major portion of his time and energy supplementing the rations issued by the commissary. A good example of the archforager was Private Walter Kittredge of the Twenty-fourth Wisconsin Regiment. Kittredge rarely passed a day in which he did not enrich army fare by trading, begging or stealing—though for stealing he substituted the euphemisms "raising," "gobbling" and "drawing over the left"—edibles not obtainable from regular sources. So great was his resourcefulness, boldness and persistence that he was able to live sumptuously when comrades were bedeviled by the gnawings of hunger.[142]

Kittredge was as brave in combat as he was adept in foraging. He remained gallantly at his post at Stone's River while scores around him took to their heels, was seriously wounded and after a period in the hospital returned to civilian life a battle-scarred hero.[143]

The forager sometimes used the same techniques as the bummer, but the latter was a far more noxious type. The bummer was a scoundrel whose main interest was pillage and who had little concern for the war's basic objectives. His favorite arena was the periphery of the army where restraint was weakest and plunder richest. He greatly preferred raids on civilian Rebels to pitched battles against those bearing arms. As a group, bummers merit a place with the rogues whose character has already been delineated.[144]

One of the most distinctive types was the mournful one. This character saturated himself in gloom, wore a dejected mien and took a pessimistic view of the future. He never laughed, rarely smiled and seemed to be pained by the joviality of others. He liked to dwell on such themes as sickness, death and the depravity of man. His enjoyment, if any, derived from contemplation of woe—past, present and future.

The mournful one wrote gloomy letters home in which he spelled out the hardships of army life, expressed grave concern over the plight of his family and made dire predictions as to his own fate. One Yank of this species sprinkled missives to his wife with such doleful statements as these:

I have Cum to the Conclusion that you hav fergot me intierly. . . . I want to get hom to see you all so bad I dont no what to do. . . . We live darnd hard.

I am so fraid that our Dear little babes will get the flux I dont know what to do Mary you must Bee very Carful of them it seemes like all the old people is diing off their in ohio but that is the Way of the World the old must die and the young may die.[145]

The wife's letters in reply were not of the sort to alleviate melancholy. On one occasion she wrote: "i am very sorry to hear that you are a marching for i am a fraid that you are going in to a battel this is a world of troubel." [146]

Another prophet of gloom addressed these doleful sentiments to his spouse:

Dear Sallie this is a hard place there is no pleasure here all is trouble and vexation this place lacks agreat deal of being at home with you and Willie. . . . god only knows when this war will be over or who will be the survivors of this war. I may have seen my home on earth with its many charms and its numerous friends the last time but dear sallie there is a home fare in the skies for you and I.[147]

This Yank was of religious bent and the same was true of some other doleful fellows. To this group, religion, instead of being a source of joy and hope, was essentially a spring of sorrow and of woe.

Some of the mournful ones were pathological cases whose chronic dejection was beyond control. No doubt some of the 278 recorded instances of suicide among wearers of the blue were of men sorely afflicted with depressive mental ailments.[148]

Closely related to the mournful one was the recluse—indeed the two were sometimes identical. Of recluses a Yank wrote after the war:

> These men were irreproachable as soldiers . . . but they seemed shut up within an impenetrable shell, and would lie on their blankets silent while all others joined in the social round; or perhaps would get up and go out of the tent as if its lively social atmosphere was uncongenial. . . . Should you address them they would answer pleasantly but in monosyllables. . . . They could not be drawn out. They would cook by themselves, eat by themselves, camp by themselves . . . in fact keep by themselves at all times as much as possible.[149]

Sometimes the recluse was a snob. New England, and especially the intellectual circles of Boston, appears to have sent more soldiers of this type than other sections. A son of the Bay State wrote from Virginia early in 1863: "This company . . . is a sad place for a cultivated gentleman, no fit associates for a collegian & a poor company for me." A Yank who entered the service from Yale expressed similar sentiments, writing his mother while on detached duty: "I managed to get away from the Company [and come] . . . here in the woods where there would be less stealing whiskey, less swearing & less of Southwick's perpetual growl," (Southwick being his regular sergeant nicknamed "old rum blossom" from the redness of his nose).[150]

Now and then a dandy was to be found among the rank and file. John D. Billings, who served as an artilleryman in the Army of the Potomac and whose *Hard Tack and Coffee* is among the most delightful of published memoirs on the Union side, referred to this type as the "paper-collar young man" and pictured him as wearing "enamelled long-legged boots and custom made clothes," looking with disdain on regulation apparel and eating "in a most gingerly way of the stern, unpoetical government rations." He further described the dandy as an only son who had been "a dry-goods clerk in the city at home, where no reasonable want went ungratified." [151]

Another type was the maladroit one, known also as the Jonah. The Jonah was a constitutional blunderer, utterly devoid of the rhythm and co-ordination that are the essence of drill. He spilled his coffee down the necks of his comrades, kicked their shins on the march and prodded them with his bayonet while executing the manual of arms.[152] Concerning one of this type, who bore the nickname of "Molasses," Charles E. Davis of the Thirteenth Massachusetts Regiment wrote:

He was homely in appearance, unshapely in form, awkward in gait and as ignorant and dirty a slouch as could be found. His gait was like that of a man who, having spent his life in a ploughed field, could not divest his mind of the idea that he was still stepping over furrows. . . . He was generally absent when his services were needed. . . . Just before we went into the battle of Manassas . . . he stopped to tie his shoe and never returned to the regiment again. . . . We were glad he never came back.[153]

Held in even more contempt than the Jonah was the mamma's boy, the helpless one, who never quite cut the home ties and who had to be wet-nursed by his comrades. Of such a soldier, Private Alonzo Miller of the Twelfth Wisconsin Regiment wrote:

I . . . would have written more but I have had to take care of Jap. He is quite a baby. He does not know how to get along. . . . I cook for Jap and myself for he does not know how to do the very least thing. . . . He eats like sixty and does not have courage to stir to exercise it off. . . . He does not take care of himself as he ought. When he left me [to go to the hospital] he was lousy.[154]

In happy contrast to the long-faced kind was the bouncing optimist, or the I-love-life species. This type greeted reveille with a resounding whoop, mirthfully ogled sleep-heavy comrades, devoured the rough breakfast as if the fare were savory, tackled camp police details with a song, performed drill in the manner of one playing a pleasant game and repeated the colorless routine day after day without a show of boredom. During a hard march this type of Yank kept up a flow of quips and chatter and around the campfire at night was full of good humor. In any kind of gathering he was the life of the party. Even in sickness and suffering he was hard to down, the theme of his existence in darkness and in light being that of the popular camp song, "Gay and Happy Still." [155]

A blood relationship of the I-love-life type was the chronic prankster whose antics ranged all the way from laying dead snakes in soldier bunks to faking honeyed missives to love-smitten comrades. One Yank who was a victim of the latter trick wrote to the lady whose script had been forged:

Such people are low-minded and mean . . . they know you & know that I correspond with you and were impudent enough to write a letter while we were at Camp Morton imitating your hand writing & signing your name to it and directing it to me. . . . I feel thankful that all they can do or say cannot seperate me from my own sweet Maggie.[156]

The Union Army also had some soldiers of fortune. Yanks of this type were usually restless characters who had roamed the world and had many exciting experiences. Most of them delighted in regaling comrades with tales of their adventures, but some were extremely reticent. Of one of these nomads who served as a corporal in the Sixth New York Cavalry a comrade wrote:

His open countenance has something of the dash and "rough-&-ready" in it which you might expect to find in the runaway boy of sixteen, the whaler for three years (during which time he twice deserted), the merchantman, the backwoodsman, the cattle dealer, the speculator, the pedlar, the grocerman, the horse jockey, the butcher & the tinker. In each of these characters he has figured besides several others that might be mentioned. He has been in the Sandwich Islands & to the North Pole, in the South Seas & on the Spanish Main. He has picked up a good deal of information & can talk sensibly on most subjects.[157]

A character not so easily defined as some of the others, but none the less distinctive, was the sensitive type—the artist-in-arms; the man whose nature was attuned to beauty and light rather than sordidness and shadow, and whose inclination and genius were for creation rather than destruction. Few of these sensitive souls had ever fired a gun before joining the army. Some of them found soldiering intolerable while others—though sometimes at considerable pain—made the adjustment to warrior life with remarkable facility.

An excellent example of the latter group was George F. Newhall of the Eleventh Massachusetts Regiment who, with four brothers, enlisted early in the conflict and served in the Army of the Potomac. George came from a cultured home, had a good education, was of gentle disposition and refined tastes, manifested a profound interest in the world of nature and worked hard at soldiering. "I came out to see the country as well as to fight," he wrote his parents from Virginia in March 1862, "which I think can be done and still be a good soldier." [158]

At every opportunity Newhall roamed the lush Virginia countryside studying the flora and fauna, listening to the songs of birds and making sketches of leaves and blossoms. While his brothers passed on to the homefolk details of marches and battles, he preferred to describe the progress of the dogwood and the coloring of the azalea.

From a picket post near Yorktown in April 1862 Newhall wrote his father:

Perhaps Edd will keep you posted on war news while I branch off on other matters. The tree in blossom of which I wrote is the Mezeron and has been mistaken by a newspaper correspondent for the peach. . . . I find also the azalea with pink flowers, garlic in abundance. As we march along a bulbous rooted plant with deep blue flowers, bell shaped, attracts attention. Narcissus is found growing in the woods and candytuff with a prettier flower than the cultivated. . . . The trees are just beginning to leave out.[159]

He found it difficult, even as the rattle of musketry ahead urged the column onward, to keep from turning aside to explore the wonders of nature, as the following excerpts from letters written during the Peninsula campaign attest:

May 20, 1862 . . . We find the Callicanthey growing in the woods about Williamsburg, also lupins and azaleas and many other flowers I noticed while filing through the woods during the battle at that place.

June 21, 1862 . . . If you have seen the *red bud* or *Judas Tree* in bloom you can imagine the rare sight it was to see the forest full of them, even the trunks of some of them were clothed in bloom. Have fell into line of battle twice since I began to write this.[160]

By the cruel caprice of Mars, this devotee of beauty who fought gallantly through the Seven Days (but whose report of that campaign told not of hardship and slaughter, but rather of hills ripe with wheat, "bigonias all in bloom—fields full of passion flowers, some very handsome vetches or wild peas and other flowers") was listed among the missing at Second Manassas and apparently was not heard of again. His brother James informed the homefolk two months later: "I have talked with the boys of his company. The last seen of him he was rushing ahead." [161]

Perhaps he had his eye on a flower as he dashed forward in the charge. The place where he was last seen was heavily wooded. If he perished there, he must have died happy, for the forest was the joy of his life.

The roll of soldier types would not be complete without inclusion of one who may be aptly termed as ever faithful. Yanks of this species, except for sickness or some other disability, never missed a formation or battle; endured hardship without murmur; and, when fate required, uncomplainingly laid down their lives for country and cause.

To this exemplary group belonged Private Day Elmore, a country lad from near Aurora, Illinois. Elmore, after much persuading of his parents who objected on the score of his youth, enlisted in Company H, Thirty-sixth Illinois Infantry, in August 1861 when he was seventeen. He was mustered in as a drummer, but at the battle of Pea Ridge discarded his drum, took up the musket and henceforth was a full-fledged fighting man. He distinguished himself at Perryville and Murfreesboro and in November 1862 was promoted corporal. During the hard times of Buell's Kentucky campaign he wrote his homefolk: "If our Regt was Discharged tomorrow [and] . . . if this war was not at an End I would Enlist again." He added that the newspapers contained rumors of peace, but that he was opposed to compromise with the Rebels because "tha comenced it, and if they have not Enough we can give it to them to thare hearts content." [162]

At Chickamauga he was wounded in the chest, fell into Rebel hands and was sent to Belle Isle prison in Richmond. After a few months he was paroled and exchanged, but even before the exchange became official he joined his regiment and resumed his military duties. Long before his three-year term of enlistment expired he re-enlisted as a "Veteran Volunteer." Shortly after signing up as a veteran, Elmore wrote his father in explanation of his action: "I can not Express my self so I will only say that my whole soul is wrapt up in this our countrys caus I ought to be at school but I feel that I am only doeing my Duty to my self and you, Pa." [163]

On May 1, 1864, the young patriot was promoted sergeant, and in the ordeals of fire that marked the Georgia campaign he conducted himself with the same fidelity and gallantry that he had displayed throughout his prior career in arms. After the fall of Atlanta he went to Tennessee with General Thomas, the "Rock of Chickamauga," and at Franklin he received a wound which led shortly to his death. A local woman who found him in a hospital after the fight and took him to her home near by, holding him bleeding in her arms to protect him from the jolts of the buggy, wrote his parents a few days after his death: "His wound bled profusely but he thought all the time he would get well. . . . He suffered a great deal but did not complain, he was perfectly conscious to the last." [164]

So, calmly, without fear and without complaint, died this noble Yank, three months before his twenty-first birthday. Behind him lay more than three years of soldiering for the Union. Few of those who wore the blue endured more of suffering and peril than Day Elmore and probably none was purer in character, loftier in patriotism or more faithful in service. Throughout his army career he gloried in hardship and in his ability to endure it. After his fate was determined the captain of his company who had known him intimately since the time the regiment was formed wrote the bereaved parents: "Among all the brave men that I have seen march to battle I have never seen a braver, cooler man than my loved comrade Day Elmore." [165]

Not all who wore the blue were men. In addition to those employed as nurses, stewardesses and laundresses, or informally attached as vivandières, a large but indeterminable number of women actually served as soldiers. A few—such as "Major" Pauline Cushman, the famous spy of Rosecrans' command, Mary E. Walker and Sarah E. Clapp who served as assistant surgeons, and a Mrs. Reynolds who held a commission of major from the Governor of Illinois—gained official recognition without concealing their sex;[166] and Ella Hobart Gibson, while denied War Department approval as such, was elected chaplain of the First Wisconsin Regiment of Heavy Artillery in 1864 and for nine months actually performed the duties of that position.[167]

But since army policy of the period restricted membership in the military fraternity to males, the overwhelming majority of women who wore the Federal uniform had to pass muster as men. Some of the gentler sex who disguised themselves and swapped brooms for muskets were able to sustain the deception for amazingly long periods of time.

One of the most celebrated of the female Yanks was Sarah Seelye of Michigan who enlisted as Franklin Thompson in Company F of the Second Michigan Infantry in May 1861 at the age of twenty. Apparently she had little difficulty passing as a man. For nearly two years she performed the full duties of a soldier, including participation in the First Battle of Manassas and the Seven Days' campaign. Stricken with malaria while serving in Kentucky early in 1863, and being unwilling to go to the hospital, Sarah applied for a furlough. When this request was denied, she revealed her sex and became a nurse, to serve in that capacity until the end of the war. After the conflict Congress granted her a pension.[168]

Even more sensational was the career in arms of a woman who was listed in War Department records as Albert Cashier, but whose real name was Hodgers. She was born in Ireland but came to the United States as a child and settled in the Midwest where she worked as a farmer and shepherd, often wearing male attire and apparently posing on occasion as a boy. In August 1862, when nineteen, she enlisted as a private in Company G, Ninety-fifth Illinois Regiment. She served a three-year term of enlistment during which time she was regarded as unusually quiet and reclusive, but withal a good soldier. She was in the Vicksburg campaign, the Gunntown fight, the Meridian raid, the Red River expedition and the battle of Nashville. She was mustered out of the service in August 1865 and continued her masculine disguise in civilian life. In 1899 she applied for a pension and none of the three surgeons who examined her in connection with the filing of the claim indicated any suspicion of her not being a man, though one of them listed in his report some minor ailments which suggested an intimate examination.[169]

Not until about 1911, when an automobile accident compelled her hospitalization, was it revealed that Albert Cashier was a woman. After her sex was made public former comrades visited her; recognition was mutual, though the visitors were unanimous in stating that they had not suspected her femininity until they read newspaper accounts revealing her closely kept secret. One of the comrades, Harry G. Weaver, when called on by the Bureau of Pensions in 1914 for an affidavit stated:

When we were examined [at induction] we were not stripped. We were examined on the same day. All that we showed was our hands and feet. I never did see Cashier go to toilet nor did I ever see any part of his person exposed by which I could determine the sex. He was of very retiring disposition and did not take part in any of the games. He would sit around and watch, but would not take part. He had very small hands and feet. He was the smallest man in the company.

Another comrade deposed: "Cashier was very quiet in her manner and she was not easy to get acquainted with." [170]

Most of the other women known to have served as soldiers were less successful in concealing their sex than Privates Seelye and Cashier. Usually the fact of their being women was detected early and they were sent home, though in some cases not without emphatic protest.

Probably the majority of women who entered the ranks in male disguise were respectable characters, motivated by patriotism or the desire to be near husbands or sweethearts. But a few were persons of easy virtue who enrolled as soldiers to further their lewd enterprises.[171] The Memphis *Bulletin* of December 19, 1862, reported: "A woman formerly extensively known in this city as 'Canadian Lou,' was arrested in this city last night dressed in men's clothes. She was put in for inebriety. She was with a Missouri regiment in its recent march from this city to Holly Springs and back." [172]

Vivandières and other feminine camp followers sometimes became so imbued with martial ardor during battle that they joined in the fighting. Thomas L. Livermore told of a laundress attached to the Irish brigade who advanced with the unit at Antietam and in true Erin fashion stood with it in the fight, "swung her bonnet around and cheered on the men." [173]

Some of the Union amazons were casualties; at least one was fatally wounded, while another was killed outright.[174]

The attitude of male Yanks toward comrades disclosed as women was usually one of amused tolerance. A typical comment was that of a Hoosier cavalryman who wrote his wife in February 1863:

We discovered last week a soldier who turned out to be a girl. She had already been in service for 21 months and was twice wounded. Maybe she would have remained undiscovered for a long time if she hadn't fainted. She was given a warm bath which gave the secret away.[175]

Freaks and distinct types, however interesting, comprised only a minority of the rank and file. The overwhelming majority of Yanks were blended into a great mass of ordinary soldiers. But Billy Yanks en masse had some well-defined traits. In the first place they were ebullient. An Illinois officer observed of his own corps that "on the march they make it a point to abuse every man or thing they see. They always feel 'bully,' will certainly march further with less straggling and make more noise whooping than any other corps in the service." [176]

The soldier historian of an Indiana unit stated:

Our regiment yelled at everything they saw or heard. When another regiment passed, they yelled at them; they scared the darkies almost to death. . . . as they tumbled out to roll-call in the morning, they yelled . . . ; after a hard day's scouting they were never too tired to hail the end of their tasks with a joyous yell. . . . A yell would start in at one end of the division, and regiment after regiment and brigade after brigade would take it up and carry it along, then send it back to the other end; few knowing what it was about, or caring less.[177]

The appearance of a stray mule or dog along the route of march was certain to elicit a chorus of whoops that would put the poor animal to panicky flight; and discovery of a rabbit in camp would produce a pandemonium comparable to that of a surprise attack by the enemy.

Animals were not the only victims of soldier ebullience. If civilians came among the men in blue wearing strange apparel, asking foolish questions or otherwise appearing naïve or peculiar, they were sure to be swamped with a tidal wave of irreverent and impudent comment. When some Yank near the head of a marching column recognized a friend along the way and addressed him with a "How are you Jake?" the greeting would sometimes go all the way down the line, gaining volume as it went along.[178] Even officers were not immune to irreverent jibes.[179]

Billy Yank's high spirits sprang largely from his kindred trait of giving a comical twist to almost every aspect of soldier life. A company commander stated that "anything short of death is a capital joke," and a Pennsylvania private wrote: "*We laugh* at everything here. You wouldn't believe that anyone could make light of some of the scenes of which we are the witnesses. The roughtest jokes I ever heard in my life were perpetrated under a heavy fire." This fun-loving quality manifested itself in many ways. Some found merriment in placarding their tents with such rakish inscriptions as "Pups for Sale," "Rat Terriers," "Bull Pups Here," "Doghole No. 1" and "Sons of Bitches Within." Others indulged their humor by applying grotesque nicknames to comrades. A ruddy-faced youth of a New England regiment was dubbed "Blossom," while a giant who marched by his side was called "Baby." In an Indiana company one soldier was known as "Billy Cat," and others as "Wolf," "Big Jig" and "Little Jig." A favorite sobriquet in many units was "Possum." [180]

Clannishness was a third trait common to most Yanks. Soon after donning the uniform soldiers of congenial character and habits gravitated to informal groups which usually became messes. These little families changed in composition with the caprices of fate and the fortunes of war, but rarely did they lose their close-knit quality. If a freak happened to be admitted to the sanctum through an error of judgment, he was usually frozen out in relatively short order. As already noted, a feeling of kinship also existed in company, regiment and larger units, but in no formal organization was loyalty as fierce as in the mess-size group of a man and his pals.

Those who wore the army uniform sometimes manifested a community consciousness as against those who did not. On visits to cities soldiers frequently helped shield spreeing comrades from the tentacles of the law, even when deploring their unseemly conduct. And Yanks were quick to gang up on any civilian who by word or deed appeared hostile to wearers of the blue.

Billy Yanks were also domestic creatures. Given even a slight prospect of an extended sojourn in a locality they would build huts, improvise furniture, decorate the walls with pictures, fashion shelves or pegs for their trappings and add to their surroundings sundry other touches of home. The Union soldiers were great fixer-uppers. Sketches of their premises show elaborately ornamented campsites and numerous improvisations for making their dwellings more attractive and comfortable. Decorative practices in some cases extended to affixing pin-up girls to the walls, but some of these, appareled after the fashion of *Godey's*, were in marked contrast to the scantily attired models favored by soldiers of later generations.[181]

Another trait manifested by Yanks en masse was wastefulness. This quality sprang in large measure from poor discipline. It was also attributable in part to American concepts of abundance, particularly as concerned the government's resources. Whatever the basis of the phenomenon, there can be no doubt that the average soldier was notoriously profligate of food, clothing, arms and other equipment issued by Uncle Sam. Lieutenant Samuel Fiske wrote after Antietam that "whole regiments threw away their overcoats and blankets and every thing that encumbered them." He added: "Just as it is said that out of the waste of an American kitchen, a French family would live comfortably, so it might almost be said, that out of the waste of an American war a European war might be carried on." [182]

Limitations of space preclude more than a brief mention of various special groups. Among these were the sharpshooters, two regiments of whom were formed among Regular Army units. The first was commanded by the famous Colonel Hiram Berdan, and numbered among its privates the fabulous character known as "California Joe." The sharpshooters were picked for their ruggedness and marksmanship and were armed with the best of rifles. They were used principally as skirmishers, but they proved very effective also in picking off Rebel artillerymen. They figured conspicuously in the Gettysburg, Mine Run and Wilderness campaigns.[183]

Another elite organization was the Pioneer Corps which served in the Army of the Cumberland. In the battle of Stone's River this unit, numbering 1,700 men detailed from infantry regiments and commanded by Captain James St. Clair Morton, Rosecrans' chief engineer, performed services comparable to that of combat engineers in World War II. In his report of Stone's River, Rosecrans paid high tribute to the Pioneer Corps, stating that "the efficiency and *esprit du corps* suddenly developed in this command, its gallant behavior in action, and the eminent services it is continually rendering the army entitle both officers and men to special public notice and thanks." [184]

"Mounted infantry" comprised another special type of troops. Soldiers of this category, as the name suggests, were doughboys on horses, though they enjoyed the luxury of riding for only a part of their service. The most famous troops of this class were those of Wilder's "Lightning Brigade" who, as already noted, were armed with repeating rifles and employed to excellent advantage in the battles about Chattanooga.[185]

Incapacitation of numerous soldiers for active service by disease, debility and wounds caused the setting up in April 1863 of the Invalid Corps. Members of this organization, the "limited service" personnel of the Civil War, were used for less strenuous duties in garrisons, prisons and hospitals, mainly as clerks, police, nurses, orderlies and cooks. In December 1863 the Invalid Corps numbered over 20,000 officers and men, organized as infantry into more than 200 companies.[186]

It naturally became a refuge for some able-bodied shirks, a circum-stance which, along with its unfortunate name, made the organization the butt of many jibes. A song entitled "The Invalid Corps" which poked fun at the group was sung by a comic vocalist of the period and published as a broadside.[187]

In March 1864 the name of the organization was changed to the Veteran's Reserve Corps. Whatever others may have thought of them, the invalid veterans were rated high by the Secretary of War who credited them with a substantial contribution to the Union cause.[188]

A group who had no separate organization, but who enjoyed high standing among soldiers, were the Veteran Volunteers. These were the seasoned Yanks who in accordance with orders promulgated in June 1863 volunteered to extend their service for "three years or the war." As an inducement to this advance re-enlistment, the War Department offered veterans bounties of $400 and thirty-day furloughs. Back of this action was a deep concern for the future effectiveness of the army. A check made in the summer of 1863 revealed that the terms of service of more than half of the units then in the field would expire before the end of 1864. The prospective loss of all this man power and experience was viewed as a disaster that might prove overwhelming; hence, a determination to avert it.[189]

With the end of the season of active campaigning in 1863 authorities high and low applied tremendous pressure on the veterans to re-enlist. As a result of the combined influences of propaganda, patriotism, bounty and furloughs, an epidemic of re-enlistment passed through the armies during the following winter, with regiment after regiment going through the "veteranizing" process of signing up, returning north amid a fanfare of public receptions, visiting homefolk and then heading south for the all-out campaigns of 1864 and 1865.

The Veteran Volunteers received as distinctive emblems service chevrons of red and blue braid to wear on their left sleeves.[190] Comments in their letters and diaries indicate that the wearers of the veteran's badge took great pride in their status. And their satisfaction was eminently justified, for the 200,000 or more Yanks who were saved to continued service by the re-enlistment program were a tremendous influence in the ultimate triumph of the Northern armies.[191]

Retention of the veterans was especially vital in view of the woeful deterioration in the quality of men recruited from civilian life in the last two years of the war. The combined effects of war-weariness, the desire to profit from boom economic conditions created by the conflict and the notoriously defective system by which the ranks were replenished resulted in the offscourings of the world being dumped into the service in the latter stages of the war.

The miserable character of the substitutes, bounty jumpers and others who were hired to bear arms in the period following Gettysburg and Vicksburg is so well known as to require no elaboration here.[192] But examples may appropriately be cited to show effects in specific units. Charles E. Davis wrote of the replenishment of his own regiment, the Thirteenth Massachusetts in August 1863:

One hundred and eighty-six recruits arrived in camp to-day. Heretofore the men who came to us reflected credit on themselves, the regiment, and the State. This lot consisted of substitutes, bounty-jumpers, and one unfortunate conscript. Most of this number were thieves and roughs who were engaged in the draft riots, and were obliged to leave New York and Boston in self-defence. . . .

Strong men, particularly soldiers, are not easily moved to tears, yet the cheeks of a good many men were wet as they gazed on these ruffians drawn up in line for assignment to companies. The pride which we felt in the membership of the Thirteenth turned to bitterness at sight of these fellows.

As the roll was called we speculated as to which company they might be assigned, though there was little choice. More than half of them were under assumed names, and it frequently happened at subsequent roll-calls that some of them were unable to remember the names under which they enlisted. Among the nationalities represented there were Frenchmen, Italians, Germans, Spaniards, Portuguese, Costa Ricans, Greeks, Maltese, and Canadians; a deserter from the "Louisiana Tigers," one from a Georgia regiment, and one from an Alabama regiment. . . .

In the last batch that were told off there were six whom it was deemed unsafe to keep together, and they were separated by placing them in different companies. Three of the number assigned to Company K disappeared at once. During the first night after their arrival forty deserted.[193]

The story was very much the same in other organizations. In June 1864 the commanding officer of a regiment stationed in South Carolina wrote his wife:

If you could only see the miserable conscripts and substitutes bought up and sent out here to fill our regiments, the dregs of every nation, paupers and thieves, fools and knaves, not one in three who can be trusted on picket for fear they will desert to the enemy. You would not wonder at the indignation of the veterans, who enlisting at the outbreak of the war have fought thus far without bounty or reward, and are ready to fight to the end, if only they can be supported and strengthened. I honestly believe, that some regiments are weaker to-day for the recruits they have received, and though largely increased in numbers they would be of less service in action.[194]

Little wonder that officers charged with delivering recruits to regiments in the field sometimes found it necessary to treat them as prisoners from the time of their induction and to lock them up at every layover point along the way. Fortunately for the units receiving them, a goodly portion of the newcomers deserted within a short time of their arrival in combat areas.[195]

Of course some of the late-comers to the ranks were good men and, as previously stated, a substantial portion of them became creditable soldiers. But in general they fell far short of compensating for the volunteers of earlier periods who were lost to the service, as casualties or otherwise, in 1863 and 1864. The fighting quality of the army as a whole seems to have reached its zenith in the early months of 1863 and to have declined thereafter until the end of the war. The deterioration was less damaging than it might have been had the Confederate Army not undergone a similar experience—and in addition suffered a hopeless dwindling of numbers.

With due allowance for fluctuations in its combat effectiveness the fact remains that the Union Army during the whole of its war career was a good army. The men who wore the blue, whatever their peculiarities and shortcomings, proved themselves effective soldiers. Their faults were in essence those of the mid-century America of which they were a part; so likewise were their virtues.

The balance of weakness and strength was a citizen soldier who reflected credit on the young democracy which he represented and whose performance in battle, by the admission of professionals sent from European armies to observe him, compared favorably with that of soldiers anywhere.

CHAPTER XIII

BILLY YANK AND JOHNNY REB

THE ATTITUDE of the men in blue toward their opponents varied greatly with individuals and circumstances. Some Yanks professed a deep and abiding hatred for their foes. A Pennsylvanian who participated in the seesaw fighting of 1864 in the Shenandoah Valley wrote his wife: "I wish we could Ketch them Some place and Kill every Son of a Bitch [as] the[y] are nothing But Regular Raiders and Thiefs." [1] Three years earlier a New Englander had written from the Northern bank of the Potomac: "all i want to do now is to licke these Sons of B—chs across the river from us that is the height of my Ambition." [2]

But these declarations were mild in comparison to that of another Yank, T. R. Keenan of the Seventeenth Massachusetts Regiment, who wrote shortly after Lee's surrender:

I am sorry the war is ended. Pray do not think me murderous. No; but all the punishment we could inflict on the rebels would not atone for one drop of blood so cruelly spilled. I would exterminate them root and branch. They have often said they preferred it before subjugation, and, with the help of God, I would give it them. I am only saying what thousands say every day.[3]

Keenan was writing with the report of Lincoln's assassination fresh in mind but, even so, there can be no doubt of the genuineness of his hatred and that of many others who wore the blue.

Antipathy toward the Rebels sprang from sundry sources. Among these was the conviction that Southerners were a haughty, hot-tempered, overbearing, bloodthirsty people who in utter disregard of Northern concessions had turned their backs on the benefits of Union and thrust the nation into war.

Soldiers of the South, while not deemed as culpable as stay-at-home politicians in fomenting the rebellion, nevertheless were condemned as representatives of the war-guilty society. Furthermore, they were the obvious instruments of carrying on the war, with all its misery and woe; and as the immediate agents of rebellion, bent on killing or being killed, they were a natural and convenient target for accumulated resentment.

In some instances hatred sprang from a belief that Confederates were semibarbarians who ignored usages of war recognized by civilized nations, tortured prisoners, mutilated the dead and engaged in various other inhuman practices. Atrocity stories began with the earliest skirmishes and were revived with almost every subsequent engagement. A Michigan soldier, in a letter dated June 21, 1861, and published in the Detroit *Free Press*, reported discovery near his tent in the District of Columbia of an infernal machine which in modern parlance would be called a booby trap. This gadget, planted presumably by the Rebels, was described as "consisting of two tin covers fitting together . . . [to resemble a] tobacco box . . . filled with percussion powder . . . [and] covered with iron caps . . . of so explosive a nature that a very slight pressure, as of a person stepping upon it, would cause an explosion . . . very destructive to a company of soldiers." This device, according to the correspondent, gave evidence that "we have to cope with an enemy who are bent upon our destruction by setting such traps and snares as these . . . without endangering their own lives. . . . They have all the craftiness and treachery of the Indian," he added, "with out any of his bravery. It is this which constitutes the boasted chivalry of the South." [4]

Other atrocities charged to Confederates at various times by their opponents included the use of poisoned bullets, the murdering of prisoners, the poisoning of cisterns and wells lying along the route of Federal advance, the maltreatment of the wounded and the desecration of the dead. After the First Battle of Bull Run a Connecticut soldier informed his sister that the "South Carolina Rebels are Barbarians and savages—the[y] yesterday bayoneted our wounded on the Battle field." Another Yank writing of the same engagement passed on as truth the report that the Rebels had set fire to a tent containing Yankee wounded and shot to death those occupants not destroyed by the flames. "Great God!" he added, "who [can] be merciful to such savages." [5]

A Massachusetts soldier reported to his homefolk in May 1862 that five skulls found in abandoned Rebel quarters near Centerville had been neatly polished and inscribed with words "Five Zouaves' Coconuts killed at Bull Run by Southern lead," while a Minnesotan told of rescuing from another Confederate campsite a cranium, supposedly of a Federal soldier, that had been "used by the Rebs for a soap dish." Still another Yank in all seriousness made the startling allegation that Confederates had used the skulls of slain Federals for soup bowls.[6]

Similar accusations were included in official reports of battles and published in the newspapers. A Northern authoress who was in Winchester, Virginia, in May 1862 when Jackson's troops captured that town was quoted by the press as stating that "the rebels . . . have no humanity. They kill our wounded soldiers and even our women nurses are said to be shot." [7]

Most of the atrocity reports were undoubtedly the products of imagination quickened by hysteria but, true or false, they had their influence in fanning the flame of hate already crackling from years of misunderstanding and controversy.

In November 1861 a chaplain of the Army of the Potomac made an address on the cruelty of Confederates to Federal wounded at Ball's Bluff, charging his listeners to remember the brutality when next they met the foe. After the service one of the audience wrote to a friend: "I believe the boys would have fought like the devil if they could have been lead into a fight after that address." [8]

During the Peninsula campaign of the next spring, some New Yorkers, infuriated by reports of Rebel atrocities on their comrades, swore that they would take no prisoners but would "bayonet every damned wounded rebel on the field." Afterward when one of their number was shot by a Confederate picket whose surrender they had demanded, they grabbed the offending sentry and, according to a soldier's report, "put a rope around his neck and hoisted him on a tree, made a target of his suspended body, then cut him down, bayoneted him in a dozen places, then dragged him to the road where they watched till long trains of wagons made a jelly of the remains." [9]

Other instances of a vengeful fury that would grant no quarter might be cited, but they were rare, as was the extreme hatred which inspired them.

While the number of Yanks who regarded the men in gray as little better than barbarians was relatively small, those who looked on their opponents as dirty and ignorant constituted a substantial portion of the Federal forces. Typical of many comments of the Union soldiers about the Rebels was that of a Wisconsin artilleryman who remarked of some Alabamians captured at Vicksburg: "I . . . found some of the greenest speciments of humanity, I think, in the universe, their ignorance being little less than the slave they despise, with as imperfect a dialect. 'They Recooned as how you'uns all would be a heap wus to we'uns all.' " [10]

A Minnesotan characterized the Confederates as "vagabonds," while a Kentucky Unionist was convinced by examining the faces of "thou-

sands" of dead Rebels at Shiloh that a "very large majority" were "ruffi-
ans and desperadoes." [11]

Some Yanks professed to dislike the Southerners because of their
fighting methods. In addition to attributing to their foes the use of hid-
den torpedoes and other trick killers, they condemned the Rebs for
making sneak attacks in Yankee uniforms, donning cowbells and creep-
ing through the sentry lines at night on hands and knees to reconnoiter
Federal positions.[12]

Others denounced the Rebels as lacking in courage, but most of those
who registered such sentiments had not been in a major battle. An
Ohioan wrote his mother during Bragg's Kentucky invasion of 1862:
"We will give the Rebels a dose that they wont like to take iff they wont
Run they wont give us a fair fight they will Run every Chance they get
. . . they have been Run all over they state." [13] About the same time
another Yank boasted: "They won't fight us, they Know we can whip
them with Mitens on." [14] The day before the capture of Jackson, Mis-
sissippi, a participant in the Vicksburg campaign observed to his wife:
"Mary if Jackson is taken I dont think I will evry be in a battel for the
rebes wont stand fight at all we have went for them three times but they
ran evry time." [15]

Some who conceded a measure of courage to the Rebs in a shooting
fight deemed them unable to withstand the near threat of cold steel.
During McClellan's campaign for Richmond in June 1862 a New Yorker
stated that the Confederates "will fight hard, but they will run at the
sight of our bayonet." [16] In similar vein a Massachusetts soldier wrote
from Virginia shortly after Chancellorsville: "They have shown they can
fight but no better than our men. They cannot stand a charge—almost
always break and run." [17]

Another Yank found the Southerners unduly cover-conscious. They
"fight well when they can hide," he stated, "but when they have to come
out into the open field, they dont come up to the scrach . . . they can
stand bullets if they can skulk behind a tree, but when the bayonets
come, they run." In this Yank's opinion the "rebles" were "as bad as the
red skins of old." [18]

When disparagers of Southern bravery were confronted by a dashing
performance which utterly contradicted their generalizations, they usu-
ally had a ready answer: The Rebels were crazy drunk on whisky and
gunpowder. This claim, which interestingly enough was also used by
Rebels to explain Yankee gallantry, was found in many soldier letters.
An Ohioan of Sherman's command reported that prisoners taken in the

battle of Atlanta "were too drunk to run back to their works," and quoted the Rebels as saying that they "were served with a pint & a half of whiskey before making the attack." A Massachusetts corporal informed his sister after Chancellorsville that he was discouraged from "fighting madmen or not men at all but whiskey & gunpowder put into a human frame." Still another Yank, a Regular who participated in the Georgia campaign, wrote of the battle of Resaca: "The rebs charged on our men 8 Different times but were repulsed every time with a Heavey loss. . . . [Their dead] lay like sheaves of wheat In a field, all very black from the Powter & Whiskey they drank to make them Brave & Bold." [19]

By no means did all those who wore the blue regard their foes with loathing or hatred. One does not have to hate to be effective in combat any more than a hunter has to despise the game he shoots on a sporting expedition. The eager expectancy, the thrill of the closing, the movement and noise and the nearness of danger get the participant's blood up and infuse him with a desire to bag his quarry. Hence, there were many instances where Yanks pitched into their foes in the spirit of adventure with little or no sense of hatred and derived immense exhilaration and even enjoyment from the experience. A young Boston blue blood wrote his father from Virginia in 1862 that skirmishing with the Rebels was very much like "hunting after some kind of animals instead of men. It may seem inhuman," he added, "but I must say that I never enjoyed anything better in my life than I do going on picket and getting a shot at the scamps." Another Yank, whose background was less cultured, put a similar reaction in earthier terms. "Went out a Skouting yesterday," he wrote his father from Western Virginia in September 1861. "We got To one House where there was Five Secessionest And they broke and Run and Arch . . . holoed out to Shoot the ornery Suns of Bitches . . . [and we] all let go . . . at them. . . . Thay may Say what they please but godamit pa It is Fun." [20]

In some instances where hatred was real and deep initially, it abated with the passing of time. Numerous factors contributed to this metamorphosis, but the most influential seems to have been the development after months of hardship of the conviction that the common soldiers of both sides were victims of political machinations. A New Yorker who early in his fighting career breathed the sentiment of "death to traitors," within a year was reporting friendly discussions with Rebel pickets. "We generally end [these sessions]," he stated, "by mutually wishing we had let those who made the quarrel be the very ones to fight. If the question was left to the two contending armies here, we would restore the Union tomorrow and hang both cabinets at our earliest convenience after-wards." [21]

One who reads extensively the literature of the war period, and espe-cially the letters and diaries of soldiers, finds numerous indications of friendly sentiment among opposing participants. If the grim fact of the contestants actually meeting now and then in desperate battle could be overlooked, it might be inferred that good feeling outweighed hostility.

Several reasons may be found for amicable inclinations of Yanks to-ward Rebs. First was their admiration of the gallantry displayed by the men in gray, for more Yanks praised their opponents for bravery than condemned them for lack of it. An Illinois participant in the Vicksburg campaign who in the early days of his service had been quite contemp-tuous of his opponents was converted to open admiration of them by their gallantry at Haines's Bluff and Arkansas Post. After the latter en-gagement he wrote his wife: "The Rebles . . . are a motly looking crew but they fight like Devills . . . they held out [under the heaviest fire of infantry and gunboats] from half past one till half past 4. . . . I hope I did not hit any person [even] if they are Rebles. We shook hands after the fight. I was hungry and they gave me some meat and bread that was good sure." Several weeks later he stated: "We have no feelings of ani-mosity toward a conquered foe; the Brave never has, as shown at the fight at the Post." [22]

At Malvern Hill, Gettysburg and other major battles featured by large-scale Confederate assaults, Yanks looked with respectful awe on the charging gray lines as they surged relentlessly onward against seemingly impenetrable walls of lead and fire. These displays of heroism had deep and lasting effect on the men in blue. In some cases the result was a gnawing doubt of the North's ability to conquer so brave a foe. After Chancellorsville one serious-minded Yank wrote: "The 'gentlemen' that used to [be] spoken of so contemptuously, the 'Southern gentlemen,' the fuming & tearing chivalry, outfight us, *outstand* us, out commonsense us, beat us in every battle. I admire the desperation, the patience too—the stern will of the South." [23]

Another factor leading to friendliness of Yanks toward their foes was the discovery among them of fine qualities of character. Generosity, honor, devotion to their cause, manliness in adversity—these were some of the virtues frequently attributed by the men in blue to opponents encountered during truces or as prisoners of war.

Sympathy also had a part in fomenting friendliness. As the Rebels captured at Port Hudson on July 9, 1863, stacked their arms in surrender one of the captors wrote: "For the first time I felt sorry for the brave fellows. If their cause is not just, they have been true to it and it must be like death itself for a brave fighter to lay his arms down before his enemy." He added: "In a twinkling we were together. The Rebs are mostly large, fine-looking men. They are about as hard up for clothes as we are. . . . They have treated the prisoners [captured during the prior siege] as well as they could, giving them the same sort of food they ate themselves." [24]

Many Yanks, especially after the tide turned against the South, registered sympathy for the deprivation and hardship suffered by the men in gray. "For a month they say they have been on half rations," wrote a Maine cavalryman from near Fredericksburg in 1863. "It does look pitiful to look across the river and see them . . . most of them are dreadful ragged so much so that they suffer a great deal with the cold." [25] Following a skirmish in Georgia in which the opposing force consisted in part of boys and old men, an Illinois captain wrote: "I hope we will never have to shoot at such men again. They knew nothing at all about fighting, and I think their officers knew as little." [26]

Good feeling of Yanks toward Rebs manifested itself in varied forms of fraternization. Whenever opposing forces came in holloing distance of each other confab was apt to become a principal activity. Often the conversation had a bantering tone, as witness the following exchange at Fredericksburg:

> Reb: What makes your folks leave us so many good clothes and fine blankets?
> Yank: We obey the injunction to clothe the naked and feed the hungry.[27]

or these dialogues at Vicksburg:

> Reb: When is Grant going to march into Vicksburg?
> Yank: When you get your last mule and dog eat up.

> Yank: Havent you Rebs got a new general—General Starvation?
> Reb: Have you Yanks all got nigger wives yet? [28]

or the pungent raillery at Mine Run:

> Reb: Why the hell didnt you charge yesterday?
> Yank: Go to hell, you Grayback S.O.B's, you're dammed glad we didnt.[29]

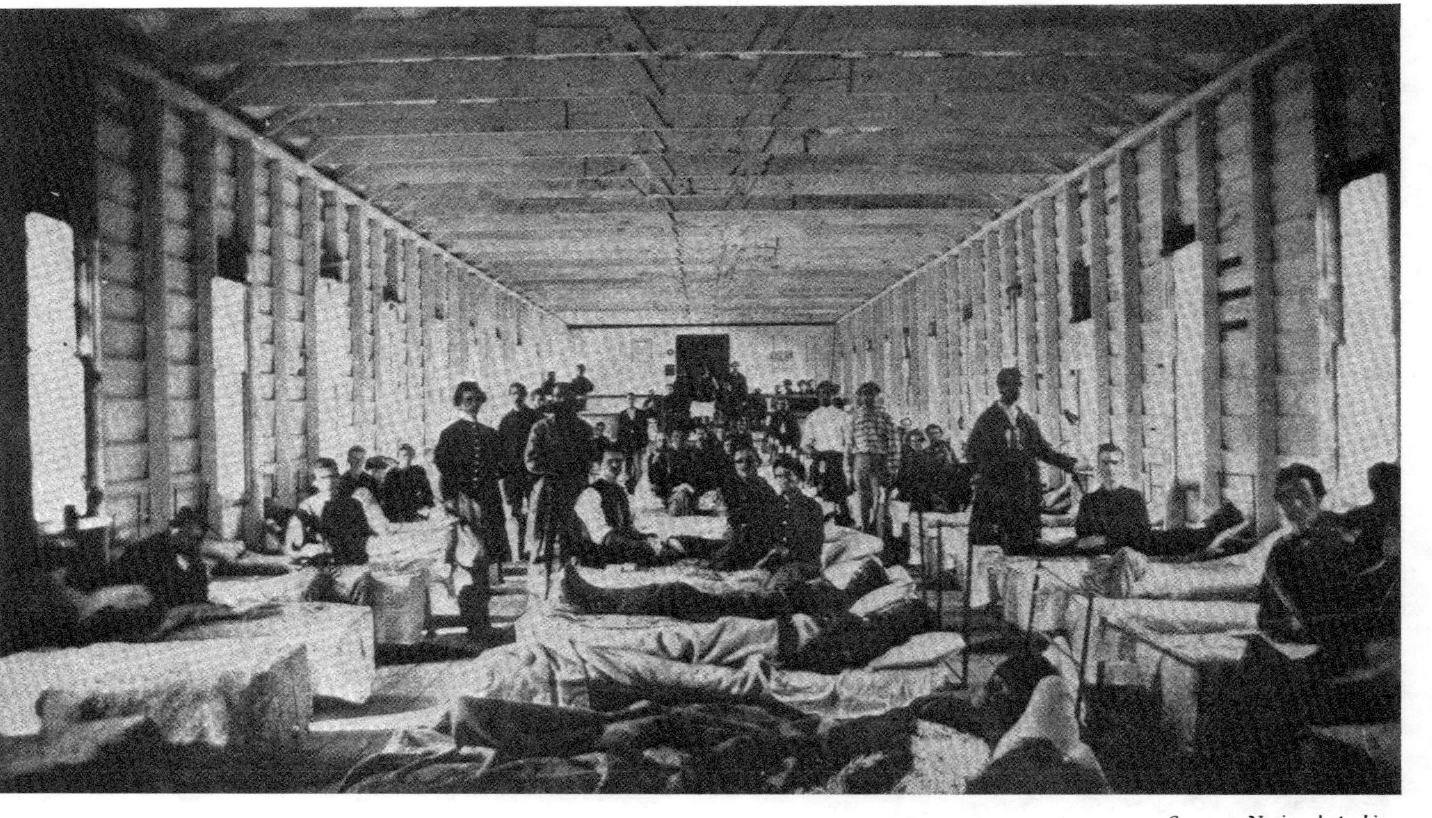

ON THE ROAD TO RECOVERY

Wounded soldiers in convalescent hospital, Alexandria, Virginia

Courtesy National Archives

DISPENSERS OF ARMY JUSTICE
Court-Martial Group, Army of the Cumberland

or the verbal jousts before Atlanta:

Yank: What is Confederate money worth?
Reb: What niggers command your brigade?
Yank: How much do you ask for your slaves?
Reb: Have the niggers improved the Yankee breed any? [30]

More frequently, however, gabfests were in the nature of friendly talk about such matters of common interest as rations, pay, the weather, lice, officers, home and peace.

During such discussions informal truces were observed. If for any reason resumption of firing became necessary, appropriate warnings would be issued and adequate time allowed for all to find cover.

Other forms of fraternization included joint swimming parties; musicals in which men of opposing camps sometimes took turns in rendering favorite selections; and gambling. On the Virginia front in 1863 a Yank and a Reb were competitors for a sheep that ventured between the lines. They finally agreed to compromise by dividing the prize, each taking half the carcass to his own camp.[31]

Sometimes pickets became so cordial that they took turns playing host at meals, and in rare instances Yanks and Rebs accepted invitations to spend the night as guests of their opponents, returning to their own quarters just before daybreak.[32]

On one occasion a Yankee lieutenant, considerately disguised by his hosts as a Southerner, was taken to a Virginia party by a group of Rebs with whom he had made a "hollering" acquaintance on the picket line.[33] The Chattanooga *Gazette* of February 17, 1864, reported a wedding at near-by Walden's Ridge in the following remarkable circumstances:

The party was composed of 1st Rebel and Union citizens; 2nd Rebel and Union soldiers; 3rd Rebel and Union deserters; 4th Rebel and Union spies; 5th Rebel and Union bushwhackers. Scarcely a harsh word was uttered during the whole night; all danced together as if nothing was wrong, and parted mutually the next morning, each party marching off separately.[34]

Strange war! But other incidents were hardly less fantastic. On several occasions soldiers of the two armies intermingled after battle to bury the dead, laying the Confederates in one big grave and the Federals in another close by, with "a chaplain of either army" administering the last rites. In one instance Rebs borrowed shovels from the Yankees to dig graves for their dead.[35]

At Chattanooga Private Ed Smith of a Pennsylvania regiment was disturbed several times one night by a Confederate picket posted near by calling for the corporal of the guard. The next morning when the Rebel officer of the guard came down the line Private Smith saluted him across the intervening creek and after the salute was returned said, "Lieutenant your Corporal on duty last night had a hard time of it. Cant you use your influence to get him to resign?" This bit of impudence produced a hearty laugh from both sides of the line.[36]

Near Fredericksburg during the second winter of the war opposing pickets on one occasion put each other through the manual of arms and then sang and danced together.[37] A few weeks later other Yanks on this front agreed while swimming with Confederates to make a temporary exchange of places. Without informing comrades on either side the Yanks then swam to the Southern bank and the Confederates to the Northern. As soon as they took their positions on the Northern shore, the Confederates, pretending to be Yankees, shouted to Southerners across the river, "How are you, pork and molasses? When are you going to pitch into us again?" After a brief period of such banter, the groups returned to their proper stations.[38]

One of the most common forms of fraternization was the bartering of small articles contributing to the comfort and convenience of soldier life. Innumerable trade sessions began with

> Hello, Yank!
> Hello, Johnny!
> Got any coffee?
> Yes.
> Got any tobacco?
> Yes, come and get it.
> Won't shoot?
> No.

The two soldiers, joined usually by a few others from either camp, would then lay down their guns, meet at a point about halfway between the lines, measure out and swap the coffee—scarce in the South—for tobacco —hard to obtain in the North—and then return to their respective positions.[39]

Another common item of barter was the newspaper. Beyond tobacco and news sheets, Confederates had little to offer in trade, but these were used extensively to obtain from Yanks such articles as canteens (more durable than those obtainable in the South), pocketknives, sugar, sardines, soap and whisky.

Many Yanks and Rebs carried on their trade by remote control. When rivers and lakes separated the lines tiny boats were loaded with commodities, fitted with sails and sent on their way. On reaching their destination the vessels were unloaded, filled with exchange cargoes as agreed on by shouting, signaling or other means of communication, and sent back to the opposite bank. On the Rappahannock early in 1863 some New Jersey soldiers received a shipment "by miniature boat six inches long" to which was attached the following note:

Gents U. S. Army
    We send you some tobacco by our Packet. Send us some coffee in return. Also a deck of cards if you have them, and we will send you more tobacco. Send us any late papers if you have them.
                                    Jas. O. Parker
                                    Co. H. 17th Regt. Miss. Vols.[40]

Dogs were also used to convey articles of trade. Alfred S. Roe who served in a New York artillery unit recalled that near Petersburg during the war's last winter "a certain canine of strictly impartial sentiments" was "taught to respond to a whistle from either side. Thus with a can of coffee suspended from his neck he would amble over to the Johnnies, and when they had replaced coffee with tobacco he would return in obedience to Union signals, intent only on the food reward both sides gave him." [41]

In the informal intermingling of the blue and the gray, whether for confab, trade, picking blackberries or burying the dead, friends of prewar days, and even close relatives separated by conflict, sometimes were brought together for brief periods of pleasant association.[42] Casual acquaintances thus initiated sometimes ripened into friendships when units were habitually opposed to each other. On June 20, 1863, a Norwegian Yank wrote from near Vicksburg:

I can inform you that we can converse with the enemy every evening. The other day when I was in the rifle pits we began to talk to them and asked them what their regiments were. Those we talked to belonged to . . . the 1st and the 3rd Missouri. They were the same regiments which were under Green in Missouri, and which we had fought at Monroe, Shelbina, and Blumelo; so you may be sure we knew them well. They inquired about Major Stone and many others whom they know. One day . . . a part of Co K and some of the enemy came together and stacked arms and talked for a long time. Our men cooked coffee and treated them and [afterward] . . . each one took up his position again and they began to fire at each other again, but not as hard as before.[43]

On the night after this episode nine Rebs deserted to the Yanks. In other instances get-togethers were followed by Yanks changing their allegiance to the Confederacy, though, owing largely to the better situation of the North with respect to food and clothing, desertion of Confederates to their foes was more common than otherwise. A more frequent consequence of fraternization than desertion was a momentary loss of enthusiasm for fighting. After a friendly meeting with opponents near Petersburg in 1865, a Yank noted in his diary: "It did not seem as though we were at war with them." [44] And in the wake of a similar occasion near Kennesaw Mountain in 1864 one of Sherman's young soldiers wrote his parents:

We made a bargain with them that we would not fire on them if they would not fire on us, and they were as good as their word. It seems too bad that we have to fight men that we like. Now these Southern soldiers seem just like our own boys. . . . They talk about . . . their mothers and fathers and their sweethearts just as we do. . . . Both sides did a lot of talking but there was no shooting until I came off duty in the morning.[45]

Officers usually discouraged fraternizing and many flatly forbade it, from considerations of intelligence and morale. Some soldiers likewise opposed friendly intercourse with their enemies, but they represented a decided minority. Among those who refused to "go the whole hog" was Sergeant Day Elmore who wrote from near Atlanta in July 1864: "The Boys have been to gather a number of times . . . traiding coffee for tobacco, but I do not love them so I could not take them by the hand as some of the Boys did." [46]

Friendliness of Yanks toward Rebs also found expression in numerous acts of kindness. Confederate prisoners often received food and water from their captors. Wounded Rebs lying between the lines were sometimes succored at considerable risk by sympathetic wearers of the blue. In field hospitals wounded of the opposing forces, lying sometimes side by side, received the same consideration from attendants and contributed as best they could to one another's comfort.[47] A Union captain who walked over the field after Gettysburg rendering aid to Confederate casualties wrote: "I was glad to do a little something for them. . . . Utterly as I detest a living active rebel, as soon as he becomes wounded and a prisoner, I dont perceive any differences in my feelings toward him and towards one of our wounded heroes." [48]

Sometimes acts of kindness were motivated by common membership in fraternal organizations, such as the Masonic Order. Again they were in reciprocation of good deeds done by the Rebels. In 1863 members of the Third Ohio Regiment en route to Richmond as prisoners of war were treated to a meal of bacon, bread and coffee by soldiers of the Fifty-fourth Virginia Regiment who happened to discover their lack of nourishment. Later the Ohioans were exchanged and sent back to duty near Chattanooga. At the battle of Missionary Ridge soldiers of the Fifty-fourth Virginia Regiment were captured and taken to Kelly's Ferry. Here their presence became known to some of the Third Ohio who rushed to their camp, gathered up all sorts of food and delicacies and gave them to their hungry benefactors of several months before.[49]

Kindly acts and friendly intercourse were, to be sure, not peculiar to the American Civil War. Every major conflict in history has been marked by fraternization of opposing troops. But owing to the fact of their speaking a common language, being of the same nationality and having a similar cultural background Yanks and Rebs fraternized more extensively than most warriors. Even so, the historian must treat the subject with care, since one incident of friendly commingling, because of the human interest and drama that it involved, was apt to receive more notice in the records than days of skirmishing and weeks of passive hostility. It must also be kept in mind that friendly get-togethers, despite concern of officers about the effect on morale, as a general rule had little if any effect on combat effectiveness. Amazing though it was to participants, and remarkable as it is to their descendants, Yanks and Rebs who met between the lines to swap coffee for tobacco, and who lingered to talk sympathetically over common problems, could in the space of a few minutes go after one another with demoniac yells and awful destructiveness. A brothers' war, this incredible war of the 1860s has been called, and instances are recorded of brother shooting brother; it has also been called a polite and a crazy war.[50] But, however incredible, polite or crazy, it *was* a war and the bloodiest one known to the world of that time.

In the light of the records and a calm and studied judgment of them nearly a century after the conflict, how does the common soldier of the Union compare with his opposite in gray? While admittedly numerous exceptions may be found, the following conclusions seem valid as broad generalizations.

First, Billy Yank was more literate than Johnny Reb. The Northern states made more adequate provision for elementary education and hence had fewer citizens who could not read and write. While it is true that the North had a considerably greater admixture of foreign-born among its population, many of the immigrants were literate. The better education of Yanks is plainly evident in their home letters. One who delves deeply into these sources encounters far fewer references to the use of amanuenses among wearers of the blue; and while spelling and grammar of the general run of correspondence on both sides left much to be desired, deficiencies of Southern soldiers were noticeably greater.

Then, one encounters among the Union ranks evidences of a healthier intellectual life. Owing to the North's better educational facilities, the more heterogeneous character of its population, the more varied pattern of its economy, the presence in its borders of more large cities, the greater prosperity of its citizens, the easier access to newspapers, books and periodicals, the greater freedom of thought and discussion and sundry other advantages, the Northern soldier manifested wider interests and greater curiosity about things past and present than his opposite in the Confederate Army. Common soldiers on either side who showed either a deep concern for philosophic aspects of the conflict or a grasp of their significance were rare, but the North appears to have had considerably more than its share of these exceptions.

Billy Yank revealed a far livelier interest in politics than Johnny Reb. On the national level this was due in large measure to the fact that on the one occasion when Rebs had an opportunity to vote for a President, Davis was without opposition, while in the North the campaign of 1864 was a real contest between aggressive candidates, with both parties making strong bids for the soldier vote. But this does not account fully for the difference. Rebs registered little concern for the outcome of Congressional and gubernatorial races, while their opponents often demonstrated an active interest in them.

The common soldier of the North was apparently less religious than his Southern counterpart. Certainly he was less emotional in his worship. Religious effusions appeared less frequently in his letters and he was considerably less susceptible to revivals. The Union Army experienced some evangelistic outbreaks, but they were small-scale phenomena rarely overleaping the boundaries of a brigade and were relatively subdued in character. The Confederate forces, on the other hand, were swept by tremendous revivals, army-wide in scope, in both the third and fourth winters of the war. These outbreaks were featured by enthusiastic praying, singing, shouting and other characteristics of rural protracted meetings.

The question naturally arises: Why this difference in armies of such similar composition and background? Several explanations may be suggested. In the first place, the Southern Army was considerably more rural in composition than the Northern, and American countryfolk historically have been more emotional in their religion than those of urban background. True, the Midwest was predominately rural, but Yanks from that area were frequently intermingled with those from Eastern cities. Then, the Southern forces probably had a heavier admixture of the frontier element than did those of the Union. In the third place, Confederates were more homogeneous than their foes, from standpoints of nativity, language and general culture; and evangelistic sects were stronger among them. A fourth basis of the difference may have been the greater emphasis which political and military leaders of the South placed on religion. Davis proclaimed more days of fasting and prayer than Lincoln did, and Lee and Jackson by example and precept did more to promote religious interest among their soldiers than Grant and Sherman. One does not find among high-ranking Northern leaders a match for Leonidas Polk, the bishop-general who habitually carried a prayer book into battle and who in the space of a few days baptized Generals Joseph E. Johnston and John B. Hood, the former an army commander at the time and the latter shortly to be elevated to that position.

Probably the most cogent factor in Johnny Reb's greater religiousness was the turn in his case of the tide of war from victory toward defeat. It is a noteworthy fact that the large-scale revivals did not occur until after Gettysburg and Vicksburg. Before these great reverses the men in gray had enjoyed a feeling of self-sufficiency. But from the summer of 1863 on, increasing doubt of their own strength caused them to look more and more to a higher power for sustenance and success. The trend among the men in blue was in the opposite direction.

Johnny Reb's greater emotionalism in religon accords with another and more basic difference between soldiers of the two armies; namely, that Billy Yank was of a more practical and prosaic bent of mind. This difference is less tangible than others, but it appears none the less real. The distinction was manifest in his greater concern with the material things of life. Northern soldiers more frequently engaged in side activities to supplement their army wages. Their letters contain far more references to financial matters—lending their earnings at interest, buying land, building up a store for the future—than those written by Confederates. It is true that Yanks had more money to write about, but the fact of better and more regular pay, important though it was, was not of sufficient moment wholly to account for the difference.

Then, Billy Yank's letters were not so rich in humor and imagination as Johnny Reb's. When he took pen in hand he did not joke or break into poetry so often. He did not have so acute a sense of the ludicrous, the dramatic or the fanciful. His descriptions of battle were not so frequent, so full or so moving. In writing to his sweetheart or wife, he was not so playful, or so gallant, or so ready in the use of small talk; nor was he so prone to use endearing terms. Still another indication of the Northern soldier's more practical bent was his greater concern about rising in the military hierarchy; certainly his letters and diaries are more replete with comment about promotion.

Soldier attitudes as revealed in their letters and diaries leave the impression that Billy Yank was not so deeply concerned with the war as Johnny Reb. Financial considerations seem to have figured more conspicuously in his participation in the conflict, and he appears to have felt less of personal commitment and responsibility. This difference was due in part to the South's being the invaded land and Confederate soldiers thus being cast in the roles of defenders of family and fireside.

Other pertinent considerations were the Confederacy's smaller and more homogeneous population and the nature of its economy, for these circumstances caused the war to make a greater impact on Southerners than on Northerners. To a large extent the war was incidental to Northern life, while to Southerners it was of transcendent importance. Billy Yank was fighting to subdue a revolt against national authority and to free the slaves; Johnny Reb was fighting to establish an independent government, but he also was fighting for a peculiar way of life, for the defense of his home, and, as it often seemed to him, for life itself. Billy Yank could lose the war, go home and hope to resume living very much as before; but Johnny Reb was inclined to view defeat as a prelude to utter ruin.

What about the fighting qualities of the opposing participants? Johnny Rebs seem to have taken more readily to soldiering from their prior mode of life, the presence among them of a recognized leadership caste, and the strength in Southern society of the martial spirit. Moreover, the men who wore the gray fought with more dash, *élan* and enthusiasm, as witness the greater spontaneity and exuberance of their battle cheers. Their penchant for recounting the details of combat in home letters suggests that they derived a greater thrill from fighting. But

Billy Yanks often displayed more of tenacity, stubbornness en masse and machinelike efficiency.

Johnny Reb made a better showing on the battlefield during the first half of the war, but his superiority was attributable in the main to better leadership. There is no reason to believe, however, that he ever possessed more of determination, courage, pride, loyalty to fellows and other basic characteristics that go to make a good soldier. Such differences as existed in combat effectiveness had disappeared by the autumn of 1863, if not sooner, and on the basis of the whole war record it cannot be said that the common soldier of one side was any better or any worse fighter than the one who opposed him. Certainly the Confederates had no braver soldiers than those blue-clad heroes who responded to Grant's order to charge the works at Vicksburg on May 22, 1863, and at Second Cold Harbor on June 3, 1864. On the latter occasion Hancock's famous Second Corps lost over 3,000 men in about twenty minutes of fighting.[51] When informed that they were to make the assault these gallant soldiers, most of them veterans tried and true, calmly wrote their names and home addresses on slips of paper and pinned them to their uniforms so that their bodies might be identified and their homefolk informed promptly of their fate.[52]

In sum, it may be stated that the similarities of Billy Yank and Johnny Reb far outweighed their differences. They were both Americans, by birth or by adoption, and they both had the weaknesses and the virtues of the people of their nation and time. For the most part they were of humble origin, but their conduct in crisis compared favorably with that of more privileged groups and revealed undeveloped resources of strength and character that spelled hope for the country's future.

While it is indeed regrettable that people so similar and basically so well-meaning found it necessary to resort to arms in settling their differences, now that their doing so is a matter of history their descendants can point with justifiable pride to the part played in the struggle by both the Blue and the Gray.

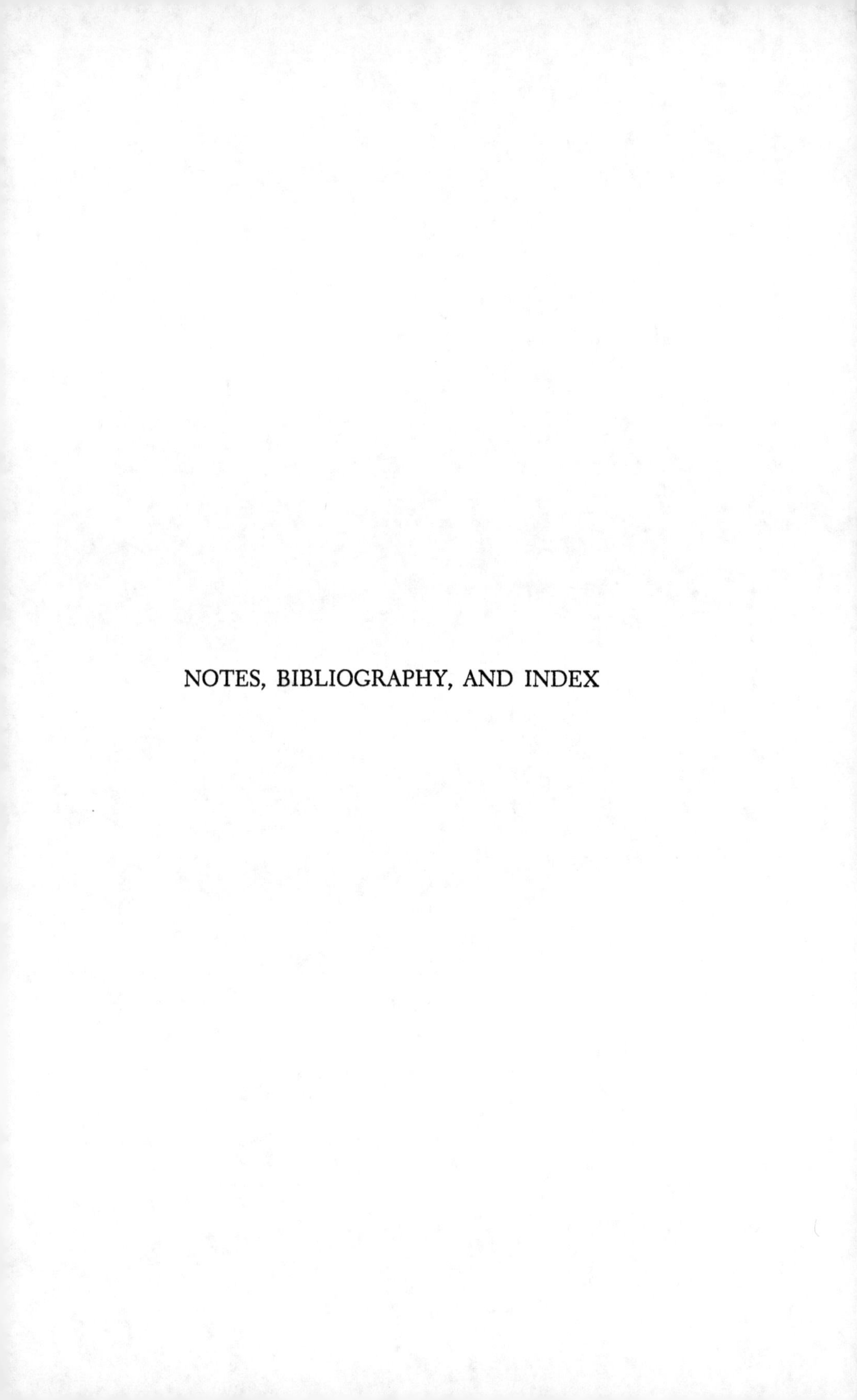

NOTES, BIBLIOGRAPHY, AND INDEX

Chapter I

SOUTHWARD HO!

[1] For able discussions of Northern sentiment in the period preceding the war see Avery O. Craven, *The Coming of the Civil War* (New York, 1942) and Howard C. Perkins, editor, *Northern Editorials on Secession* (2 vols., New York, 1942).

[2] Detroit *Free Press*, April 19, 1861.

[3] Portland, Maine, *Transcript*, April 27, May 18, 1861.

[4] For examples see Detroit *Free Press*, April 15-30, 1861.

[5] *Ibid.*, April 18, 1861.

[6] Portland, Maine, *Transcript*, May 4, 1861; diary of Harvey Reid, April 22, 1861, manuscript, Univ. of Wis.

[7] Portland, Maine, *Transcript*, April 27, 1861.

[8] David P. Jackson, editor, *The Colonel's Diary* (Sharon, Pa., 1922), 39. The Detroit *Free Press* of June 4, 1861, reported: "On every corner squads of urchins armed with wooden guns and swords of tin make their mighty drill. . . . Every boy is the possessor and sole proprietor of a drum and many a home groans under its continued rub-a-dub . . . while many a head is caused to ache at the persevering efforts of sonny with his new fife."

[9] Portland, Maine, *Transcript*, May 25, 1861.

[10] *Ibid.*, April 27, 1861.

[11] Philip D. Jordan and Charles M. Thomas, editors, "Reminiscences of an Ohio Volunteer," *Ohio State Arch. and Historical Quarterly*, XLVIII (1939), 304-308. The Twentieth Ohio was an infantry regiment. Regiments mentioned throughout this study unless otherwise designated are infantry.

[12] Harvey Reid to his homefolk, April 20, 1861, and diary entry of April 24, 1861, manuscripts, Wis. Historical Society; Detroit *Free Press*, April 28, 1861.

[13] Robert S. Fletcher, *History of Oberlin College* (Oberlin, Ohio, 1943), II, 845, 881.

[14] Dewitt Mead to Aaron Mead, July 16, 1861, manuscript, Chicago Historical Society.

[15] H. C. Hawes, *Experiences of a Union Soldier* (Atlanta, Ill., 1928), 2; Col. H. Van Rensselaer, Report of Inspection, Dept. of the Missouri, dated Feb. 10, 1862, AGO Records, 1862, file 14-I, Nat'l Archives.

[16] *Dictionary of American Biography* (New York, 1928-1937), IX, 272. To be cited hereafter as *DAB*.

[17] Edward R. Perkins, "A Soldier's Memory of Abraham Lincoln," manuscript, Minn. Historical Society.

[18] *War of the Rebellion: A Compilation of the Official Records of the Union and Confederate Armies* (Washington, D. C., 1880-1901), series 3, I, 107, 140. To be cited hereafter as *O. R.*

[19] *Ibid.,* 101.

[20] *Ibid.,* II, 298-300.

[21] *Ibid.,* I, 824.

[22] For description of a typical recruiting meeting, see James S. Clark, *Life in the Middle West* (Chicago, 1916), 44-47.

[23] Oscar O. Winther, editor, *With Sherman to the Sea: The Journal of Theodore F. Upson* (Baton Rouge, 1943), 19. To be cited hereafter as *With Sherman to the Sea.*

[24] Capt. T. J. Wright, *History of the Eighth Kentucky Regiment Volunteer Infantry* (St. Joseph, Mo., 1880), 19.

[25] Cyril B. Upham, "Arms and Equipment for the Iowa Troops in the Civil War," *Iowa Journal of History and Politics,* XVI (1918), 35-36.

[26] Selden Connor, "The Boys of 1861," Military Order of the Loyal Legion of the United States, Maine Commandery, *War Papers,* I (Portland, Maine, 1898), 323-343; Fred A. Shannon, *Organization and Administration of the Union Army* (Cleveland, 1928), I, 90 ff.

[27] *O. R.,* series 1, II, 369-370; "The Fourteenth Indiana on Cheat Mountain," *Indiana Magazine of History,* XXIX (1933), 352.

[28] *O. R.,* series 1, III, 97.

[29] *Ibid.,* X, pt. 1, 84.

[30] Elizabeth Ring, "Reveille in Limington, 1861-1865," manuscript in possession of its author, to whom I am indebted for assistance in locating Maine materials; Charles E. Davis, *Three Years in the Army: The Story of the Thirteenth Massachusetts Volunteers* (Boston, 1894), xxviii, to be cited hereafter as *Three Years in the Army;* Shannon, *Organization and Administration of the Union Army,* I, 107 ff; Bell Irvin Wiley, *The Life of Johnny Reb: The Common Soldier of the Confederacy* (Indianapolis, 1943), 311.

[31] Herman C. Newhall to his brother, Aug. 4, 1861, manuscript, Boston Public Library.

[32] *O. R.,* series 1, V, 81; *Revised Regulations for the Army of the United States, 1861* (Philadelphia, 1861), paragraph 1261. To be cited hereafter as *Army Regulations.*

[33] Charles A. Barker to his parents, Nov. 10, 1861, manuscript, Essex Institute.

[34] Leander Stillwell, *The Story of a Common Soldier* (Erie, Kan., 1920), 15.

[35] See chapter XII.

[36] *O. R.,* series 3, II, 236.

[37] *Ibid.,* III, 136-140, 1071-1073; IV, 6 ff, 660 ff.

[38] For various nicknames of volunteer organizations see Richard C. Drum, *List of Synonyms of Organizations in the Volunteer Service of*

the United States during the Years 1861, '62, '63, '64, and '65 (Washington, D. C., 1885).

[39] C. Barney, *Recollections of Field Service with the Twentieth Iowa Infantry Volunteers* (Davenport, 1865), 33-35. A visitor to a regimental camp near Washington in July 1861 reported: "The colonel had his wife, one lieutenant his, many of the soldiers theirs. . . ." U. S. Sanitary Commission *Documents*, No. 17, "Report of a Preliminary Survey of the Camps of a Portion of the Volunteer Forces near Washington" (dated July 9, 1861), 18.

[40] Diary of Sgt. Henry A. Buck, Jan. 20, 1862, manuscript, Univ. of Mich.

[41] Eli R. Pickett to his wife, Sept. 6, 1862, manuscript, Minn. Historical Society; S. F. Fleharty, *Our Regiment: A History of the 102nd Illinois Infantry Volunteers* (Chicago, 1865), 8-9.

[42] A. Davenport to his homefolk, May 1, 1861, manuscript, N. Y. Historical Society.

[43] *O. R.*, series 3, II, 609 ff.

[44] Wirt A. Cate, editor, *Two Soldiers* (Chapel Hill, N. C., 1938), 222.

[45] A U. S. Sanitary Commission representative who inspected more than a score of regiments in the vicinity of Cairo in the latter part of 1861 commented on the "immense number" of photographs which the volunteers had made of themselves after drawing their uniforms. U. S. Sanitary Commission *Documents*, No. 36, 28.

[46] Detroit *Free Press*, June 20, Sept. 12, 1861.

[47] *Ibid.*, May 23, 1861; Winther, *With Sherman to the Sea*, 30-31. Accidental shooting was woefully prevalent among early volunteers. W. H. Russell reported after a visit to camps about Washington, D. C., in July 1861: "The number of accidents from the carelessness of the men is astonishing; in every day's paper there is an account of deaths and wounds caused by the discharge of firearms in the tents." *My Diary North and South* (Boston, 1863), 396.

[48] W. H. Darlington to his mother, July 25, Aug. 1, 1861, manuscript, Harvard.

[49] O. W. Norton, *Army Letters, 1861-1865* (Chicago, 1903), 16.

[50] Ellis Spear, "The Story of the Raising and Organization of a Regiment of Volunteers in 1862," Loyal Legion, District of Columbia Commandery, *War Papers*, No. 46 (Washington, D. C., 1903), 1 ff.

[51] Notation in back of diary of James P. Snell, manuscript, Illinois State Historical Library.

[52] Henry Crydenwise to his parents, Oct. 9, 1861, manuscript, Emory. In addition to the Crydenwise collection at Emory are a few letters at Duke. Charles W. Wills, *Army Life of an Illinois Soldier* (Washington, 1906), 14.

[53] Ruth A. Gallaher, editor, "Peter Wilson in the Civil War," *Iowa Journal of History and Politics*, XL (1942), 158, 163.

[54] Norton, *op. cit.*, 15-16.

[55] J. G. Fraser to his homefolk, April 25, 1864, manuscript, Indiana Historical Society.

[56] Detroit *Free Press,* June 23, 1861.

[57] *Ibid.,* Oct. 24, 1861.

[58] J. W. Rich, "The Color Bearer of the 12th Iowa," *Iowa Journal of History and Politics,* VI (1908), 95-99.

[59] Lt. F. M. Abbott to his brother, July 22, 1861, manuscript, Harvard.

[60] Diary of Harvey Reid, April 24, 1861.

[61] Detroit *Free Press,* Aug. 31, 1861.

[62] Everett W. Pattison, "Some Reminiscences of Army Life," Loyal Legion, Commandery of Missouri, *War Papers and Personal Reminiscences* (St. Louis, 1892), I, 248.

[63] Diary of Lt. T. Waldo Denny, April 17, 1861, manuscript, Veterans' Records, Nat'l Archives.

[64] Cyrus Stone to his mother, Oct. 22, 1861, manuscript, Minn. Historical Society.

[65] Urich N. Parmelee to his father, April 11, 1863, manuscript, Duke.

[66] Henry C. Hall to his brother, Nov. 6, 1861, manuscript, Duke.

[67] W. H. Darlington to his mother, July 23, 1861.

[68] William McCarter, "My Life in the American Army," I, 7-8, manuscript, N. Y. Public Library; Carl Wittke, "The Ninth Ohio Volunteers," *Ohio State Arch. and Historical Quarterly,* XXXV (1926), 402-417.

[69] For an example see William H. Bentley, *History of the 77th Illinois Volunteer Infantry* (Peoria, 1883), 16.

[70] This song's popularity among departing units is based on study of innumerable letters and diaries. A good example is afforded in a letter of Sgt. William T. Pippey, Jan. 15, 1862: "We had a jolly time in the cars singing 'John Brown.'" Manuscript, Duke.

[71] Edward Louis Edes to his father, Oct. 1, 1863, manuscript, Mass. Historical Society.

[72] C. A. Whittier, "Reminiscences of the War, 1861-1865," typescript, Boston Public Library.

[73] Journal of William E. Chase, Oct. 15, 1864, manuscript, Maine Historical Society.

[74] J. Bendernagel to William D. Murphy, April 29, 1861, manuscript, N. Y. Historical Society.

[75] J. H. Kendig to his brother, Dec. [no day], 1861, manuscript, Historical Society of Pa.

[76] C. B. Thurston to his parents, March 27, 1862 [misdated, 1861], manuscript, Emory.

[77] Capt. Charles A. Barnard to his wife, Feb. 13-19, 1862, manuscript, Maine Historical Society.

[78] Diary of Rufus Kinsley, March 12—April 5, 1862, manuscript, Vt. Historical Society.

[79] Lt. Roswell Farnham to his wife, May 2, 9, 10, 1861, typescript, Vt. Historical Society.

[80] Hercules Stanard to his sister, from Washington, D. C., June 13, 1861, manuscript, Univ. of Mich.

[81] Jasper Newton Searles to his homefolk, June 27, 1861, manuscript, Minn. Historical Society.

[82] "J.F.W.W.," "Our Hospital and the Men in Them," *Monthly Religious Magazine*, XXIX (1863), 241-242.

[83] Ransom E. Hawley to his sister, Sept. 21 [1863], manuscript, Ind. State Library.

[84] Franc B. Wilkie, *Pen and Powder* (Boston, 1888), 14-15.

[85] Joseph H. Diltz to B. F. Maden, Feb. 2, 1862, manuscript, Duke.

[86] "Letters of a Badger Boy in Blue," *Wis. Magazine of History*, IV (1920-21), 209.

[87] Henry Crydenwise to his parents, Oct. 20, 1861.

[88] Diary of William B. Gaskins, Sept. 20, 1861, manuscript, Duke.

[89] Wesley H. Day to Dudley Tillison, June 9 [1861], manuscript, Vt. Historical Society.

[90] Samuel C. Evans to his sister, Dec. 29, 1863, manuscript, Minn. Historical Society.

[91] Enoch T. Baker to his wife, Nov. 10, 1861, manuscript, Historical Society of Pa.

[92] William O. Wettleson to his parents, Oct. 12, 1861, manuscript, Luther College Library. I am indebted to Inga B. Norstog for translating and transcribing this and other Norwegian items in the Luther College collection.

[93] Arthur C. Cole, *The Era of the Civil War* (vol. 3, *Centennial History of Illinois*, Springfield, Ill., 1919), 278.

[94] Diary of W. H. Jackson, Aug. 18, 1862, manuscript, N. Y. Public Library.

[95] Detroit *Free Press*, April 19, 1861. W. H. Russell, the London *Times* correspondent, noted after a visit to an Illinois camp in June 1861: "During my short sojourn in this country I have never yet met any person who could show me where the sovereignty of the Union resides. General Prentiss, however, and his Illinois volunteers are quite ready to fight for it." *My Diary North and South*, 338.

[96] Diary of Philip Smith, July 22, 1861, bound series of articles from Peoria *Evening Star*, filed in Veterans' Records, Nat'l Archives.

[97] Samuel Storrow to his father, Oct. 12, 1862, manuscript, Mass. Historical Society.

[98] For an excellent discussion of motivations of World War II soldiers, see Samuel A. Stouffer and others, *The American Soldier* (New York, 1949), I, 430-485.

[99] John P. Moulton to his mother, Nov. 4, 1861, manuscript, Western Reserve Historical Society.

[100] For a further discussion of soldier attitudes toward slavery and the Negro, see chapter V.

[101] James Ford Rhodes, *History of the United States from the Compromise of 1850* (New York, 1892-1906), I, 278-285.

[102] "Letters of a Badger Boy in Blue," *Wis. Magazine of History*, IV (1920-1921), 90 ff.

[103] *Ibid.*

[104] *Ibid.*

[105] *Emigranten* (Norwegian newspaper published at Madison, Wis.), Oct. 7, 1861.

[106] Diary of Rufus Kinsley, Jan. 21, 1863.

[107] John P. Sheahan to his father, Oct. 14, 1862, manuscript, Maine Historical Society.

[108] Urich N. Parmelee to his mother, Sept. 8, 1862.

[109] *Ibid.*, March 29, 1863.

[110] This sketch is based on the Parmelee Papers.

[111] The *Cavalier*, published by the Fifth Pennsylvania Cavalry, June 25, 1862.

[112] A. Davenport to his homefolk, Sept. 26, 1862, Feb. 7, 1863.

[113] Henry L. Joslin to his mother, July 20, 1862, manuscript, American Antiquarian Society.

[114] A. Davenport to his homefolk, July 12, 1862.

[115] Charles D. Babbott to his father, Dec. 14, 1862, manuscript, Rutherford B. Hayes Memorial Library.

[116] William T. Pippey to "A.H. and B.Y.," July 31, 1862.

[117] Daniel E. Burbank to his parents, Aug. 11, 1861, manuscript, American Antiquarian Society.

[118] Samuel C. Evans to James Peet, July 27, 1863.

[119] Sgt. Eli R. Pickett to his wife, March 27, 1863.

Chapter II

FROM REVEILLE TO TAPS

[1] All the infantry calls are listed, with music for both drum and bugle, in Silas Casey, *Infantry Tactics* (N. Y., 1862), I, 227 ff. Those most frequently used, with music and accompanying remarks, are to be found also in the appendix of "Transcripts from the Letters and Diaries of Herbert E. Valentine, 1861-1864," manuscript, Essex Institute. To be cited hereafter as Valentine letters and diaries. Valentine was a musician in the 23rd Mass. Regt.

[2] For an excellent discussion of artillery routine and for camp life in general, see John D. Billings, *Hard Tack and Coffee* (Boston, 1888), 164 ff.

[3] David Leigh to "Mr. Drumgold," Aug. 1, 1863, manuscript, Dartmouth.

[4] Actually the signal which headed the official list of calls was a preliminary one known as the "assembly of buglers." But soldier narratives leave the impression that this was rarely used. The overwhelming ma-

jority of these accounts state that the notes of the reveille were the first heard by the men.

[5] See the delightfully human illustration (by the soldier artist Charles W. Reed) in Billings, *op. cit.*, 167.

[6] George A. Townsend, *Rustics in Rebellion* (Chapel Hill, 1950), 10.

[7] Valentine letters and diaries, appendix.

[8] Camp routine was outlined by innumerable diarists and letter writers, and the account here given of a typical day's activity, and the sections on training and equipment which follow, are drawn from so many different sources as to make it impractical to list them all. Important variations and details of special interest are cited at appropriate points in the narrative.

[9] Charles Ward to his brother, Oct. 2, 1862, manuscript, American Antiquarian Society; Jesse A. Wilson to his father, Sept. 13, 1862, manuscript in possession of Mrs. Fred A. Johnson, Belfast, Maine.

[10] Thomas L. Livermore, *Days and Events* (Boston, 1920), 35.

[11] G. Haven, "Camp Life at the Relay," *Harper's New Monthly Magazine*, XXIV (1861-1862), 631.

[12] Valentine letters and diaries, appendix.

[13] See poetic description of camp life in Ruth A. Gallaher, editor, "Peter Wilson in the Civil War," *Iowa Journal of History and Politics*, XL (1942), 298.

[14] For an unusually good description of Sunday inspection, see Livermore, *op. cit.*, 39.

[15] Leander Stillwell, *The Story of a Common Soldier*, 90-91; Max H. Guyer, editor, "The Journal and Letters of William O. Gulick," *Iowa Journal of History and Politics*, XXVIII (1930), 215.

[16] Billings, *op. cit.*, 77.

[17] Haven, *op. cit.*, 632-633; Lawrence Van Alstyne, *Diary of an Enlisted Man* (New Haven, 1910), 56-57; Edward L. Edes to his father, July 13, 1862, manuscript, Mass. Historical Society; M. P. Larry to his sister, Jan. 31, 1863, manuscript, Maine Historical Society.

[18] *Ibid.*

[19] *Army Regulations, 1861*, article XXXI.

[20] *Ibid.*

[21] At the outbreak of the war, pay of artillery and infantry privates was $11 per month and that of cavalry $12. Herbert E. Valentine letters and diaries, I, 8. On Aug. 6, 1861, Congress increased the rate to $13 per month for all arms, and on June 20, 1864, to $16 per month. War Department Adjutant General's Office *General Orders*, 1861, No. 54, and 1864, No. 216.

[22] Assignment of pay to relatives was provided by Congress on July 22, 1861. See W.D.A.G.O. *General Orders*, 1861, No. 81. Cpl. Day Elmore wrote his father Sept. 30, 1862: "I signed . . . [the allotment roll] for sending you $16 evry 2 months." Manuscript in possession of Mrs. Hall Mosher, Memphis, Tenn. For an explanation of the allotment system see Billings, *op. cit.*, 97-98.

[23] Charles E. Davis, *Three Years in the Army*, 15.

[24] Details of training procedure on the various levels are given in Casey's, Hardee's and Scott's manuals of tactics; a convenient digest of all three is William Gilham, *Manual of Instruction for the Volunteers and Militia of the United States* (Philadelphia, 1861). The Civil War papers at Emory University of Capt. C. S. Wortley, 20th Michigan Regiment, contain in addition to Casey the following training guides: *Instructions for Officers and Non-Commissioned Officers on Outpost and Patrol Duty and Troops in Campaign* (Washington, 1863); *A System of Target Practice for the Use of Troops* (Washington, 1862); *Rules for the Management and Cleaning of the Rifle Musket, Model 1863* (Washington, 1863); and *Instructions to Mustering Officers and Others of Kindred Duties* (Washington, 1863).

[25] Diary of William Boston, Feb. 5, 1863, typescript, Univ. of Mich.

[26] George B. Turner to his father, Dec. 21, 1862, typescript, Ohio State Arch. and Historical Society.

[27] For example see John Beatty, *The Citizen Soldier; or, Memoirs of a Volunteer* (Cincinnati, 1879), 77.

[28] Gallaher, *op. cit.*, 174; diary of Cpl. Henry Clay Scott, Sept. 21, Oct. 21, 1861, manuscript, N. Y. Public Library.

[29] Fritz Haskell, editor, "Diary of Col. William Camm," Ill. State Historical Society *Journal*, XVIII (1926), 813.

[30] Donald Gordon, editor, *M. L. Gordon's Experiences in the Civil War* (Boston, 1922), 32.

[31] O. W. Norton, *Army Letters, 1861-1865*, 37-38.

[32] Lt. Col. Lucius Fairchild, acting commander of the 2nd Wis. Regt., and an unusually able officer, wrote to his sister, Dec. 20, 1861: "Day before yesterday Gen. McDowell had another of his division drills —& sham battle—It was a very fine affair, and a good drill for the soldiers . . . better still for the field officers . . . giving them practice in handling men for a definite purpose. I have been in command on all of our big division drill, & feel that I have learned a great deal—feel more confidence in being able to conduct a regt through battle—if I should ever be called on to do so." Manuscript, Wis. Historical Society. McDowell seems to have been one of the very few commanders who early in the war laid great stress on maneuvers by division. See *O. R.*, series 1, XII, pt. 1, 91.

[33] Oscar O. Winther, editor, *With Sherman to the Sea*, 31.

[34] George W. Landrum to his sister, January [no day] 1862, typescript, Western Reserve Historical Society.

[35] Lt. Charles H. Salter to Mrs. Isabella G. Duffield [n.d., but 1861], manuscript among Duffield Papers, Detroit Public Library.

[36] *O. R.*, series 1, XXXII, pt. 3, 323.

[37] Edward L. Edes to his father, Jan. 10, 1864.

[38] *O. R.*, series 1, XII, pt. 3, 346. A camp of instruction, resembling the casual camp of World War II, was set up in Nashville, 1864. See *ibid.*, XXXII, pt. 3, 505. Early in the war a central signal camp of instruction was established at Georgetown, D. C., *ibid.*, V, 70. For reference to an artillery camp of instruction, which seems to have resembled a

World War II unit-training center, see Rhode Island Soldiers' and Sailors' Historical Society, *Personal Narratives*, 2nd Series, No. 11 (Providence, 1881), 36-37.

[39] O. R., series 1, XXXVIII, pt. 5, 408.

[40] For example of a veteran first sergeant drilling a score of recruits that joined his company at Atlanta just before the beginning of Sherman's march to the sea, see diary of N. L. Parmater, Oct. 30, 31, Nov. 1, 5, 1864, typescript in possession of Dr. A. M. Giddings, Battle Creek, Mich. In the 16th N. Y. Regt., recruits received after Antietam seem to have been trained by themselves in the morning and with the old troops in the afternoon. See Cyrus R. Stone to his parents, Oct. 7, 1862, manuscript, Minn. Historical Society.

[41] R. G. Carter, *Four Brothers in Blue* (Washington, 1913), 315.

[42] Norton, *op. cit.*, 28.

[43] George Milledge to his brother, Joseph Diltz, June 9, 1863, manuscript, Duke.

[44] For example, on July 19, 1862, after participating in the Seven Days' campaign, James O. Newhall wrote his father from Harrison's Landing, Va.: "We have resumed drilling again. Some of the boys dislike it much, thinking they are well enough drilled already, but there is nothing like discipline, after all." Manuscript, Boston Public Library.

[45] *Army Regulations*, 1861, article XXXVI. Officer latrines were back of the baggage train. Enlisted men's latrines were at the opposite end of the camp.

[46] U. S. Sanitary Commission *Documents*, No. 26, 10.

[47] For illustrations of the various types of shelter, see Billings, *op. cit.*, 45 ff.

[48] A. C. Hawes, *The Experiences of a Union Soldier*, 10.

[49] Billings, *op. cit.*, 47.

[50] *Ibid.*, 48-50.

[51] *Ibid.*, 50-51.

[52] *Ibid.*, 52-53; Samuel Storrow to his parents, March 17, 23, 1863, manuscript, Mass. Historical Society.

[53] Billings, *op. cit.*, 54; Gilham, *op. cit.*, 643.

[54] Billings, *op. cit.*, 54; Lt. Roswell Farnham to his wife, May 25, 1861, manuscript, Vt. Historical Society.

[55] Asa Ward Brindle to "Frank and Flora," Oct. 25, 1862, manuscript (microfilm), Detroit Public Library.

[56] John P. M. Green, "Belated Diary of a Civil War Soldier in the First N. H. Light Battery," 2, 5, 6, typescript, N. H. Historical Society.

[57] Lt. Col. Roswell Farnham to his wife, Nov. 28, 1862.

[58] Frank M. Rood to his parents, Jan. 3, 1863, manuscript in possession of Frank M. Rood, Poultney, Vt.; Billings, *op. cit.*, 54-58, 66, 73-79.

[59] Mrs. Roswell Farnham to her brother, Dec. 24, 1862. Mrs. Farnham was visiting her husband in camp when she wrote the letter. For an excellent photograph showing many barrel-topped chimneys, see F. T. Miller, editor, *Photographic History of the Civil War*, (N. Y., 1911), VIII, 225.

[60] Billings, *op. cit.*, 56.

[61] *Ibid.*, 75-76.

[62] *Ibid.*, 77-80; diary of Ezra G. Huntley, Dec. 30, 1864, manuscript, Dartmouth.

[63] Urich N. Parmelee to his mother, Dec. 13, 1863, manuscript, Duke.

[64] Billings, *op. cit.*, 57; Edwin E. Newhall to his homefolk, Jan. 8, 1862; Miller, *Photographic History of the Civil War*, VIII, 258-259.

[65] Edwin E. Newhall to his parents, Jan. 8, 1862.

[66] Billings, *op. cit.*, 276-278, 316-320; *Revised U. S. Army Regulations*, 1861, article LI; W.D.A.G.O. *General Orders*, No. 108, Dec. 16, 1861, changed the color of trousers from dark blue to sky blue. Colored illustrations of various uniforms may be found in the *Atlas to Accompany the Official Records of the Union and Confederate Armies, 1861-1865* (Washington, 1890-1895), plate 172. The illustrations are too artistic to be realistic, except in representing prescribed modes.

[67] Henry L. Joslin to his mother, Nov. 11, 1861, manuscript, American Antiquarian Society.

[68] Winther, *op. cit.*, 25.

[69] See Miller, *Photographic History of the Civil War*, especially volume VIII.

[70] O. B. Clark, editor, *Downing's Civil War Diary* (Des Moines, Iowa, 1916), 16; "Remarks by Capt. J. B. Molyneaux at a Dinner Given by the Cleveland Contingent, Ohio Commandery Military Order of the Loyal Legion . . . April 2, 1913," typescript, Duke.

[71] Billings, *op. cit.*, 316.

[72] Winther, *op. cit.*, 26.

[73] *Ibid.*

[74] John A. Cockerill, "What a Boy Did at Shiloh," in Portland, Maine, *Daily Express*, Jan. 21, 1890, supplement.

[75] O. R., series 1, XXXI, pt. 3, 392; G. W. Adams, "Health and Medicine in the Union Army, 1861-1865" (Ph.D. Dissertation, Harvard, 1946), II, 645.

[76] *Army Regulations*, 1861, article LI; O. R., series 1, XXV, pt. 2, 152, XLVI, pt. 3, 33, XLVII, pt. 2, 419. For colored illustrations of corps badges see *Atlas to Accompany O. R.*, plate 175. Insignia of rank and also buttons are shown in *ibid.*, plate 172.

[77] See Fred A. Shannon, *Organization and Administration of the Union Army*, I, 53 ff.

[78] O. R., series 1, XIX, pt. 1, 12.

[79] A. Davenport to his homefolk, April 19, 1863, manuscript, N. Y. Historical Society.

[80] *Ibid.*

[81] Asst. Surgeon Benj. S. Catlin to his parents, Dec. 9, 1862, manuscript, Conn. State Library; David Leigh to "Mr. Drumgold," Nov. 10, 1863.

[82] Diary of John H. Markley, manuscript, Historical Society of Pa.; Edward L. Edes to his father, July 26, 1863.

[83] N. Y. *Tribune*, June 6, 1864.

[84] Jacob E. Beltzer to William R. Keran, May 18, 1862, manuscript, Ohio State Arch. and Historical Society.

[85] Albert G. Hart to his wife, Sept. 26, 1862, manuscript, Western Reserve Historical Society.

[86] *O. R.*, series 1, XX, pt. 2, 118.

[87] Van Alstyne, *op. cit.*, 155.

[88] *O. R.*, series 1, XLVII, pt. 1, 257.

[89] *Ibid.*, XXXI, pt. 2, 262, 580-581, and pt. 3, 392.

[90] William H. Lloyd to his wife, Dec. 21, 1863, manuscript, Western Reserve Historical Society.

[91] For example, see *O. R.*, series 3, II, 804-805.

[92] See chapter III.

[93] Shannon, *op. cit.*, I, 113 ff; Comte de Paris, *History of the Civil War in America* (Philadelphia, 1875), I, 298-299; Bell Irvin Wiley, *The Life of Johnny Reb*, 291-292; DAB, XX, 209. For illustrations of the various types of guns, see *Atlas to Accompany O. R.*, plate 173.

[94] Winther, *op. cit.*, 107, 157-158.

[95] Daniel E. Burbank to his parents, Oct. 17, 1861, manuscript, American Antiquarian Society. Accuracy at 1500 yards by an average Yank seems an exaggeration.

[96] For an indication of the conservative attitude of the Chief of Ordnance late in the conflict, see *O. R.*, series 3, IV, 802. Opposing viewpoints on culpability with reference to arms development are presented in Shannon, *op. cit.*, I, 107-148 and Kenneth P. Williams, *Lincoln Finds a General* (N. Y., 1949), II, 784-785, 798-800.

[97] For drawings of various types of cannon, see *Atlas to Accompany O. R.*, plate 173. The Comte de Paris discusses artillery pieces and projectiles at length in *op. cit.*, I, 300-307.

[98] Several makes of carbines and pistols are illustrated in *Atlas to Accompany O. R.*, plate 173. For references to types in the possession of soldiers, see Report of Col. H. Van Rensselaer, Inspector General's Office, Washington, D. C., on inspection of the Dept. of Mo., dated Feb. 12, 1862, manuscript, A.G.O. Records, file 14-I, Nat'l Archives; Flavius J. Bellamy, 3rd Ind. Cav., to his homefolk, Jan. 4, Aug. 12, 1862, Aug. 16, 1863, manuscript, Ind. State Library; William Blackburn to his brother, Feb. 11, 1862, manuscript, Historical Society of Pa.; Franklin H. Bailey to his father, Dec. 26, 1864, manuscript, Univ. of Mich.

[99] Franklin H. Bailey to his parents, March 16, 1864.

[100] Billings, *op. cit.*, 76-79, 86, 126, 134, 272-278.

[101] A. Davenport to his homefolk, April 18, 1862.

[102] Samuel Storrow to his mother, Nov. 16, 1862. For other comment on individual equipment and its weight, see C. B. Thurston to his parents, July 20, 1862, manuscript, Duke; Clarence F. Cobb, *The Maryland Campaign, 1862* (Washington, 1891), 15-16.

[103] Billings, *op. cit.*, 343.

[104] Directives specified whether troops were to proceed "in heavy marching order"—*i.e.*, carrying all their equipment—or "in light marching order," with only essentials. Henry S. Commager, *The Blue and the*

Gray (Indianapolis, 1950), I, 289, quoting Joel Cook, *The Siege of Richmond.*

Chapter III

THE SUPREME TEST

[1] O. R., series 1, XVI, pt. 1, 918.

[2] The account which begins here of preliminaries to battle and the action which followed is based on a mass of official and personal material. Specific citations are given only in the instance of direct quotations or where other considerations seem to make references desirable. The narrative is not of any particular engagement but all the incidents cited actually occurred in connection with some action.

[3] For examples of prebattle speeches and instructions see O. R., series 1, XX, pt. 1, 183, XXI, 241, XXXVIII, pt. 4, 41-42; Thomas W. Hyde, *Following the Greek Cross* (N. Y., 1894), 125-126; A. Davenport to his homefolk, June 4, 1862, manuscript, N. Y. Historical Society.

[4] Thomas L. Livermore, *Days and Events*, 133.

[5] A. H. Pickel to his father, Dec. 19, 1862, manuscript, Duke University.

[6] William D. Bickham, *Rosecrans' Campaign with the Fourteenth Army Corps* (Cincinnati, 1863), 362.

[7] Cyrus R. Stone to his parents, Dec. 20, 1862, manuscript, Minn. Historical Society; Harold A. Small, editor, *The Road to Richmond: The Civil War Memoirs of Major Abner R. Small* (Berkeley, Calif., 1939), 84-85; Chaplain Joseph H. Twichell to his father, June 2, 1862, manuscript, Yale.

[8] A. H. Pickel to his father, Dec. 19, 1862.

[9] M. P. Larry to his sister, Dec. 18, 1862, manuscript, Maine Historical Society.

[10] Ruth A. Gallaher, editor, "Peter Wilson in the Civil War," *Iowa Journal of History and Politics*, XL (1942), 298-299.

[11] Edward L. Edes to his father, April 14, 1863, manuscript, Mass. Historical Society.

[12] O. R., series 1, X, pt. 1, 332-333.

[13] One soldier recalled after the war that he thought of death when going into battle only as something that might befall "the other fellow." S. H. M. Byers, "How Men Feel in Battle," *Harper's Monthly Magazine*, CXII (1906), 931.

[14] M. P. Larry to his sister, Feb. 26, 1864.

[15] Thomas B. Barker to his brother, July 20, 1861, manuscript, Maine Historical Society.

[16] Undated note added to *ibid.*, signed: "A Surgeon C.S.A."

[17] Edgar L. Erickson, "With Grant at Vicksburg, From the Civil

War Diary of Capt. James F. Wilcox," Ill. State Historical Society *Journal*, XXX (1938), 479-480.

[18] James H. Croushore, editor, *A Volunteer's Adventures, A Union Captain's Record of the Civil War*, by John William De Forest (New Haven, 1946), 63. To be cited hereafter, De Forest, *A Volunteer's Adventures*; a lieutenant who went to the rear for ammunition at Winchester, Va., Sept. 19, 1864, told on his return to ranks of seeing file closers performing their work in dead earnest. "By Gad," he said, "I never saw such spanking and ferruling since I was at school." *Ibid.*, 186.

[19] *Ibid.*, 64.

[20] Herbert E. Valentine to his mother, Jan. 2, 1863, manuscript, Essex Institute.

[21] Franklin H. Bailey to his parents, April 8, 1862, typescript, Univ. of Mich.

[22] De Forest, *A Volunteer's Adventures*, 65; Small, *op. cit.*, 64; journal of Charles F. Johnson, Sept. 17, 1862, manuscript, Minn. Historical Society; Lt. W. Henry Clune to his wife, April 13, 1862, manuscript, Shiloh National Park.

[23] De Forest, *A Volunteer's Adventures*, 185-186.

[24] John P. Sheahan to his father, July 10, 1863, manuscript, Maine Historical Society; Mrs. J. D. Wheeler, compiler, *In Memoriam: Letters of William Wheeler of the Class of 1855, Y. C.* (Cambridge, Mass., 1875), 418.

[25] R. G. Carter, *Four Brothers in Blue*, 318.

[26] Franklin H. Bailey to his parents, April 8, 1862.

[27] O. W. Norton, *Army Letters, 1861-1865*, 93, 106-109.

[28] John P. Sheahan to his father, June 10, 1863.

[29] John N. Moulton to his sister, Jan. 29, 1863, manuscript, Western Reserve Historical Society; William Hamilton to his mother, Dec. 24, 1862, manuscript, Library of Congress.

[30] William O. Wettleson to his father, March 15, 1865, manuscript, Luther College Library. Translated from the Norwegian by Inga B. Norstog.

[31] For a discussion of the Rebel yell, see Bell Irvin Wiley, *The Life of Johnny Reb*, 71-72.

[32] O. R., series 1, XII, pt. 2, supplement, 1012.

[33] Albert G. Hart to his sons, Oct. 27, 1863, manuscript, Western Reserve Historical Society.

[34] Almon Clarke, "In the Immediate Rear: Experiences and Observations of a Field Surgeon," Mil. Order of the Loyal Legion, Wis. Commandery, *War Papers*, II (Milwaukee, 1896), 91.

[35] H. Allen Gosnell, *Guns on the Western Waters* (Baton Rouge, 1949), 228.

[36] O. R., series 1, XXXIV, pt. 3, 169; Livermore, *Days and Events*, 141; Cyrus R. Stone to his parents, Sept. 16, 1862.

[37] O. R., series 1, XX, pt. 1, 335; "G.S.G.," to William Wheatcraft, Jan. 11, 1863, manuscript, Misc. Civil War Letters, Ill. State Historical Library.

[38] For references to uninhibited yelling see Edgar L. Erickson, *op. cit.*, entry of May 1, 1863 and O. R., series 1, XII, pt. 2, 441, XVI, pt. 1, 804, XXX, pt. 1, 657, XXXVI, pt. 1, 668, XXXVIII, pt. 2, 371.

[39] Livermore, *Days and Events*, 141.

[40] Stephen A. Miller to his sister, Nov. 27, 1863, manuscript, Indiana Historical Society; Robert W. Rickard to his uncle, Aug. 14, 1863, manuscript. Ill. State Historical Library.

[41] Frank Wilkeson, *Recollections of a Private Soldier in the Army of the Potomac* (N. Y., 1887), 71-72.

[42] R. G. Carter, *Four Brothers in Blue*, 314.

[43] O. R., series 1, XXVII, pt. 1, 330-331, 446.

[44] Felix Brannigan to his sister May 15, 1862, typescript, Library of Congress; O. R., series 1, XXX, pt. 1, 60, 855.

[45] Small, *op. cit.*, 64 ff; O. R., series 1, XI, pt. 2, 391, XXVII, pt. 1, 234, XXXVI, pt. 1, 335-336, 358-359, 410, 704, XXXVIII, pt. 1, 710-711, pt. 3, 556-557; diary of Lt. Col. Allen L. Fahnestock, June 27, July 1, 1864, manuscript, Ill. State Historical Library.

[46] Unsigned letter, March 2, 1862 (erroneously dated March 2, 1861), manuscript in possession of Charles N. Owen, Chicago, who generously made available to me many rewarding letters.

[47] Gen. John Gibbon in his report of the second day's fighting at Gettysburg stated: "The smoke was at this time so dense that but little could be seen of the battle, and I directed some of the guns to cease firing fearing they might injure our own men." O. R., series 1, XXVII, pt. 1, 417. A soldier wrote after the Iuka, Miss., fight: "The smoke hung over the battlefield like a cloud, obscuring every object ten feet off." J. H. Greene, *Reminiscences of the War: Extracts from Letters Written Home from 1861 to 1865* (Medina, Ohio, 1886), 29.

[48] Small, *op. cit.*, 19-23.

[49] William H. Brearley to his father, Sept. 26, 1862, manuscript, Detroit Public Library.

[50] Small, *op. cit.*, 23.

[51] Edward L. Davis to "Friend Emma," July 27, 1861, manuscript, Wis. Historical Society.

[52] O. W. Norton wrote of his experiences at Malvern Hill: "We were so worn out by excitement, fatigue and want of sleep that there was not the spirit in the movement of the men that usually characterized them." *Army Letters*, 108.

[53] E. W. Robie to "Friend Lou," July 12, 1862, manuscript, Univ. of Vt.

[54] William H. Brearley to his father, Sept. 26, 1862.

[55] Diary of Matthew Marvin, Dec. 15, 1862, manuscript, Minn. Historical Society.

[56] An artillery private who was at Chancellorsville wrote: "We were all deaf for quite a while after the fight." Mrs. B. A. White, editor, *Richmond and Way Stations* (Milford, Mass., 1889), 43.

[57] Journal of Charles F. Johnson, Sept. 17, 1862.

[58] Mark De Wolfe Howe, editor, *Touched with Fire: Letters and*

Diary of Oliver Wendell Holmes, Jr. (Cambridge, Mass., 1946), 50-51.

[59] S. F. Fleharty, *Our Regiment: A History of the 102nd Ill. Inf. Vols.*, 83.

[60] Philip D. Jordan, editor, "Forty Days with the Christian Commission: A Diary of William Salter," *Iowa Journal of History and Politics*, XXXIII (1935), 147; unidentified officer of Grant's army to "Dear Henry," May, 28, 1863, manuscript in Lucian B. Case Papers, Chicago Historical Society; Herbert E. Valentine letters and diaries, June 22, July 2, Aug. 3, 1864.

[61] Edwin Hutchinson to his mother, Sept. 18, 1862, manuscript, La. State Univ.

[62] Joseph H. Diltz to his father, Oct. 10, 1862, manuscript, Duke.

[63] Henry J. H. Thompson to his wife, April 4, 1862, manuscript, Duke.

[64] A. Davenport to his homefolk, Dec. 17, 1862.

[65] *Ibid.*, June 11, 1861.

[66] Thomas N. Lewis to his uncle, April 10, 1862, manuscript among Moulton Letters, Western Reserve Historical Society.

[67] Alfred S. Roe, *The Ninth New York Heavy Artillery* (Worcester, Mass., 1899), 181; Nashville *Daily Union*, April 7, 1863.

[68] Lt. W. Henry Clune to his wife, April 13, 1862.

[69] Greene, *op. cit.*, 20; David McLain, who claimed that he carried Old Abe through the Corinth fight, while not specifically contradicting Greene's account, gives a much less spectacular version of the eagle's performance. See David McLain, "The Story of Old Abe," *Wis. Magazine of History*, VIII (1925), 410-411.

[70] Bickham, *op. cit.*, 363.

[71] Howe, *op. cit.*, 115.

[72] O. R., series 1, XXXVIII, pt. 3, 583.

[73] *Ibid.*, XXX, pt. 1, 769.

[74] Wilkeson, *op. cit.*, 95.

[75] R. G. Carter, *Four Brothers in Blue*, 253.

[76] Jasper Packard, *Four Years of Camp, March and Battle* (Washington, 1870), 5.

[77] Alfred Davenport, *Camp and Field Life of the Fifth New York Volunteer Infantry* (N. Y., 1879), 229.

[78] M. P. Larry to his sister, June 28, 1863.

[79] *Ibid.*, Dec. 8, 1863; John McMeekin to his mother, Jan. 15, 1863, manuscript, Western Reserve Historical Society.

[80] John McMeekin to his mother, Jan. 15, 1863.

[81] George Milledge to Mrs. J. H. Diltz, July 7, 1863, manuscript, Duke.

[82] W. O. Lyford to his father, July 22, 1861, manuscript in possession of Charles N. Owen, Chicago.

[83] For an example, see Lydia Minturn Post, editor, *Soldiers' Letters* (N. Y., 1865), 404-405.

[84] A. Davenport to his homefolk, June 1, 1862; Cyrus R. Stone to his parents, Sept. 23, 1862.

[85] John P. Sheahan to his father, Oct. [no day] 1863.

[86] William Hamilton to his mother, Dec. 24, 1862.

[87] Thomas N. Lewis to his uncle, April 10, 1862.

[88] *Indiana Magazine of History*, XXXIII (1937), 340.

[89] For example, see Lt. Henry W. Clune to his wife, April 16, 1862.

[90] Edwin Horton to his wife, Dec. 4, 1863, manuscript, Vt. Historical Society.

[91] William H. Lloyd to his wife, May 21, 1864, manuscript, Western Reserve Historical Society.

[92] Unidentified soldier (but apparently Sewell Welch) to Ansel Hawkes, Oct. 24, 1864, manuscript in possession of Delmont Hawkes, Sebago Lake, Maine, to whom I am indebted for its use.

[93] William H. Brearley to his father, Sept. 26, 1862.

[94] O. R., series 1, XXIV, pt. 2, 170-177.

[95] *Ibid.*, 186.

[96] For example, see *ibid.*, XXXVI, pt. 1, 366-367, 952.

[97] Brig. Gen. J. J. Bartlett to Col. Joseph Howland, June 25, 1864, manuscript, N. Y. Historical Society.

[98] O. R., series 1, XXXVIII, pt. 1, 77.

[99] *Ibid.*, 226.

[100] *Ibid.*, XXXVI, pt. 3, 240.

[101] Diary of S. E. Thomason, June 23, 1861, manuscript in possession of Charles N. Owen, Chicago.

[102] Judge Advocate General Records, MM1071, manuscript, Nat'l Archives.

[103] After Haines's Bluff a soldier wrote: "Lots of our best men run like thunder thar is som in our company run them big brags the cordley devils." John McMeekin to his mother, March 16, 1863.

[104] Small, *op. cit.*, 70.

[105] Livermore, *Days and Events*, 205.

[106] David P. Jackson, editor, *The Colonel's Diary*, 82.

[107] Hazel C. Wolf, editor, *Campaigning with the First Minnesota* (St. Paul, 1944), 349.

[108] O. R., series 1, X, pt. 1, 135.

[109] *Ibid.*, 203.

[110] *Ibid.*, 324.

[111] *Ibid.*, 333.

[112] *Ibid.*, XI, pt. 1, 843, 852, 878; pt. 2, 111.

[113] *Ibid.*, XII, pt. 2, 445, 482 and supplement, 1065.

[114] *Ibid.*, XIX, pt. 2, 348.

[115] Lt. Henry Ropes to his father, Dec. 16, 1862, manuscript (copy), Boston Public Library.

[116] Capt. Henry Abbott to his brother, Dec. 17, 1862, manuscript, Harvard.

[117] O. R., series 1, XVII, pt. 1, 76. The regiment redeemed itself at Corinth. See *ibid.*, 171.

[118] Lt. George W. Landrum to his sister, Oct. 12, 1862, typescript, Western Reserve Historical Society.

[119] *Ibid.*

[120] *Ibid.*, Dec. 31, 1862, and Jan. (no day) 1863; *O. R.*, series 1, XX, pt. 1, 289, 547-548; Albert G. Hart to his wife, Jan. 7, 9, 1863.

[121] *O. R.*, series 1, XX, pt. 1, 548.

[122] For examples of soldier comment on the Chancellorsville rout, see R. G. Carter, *Four Brothers in Blue*, 249, and David Leigh to "Mr. Drumgold," May 20, 1863, manuscript, Dartmouth. For a recent study of the Chancellorsville campaign, see K. P. Williams, *Lincoln Finds a General*, II, 589 ff.

[123] *O. R.*, series 1, XXVII, pt. 1, 380.

[124] Knute Nelson to his brother, May 22—June 3, 1863, manuscript, Minn. Historical Society; Henry Crydenwise to his parents, July 9, 1863, manuscript, Emory.

[125] *O. R.*, series 1, XXIV, pt. 2, 257-258.

[126] *Ibid.*, XXX, pt. 1, 192-193.

[127] *Ibid.*, XXXIV, pt. 1, 399, 416; pt. 3, 169-171.

[128] Diary of John Merrilies, June 10, 11, 1864; Robert S. Henry, *First with the Most Forrest* (Indianapolis, 1944), 293-298.

[129] De Forest, *A Volunteer's Adventures*, 210-211.

[130] *O. R.*, series 1, XLVI, pt. 1, 846 and XLVII, pt. 1, 435; diary of William C. Meffert, March 13 [19], 1865.

[131] *Medals of Honor Issued in the War Department up to and Including Oct. 31, 1897* (Washington, 1897), 43.

[132] *O. R.*, series 1, VIII, 339.

[133] *Ibid.*, XI, pt. 1, 732-733.

[134] *Ibid.*, 812.

[135] *Ibid.*

[136] *Ibid.*, XVII, pt. 1, 275-276.

[137] Felix Brannigan to his sister, n.d., but early 1863.

[138] *O. R.*, series 1, XXX, pt. 1, 431.

[139] *Ibid.*, XXI, 309.

[140] *Ibid.*, XXIII, pt. 1, 492, 497.

[141] *Ibid.*, XXXI, pt. 2, 169.

[142] For example, see *ibid.*, XI, pt. 2, 373.

[143] *Ibid.*, XXX, pt. 1, 317.

[144] *Ibid.*, XXVII, pt. 1, 451-452.

[145] J. W. Rich, "The Color Bearer of the Twelfth Iowa Volunteer Infantry," *Iowa Journal of History and Politics*, VI (1908), 96-102.

[146] *O. R.*, series 1, XXIV, pt. 1, 630-631.

[147] *Ibid.*, 720.

[148] *Ibid.*, XXVII, pt. 1, 446.

[149] *Ibid.*, XXX, pt. 1, 62, 695.

[150] Confederates noted the improvement in Billy Yank's fighting qualities. After Gettysburg Gen. A. P. Hill was said to have remarked that he "had never known the Federals to fight so well" as they did on the first day of the fight. *O. R.*, series 1, XXVII, pt. 1, 272. Long after the war a veteran, commenting on the repeated charges made by the Federals against heavy opposition at Fredericksburg, remarked to a young

relative: "Up until then, son, I felt we had them licked. After that I never was sure. They hadn't learned to fight by Fredericksburg, but they had learned to get killed and not to run. I knew they'd come back some other time." Ellis G. Arnall, *The Shore Dimly Seen* (N. Y., 1946), 125.

Chapter IV

IN DIXIE LAND

[1] J. W. Evans to James Peet and wife, May 25, 1862, Peet Papers, manuscript, Minn. Historical Society; Daniel E. Burbank to his parents, Aug. 11, 1861, manuscript, American Antiquarian Society.

[2] William O. Wettleson to his homefolk, Nov. 27, 1864, manuscript, Luther College Library, translated from the Norwegian by Inga B. Norstog.

[3] William F. Lerich to his father, Jan. 26, 1862, manuscript, Univ. of Mich.

[4] Francis S. Flint to Jennie Russell, Oct. 30, 1864, manuscript, Minn. Historical Society.

[5] Louis Westacott to B. F. Moulton, Jan. 18, 1862, manuscript, Western Reserve Historical Society; D. B. Bates to William P. Corthell, March 7 [1864], manuscript, American Antiquarian Society; J. F. Morris to Clarissa Butler, May 7, 1863, manuscript among Miscellaneous Civil War Letters, American Antiquarian Society.

[6] Jesse A. Wilson to his mother, June 23, 1863, manuscript in possession of Mrs. Fred A. Johnson, Belfast, Maine.

[7] L. Marion Moulton to his uncle and aunt, Dec. 10, 1864, Western Reserve Historical Society; Henry C. Hall to his sister, Aug. 10, 1862, manuscript, Duke; Eli R. Pickett to his wife, June 23, 1864, manuscript, Minn. Historical Society.

[8] R. G. Carter, *Four Brothers in Blue*, 260.

[9] John P. Sheahan to his father, Oct. 14, 1862, manuscript, Maine Historical Society; Frederick A. Dickinson to "Dear George," Aug. 14, 1861, manuscript, American Antiquarian Society.

[10] Henry J. H. Thompson to his wife, Oct. 17, 1863, manuscript, Duke.

[11] W. C. Lusk, editor, *War Letters of William Thompson Lusk* (N. Y., 1911), 66.

[12] William B. Stanard to his homefolk, Feb. 22, 1862, manuscript, Univ. of Mich.

[13] John H. B. Kent to George Baxter, Dec. 27, 1862, manuscript, Mass. Historical Society; James L. Sellers, editor, "The Richard H. Mockett Diary," *Miss. Valley Historical Review*, XXVI (1939), 240; C. Parrish to his brother, Sept. 23, 1864, manuscript among Stanard Papers, Univ. of Mich.

[14] Lt. George W. Landrum to his sister, March 28, April 23, April 28, 1862, typescript, Western Reserve Historical Society.

[15] George W. Driggs, *Opening of the Mississippi: or Two Years Campaigning in the Southwest* (Madison, Wis., 1864), 100-101; Willis D. Maier to Annie F. Howells, June 19, 1863, manuscript, Howells Letters, Hayes Memorial Library.

[16] Andrew K. Rose, Aug. 9, 1863, manuscript, Duke University; Henry S. Simmons to his wife, Nov. 16, 1862, manuscript, Lowdermilk's Bookstore, Washington, D. C. I am greatly indebted to P. P. Jones, manager of Lowdermilk's Bookstore, for permission to use this excellent source.

[17] Cyrus R. Stone to his parents, April 12, 1862, manuscript, Minn. Historical Society.

[18] D. H. Dodd to his father, Dec. 30, 1862, manuscript, Ind. Historical Society.

[19] William R. Hartpence, *History of the Fifty-first Indiana Veteran Volunteer Infantry* (Cincinnati, 1894), 49.

[20] Charles W. Wills, *Army Life of an Illinois Soldier*, 215; Surg. Humphrey H. Hood to his wife, Dec. 20, 1862, manuscript, Ill. State Historical Library.

[21] Edward L. Edes to his sister, March 6, 1864, manuscript, Mass. Historical Society; John Tallman to his sister, April 12, 1864, manuscript, Chicago Historical Society.

[22] Wills, *Army Life of an Illinois Soldier*, 99-101.

[23] *Ibid.*, 228.

[24] James E. Bates to "Brothers and Sisters of the Old Social," manuscript among William P. Corthell Letters, American Antiquarian Society; Frederick A. Dickinson to his father, Feb. 26, 1862.

[25] Diary of Charles W. Wills, June 14, 1864, manuscript, Ill. State Historical Library; *Diary of E. P. Burton* (Des Moines, 1939), 5; James K. Hosmer, *The Color-Guard* (Boston, 1864), 118.

[26] Capt. Hans Mattson to his wife, Jan. 1, 1862, manuscript, Minn. Historical Society; David P. Conyngham, *Sherman's March through the South* (N. Y., 1865), 149-152.

[27] Lt. F. M. Abbott to his father, March 12, 1862, manuscript, Harvard.

[28] J. H. Greene, *Reminiscences of the War*, 51-52; Lusk, *Letters of William Thompson Lusk, 1861-1863*, 110.

[29] Diary of Maj. Oliver L. Spaulding, June 22, 1863, manuscript, Univ. of Mich.

[30] J. R. Barney to his brother, Oct. 24, 1862, manuscript, Dinsmore Letters, Ill. State Historical Library.

[31] Diary of E. J. Sherlock, Aug. 25, 1863, manuscript, Ind. Historical Society.

[32] John Herr to his sister, Feb. 5, 1865, manuscript, Duke; D. H. Dodd to his sister, Dec. 24, 1862.

[33] Diary of William E. Limbarker, Jan. 16, 1862, manuscript, Univ. of Mich.

[34] Edward Whitaker to his sister, June 24, 1861, manuscript, Conn. State Library.

[35] Elitha House to "Dear Jennie," April 18, 1863, manuscript, Miscellaneous Civil War Letters, Western Reserve Historical Society.

[36] Diary of John Merrilies, Dec. 18, 1862, manuscript, Chicago Historical Society.

[37] Hosmer, *The Color-Guard*, 118-119; Henry Crydenwise to his parents, Jan. 22, 1862, manuscript, Emory.

[38] Henry Crydenwise to his parents, Feb. 25, 1862, March 10, April 6, 1863; Harold A. Small, editor, *The Road to Richmond*, 200-201; Robert J. Kerner, editor, "Diary of Edward W. Crippin, Private 27th Ill. Vols.," Ill. State Historical Society *Transactions*, 1909 (Springfield, Ill., 1910), 250; "Journal of Melvin Cox Robertson," *Ind. Magazine of History*, XXVIII (1932), 127.

[39] Diary of Capt. E. J. Sherlock, Feb. 2, 1865, typescript, Nat'l Archives. The manuscript of this diary is at the Ind. Historical Society. References to it from here on will be to the manuscript unless otherwise indicated. Clara A. Glenn, editor, *Letters of Robert Walker* (Viroqua, Wis., 1917), 22; George F. Newhall to "Dear Friends," March 14, 1862, manuscript, Boston Public Library.

[40] Frances A. Tenney, editor, *War Diary of Luman Harris Tenney, 1861-1865* (Cleveland, 1914), 34, 38; John McMeekin to his sister, Dec. 15, 1862, manuscript, Western Reserve Historical Society; "The Fourteenth Indiana in the Valley of Virginia," *Ind. Magazine of History*, XXX (1934), 294.

[41] Hazel C. Wolf, editor, *Campaigning with the First Minnesota*, 251.

[42] Diary of Charles W. Wills, Jan. 10, 1864 [1865]. At this time Wills was writing his diary in installments and sending them home as letters to his sister. For the printed version of this entry, see *Army Life of an Illinois Soldier*, 336.

[43] Wills, *Army Life of an Illinois Soldier*, 29; diary of Oliver L. Spaulding, Nov. 4, 1862.

[44] Diary of James P. Snell, July 26, 1862, manuscript, Ill. State Historical Library.

Chapter V

ALONG FREEDOM ROAD

[1] Artemas Cook to Curtis Babbott, Jan. 3, 1864, manuscript, Hayes Memorial Library; A. Davenport to his homefolk, June 19, 1861, manuscript, N. Y. Historical Society.

[2] Capt. F. M. Abbott to his brother, Feb. [no day or year, but 1863], manuscript, Harvard.

³ Diary of Ezra G. Huntley, Dec. 29, 1864, manuscript (copy), Dartmouth.

⁴ Diary of Sgt. Matthew Marvin, Jan. 12, 1863, manuscript, Minn. Historical Society.

⁵ John B. Cuzner to Elsie Vandorn, Feb. 15, 1863, manuscript, Conn. Historical Society; John P. Sheahan to his homefolk, Sept. 22, 1862, manuscript, Maine Historical Society; A. Davenport to his homefolk, April 18, 1862.

⁶ C. B. Thurston to his brother, Feb. 24, 1863, manuscript, Emory; Samuel W. Peter to his sister and brother, Oct. 27, 1862, manuscript, Ill. State Historical Library; Lt. Charles B. Stoddard to his aunt, Jan. 7, 1863, manuscript, Harvard.

⁷ Capt. Gilmore Jordan to his homefolk, Aug. 17, 1862, manuscript, Ind. Historical Society.

⁸ Diary of Capt. Oliver Lyman Spaulding, Dec. 25, 1862, manuscript, Univ. of Mich.

⁹ John Hope Franklin, editor, *The Diary of James T. Ayers* (Springfield, Ill., 1947), 46.

¹⁰ N. B. Bartlett to his brother, Aug. 2 [1864], manuscript, Chicago Historical Society; Henry J. H. Thompson to his wife, Sept. 7, 1864, manuscript, Duke.

¹¹ Capt. W. A. Walker to "Dear James," Jan. 16, 1864, manuscript, Princeton.

¹² Stephen A. Miller to his sister, Jan. 31, 1863, manuscript, Ind. Historical Society.

¹³ J. R. Barney to his brother, Oct. 24, 1862, manuscript among Dinsmore Letters, Ill. State Historical Library.

¹⁴ Samuel S. Hoyt to his brother, March 8, 1863, manuscript among Lucian B. Case Papers, Chicago Historical Society; John McMeekin to his mother, March 16, 1863, manuscript, Western Reserve Historical Society.

¹⁵ Lt. Samuel Storrow to his mother, Dec. 24, 1864, manuscript, Mass. Historical Society; Abraham Kendig to his sister, May 16, 1862, manuscript, Historical Society of Pa.; George Newhall to his homefolk, Feb. 24, 1862, manuscript, Boston Public Library.

¹⁶ John McMeekin to his mother, March [no day], 1863.

¹⁷ John Beatty, *The Citizen Soldier*, 141-142.

¹⁸ Chauncey H. Cooke to his homefolk, March 5, 1863, in "Letters of a Badger Boy in Blue," *Wis. Magazine of History*, IV (1920-1921), 324-327; James B. Loughney to Marie Brogan, Feb. 26, 1863, manuscript, Wis. Historical Society.

¹⁹ Henry J. H. Thompson to his wife, June 20, 1863.

²⁰ A. Davenport to his homefolk, June 14, 1861; Thomas N. Lewis to his uncle, Nov. 14, 1862, manuscript among Moulton Letters, Western Reserve Historical Society; for an example of soldiers shooting Negroes, see diary of Matthew Marvin, Jan. 12, 1863.

²¹ J. S. McCulloch, "Reminiscences of Life in the Army and as a Prisoner of War," manuscript (photoduplicate), Washington and Jef-

ferson College Library. I am indebted to C. M. Ewing of that college for locating this item and making it available to me.

[22] John Bessemer to John Weissert, Nov. 17, 1861, manuscript, Univ. of Mich. This letter is in German script.

[23] John McMeekin to his mother, Dec. 15, 1862.

[24] O. R., series 1, XLVII, pt. 2, 33, 184; Bell Irvin Wiley, *Southern Negroes, 1861-1865* (New Haven, 1938), 235.

[25] J. F. Morris to Clarissa Butler, May 7, 1863, manuscript among Miscellaneous Civil War Letters, American Antiquarian Society. An Indiana colonel wrote on one occasion that in Buell's army "some of the regiments seem to have as many servants as soldiers." A. T. Volwiler, editor, "Letters from a Civil War Officer," *Miss. Valley Historical Review*, XIV (1928), 509.

[26] Lawrence Van Alstyne, *Diary of an Enlisted Man*, 213-214.

[27] Diary of Rufus Kinsley, June 17, Aug. 26, 1862, manuscript, Vt. Historical Society.

[28] Wiley, *Southern Negroes, 1861-1865*, 77.

[29] For example, see *Diary of E. P. Burton*, 20.

[30] Samuel Storrow wrote his homefolk, Feb. 4, 1863: "Oh many's the good meal I've had in an old 'nigger hut.' Their hoecakes are big things I tell you. The darkies are always very civil, obliging and ready to do anything in their power for one."

[31] Henry Crydenwise to his parents, Feb. 5, 1862, manuscript, Emory.

[32] Henry E. Simmons to his wife, June 6, 1863, manuscript, Lowdermilk's Bookstore, Washington, D. C.

[33] Robert S. Fletcher, *History of Oberlin College*, II, 864.

[34] Abraham Kendig to his brother, Jan. 4, 1864; Alfred S. Roe, *The Ninth New York Heavy Artillery*, 246-247.

[35] Joseph F. Shelley to his wife, Nov. 6, 1863, in Fanny J. Anderson, editor, "The Shelley Papers," *Indiana Magazine of History*, XLIV (1948), 197.

[36] Most of the instances were noted in manuscript court-martial proceedings, Nat'l Archives. An example of apparent concubinage is recorded in *The Soldier's Friend* of Aug. 8, 1868.

[37] Nashville *Dispatch*, June 17, 1864. An instance of what appears to be marriage of a Negro woman to a white soldier was found in a provost marshal's report dated Newport News, Va., June 6, 1861, filed with the Roswell Farnham Letters, typescript, Vt. Historical Society.

[38] Edward E. Newhall to his homefolk, Dec. 19, 1861, and Henry A. Newhall to his homefolk, Feb. 2, 1862, manuscripts, Boston Public Library.

[39] Edward E. Newhall to his homefolk, June 22, 1862.

[40] William R. Hartpence, *History of the Fifty-first Indiana Veteran Volunteer Infantry*, 72. Chaplain Arnold T. Needham on March 6, 1864, gave his wife the following version of an Alabama Negro preacher's account of the crucifixion: "Dey put him up on de cross, dey drove de ten-penny nails troo his hands, and dey stick de spear in his

side, and de blood run down on de ground, until as de Scripture saith it roared like a bull in de pen." Manuscript, Chicago Historical Society.

[41] Henry E. Simmons to his wife, Nov. 23, 1862, and June 6, 1863.

[42] G. F. Jourdan to his wife, May 3, 1863, manuscript among Miscellaneous Civil War Letters, American Antiquarian Society.

[43] James W. Smith to Mattie C. Howard, Nov. 4, 1862, manuscript, Ill. State Historical Library; Henry Warren Howe to his homefolk, June 19, 1861, in Henry Warren Howe, *Passages from the Life of Henry Warren Howe* (Lowell, Mass., 1899), 93.

[44] Michael R. Dresbach to his wife, Dec. 14, 1864, manuscript, Minn. Historical Society.

[45] Enoch T. Baker to his wife, July 27, 1862, manuscript, Historical Society of Pa.

[46] Henry J. H. Thompson to his wife, March 6, 1863.

[47] Wiley, *Southern Negroes, 1861-1865*, 325.

[48] *Ibid.*, 305.

[49] Diary of Sgt. William D. Evans, Jan. 11, 1865, manuscript, Western Reserve Historical Society; Wiley, *Southern Negroes, 1861-1865*, 324-325.

[50] Diary of Rufus Kinsley, Sept. 21, 1862.

[51] *Ibid.*, June 1, 1864.

[52] Henry Crydenwise to his parents, Nov. 28, 1863.

[53] *Ibid.*, April 10, 1865.

Chapter VI

THE DEPTHS OF SUFFERING

[1] Benjamin F. Green to William D. Murphy, Dec. 15, 1861, manuscript, N. Y. Public Library; Andrew K. Rose to his parents [July 1863], manuscript, Duke.

[2] After this chapter was drafted the writer had the privilege of reading G. W. Adams' "Health and Medicine in the Union Army, 1861-1865" (Ph.D. Dissertation, Harvard, 1946). This study by a competent historian of Civil War medicine is by far the best work on the subject. It is scheduled for publication in revised form by Henry Schuman of New York under the title *Doctors in Blue: An Account of Health and Medicine in the Union Army, 1861-1865*. Several references to the dissertation, particularly in instances where Mr. Adams' treatment is much fuller than that permitted here, were added to the notes of this chapter.

[3] Surgeon General of the U. S. Army, *Medical and Surgical History of the War of the Rebellion* (Washington, D. C., 1870-1888), Medical Volume, pt. 1, xxxvii, xliii, pt. 2, 3, and pt. 3, 3 ff. Hereafter this source will be cited as *Med. and Surg. Hist.*

⁴ *Ibid.*, pt. 1, xxxvii and pt. 2, 3.

⁵ *Ibid.*, pt. 3, 18 and diagram opposite p. 24. The figures cited in this paragraph are for white troops.

⁶ *Ibid.*, 6.

⁷ U. S. Sanitary Commission *Documents*, No. 40, 9, No. 43, 2.

⁸ *Ibid.*, No. 36, 32; *O. R.*, series 1, V, 81, XXXVI, pt. 1, 213.

⁹ *Med. and Surg. Hist.*, Medical Vol., pt. 3, 626; U. S. Sanitary Comm. *Documents*, No. 36, 19; *O. R.*, series 1, V, 85; vaccination was required by paragraph 1261, *Army Regulations*, 1861.

¹⁰ W. W. Keen, "Military Surgery in 1861 and 1918," *Annals of the American Academy of Political and Social Science*, LXXX (1918), 12, 18.

¹¹ U. S. Sanitary Comm. *Documents*, No. 26, 5, 6, 11.

¹² *Ibid.*, 5.

¹³ For example see *ibid.*, No. 17, 5; No. 26, 5; and No. 36, 28. W. H. Russell in a tour of the Army of the Potomac shortly before First Manassas found "the camps . . . dirty to excess." *My Diary North and South*, 403.

¹⁴ U. S. Sanitary Comm. *Documents*, No. 17, 4.

¹⁵ *Ibid.*, No. 40, 16.

¹⁶ *Army Regulations*, 1861, paragraphs 100-101; U. S. Sanitary Comm. *Documents*, No. 17, 4-5; No. 40, 18-20.

¹⁷ "Desiccated," or processed, foods are discussed in chapter IX.

¹⁸ *Army Regulations*, 1861, paragraph 1191; U. S. Sanitary Comm. *Documents*, No. 17, 8-13; No. 26, 7; No. 40, 21-24; Capt. Edward S. Redington to his wife, March 28, 1863, manuscript, Wis. Historical Society; C. Barney, *Recollections of Field Service with the Twentieth Iowa Infantry Volunteers*, 27-28.

¹⁹ U. S. Sanitary Comm. *Documents*, No. 36, 20.

²⁰ *Ibid.*, No. 24, 3; No. 26, 2; No. 36, 30-31; W. H. Russell, *My Diary North and South*, 404.

²¹ *Ibid.*

²² U. S. Sanitary Comm. *Documents*, No. 24, 2.

²³ P. M. Ashburn, A *History of the Medical Department of the United States Army* (Boston, 1929), 72 ff; Francis R. Packard, *History of Medicine in the United States* (N. Y., 1931), 639 ff; G. W. Adams has an excellent discussion of medical administration at the beginning of the war and its subsequent reform in *op. cit.*, chaps. 1-2.

²⁴ Charles J. Stille, *History of the U. S. Sanitary Commission* (Philadelphia, 1886), 124-137; Ashburn, *op. cit.*, 72-73; Packard, *op. cit.*, 641.

²⁵ Ashburn, *op. cit.*, 74-75, 85-86; Evelyn S. Drayton, "William Alexander Hamond 1828-1900," *Military Surgeon*, CIX (1951), 559-565.

²⁶ U. S. Sanitary Comm. *Documents*, No. 36, 32; No. 40, 53; *O. R.*, series 1, XI, pt. 1, 192.

²⁷ U. S. Sanitary Comm. *Documents*, No. 40, 33.

²⁸ *Ibid.*, No. 17, 17.

²⁹ *O. R.*, series 1, XI, pt. 1, 189. Known as acting assistant surgeons,

contract surgeons employed during the war aggregated 5,532. *Ibid.*, series 3, V, 150.

[80] U. S. Sanitary Comm. *Documents*, No. 26, 12; No. 38, 7.

[81] O. R., series 1, VII, 242-243; Hq. Army Dept. and Army of the Tenn. G. O. No. 8, June 11, 1864.

[82] Surgeon Henry P. Strong to his wife, Jan. 19, 24, 1862, typescript, Wis. Historical Society; Adjutant Richard L. Ashhurst to his homefolk, March 21, 1863, typescript, Historical Society of Pa.; J.A.G. Records MM-756, manuscript, Nat'l Archives.

[83] O. R., series 1, XXXVIII, pt. 3, 57; series 3, V, 150. If contract physicians, hospital surgeons and all other classes are included, the number of doctors serving in the army by April 1865 exceeded 12,000. For an extensive discussion of army doctors and their practice, see Adams, *op. cit.*, especially chap. 3.

[84] For two examples see O. R., series 1, III, 70 and X, pt. 1, 361.

[85] Harvey E. Brown, *History of the Medical Department of the United States Army* (Washington, 1875), 254.

[86] Capt. Edward G. Abbott to his father, Dec. 13, 1861, manuscript, Harvard.

[87] Alfred Davenport, *Camp and Field Life of the Fifth New York Volunteer Infantry*, 134; David Lathrop, *History of the 59th Regiment Illinois Volunteers* (Indianapolis, 1865), 169; John D. Billings, *Hard Tack and Coffee*, 310-311.

[88] Thomas N. Lewis to his uncle, June 7, 1861, manuscript among Moulton Letters, Western Reserve Historical Society; Thomas M. Moulton to his brother, May 22, 1865; A. Davenport to his homefolk, June 17, 1862, manuscript, N. Y. Historical Society.

[89] John McMeekin to his mother, March [no day], 1863, manuscript, Western Reserve Historical Society; diary of M. F. Roberts, May 3, 1864, manuscript, Western Reserve Historical Society.

[40] William N. Price, *One Year in the War* (n.d., n.p.), 42; Edward L. Edes to his father, Aug. 12, 1863, manuscript, Mass. Historical Society.

[41] Jacob Weidensall to his brother, March 1, 1862; Ill. Historical Records Survey, *Calendar of the Robert Weidensall Correspondence, 1861-1865 at George Williams College, Chicago, Illinois* (Chicago, 1940), 2.

[42] U. S. Sanitary Comm. *Documents*, No. 35, 5.

[43] Richard L. Ashhurst to his homefolk, Sept. 18, 1862.

[44] Joseph J. Woodward, *Outlines of the Camp Diseases of the United States Armies* (Philadelphia, 1863), 268. To be cited hereafter as Woodward, *Camp Diseases. Med. and Surg. Hist.*, Medical Vol., pt. 3, 649 ff. Figures given in *Med. and Surg. Hist.* for measles and all other diseases must be regarded as only approximate. See introductory statement, Medical Volume, pt. 1, i-xliii.

[45] Ruth A. Gallaher, editor, "Peter Wilson in the Civil War," *Iowa Journal of History and Politics*, XL (1942), 180-181.

[46] *Med. and Surg. Hist.*, Medical Vol., pt. 3, 650; John McMeekin to his mother, Feb. 5, 1863.

[47] Charles W. Wills, *Army Life of an Illinois Soldier*, 8.

[48] *Med. and Surg. Hist.*, Medical Vol., pt. 3, 77; Woodward, *Camp Diseases*, 28 ff; C. B. Thurston to his father, Nov. 23, 1863, manuscript, Emory.

[49] *Med. and Surg. Hist.*, Medical Vol., pt. 3, diagram opposite p. 90.

[50] *Ibid.*, 11, 192, 196.

[51] *Ibid.*, 199, and diagram opposite p. 199.

[52] O. R., series 1, VII, 513.

[53] John W. De Forest, *A Volunteer's Adventures*, 152-154.

[54] Elias R. Goad to a friend, Nov. 7 [1861], manuscript in possession of Charles N. Owen, Chicago.

[55] Lucius F. Hubbard, "Minnesota in the Battle of Corinth," Minn. Historical Society *Collections*, XII (1905-08), 533. Theodore Upson wrote in his journal July 27, 1863: "It is fearfully hot and there is a great amount of sickness . . . so many are in the hospitals that we are not allowed to fire volleys over the graves for fear it will discourage the sick ones." Oscar O. Winther, editor, *With Sherman to the Sea*, 65-66.

[56] *Med. and Surg. Hist.*, Medical Vol., pt. 3, 662, 675-679; O. R., series 3, V, 151.

[57] *Med. and Surg. Hist.*, Medical Vol., pt. 1, 636-641, 710-711. Figures for Negro troops are for the period June 30, 1864—June 30, 1866.

[58] J. J. Moulton to his homefolk [n.d., but May or June 1861]. Diarrhea and dysentery, owing possibly to poorer discipline, were considerably greater among Western troops than among Eastern. *Med. and Surg. Hist.*, Medical Vol., pt. 2 (which is devoted to the "fluxes"), 9.

[59] William T. Pippen to "A. H. and B. G.," July 11, 1862, manuscript, Duke; diary of Henry Clay Scott, July 18, 1861, manuscript, N. Y. Public Library.

[60] Henry J. H. Thompson wrote his homefolk March 6, 1863: "I am alive and moveing & lively to[o] last Night for I had the Virginia Quickstep I had to ease myself 2 times." Manuscript, Duke.

[61] *Med. and Surg. Hist.*, Medical Volume, pt. 2, diagram opposite p. 22.

[62] *Ibid.*, 2-3.

[63] *Ibid.*, 6.

[64] *Ibid.*, 6-7.

[65] Ashburn, *op. cit.*, 82 states: "Unhappily, not much progress had been made in the prevention of disease, which is fully explained by the fact that bacteriology and its twin, modern hygiene, were yet unborn."

[66] U. S. Sanitary Comm. *Documents*, No. 27, 5.

[67] *Med. and Surg. Hist.*, Medical Vol., pt. 2, 661 ff, 718, 808, 818.

[68] *Ibid.*, pt. 3, 112 ff.

[69] *Ibid.*, 115.

[70] *Ibid.*, 369, 371. For numerous clinical records, many of which specify treatment in detail, see *ibid.*, 216-267.

[71] *Ibid.*, pt. 2, 718-722.

[72] Harold A. Small, editor, *The Road to Richmond*, 188.

[73] Henry J. H. Thompson to his wife, Aug. 15, 1863.

[74] Daniel Beidelman to his mother, Sept. 18, 1862, manuscript, Duke; Leland O. Barlow to his sister, Jan. 26, 1863, manuscript, Conn. State Library; diary of Stillman H. Budlong, Oct. 31, 1861, manuscript, Westerly, R. I., Public Library.

[75] Capt. Edward S. Redington to his wife, June 16, 1863.

[76] Henry J. H. Thompson to his wife, April 5, 1863; Edward L. Edes to his mother, Sept. 25, 1862; Benjamin E. Sweetland to his wife, Nov. 15 [1862], manuscript, Boston Public Library.

[77] *Med. and Surg. Hist.*, Medical Vol., pt. 1, appendix, 40.

[78] *Ibid.*

[79] Stille, *op. cit.*, 153 ff; [Frederick Law Olmsted] *Hospital Transports, A Memoir of the Embarkation of the Sick and Wounded from the Peninsula of Virginia in the Summer of 1862* (Boston, 1863), 18 ff; to be cited hereafter as Olmsted, *Hospital Transports*; George T. Stevens, *Three Years in the Sixth Corps* (N. Y., 1870), 44, 46. Stevens was surgeon of the 77th N. Y. Regt.

[80] *Med. and Surg. Hist.*, Medical Vol., pt. 1, appendix, 92; Stevens, *op. cit.*, 114.

[81] *Med. and Surg. Hist.*, Medical Vol., pt. 1, appendix, 148 ff, 253, 255; U. S. Sanitary Comm. *Documents*, No. 75, 3; Stille, *op. cit.*, 277, 393-400; U. S. Sanitary Comm. *Bulletin*, I (1864), 424.

[82] This statement is based primarily on a study of medical reports in *Med. and Surg. Hist.*, pt. 1, appendix, and U. S. Sanitary Commission *Documents*. All materials used point to general improvement, especially after 1862 when the reforms of Hammond and Letterman began to bear fruit.

[83] U. S. Sanitary Comm. *Documents*, No. 23, 1 ff, No. 36, 5 ff and No. 41, 3 ff; *Med. and Surg. Hist.*, Medical Vol., pt. 3, 896 ff.

[84] Stille, *op. cit.*, 153.

[85] Ashburn, *op. cit.*, 70; *Med. and Surg. Hist.*, Medical Vol., pt. 3, 896-909. James A. Tobey, *The Medical Department of the Army: Its History, Activities and Organizations* (Baltimore, 1927), 15-17.

[86] *Ibid.*

[87] U. S. Sanitary Comm. *Documents*, No. 23, 3.

[88] *Med. and Surg. Hist.*, Medical Vol., pt. 3, 908-909.

[89] *Ibid.*; Ashburn, *op. cit.*, 79-80.

[90] *Ibid.*

[91] *Med. and Surg. Hist.*, Medical Vol., pt. 3, 943-945.

[92] *Ibid.*, Surgical Vol., pt. 3, 923-935; Medical Vol., pt. 1, appendix, 78; U. S. Sanitary Comm. *Bulletin*, I (1864), 520.

[93] *Med. and Surg. Hist.*, Surgical Vol., pt. 3, 923-935; Medical Vol., pt. 1, appendix, 78.

[94] U. S. Sanitary Comm. *Documents*, No. 48, 12-13; *Med. and Surg. Hist.*, Surgical Vol., pt. 3, 931-935; J. S. Newberry, *The U. S. Sanitary Commission in the Valley of the Mississippi* (Cleveland, O., 1871), 66. This is U. S. Sanitary Comm. *Documents*, No. 96.

[95] *Med. and Surg. Hist.*, Medical Vol., pt. 1, appendix, 49; Stille, *op. cit.*, 157-158.

[96] Stille, *op. cit.*, 150-153; *Med. and Surg. Hist.*, Medical Vol., pt. 1, appendix, 30.

[97] U. S. Sanitary Comm. *Documents*, No. 23, 5; No. 40, 79; *O. R.*, series 1, III, 274-275; *Med. and Surg. Hist.*, Medical Vol., pt. 1, appendix, 19.

[98] *Med. and Surg. Hist.*, Medical Vol., pt. 1, appendix, 31.

[99] *Ibid.*

[100] *Ibid.*, 70, 78.

[101] *Ibid.*, 88; Mrs. E. N. Harris to Mrs. Joel Jones, June 5, 1862, in "Anecdotes of our Wounded and Dying Soldiers in the Rebellion," manuscript, Historical Society of Pa.

[102] Stille, *op. cit.*, 161.

[103] *Ibid.*, 161-164; *Med. and Surg. Hist.*, Surgical Vol., pt. 3, 958 ff.

[104] *Med. and Surg. Hist.*, Medical Vol., pt. 1, appendix, 88, 93; Olmsted, *Hospital Transports*, 98-110, 166.

[105] *Med. and Surg. Hist.*, Medical Vol., pt. 1, appendix, 117, 125-127, 129.

[106] *Ibid.*, 127; a U. S. Sanitary Commission representative reported on May 8, 1864, concerning removal of the wounded from the Wilderness: "The sufferings of these men cannot in any degree be realized. The road —an old plank road—was in a wretched condition, and the groans and shrieks of the sufferers were truly heart-rending." U. S. Sanitary Comm.

[107] Newberry, *op. cit.*, 63 ff; *Med. and Surg. Hist.*, Medical Vol., pt. 1, *Bulletin*, I (1864), 425.
appendix, 253.

[108] *Med. and Surg. Hist.*, Medical Vol., pt. 1, appendix, 140 ff; 268, 283 ff.

[109] Ashburn, *op. cit.*, 73 ff; Packard, *op. cit.*, 641-655; *Time* magazine, Nov. 24, 1947; *Med. and Surg. Hist.*, Surgical Vol., pt. 3, 933 ff.

[110] *Ibid.*; U. S. Sanitary Comm. *Documents*, No. 57, 5-10, 23-24. The ambulance and field-hospital systems are treated in detail in Adams, *op. cit.*, chapters 6 and 7.

[111] *Med. and Surg. Hist.*, Surgical Vol., pt. 3, 933-934, 938, 941-943. Letterman had issued an order on Aug. 24, 1863, improving the ambulance system. See U. S. Sanitary Comm. *Bulletin*, I (1864), 151-152.

[112] *Med. and Surg. Hist.*, Surgical Vol., pt. 3, 902.

[113] Ashburn, *op. cit.*, 80; *Time* magazine, Nov. 24, 1947.

[114] Stille, *op. cit.*, 161 ff; *Med. and Surg. Hist.*, Medical Vol., pt. 1, appendix, 1 ff; Surgical Vol., pt. 3, 916 ff.

[115] This was provided by Letterman's reorganization circular of Oct. 30, 1862. Copy in U. S. Sanitary Comm. *Documents*, No. 57, 6-8.

[116] For an example, see *O. R.*, series 1, XXXVIII, pt. 2, 526-527.

[117] Many of these specimens were reproduced, some in color, in the surgical volumes of the *Med. and Surg. Hist.*

[118] *Med. and Surg. Hist.*, Medical Vol., pt. 1, appendix, 70 and Surgical Vol., pt. 3, 887-898; U. S. Sanitary Comm. *Documents*, No. 40, 53-54; *O. R.*, series 1, XI, pt. 1, 192, XXV, pt. 1, 400; Adams, *op. cit.*, chaps. 8-9.

[119] Col. T. D. Kingsley to H. D. Rallion, June 25, 1863, manuscript in possession of Towner K. Webster, Chicago, photostat obtained through kindness of Monroe F. Cockrell.

[120] O. R., series 1, XXXVIII, pt. 2, 526-527. For statistics and other information on amputations see *Med. and Surg. Hist.*, Surgical Vol., pt. 3, 869-886. Gangrene is discussed in *ibid.*, 824-851. For a gory illustration of gangrene effects, see colored picture, *ibid.*, 850.

[121] Billings, *Hard Tack and Coffee*, 310-311.

[122] Col. T. D. Kingsley to H. D. Rallion, June 25, 1863.

[123] Keen, "Military Surgery in 1861 and 1918," *Annals of the American Academy of Political and Social Science*, LXXX (1918), 14, 15.

[124] For criticisms of civilian agencies by medical authorities, see O. R., series 1, X, pt. 2, 62, XI, pt. 1, 177-178, XXXVIII, pt. 5, 7.

[125] B. B. Brown to his sister, Oct. 28, 1862, "Civil War Letters," *North Dakota Historical Quarterly*, I (1927), 66.

[126] Diary of Lt. Henry A. Kircher, June 8, 1863, manuscript, Ill. State Historical Library.

[127] "Prock's Letters from Camp, Battlefield and Hospital," *Indiana Magazine of History*, XXXIV (1938), 96.

[128] Commendation of the Sisters of Charity was found in a number of soldier letters and no criticism was found. Adams, *op. cit.*, II, 562, notes that soldiers referred to several nun groups as "Sisters of Charity." Work of the Christian and Sanitary Commissions also elicited a considerable amount of favorable comment, though the U. S. Sanitary Commission was condemned by some on the score of partiality to officers. The Christian Commission differed from the Sanitary Commission in that its primary function was the spiritual care of the soldiers, though it did distribute delicacies and reading materials to the sick and wounded. For a commendatory statement by a soldier concerning the Christian and the U. S. Sanitary Commissions see [David Lane], *A Soldier's Diary* (n.d., n.p., but 1905), 150-151.

[129] The work of the Christian Commission is related in the published *Annual Reports* of that organization, and in manuscript reports of its agents filed in the National Archives. The United States Sanitary Commission issued a series of ninety-six *Documents* (N. Y., 1866-1871), a *Bulletin* (3 vols., N. Y., 1864-1866), and various other publications. Charles J. Stille wrote a contemporary account of its work, and the Western phase was treated by J. S. Newberry in U. S. Sanitary Comm. *Documents*, No. 96. Recent studies include Marjorie B. Greenbie, *Lincoln's Daughters of Mercy* (N. Y., 1944) and an unpublished Ph.D. dissertation at Columbia University by William Maxwell. The Western Sanitary Commission, a separate organization, is treated in J. G. Forman, *The Western Sanitary Commission. A Sketch of Its Origin, History, Labors for the Sick and Wounded .... with Incidents of Hospital Life* (St. Louis, 1864). The work of all civilian defense agencies is ably discussed by Adams, *op. cit.*, chap. 5.

[130] See Stille, *op. cit.*, Newberry, *op. cit.*, and U. S. Sanitary Comm. *Documents*.

[181] E. A. Peterson wrote his homefolk from Chattanooga June 21, 1864: "The blamed Sanitary & Christian [Commissions] will not help a fellow unless he has shoulder straps." Manuscript, Duke; C. B. Thurston wrote his father July 1, 1863, from Fort St. Phillip, La.: "The Sanitary Commission in this department . . . has been a humbug."

[182] Bell Irvin Wiley, *The Life of Johnny Reb*, 244-269.

Chapter VII

GAY AND HAPPY STILL

[1] A. Davenport to his homefolk, Jan. 26, 1863, manuscript, N. Y. Public Library; Edmund English to his mother, Jan. 27, 1863, microfilm of manuscript, Huntington Library.

[2] A. Davenport to his homefolk, March 27, 1863; L. Marion Moulton to his homefolk, Dec. 13, 1864, manuscript, Western Reserve Historical Society.

[3] John Milledge to Mrs. Joseph H. Diltz, May 20, 1863, manuscript, Duke; Lt. Widwey to "Dear Friend," Sept. 8, 1861, in *Emigranten* (a Norwegian newspaper published at Madison, Wis.), Oct. 7, 1861. Translation by Inga B. Norstog.

[4] O. R., series 1, XXIX, pt. 2, 26.

[5] Cyrus R. Stone to his parents, June 24, July 15, 1862, manuscripts, Minn. Historical Society.

[6] Frank Leslie published both *Frank Leslie's Illustrated Newspaper* and *Frank Leslie's Monthly*.

[7] For an example of a severe soldier criticism of Frank Leslie's battle artists, see Sgt. Henry C. Hall to his sister, Oct. 5 [1862], manuscript, Duke.

[8] Hazel C. Wolf, editor, *Campaigning with the First Minnesota*, 250; Samuel Storrow to his parents, Feb. 15, 1863, manuscript, Mass. Historical Society.

[9] Bishop Crumrine to his brother, Nov. 12, Dec. 17, 1863; Feb. 12, March 6, March 24, 1864, manuscripts, Washington and Jefferson Library. Copies furnished by the courtesy of Charles M. Ewing. The Mrs. Hentz referred to was Caroline Lee Whiting Hentz (1800-1856) and the book, *Ernest Linwood*. See DAB, VIII, 565-566.

[10] U. S. Christian Commission, Daily Record Book for 9th Corps, 1864, manuscript, Nat'l Archives. Knute Nelson, "Civil War Notes and Memoranda," manuscript, Minn. Historical Society.

[11] Urich N. Parmelee to his mother, Oct. 26, 1863, manuscript, Duke.

[12] For an extensive discussion and full cataloguing of Beadle publications, see Albert Johannsen, *The House of Beadle and Adams* (2 vols., Norman, Okla., 1950). Johannsen discusses the popularity of Beadle books in the Union Army on p. 39 of vol. 1.

[13] Asbury L. Kerwood, *Annals of the Fifty-Seventh Regiment Indiana Volunteers* (Dayton, Ohio, 1868), 188-189.

[14] Edward L. Edes to his mother, Feb. 5, 1864, manuscript, Mass. Historical Society; C. W. Bardeen, *A Little Fifer's War Diary* (Syracuse, 1910), 291; diary of Florison D. Pitts, Sept. 29, 1863, manuscript, Chicago Historical Society; the author of *East and West* was Mrs. Frances F. Barritt, Johannsen, *op. cit.*, II, 29-30. *The Gold Fiend* was not a Beadle publication.

[15] U. S. Christian Commission, *Third Annual Report* (Philadelphia, 1865), 50-51.

[16] For examples, see U. S. Christian Commission, Daily Record Book, 5th Corps, entries of Dec. 30, 1864, by Samuel Hopley and Feb. 8, 1865, by W. M. Lisle, manuscript, Nat'l Archives.

[17] Edward L. Edes to his mother, Feb. 5, 1864.

[18] U. S. Christian Commission, *Third Annual Report*, 47-50.

[19] E. A. Johnson, editor, *The Hero of Medfield. The Journals and Letters of Allen Alonzo Kingsburg* (Boston, 1862), 62.

[20] Diary of Horton P. Rugg, March 12, 1863, manuscript (hand copy), Conn. State Library.

[21] For example, see Edward L. Edes to his mother, March 29, 1863.

[22] Jenkin Lloyd Jones, *An Artilleryman's Diary* (Madison, Wis., 1914), 85; C. B. Thurston to his brother, October 21, 1862, manuscript, Emory; Samuel Storrow to his parents, Dec. 26, 1862.

[23] U. S. Christian Commission, Daily Record Book, 9th Corps, entry of Sept. 20, 1864, by A. J. Wilcox and Sept. 25, 1864, by a Mr. Petty.

[24] Hq. Army of the Potomac, G. O. No. 151, Aug. 4, 1862. A number of references were found in soldier accounts to regiments having bands after their discontinuance was ordered. See for example, James K. Hosmer, *The Color-Guard*, 37.

[25] "John" to Fannie L. Partridge, April 19, 1862, manuscript, Chicago Historical Society. The band leader referred to was Patrick Sarsfield Gilmore, famous Irish-born bandmaster and composer of the period 1850-1890. After directing the 24th Mass. band, 1861-1863, he was put in charge of all army bands in the Department of the Gulf, where, at Governor Hahn's inauguration in 1864, he inaugurated a type of mammoth concert for which he later became nationally famous. While in New Orleans, Gilmore composed, under the pseudonym Louis Lambert, the popular war song "When Johnny Comes Marching Home." *DAB*, VII, 312.

[26] *DAB*, VII, 312.

[27] Journal of Maj. Charles B. Fox, Nov. 7, 1863, Mass. Historical Society.

[28] Col. John A. Cockerill, "What a Boy Did at Shiloh," Portland, Maine, *Daily Express*, Jan. 21, 1890, supplement; O. R., series 1, XI, pt. 1, 458-459; Charles Ward to his brother, May 11, 1863, manuscript, American Antiquarian Society; Leander Stillwell, *The Story of a Common Soldier*, 62; E. T. Baker to his wife, Sept. 9, 1862, manuscript, Historical Society of Pa.

[29] J. M. Roberts, *The Experience of a Private in the Civil War* (privately printed, 1924), 10.

[30] Lt. Col. Charles B. Fox to his wife, Jan. 10, 1864, manuscript, Mass. Historical Society.

[31] Bell Irvin Wiley, *The Life of Johnny Reb*, 318.

[32] Capt. T. J. Wright, *History of the Eighth Regiment Kentucky Volunteer Infantry*, 146.

[33] The New York Public Library, the Library of Congress, the Historical Society of Pennsylvania, Brown University and the American Antiquarian Society have especially good collections of Civil War Songs and Music.

[34] The three Beadle titles cited are in the New York Public Library Music Division Collection. For other Beadle songbooks, see Johannsen, *op. cit.*, I, 41, 43, 48, 49.

[35] The first seven songsters listed in this sentence were found in the New York Public Library. The others used were in the Historical Society of Pennsylvania, except "The Yankee Doodle Songster" which was seen in the Burton Collection of the Detroit Public Library.

[36] For a palmetto tree version, see copy of the song in George B. Sprague Papers, Wis. Historical Society. Leland O. Barlow in a letter to his sister, July 24, 1863, mentions a crab-apple tree version. Manuscript, Conn. State Library. The origin of "John Brown's Body" has been the subject of considerable discussion. Katherine Little Bakeless in *Glory Hallelujah: The Story of the Battle Hymn of the Republic* (Philadelphia, 1944), accepts the claim of T. Brigham Bishop, minstrelman and composer, that he wrote the words and music in 1858. Most earlier writers incline to the view that the tune was based on a plantation or campmeeting melody and that the words originated among members of a Boston militia organization which became a part of the 12th Mass. Regt. The regiment was said to have sung the song as it marched down Broadway in New York en route to Virginia in the summer of 1861. See Nicholas Smith, "The Battle Hymns of Nations," Military Order of the Loyal Legion of the United States, Wisconsin Commandery, *War Papers*, III (Milwaukee, 1903), 471 ff; Brander Matthews, "Songs of the War," *Century Magazine*, XXXIV (August 1887), 619-629; *Our War Songs North and South* (Cleveland, 1887), 7-9; and Philip D. Jordan, *Singin' Yankees* (Minneapolis, 1946), 229-230.

[37] "Civil War Diary of William C. Benson," *Indiana Magazine of History*, XXIII (1927), 360; DAB, VI, 110.

[38] A copy of this parody was found in the front of the diary of Sgt. William H. Tyner, 38th Ill. Regt. This manuscript is in possession of Mrs. Richard Alison of Jackson, Tennessee, to whom I am indebted for its use.

[39] Colonial Dames of America, *American War Songs* (Philadelphia, 1925), 70-72. For a full account of the song's origin, see Bakeless, *op. cit.*

[40] Nicholas Smith, *op. cit.*, 484-486.

[41] *Ibid.*

[42] It is interesting to note that a German soldier, Franz Eder of the

119th N. Y. Regt., who kept his diary in his native tongue copied this song in the back in neatly written English. Manuscript, N. Y. Public Library. The words of this song, along with many other war lyrics, may be found in F. T. Miller, editor, *Photographic History of the Civil War*, IX, 342-352.

[43] Capt. C. Barney, *Recollections of Field Service with the Twentieth Iowa Infantry*, 38. For the complete lyrics of "Gay and Happy Still," see Miller, *op. cit.*, IX, 349.

[44] William R. Hartpence, *History of the Fifty-first Indiana Veteran Volunteer Infantry*, 251-252.

[45] For a discussion of folk songs of the era, see Alfred M. Williams, "Folk Songs of the Civil War," *Journal of American Folklore*, V (1892), 265-283.

[46] Most of the war songs listed here may be found, along with sketches of the principal composers, in *Our War Songs North and South*, published by S. Brainards' Sons. Good collections of folk and sentimental songs have been published by Carl Sandburg, *The American Songbag* (N. Y., 1927), John A. and Alan Lomax, *American Ballads and Folk Songs* (N. Y., 1934), and Philip D. Jordan and Lillian Kessler, *Songs of Yesterday* (Garden City, 1941). But one interested in lyrics used in Civil War times should consult original sheet music of the period which is obtainable in most major libraries. The Library of Congress and the New York Public Library collections are especially good. Sigmund Spaeth's *A History of Popular Music in America* (N. Y., 1948), 153-161, contains a brief but able discussion of Northern songs and composers of the war period.

[47] For comment on the popularity of "Wait for the Wagon," see "Songs of the Long Ago" in Chicago *Tribune*, Nov. 26, 1887. Lloyd D. Harris in "Army Music," Military Order of the Loyal Legion, Commandery of Missouri, *War Papers and Personal Reminiscences*, I (St. Louis, 1892), 291, stated: "Every officer in our regiment who sang the solo of 'Benny Havens, O!' was killed in battle."

[48] Stephen A. Miller to his sister, Oct. 16, 1863, manuscript, Ind. Historical Society; Harvey Reid to his homefolk, June 3, 1863, manuscript, Wis. Historical Society; William Bircher, *Diary of a Drummer Boy* (St. Paul, Minn.. 1889), 161; diary of Oliver L. Spaulding, Nov. 4, 1862, manuscript, Univ. of Mich.; J. H. Greene, *Reminiscences of the War*, 41. A copy of the "Homespun Dress" made by a soldier, and apparently sent to his homefolk, is in the Ezra Rickett Collection, manuscripts, Ohio State Arch. and Historical Society.

[49] Spaeth, *op. cit.*, 154; Wiley, *The Life of Johnny Reb*, 318. The best study of Southern songs of the war years is Richard B. Harwell, *Confederate Music* (Chapel Hill, 1950). The same author has also compiled a handsome book of facsimiles of Confederate sheet music under the title *Songs of the Confederacy* (N. Y., 1951).

[50] For a splendid discussion of the origin and history of "Dixie," see Hans Nathan, "Dixie," *The Musical Quarterly*, XXXV (1949), 60-84.

[51] George T. Stevens in *Three Years in the Sixth Corps*, 268, states

that as the Sixth Corps, returning south from the Gettysburg campaign, crossed the Potomac the bands played "Oh, Carry Me Back to Ole Virginia," thus bearing out the claim that while Bland's song of that title was not published until 1878, an earlier version was in circulation during Civil War times. See letter to the editor by Henry S. Commager in New York *Herald-Tribune* Book Review section, Jan. 22, 1950, 13.

[52] Richard B. Harwell, "Confederate Carrousel: Southern Songs of the Sixties," *Emory University Quarterly*, VI (1950), 90-91; S. J. Adair Fitz-Gerald, *Stories of Famous Songs* (Philadelphia and London, 1906), I, 131.

[53] Cyrus R. Stone to his wife, Jan. 12, 1863. Members of the 138th New York Regiment, many of whom were from Wayne County, N. Y., while digging ditches near Washington in 1862, sang it thus:

> I wish I was in Old Wayne County,
> My three years up, and I had my bounty,
> Look away, look away . . .

Alfred S. Roe, *History of the Ninth New York Heavy Artillery*, 39. For a parody called the Jay Hawker's Dixie, sung by the Seventh Kansas Regiment, see Theodore C. Blegen, editor, *Civil War Letters of Colonel Hans C. Heg* (Northfield, Minn., 1936), 94-97.

[54] O. W. Norton, *Army Letters, 1861-1865*, 324. For a slightly different version, see Roe, *op. cit.*, 68 and John D. Billings, *Hard Tack and Coffee*, 168-169.

[55] Norton, *op. cit.*, 324. For other versions, see Billings, *op. cit.*, 172 and Roe, *op. cit.*, 68.

[56] Roe, *op. cit.*, 69.

[57] Norton, *op. cit.*, 325.

[58] Roe, *op. cit.*, 68.

[59] Norton, *op. cit.*, 325.

[60] William H. Bentley, *History of the 77th Illinois Volunteer Infantry*, 138.

[61] Billings, *op. cit.*, 118.

[62] *The Good Old Songs We Used to Sing '61 to '65* (Washington, D. C., 1902), 11.

[63] Charles E. Davis, *Three Years in the Army*, 156.

[64] Broadside among Civil War Lyrics, Emory.

[65] Journal of David H. Haines, Oct. 20, 1863, manuscript, Detroit Public Library.

[66] Broadside among Civil War Songs, Maine Historical Society.

[67] Reference to "Chickamauga" was found in a letter of William H. Lloyd to his wife, Sept. 13, 1864, manuscript, Western Reserve Historical Society, and a hand copy of this and of "An Epick" on Murfreesboro and on Chattanooga are in the Ezra E. Rickett Collection. A song glorifying the exploits of the 2nd Division, 20th Corps, in the battles about Chattanooga of November 23-25, 1863, was sent home by William H. Lloyd on Aug. 23, 1861.

[68] See *Our War Songs North and South*, 42-44, 310-311. "We Are Marching Down to Dixie" was copied by Sgt. Will H. Tyner, 38th Ill. Regt. and preserved with his papers.

[69] Hand copy in Ezra E. Rickett Collection.

[70] "Extracts from the War Diary of John V. Ruehle," manuscript, Detroit Public Library.

[71] Broadside in Ill. State Historical Library.

[72] The 69th New York Regiment provided the theme for a number of ballads. Alfred M. Williams, "Folk Songs of the Civil War," *Journal of American Folklore*, V (1892), 268.

[73] *Our War Songs North and South*, 179-185.

[74] A hand copy of "A New Ballad of Lord Lovel" was found in the Ezra E. Rickett Collection. For a discussion of the original ballad and various adaptations, including two of the Civil War period, see H. M. Belden, editor, "Ballads and Songs Collected by the Missouri Folk Lore Society," University of Missouri *Studies*, XV (1940), 52-54.

[75] Copy from front of diary of Sgt. William B. Tyner. A note by Tyner credits the song to E. W. Locke. The ballad "Chattanooga," adapted to the air "Nelly Bly," began:

> General Bragg, how do you like
> The looks of General Grant?

Copy in Ezra E. Rickett Collection.

[76] John Beatty, *The Citizen Soldier*, 64.

[77] Broadside, Emory. "The Yankee Doodle Songster" contains "Jefferson D" by H. S. Cornwall and "O! Jeff Davis" by H. Angelo.

[78] *Ibid.*

[79] Vance Randolph, in *Ozark Folk Songs* (Columbia, Mo., 1948), II, 352, says that "Shoo, Fly, Shoo" was "one of the most popular nonsense songs of the Civil War period."

[80] Billings, *op. cit.*, 215. For the original version of "Abraham's Daughter," see *Our War Songs North and South*, 461-463.

[81] *Our War Songs North and South*, 10.

[82] John Beatty, *op. cit.*, 119. "I Am Jesus' Little Lamb" was heard by the writer in a World War II training center.

[83] Diary of an unidentified soldier of the 24th Conn. Regt., Jan. 17, 1863, manuscript, Conn. State Library.

[84] Lloyd D. Harris, *op. cit.*, I, 289-291; Henry M. McIntire to his parents, Sept. 8, 1861, manuscript, Mass. Historical Society; Hq. Dept. of the Gulf, G. O. No. 19, Feb. 26, 1863.

[85] Asst. Surg. Humphrey H. Hood to his wife, Dec. 6, 1862, manuscript, Ill. State Historical Library.

[86] Diary of Charles E. Bolton, Aug. 1, 1864, manuscript, Mass. Historical Society.

[87] See especially letters of Fox to his wife, Jan. 13, Sept. 5, and Nov. 1, 1864.

[88] *Ibid.*, Oct. 16, 1864.

[89] Frank M. Rood to "Friend Elvira," Aug. 31, 1863, manuscript in possession of Harry Rood, Poultney, Vt.; Mrs. J. D. Wheeler, compiler, *In Memoriam: Letters of William Wheeler of the Class of 1855 Y. C.*, 30.

[90] Carl Wittke, "The Ninth Ohio Volunteers," *Ohio State Archaeological and Historical Quarterly*, XXXV (1926), 415; Walter Koempel, editor, *Phil Koempel's Diary* (n.p., n.d.), 41. The diarist, a member of Co. B, 1st Conn. Cav., quotes a portion of the song.

[91] Lt. Col. Charles B. Fox to his mother, Feb. 6, 1864; Adam Muenzenberger to his homefolk, April 20, 1863, manuscript (typescript translation), Wis. Historical Society.

[92] Regis de Trobriand, *Four Years with the Army of the Potomac* (Boston, 1889), 95.

[93] See for example, Beatty, *op. cit.*, 64; Lloyd D. Harris, *op. cit.*, 289-291.

[94] Blegen, editor, *Civil War Letters of Colonel Hans C. Heg*, 140.

[95] Diary of James F. Williams, Feb. 20, 1864, manuscript, N. Y. Public Library; Josiah S. Chandler, "What a Private Saw Thought and Did during the War of the Rebellion," 120-121, manuscript, Western Reserve Historical Society; diary of James F. Williams, Feb. 6, 1864; diary of Charles F. Johnson, March 4, 8, 1863, manuscript, Minn. Historical Society; Edward L. Edes to his father, April 3, 1864.

[96] Stevens, *Three Years in the Sixth Corps*, 183.

[97] A Vermonter who recorded a rough-and-tumble affair in his unit reported that the "Conal broak one Lieutenant's nose." Albert Harris to his brother, March 1, 1863, manuscript, Vt. Historical Society.

[98] David Lathrop, *History of the 59th Regt. Illinois Vols.*, 184-185.

[99] Wiley, *The Life of Johnny Reb*, 319.

[100] Henry P. Whipple, *The Diary of a Private Soldier* (Waterloo, Wis., 1906), 12.

[101] Oscar O. Winther, editor, *With Sherman to the Sea*, 47.

[102] Diary of Charles W. Wills, Oct. 7, 1864, manuscript, Ill. State Historical Library.

[103] Billings, *op. cit.*, 204.

[104] Norton, *op. cit.*, 32-33.

[105] *Ibid.*, 18; Capt. Lucius Fairchild to his mother, May 25, 1861, manuscript, Wis. Historical Society.

[106] Roe, *op. cit.*, 74.

[107] *Ibid.*, 258-259.

[108] Diary of Charles W. Wills, May 2, 1864.

[109] Winther, *op. cit.*, 93-94.

[110] Herbert E. Valentine to his homefolk, Dec. 10, 1861.

[111] C. B. Thurston to his brother, March 29, 1863; journal of Charles F. Johnson, July 4, 1862; Edward E. Newhall to his homefolk, Nov. 21, 1861, manuscript (typescript), Boston Public Library; diary of Philip H. Smith, Dec. 26, 1861, bound series of articles from Peoria *Evening Star*, 1917, in Veterans' Records, Nat'l Archives; George Monteith to his mother, Jan. 2, 1862, manuscript, Univ. of Mich.

[112] Lt. John R. Wintherbotham to his homefolk, March 21 and Dec. 28, 1863, manuscripts, Chicago Historical Society; Wesley A. Brown to his wife, Dec. 25, 1861, manuscript in possession of Alice L. Pendleton, Isleboro, Maine, to whom I am indebted for the use of a number of excellent letters.

[113] Abraham Kendig to his father, Dec. 23, 1862, manuscript, Historical Society of Pa.; diary of an unidentified Union sergeant, Jan. 1, 1863, quoted in Charleston, S. C., *Daily Courier*, July 18, 1863; Lt. Charles B. Stoddard to his parents (n.d., but Dec., 1862), manuscript, Harvard University.

[114] Fred A. Shannon, editor, *Civil War Letters of Sgt. Onley Andrus* (Urbana, Ill., 1947), 72; William H. Lloyd to his wife, Jan. 1, 1865.

[115] Diary of John N. Williams, June 5, 1863; John J. Wyeth, *Leaves from a Diary* (Boston, 1878), 33; Bardeen, *A Little Fifer's War Diary*, 295; Hazel C. Wolf, *op. cit.*, 236; George T. Stevens, *op. cit.*, 183.

[116] Charles Fairchild to his mother, May 27, 1861.

[117] Felix Brannigan to his homefolk, Oct. 29, 1861, typescript, Library of Congress.

[118] John Beatty, *op. cit.*, 121-122.

[119] Wyeth, *Leaves from a Diary*, 31.

[120] James M. Nichols, *Perry's Saints, or the Fighting Parson's Regiment in the War of the Rebellion* (Boston, 1886), 147.

[121] Journal of Charles F. Johnson, June 30, 1862.

[122] Urich N. Parmelee to his brother, Aug. 6, 1863.

[123] Rebecca R. Usher to her sister, Nov. 23, 1862, and an undated letter apparently written in Jan. 1863, typescripts, Maine Historical Society.

[124] Jordan, *op. cit.*, 230-244; Carol Brink, *Harps in the Wind: The Story of the Singing Hutchinsons* (N. Y., 1927), 204-219; the Hutchinsons (John's group) were barred by McClellan from the Army of the Potomac early in 1862, because a program which they gave soon after receiving a pass from Cameron to sing in Union camps provoked a minor disturbance among those hostile to abolitionism.

[125] E. W. Locke, *Three Years in Camp and Hospital* (Boston, 1870), 33; *DAB*, XIII, 341 and XV, 431-432.

[126] Beatty, *op. cit.*, 225-226.

[127] *Ibid.*, 85-86.

[128] Diary of James E. Graham, April 21, 1863, manuscript, Ohio State Arch. and Historical Society.

[129] Diary of Florison D. Pitts.

[130] *Ibid.*, Oct. 4, 1863.

[131] Jacob H. Kendig to his parents, May 9, 1864.

[132] Diary of O. B. Hinckley, May 5, 1865, manuscript, Duke University.

[133] Hazel C. Wolf, *op. cit.*, 230.

[134] Diary of Florison D. Pitts, Sept. 16, 17, 25, and Oct. 20, 1863.

[135] *Iowa Historical Record*, XVI (Iowa City, 1900), 138; diary of George N. Champlin, Jan. 4, 11, 18, and March 1, 1864, typescript, Conn. State Library.

[186] Flavius J. Bellamy to his homefolk, Feb. 11, 1864, manuscript, Ind. State Library.

[187] The writer is planning a special study of soldier newspapers of the Civil War. To this end he has collected photographic reproductions of well over 100 titles of camp newspapers located in public depositories and in private possession.

[188] The Historical Society of Pennsylvania and Duke University have runs of the *New South* and the *Free South*. An excellent file of the *Union Appeal* is in the Cossitt Library in Memphis.

[189] The prison paper is reproduced in *Stars and Stripes in Rebeldom* (Boston, 1862). Two issues of *Stars and Stripes* published at Thibodaux, La., are in the American Antiquarian Society; another paper of that name, published in Missouri, is in the William L. Clements Library.

[140] Issues of these papers are, in the order listed, in the Kansas State Historical Society, the G.A.R. Memorial Hall, Scranton, Pa., the New York Historical Society and the Library of Congress. The Massachusetts Historical Society and the Chicago Historical Society also have some issues of the *Camp Kettle*.

[141] Copies of the *First Minnesota* may be found in several libraries, including the Minnesota Historical Society, the Confederate Museum, the American Antiquarian Society and Western Reserve Historical Society. Other items in this sentence, in the order listed, may be found at the Kansas State Historical Society, the Connecticut State Library, the Huntington Library, Western Reserve Historical Society, the American Antiquarian Society, the Wisconsin Historical Society, the Illinois State Historical Library, private collection of Foreman Lebold, Chicago (to whom I am indebted for a photographic copy), the Chicago Historical Society and the Western Reserve Historical Society.

[142] Issues of these papers, in the order listed, are in the American Antiquarian Society, the Wisconsin Historical Society, the Chicago Historical Society, the Minnesota Historical Society and the Missouri Historical Society of St. Louis.

[143] Issues of *Unconditional S. Grant* are in the Chicago Historical Society and the Massachusetts Historical Society; *Grant's Petersburg Progress* in the Minnesota Historical Society; and *Lauman's Own* in the Chicago Historical Society.

[144] Best file of the *Cripple* is in the Connecticut State Library. The *Crutch* and the *Cartridge Box* are in the Library of Congress.

[145] This item is in the Library of Congress.

[146] A. M. Stewart, *Camp, March and Battlefield* (Philadelphia, 1865), 102.

[147] Charles E. Goddard to his mother, March 18, 1862, manuscript, Minn. Historical Society; Edward C. Culp, *The 25th Ohio Veteran Volunteer Infantry in the War for the Union* (Topeka, Kan., 1885), 122-126.

[148] *The American Patriot*, June 18, 1861, Mo. Historical Society.

[149] Corinth *Chanticleer*, July 31, 1863, Minn. Historical Society; *Union Advance Picket*, May 15, 1862, Western Reserve Historical So-

ciety; *Battery Reveille*, June 7, 1861, Western Reserve Historical Society.

[150] This item is in the Wisconsin Historical Society.

[151] This paper is in the Kansas State Historical Society.

[152] For an example, see "The Veteran Banner," April, 1865, in the Ohio State Archaeological and Historical Society.

[153] *Yazoo Daily Yankee*, July 20, 1863, Ohio State Arch. and Historical Society.

[154] *The Volunteer*, Nov. 7, 1863, Washington County Indiana Historical Society. I am indebted to Prof. Chase Mooney, Univ. of Ind., for a photostatic copy of this item.

[155] Issue of Oct. 21, 1863, New Iberia, La.

[156] Issue of Jan. 22, 1862, Somerset, Ky., in Wis. Historical Society.

[157] Charles A. Partridge, *History of the 96th Illinois Regiment Volunteer Infantry* (Chicago, 1887), 71; William Todd, editor, *History of the 9th Regiment New York State Militia* (N. Y., 1889), 148-152; Hyde, *op. cit.*, 267.

[158] The Kansas State Historical Society has a good file of the *Soldier's Letter* of the 2nd Colorado Cavalry. The *Soldier's Letter* published in the 96th Illinois Regiment is in the Illinois State Historical Library.

[159] U. S. Sanitary Comm. *Documents*, No. 40, 29.

[160] Simon B. Hulbert, Monthly Record for 1863, manuscript, N. Y. Historical Society.

[161] Abraham Kendig to his homefolk, Nov. 28, 1861; Bishop Crumrine to his brother, Aug. 23, 1862; Edwin Horton to his wife, March 30, 1864, manuscript, Vt. Historical Society.

[162] Richard Puffer to his sister, May 28, 1863, manuscript, Chicago Historical Society; John N. Moulton to his mother, Aug. 7, 1864.

[163] This sample is a composite based on many letters; all of the phrases are authentic.

[164] H. R. Leonard to Elizabeth Davis, Oct. 5 [1861], manuscript among Miscellaneous Civil War Letters, Western Reserve Historical Society; William A. Harper to his wife, Jan. 13, 1865, manuscript, Ind. Historical Society.

[165] For examples of uninhibited comments on amorous activities, see Patrick Heffron to "Dear Friend John," Dec. 4, 1862, and "Jake" to "Friend Page," Aug. 11, 1863, manuscripts in possession of Beverly DuBose, Jr., Atlanta; Isaac Mertz to Jefferson Hartman, March 8, 1865, manuscript, Duke; Frank R. Lyman to Royale E. Cook, Oct. 9, 1864, manuscript, Dartmouth.

[166] "Jake" to "Friend Page," Aug. 11, 1863; W. H. Campbell to his sweetheart, March 4, 1862, manuscript in private possession.

[167] D. H. Dodd to his homefolk, Jan. 8, 1863, manuscript, Ind. Historical Society.

[168] John C. Arnold to his wife, May 28, 1864, typescript, Nat'l War College.

[169] Calvin B. Crandall to his parents, Feb. 9, 1863, typescript of original manuscript, Neb. Historical Society.

[170] John McMeekin to his sister, Nov. 13, 1862, manuscript, Western Reserve Historical Society.

[171] Charles Babbott to his father, Jan. 1, 1863, manuscript, Hayes Memorial Library; Henry J. H. Thompson to his wife, n.d., but summer of 1861, manuscript, Duke.

[172] Robert M. Atkinson to his homefolk, Dec. 16, 1863, manuscript, Ohio State Arch. and Historical Society.

[173] Henry Warren Howe, *Passages from the Life of Henry Warren Howe*, 174.

[174] James Rich to his wife, n.d., but spring of 1863, typescript in possession of Dr. A. M. Giddings, Battle Creek, Mich.; Thomas Wall to Andrew Weld, March 21, 1864 [1865], manuscript, Wis. Historical Society; Michael R. Dresbach to his wife, Aug. 22, 1864, manuscript, Minn. Historical Society.

[175] Francis S. Flint to "Darling Jennie," Aug. 24, 1863, manuscript, Minn. Historical Society.

[176] Unidentified soldier to Margaret McMeekin, letter not dated.

[177] Albert E. Trumble to Amelia Boyce, Dec. 17, 1861, Aug. 19, 1862, May 25, 1863, and Aug. 5, 1864, manuscripts in possession of Faith Wirsching Lemmer, San Francisco.

[178] For examples of an advertisement for correspondents, see New York *Herald*, Jan. 16, 1864, section headed "Matrimonial," and Chattanooga *Daily Gazette*, March 6, 1864.

[179] F. F. Dean to Will Robinson, Jan. 2, 1861, manuscript, Ind. State Library; William H. Crawford to his homefolk, n.d., but 1861, typescript, Univ. of Missouri; Bailey Sutherland to his sister, June 22, 1862, manuscript, Univ. of Ky.; Charles C. Garrett to his cousin, Jan. 29, 1862, manuscript, Ohio State Arch. and Historical Society.

[180] William Worthington to his homefolk, various dates, manuscripts in private possession; John Herr to his sister, Nov. 6, 1863, manuscript, Duke.

[181] John Herr to his sister, Nov. 6, 1862; Franklin H. Bailey to his parents, Dec. 14, 1861, manuscript, Univ. of Mich.

[182] William O. Wettleson to his parents, March 13, 1865, manuscript, Luther College. Translated from the Norwegian by Inga B. Norstog.

[183] Charles M. Anson, "Reminiscences of an Enlisted Man," Military Order of the Loyal Legion, *Wis. Commandery*, IV (Milwaukee, 1914), 279-290.

[184] For a discussion of the origin and circulation of the poem, see chapter X and Wiley, *The Life of Johnny Reb*, 305.

[185] This version is from an undated note of Henry J. H. Thompson to his wife. It differs from most others in that the last line usually was "For the space of three years."

Chapter VIII

TOEING THE MARK

[1] Amory K. Allen to his wife, Sept. 20, 1863. "Letters of Amory K. Allen," *Indiana Magazine of History*, XXXI (1935), 374.

[2] For basic provisions concerning courts-martial, see *Army Regulations* for the war years (to be cited from here on as A. R.), especially Article XXXVIII and "The Articles of War" (to be cited hereafter as A. W.) in the appendix. A useful commentary on the articles of war and the system of military discipline is George W. Davis, *A Treatise on the Military Law of the United States* (N. Y., 1901).

[3] For a full report of this affair, see O. R., series 1, XXVI, pt. 1, 262-272.

[4] J. Albert Monroe, "Reminiscences of the War of the Rebellion," Soldiers and Sailors Historical Society of Rhode Island, *Personal Narratives*, 2nd series, No. 11 (Providence, 1881), 11-12; diary of George W. Little, entry of Dec. 17, 1862, manuscript, Chicago Historical Society; Stephen M. Weld to his father, March 25, 1864, *War Diary and Letters of Stephen M. Weld 1861-1865* (Cambridge, Mass., 1912), 266-268; Lt. Col. Charles B. Fox to his wife, Sept. 16, 1864, manuscript, Mass. Historical Society.

[5] 66 and 67 A. W.

[6] Hq. Dept. of the Gulf, Office of J.A.G., circular dated Oct. 12, 1863.

[7] 64, 65 A. W.; A. R., 1861, Article 38; George B. Davis, *op. cit.*, 524.

[8] For a discussion of the character and jurisdiction of military commissions, see Davis, *op. cit.*, 309-311.

[9] For details of court-martial procedure, see A. R., 1861, Article 38.

[10] Manuscript copies of proceedings of cases referred to the Judge Advocate General are filed in the J.A.G. Records Division of the Nat'l Archives. These will be cited hereafter as J.A.G. Records. Findings and sentences of courts-martial were published in appropriate general orders, cited as G. O.

[11] For examples of wholesale invalidation of court-martial actions in 1863 for procedural defects, see War Dept. Adjutant General's Office (cited hereafter as W.D.A.G.O.) G. O. 292, Aug. 22, 1863, and 297, Sept. 3, 1863.

[12] Hq. Army of Potomac, G. O. 38, April 2, 1863.

[13] J.A.G. Records MM 752.

[14] A. R., 1863 (Washington, 1863), 538.

[15] *Ibid.*; Hq. Dept. of the Gulf, office of J.A.G., circular dated Oct. 12, 1863.

[16] J.A.G. Records MM 752.

[17] A. R., 1863, 538.

[18] Lt. Col. Charles B. Fox, commanding officer of the 66th Mass. Inf.

Regt., wrote to his father, Aug. 18, 1864, that a field officer's court could decide on cases "in the same day that the crime is committed and the sentence goes at once into effect."

[19] Diary of A. W. Tower, entry of July 16, 1863, manuscript, N. Y. Public Library.

[20] John D. Billings, *Hard Tack and Coffee*, 145.

[21] William H. White to his mother, Oct. 9, 1861, manuscript, Hager Family Papers, Univ. of Mich.

[22] Clothing, Order, Descriptive and Morning Report Book, Company B, 7th Mass. Inf. Regt., manuscript, Nat'l Archives.

[23] Edward L. Edes to "Robert," March 1, 1864, manuscript, Mass. Historical Society.

[24] 45 A. W.

[25] Richard L. Ashhurst to his homefolk, Nov. 6, 1862, typescript, Historical Society of Pa.

[26] Manuscript, N. Y. Public Library.

[27] O. R., series 1, XI, pt. 3, 83-84 and XLIV, 596.

[28] Charles A. Barker to his homefolk, March 30, 1862, Aug. 17, 1863, manuscripts, Essex Institute; George Gray Hunter to his brother, Feb. 20, 1864, manuscript in possession of Wm. A. Hunter, Harrisburg, Pa.

[29] Hq. Dept. of the Gulf, G. O. 11, April 14, 1862; Hq. Army of the Potomac, G. O. 58 and 87, Feb. 18, March 4, 1862; J.A.G. Records MM 219, manuscript, Nat'l Archives.

[30] Surgeon Albert G. Hart to his wife (n.d., n.p., but apparently Louisville, Ky., Sept., 1862), manuscript, Western Reserve Historical Society; J.A.G. Records MM 512, 989, manuscripts, Nat'l Archives. For an instance of a colonel having his skull crushed after return to civilian life by a soldier who bore a lingering grudge, see Barbara Burr, editor, "Letters from Two Wars," Ill. State Historical Society *Journal*, XXX (1937-1938), 157.

[31] Humphrey H. Hood to his wife, Oct. 8, 1864, manuscript, Ill. State Historical Library.

[32] John P. Moulton to his sister, Nov. 15, 1861, manuscript, Western Reserve Historical Society.

[33] A. Davenport to his homefolk, Jan. 17, 1863, manuscript, N. Y. Historical Society.

[34] 9 A. W.; George B. Davis, *op. cit.*, 378.

[35] *List of the U. S. Soldiers Executed by United States Military Authorities during the Late War* (n.p., n.d.), pamphlet in War Records Division, Nat'l Archives. Fourteen of the soldiers executed for mutiny were Negroes.

[36] Hq. Army of the Potomac, G. O. 12, Jan. 17, 1862; Hq. Dept. of Kansas, G. O. 15, April 5, 1864; Hq. Dept. of the Gulf, G. O. 11, April 14, 1862.

[37] Hq. Army of the Potomac, G. O. 33, Jan. 29, 1862; J.A.G. Records NN 3798.

[38] *Ibid.*, MM 1137.

[39] Hq. 17th Corps, G. O. 26, Sept. 15, 1863 and G. O. 37, Oct. 29, 1863; J.A.G. Records MM 923.

[40] Billings, *Hard Tack and Coffee*, 155.

[41] For example see Susan R. Jervey and Charlotte St. J. Ravenel, *Two Diaries* (n.p., 1921), 13, 21.

[42] Hq. Army of the Potomac, G. O. 15, Sept. 20, 1861.

[43] For example, see Hq. Dept. of the Gulf, G. O. 85, Oct. 25, 1862.

[44] Hq. Army of the Potomac, G. O. 74, Feb. 26, 1862.

[45] J.A.G. Records NN 2158.

[46] Hq. Army of the Potomac, G. O. 6, Sept. 4, 1861, and G. O. 8, Sept. 8, 1861; George T. Stevens, *Three Years in the Sixth Corps*, 42-43.

[47] Josiah S. Chandler, "What a Private Saw, Thought and Did during the War of the Rebellion," 196, manuscript, Western Reserve Historical Society; Cyrus R. Stone to his parents, Jan. 4, 1863, manuscript, Minn. Historical Society; Hazel C. Wolf, editor, *Campaigning with the First Minnesota*, 233; Billings, *Hard Tack and Coffee*, 155-156; Joseph T. Embree to his homefolk, Dec. 25, 1862, manuscript, Ind. State Library.

[48] Josiah S. Chandler, "What a Private Saw, Thought and Did during the War of the Rebellion," 158-159.

[49] *Ibid.*

[50] *List of U. S. Soldiers Executed by United States Military Authorities during the Late War; O. R.*, series 1, XLVI, pt. 2, 56.

[51] The only other instance of execution by a drumhead court-martial recorded in the War Department list is that of a white soldier convicted of desertion.

[52] The soldier was a private of the 18th Ill. Inf., executed on Oct. 2, 1861.

[53] The culprit was a private of the 2nd Colorado Cav., hanged on Nov. 10, 1864.

[54] Hq. Dept. of the Gulf, G. O. 46, June 2, 1863; J.A.G. Records NN 3900.

[55] Ella Lonn, best authority on the subject, estimates total Union desertions at 200,000. *Desertion during the Civil War* (N. Y., 1928), 154.

[56] Gen. George G. Meade, "Report of the Number of Men in the Army of the Potomac tried for desertion from July 1 to date, number guilty and shot," dated Nov. 30, 1863. Manuscript among Robert T. Lincoln Papers, Library of Congress. I am indebted to Helen Bullock of the National Council for Historic Sites and Buildings for calling this item to my attention.

[57] *List of U. S. Soldiers Executed by the United States Military Authorities during the Late War.* Helen Bullock, from a study of cases referred to Lincoln, found for all offenses four executions not included in the W.D. list. Helen Bullock to the writer, March 7, 1950.

[58] For typical comment on execution, see letters of Thomas Clark to his sister from Fernandina, Fla., Feb. 29, 1864, manuscript, Historical Society of Pa.; Henry J. H. Thompson to his wife from New Bern, N. C.,

Aug. 13, 1864, manuscript, Duke; Calvin B. Crandall to his parents, Aug. 29, 1863, manuscript, Neb. Historical Society.

[59] W. C. Ford, editor, *War Letters, 1862-1865 of John C. Gray and John C. Ropes* (Boston, 1927), 165-166.

[60] Diary of John M. Hawkes, entry of Feb. 29, 1864, manuscript, Boston Public Library; M. S. Schroyer, "Company G. History," *Snyder County Historical Society Bulletin*, II (1939), 97; diary of Sgt. James F. Williams, entry of Dec. 2, 1864, manuscript, N. Y. Public Library.

[61] Diary of Wm. H. Tyner, entry of Feb. 11, 1863, manuscript in possession of Mrs. Richard Alison, Jackson, Tenn. The fourth soldier was shot and so badly wounded by the father of the girl that he was spared the flogging. For an instance of a colonel having three colored soldiers tied to stakes and flogged with horsewhips in March 1864, see W.D. A.G.O. *General Court Martial Orders*, No. 265, Aug. 30, 1864.

[62] J.A.G. Records NN 2156.

[63] William R. Hartpence, *History of the Fifty-first Indiana Veteran Volunteer Infantry*, 86; David Lathrop, *History of the 59th Regiment Illinois Volunteers*, 187.

[64] Edwin C. Bennett, *Music, Musket and Sword, or the Camp, March and Firing Line in the Army of the Potomac* (Boston, 1900), 13.

[65] "Captain Samuel A. Craig's Memoirs of the Civil War and Reconstruction," *West Pennsylvania Historical Magazine*, XIII (1930), 231.

[66] Diary of Isaac Walker, entry of July 24, 1862, typescript, Dartmouth; Billings, *Hard Tack and Coffee*, 148-149; Frank Wilkeson, *Recollections of a Private Soldier in the Army of the Potomac*, 32-35.

[67] Frank Wilkeson, *op. cit.*, 32-33.

[68] Billings, *Hard Tack and Coffee*, 148; E. R. Hutchins, compiler, *The War of the 'Sixties* (N. Y., 1912), 327-328.

[69] Hq. Army of the Potomac, G. O. 36, Oct. 31, 1861.

[70] *Ibid.*, G. O. 40, Feb. 4, 1862, and G. O. 87, March 4, 1862.

[71] G. A. Hanson to "Dear Uncle," March 4, 1863, manuscript, Luther College Library. Translation from the Norwegian by Inga B. Norstog.

[72] John W. De Forest, A *Volunteer's Adventures*, 45; Gen. J. J. Bartlett to Col. Joseph Howland, Feb. 12, 1863, manuscript among Howland Letters, N. Y. Historical Society.

[73] A. Davenport to his homefolk, March 9, 1862.

[74] Hq. Dept. of the Gulf, G. O. 129, Sept. 13, 1864.

[75] Hq. Army of the Potomac, G. O. 34, Jan. 30, 1862.

[76] O. R., series 1, XXVI, pt. 1, 456-479.

[77] Hq. Army of the Potomac, G. O. 29, Jan. 28, 1862.

[78] Diary of George O. Hand, entry of Sept. 16, 1862, manuscript (photostat), Library of Congress; diary of Private Johnson, entry of March 21, 1863, manuscript, Historical Society of Pa.

[79] Hq. Army of the Potomac, G. O. 57, Feb. 17, 1862, and G. O. 18, May, 1864.

[80] *Ibid.*, G. O. 11, Sept. 14, 1861.

[81] Hq. Army of the Potomac, G. O. 73, Feb. 26, 1862; 83 A. W.

[82] J.A.G. Records MM 189.

[83] *Ibid.*

[84] J.A.G. Records MM 672.

[85] For a specific example of a witness' forgetfulness, see J.A.G. Records MM 189.

[86] A. Davenport to his homefolk, Aug. 12, 1861; Peter Wilson to his brother, Jan. 28, 1863. Ruth A. Gallaher, editor, "Peter Wilson in the Civil War," *Iowa Journal of History and Politics*, XL (1942), 346-347.

[87] Thomas H. Parker, *History of the 51st Regiment Pennsylvania Vols.* (Philadelphia, 1869), 172-173; Hq. Army of the Potomac, G. O. 58, Feb. 18, 1862.

[88] Diary of Joseph Isaacs, entry of Aug. 23, 1861, manuscript, N. Y. Public Library; a New Yorker confined in Elmira wrote his colonel Oct. 21, 1863: "This Guard House is a horrible, filthy, dirty hole, and full of lice and is a place that I can leave with pleasure." J.A.G. Records LL 1431. For unfavorable comments on guardhouses by inspecting officers, see report by Col. H. Van Rensselaer of inspection of the Dept. of Missouri, dated Feb. 10, 1862, in A.G.O. Records, 1862, file 14-I, and report by Col. D. B. Sackett, of inspection of Dept. of the Cumberland, dated Aug. 10, 1864, in I.G.O. Letters Received, Box 5, manuscripts, Nat'l Archives.

[89] A. Davenport to his homefolk, Jan. 3, 1862.

[90] Hq. Army of the Potomac, G. O. 58, Feb. 18, 1862; C. W. Bardeen, A *Little Fifer's War Diary*, 169; A. Davenport to his homefolk, July 21, 1862.

[91] David Lathrop, *op. cit.*, 88-89.

[92] "Reminiscences of John Culbertson," 69-71, typescript in possession of Gladys Culbertson, Detroit.

[93] Bell Irvin Wiley, "Billy Yank and Abraham Lincoln," *Abraham Lincoln Quarterly*, VI (1950), 106; O. R., series 3, IV, 418; W.D.A.G.O. *General Court Martial Order* No. 89, May 9, 1864 (copy filed in J.A.G. Records MM 950).

[94] These statements are based on an interview, March 30, 1949, with Helen Bullock who has made an intensive study of courts-martial cases referred to the President, and on the writer's own research in the manuscript courts-martial proceedings in the Nat'l Archives.

[95] J.A.G. Records MM 922.

[96] *Ibid.*

[97] J.A.G. Records LL 1431.

[98] O. R., series 1, V, 637; VII, 511-512; VIII, 409.

[99] Col. H. Van Rensselaer, Report of Inspection, Dept. of the Missouri, dated Feb. 10, 1862, A.G.O. Records, 14-I, manuscripts, Nat'l Archives.

[100] Willoughby M. Babcock, editor, *Selections from the Letters and Diaries of Brevet Brigadier General of the 75th N. Y. Volunteers* (n.p., 1922), 87. W. H. Russell, London *Times* correspondent who observed many soldiers in camp and in Washington in the summer of 1861, made frequent reference to poor discipline and incompetent officers. For ex-

amples, see *My Diary North and South*, 340, 482, 561, 586. Russell leaves the impression that saluting, even of top-ranking generals, was exceptional and that volunteer officers knew little about their duties and had little control over their men.

[101] Charles Ward to his folk, n.d., n.p., but apparently from near Falls Church, Va., Sept. 1862, manuscript, American Antiquarian Society; Asa Ward Brindle to his aunt, Sept. 7, 18, 1862, manuscripts (microfilm), Detroit Public Library.

[102] Col. James A. Hardie to Halleck, Oct. 27, 1864, Hq. of the Army Records, Document File, Inspections, Box 131, manuscripts, Nat'l Archives.

[103] Maj. E. H. Ludington to Secretary E. M. Stanton, Jan., 1865, item L-4, 1865, Box 8, Letters Received, I.G.O. Papers, manuscripts, Nat'l Archives.

[104] Report dated Jan. 13, 1865, item S-17, 1865, Box 10, Letters Received, I.G.O. Papers.

[105] Report dated Sept. 19, 1864, Box 5, Letters Received, I.G.O. Papers.

[106] Hq. 3rd Div., 19th Corps, Dept. of Gulf, G. O. 3, Aug. 29, 1864, 19th Army Corps Records, Misc. Papers and Reports, manuscripts, Nat'l Archives.

[107] Col. James A. Hardie to Halleck, April 23, 1864, submitting extracts from inspection reports, Dept. of the South. Hq. of the Army Records, Document File, Inspections, Box 130.

[108] Maj. M. Hazen White, A.A.I.A. to Brig. Gen. J. R. West, Sept. 29, 1864, manuscript, Hq. of the Army Records, Document File, Inspections, Box 131.

[109] Hardie to Halleck, Sept. 2, 1864, submitting extracts from inspection reports, Dept. of Arkansas and Dept. of the Gulf, Hq. of the Army Records, Document File, Inspections, Box 131.

[110] J. F. Rhodes, *History of the United States Since the Compromise of 1850*, V, 89.

Chapter IX

HARDTACK, SALT HORSE AND COFFEE

[1] Nashville *Daily Union*, April 16, 1863.

[2] A. R., 1863, article 43, paragraph 1190.

[3] G. W. Adams, "Health and Medicine in the Union Army" (Ph.D. dissertation, Harvard, 1946), II, 619. For a comparison of the Federal ration with that of other nations, see Austin Flint, editor, *Contributions Relating to the Causation and Prevention of Disease* (N. Y., 1867), 73 ff. This book was published under the auspices of the U. S. Sanitary Commission as a part of its "Sanitary Memoirs."

[4] Bell Irvin Wiley, *The Life of Johnny Reb*, 91; O. R., series 3, I, 399; Adams, "Health and Medicine in the Union Army," II, 619.

[5] Col. A. B. Eaton, Report to the Secretary of War on Inspection of Disbursing Branches of the Department of the South, dated June 2, 1864. I.G.O. Letters Received, Box 2, manuscripts, Nat'l Archives; O. R., series 1, XI, pt. 1, 175-176; *ibid.*, series 3, IV, 481-482; *Med. and Surg. Hist.*, Medical Volume, pt. 3, 711.

[6] U. S. Sanitary Comm. *Documents*, No. 40, 21. In reviewing a court-martial case in 1862, McClellan stated: "It has been made painfully apparent during the last few months that under the name of *Company Savings* large quantities of stores belonging to the U. S. have been embezzled by dishonest men entrusted with their keeping." Hq. Army of the Potomac, G. O. 89, March 5, 1862.

[7] John D. Billings, *Hard Tack and Coffee*, 112.

[8] E. A. Johnson, editor, *The Hero of Medfield*, 33.

[9] John N. Moulton to his homefolk, July 16, 1862, manuscript, Western Reserve Historical Society.

[10] Charles K. Bailer to his parents, Feb. 8, 1862, typescript, Western Reserve Historical Society.

[11] Levi A. Ross to his father, Oct. 26, 1862, manuscript, Ill. State Historical Library; George W. Kimball to his wife, Dec. 28, 1862, manuscript in possession of Stetson Conn, Washington, D. C.

[12] O. R., series 1, XI, pt. 1, 207-209, 214; XII, pt. 3, 379-381.

[13] Herman C. Newhall to his father, Nov. 28, 1862, manuscript, Boston Public Library; Leland O. Barlow to his sister, Dec. 1, 1862, manuscript, Mass. Historical Society; John B. Cuzner to Ellen Vandorn, Jan. 8, 1863, manuscript, Conn. Historical Society.

[14] For one soldier's reaction to the changed order, see A. Davenport to his parents, Jan. 30, Feb. 15, March 27, 1863, manuscript, N. Y. Historical Society.

[15] Diary of Stephen W. Gordon, typescript in possession of Fred L. Williams, Atlanta, to whom I am indebted for its use. The original is in the headquarters of the National Military Park, Fredericksburg, Va.

[16] For example, see A. Davenport to his parents, March 27, 1863.

[17] Adams, "Health and Medicine in the Union Army," II, 620.

[18] Frank M. Rood to "Friend Elvira," Nov. 18, 1863, manuscript in possession of Harry Rood, Poultney, Vt.

[19] Henry C. Bear to his wife, Dec. 7, 1862, manuscript in possession of Mrs. Stanley B. Hadden, Urbana, Ill.

[20] Leander Stillwell, *The Story of a Common Soldier*, 124.

[21] Diary of David J. Brothers, Dec. 10, 1862, manuscript, Wis. Historical Society.

[22] On June 19, 1863, an unidentified Norwegian soldier wrote Magnus Anderson Linnevolden from near Vicksburg: "We got to the Black River on the 17th. . . . We had long been on half rations and on the last days we had had only one cracker a day." Manuscript, Luther College Library, translation by Inga B. Norstog. For evidence of excessive

foraging and plundering during the Vicksburg campaign, see diary of John Merrilies, May 6, 9, 15, 1863, manuscript, Chicago Historical Society.

[23] O. R., series 1, XXIII, pt. 1, 461, 478; XXX, pt. 3, 247; Flint, *Contributions Relating to the Causation and Prevention of Disease*, 60-62. Robert S. Henry, *The Story of the Confederacy* (Indianapolis, 1931), 316.

[24] Willis D. Maier to Annie F. Howells, Oct. 22, 1863, manuscript, Hayes Memorial Library.

[25] Charles K. Bailer to his sister, Jan. 18, 1864.

[26] O. R., series 1, XXXI, pt. 2, 262, 580-581, pt. 3, 392; *Med. and Surg. Hist.*, Medical Vol., pt. 1, appendix, 286. Only a part of the troops made the return trip to Chattanooga.

[27] For example, see Michael R. Dresbach to his wife, Oct. 16, 1864, manuscript, Minn. Historical Society.

[28] Diary of Reuben Sweet, entry of Oct. 18, 1864. This diary was published in the Antigo, Wis., *Daily Journal*, March 9—May 25, 1939; clippings of the articles are in a scrapbook in the library of the Wis. Historical Society.

[29] For example, see George Sharland, *Knapsack Notes* (Springfield, Ill., 1865), 49-53.

[30] O. B. Clark, editor, *Downing's Civil War Diary*, 237.

[31] Col. James A. Hardie to Gen. H. W. Halleck, Feb. 24, 1865, Hq. of the Army Records, Documents File, Inspections, Box 131, manuscripts, Nat'l Archives; Michael R. Dresbach to his wife, March 12, 1865.

[32] U. S. Sanitary Comm. *Documents*, No. 40, 21; Col. James A. Hardie to Gen. H. W. Halleck, Feb. 9, 24, 1865.

[33] Hq. Army of the Potomac, G. O. 85, March 5, 1862.

[34] Charles J. Stille, *History of the U. S. Sanitary Commission*, 326. Officers were following authorized procedure in purchasing provisions from commissary stocks; their offense was in taking nearly all the vegetables before the enlisted men had a chance to draw them.

[35] Lt. Col. E. G. Beckwith to Gen. A. B. Eaton, No. 5, 1864, and accompanying paper, I.G.O. Letters Received, Box 2, manuscripts, Nat'l Archives.

[36] *Ibid.*

[37] Calvin B. Crandall to his parents, Oct. 21, 1862, typescript of original in Neb. Historical Society.

[38] *Ibid.*

[39] Stille, *op. cit.*, 327; Rebecca Usher to her sister, Feb. 8, 1865, manuscript, Maine Historical Society.

[40] Diary of Capt. E. J. Sherlock, entry of Jan. 7, 1865, typescript, Nat'l Archives.

[41] William Blackburn to his brother, Feb. 26, 1862, manuscript, Historical Society of Pa.

[42] See chapters IV and V.

[43] Henry Crydenwise to his parents, May 19, 1862, manuscript, Emory.

[44] Diary of Lorenzo S. Leavitt, entry of March 17, 1863, manuscript in possession of Harry C. Leavitt, Turner, Maine.

[45] Franklin J. Hubbard to his brother, June 18, 1862, manuscript, Univ. of Vt.

[46] This statement is based on a study of correspondence and reports in O. R., series 1, XXXVIII, XXXIX, XLIV and XLVII.

[47] For examples of officers actively participating in pillage, see: Proceedings and Report of Court of Inquiry on Sale of Cotton and Produce, held at St. Louis in March, 1863, Gen. Irvin McDowell, President, manuscripts, I.G.O. Papers, Nat'l Archives; Susan R. Jervey and Charlotte St. J. Ravenel, *Two Diaries*, 10, 20.

[48] Leland O. Barlow to his sisters, Nov. 1, 1862.

[49] Samuel Storrow to his parents, Nov. 19, 1862, manuscript, Mass. Historical Society.

[50] For example, see letters of Andrew K. Rose, 1862-1863, manuscripts, Duke.

[51] John W. De Forest, A *Volunteer's Adventures*, 74.

[52] Diary of Jenkins Lloyd Jones, entry of Nov. 3, 4, 1863, manuscript, Wis. Historical Society.

[53] For examples, see diaries of Florison D. Pitts and John Merrilies, both in the Chicago Mercantile Battery, for the period of these campaigns, manuscripts, Chicago Historical Society.

[54] Fred A. Shannon, editor, *Civil War Letters of Sgt. Onley Andrus*, 42.

[55] William Henry Peter to his brother, Dec. 3, 1862, manuscript, Ill. State Historical Library.

[56] Surgeon Henry P. Strong to his wife, Jan. 22, 1863, typescript, Wis. Historical Society.

[57] Willie H. Barnes to Annie F. Howells, May 3, 1863, manuscript, Hayes Memorial Library.

[58] R. G. Carter, *Four Brothers in Blue*, 411.

[59] Alfred S. Roe, *The Ninth New York Heavy Artillery*, 164-166; O. R., series 1, XLIV, 726-727, 792-793.

[60] Diary of William D. Evans, Feb. 13, 1865, manuscript, Western Reserve Historical Society.

[61] Billings, *Hard Tack and Coffee*, 113; Daniel Beidelman, Jr., to his father, Nov. 12, 1862, manuscript, Duke.

[62] John C. Arnold to his wife, June 12, 1864, typescript, National War College (Arnold's spelling made it "teeth dollers"); J. W. Danford to Amanda Wright, Oct. 24, 1861, manuscript among Miscellaneous Civil War Letters, Western Reserve Historical Society; George B. Sprague to his mother, Oct. 7, 1862, typescript of original furnished through courtesy of Hazel Wolf, Peoria, Ill.; Charles Babbott to his father, Dec. 16, 1862, manuscript, Hayes Memorial Library; extracts from the war diary of John V. Ruehle, Jr., Dec. 13, 1862, manuscript, Detroit Public Library; William B. Stanard to his sister, Jan. 12, 1862, manuscript, Univ. of Mich.

[63] J. W. Danford to Amanda Wright, Dec. 21, 1861.

[64] S. M. Fox, "Story of the Seventh Kansas," Kansas State Historical Society *Transactions*, VIII (1903-1904), 46.

[65] William F. Goodhue to his parents, Jan. 10, 1863, manuscript, Ill. State Historical Library.

[66] Billings, *Hard Tack and Coffee*, 117; William Bircher, A *Drummer Boy's Diary*, 125-127.

[67] Bircher, A *Drummer Boy's Diary*, 125-127. Bircher's description of hardtack pudding is almost word for word the same as that given by Henry M. Kieffer in *The Recollections of a Drummer Boy* (6th edition, Boston, 1889), 223-225, but I do not know which one of the authors deserves credit for the original account.

[68] Bircher, A *Drummer Boy's Diary*, 125.

[69] Samuel Storrow to his parents, Nov. 26, 1862; Charles A. Barker to his mother, Aug. 2, 1863, manuscript, Essex Institute; Billings, *Hard Tack and Coffee*, 116; Harold A. Small, editor, *The Road to Richmond*, 51.

[70] Reminiscences of Daniel H. Rowe, 34, manuscript, Ind. Historical Society; Cyril B. Upham, "Arms and Equipment for the Iowa Troops in the Civil War," *Iowa Journal of History and Politics*, XVI (1918), 47; W. H. Darlington to his mother, Sept. 6, 1861, manuscript, Harvard.

[71] Billings, *Hard Tack and Coffee*, 136.

[72] *Ibid.*, 135; Bircher, A *Drummer Boy's Diary*, 126.

[73] Shannon, *Civil War Letters of Sgt. Onley Andrus*, 95.

[74] Billings, *Hard Tack and Coffee*, 135.

[75] G. W. Adams, "Health and Medicine in the Union Army," II, 622; N. B. Bartlett to his mother, April 3 [1864], manuscript, Chicago Historical Society.

[76] Richard B. Irwin, *History of the Nineteenth Army Corps* (N. Y., 1893), 127; Samuel Storrow to his parents, Dec. 2, 1862; diary of John H. Markley, entry of July 10, 1863, manuscript, Historical Society of Pa.

[77] Joseph H. Diltz to B. F. Maden, Feb. 2, 1862, manuscript, Duke; Charles Anderson to his sister, Aug. 26, 1861, manuscript among Miscellaneous Civil War Letters, Western Reserve Historical Society; Stillwell, *The Story of a Common Soldier*, 124.

[78] *Tri-Weekly Camp Journal* (Somerset, Ky.), Jan. 22, 1862; Billings, *Hard Tack and Coffee*, 135; Johnson, *The Hero of Medfield*, 26.

[79] Billings, *Hard Tack and Coffee*, 124.

[80] F. Y. Hedley, *Marching through Georgia* (Chicago, 1890), 82.

[81] William Hamilton to his mother, Nov. 15, 1862, manuscript, Library of Congress; Isaac Jackson to his brother, Oct. 21, 1862, typescript, in possession of J. O. Jackson, Highland Park, Mich.

[82] Felix Brannigan to an unidentified correspondent, June 18, 1861, typescript, Library of Congress.

[83] Hedley, *Marching through Georgia*, 82-83; O. R. series 1, XI, pt. 1, 175.

[84] O. R., series 3, IV, 481; *Med. and Surg. Hist.*, Medical Volume, pt. 3, 711; *Med. and Surg. Hist.*, Medical Volume, pt. 2, 627.

[85] Stillwell, *The Story of a Common Soldier*, 266; G. W. Adams, "Health and Medicine in the Union Army," II, 638.

[86] Stillwell, *The Story of a Common Soldier*, 266; C. W. Bardeen, *A Little Fifer's War Diary*, 198-199; M. S. Schroyer, "Company 'G' History," Snyder County Pennsylvania Historical Society *Bulletin*, II (1939), 74.

[87] Small, *The Road to Richmond*, 197; G. W. Adams, "Health and Medicine in the Union Army," II, 638.

[88] William Henry Peter to his sister, March 18, 1863.

[89] *Il Recruito: A Comic Opera* (n.d., n.p.), 6. This rare item is at Emory.

[90] Charles Goddard to his mother, Jan. 24, 1864, manuscript among Orrin F. Smith Papers, Minn. Historical Society.

[91] Lt. Col. Roswell Farnham to his sister, Oct. 3, 1862, typescript, Vt. Historical Society.

[92] Diary of Joseph Isaacs, entry of July 13, 1861, manuscript, N. Y. Public Library; Charles Ward Newton to his brother, Oct. 2, 1862, manuscript, American Antiquarian Society; Abraham Kendig to his sister, Dec. 4, 1864, manuscript, Historical Society of Pa.

[93] De Forest, *A Volunteer's Adventures*, 155.

[94] Henry A. Buck to his homefolk, July 29, 1863, manuscript, Univ. of Mich.; Jasper N. Barritt to his brother, Jan. 18, 1864, manuscript, Library of Congress.

[95] Shannon, *Civil War Letters of Sgt. Onley Andrus*, 54.

[96] Charles W. Wills, *Army Life of an Illinois Soldier*, 34. The writer in his boyhood knew a Union veteran, G. W. Bunker, in West Tennessee, who ate pawpaw apples, much to the amazement of the natives. Bunker said that he acquired a taste for the fruit while serving in the army.

[97] Lt. J. S. Pierson to Emma Harris, Aug. 23, 1864, manuscript, Ohio State Archaeological and Historical Society; Billings, *Hard Tack and Coffee*, 131.

[98] O. R., series 3, III, 94.

[99] Lt. Col. Roswell Farnham to his sister, June 19, 1863; S. H. M. Byers, "How Men Feel in Battle," *Harpers Monthly Magazine*, CXII (1906), 933; diary of Capt. E. J. Sherlock, Jan. 1, 1865.

[100] H. Holden to his brother, Aug. 30, 1862, manuscript among Miscellaneous Civil War Letters, American Antiquarian Society; C. B. Thurston to his brother, March 30, 1863, manuscript, Emory; Henry J. H. Thompson to his wife, Sept. 29, 1864, manuscript, Duke.

[101] Joseph H. Diltz to B. F. Maden, Feb. 2, 1862; "Letters of a Badger Boy in Blue," *Wisconsin Magazine of History*, IV (1920-1921), 216.

[102] Edward L. Edes to his uncle, July 1, 1862, manuscript, Mass. Historical Society; Albert Harris to his sister, Jan. 18, 1863, manuscript, Vt. Historical Society; John McMeekin to his mother, Jan. 15, 1863, manuscript, Western Reserve Historical Society.

[103] John C. Arnold to his wife, March 10, 1864.

Chapter X

EVIL AND GOODNESS

[1] J. E. Hart to his wife, June 16, 1861, manuscript, Vt. Historical Society; "On the March with Sibley in 1863: The Diary of Private Henry J. Hagadorn," *North Dakota Historical Quarterly*, V (1930), 125; David Lathrop, *History of the Fifty-ninth Regiment Illinois Volunteers*, 126-127.

[2] A. Davenport to his homefolk, Dec. 13, 1861, manuscript, N. Y. Historical Society; *ibid.*, Dec. 6, 1862, March 9, 1863.

[3] Delos W. Lake to Calvin Lake, Feb. 12, 1864, microfilm of manuscript, Huntington Library.

[4] Urich N. Parmelee to his brother, Oct. 22, 1861, manuscript, Duke; diary of John Merrilies, general entry covering period Sept. 3—Nov. 26, 1862, manuscript, Chicago Historical Society.

[5] 3 A. W.

[6] Oscar O. Winther, *With Sherman to the Sea*, 38; Albert G. Hart to his wife, Dec. 15, 1861, manuscript, Western Reserve Historical Society; John W. De Forest, *A Volunteer's Adventures*, 43.

[7] Diary of Capt. Van S. Bennett, entry of Jan. 6, 1864, manuscript, Wis. Historical Society; John Hope Franklin, editor, *The Diary of James T. Ayers*, 16.

[8] W.D.A.G.O. G. O. 225, July 22, 1863; Hq. Army of Potomac, G. O. 91, March 6, 1862.

[9] For a soldier's comment on the nature of profanity used in camp, see Winther, *With Sherman to the Sea*, 103-104.

[10] [David Lane], *A Soldier's Diary*, 217; Thomas L. Livermore, *Days and Events*, 182.

[11] A. S. Roe, *The Ninth New York Heavy Artillery*, 102.

[12] Reminiscences of John Newton Culbertson, 78, typescript in possession of Gladys Culbertson, Detroit Public Library; Winther, *With Sherman to the Sea*, 123; M. S. Schroyer, "Company 'G' History," Snyder County Historical Society *Bulletin*, II (1939), 97.

[13] C. W. Bardeen, *A Little Fifer's War Diary*, 263; diary of John Merrilies, March 21, 1863.

[14] John Beatty, *The Citizen Soldier*, 150. For another instance of a unit-sponsored cockfight, see diary of Stephen Gordon, March 16, 1864, typescript in possession of Fred L. Williams, Atlanta.

[15] Michael R. Dresbach to his wife, Jan. 7, 1865, manuscript, Minn. Historical Society; diary of William D. Evans, entry of Dec. 3, 1864, manuscript, Western Reserve Historical Society.

[16] John P. M. Green, "Belated Diary of a Civil War Soldier in the First N. H. Light Battery," 2, typescript, N. H. Historical Society; [Thomas W. Fanning], *The Adventures of a Volunteer* (Cincinnati, 1863), 27-28.

[17] Bardeen, *A Little Fifer's War Diary*, 181-182, 262-275, 290-299.

[18] Diary of Jacob E. Hyneman, Feb. 20, 1864, typescript in possession of Charles N. Owen, Chicago.

[19] De Forest, *A Volunteer's Adventures*, 30.

[20] Hq. Army of Potomac, G. O. 40, Feb. 4, 1862.

[21] James M. Nichols, *Perry's Saints*, 113.

[22] Theodore C. Blegen, editor, *Civil War Letters of Colonel Hans C. Heg*, 60.

[23] "Prock's Letters from Camp, Battle-field and Hospital," *Indiana Magazine of History*, XXXIV (1938), 87; diary of Jacob E. Hyneman, Dec. 26, 1864; diary of Jacob H. Mechling, Feb. 26, 1863; D. J. Miller to Fielding Beeler, March 27, 1864; manuscript, Ind. State Library; diary of N. L. Parmater, Oct. 10, 1861, typescript in possession of Dr. A. M. Giddings, Battle Creek, Mich.

[24] Charles E. Goddard to his mother, Dec. 2, 1861, manuscript among Orrin F. Smith Papers, Minn. Historical Society; Edward E. Newhall to his homefolk, Nov. 21, 1861, manuscript, Boston Public Library.

[25] Abner Doubleday, "Some Experiences of Wit, Humor and Repartee in Army and Navy Life," manuscript, N. Y. Historical Society.

[26] James G. Nash to his homefolk [undated fragment, but 1864]. This manuscript is among the John P. Bannon Papers, N. Y. Historical Society.

[27] William Blackburn, to his brother, Feb. 26, 1862, manuscript, Historical Society of Pa.

[28] Portland, Maine *Transcript*, April 23, 1864.

[29] Leonard E. Wilder of the 7th Ohio Regt. wrote his homefolk Nov. 27, 1861: "The *Glorious Army* is an awful place to keep anything. You must freeze to it or it will be gone." Manuscript among Franklin J. Hubbard Letters, Univ. of Vt.; Cyrus R. Stone of the 16th N. Y. Regt. wrote his parents Sept. 27, 1862: "Anyone have got to take care of his things if he do not want them stole. There are those in the army who would steal at home and there are those who steal here who would not at home. I would hate to have an army in the vicinity where I live." Manuscript, Minn. Historical Society.

[30] J. H. Greene, *Reminiscences of the War*, 35. For a detailed discussion of plunder by Union forces, see E. M. Coulter, *The Confederate States of America, 1861-1865* (Baton Rouge, 1950), 363-370.

[31] Diary of Capt. Heber S. Thompson, entry of July 23, 1864, manuscript in possession of Dr. A. M. Giddings, Battle Creek, Mich.

[32] For a vivid description of pillage in South Carolina, see Susan R. Jervey and Charlotte St. J. Ravenel, *Two Diaries*, 8 *et passim*.

[33] Works Progress Administration, "Indian Pioneer History," XIV, 12 (interview of Christian Bates by Lula Austin, March 27, 1937), bound transcript, Foreman Collection, Okla. Historical Society.

[34] See chapter VII.

[35] Chattanooga *Daily Gazette*, Sept. 1, 1864.

[36] A broadside copy of the advertisement and accompanying verses

is in the Alabama Department of Archives and History, Montgomery, Ala.

37 A copy of the advertisement and verses in the handwriting of Florison D. Pitts, bugler in the Chicago Mercantile Battery, was found among the Civil War letters of Florison D. Pitts; at the bottom of the page containing the poetry, Pitts wrote for the information of his homefolk: "The above was found on the person of a rebel prisoner taken near Chattanooga in Jan. 1864." Manuscript, Chicago Historical Society.

38 E. L. Rudolph, *Confederate Broadside Verse* (New Braunfels, Texas, 1950), 15.

39 Manuscript, dated Nov. 23, 1863, among Keran Collection, Ohio State Arch. and Historical Society.

40 John B. Cuzner to Ellen Vandorn, Aug. 28, 1863, manuscript, Conn. Historical Society; Enoch T. Baker to his wife, Nov. 10, 1861, manuscript, Historical Society of Pa.; Henry J. H. Thompson to his wife, June 20, 1863, manuscript, Duke.

41 Cincinnati *Enquirer*, Jan. 2, 1864, quoted in A. C. Cole, *The Irrepressible Conflict* (N. Y., 1934), 366-367; Annual Report of N. Y. Police Commissioner for 1863 in New York *Herald*, Jan. 5, 1864.

42 Margaret Leech, *Reveille in Washington, 1860-1865* (N. Y., 1941), 261 ff; Franc B. Wilkie, *Pen and Powder*, 198-199.

43 Leech, *Reveille in Washington*, 262-264.

44 Eli Veazie to Jeremiah Norris, April 20, 1863, manuscript among George E. Norris Letters, Duke.

45 J. L. Bassett to "Friend George," Feb. 22 [1864], manuscript among Miscellaneous Civil War Letters and Documents, Essex Institute. For a thinly disguised account of a homebound Yank's three-day spree with a *nymph du monde* of Memphis, see diary of John B. Fletcher, Dec. 18-20, 1863, manuscript, Ill. State Historical Library.

46 Henry J. H. Thompson to his wife, Dec. 4, 1863 and Jan. 16, 1865.

47 Frank R. Lyman to Royal E. Cook, Oct. 9 [1864], manuscript among uncataloged Civil War Personal Narratives, Dartmouth.

48 Samuel Jarrett to Jefferson Hartman, Jan. 15, 1865, manuscript, Duke.

49 For vice conditions in the cities named, see local and police news columns for the occupation period of the Chattanooga *Daily Gazette*, Nashville *Dispatch*, Memphis *Bulletin* and Memphis *Union Appeal*.

50 Surgeon W. M. Chambers, "Sanitary Report of the Condition of the Prostitutes of Nashville, Tenn.," Jan. 31, 1865, manuscript, Western Reserve Historical Society, file P-188.

51 *Ibid.*; Nashville *Dispatch*, July 8, 10, 26 and 28, 1863.

52 Nashville *Dispatch*, Dec. 22, 1864.

53 Memphis *Bulletin*, April 30, 1863; David P. Jackson, editor, *The Colonel's Diary*, 98-99.

54 Memphis *Bulletin*, May 1, 1863.

55 *Ibid.*

56 *Ibid.*, May 3, 1863, and various subsequent issues, especially that of Aug. 12, 1863.

[57] Leech, *Reveille in Washington*, 265.

[58] *Med. and Surg. Hist.*, Medical Volume, pt. 1, 636-637, 710-711; pt. 3, 891-896.

[59] *Ibid.*, pt. 3, 891; J. J. Woodward, *Outlines of Camp Diseases of the U. S. Army*, 21-22; for a graph showing the venereal trend July 1861 —June 1866, see *Med. and Surg. Hist.*, Medical Volume, pt. 3, plate opposite p. 890.

[60] A sampling of regiments in the Army of the Potomac for the period July—October 1861 showed 308 cases of gonorrhea as against 224 cases of measles. U. S. Sanitary Comm. *Documents* No. 40, 41.

[61] For a discussion of venereal disease in the Confederate Army, see Bell Irvin Wiley, *The Life of Johnny Reb*, 55-57.

[62] *Med. and Surg. Hist.*, Medical Volume, pt. 3, 893-896; W. M. Chambers, "Sanitary Report of the Condition of the Prostitutes of Nashville, Tenn."

[63] William F. Goodhue to his parents, Oct. 1, 1864, manuscript, Ill. State Historical Library.

[64] Winther, *With Sherman to the Sea*, 20 *et passim*.

[65] Ella Lonn, "The Forty-Eighters in the Civil War," in A. E. Zucker, editor, *The Forty-Eighters: Political Refugees of the German Revolution of 1848* (N. Y., 1950), 215-216.

[66] George W. Landrum to his sister, May 15, 1863, typescript, Western Reserve Historical Society.

[67] *United States Statutes at Large*, chap. IX, sec. 9; William R. Eastman, "The Army Chaplain of 1863," Military Order of the Loyal Legion of the U. S., N. Y. Commandery, *Personal Recollections of the Rebellion*, IV (N. Y., 1912), 339-340; O. R., series 3, I, 154, 157, II, 223, III, 175-176; Bertram W. Korn, "Jewish Chaplains during the Civil War," American Jewish Archives, I (Cincinnati, 1948), 8-12; Edwin C. Bennett, *Musket and Sword, on the Camp, March and Firing Line in the Army of the Potomac*, 178-179. The pay of Chaplains was $100 per month plus allowances that brought annual compensation to about $1400.

[68] C. B. Thurston to his parents, March 7, 1863, manuscript, Emory; Edward L. Edes to his father, Dec. 19, 1862, manuscript, Mass. Historical Society; J. D. Barnhart, editor, "A Hoosier Invades the Confederacy," *Indiana Magazine of History*, XXXIX (1943), 151.

[69] Albert Harris to his sister, Feb. 14, 1863, manuscript, Vt. Historical Society.

[70] Thomas N. Lewis to his uncle, June 7, 1861, manuscript among Moulton Letters, Western Reserve Historical Society; Charles E. Goddard to his mother, Jan. 12, 1864.

[71] Doubleday, "Some Experiences of Wit, Humor, and Repartee in Army and Navy Life."

[72] Charles Barnard to his wife, Dec. 8, 1862, manuscript, Maine Historical Society.

[73] Edward Gardner Abbott to his father, June 10, 1862, manuscript, Harvard.

[74] Fritz Haskell, editor, "Diary of Col. William Camm," Ill. State Historical Society *Journal*, XVIII (1926), 825; S. M. Fox, "Story of the 7th Kansas," Kansas Historical Society *Transactions*, VIII (1903-1904), 47.

[75] H. Clay Trumbull, *War Memories of an Army Chaplain* (N. Y., 1898), 8; Bardeen, *A Little Fifer's War Diary*, 294; O. W. Norton, *Army Letters*, 100; W. C. Ford, editor, *War Letters, 1862-1865, of John C. Gray and John C. Ropes*, 217; Herbert E. Valentine to his mother, Sept. 7, 1862, manuscript, Essex Institute; Charles W. Oleson to C. B. Thurston, April 15 [1863].

[76] Cyrus R. Stone to his parents, Dec. 20, 1862; diary of William E. Limbarker, Jan. 17, 1862, manuscript, Univ. of Mich.

[77] Winther, *With Sherman to the Sea*, 87; Henry Crydenwise to his parents, April 13, 1865, manuscript, Emory.

[78] Henry Crydenwise to his parents, March 13, 1862; Harold A. Small, editor, *The Road to Richmond*, 32, 142; Samuel Storrow to his parents, Dec. 6, 1862, manuscript, Mass. Historical Society; Chaplain Joseph Hopkins Twichell to his father, Aug. 4, 7, 1861, and Aug. 28, 1862, manuscript, Yale.

[79] For difficulties encountered by chaplains, see Ethel Lowerre Phelps, editor, "Diary of Winthrop Henry Phelps," May 24, 1862, and subsequent entries, typescript, Minn. Historical Society; "A Chaplain's Experience in the Army," *Monthly Religious Magazine*, XXIX (1863), 223-232.

[80] Henry A. Buck to his sister, letter-journal covering period Oct. 4—Nov. 12, 1862, manuscript, Detroit Public Library; see also Lathrop, *History of the 59th Regt. Ill. Vols.*, 205-206.

[81] Diary of Uriah McCracken, May 31, 1863, manuscript in possession of George McCracken, Davenport, Iowa.

[82] O. R., series 1, XX, pt. 2, 203; Hq. Army of the Potomac, *G. O.*, 7, Sept. 6, 1861; John D. Gaylord to his homefolk, Nov. 10, 1862, manuscript, Duke.

[83] Diary of Rufus Kinsley, April 10, 1864, manuscript, Vt. Historical Society.

[84] For details on activities of Christian Commission, see the published annual reports of the organization and the Daily Record Books of its representatives, manuscripts, Nat'l Archives. For typical reactions of soldiers to the Commission and its agents, see Diary of George Rolfe, Jan. 19, 1865, typescript, Saratoga National Military Park; Edmund Newsome, *Experience in the War of the Great Rebellion* (Carbondale, Ill., 1880), 136-137; Day Elmore to his mother, May 2, 1864, manuscript in possession of Mrs. Hall Mosher, Memphis, Tenn.

[85] Most of these hymns, and many others, were included in *The Soldier's Hymn Book*, published by the Chicago Y.M.C.A. in 1864, a copy of which is in the Chicago Historical Society. I am indebted to Betty Baughman of the Chicago Historical Society for calling this item to my attention and providing a table of contents.

[86] Diary of George Rolfe, Jan. 24, 1864—April 16, 1865; diary of

Rodney Seaver, June 15, 1864, manuscript, Western Reserve Historical Society; Alonzo Miller to his homefolk, Feb. 14, 1864, typescript, Kennesaw Mountain National Park.

[87] M. P. Larry to his sister, Jan. 31, 1863, manuscript, Maine Historical Society; diary of George Rolfe, March 27, April 24, May 22, June 12, July 2, July 3, 1864.

[88] "Capt. Samuel Craig's Memoirs of Civil War and Reconstruction," *Western Pa. History Magazine*, XIII (1930), 233; Col. F. Quinn to Gov. Austin Blair, April 26, 1862, manuscript, Detroit Public Library.

[89] Diary of Joseph D. Galloway, Dec. 15, 1861, manuscript, N. Y. Public Library; M. P. Larry to his sister, Dec. 20, 1863.

[90] Delos W. Lake to his homefolk, Nov. 9, 1862.

[91] Diary of Jenkins Lloyd Jones, Feb. 1, 1863, manuscript, Wis. Historical Society; Small, *Road to Richmond*, 145.

[92] U. S. Christian Commission, *Third Annual Report* (Philadelphia, 1865), 28. For a description of large-scale outdoor meetings in North Carolina late in the war, see Delos W. Lake to his mother, April 7, 1865.

[93] Hazel C. Wolf, editor, *Campaigning with the First Minnesota*, 32-33; Isaac Jackson to his sister Sallie, May 27, 1863, typescript in possession of J. O. Jackson, Highland Park, Mich.

[94] Nashville *Daily Union*, April 7, 15, 1863; A. M. Stewart, *Camp, March and Battlefield*, 98; diary of George N. Champlin, Jan. 4, 11, 1864, typescript, Conn. State Library.

[95] Diary of George N. Champlin, Jan. 18, 20, 1864.

[96] For detailed information on religious periodicals distributed in the army, see "Religious Newspapers ordered for 1865," manuscript, among U. S. Christian Commission Papers, Nat'l Archives.

[97] Ethel Lowerre Phelps, "Diary of Winthrop Henry Phelps," Jan. 1, 1865 (citing *Thirty Ninth Annual Report of American Tract Society, 1864*).

[98] *Second Report of the Maryland Committee, U. S. Christian Commission* (Baltimore, 1863), 45, 72; *A Memorial Record of the U. S. Christian Commission* (N. Y., 1866), 54; A. M. Stewart, *Camp, March and Battlefield*, 60.

[99] *Second Report of the Maryland Committee, U. S. Christian Commission*, 72.

[100] *Ibid.*

[101] "Publications Received, 1864-1865," ledgers 1 and 3.

[102] Emily Adams Bancroft, compiler, *Memorial and Letters of Rev. John R. Adams* (Cambridge, Mass., 1890), 87-88; diary of E. J. Sherlock, Aug. 8, 1863, manuscript, Ind. Historical Society.

[103] John W. Clark to his sister, Jan. 29, 1861, manuscript in possession of the writer; *A Memorial Record of the New York Branch of the U. S. Christian Commission*, 52-53.

Chapter XI

THE SPIRITS EBB AND FLOW

[1] O. W. Norton, *Army Letters, 1861-1865*, 23.

[2] J. J. Moulton to his homefolk, n.d., but summer of 1861, manuscript, Western Reserve Historical Society.

[3] Vance Nelson to Amanda Wright, Dec. 12, 1861, manuscript among Miscellaneous Civil War Letters, Western Reserve Historical Society.

[4] Edward Whitaker to his homefolk, Feb. 24, 1862, manuscript, Conn. State Library; Hazel C. Wolf, editor, *Campaigning with the First Minnesota*, 28; William A. Harper to his wife, March 26, 1862, manuscript, Ind. Historical Society.

[5] A. Davenport to his homefolk, May 23, June 1, July 8, July 12, 1862, manuscripts, N. Y. Historical Society.

[6] Ella Lonn, *Desertion during the Civil War*, 145; Herman Chauncey Newhall to his homefolk, Dec. 18, 1862, manuscript, Boston Public Library; Henry S. Abbott to his brother, Dec. 17, 1862, manuscript, Harvard.

[7] Surgeon Humphrey H. Hood to his wife, March 26, 1863, manuscript, Ill. State Historical Library; Hq. Dept. of Tenn., G. O. 12, Feb. 1, 1863.

[8] John N. Tallman to his brother, March 3, 1863, manuscript, Chicago Historical Society; diary of John H. Williams, Dec. 9, 1862, typescript translation from the Welsh, Vt. Historical Society; Samuel Storrow to his parents, Dec. 23, 1862, manuscript, Mass. Historical Society; C. W. Bardeen, *A Little Fifer's War Diary*, 169.

[9] M. N. Collins to C. H. Bell, Dec. 22, 1862, manuscript, Dartmouth.

[10] Edward L. Edes to "Charlotte," Dec. 28, 1862, manuscript, Mass. Historical Society.

[11] John N. Moulton to his homefolk, Feb. 1, 1863.

[12] *Ibid.*, March 16, March 19, 1863.

[13] Levi Ross to his father, Feb. 3, 1863, manuscript, Ill. State Historical Library.

[14] M. P. Larry to his sister, Dec. 23, 1862, manuscript, Maine Historical Society.

[15] Bell Irvin Wiley, "Billy Yank and the Brass," Ill. State Historical Society *Journal*, XLIII (1950), 250.

[16] Samuel W. Croft to his sister, Dec. 21, 1862, and Feb. 3, 1863, manuscripts, Washington and Jefferson College. I am indebted to C. M. Ewing for calling these manuscripts to my attention and lending me copies of them. Herman Chauncey Newhall to his father, Dec. 28, 1862.

[17] A. H. Pickel to his father, Feb. 22, 1863, manuscript, Duke;

Richard Puffer to his sister, Feb. 12, 1863, manuscript, Chicago Historical Society.

[18] Levi Ross to his father, March 25, 1863.

[19] A. Davenport to his homefolk, March 27, 1863; diary of Stephen W. Gordon, Feb. 7—May 6, 1863, typescript in possession of Fred L. Williams, Atlanta; Edmund English of the 2nd N. J. Regiment wrote, after the war, of the period following Burnside's removal: "I did not think it possible that such a change could have taken place for the better as has been effected in the short space of two months. From a dissatisfied and almost mutinous mob, we have become a good and well-disciplined army second to none." "Memoirs of Campaign Life," manuscript among the Edmund English Papers. I am indebted to the Huntington Library for lending me a microfilm copy of these papers.

[20] The Provost Marshal General's Bureau was created on March 3, 1863. National Archives *Guide* (Washington, 1948), 395.

[21] For one soldier's comment on the effect of improving health on morale, see Isaac Jackson to his brother, March 23, 1863, typescript in possession of J. O. Jackson, Highland Park, Mich.

[22] Edmund English to his mother, Jan. 27, April 12, 1863; Jesse A. Wilson to his parents, Feb. 10, April 12, 1863, manuscripts in possession of Mrs. Fred A. Johnson, Belfast, Maine; M. P. Larry to his sister, April 12, 1863.

[23] Isaac Jackson to his brother, March 19, 1863.

[24] Wolf, *Campaigning with the First Minnesota*, 347.

[25] Surgeon Edwin Hutchinson to his mother, July 1, 1863, manuscript, La. State Univ.

[26] On Dec. 28, 1862, one soldier wrote from Falmouth, Virginia: "I want just one *good show*, one hack at them, where I can reach them; when our army can be victorious; and that's what we want—a victory!" R. G. Carter, *Four Brothers in Blue*, 324.

[27] Of Gettysburg one Yank later wrote: "I hesitate to say how much it meant to our army, but as I am telling everything else I may as well tell this, that if the battle had gone against us, I should have made straight for Fitchburg [his home] and I should have had lots of company. We had lost battle after battle, by blunder after blunder, of commander after commander, and we had lost all confidence. It was common talk in the ranks, 'We'll do our level best here, but if we cant lick the rebs on Yankee soil, that's the end of it for us.'" Bardeen, *A Little Fifer's War Diary*, 214.

[28] C. B. Thurston to his father, July 10, 1863, manuscript, Emory.

[29] Frank Wilkeson, *Recollections of a Private*, 185-187.

[30] Private E. W. Chase of Sherman's army wrote in his journal on April 12, 1865: "News reached us that Lee had surrendered his army. The tumult of joy was indescribable." Manuscript, Maine Historical Society.

[31] In one instance, at least, the burial routine was given a lightening touch. In relating the death and interment of a comrade who died on a march from Kentucky to Tennessee in 1863, a Michigan soldier

stated: "A prayer over the grave and three volleys completed the ceremony. The band played the death march while going towards the grave and Yankee doodle comming back." William H. Brearley to his sister, Oct. 17, 1863, manuscript, Detroit Public Library.

[32] William A. Harper to his wife, Feb. 16, 1863, manuscript, Ind. Historical Society.

[33] J. J. Moulton to his homefolk, Jan. 25, 1863; Charles K. Bailer to his sister, April 25, 1864, manuscript, Western Reserve Historical Society.

[34] David Williams to John R. Corrie, March 9, 1863, manuscript in possession of Mrs. Lester L. Corrie, Urbana, Illinois.

[35] H. C. Bear to his wife, Dec. 7-14, 1862, manuscript in possession of Mrs. Stanley B. Hadden, Urbana, Illinois.

[36] Levi Ross to his parents, June 26, 1863.

[37] David Leigh to "Mr. Drumgold," March 3, Aug. 1, 1863, manuscript, Dartmouth.

[38] John McMeekin to his mother, from near Young's Point, La., Feb. 11, 1863, manuscript, Western Reserve Historical Society.

[39] *Ibid.*, Jan. 15, March 16, 1863; Lonn, *Desertion during the Civil War*, 204-205; Wood Gray, *The Hidden Civil War* (N. Y., 1942), 132-135, 154-155.

[40] Anson W. Bristol to Lucian B. Case, May 17, 1863, manuscript, Chicago Historical Society; Seth H. Cook to Curtis Babbott, Dec. 10, 1862, manuscript, Hayes Memorial Library.

[41] John W. Clark to his sister, April 3, 1864, manuscript in possession of the writer; Thomas N. Lewis to his aunt, Jan. 24, 1862, manuscript, Western Reserve Historical Society.

[42] H. R. Leonard to Jennie Davis, Nov. 23 [1861], manuscript among Miscellaneous Civil War Letters, Western Reserve Historical Society.

[43] C. B. Thurston to his brother, March 30, 1863, and to his father, June 3, 1863.

[44] Vance Nelson to Amanda Wright, Dec. 12, 1861.

[45] Lucretia E. Thompson to Henry J. H. Thompson, Jan. 14, 1863, manuscript, Duke. She headed this letter appropriately, "Camp Lonely."

[46] William H. Lloyd to his wife, various dates, 1863-1865, manuscripts, Western Reserve Historical Society. The letters quoted are those of Sept. 24, Oct. 3, Oct. 10, Dec. 21, Dec. 23, 1863.

[47] John N. Henry to his wife, Jan. 2, 1863, manuscript, Minn. Historical Society.

[48] Diary of M. F. Roberts, April 12, 1864, manuscript, Western Reserve Historical Society; Portland, Maine, *Transcript*, May 2, 1863.

[49] Willis D. Maier to Annie F. Howells, Nov. 21, 1863, Jan. 6, 1864, manuscripts, Hayes Memorial Library. His three-year term was to expire in eight months.

[50] O. R., series 1, XII, pt. 3, 410.

[51] Hercules Stanard to his father, Nov. 17, 1862, manuscript, Univ. of Mich.

[52] W. O. Lyford to his homefolk, July 31, Aug. 31, 1861; Feb. 14,

March 8, Oct. 8, 1862, manuscripts in possession of Charles N. Owen, Chicago.

[53] John W. De Forest, A *Volunteer's Adventures*, 165. For the superior discipline of De Forest's regiment and the triumph of good morale over hardship, see *ibid.*, 151.

[54] See chapter XII.

[55] Charles Ward to his homefolk, Sept. 14, Sept. 22, Nov. 14, 1862; May 7, July 7, 1863, manuscripts, American Antiquarian Society.

[56] "Correspondence of Ira Butterfield," *North Dakota Historical Quarterly*, III (Jan., 1929), 130.

Chapter XII

THE MEN WHO WORE THE BLUE

[1] *O. R.*, series 3, V, 130.

[2] Diary of William C. Richardson, 1862-1865, 4 vols., *passim*, manuscript, Western Reserve Historical Society; J. H. Kendig to his brother, Aug. 10, 1863, manuscript, Historical Society of Pa.

[3] F. T. Miller, editor, *Photographic History of the Civil War*, VIII, 195; Frances A. Tenney, editor, *War Diary of Luman Harris Tenney, 1861-1865*, 65.

[4] Harvey Reid to his brother Charles [n.d., but 1862], manuscript, Wis. Historical Society.

[5] Ray H. Mattison, "The Drummer Boy of Shiloh," manuscript, Shiloh National Park. Mattison was historian of the Shiloh Park at the time he made this study. I am indebted to Superintendent James Holland of the Shiloh Park for making it available to me and for furnishing additional information; also to E. J. Pratt, his assistant, for showing me the "doctored" cemetery roll. The collection at Shiloh contains a copy of the Hays song, "The Drummer Boy of Shiloh" (Louisville and Chicago, 1862), and a play, "The Drummer Boy: Or the Battle-field of Shiloh, a New Military Allegory in Six Acts" (Pittsburgh, 1870) by Comrade Samuel J. Muscroft. Neither Hays nor Muscroft mention a drummer boy by name. Various depositories other than Shiloh have files on the drummer boy of Shiloh.

[6] This account of Clem's service, except as otherwise indicated, is based on John L. Clem, "From Nursery to Battlefield," *Outlook* magazine, CVII (1914), 546-547. At one place in the article Clem states that it was to the 23rd Michigan Regiment that he attached himself as drummer, but this is obviously an error.

[7] Prints of this photograph are at the Chickamauga-Chattanooga National Military Park and Shiloh National Military Park.

[8] For details of Clem's career, other than those contained in his own article cited above, see Miller, *Photographic History of the Civil*

War, VIII, 192; *Who's Who in America,* 1912-1913 (Chicago, 1912), 400; Indianapolis *Star,* May 24, 1936 and May 15, 1937; A. S. Roe, *The Youth in the Rebellion* (Worcester, Mass., 1883), 10-11. I am indebted to Caroline Dunn of the William Henry Smith Memorial Library, Indiana Historical Society, for finding important information about Clem and other drummer boys.

[9] O. R., series 1, XVI, pt. 1, 1086.

[10] *Medals of Honor Issued by the War Department up to and Including October 31, 1897,* 66. See also O. R., series 1, XXXVIII, pt. 3, 192. Samuel Scoville in *Brave Deeds of Union Soldiers* (Philadelphia, 1910), 54, 63, tells of heroic deeds by Johnny McLaughlin and Eddie Lee at Shiloh and Wilson's Creek, respectively. But the tone of the account is not such as to create confidence in its reliability. A check of the records of Indiana and Iowa, states from which these boys were supposed to have entered the army, failed to reveal any trace of them or their careers. Moreover, the units to which they were said to have belonged did not take part in the actions with which their heroism allegedly was connected. For ten interesting letters by a young musician, see Don Russell, "Letters of a Drummer Boy," *Indiana Magazine of History,* XXXIV (1938), 324-339.

[11] O. R., series 3, I, 454 and II, 236, 612.

[12] Benjamin A. Gould, *Investigations in the Military and Anthropological Statistics of American Soldiers* (N. Y., 1869), 38. This volume, to be cited hereafter as Gould, *Anthropological Statistics,* was published by the United States Sanitary Commission in the series, "Sanitary Memoirs of the War of the Rebellion."

[13] The lists examined by the writer are in the manuscript Regimental Descriptive Books, Nat'l Archives. Selection was made in such a way as to obtain a sample representative of the three principal branches (infantry, cavalry and artillery), the various states, and organizations formed at different stages of the war. The lists include both original enlistees and recruits added throughout the war. This tabulation will be cited hereafter as Regimental Descriptive Lists. For an example of drummer boys graduating to the fighting ranks, other than that of Clem, see Charles E. Davis, *Three Years in the Army,* 110-111.

[14] G. L. Kilmer, "Boys in the Union Army," *Century Magazine,* LXX (1905), 269.

[15] Martha N. McLeod, editor, *Brother Warriors, The Reminiscences of Union and Confederate Veterans* (Washington, 1940), 47.

[16] Chauncey H. Cooke, *A Soldier Boy's Letters to his Father and Mother* (n.d., n.p., but 1912), 2. These letters were also published serially in the *Wisconsin Magazine of History,* IV (1920-1921), 75-100, 208-217, 322-344, 431-456, and V (1921-1922), 63-98.

[17] Miller, *Photographic History of the Civil War,* IX, 67.

[18] Portland, Maine, *Transcript,* Sept. 6, 1862.

[19] For a court-martial case involving desertion of a soldier who was younger than eighteen, see Hq. Army of the Potomac, G. O. 71, Feb. 21,

1861. McClellan approved discharge of the youth and issued a rebuke to recruiting officers who enlisted minors. *Ibid.*

[20] Urich N. Parmelee to his brother, April 4, 1864, and to his mother, Dec. 11, 1864, manuscripts, Duke.

[21] *O. R.*, series 1, XI, pt. 1, 896; Francis M. Field to his parents, Jan. 28, 1863, manuscript, Ohio State Arch. and Historical Society.

[22] Roe, *The Youth in the Rebellion*, 10-11; *O. R.*, series 1, X, pt. 1, 376 and XI, pt. 1, 896; *Medals of Honor Awarded by the War Department up to and Including October 31, 1897*, 56.

[23] Kilmer, "Boys in the Union Army," 271.

[24] Charles E. Goddard to his mother, especially letters of Dec. 2, 1861, Aug. 7, 1862, Sept. 28, 1862, and Dec. 4, 1863, manuscripts, Minn. Historical Society.

[25] Robert U. Johnson and Clarence C. Buel, editors, *Battles and Leaders of the Civil War* (N. Y., 1888), III, 624; Kilmer, "Boys in the Union Army," 275.

[26] *O. R.*, series 3, II, 236, 612; W.D.A.G.O. G. O. 104, Dec. 2, 1861.

[27] Gould, *Anthropological Statistics*, 34-35.

[28] *Ibid.*, 34.

[29] Regimental Descriptive Lists.

[30] Descriptive Book, 1st Mo. Inf. Regt., manuscript, Nat'l Archives.

[31] *A Memorial Record of the New York Branch of the U. S. Christian Commission* (N. Y., 1866), 56.

[32] Office of the Iowa Adjutant General, *Roster and Record of Iowa Soldiers* (Des Moines, 1911), V, 786, 788. I am indebted to Mildred Throne of the State Historical Society of Iowa for providing data concerning King. The oldest Confederate known to the writer was E. Pollard who enlisted in the 5th North Carolina Infantry at 73. See Bell Irvin Wiley, *The Life of Johnny Reb*, 332.

[33] W. W. Gist, "The Ages of Soldiers in the Civil War," *Iowa Journal of History and Politics*, XVI (1918), 396.

[34] Gould, *Anthropological Statistics*, 34; G. D. Kilmer, "Boys in the Union Army," *Century Magazine*, XII (1905), 269.

[35] Gould, *Anthropoligcal Statistics*, 34.

[36] *Ibid.*, 86-88.

[37] The degree of youthfulness has been grossly exaggerated on the basis of false statistics circulated in the early 1900s. As late as 1918 a religious periodical stated that the average age of Civil War soldiers at the end of the conflict was 19, and a G. A. R. speaker declared that the armies of the sixties contained a million soldiers who were under 16! W. W. Gist, "The Ages of Soldiers in the Civil War," *Iowa Journal of History and Politics*, XVI (1918), 387.

[38] Gould, *Anthropological Statistics*, 88.

[39] Regimental Descriptive Lists; Descriptive Book, 15th Ohio Infantry Regt. (Company A), manuscript, Nat'l Archives.

[40] Regimental Descriptive Lists.

[41] Detroit *Free Press*, May 31, 1861.

[42] Frank Moore, editor, *The Rebellion Record*, I (N. Y., 1861), 148-154, quoted in Henry S. Commager, editor, *The Blue and the Gray*, I, 86-87.

[43] Reid's manuscript diary is in the Ill. State Historical Library. The first quotation is from the entry of July 30, 1861.

[44] Samuel Storrow to his parents, May 12, 1863, manuscript, Mass. Historical Society.

[45] Thomas L. Livermore, *Days and Events*, 400-401.

[46] Edward L. Edes to his father, Feb. 20, 1863, manuscript, Mass. Historical Society; Urich N. Parmelee to his brother, Aug. 4, 1862; Leland O. Barlow to his sister, Sept. 4, 1863, manuscript, Conn. State Library.

[47] Mrs. J. D. Wheeler, compiler, *In Memoriam: Letters of William Wheeler of the Class of 1855 Y.C.*, 423.

[48] When after six months the case came to Lincoln's attention the sentence was remitted and the soldier restored to duty. J.A.G. Records NN 1844, manuscript, Nat'l Archives.

[49] Francis M. Field to his homefolk, Dec. 23, 1862.

[50] Regimental Descriptive Lists.

[51] As recently as a year ago an author whose history has a decided Southern slant asserted very positively in a meeting attended by the writer that "the majority of Yankee soldiers were foreign hirelings."

[52] Regimental Descriptive Books.

[53] Ella Lonn, *Foreigners in the Union Army and Navy* (Baton Rouge, 1951), 90-110, 146, 578, 663-672; Regimental Descriptive Books.

[54] Lonn, *Foreigners in the Union Army and Navy*, 44-56, 485-545, 648-651; letters of Adam Muenzenberger to his wife, typescript translation from the German, Wis. Historical Society; Rebecca R. Usher to her sister Ellen, March 31, 1865, typescript, Maine Historical Society; diary of Calvin Fletcher, Sept. 5, 1861, manuscript, Ind. Historical Society; Urich N. Parmelee to his mother, Jan. 26, 1863.

[55] *The Reminiscences of Carl Schurz* (N. Y., 1908), I, 25.

[56] Lonn, *Foreigners in the Union Army and Navy*, 116-126, 510-512, 578, 672-674.

[57] *Ibid.*, 645-648.

[58] Charles Ward to his brother, Oct. 2, 1862, manuscript, American Antiquarian Society.

[59] For a penetrating discussion of Irish fighting characteristics, see Lonn, *Foreigners in the Union Army and Navy*, 645-648.

[60] Thomas L. Livermore relates an amusing incident of an Irishman who, feeling the need of a spree, requested permission of his commanding officer to get drunk. *Days and Events*, 215.

[61] Lonn, *Foreigners in the Union Army and Navy*, 383 ff.

[62] Gould, *Anthropological Statistics*, 27; Lonn, *Foreigners in the Union Army and Navy*, 578-579.

[63] Gould, *op. cit.*, 27; Theodore C. Blegen, editor, *Civil War Letters of Colonel Hans C. Heg*, 21 et passim; Lonn, *Foreigners in the Union Army and Navy*, 131-132, 576-580, 674.

[64] Blegen, *op. cit.*, 25-26.

[65] The Knute Nelson manuscripts are in the Minn. Historical Society. The letters quoted are dated June 10, 1862, and Feb. 3, 1864. Revealing also as to Scandinavian characteristics and experience are the Hans Mattson letters in the Minn. Historical Society and a Miscellaneous Scandinavian Collection at Luther College, soldier items of which were translated for the writer by Inga B. Norstog.

[66] Regimental Descriptive Lists; Lonn, *Foreigners in the Union Army and Navy*, 674-675.

[67] Lonn, *Foreigners in the Union Army and Navy*, 155, 436-478.

[68] *Ibid.*, 162, 347-405.

[69] Wheeler, *In Memoriam: Letters of William Wheeler*, 305, 313, 316.

[70] Hq. Army of the Potomac, G. O. 38, 41, Feb. 1, 6, 1862; J.A.G. Records MM 672, manuscript, Nat'l Archives.

[71] Charles W. Wills, *Army Life of an Illinois Soldier*, 20.

[72] *O. R.*, series 3, V, 662. Some of the Negroes credited to the Northern states actually were recruited in the South. *Ibid.*

[73] *Ibid.*, 660-661; Joseph T. Wilson, *The Black Phalanx* (Hartford, Conn., 1891), 464-480. The artillery brigade of the 25th Corps was white.

[74] *O. R.*, series 1, XXVI, pt. 1, 689; Wilson, *Black Phalanx*, 195; R. B. Marcy, Report of an Inspection of the Dept. of Miss. and the Gulf, March—June, 1865. Item M-63, I.G.O. Letters Received, manuscripts, Nat'l Archives; Thomas W. Higginson to his wife, May 9, 1863, manuscript, Harvard.

[75] U. S. Christian Commission, Daily Record Book, entry by A. B. Peffers, Wild's Station, March 29, 1865, manuscript, Nat'l Archives.

[76] This summary of the Negroes' combat performance is based mainly on Bell Irvin Wiley, *Southern Negroes, 1861-1865*, 295-344 and on battle reports in the *Official Records*.

[77] W. C. Ford, editor, *War Letters, 1861-1865 of John C. Gray and John C. Ropes*, 184.

[78] Wiley, *Southern Negroes*, 313 ff.

[79] The inspection reports, filed in the I.G.O. Records, Nat'l Archives, of R. B. Marcy, D. B. Sackett and James A. Hardie, are especially valuable. Comments of officers that are particularly revealing, in addition to Higginson's, are those of Charles B. Fox (manuscripts, Mass. Historical Society), Henry Crydenwise (manuscripts, Duke and Emory), and Rufus Kinsley (manuscripts, Vt. Historical Society).

[80] Wiley, *Southern Negroes, 1861-1865*, 313 ff; Edward Whitaker to his sister, June 26, 1862, manuscript, Conn. State Library; Urich N. Parmelee to his brother, May 22, 1864.

[81] Diary of Lt. H. S. Adams, Sept. 16, 1863, manuscript, N. Y. Public Library.

[82] John W. De Forest, A *Volunteer's Adventures*, 26.

[83] *Ibid.*, 40.

[84] *O. R.*, series 1, XXX, pt. 3, 336.

[85] *Ibid.*, XXII, pt. 2, 56-58; R. B. Marcy, Report of an Inspection of the Dept. of Arkansas made in June and July 1864, I.G.O. Letters Received, Item M-69, manuscript, Nat'l Archives. For extensive accounts of the role of the red man in the Union Army, see Annie Heloise Abel, *The American Indian as Participant in the Civil War* (Cleveland, 1919), and Wiley Britton, *The Union Indian Brigade in the Civil War* (Kansas City, 1922).

[86] Muster-out Rolls, Co. C, Second Indian Regt. and Co. B, Third Indian Regt., manuscripts (photostats), Okla. Historical Society. Originals of these rolls are in the Nat'l Archives; Record Book of Co. A (clothing account), Third Indian Regiment, manuscript, Okla. Historical Society.

[87] Descriptive Book, Co. F, Third Indian Regt., manuscript, Okla. Historical Society.

[88] Capt. J. H. Greene, *Reminiscences of the War*, 54.

[89] Wiley Britton, "Union and Confederate Indians in the Civil War," in *Battles and Leaders of the Civil War* I, 335.

[90] O. R., series 1, XIII, 894 and XXII, pt. 1, 447-462; Wiley, *The Life of Johnny Reb*, 326. An Arkansas pioneer in 1937 told of seeing Union Cherokee soldiers scalp Rebel opponents after a Civil War engagement in the Indian country. W.P.A. "Indian Pioneer History," XII, 390, interview of James Robert Barnes, bound typescript, Foreman Collection, Okla. Historical Society.

[91] O. R., series 1, XXII, pt. 2, 56-58 and XXXIV, pt. 2, 754-755. James Hardie, Extracts from Inspection Reports, District of the Frontier, for June 1864, Department of the Army Records, Document File, manuscript, Nat'l Archives.

[92] O. R., series 1, XXII, pt. 1, 94.

[93] *Ibid.*, 314-315, 337-338, 378-382, 447-456; pt. 2, 56-58, 371, 465; XXXIV, pt. 2, 754-755; R. B. Marcy, Report of an Inspection of the Dept. of Arkansas Made in June and July, 1864.

[94] O. R., series 1, XXII, pt. 2, 283-284; James Hardie, Extracts from Inspection Reports, District of the Frontier for June, 1864; R. B. Marcy, Report, Aug. 15, 1864, of a Special Inspection of the Dept. of Arkansas, I.G.O. Letters Received, item M-64, manuscript, Nat'l Archives. For a dramatic account of Cherokee participation and suffering in the Civil War, and of pillage of loyal Indians by Union soldiers, see T. W. Wright, Attorney for Cherokees, to Col. Garrett, Commanding Officer, Fort Gibson [July 31, 1865], manuscript, Indian Archives, Okla. Historical Society.

[95] Branches represented in the Union Army included infantry, cavalry, artillery, engineers, signal corps, adjutant general's department, medical service, ordnance, quartermaster, subsistence and finance; M. J. O'Brien, translator, *The American Army in the War of Secession*, by General DeChanal (Leavenworth, Kan., 1894), 5.

[96] Frederick Phisterer, *Statistical Record of the Armies of the United States* (Supplementary Volume, *Campaigns of the Civil War*, N. Y., 1883), 22-23.

[97] *Ibid.*, 11; James G. Randall, *Civil War and Reconstruction* (N. Y., 1937), 266, 411. For a full discussion of substitution see Fred A. Shannon, *Organization and Administration of the Union Army*, II, 49-99.

[98] W.D.A.G.O. G. O. 110, April 29, 1863; O. R., series 3, I, 153 and II, 518-520; Silas Casey, *Infantry Tactics*, I, 11; Phisterer, *Statistical Record*, 55.

[99] See chapter II.

[100] O. R., series 1, XXV, pt. 2, 152; for colored illustrations of corps badges, see *Atlas to Accompany O. R.*, plate 175, and Billings, *Hard Tack and Coffee*, 250-268.

[101] O. R., series 3, II, 518-520; W.D.A.G.O. G. O. 110, April 29, 1863.

[102] Thomas L. Livermore, *Numbers and Losses during the Civil War* (Boston, 1900), 68.

[103] Matthew Marvin to his brother, Dec. 24, 1862, manuscript, Minn. Historical Society; E. A. Johnson, editor, *The Hero of Medfield*, 72.

[104] For examples of interregimental brawls, see Enoch T. Baker to his wife, Nov. 18, 1861, manuscript, Historical Society of Pa.; Lawrence Van Alstyne, *Diary of an Enlisted Man*, 85; Leland O. Barlow to his sister, Feb. 1, 1863.

[105] Van Alstyne, *Diary of an Enlisted Man*, 169.

[106] Wills, *Army Life of an Illinois Soldier*, 218; Frank E. Lansing to his mother, Feb. 13, 1864, manuscript, Detroit Public Library.

[107] "The Fourteenth Indiana in the Valley of Virginia," *Indiana Magazine of History*, XXX (1934), 293.

[108] Wills, *Army Life of an Illinois Soldier*, 144.

[109] Willis D. Maier to Annie F. Howells, July 20, 1863 and Dec. 15, 1863, manuscript, Hayes Memorial Library.

[110] Ransom Bedell to his cousin, Aug. 24, 1864, manuscript, Ill. State Historical Library.

[111] Alonzo Miller to his sister, May 21, 1865, typescript, Kennesaw Mountain National Park.

[112] William Benjamin Johnson, *Union to the Hub and Twice Around the Tire: Reminiscences of William Benjamin Johnson* (n.d., n.p., but privately printed, 1950), 108; excerpts from the diary of Osborn H. Oldroyd, June 13, 1863, typescript, Vicksburg National Park; diary of Charles W. Wills, May 1, 1864, manuscript, Illinois State Historical Library.

[113] Wills, *Army Life of an Illinois Soldier*, 218. Wills stated that the Westerners were usually the aggressors in the oral jousts.

[114] Henry P. Whipple, *The Diary of a Private Soldier*, 27.

[115] Capt. Charles H. Salter to Mrs. I. G. Duffield, June 12, 1864, manuscript, Detroit Public Library.

[116] Thomas H. Parker, *History of the 51st Regiment Pennsylvania Vols.*, 362.

[117] Willis D. Maier to Annie F. Howells, June 19, 1863.

[118] Abraham Kendig to his homefolk, March 29, 1862.

[119] Lt. Roswell Farnham to "Friend Harding," June 3, 1861, typescript, Vt. Historical Society.

¹²⁰ *Statistics, Medical and Anthropological of the Provost Marshal General's Bureau* (Washington, 1875), I, 29.

¹²¹ Nashville *Dispatch*, Nov. 27, 1864.

¹²² R. G. Carter, *Four Brothers in Blue.*

¹²³ For one of many tributes to the Regulars' combat performance, see O. R., series 3, III, 1110.

¹²⁴ Frank E. Lansing to his mother, Nov. 13, 1863; William F. Goodhue to his parents, March 13, 1863, manuscript, Ill. State Historical Library.

¹²⁵ Diary of John Merrilies, May 8, 1864, manuscript, Chicago Historical Society.

¹²⁶ Davis, *Three Years in the Army,* 191-192.

¹²⁷ Diary of Philip Smith, Oct. 22, 1863, bound volume of articles from Peoria *Evening Star,* 1917, in the Veterans' Records Division of the Nat'l Archives.

¹²⁸ Diary of Charles W. Wills, Feb. 1, 1865.

¹²⁹ Hazel C. Wolf, editor, *Campaigning with the First Minnesota,* 229-230.

¹³⁰ Diary of an unidentified soldier of Co. B, 24th Conn. Regt., Jan. 27, 1863, manuscript, Conn. State Library.

¹³¹ Davis, *Three Years in the Army,* 183-184; Charles Ward to his parents, n.d., n.p., but near Falmouth, Va., April, 1863; Capt. Charles Barnard to his wife, Sept. 25, 1862, manuscript, Maine Historical Society; John D. Billings, *Hard Tack and Coffee,* 95 ff.

¹³² John Beatty, *The Citizen Soldier,* 40.

¹³³ Billings, *Hard Tack and Coffee,* 101.

¹³⁴ Lt. Henry A. Buck to his sister, April 1, 1863, manuscript, Detroit Public Library.

¹³⁵ Eli R. Pickett to his wife, Dec. 29, 1862, manuscript, Minn. Historical Society.

¹³⁶ Henry M. Crydenwise to his parents, Dec. 18, 1861, manuscript, Duke.

¹³⁷ Charles Tillison to his homefolk, Oct. 22, 1862, manuscript, Vt. Historical Society.

¹³⁸ *Ibid.,* various home letters in the winter of 1862-1863; T. J. Tillison to Dudley Tillison, May 15, 1863.

¹³⁹ Charles Tillison to Dudley Tillison, Feb. 21, 24, 1864.

¹⁴⁰ W. J. Jackson to Dudley Tillison, June 4, 1863; Dudley Tillison to Charles Tillison, Dec. 25, 1863; Vermont Adjutant General's Office, *Revised Roster of Vermont Volunteers* (Montpelier, 1892), 49.

¹⁴¹ A. S. Roe, *The Ninth New York Heavy Artillery,* 274; Joseph H. Diltz to his wife, Nov. 24, 1862, manuscript, Duke.

¹⁴² Diary of Walter F. Kittredge for 1862, especially entries of Oct. 29, 31, Nov. 2, 8, 14, 19, 20, 27, Dec. 3, 12, manuscript in possession of Robert B. Holtman, La. State Univ.

¹⁴³ *Ibid.,* entries for Jan. and Feb. 1863.

¹⁴⁴ For a full description of the bummer type, see George Sharland, *Knapsack Notes,* 46-47.

[145] Joseph H. Diltz to his wife, Jan. 24, 1862 and Aug. 10, 1863.

[146] Mary Diltz to Joseph Diltz, May 3, 1863.

[147] Thomas L. Pankey to his wife, July 18, 1863, manuscript, Ill. State Historical Library.

[148] *Med. and Surg. Hist.*, Surgical Volume, pt. 3, 641.

[149] Billings, *Hard Tack and Coffee*, 67.

[150] Edward L. Edes to his uncle, Feb. 10, 1863; Urich N. Parmelee to his mother, June 25, 1862.

[151] Billings, *Hard Tack and Coffee*, 105.

[152] *Ibid.*, 91-95.

[153] Davis, *Three Years in the Army*, 177-178.

[154] Alonzo Miller to his homefolk, April 22, April 27, July 9, 1864.

[155] O. W. Norton, *Army Letters, 1861-1865*, 75-76.

[156] "Letters of Privates Cook and Ball," *Indiana Magazine of History*, XXVII (1931), 256.

[157] Urich N. Parmelee to his mother, Nov. 20, 1862. For a brief history of another interesting soldier of fortune, killed at Antietam, see diary of Thomas Francis Galwey, Sept. 17, 1862, typescript in possession of Col. Geoffrey Galwey, Washington, D. C.

[158] George F. Newhall to his father, March 28, 1862, manuscript, Boston Public Library.

[159] *Ibid.*, April 22, 1862.

[160] *Ibid.*, May 20, June 21, 1862.

[161] *Ibid.*, July 4, 1862; James D. Newhall to his parents, Nov. 5, 1862, manuscript, Boston Public Library.

[162] Day Elmore to his parents, Sept. 29, 1862, manuscript in possession of Mrs. Hall Mosher, Memphis, to whom grateful acknowledgment is made for the use of these letters. In preparing this sketch of Elmore's war service, I have drawn on an unidentifiable newspaper obituary and several official documents filed with the letters.

[163] *Ibid.*, Feb. 3, 1864.

[164] Mrs. William Hume Harris, Franklin, Tenn., to Daniel Elmore, Dec. 14, 1862, manuscript among Day Elmore letters.

[165] Capt. Horace Hittenden to Daniel Elmore, Dec. 8, 1864, manuscript among Day Elmore letters.

[166] Miller, *Photographic History of the Civil War*, VIII, 273; file no. 184934Y-1, "Women Who Served in Wars of the United States," Record and Pension Branch, A.G.O. Records, Nat'l Archives; file 132D, A.G.O. Records, "Remarkable Cases and Names," Nat'l Archives; Adjutant General, U. S. Army to John Hix, June 27, 1932, A.G.O. file AG291.9 (6-17-32) ORD; George W. Driggs, *Opening of the Mississippi*, 95.

[167] File W3370, 1864, Record and Pension Branch, A.G.O., Nat'l Archives.

[168] "Women Who Served in Wars of the United States"; Office of Adjutant General of Michigan, *Record of Service of Michigan Volunteers in the Civil War, 1861-1865* (Kalamazoo, 1902), II, 170; diary of William Boston, April 22, 1863, typescript, Univ. of Mich.

169 Pension file of Albert D. J. Cashier (certificate no. 1,001,132), manuscripts, Veterans Administration's Records, Nat'l Archives.

170 *Ibid.*

171 For example see Nashville *Dispatch*, Aug. 29, 1862, and Henry C. Bear to his wife, Dec. 7-14, 1862, manuscript in possession of Mrs. Stanley B. Hadden, Urbana, Illinois.

172 Memphis *Bulletin*, Dec. 19, 1862.

173 Livermore, *Days and Events*, 146.

174 New York *Tribune*, Feb. 20, 1864, quoting Detroit *Advertiser*; William F. Fox, *Regimental Losses in the Civil War* (Albany, N. Y., 1889), 60.

175 Fanny J. Anderson, editor, "The Shelley Papers," *Indiana Magazine of History*, XLIV (1948), 186.

176 Wills, *Army Life of an Illinois Soldier*, 218.

177 William R. Hartpence, *History of the Fifty-first Indiana Veteran Volunteer Infantry*, 68-69.

178 "The Fourteenth Indiana in the Valley of Virginia," *Indiana Magazine of History*, XXX (1934), 293.

179 Wills, *Army Life of an Illinois Soldier*, 233.

180 *Ibid.*; Donald Gordon, editor, *M. L. Gordon's Experiences in the Civil War*, 34; Beatty, *op. cit.*, 231-232; Thomas L. Livermore, "The Northern Volunteers," *Granite Monthly*, X (1887), 247; Hartpence, *History of the Fifty-first Indiana Veteran Volunteer Infantry*, 208; see Oscar O. Winther, editor, *With Sherman to the Sea*, 115.

181 For a sketch of the interior of a soldier's hut, showing pin-up girls on wall, see diary of Thomas Francis Galwey.

182 [Samuel Fiske], *Mr. Dunn Brown's Experiences in the Army* (Boston, 1866), 50-51.

183 C. A. Stevens, *Berdan's United States Sharpshooters in the Army of the Potomac, 1861-1865* (St. Paul, Minn., 1892), *passim*; Fox, *Regimental Losses in the Civil War*, 418-419; Wesley Bradshaw (pseud. for Charles W. Alexander), *The Volunteer's Roll of Honor* (Philadelphia, 1863), 40-42.

184 O. R., series 1, XX, pt. 1, 197-198.

185 See chapter II; Fox, *Regimental Losses in the Civil War*, 503, 507.

186 O. R., series 3, III, 999, 1002, 1052, 1131-1132.

187 A broadside copy of the song is in the Ezra E. Rickett Collection, Ohio State Arch. and Historical Society. The composer was Matt Gebler and the printer J. H. Johnson of Philadelphia.

188 O. R., series 3, III, 1132, IV, 188.

189 *Ibid.*, III, 414-416, 997-999, V, 650.

190 Hartpence, *History of the Fifty-first Indiana Veteran Volunteer Infantry*, 201.

191 O. R., series 3, IV, 930, 1214, V, 651; Livermore, *Numbers and Losses in the Civil War in America*, 1.

192 For a discussion of substitutes, bounty jumpers and other evils attendant on raising and maintaining the Union forces, see Fred A.

Shannon, *Organization and Administration of the Union Army*, especially II, 54 ff.

[193] Davis, *Three Years in the Army*, 263-264.

[194] Lt. Col. Charles B. Fox to his wife, June 25, 1864.

[195] Maj. George Blagden, Report of a Special Inspection of the Recruiting Service at Pottsville, Pa., May 9, 1864, I.G.O. Letters Received, manuscripts, Nat'l Archives.

Chapter XIII

BILLY YANK AND JOHNNY REB

[1] John C. Arnold to his wife, Aug. 7, 1864, typescript, National War College.

[2] Henry Wilson to Jeremiah Norris, Dec. 29, 1861, manuscript, Duke.

[3] Lydia Minturn Post, editor, *Soldiers' Letters*, 468-469.

[4] Detroit *Free Press*, June 28, 1861.

[5] Edward Whitaker to his sister, July 19, 1861, manuscript, Conn. State Library; Samuel W. Croft to his sister, July 26, 1861, typescript, Washington and Jefferson College.

[6] Edward E. Newhall to his homefolk, March 12, 1862, manuscript, Boston Public Library; Charles E. Goddard to his mother, Nov. 13, 1863, manuscript, Minn. Historical Society; Charles W. Wills, *Army Life of an Illinois Soldier*, 60-61.

[7] Portland, Maine, *Transcript*, June 7, 1862.

[8] Frederick C. Dickinson to "Dear George," Nov. 2, 1861, manuscript, American Antiquarian Society.

[9] Felix Brannigan to his sister, June 17, 1862, typescript, Library of Congress.

[10] Diary of Jenkins Lloyd Jones, July 8, 1863, manuscript, Wis. Historical Society.

[11] Lt. L. Muller to his cousin, Oct. 14, 1861, typescript translation from the German original, Minn. Historical Society; Maj. B. F. Buckner to Helen Martin, April 18, 1862, manuscript, Univ. of Ky.

[12] Diary of Jacob E. Hyneman, Oct. 31, 1864, typescript in possession of Charles N. Owen, Chicago; Cyrus R. Stone to his homefolk, Dec. 11, 1861, manuscript, Minn. Historical Society.

[13] John Herr to his mother, Oct. 5, 1862, manuscript, Duke.

[14] Unidentified Indiana soldier to his sister, Sept. 26, 1862, manuscript, Ransom T. Young Papers, Ind. State Library.

[15] Joseph H. Diltz to his wife, March 13, 1862, manuscript, Duke.

[16] Cyrus R. Stone to his parents, June 7, 1862.

[17] Charles Ward to his sister, May 23, 1863, manuscript, American Antiquarian Society.

[18] Daniel E. Burbank to his brother [July 21], 1861, manuscript, American Antiquarian Society.

[19] Diary of William D. Evans, July 29, 1864, manuscript, Western Reserve Historical Society; Edward L. Edes to his sister, May 10, 1863, manuscript, Mass. Historical Society; Charles K. Bailer to his sister, May 20, 1864, typescript, Western Reserve Historical Society.

[20] F. M. Abbott to his father, April 10, 1862, manuscript, Harvard; Felix William Worthington to his father, Sept. 11, 1861, manuscript in private possession.

[21] Felix Brannigan to his sister, undated fragment, but written shortly after Gettysburg.

[22] Henry C. Bear to his wife, Dec. 14, 1862, Jan. 4, Jan. 13, April 14, 1863, manuscripts in possession of Mrs. Stanley B. Hadden, Urbana, Ill.

[23] Urich N. Parmelee to his brother, May 21, 1863, manuscript, Duke.

[24] Lawrence Van Alstyne, *Diary of an Enlisted Man*, 146-147.

[25] John P. Sheahan to his father, April 8, 1863, manuscript, Maine Historical Society.

[26] Diary of Charles W. Wills, Nov. 22, 1864, manuscript, Ill. State Historical Library.

[27] Martin Haynes, *History of the Second Regiment New Hampshire Volunteers* (Manchester, N. H., 1865), 124.

[28] M. Ebenezer Wescott, *Civil War Letters* (n. p., 1909), 14; diary of Maurice K. Simons, May 25, 1863, manuscript, Univ. of Texas.

[29] Diary of Francis Galwey, Dec. 1, 1863, typescript in possession of Col. Geoffrey Galwey, Washington, D. C.

[30] A. S. Neal to his father, May 15, 1864, typescript, Ga. Archives.

[31] Charles E. Davis, *Three Years in the Army*, 289.

[32] John P. Sheahan to his parents, Feb. 18, 1863; Bell Irvin Wiley, *The Life of Johnny Reb*, 321.

[33] Wiley, *The Life of Johnny Reb*, 321.

[34] Chattanooga *Daily Gazette*, March 6, 1864.

[35] Oscar O. Winther, editor, *With Sherman to the Sea*, 116-117; Wiley, *The Life of Johnny Reb*, 317.

[36] M. S. Schroyer, "Company 'G' History," Snyder County Historical Society *Bulletin*, II (1939), 107.

[37] Hazel C. Wolf, editor, *Campaigning with the First Minnesota*, 251.

[38] Portland, Maine, *Transcript*, June 13, 1863.

[39] Diary of Capt. James Biddle, Aug. 13, 1864, typescript, Detroit Public Library.

[40] Benjamin Borton, *A While with the Blue: Memories of War Days* (Passaic, N. J., 1898), 76-77.

[41] A. S. Roe, *The Ninth New York Heavy Artillery*, 216.

[42] For examples, see Richard Puffer to his sister, May 28, 1863, and diary of John Merrilies, May 25, 1863, manuscripts, Chicago Historical Society; *Publications of the Mississippi Historical Society*, Centenary Edition, V (Jackson, Miss., 1925), 273.

[43] H. A. Nelson to "Good Friend Harway," June 20, 1863, manuscript, Luther College Library. I am indebted to Inga B. Norstog for translating this item from the Norwegian.

[44] Diary of Ezra G. Huntley, March 20, 1865, manuscript, Dartmouth.

[45] "Letters of a Badger Boy in Blue," *Wisconsin Magazine of History*, V, 81-82.

[46] Day Elmore to his parents, July 2, 1864, manuscript in possession of Mrs. Hall Mosher, Memphis.

[47] George G. Agassiz, editor, *Meade's Headquarters, 1863-1865: Letters of Colonel Theodore Lyman from the Wilderness to Appomattox* (Boston, 1922), 106.

[48] Mrs. J. D. Wheeler, compiler, *In Memoriam: Letters of William Wheeler of the Class of 1855, Y.C.*, 414.

[49] Portland, Maine, *Transcript*, Jan. 23, 1864.

[50] Frank E. Smith, "The Polite War," *Coronet*, III (1937), 44-46. For an instance of a Confederate killing a Yankee brother at Fredericksburg and his shock on discovering the identity of the man he had slain, see Nashville *Daily Union*, April 7, 1863. *Grant's Petersburg Progress*, April 7, 1865, reported the case of a Yankee lieutenant capturing his Rebel father in one of the final actions near Petersburg.

[51] *O. R.*, series 1, XXXVI, pt. 1, 345, 366-367; James Ford Rhodes, *History of the United States from the Compromise of 1850*, IV, 446. The entire action lasted about an hour, but the assault phase in which most of the casualties were suffered was completed in about twenty minutes.

[52] *Century Magazine*, LIII (1897), 720. Yanks ordered to make a desperate assault at Mine Run in November 1863 were also said to have pinned their names on their uniforms to facilitate identification. See G. Albert Monroe, "Reminiscences of the War of the Rebellion," Rhode Island Soldiers and Sailors Historical Society *Personal Narratives*, 2nd Series, No. 11 (Providence, 1881), 42-43.

BIBLIOGRAPHICAL NOTES

The quantity of material on soldier life in the Union Army is so enormous as to make impractical a listing of all the items used in the preparation of this work. The following brief note is intended as a general guide to the principal types of sources, with emphasis on relevancy to soldier life. Full information on specific references will be found in the footnotes; for the convenience of the reader location of each manuscript is given the first time it is cited in every chapter.

MANUSCRIPTS

The most revealing and interesting of the manuscripts are the letters of the rank and file. Extant letters of Union soldiers greatly outnumber those on the Confederate side, owing to the larger size of the Federal army, the North's higher rate of literacy and the greater effectiveness of Billy Yanks and their descendants in collecting and preserving war correspondence. The most extensive letter collections are those at Duke University, the Western Reserve Historical Society, the University of Michigan, the Wisconsin Historical Society, the Minnesota Historical Society, the Illinois State Historical Library and the Indiana State Library and Historical Society. Smaller, but still highly rewarding, are the holdings of the Maine Historical Society, the Vermont Historical Society, the Baker Library of Dartmouth College, the Boston Public Library, the Essex Institute, the American Antiquarian Society, the Connecticut Historical Society, the Connecticut State Library, the New York Historical Society, the New York Public Library, the Historical Society of Pennsylvania, the Burton Collection of the Detroit Public Library, the Hayes Memorial Library, the Ohio State Archaeological and Historical Society, the Chicago Historical Society and the Library of Congress.

Some valuable nuggets were found in the Massachusetts Historical Society, but soldier materials at this depository could not be fully exploited because of the name system of filing and the lack of a descriptive guide. A number of the National Military Parks have acquired respectable collections of manuscripts and these were generously made available to the writer by the National Park Service.

Several hundred unpublished diaries were read, but since many diarists wrote with one eye on posterity, these sources are generally not so revealing as letters composed in the spirit of the moment with little or no thought of their being read by anyone except the recipients. A few diaries are so exceptional in their tone and content, however, as to merit special mention. Those of Florison D. Pitts and John Merrilies in the Chicago Historical Society are frank, sprightly accounts of service in Western commands of two gay young artillerymen from Chicago. That of Charles W. Wills, in the Illinois State Library, is an excellent source.

This account was printed, along with other journals, in *Reminiscences of the Civil War from Diaries of Members of the 103rd Illinois Infantry* (Chicago, 1904) and again, with letters added, as a separate volume under the title *Army Life of an Illinois Soldier* (Washington, 1906); but the sister of Wills who prepared the work for publication in its latter form deleted some of the most revealing passages. Sergeant Matthew Marvin's diary, in the Minnesota Historical Society, throws valuable light on many phases of soldier life in the Army of the Potomac. The diary in the Western Reserve Historical Society of another sergeant, M. F. Roberts, records interesting details of Sherman's march through Georgia and the Carolinas. The journal of Stephen Gordon, the original of which is in the Fredericksburg National Military Park, and a copy of which was generously placed at my disposal by Fred L. Williams, Jr., of Atlanta, is of outstanding value for the detailed information it gives about food and commissary operations on the Virginia front. In the main library of the University of Michigan is a diary which startles by its very appearance, for this journal, kept by Henry A. Buck, was completely penetrated by a bullet on December 31, 1862, at Stone's River. A note by Buck bearing the date of January 1, 1863, states: "The faithful record saved my life."

Other manuscript records used in large quantity included regimental descriptive books, courts-martial proceedings, inspection reports, and United States Christian Commission papers. By far the richest collections of these materials are those in the National Archives. The courts-martial proceedings, which exist in formidable quantity, proved to be especially valuable social documents.

PRINTED CORRESPONDENCE AND DIARIES: BOOKS

Officers are better represented in this category of sources than are the men of the ranks, but even so a considerable quantity of soldier letters and diaries has been published in book form. One of the most interesting is *A Little Fifer's War Diary* by C. W. Bardeen (Syracuse, 1910) which, contrary to many works of this type, records the evil as well as the good of camp life. Excellent also is Robert Goldthwaite Carter, compiler, *Four Brothers in Blue, or Sunshine and Shadows of the War of the Rebellion* (Washington, 1913) which consists largely of the home letters of four Massachusetts soldiers who served in the Army of the Potomac. *The Civil War Diary of James T. Ayers* edited by John Hope Franklin (Springfield, Ill., 1947) is a pungent, forthright and extremely readable account of an unpolished Yank who recruited Negroes in Alabama. *The Hero of Medfield: Containing the Journals and Letters of Allen Alonzo Kingsbury* edited by E. A. Johnson (Boston, 1862), while covering a relatively brief period, is an interesting, informative, undoctored account of a bugler's service in Virginia during the early part of the conflict. One of the very best of all the published journals is Jenkins Lloyd Jones, *An Artilleryman's Diary* (Madison, Wis., 1914). O. W. Norton's *Army Letters, 1861-1865* (Chicago, 1903), while bearing the earmarks of prepublication polishing, is a superior record of one who served as a private in the Army of the Potomac until November 1863, when he became a lieutenant of colored troops. More readable than Norton's letters and excellent in every respect are the *Civil War Letters of Sgt. Onley Andrus*, edited by Fred Albert Shannon (Urbana, 1947). Most of Andrus' service was in Tennessee, Mississippi and Louisiana. Lawrence Van Alstyne's *Diary of an Enlisted Man* (New Haven, 1910) gets off to a slow start but the author's style, like that of some other diarists, improves with practice and the end product of his efforts is an absorbing book. The account is a memoir rather than a diary for the period after June 15, 1864. Mrs. J. D. Wheeler, compiler, *In Memoriam: Letters of William Wheeler of the Class of 1865, Y[ale] C[ollege]* (Cambridge, Mass., 1875) is an unusually fine collection of letters written by a graduate of Yale who served three months as an infantry private in 1861, then became an artillery officer and died from a sharpshooter's bullet before Atlanta in June 1864. Another Yank killed during the conflict (at Gettysburg) who left a full and frank record of his service was Isaac Lyman Taylor whose diary, edited by Hazel C. Wolf, was printed first as a series of articles in *Minnesota History*, volume 25, and then in book form under the title *Campaigning with the First Minnesota* (St. Paul, 1944). Perhaps the most readable of all the common-soldier journals is that of the young Hoosier Theodore F. Upson, edited by Oscar O. Winther under the title *With Sherman to the Sea* (Baton Rouge, 1943). This work, however, is not strictly a journal, but rather a postwar adaptation by Upson of letters and diaries written during the conflict.

Some of the published papers of officers give exceedingly valuable information about the life of the men. Especially outstanding in this respect, and thoroughly fascinating in general, are the letters and journal of John William De Forest, edited by James H. Croushore under the title *A Volunteer's Adventures, A Union Captain's Record of the Civil War* (New Haven, 1946). Other outstanding letter or diary accounts of officers issued in book form include: Willoughby M. Babcock, Jr., *Selections from the Letters and Diaries of Brevet-Brigadier General Willoughby Babcock of the Seventy-fifth New York Volunteers: A Study of Camp Life in the Union Armies during the Civil War* (Albany, 1922); Theodore C. Blegen, editor, *The Civil War Letters of Colonel Hans Christian Heg* (Northfield, Minn., 1936); W. C. Fotd, editor, *War Letters, 1862-1865 of John Chipman Gray and John Codman Ropes* (Boston, 1927); J. H. Greene, *Reminiscences of the War. Bivouacs, Marches, Skirmishes, and Battles. Extracts from Letters Written Home from 1861 to 1865* (Medina, Ohio, 1886); Mark De Wolfe Howe, editor, *Touched with Fire, Civil War Letters and Diary of Oliver Wendell Holmes, Jr., 1861-1864*; and W. C. Lusk, editor, *War Letters of William Thompson Lusk* (New York, 1911).

PRINTED CORRESPONDENCE AND DIARIES: PERIODICALS

Some excellent letter and diary accounts by common soldiers have appeared in the journals and occasional publications of state historical societies. The files of the *Indiana Magazine of History* are especially rich in this type of material. John D. Barnhart, editor, "A Hoosier Invades the Confederacy: Letters and Diaries of Leroy S. Mayfield," *Indiana Magazine of History*, XXXIX (1943), 144-191, traces the career of a young Hoosier who served both as a private and a junior officer under Sherman. "The Shelley Letters," edited by Fanny J. Anderson, *Indiana Magazine of History*, XLIV (1948), 181-198, relate the experiences of a German native who went to war as a substitute and who was stationed in Tennessee during most of his service. Max Hedrick Guyer, editor, "Journal and Letters of Corporal William O. Gulick" and Ruth A. Gallaher, editor, "Peter Wilson in the Civil War," in the *Iowa Journal of History and Politics*, XXVIII (1930), 194-268, 390-456, 534-604 and XL (1942), 153-204, 261-321, 339-415, are full and interesting reports of Iowa soldiers, one a cavalryman and the other a foot soldier, who fought in Western commands. Unusual, though disappointingly few, are the "Edgar Dinsmore Letters" written by a Negro soldier of the Fifty-fourth Massachusetts Regiment and edited by Richard B. Harwell for the *Journal of Negro History*, XXV (1940), 363-371. The best collection of soldier correspondence published in any of the historical journals is "A Badger Boy in Blue: The Letters of Chauncey H. Cooke" in the *Wisconsin Magazine of History*, IV (1920-1921) and V (1921-1922). Cooke was a Wisconsin farm boy who served first against the Indians in Minnesota and then with Grant and Sherman in Mississippi, Tennessee and Georgia. Before their appearance in the *Wisconsin Magazine of History* these letters were published in a newspaper and then in book form under the title *Soldier Boy's Letters to his Father and Mother* (Independence, Wis., 1915).

Among the better officer collections appearing in historical society publications are: "The Civil War Letters of Major James Zearing, M.D. 1861-1865" and "Major Connolly's Diary and Letters to his Wife, 1862-1865" in the Illinois State Historical Society *Transactions* for 1921 and 1928 respectively (Springfield, 1922 and 1928); Fritz Haskell, editor, "Diary of Colonel William Camm in the *Journal* of the Illinois State Historical Society, XVIII (1926), 793-980; and Willie D. Halsell, editor, "The Sixteenth Indiana Regiment in the Last Vicksburg Campaign," *Indiana Magazine of History*, XLIII (1947), 67-82. The letters of "Prock" (William Landon) published in volumes 29, 30, 33 and 34 of the *Indiana Magazine of History* are interesting communications of a Hoosier who served as an enlisted man and an officer in the Army of the Potomac.

PRINTED MEMOIRS

In the years following Appomattox hundreds of Yanks wrote memoirs of their war experiences and hopefully issued them as books or pamphlets. The total output fills several shelves of the Library of Congress. The quality of these accounts varies greatly and all have to be used with care. In this work, as in *The Life of Johnny Reb*, I have followed the policy of accepting only those reminiscent items which accorded with records of a more substantial character. In my judgment the best memoir by an enlisted participant on either side is Leander Stillwell's *The Story of a Common Soldier of Army Life in the Civil War, 1861-1865* (second edition, Erie, Kansas, 1920). The author, an Illinoisan of humble background, enlisted in January 1862 at eighteen and served for nearly four years, mainly in Mississippi and Tennessee. This account, based largely on wartime diaries and letters, was begun with a view of informing young Jeremiah Stillwell of his father's soldier experience. As the writing progressed a larger audience was envisioned, but the narrative retained the simple, straightforward quality of a story told by a parent of "what I saw and did during the war." Another superb memoir is *Hard Tack and Coffee, or the Unwritten Story of Army Life* by John D. Billings (Boston, 1888). Billings' work is in essence a depiction of soldier life in the Army of the Potomac built around his personal experience and observations as an artilleryman. It is rich in humor, franker than most reminiscences and has the flavor of authenticity. Its value is greatly enhanced by more than 200 realistic illustrations from the gifted pen of Charles W. Reed, many of which were sketched during the artist's service with the Ninth Massachusetts Battery. Frank Wilkeson's *Recollections of a Private Soldier in the Army of the Potomac* (New York, 1887) is the account of another artilleryman who served in the East, but he did not enter the army until the third winter of the war and most of his service was as an officer. The narrative is readable but the author seems a bit reckless in the use of quotation and anecdote. Certainly the book is not in the same class with that of Stillwell or Billings. Warren Lee Goss's *Recollections of a Private: A Story of the Army of the Potomac* (New York, 1890) is apparently more a secondary account than of Goss's own experiences. The author, like some other professional writers who reported the conflict, is overly free with the use of the first person and seems more interested in telling a good story than an authentic one.

A better than average memoir, though restricted in scope, is John A. Cockerill, "A Boy at Shiloh," published by the Ohio Commandery of the Military Order of the Loyal Legion of the United States in its *Sketches of the War*, VI (1908), 14-34. In general the publications of the various components of the Loyal Legion were less rewarding for my purposes than were *Personal Narratives of the Rhode Island Soldiers' and Sailors' Historical Society* (six series in six volumes, Providence, 1878-1905). Both were disappointing but the same may be said of memoir literature in general. Striking exceptions to the general rule, in addition to the narratives of Stillwell and Billings, are three officer accounts of outstanding merit. Thomas L. Livermore, *Days and Events, 1860-1866* (Boston, 1920) is a fascinating memoir written soon after the conflict by an interesting participant who enlisted as a private at seventeen but whose ability pushed him upward so rapidly that he was a colonel before his twenty-second birthday. He wrote frankly, accurately and attractively of many phases of his experience in the Army of the Potomac. John Beatty's *The Citizen Soldier; or Memoirs of a Volunteer,* (Cincinnati, 1879) is an equally admirable record of service in Kentucky and Tennessee of an Ohio banker who rose to the command of a brigade before leaving the service early in 1864. Beatty's narrative is honest and realistic and tells far more about the common soldiers than most writings of general officers. Even better in some respects than Beatty's and Livermore's books is Harold A. Small, editor, *The Road to Richmond; The Civil War Memoirs of Abner R. Small of the Sixteenth Maine Volunteers: Together with the Diary Which He Kept When He Was a Prisoner of War* (Berkeley, Calif., 1939). Small's narrative, which apparently follows closely notes jotted down during the war, is a thoroughly delightful commentary by a close observer and talented writer. His service included most of the major campaigns in Virginia.

Of journalistic accounts of the war, the one richest in information about soldier life is George Alfred Townsend, *Campaigns of a Non-Combatant* (New York, 1866), which has been recently reproduced with an introduction by Lida Mayo under the title *Rustics in Rebellion* (Chapel Hill, 1950).

UNIT HISTORIES

Histories of Federal units exist in large quantity, with those of regiments being most numerous. These works, like those on the Confederate side, vary greatly in character and scope. Charles E. Davis, *Three Years in the Army: The Story of the Thirteenth Massachusetts Volunteers from July 16, 1861 to August 1, 1864* (Boston, 1894) is one of the best regimental histories. Based in large part on diaries of five members of the organization, it is unusually rich in details of camp life and in descriptions of the Southern country and people. A valuable feature is a descriptive roll of the whole regiment for the entire period of the war. Another unit history of rare excellence is Alfred Seelye Roe, *The Ninth New York Heavy Artillery* (Worcester, Mass., 1899). In preparing this history the author, who was a member of Company A, drew heavily on letters and diaries of comrades and his own experience. A felicitous style, an abundance of human-interest detail and an appealing format make this an attractive volume. *Camp and Field Life of the Fifth New York Volunteer Infantry (Duryee Zouaves)*, by Alfred Davenport, draws heavily on the author's fascinating home letters written while a member of the unit. Manuscript copies of these letters are in the New York Historical Society. In writing up the Peninsula campaign of 1862, Davenport also borrowed freely from Samuel Tiebout's diary. The generous use of this excellent source material and the fact of the account being drafted soon after the war combine with Davenport's gifts as a reporter to make this a readable and valuable work. Other organizational histories of exceptional merit are: Richard B. Irwin, *History of the Nineteenth Army Corps* (New York, 1893); James Dugan, *History of Hurlbut's Fighting Fourth Division* (Cincinnati, 1863); Stephen F. Fleharty, *Our Regiment: A History of the 102nd Illinois Infantry Volunteers* (Chicago, 1865); William R. Hartpence, *History of the Fifty-first Indiana Veteran Volunteer Infantry* (Harrison, Ohio, 1894); David Lathrop, *History of the Fifty-ninth Regiment Illinois Volunteers* (Indianapolis, 1865);

Thomas H. Parker, *History of the Fifty-first Pennsylvania Volunteers and Veteran Volunteers* (Philadelphia, 1869); and Thomas J. Wright, *History of the Eighth Regiment Kentucky Volunteer Infantry* (St. Joseph, Mo., 1880). In a class by itself is Sergeant M. S. Schroyer, "Company 'G' History" in the Snyder County Historical Society *Bulletin*, II (1939), 64-156. This work abounds with human-interest detail and colorful anecdote, but the tone is such as to make one wonder if the author did not at times confuse recollection with imagination.

A useful though old list of unit histories and personal narratives is contained in *Bibliography of State Participation in the Civil War, 1861-1866* (Washington, 1913). Much extremely valuable information about this type of literature is given by E. Merton Coulter in *Travels in the Confederate States* (Norman, Okla., 1948). Henry S. Commager's *The Blue and the Gray* (2 vols., Indianapolis, 1950) is a mine of bibliographical data for both sides.

PERIODICALS AND NEWSPAPERS

The richest periodical sources, as previously noted, are the publications of the state historical societies. Some valuable material is also to be found in the *American Historical Review* and organs of regional societies such as the *Mississippi Valley Historical Review*. The *Century Magazine, Scribner's, Atlantic Monthly, Harper's* and similar periodicals printed many articles about the Civil War, but most of these have an officer slant and are concerned mainly with general operations. One article that deserves special mention for the valuable light which it throws on the common soldier is Thomas L. Livermore, "The Northern Volunteers," *Granite Monthly*, X (1887), 239-247, 257-266. Also valuable, for its analysis of soldier reaction to combat, is S. H. M. Byers, "How Men Feel in Battle," *Harper's*, CXII (1906), 931-936. Interesting sidelights on religious life are given in "A Chaplain's Experience in the Army," *Monthly Religious Magazine*, XXIX (1863), 223-232, 343-352. C. King's meaty article, "The Volunteer Soldier of 1861," which appeared in *Review of Reviews*, XLIII (1911), 709-720, was also published in Francis Trevelyan Miller, editor, *Photographic History of the Civil War* (New York, 1911), VIII, 58-104.

A sampling of newspapers confirmed prior experience that, while not without value, these sources for study of soldier life are so far inferior to unpublished letters and diaries as to justify only a limited use of them. Newspaper files surveyed in this study included those of Portland, Maine, New York City, Detroit and, for the period of Federal occupation, those of Memphis, Nashville, Chattanooga and New Orleans. In addition, many regimental newspapers printed by and for soldiers, usually on captured presses, were consulted.

GOVERNMENT AND INSTITUTIONAL DOCUMENTS

By far the richest source among government publications is the monumental *War of the Rebellion: Official Records of the Union and Confederate Armies* (Washington, 1880-1910) which, owing to limitations of the index, has to be leaved for a study of this sort. Useful also are the various editions of *Army Regulations* which as a rule contain the articles of war; some of the later editions also include in appendices important legislation affecting the army. The *General Orders* both of the War Department Adjutant General's Office and of lower commands contain a wealth of information bearing on soldier life. Orders convening courts-martial and announcing their findings are usually included in the regular series of general orders, but beginning in 1864 the Adjutant General's Office at Washington began publishing *General Court-Martial Orders* as a separate series. The best collection of general orders known to the writer is that in the National Archives. A vast amount of information on health and medical treatment is contained in the *Medical and Surgical History of the War of the Rebellion* issued by the Surgeon General's office in six large books (Washington, 1870-1888). Of institutional publications the most useful in this study were the *Documents* of the United States Sanitary Commission (2 vols., New York, 1866) and the *Annual Reports* of the United States Christian Commission (Philadelphia, 1863-1865).

SPECIAL STUDIES AND OTHER SECONDARY WORKS

Fred Albert Shannon's *Organization and Administration of the Union Army, 1861-1865* (2 vols., Cleveland, 1928) was enormously helpful in the planning of this study and provided indispensable information about high-level policy and its bearing on the fighting forces.

Ella Lonn's recent *Foreigners in the Union Army and Navy* (Baton Rouge, 1951) is a remarkably thorough and penetrating study by the author of *Foreigners in the Confederacy* (Chapel Hill, 1940). The medical aspect of army life is definitively treated in George W. Adams' *Doctors in Blue: Health and Medicine in the Union Army, 1861-1865* (New York, 1952) which the author very generously permitted me to read in manuscript.

PICTURES

The National Archives and the Library of Congress have immense collections of Civil War photographs taken for the most part by Matthew B. Brady and assistants. Several thousand pictures in the National Archives file were examined. Some of the state historical societies also have good picture collections, as does the American Antiquarian Society, many of which were taken by local "daguerrean artists." In the Prints and Photographs Division of the Library of Congress are drawings of a number of Civil War artists, including A. R. Waud, Edwin Forbes and Winslow Homer.

Filed with the personal papers of Charles W. Reed in the Manuscripts Division of the Library of Congress are many sketches by that talented soldier-artist who, as previously noted, was the illustrator for John D. Billings' *Hard Tack and Coffee.* Some of the most authentic sketches of soldier equipment and surroundings found by the writer are those with which Herbert E. Valentine, a Massachusetts soldier, illustrated his manuscript letters and diary; this interesting item is in the library of the Essex Institute. Published collections of war pictures usually do not feature the common soldier, but a number of soldier likenesses and camp scenes are to be found in Miller's *Photographic History of the Civil War* (10 vols., New York, 1911); *Battles and Leaders of the Civil War* (4 vols., New York, 1887-1888), Roy Meredith, *Mr. Lincoln's Camera Man* (New York, 1946); and Edwin Forbes, *Life Studies of the Great Army* (New York, 1876). *Frank Leslie's Illustrated Newspaper* contains many camp scenes, but these, like many reproduced in popular periodicals of the time, often give distorted impressions of the subjects depicted.

The most delightful of published drawings are those of the talented Winslow Homer, an army artist for *Harper's*. In 1864 L. Prang of Boston issued a group of Winslow Homer sketches under the title *Life in Camp*. This firm also issued a series of separate lithographs made from Homer drawings (Boston, n.d.). Homer's pictures are exceptional for their emphasis on the common soldier and their authentic representation of soldier life.

INDEX

Abbott, Captain E. G., 131
Abbott, Captain Henry, 89, 94
Absence without leave, 197-198, 277
Adams Express Company, 156
Adrian, Michigan, 28 f.
Age, 296, 298-303
Aiken, Private John, Jr., 300
Alexandria Hospital, 141
Ambulance system, 146-147
American Bible Society, 272
American Tract Society, 272
Ammen, Colonel Jacob, 69, 88
Ammunition, 66-67, 78-79
Amphibious training, 51
Andrus, Sergeant Onley, 174, 235 f., 244
Antietam, battle of, 27, 61, 74, 89
Arkansas, troops of, 22; First Regiment, 165
Armfield, Private Wesley, 215
Arms, 22-23, 50-51, 62-64, 94
Army Medical Department, 124, 134, 136
Army Medical Museum, 147
Army of the Cumberland, 156, 231, 272
Army of the Ohio, 143
Army of the Potomac, 206, 219, 220, 226-227, 254, 321-322
Army of the Tennessee, 143, 146
Artillery, training, 51, 52; progress, 94; punishments, 209; numbers, 319; organization, 319, 320; interbranch rivalry, 327
Ashhurst, Richard L., 198
Atlantic Monthly, 154
Atrocity stories, 347-348
Ayers, James T., 111

Babbott, Private Charles, 186

Bailey, Private Franklin, 71, 72
Baltimore, Maryland, 35
Bangor, Maine, 17
Banks, General N. P., 193, 195, 196
Bardeen, C. W., 251
Barker, Private Charles, 23, 198
Barker, Thomas B., 70
Barney, J. R., 112
Bartlett, General J. J., 210
Baseball, 170
Bath, Maine, 18
Battle conduct, 66-95
Battle cry, 73-75
Beatty, General John, 250
Beinstick, Samuel, 317
Belfast, Maine, 18
Belknap, Colonel, 81
Bellows, Henry W., 150
Bellows Falls, Vermont, 34
Belmont, battle of, 143
Benge, Sergeant Harrison, 317
Bentonville, Virginia, 90
Berdan, Colonel Hiram, 341
Billings, John D., 332
Billy Yank, origin of expression, 13; volunteers, 17-24; training, 24-29; transportation, 30-36; reception of, 34-36; camp life, 45-58; clothing, 58-62; arms, 62-64; impedimenta, 64-65; conduct in battle, 66-95; opinion of South and Southerners, 96-108; attitude toward Negroes, 109-123; health, 124-151; recreation, 152-191; military justice and discipline, 192-223; food, 224-246; morals, 247-274; morale, 275-295; age, 296-303; occupations, 303-304; education, 304-306; nationality, 306-313; race, 313-319;

branches of army, 319-320; regimental loyalty, 320-324; state pride, 324; volunteers vs. regulars, 324-326; personality types, 327-337; women soldiers, 337-339; traits of, 339-341; special groups, 341-344; and Johnny Reb, 346-357; compared to Johnny Reb, 358-361
Black, William, 300
Blitz, Antonio, 176
Blunt, General James G., 318
Boner, Joe, 328
Boston *Transcript*, 153
Bowdoin College, 18
Boyce, Amelia, 188 *f.*
Bragg, General Braxton, 166
Brearley, Private William, 77-78, 84
Brice's Cross Roads, Mississippi, 90
Brinton, J. H., 143
Brisbane, Reverend William, 18
Brouse, Chaplain John A., 267
Brown, Augustus, 17
Browne, Junius, 74
Buck, Sergeant Henry A., 244
Buell, General D. C., 145, 218
Bugle calls, 45, 163-164
Burgess, president of Eureka College, 19
Burke, Henry, 297
Burnett, Alf, 263
Burns, Private David, 82
Burnside, General Ambrose, 226, 268
Bushong, Joseph T., 299
Butler, General B. F., 265, 313
Butterfield, Ira, 295

Caleb, Iola, 82
Camp, Private David W., 300
Canadian soldiers, 309
Carson, Private William J., 93
Casey, Silas, 25
Cashier, Albert, 337-338
Catholics, 263
Cavalry, training, 51, 52; guns, 63-64; punishments, 209; lack of discipline, 221-223; numbers, 319; organization, 320; interbranch rivalry, 326-327
Cedar Creek, Virginia, 90
Cedar Mountain, battle of, 158
Chancellorsville, battle of, 89, 158
Chaplains, 155-156, 263-268, 269, 272, 337
Cheat Mountain, battle of, 22
Chickamauga, battle of, 90
Chippewa Indians, 20
Christian Associations, 272
Christian Commission, 150, 154, 155-156, 255, 269, 271, 272, 273
Cincinnati *Commercial*, 153
Civilians, 286
Clapp, Sarah E., 337
Clem, John L., 297-298
Clemens, William, 91
Clemmons, Leonidas, 23
Clune, Lieutenant Henry, 80
Cole, Buck, 265-266
Colleges, reaction to Fort Sumter, 18-19
Collins, M. N., 279
Common, Charley, 298
Connecticut, Sixteenth Regiment, 272
Conscription, 275, 281, 282
Conversation, 190-191
Cooke, Chauncey H., 40-41, 299
Cooper's Shop, 35
Copperheads, 286-288
Corps d'Afrique, 122-123
Council of Chaplains of the Army of the Cumberland, 272
Courts-martial, 193-223 *passim*
Cowardice, 86-91
Croft, Private Samuel, 281
Cross, Colonel, 74, 87
Crumrine, Bishop, 184
Crydenwise, Henry, 122-123
Cuddy, Sergeant Michael, 93
Cushman, "Major" Pauline, 337
Cuzner, John B., 256

Dana, Charles A., 90

Dancing, 175
Danville, Virginia, 117
Davenport, Alfred, 83, 247, 277
Davis, Charles E., 332, 343
Davis, Jefferson, 104, 166
Debating, 178-179
De Forest, John William, 135, 210, 235, 252, 293-294, 316
De Marsan, H., 256
Dennison, governor of Ohio, 20
Desertion, 92, 205-207, 277. *See also* Cowardice
Detroit *Free Press*, 18
Dexter, Maine, 17
Diarrhea, 124, 136-137, 228
Dime novels, 155
Dimick, Christopher, 124
Discipline, 128-129, 192-194, 218-223, 293
Disease, 124-140. *See also* Dysentery, Scurvy, Venereal disease
Dodds, Ozra J., 18 *f.*
Dodson, Jacob, 19
Donelson campaign, 152
Draft riots, 287
Dramatic entertainments, 175-177
Dresbach, Private Michael, 187
Dress parade, 46-47
Drill, 49-54
Drinking, general discussion of, 252-254; mentioned, 31-32, 102, 130-131, 137, 138, 144, 174, 177-178, 198, 231, 269, 330, 349-350
Drummer boys, 296-298
Dry Tortugas, 215
Duffield, George, 29
Duffield, Colonel W. W., 29
Dutton, W. W., 301
Dysentery, 124, 136-137, 228

Eddy, Private Samuel E., 91
Edes, Private Edward, 69, 198, 264, 279
Elmore, Day, 293, 335-337
Emancipation Proclamation, 41, 42-43, 281
English soldiers, 309
Equipment, 22-23, 64-65

Eureka College, 19
Executions, 205, 206-207, 217-218

Fernandina, Florida, 117
Fiske, Lieutenant Samuel, 341
Flags, 28-30, 93-94
Flint, Francis S., 187
Florence Nightingale Association, 19
Foley, William, 300
Food, 66, 127-128, 164, 224-246
Football, 170
Foraging, 233-236
Foreign-born soldiers, 306-313
Foreman, Corporal, 91
Forman, Colonel James B., 302
Fort Snelling, 19
Fort Wayne, 26
Forty-eighters, 308
Fox, Lieutenant Colonel Charles B., 168
Frank Leslie's, 154
Fraternization, 178, 353-357
Fredericksburg, campaign of, 61, 68, 89, 145, 152
French, Private Samuel, 91
French soldiers, 169
Furloughs, 292

Galloway, Joseph D., 198
Gambling, 212, 247, 249-252
Games, 169, 171
Gates, George, 73
Geary, John W., 193
German soldiers, 169, 273, 307-308
Gettysburg campaign, 61, 89, 145
Gibson, Ella Hobart, 337
Goddard, Charles, 301
Goldsboro expedition, 226
Goodhue, Private William F., 262
Gordon, Private M. L., 51
Gould, Benjamin A., 298 *f.*, 302, 303
Graham, Corporal N. B., 161
Grannis, Sergeant Henry J., 30, 93-94
Grant, General Ulysses S., 22, 143, 146, 164, 322, 323

Greybeards, 303
Groves, Simon, 133
Grub, Corporal Philip, 92
Guard duty, 46
Gwynne, Private Nathaniel, 301

Halleck, General H. W., 140, 146, 193, 218
Hammond, William A., 129, 142, 145, 146, 147, 224
Handicraft, 179
Haralson, Captain Jonathan, 256
Hardee, William J., 25
Hardie, Colonel James, 220, 222
Hardtack, 237-238
Hard Tack and Coffee, 332
Harper, William A., 285-286
Harper's Magazine, 154
Haviland, Laura S., 268
Hays, Will S., 297
Hazen, Colonel W. B., 89
Health, 124-151, 285. *See also* Dysentery, Medical care, Physical examinations, U. S. Sanitary Commission, Venereal disease
Heath, Private Charles N., 249
Heg, Colonel Hans C., 169, 253, 309
Henry, John N., 291
Heroism, 91-94
Herr, Private John, 190
Higginson, Colonel Thomas Wentworth, 314
Hill, Senator Benjamin, 328
History of the First Year of the War, Pollard, 157
Hodgers, *see* Cashier, Albert
Hole-in-the-Day, Chief, 20
Holidays, 174 f.
Holmes, Captain Oliver Wendell, 78, 80
Honey Springs, Indian Territory, 317-318
Hood, General John B., 359
Hooker, General Joseph, 153, 218, 226-227, 281
Hospitals, 140-147, 150, 156

Hovey, president of Illinois State Normal College, 19
Howard, General O. O., 114, 268
Howe, Julia Ward, 160
Howe, Orion P., 298
Humor, 190-191
Hunter, Alexander, 14
Hunter, George Gray, 199
Hunting, 170-171
Hurlbut, General Stephen A., 88
Hyneman, Jacob E., 252

Illinois, Second Cavalry, 222; Thirty-third Infantry, 19; Fifty-fifth, 298; Fifty-ninth, 208; Eighty-second, 27; Eighty-sixth, 280; Ninety-sixth, 183
Illinois State Normal College, 19
Indiana, Eighth Regiment, 219; Ninth, 81; Thirteenth, 22; Eighteenth, 219; Twenty-second, 219; Twenty-third, 219; Twenty-fifth, 219; Forty-third, 220
Indians, 20, 316-319
Infantry, training, 51; guns, 62-63; progress, 94; numbers, 319; organization, 319; interbranch rivalry, 326-327; mounted, 342
Inspection, 47-48
Insubordination, 198-202
Invalid Corps, 342
Iowa, Second Regiment, 181; Fourth, 225; Eighth, 239; Twelfth, 30, 219; Fifteenth, 80 f.; Seventeenth, 89; Thirty-fourth, 279
Irish soldiers, 169, 284, 308-309
Iuka, Mississippi, 89

Jews, 263, 264
Johnny Reb and Billy Yank, 14
Johnson, Private E. A., 320
Johnston, General Joseph E., 359
Judge Advocate General, 195, 196, 214

Kansas, First Cavalry, 318; Ninth, 222; Eleventh, 181; Fourteenth, 317

Keenan, T. R., 346
Kendig, Abraham, 183 f.
Kentucky, Eighth Regiment, 21
Killeen, Private John, 249
King, Curtis, 303
Kinsley, Rufus, 121-122
Kistler, Private John, 92
Kittredge, Private Walter, 162, 330

Lake, Delos W., 247
Lamb, John M., 153
Lampley, Colonel, 81
Larry, M. P., 270
Lawton, Henry W., 302
Leech, Margaret, 257 f.
Leland, Private, 91
Leonard, H. R., 288 f.
Letterman, Jonathan, 129, 142, 145
Letter writing, 82 f., 183-189, 360
Lewis, Private Thomas W., 79
Libraries, 156-157
Life of Johnny Reb, The, 13
Lightning Brigade, 341
Limbarker, W. E., 104
Lincoln, Abraham, and Fort Sumter, 17; commutes sentence, 202; disciplinary actions, 216; Billy Yank's opinion of, 280
Literacy, 98-99, 116, 305-306, 358
Livermore, Thomas L., 87, 320, 339
Lock, E. W., 165
Logan, General John A., 326
Louisiana, troops of, 22
Louisiana invasion, 33
Lovell, General Mansfield, 166
Lyceums, 179
Lyford, Private W. O., 83, 292-293

MacArthur, Arthur, 301-302
McClellan, General George B., 26, 164, 203, 210, 213, 226, 252, 268, 276, 281
McDougall, Surgeon Charles, 140
McMeekin, Private John, 133
McMeekin, Margaret, 188

Madison, Wisconsin, 18, 19, 31
Mail, 189-190
Maine, Fifth Regiment, 254, 274
Maine State Agency, 232
Malaria, 133-134, 137
Manassas, first battle of, 22, 88, 275
Manassas, second battle of, 88
Marcy, Colonel R. B., 313
Marvin, Sergeant Matthew, 78, 320
Mascots, 80
Massachusetts, troops of, 22, 41; Second Regiment, 31; Sixth, 31, 35; Ninth, 309; Forty-fourth, 175, 242; Sixty-sixth, 168 f.
Meagher, General Thomas F., 308
Measles, 133
Medical care, 46, 124-151
Memphis, Tennessee, 259, 260, 262
Michigan, troop training in, 26; Second Regiment, 34 f., 165; Fourth, 26, 28, 325; Sixth, 26, 31, 197; Seventh, 26; Ninth, 29; Twenty-second, 297
Michigan, University of, 19
Military commissions, 194-195
Military justice, 192-223
Militia companies, 20
Milledge, Private George, 83
Miller, Private Alonzo, 333
Minnesota, First Regiment, 35, 180
Minstrel shows, 176, 177
Mississippi, the, 33
Missouri, Second Regiment, 219; Thirty-fifth, 220
Mitchel, General Ormsby, 250
Moody, Sergeant, 91
Moody, Reverend Granville, 268
Morale, 275-295
Morals, 247-274
Morton, Captain James St. Clair, 341
Moulton, Private John M., 279-280
Murdoch, James Edward, 176-177
Murfreesboro, battle of, 68, 89
Murphy, Dave, 107

Murray, Private, 91-92
Music, 46, 119, 157-169, 178. *See also* Songs

Nashville, Tennessee, 259, 262
Nebraska, Cavalry, 219
Negroes, volunteers, 19; treatment of, 103, 172; Billy Yank's attitude toward, 109-123; health, 124-125, 134, 135, 136, 137; literacy, 157, 305, 306, 313-314; First Arkansas, 165-166; and music, 168; as sutlers, 232; hospitality of, 233; recruiting of, 313; evaluation of performance, 314-315; civilians with army, 315. *See also* Slavery
Nelson, Knute, 310
Nelson, Vance, 289
Nelson, General William, 88
Newberry, J. S., 137, 150
Newhall, George F., 333
Newhall, Herman Chauncey, 281
New Hampshire, Second Cavalry, 221; Fifth, 74
New Jersey, Twenty-sixth Regiment, 170
Newspapers, 153; camp, 179-183
New York, Ninth Regiment, 170, 176, 183, 308; Eighteenth Cavalry, 222; Twentieth Regiment, 169; Forty-eighth, 176, 252-253; Fifty-first, 170; Sixty-third, 308; Eighty-eighth, 308
New York *Herald*, 153
New York *Tribune*, 43, 153
Nineteenth Corps, 221
"Normal Regiment," 19
North American Review, 154
Norton, Private O. W., 28, 73
Nursing, 149-150

Oberlin College, 19
Occupations, 303-304
Offenses, military, 192-223
Officers, choosing of, 24; training of, 25-26, 50; training duties of, 50; lack of training, 53

Ohio, troops of, 22; Third Regiment, 250; Tenth, 250; Thirteenth Battery, 88; Twentieth Regiment, 19; Twenty-fourth, 69; Twenty-fifth, 180; Fifty-second, 298; 104th, 296
Olmsted, Frederick Law, 23, 128, 150
Oxford, Ohio, 18 f.

Paducah, Kentucky, 106-107
Parmelee, Urich N., 41-42
Pay, 48-49, 291
Pembroke, Maine, 17
Pennsylvania, troops of, 32; Ninth Regiment, 325; Thirteenth, 180, 272
Perry, Colonel James M., 252
Perryville, battle of, 89, 145
Philadelphia, Pennsylvania, 35
Phillips, Colonel William A., 318
Photography, 13, 25
Physical examinations, 23, 125
Pillaging, 203
Pioneer Corps, 341
Poetry, 187-189, 191; off-color, 256
Polk, General Leonidas, 359
Pollard, *History of the First Year of the War*, 157
Porter, Admiral David D., 90
Port Hudson, battle of, 90
Practical jokes, 171-173
Prime, Captain Frederick, 85
Profanity, 102, 248-249. *See also* Insubordination
Prostitution, 168, 177, 257-262
Protestant Episcopal Book Society, 273
Provost Marshal General's Bureau, 282
Punishments, 192-223

Read, Thomas Buchanan, 176-177
Reading, 153-157
Recreation, 152-191
Recruits, large numbers of, 18-20; organization of, 20-23; training of, 24-29; departures of, 30-31;

travel, 31-36; reception of, 34-36; motives, 37-44; camp life, 45-65; Negro, 120-121, 281; poor quality of, 284
Redington, Captain Edward S., 139
Regular Army, use in training, 26; and courts-martial, 196; numbers of, 319; organization, 320; rivalry with volunteers, 324-326; sharpshooters, 341
Reid, Edward F., 304-305
Reid, Private Harvey, 296 f.
Religion, general discussion of, 262-274; mentioned, 32, 69-70, 73, 116-117, 118-119, 154, 155-156, 177, 247, 251, 331, 358-359
Replacements, 53-54
Reynolds, Mrs., 337
Rhode Island, Second Cavalry, 192
Rhodes, James Ford, 40
Richardson, William C., 296
Riley, Private, 80
"Rip Raps," 215
Robinson, Lieutenant Colonel H., 192
Roe, Alfred S., 355
Root, George F., 160, 161
Ropes, Lieutenant Henry, 89
Rosecrans, General William S., 89, 165, 268

Sabbath, observance of, 47-48, 269-270
Sabine Cross Roads, battle of, 90
Sacket, Colonel D. B., 220
Salter, Sergeant William, 54
Sanitation, 125-127, 128, 141
Savage, Private, 92
Sawyer, Charles Carroll, 162
Scandinavian soldiers, 169, 309
Schurz, Carl, 226
Scott, Private William, 204
Scott, General Winfield, 25
Scurvy, 230
Sectionalism, 96 ff.
Seelye, Sarah, 337
Self-mutilation, 86, 278

Seven Days campaign, 88, 226
Seven Pines, battle of, 88, 144
Sheahan, John P., 98
Shelter, 55-58, 127
Shenango, Pennsylvania, 18
Sheridan, General Philip H., 205
Sherman, General W. T., 26, 53, 85, 316
Shields, General Joseph, 292
Shiloh, battle of, 88, 158
Ship Island, Mississippi, 121
Sinclair, Sergeant George G., 92
Sinclair, William, 221
Sisters of Charity, 149
Skowhegan, Maine, 18
Slade, Captain James H., 168
Slavery issue, as regarded by Billy Yank, 40-44, 281. See also Negroes
Small, Abner R., 87
Smith, Private Ed, 354
Smith, Captain Frank C., 92
Smith, Philip, 39
Snell, Private James, 27
Snow battles, 170
Snuff, 101-102
Songs, 32, 44, 118-119, 157-169, 182, 297, 342
South, Yanks' opinion of, 96-108
Southern soldiers, 346-361
Souvenirs, 79, 118
Sports, 169-171
Stanard, Private William B., 99
Stanton, Edwin M., 129
"Star-Spangled Fever," 18
Stilwell, Leander, 23
Stone, Private Cyrus, 83, 267
Stone, Colonel W. M., 94
Storrow, Corporal Samuel, 39, 157, 305
Suman, Colonel Isaac, 81
Surgery, 147-148

Tallman, John, 101
Taylor, Private Isaac, 106
Tennessee, First Cavalry, 263
Tents, 55-56
Thievery, 202, 254

Thomas, George H., 202
Thompson, Henry, 187
Thornton, Private Clark, 92
Thurston, Private C. B., 110, 264, 289
Tobacco, 101-102
Todd, Private, 91
Townsend, George, 45
Trench fighting, 85-86
Troy, New York, 34
Trumble, Albert E., 188-189
Turners, society of, 169
Twentieth Corps, 165
Typhoid fever, 134-135, 138

Uncle Tom's Cabin, Stowe, 40, 273
Uniforms, 21-22, 58-62, 319
Union Medical Corps, 125 *ff.*, 145, 261
United States Colored Troops, 121-122, 313
United States Sanitary Commission, 125, 126, 129, 130, 133, 142, 149-150, 232, 298
"University Recruits, The," 30
Upper Iowa University, 30
Upson, Theodore, 263
Usher, Rebecca, 232

Venereal disease, 261
Vermont, First Regiment, 34; Eighth, 170; 114th, 170
Veteran's Reserve Corps, 342
Veteran Volunteers, 342-343
Vicksburg, siege of, 62, 70, 85, 90
Vulgarity, 255-257

Walker, Johnnie, 296 *f.*
Walker, Mary E., 337
Wall, Private W. C., Jr., 300
Wallace, the, 34
Walsh, president of Board of Aldermen, New York City, 217

Ward, Charles, 293 *f.*, 309
Ward, Private Joshua, 203-204
Washington, Henry George General, 168
Wayzata, Minnesota, 19
Weaver, Harry G., 338
Weld, Stephen, 193
Wetmore, Thomas B., 256
Wettleson, William O., 38, 73
White Oak Roads, Virginia, 90
Wilcox, Josephine, 29
Wilkeson, Private Frank, 81, 284
Williams, General A. S., 114
Williams, Private John, 201
Williamsburg, Virginia, 42
Wills, Private Charles, 312
Wilson, George H., 300
Wilson's Creek, battle of, 22
Wisconsin, Second Regiment, 22; Third, 262, 310; Fifth, 317; Eighth, 80; Fifteenth, 309, 310; Twenty-second, 296 *f.*; Twenty-fourth, 302
Wisconsin, University of, 19
Withington, Colonel, 84
Women, patriotism of, 18, 19; influence on recruiting, 21; make uniforms, 22; pose as men, 23, 337-339; flag making, 28, 30; flag presentation, 28, 29, 30; Yanks' opinion of Southern, 100-102, 106-107; work in hospitals, 149; Yanks' correspondence with, 187-189; prostitution, 257-262; as soldiers, 337-339
Woodbury, Colonel, 29
Work, Henry Clay, 162, 165
Wounded, 141-151

Yellow fever, 135
Young Men's Christian Association, 273

Zouaves, 22